Johns Hopkins
Symptoms & Remedies

JOHNS HOPKINS

SYMPTOMS
AND
REMEDIES

THE COMPLETE HOME
MEDICAL REFERENCE

Medical Editor
Simeon Margolis, M.D., Ph.D.

Prepared by the Editors of
The Johns Hopkins Medical Letter
HEALTH AFTER 50

REBUS • NEW YORK
DISTRIBUTED BY RANDOM HOUSE

THE JOHNS HOPKINS MEDICAL LETTER
HEALTH AFTER 50

JOHNS HOPKINS SYMPTOMS AND REMEDIES *is published in association with* THE JOHNS HOPKINS MEDICAL LETTER HEALTH AFTER 50. *This monthly eight-page newsletter provides practical, timely information for anyone concerned with taking control of his or her own health care. The newsletter is written in clear, nontechnical, easy-to-understand language and comes from the century-old tradition of Johns Hopkins excellence. For information on how to subscribe to this newsletter, please write to Medletter Associates, Inc., Department 1106, 632 Broadway, New York, New York 10012.*

This book is not intended as a substitute for the advice of a physician. Readers who suspect they may have specific medical problems should consult a physician about any suggestions made in this book.

Johns Hopkins was ranked America's best overall hospital in a survey conducted by *U.S. News and World Report*, published July 18, 1994.

Library of Congress Cataloging-in-Publication Data

Johns Hopkins symptoms and remedies: the complete home medical reference / medical editor, Simeon Margolis; prepared by the editors of the Johns Hopkins medical letter health after 50.
p. cm.
Includes index.
ISBN 0-929661-19-2 (Hardcover)
1. Medicine, Popular—Handbooks, manuals, etc. 2. Symptomatology—Handbooks, manuals, etc.
I. Margolis, Simeon, 1931- . II. Johns Hopkins Medical Institutions. III. Johns Hopkins medical letter health after 50. IV. Title: Symptoms and remedies.
  [DNLM: 1. Medicine—handbooks. 2. Self Medication—methods—handbooks. WB 39 J655 1995]
RC81.J66 1995
616.02'4—dc20
DNLM/DLC
for Library of Congress   95-2185
                    CIP

Printed in the United States of America
10 9 8 7 6
Distributed by Random House, Inc.

The Johns Hopkins Medical Institutions
Baltimore, Maryland 21205

How to use this book

This book is divided into two distinct sections: The first is a collection of charts, each of which covers a specific symptom and indicates one or more of the disorders commonly associated with it. You can then look up any one of these potential diagnoses in the second half of the book, which provides a comprehensive explanation of each disorder, what to do about it, whether or not you can treat it yourself (and how), and when to call a doctor.

Suppose, for example, that you are suffering from eye pain. When you look this up in the symptoms charts, you find 18 possible diagnoses listed. However, you see that only eight of these also involve the associated symptom "with eye discharge or copious tearing," which, in your case, is applicable. After reading the distinguishing features of each of these eight disorders, you determine that perhaps only three of them produce a profile of symptoms that resembles your own. You may then refer to the Disorders section to read more about these ailments—and to help you determine what to do next. (This book is not, however, intended as a substitute for the advice and expertise of a physician. Readers should always consult a doctor about any suggestions made in these pages.) The Disorder section can also serve as a valuable resource when you already know the diagnosis and simply want more information.

SYMPTOMS

In this section of the book, you will find charts covering a wide range of common symptoms. These charts are designed to help you narrow down the number of disorders that may be associated with a given symptom. You can then find further information on any potential diagnosis in the Disorder section. Please bear in mind, however, that these charts are not intended to establish a definitive diagnosis—only your doctor can do that after performing a physical examination and conducting the appropriate tests. Indeed, some of the less common disorders that can cause a specific symptom may not be covered in this book, and some symptoms (such as dry skin, for example) may develop even when no underlying disease is involved.

THE EDITORS

Abdominal pain

Associated Symptoms	Possible Diagnosis	Distinguishing Features
	Amyloidosis *Accumulation of amyloid, a starchy protein, in tissues and organs*	Symptoms vary greatly depending on the body parts affected and may include heart palpitations; shortness of breath; swelling of the legs; diarrhea; abdominal pain; raised spots on the armpits, groin, face, and neck; fatigue and weakness; numbness of the hands or feet; dizziness on standing; joint pains.
	Appendicitis, acute	Pain near the navel, spreading to the lower right abdomen; nausea and vomiting; constipation; possibly diarrhea; low-grade fever; loss of appetite.
	Cirrhosis *Chronic damage to the cells of the liver.*	No symptoms in early stages; loss of weight and appetite; nausea; swollen legs, ankles and abdomen; itching; jaundice; black stools; vomiting blood; fatigue; impotence; memory loss; confusion.
	Colitis, ulcerative *Inflammation of the lining of the colon*	Pain on the left side of the abdomen that lessens after bowel movements; bloody diarrhea; pain in the rectal area; possibly, fever, rapid heartbeat, nausea and vomiting, loss of appetite, dehydration with severe attacks.
	Colon Polyps	Rectal bleeding; blood in the stool; abdominal pain; change in bowel habits.
	Crohn's disease *Inflammation of the lining of the small intestine*	Episodes of abdominal pain or cramps in lower abdomen; nausea; diarrhea; loss of weight and appetite; possibly, fever; rectal bleeding or blood in stools; fatigue; anal fissures; joint pains; inflammation of the eyes.
	Diarrhea, acute	Loose, watery stools; increased frequency of bowel movements; abdominal cramping and pain. In infants, possibly drowsiness, slack skin, dry, sticky mouth and tongue, or persistent crying.
	Diverticular disorders *Swellings in the wall of the colon*	Usually no symptoms unless diverticulae become inflamed. Tenderness or pain in the lower left abdomen relieved by passing stools or gas; constipation or diarrhea; blood in the stool; severe, spasmodic abdominal pain that becomes constant; possibly, fever and nausea.
	Dysentery, bacillary	Watery diarrhea that may contain pus or blood; abdominal pain; rapid dehydration and weight loss; nausea and vomiting.
	Food poisoning	Symptoms vary greatly depending on the type and extent of poisoning and may include nausea, vomiting, diarrhea, bloody stools, abdominal pain, and collapse.

Abdominal pain *continued*

Associated Symptoms	Possible Diagnosis	Distinguishing Features
	Gallbladder disorders	Moderate to severe pain in the upper right side of the abdomen, chest, upper back, or right shoulder. Pain often follows the ingestion of high-fat foods and is episodic, lasting 20 minutes to several hours. Nausea and vomiting; low-grade fever; belching; heartburn; gas; possibly, jaundice, pale stools, and itchy skin.
	Hepatitis, acute viral	Fever; fatigue; loss of appetite; aching muscles and joints; abdominal pain or discomfort; jaundice; dark urine and pale stools.
	Hepatitis, chronic	Fatigue; nausea; vomiting; loss of appetite; jaundice; dark urine; clay-colored stools; depression; pain or discomfort in the upper right abdomen; abdominal swelling; fever; in women, cessation of menstruation, acne, and the appearance of male pattern facial hair.
	Intestinal obstruction	Abdominal pain and cramps; nausea; vomiting; weakness; gas; abdominal bloating; possible diarrhea; progressive constipation culminating in inability to pass stools or gas.
	Irritable bowel syndrome	Cramps in the middle or to one side of the lower abdomen that are usually relieved with bowel movements; nausea; bloating; gas; alternating diarrhea and constipation.
	Leukemias	Symptoms vary depending on the type of leukemia and may include: loss of appetite and weight; increased bruising and bleeding; bone pain, especially in the legs; abdominal pain and distention; nausea; heart palpitations; severe fatigue; pallor; breathing difficulty; fever; night sweats; headache; enlarged lymph nodes; joint pains (due to gout).
	Liver tumors	Pain or discomfort in the upper right portion of the abdomen; abdominal swelling; loss of weight and appetite; nausea and vomiting; fever; excessive perspiration; jaundice; pallor; severe fatigue.
	Malabsorption, digestive *A failure of the small intestine to absorb nutrients in the diet*	Diarrhea; weight loss; yellowish, foul-smelling stools; abdominal cramps, gas, and bloating; weakness and lethargy.
	Myelofibrosis *An increase of fibrous scar tissue within the bone marrow*	Weakness and fatigue; abdominal fullness; a tendency to bleed easily; bone pain; pallor; shortness of breath during physical exertion; increased susceptibility to bruising and infections; jaundice; weight loss.

Abdominal pain *continued*

Associated Symptoms	Possible Diagnosis	Distinguishing Features
	Ovarian cysts	In many cases, no symptoms. Painless swelling in the lower abdomen; possibly, pain during intercourse; brown vaginal discharge; lack of or heavier than usual menstrual periods; vomiting; unusual hair growth on face or body.
	Pancreatitis *Inflammation of the pancreas*	Sudden, extreme abdominal pain; nausea and vomiting; weakness; fever; clammy skin; abdominal bloating and tenderness.
	Peritonitis *Inflammation of the abdominal membrane.*	Sudden abdominal pain, rigidity, and swelling; chills and fever; weakness; rapid heartbeat; nausea and vomiting; extreme thirst; low urine output.
	Rheumatoid arthritis, juvenile	Fever; rash; abdominal pain; weight loss; swelling, stiffness, and pain in the affected joints; enlarged lymph glands; fatigue; pallor; red, painful eyes; morning stiffness.
	Stomach cancer	Discomfort in the upper abdomen; black, tarry stools; vomiting of blood; loss of appetite and weight; vomiting after meals.
	Systemic lupus erythematosus *Inflammation of connective tissues throughout the body*	Red, blotchy, butterfly–shaped rash on the cheeks and bridge of the nose; fatigue; fever; loss of appetite and weight; nausea; joint and abdominal pain; headaches; blurred vision; increased sensitivity to sun exposure; depression; psychosis; mental confusion.
	Tapeworm infestation	Often asymptomatic. Unexplained weight loss; presence of white eggs or ribbon-like segments of worm in the stool, bedding, or clothing; symptoms of pernicious anemia.
	Testicular torsion *Twisting of the spermatic cord*	Severe pain and swelling on one side of the scrotum; skin on the scrotum may appear red or purple; light-headedness or fainting; possibly, abdominal pain, nausea and vomiting.
with chest pain	Aortic aneurysm *A sac-like ballooning at a weak spot in the wall of the aorta, the body's primary artery*	Usually asymptomatic; occasionally, severe abdominal and back pain; chest pain; swallowing difficulty; dizziness and fainting; hoarseness; cough.
	Congestive heart failure	Shortness of breath; fatigue; need to sleep on several pillows; weakness; cough; heart palpitations; swelling in the legs, ankles, and abdomen; frequent urination at night; indigestion; nausea and vomiting; loss of appetite.

Abdominal pain *continued*

Associated Symptoms	Possible Diagnosis	Distinguishing Features
with chest pain *continued*	Peptic ulcer	Intermittent, burning or gnawing pain in the upper abdomen or lower chest; indigestion; loss of appetite and weight. Pain may be relieved by eating or antacids. Possible nausea and vomiting. Black, tarry stools, vomiting blood.
	Pleurisy *Inflammation of the membranes lining the lungs and chest cavity*	Sudden chest pain worse on inspiration that may also radiate into the shoulder or abdomen; rapid breathing; coughing; sneezing; possibly, fever.
	Pneumothorax *Accumulation of air between the two membranes lining the lungs and the chest cavity*	Chest pain that may radiate into the abdomen or shoulder; shortness of breath; dry cough.
	Uterine cancer	Heavy bleeding during menses; bleeding between menses or after intercourse; postmenopausal bleeding; abnormal vaginal discharge usually watery and blood-streaked; weight loss.
with back pain	Bladder infection *Cystitis*	Burning during urination; frequent and urgent urination with only small amounts of urine passed; blood in the urine; lower abdominal pain; low-grade fever; pain during sexual intercourse and, in men, during ejaculation.
	Endometriosis *The migration of the uterine lining to other reproductive or abdominal organs*	Pain in the lower abdomen, vagina, and lower back beginning just prior to menses and intensifying after blood flow has ceased; heavy bleeding during periods; pain during intercourse; diarrhea; constipation; pain during bowel movements; bleeding from the rectum; bloody urine during menses; nausea and vomiting prior to menses; infertility.
	Kidney cancer	Blood in the urine; abdominal and lower back pain; low-grade fever; fatigue; nausea and vomiting; loss of weight and appetite.
	Pancreatic cancer	Often, no symptoms until far advanced. Upper abdominal pain which spreads to the back; loss of weight and appetite; jaundice; nausea, vomiting, and indigestion; diarrhea; fatigue; depression.
	Pelvic inflammatory disease	Initially, lower pelvic pain; pain during intercourse; irregular menstrual bleeding; vaginal discharge with abnormal color or odor; low-grade fever; chills; frequent urination; fatigue; loss of appetite; later, severe abdominal pain and high fever.

Abdominal pain *continued*

Associated Symptoms	Possible Diagnosis	Distinguishing Features
with back pain *continued*	Prostate cancer	Difficulty urinating; frequent urination with decreased urine output; pain in the pelvic area and lower back; painful ejaculation or bowel movements.
	Prostatitis *Inflammation of the prostate gland*	Burning during urination; urgent and frequent urination; fever and chills; discharge from the penis; lower abdominal and back pain; blood in the urine.
	Renal calculi *Kidney stones*	Intermittent spasms of pain in the back and flanks, radiating through the lower abdomen towards the groin; nausea and vomiting; blood in the urine; urge to urinate but only small amounts of urine are passed.

Abdominal swelling

Associated Symptoms	Possible Diagnosis	Distinguishing Features
with swollen legs/ankles (edema)	Cirrhosis *Chronic damage to the cells of the liver*	No symptoms in early stages; loss of weight and appetite; nausea; swollen legs, ankles and abdomen; itching; jaundice; black stools; vomiting blood; fatigue; impotence; memory loss; confusion.
	Congestive heart failure	Shortness of breath; fatigue; need to sleep on several pillows; weakness; cough; heart palpitations; swelling in the legs, ankles, and abdomen; frequent urination at night; indigestion; nausea and vomiting; loss of appetite.
	Diverticular disorders *Swellings in the wall of the colon*	Usually no symptoms unless diverticulae become inflamed. Tenderness or pain in the lower left abdomen relieved by passing stools or gas; constipation or diarrhea; blood in the stool; severe, spasmodic abdominal pain that becomes constant; possibly, fever and nausea.
	Glomerulonephritis, acute *Sudden or intense inflammation of the glomeruli, tiny structures that filter blood in the kidneys*	Blood in the urine; passing only small amounts of urine; swelling of the ankles or the tissues around the eyes; shortness of breath; possibly, fatigue, nausea and vomiting, loss of appetite, itching, headaches, fever, impaired vision.
	Glomerulonephritis, chronic *Persistent inflammation of the glomeruli, tiny structures that filter blood in the kidneys*	Blood in the urine; passing only small amounts of urine; swelling of the ankles or the tissues around the eyes; shortness of breath; possibly, fatigue, nausea and vomiting, loss of appetite, itching, headaches, fever, impaired vision.
	Nephrotic syndrome *Damage to the filtering units of the kidneys*	Swelling in the ankles and around the eyes; weight gain, due to fluid retention throughout the body; shortness of breath; passing only small amounts of urine that has an unusually foamy appearance; fatigue; diarrhea; loss of appetite.
	Pericarditis *Inflammation of the membrane surrounding the heart*	Sharp chest pain that may spread to the neck and shoulders; pain may be relieved by sitting up and leaning forward; swollen legs and abdomen; breathing difficulty; chills; fever; fatigue.
	Renal failure, acute *Severe kidney failure*	Initially, decreased urine output, weight gain and swelling due to edema, loss of appetite, nausea and vomiting, fatigue. If untreated, confusion, seizures, and drowsiness.
	Renal failure, chronic *Persistent, mild kidney failure*	Asymptomatic in early stages. Possibly, mental confusion; shortness of breath; abdominal pain; decreased sex drive; fatigue; muscle and bone pain; numbness in the legs and feet; headache; impaired mental acuity; bad breath.

Abdominal swelling *continued*

Associated Symptoms	Possible Diagnosis	Distinguishing Features
without swollen legs/ankles	Appendicitis, acute	Pain near the navel, spreading to the lower right abdomen; nausea and vomiting; constipation; possibly diarrhea; low-grade fever; loss of appetite.
	Colitis, ulcerative *Inflammation of the lining of the colon*	Pain on the left side of the abdomen that lessens after bowel movements; bloody diarrhea; pain in the rectal area; possibly, fever, rapid heartbeat, nausea and vomiting, loss of appetite, dehydration with severe attacks.
	Constipation, chronic	Infrequent and possibly painful bowel movements; straining during bowel movements; hard, dry stool; abdominal swelling; continued sensation of fullness after evacuating bowels.
	Gallbladder disorders	Moderate to severe pain in the upper right side of the abdomen, chest, upper back, or right shoulder. Pain often follows the ingestion of high-fat foods and is episodic, lasting 20 minutes to several hours. Nausea and vomiting; low-grade fever; belching; heartburn; gas; possibly, jaundice, pale stools, and itchy skin.
	Hepatitis, chronic	Fatigue; nausea; vomiting; loss of appetite; jaundice; dark urine; clay-colored stools; depression; pain or discomfort in the upper right abdomen; abdominal swelling; fever; in women, cessation of menstruation, acne, and the appearance of male pattern facial hair.
	Intestinal obstruction	Abdominal pain and cramps; nausea; vomiting; weakness; gas; abdominal bloating; possible diarrhea; progressive constipation culminating in inability to pass stools or gas.
	Irritable bowel syndrome	Cramps in the middle or to one side of the lower abdomen that are usually relieved with bowel movements; nausea; bloating; gas; alternating diarrhea and constipation.
	Kidney cancer	Blood in the urine; abdominal and lower back pain; low-grade fever; fatigue; nausea and vomiting; loss of weight and appetite.
	Lactose intolerance *Difficulty digesting milk and dairy products*	Abdominal cramps; diarrhea; nausea; bloating; flatulence.

Abdominal swelling *continued*

Associated Symptoms	Possible Diagnosis	Distinguishing Features
	Leukemias	Symptoms vary depending on the type of leukemia and may include: loss of appetite and weight; increased bruising and bleeding; bone pain, especially in the legs; abdominal pain and distention; nausea; heart palpitations; severe fatigue; pallor; breathing difficulty; fever; night sweats; headache; enlarged lymph nodes; joint pains (due to gout).
	Liver tumors	Pain or discomfort in the upper right portion of the abdomen; abdominal swelling; loss of weight and appetite; nausea and vomiting; fever; excessive perspiration; jaundice; pallor; severe fatigue.
	Megacolon *Distention of the colon*	Severe constipation; abdominal bloating; loss of weight and appetite; possible diarrhea; in newborns, failure to pass a stool within 48 hours after birth; in children, slow growth from infancy to age five.
	Mesenteric ischemia *A blood clot blocking blood flow to the intestine*	Severe abdominal cramping, usually around the navel, that is exacerbated by eating and alleviated by fasting. Possibly, bloody stools.
	Ovarian cancer	Often asymptomatic until widespread. Possibly, abdominal swelling or discomfort, nausea, and vomiting. In advanced stages, excessive hair growth, unexplained weight loss, abnormal menstrual bleeding or postmenopausal bleeding; urinary frequency.
	Ovarian cysts	In many cases, no symptoms. Painless swelling in the lower abdomen; possibly, pain during intercourse; brown vaginal discharge; lack of or heavier than usual menstrual periods; vomiting; unusual hair growth on face or body.
	Peritonitis *Inflammation of the abdominal membrane*	Sudden abdominal pain, rigidity, and swelling; chills and fever; weakness; rapid heartbeat; nausea and vomiting; extreme thirst; low urine output.

Agitation

Associated Symptoms	Possible Diagnosis	Distinguishing Features
	Alzheimer's disease	Symptoms vary greatly in different individuals. Initially, minor forgetfulness gradually developing into severe, short-term memory loss, disorientation, an inability to concentrate, and sudden mood and personality changes. In later stages, severe confusion, possible hallucinations or paranoid delusions, loss of social and sexual inhibitions, impaired judgment, anxiety, depression, agitation and combativeness, wandering and getting lost, inability to write, urinary and fecal incontinence.
	Hypoglycemia *Low blood sugar*	Anxiety; hunger; trembling; headache; palpitations; perspiration; confusion; irritability; loss of coordination; possibly, double vision, seizures, or coma.
	Rabies	Low-grade fever; headache; loss of appetite; tingling at site of animal bite; intense thirst exacerbated by the inability to drink without violent, painful throat spasms; paralysis of facial muscles; drooling. Agitation and violent behavior, confusion, convulsions, coma.
	Renal failure, chronic *Persistent, mild kidney failure*	Asymptomatic in early stages. Possibly, mental confusion; shortness of breath; abdominal pain; decreased sex drive; fatigue; muscle and bone pain; numbness in the legs and feet; headache; impaired mental acuity; bad breath.
	Septic shock *Severe drop in blood pressure due to the presence of microorganisms or their toxins in the bloodstream*	Nausea and vomiting; prostration; diarrhea; sudden high fever; chills; rapid breathing; headache; mental confusion or agitation; decreased urine output; possible jaundice or skin rash; hands and feet may be unusually cold.

Ankle pain

Associated Symptoms	Possible Diagnosis	Distinguishing Features
	Ankylosing spondylitis *Inflammation of the joints between the spine and the pelvis*	Initially, pain and stiffness in the lower back and hips that becomes worse after resting; neck or chest pain; fatigue; possible pain in the hip, knee, and ankle joints; pain in the heel of the foot; eye pain; blurred vision.
	Bone cancer	Pain, tenderness, and swelling in the affected bones and joints, often intensifying at night; a noticeable tumor or mass; increased susceptibility to bone fractures.
	Bone fractures	Pain in the affected bone which intensifies with movement or the application of pressure; swelling, bruising, or bleeding around the site of an injury; in a compound fracture, protrusion of bone through skin; possible loss of function or feeling in the injured area; local deformity.
	Bursitis *Inflammation of the bursas, the lubricant-filled sacs in and around the joints*	Pain and swelling around a joint, usually the elbow, knee, or shoulder; painful movement in the affected joint; possibly, fever.
	Dislocations/subluxations	Deformity of the affected joint; joint pain and tenderness; difficulty moving a joint; swelling and stiffness within 30 minutes after joint injury.
	Gout	Most commonly affects the joints of the big toe. Affected joints are red, swollen, hot, and severely painful. In late stages, joint deformity. Kidney stones.
	Infectious arthritis	Pain, swelling, stiffness, and redness, usually in one joint. Fever. Severity varies from a mild ache to severe, debilitating pain and eventual joint deformity.
	Osteoarthritis *Degeneration of the cartilage that lines the joints*	Pain, swelling, and stiffness in one or more joints; enlargement and distortion of affected joints.
	Osteomalacia and Rickets *Softening and weakening of the bones, usually due to poor calcification*	Bone pain, especially in the neck, legs, hips and ribs. Muscle weakness, numbness, or spasms in the hands, feet, and throat; increased susceptibility to bone fractures.
	Peripheral vascular disease *Narrowing of blood vessels in the legs or arms*	Muscle pain on one or both legs that occurs with exercise and subsides with rest; possible pain in the fingers, arms, buttocks, lower back, or the arch of the foot; impotence. Severe symptoms include: muscle pain at rest that intensifies at night; discolored or blue toes; cold or numb feet; open sores; heightened sensitivity to cold; weak or absent pulse in the affected limb; scaly or hairless skin over the affected area.

Ankle pain *continued*

Associated Symptoms	Possible Diagnosis	Distinguishing Features
	Rheumatoid arthritis	Fatigue and weakness; joint pain, stiffness, and inflammation, especially in the hands, feet, and arms; joint deformity; dry mouth; dry, painful eyes. Morning stiffness.
	Rheumatoid arthritis, juvenile	Fever; rash; abdominal pain; weight loss; swelling, stiffness, and pain in the affected joints; enlarged lymph glands; fatigue; pallor; red, painful eyes; morning stiffness.
	Sprains and strains	Swelling, pain or tenderness in the affected joints; impaired joint function.
	Tendinitis *Inflammation of a tendon*	Pain and tenderness over a tendon anywhere in the body; if involved tendon is near or part of a joint, restricted movement of the joint.

Ankles swollen Edema

Associated Symptoms	Possible Diagnosis	Distinguishing Features
with shortness of breath	Amyloidosis *Accumulation of amyloid, a starchy protein, in tissues and organs*	Symptoms vary greatly depending on the body parts affected and may include heart palpitations; shortness of breath; swelling of the legs; diarrhea; abdominal pain; raised spots on the armpits, groin, face, and neck; fatigue and weakness; numbness of the hands or feet; dizziness on standing; joint pains.
	Chronic obstructive pulmonary disease	Shortness of breath; wheezing; persistent, mucus-producing cough, especially in the morning; possibly, chest pain, swollen legs and ankles.
	Congestive heart failure	Shortness of breath; fatigue; need to sleep on several pillows; weakness; cough; heart palpitations; swelling in the legs, ankles, and abdomen; frequent urination at night; indigestion; nausea and vomiting; loss of appetite.
	Glomerulonephritis, acute *Sudden or intense inflammation of the glomeruli, tiny structures that filter blood in the kidneys*	Blood in the urine; passing only small amounts of urine; swelling of the ankles or the tissues around the eyes; shortness of breath; possibly, fatigue, nausea and vomiting, loss of appetite, itching, headaches, fever, impaired vision.
	Glomerulonephritis, chronic *Persistent inflammation of the glomeruli, tiny structures that filter blood in the kidneys*	Blood in the urine; passing only small amounts of urine; swelling of the ankles or the tissues around the eyes; shortness of breath; possibly, fatigue, nausea and vomiting, loss of appetite, itching, headaches, fever, impaired vision.
	Nephrotic syndrome *Damage to the filtering units of the kidneys*	Swelling in the ankles and around the eyes; weight gain, due to fluid retention throughout the body; shortness of breath; passing only small amounts of urine that has an unusually foamy appearance; fatigue; diarrhea; loss of appetite.
	Pericarditis *Inflammation of the membrane surrounding the heart*	Sharp chest pain that may spread to the neck and shoulders; pain may be relieved by sitting up and leaning forward; swollen legs and abdomen; breathing difficulty; chills; fever; fatigue.
	Renal failure, acute *Severe kidney failure*	Initially, decreased urine output, weight gain and swelling due to edema, loss of appetite, nausea and vomiting, fatigue. If untreated, confusion, seizures, and drowsiness.
	Renal failure, chronic *Persistent, mild kidney failure*	Asymptomatic in early stages. Possibly, mental confusion; shortness of breath; abdominal pain; decreased sex drive; fatigue; muscle and bone pain; numbness in the legs and feet; headache; impaired mental acuity; bad breath.

Ankles swollen Edema *continued*

Associated Symptoms	Possible Diagnosis	Distinguishing Features
with shortness of breath *continued*	Systemic lupus erythematosus *Inflammation of connective tissues throughout the body*	Red, blotchy, butterfly-shaped rash on the cheeks and bridge of the nose; fatigue; fever; loss of appetite and weight; nausea; joint and abdominal pain; headaches; blurred vision; increased sensitivity to sun exposure; depression; psychosis; mental confusion.
without shortness of breath	Bone fractures	Pain in the affected bone which intensifies with movement or the application of pressure; swelling, bruising, or bleeding around the site of an injury; in a compound fracture, protrusion of bone through skin; possible loss of function or feeling in the injured area; local deformity.
	Cirrhosis *Chronic damage to the cells of the liver*	No symptoms in early stages; loss of weight and appetite; nausea; swollen legs, ankles and abdomen; itching; jaundice; black stools; vomiting blood; fatigue; impotence; memory loss; confusion.
	Dislocations/subluxations	Deformity of the affected joint; joint pain and tenderness; difficulty moving a joint; swelling and stiffness within 30 minutes after joint injury.
	Gout	Most commonly affects the joints of the big toe. Affected joints are red, swollen, hot, and severely painful. In late stages, joint deformity. Kidney stones.
	Sprains and strains	Swelling, pain or tenderness in the affected joints; impaired joint function.
	Thrombophlebitis *Inflammation associated with a blood clot*	Redness, swelling, pain, and tenderness in the affected area; most often occurs in the leg; swelling of the affected leg; prominent superficial veins around affected area; possibly, fever.
	Varicose veins	Blue or purplish, knotted veins, usually in the legs; itching or discomfort in the affected area; swollen feet and ankles. Possible scaly skin, muscle cramps, or skin ulcers.

Anxiety

Associated Symptoms	Possible Diagnosis	Distinguishing Features
	Anxiety states	Sudden attacks of unreasonable fear and panic; rapid heartbeat or palpitations; perspiration; dry mouth; irritability; muscle tension; trembling; palpitations; shortness of breath; restlessness; poor concentration; insomnia; fatigue; weakness.
	Chronic obstructive pulmonary disease	Shortness of breath; wheezing; persistent, mucus-producing cough, especially in the morning; possibly, chest pain, swollen legs and ankles.
	Congestive heart failure	Shortness of breath; fatigue; need to sleep on several pillows; weakness; cough; heart palpitations; swelling in the legs, ankles, and abdomen; frequent urination at night; indigestion; nausea and vomiting; loss of appetite.
	Hyperthyroidism *Overactivity of the thyroid gland*	Protruding eyes; weight loss despite increased appetite; intolerance to heat; excessive perspiration; nervousness or restlessness; possibly, swelling in the neck (goiter); palpitations; tremor; diarrhea.
	Hypoglycemia *Low blood sugar*	Anxiety; hunger; trembling; headache; palpitations; perspiration; confusion; irritability; loss of coordination; possibly, double vision, seizures, or coma.
	Myocardial infarction *Heart attack*	Sudden chest pain or pressure that may spread to the arm, shoulder and jaw; excessive perspiration; shortness of breath. Possible nausea and vomiting.
	Pheochromocytoma *Tumor in central part of the adrenal, the glands above the kidneys*	Headaches, sometimes severe; rapid heartbeat or heart palpitations; excessive perspiration; faintness, especially when standing up; chest pain; abdominal pain; constipation; weight loss; nervousness, irritability, or anxiety; mental confusion or psychosis.
	Pulmonary edema *An accumulation of fluid in the lungs*	Severe shortness of breath; rapid breathing; pallor; excessive perspiration; bluish nails and lips; cough with frothy sputum; wheezing; anxiety and restlessness.
	Pulmonary embolism *A blood clot travelling from legs or heart that lodges in an artery supplying the lungs*	Sudden shortness of breath and severe breathing difficulty; chest pain worse on inspiration; rapid heartbeat; cough, possibly with bloody sputum; wheezing; excessive perspiration.
	Rabies	Low-grade fever; headache; loss of appetite; tingling at site of animal bite; intense thirst exacerbated by the inability to drink without violent, painful throat spasms; paralysis of facial muscles; drooling. Agitation and violent behavior, confusion, convulsions, coma.

Appetite loss Anorexia

Associated Symptoms	Possible Diagnosis	Distinguishing Features
	Ankylosing spondylitis *Inflammation of the joints between the spine and the pelvis*	Initially, pain and stiffness in the lower back and hips that becomes worse after resting; neck or chest pain; fatigue; possible pain in the hip, knee, and ankle joints; pain in the heel of the foot; eye pain; blurred vision.
	Hepatitis, chronic	Fatigue; nausea; vomiting; loss of appetite; jaundice; dark urine; clay-colored stools; depression; pain or discomfort in the upper right abdomen; abdominal swelling; fever; in women, cessation of menstruation, acne, and the appearance of male pattern facial hair.
	Lymphoma, Hodgkin's *Cancer of the lymph nodes and lymphoid tissue*	Painless swelling of the lymph nodes usually in the neck or armpits; loss of appetite; night sweats.
	Lymphoma, non-Hodgkin's *Cancer of the lymph nodes and lymphoid tissue*	Painless swelling of lymph nodes in the neck or groin; possible abdominal pain, vomiting of blood, headache.
	Renal failure, acute *Severe kidney failure*	Initially, decreased urine output, weight gain and swelling due to edema, loss of appetite, nausea and vomiting, fatigue. If untreated, confusion, seizures, and drowsiness.
	Tuberculosis	Often, asymptomatic. Possibly, low-grade fever; excessive perspiration; cough producing sputum or blood; weight loss; chronic fatigue; chest pain; shortness of breath; night sweats.
with abdominal pain	Appendicitis, acute	Pain near the navel, spreading to the lower right abdomen; nausea and vomiting; constipation; possibly diarrhea; low-grade fever; loss of appetite.
	Colorectal cancer *A growth of malignant cells in the colon or rectum*	Change in bowel habits; diarrhea; constipation; narrow stools; bloody or dark stools; lower abdominal pain; bloating; cramps; gas; loss of weight and appetite; fatigue and heart palpitations due to anemia.
	Crohn's disease *Inflammation of the lining of the small intestine*	Episodes of abdominal pain or cramps in lower abdomen; nausea; diarrhea; loss of weight and appetite; possibly, fever; rectal bleeding or blood in stools; fatigue; anal fissures; joint pains; inflammation of the eyes.
	Hepatitis, acute viral	Fever; fatigue; loss of appetite; aching muscles and joints; abdominal pain or discomfort; jaundice; dark urine and pale stools.
	Kidney cancer	Blood in the urine; abdominal and lower back pain; low-grade fever; fatigue; nausea and vomiting; loss of weight and appetite.

Appetite loss Anorexia *continued*

Associated Symptoms	Possible Diagnosis	Distinguishing Features
with abdominal pain *continued*	Leukemias	Symptoms vary depending on the type of leukemia and may include: loss of appetite and weight; increased bruising and bleeding; bone pain, especially in the legs; abdominal pain and distention; nausea; heart palpitations; severe fatigue; pallor; breathing difficulty; fever; night sweats; headache; enlarged lymph nodes; joint pains (due to gout).
	Liver tumors	Pain or discomfort in the upper right portion of the abdomen; abdominal swelling; loss of weight and appetite; nausea and vomiting; fever; excessive perspiration; jaundice; pallor; severe fatigue.
	Megacolon *Distention of the colon*	Severe constipation; abdominal bloating; loss of weight and appetite; possible diarrhea; in newborns, failure to pass a stool within 48 hours after birth; in children, slow growth from infancy to age five.
	Mesenteric ischemia *A blood clot blocking blood flow to the intestine*	Severe abdominal cramping, usually around the navel, that is exacerbated by eating and alleviated by fasting. Possibly, bloody stools.
	Pancreatic cancer	Often, no symptoms until far advanced. Upper abdominal pain which spreads to the back; loss of weight and appetite; jaundice; nausea, vomiting, and indigestion; diarrhea; fatigue; depression.
	Pelvic inflammatory disease	Initially, lower pelvic pain; pain during intercourse; irregular menstrual bleeding; vaginal discharge with abnormal color or odor; low-grade fever; chills; frequent urination; fatigue; loss of appetite; later, severe abdominal pain and high fever.
	Stomach cancer	Discomfort in the upper abdomen; black, tarry stools; vomiting of blood; loss of appetite and weight; vomiting after meals.
	Tapeworm infestation	Often asymptomatic. Unexplained weight loss; presence of white eggs or ribbon-like segments of worm in the stool, bedding, or clothing; symptoms of pernicious anemia.
with rash/spots	AIDS *Acquired immunodeficiency syndrome*	Recurrent infections affecting the skin and respiratory system; cough; shortness of breath; loss of appetite; weight loss; fatigue; diarrhea; fever; dementia; malignant skin lesions; swollen lymph glands throughout the body; purplish skin nodules; memory loss; confusion; personality changes.

Appetite loss Anorexia *continued*

Associated Symptoms	Possible Diagnosis	Distinguishing Features
with rash/spots *continued*	Measles	Cough; fever; watery nasal discharge; loss of appetite; red, watering eyes; sore throat; body aches; red, slightly itchy rash that gradually spreads all over the body.
	Rocky Mountain spotted fever	Within a week after exposure, high fever, loss of appetite, headache, muscle aches, nausea and vomiting; dry cough; sensitivity to light. Within six days, the appearance of small pink spots on wrists and ankles, eventually spreading over the entire body, where they then grow, darken in color, and bleed.
	Sarcoidosis *Accumulation of inflammatory cells in the lymph nodes and other tissues throughout the body*	Often no symptoms. Swollen lymph nodes in the neck or armpits; muscle aches; fever; breathing difficulty; possibly, purple rash on the face; reddish skin; bumps on the legs; numbness; joint pain or stiffness; a painful, red eye; blurred vision; loss of appetite and weight.
	Syphilis	Initially, painless, ulcerated, red sore on the genitals, mouth, or rectum; swollen glands in the neck, armpit, or groin; rash with small, red, scaly bumps; fever; headache. If left untreated, damage to heart valves leading to congestive heart failure; mental deterioration; loss of balance; seizures; dementia; personality changes.
	Systemic lupus erythematosus *Inflammation of connective tissues throughout the body*	Red, blotchy, butterfly-shaped rash on the cheeks and bridge of the nose; fatigue; fever; loss of appetite and weight; nausea; joint and abdominal pain; headaches; blurred vision; increased sensitivity to sun exposure; depression; psychosis; mental confusion.
	Typhoid fever	Headache; fever, loss of appetite; abdominal pain and tenderness; extreme weakness; constipation followed by diarrhea; drowsiness, stupor, or coma; raised, pink skin eruptions on the chest and abdomen; joint aches; sore throat.
with swollen legs/ankles (edema)	Cirrhosis *Chronic damage to the cells of the liver*	No symptoms in early stages; loss of weight and appetite; nausea; swollen legs, ankles and abdomen; itching; jaundice; black stools; vomiting blood; fatigue; impotence; memory loss; confusion.
	Glomerulonephritis, acute *Sudden or intense inflammation of the glomeruli, tiny structures that filter blood in the kidneys*	Blood in the urine; passing only small amounts of urine; swelling of the ankles or the tissues around the eyes; shortness of breath; possibly, fatigue, nausea and vomiting, loss of appetite, itching, headaches, fever, impaired vision.

Appetite loss Anorexia *continued*

Associated Symptoms	Possible Diagnosis	Distinguishing Features
with swollen legs/ankles *continued*	Glomerulonephritis, chronic *Persistent inflammation of the glomeruli, tiny structures that filter blood in the kidneys*	Blood in the urine; passing only small amounts of urine; swelling of the ankles or the tissues around the eyes; shortness of breath; possibly, fatigue, nausea and vomiting, loss of appetite, itching, headaches, fever, impaired vision.
	Nephrotic syndrome *Damage to the filtering units of the kidneys*	Swelling in the ankles and around the eyes; weight gain, due to fluid retention throughout the body; shortness of breath; passing only small amounts of urine that has an unusually foamy appearance; fatigue; diarrhea; loss of appetite.
	Renal failure, chronic *Persistent, mild kidney failure*	Asymptomatic in early stages. Possibly, mental confusion; shortness of breath; abdominal pain; decreased sex drive; fatigue; muscle and bone pain; numbness in the legs and feet; headache; impaired mental acuity; bad breath.
with headache	Anemia, folic acid deficiency	Fatigue and weakness; pallor; shortness of breath, heart palpitations, or noticeably rapid heartbeat on exertion; sore, red, and glazed looking tongue; loss of weight and appetite; nausea and diarrhea; abdominal distention.
	Anemia, pernicious	Fatigue; inability to concentrate; sore, red tongue; weakness; dizziness; pallor; shortness of breath on exertion; palpitations; numbness and tingling in extremities; incoordination; headache; loss of weight and appetite; possibly, jaundice.
	Hydrocephalus *Overaccumulation of cerebrospinal fluid, the liquid surrounding the brain*	In infants, an enlarged head, rigidity of the legs, irritability, projectile vomiting, drowsiness, seizures, and lethargy. In older persons, headache, vomiting, loss of coordination, deterioration of mental faculties, speech difficulty, and loss of appetite.
	Influenza *Flu*	Chills, muscle aches, and loss of appetite followed by a cough, sore throat, nasal congestion, and fever; possible chest pain.
	Mononucleosis, infectious	Headache; high fever; swollen glands in the neck, groin, and armpits; severe sore throat; swallowing difficulty.
	Rabies	Low-grade fever; headache; loss of appetite; tingling at site of animal bite; intense thirst exacerbated by the inability to drink without violent, painful throat spasms; paralysis of facial muscles; drooling. Agitation and violent behavior, confusion, convulsions, coma.

Appetite, voracious Polyphagia

Associated Symptoms	Possible Diagnosis	Distinguishing Features
	Diabetes mellitus *Insufficiency of or resistance to insulin*	Fatigue; excessive thirst; frequent urination; weight loss despite increased appetite; blurred vision; numbness and tingling of feet and hands; impotence.
	Hyperthyroidism *Overactivity of the thyroid gland*	Protruding eyes; weight loss despite increased appetite; intolerance to heat; excessive perspiration; nervousness or restlessness; possibly, swelling in the neck (goiter); palpitations; tremor; diarrhea.
	Hypoglycemia *Low blood sugar*	Anxiety; hunger; trembling; headache; palpitations; perspiration; confusion; irritability; loss of coordination; possibly, double vision, seizures, or coma.
	Tapeworm infestation	Often asymptomatic. Unexplained weight loss; presence of white eggs or ribbon-like segments of worm in the stool, bedding, or clothing; symptoms of pernicious anemia.

Arm pain

Associated Symptoms	Possible Diagnosis	Distinguishing Features
	Bone cancer	Pain, tenderness, and swelling in the affected bones and joints, often intensifying at night; a noticeable tumor or mass; increased susceptibility to bone fractures.
	Bone fractures	Pain in the affected bone which intensifies with movement or the application of pressure; swelling, bruising, or bleeding around the site of an injury; in a compound fracture, protrusion of bone through skin; possible loss of function or feeling in the injured area; local deformity.
	Bursitis *Inflammation of the bursas, the lubricant-filled sacs in and around the joints*	Pain and swelling around a joint, usually the elbow, knee, or shoulder; painful movement in the affected joint; possibly, fever.
	Carpal tunnel syndrome	Numbness, tingling, and pain in the hand and wrist, often intensifying at night; weakness of the fingers and hand.
	Dislocations/subluxations	Deformity of the affected joint; joint pain and tenderness; difficulty moving a joint; swelling and stiffness within 30 minutes after joint injury.
	Hypoparathyroidism *Underactivity of the parathyroid glands*	Numbness and tingling and painful, cramp-like spasms of the face, hands, arms, and feet; cataracts; possible seizures.
	Infectious arthritis	Pain, swelling, stiffness, and redness, usually in one joint. Fever. Severity varies from a mild ache to severe, debilitating pain and eventual joint deformity.
	Intervertebral disk, herniated	Severe lower back or neck pain that is exacerbated by movement or lifting heavy objects, sneezing, coughing, straining at stool. Pain, tingling, or numbness in a leg or an arm, usually on one side.
	Myocardial infarction *Heart attack*	Sudden chest pain or pressure that may spread to the arm, shoulder and jaw; excessive perspiration; shortness of breath. Possible nausea and vomiting.
	Osteoarthritis *Degeneration of the cartilage that lines the joints*	Pain, swelling, and stiffness in one or more joints; enlargement and distortion of affected joints.
	Osteomalacia and Rickets *Softening and weakening of the bones, usually due to poor calcification*	Bone pain, especially in the neck, legs, hips and ribs. Muscle weakness, numbness, or spasms in the hands, feet, and throat; increased susceptibility to bone fractures.

Arm pain *continued*

Associated Symptoms	Possible Diagnosis	Distinguishing Features
	Osteomyelitis *Infection of bone and bone marrow*	Fever; severe pain in the affected bone; inflammation and swelling of the skin over the affected area; deformity. In children, arrested growth of the affected bone.
	Peripheral vascular disease *Narrowing of blood vessels in the legs or arms*	Muscle pain on one or both legs that occurs with exercise and subsides with rest; possible pain in the fingers, arms, buttocks, lower back, or the arch of the foot; impotence. Severe symptoms include: muscle pain at rest that intensifies at night; discolored or blue toes; cold or numb feet; open sores; heightened sensitivity to cold; weak or absent pulse in the affected limb; scaly or hairless skin over the affected area.
	Rheumatoid arthritis	Fatigue and weakness; joint pain, stiffness, and inflammation, especially in the hands, feet, and arms; joint deformity; dry mouth; dry, painful eyes. Morning stiffness.
	Rotator cuff injury	Pain in the shoulder; difficulty raising and lowering the arm; recurring dull ache in the shoulder; pain after sleeping on the shoulder; shoulder weakness.
	Sprains and strains	Swelling, pain or tenderness in the affected joints; impaired joint function.
	Tendinitis *Inflammation of a tendon*	Pain and tenderness over a tendon anywhere in the body; if involved tendon is near or part of a joint, restricted movement of the joint.

Back pain

Associated Symptoms	Possible Diagnosis	Distinguishing Features
with abdominal pain/discomfort	Aortic aneurysm *A sac-like ballooning at a weak spot in the wall of the aorta, the body's primary artery*	Usually asymptomatic; occasionally, severe abdominal and back pain; chest pain; swallowing difficulty; dizziness and fainting; hoarseness; cough.
	Bladder infection *Cystitis*	Burning during urination; frequent and urgent urination with only small amounts of urine passed; blood in the urine; lower abdominal pain; low-grade fever; pain during sexual intercourse and, in men, during ejaculation.
	Bladder stones	Interruption of urine stream; inability to urinate except in certain positions; frequent and urgent urination with only small amounts of urine passed; blood in the urine; pain in the genitals, lower back, or abdomen; low-grade fever.
	Cervical cancer	Initially, asymptomatic. In later stages, unexpected vaginal bleeding or discharge between periods, after intercourse, or after menopause. If untreated, pelvic pain.
	Cervical disorders, non-malignant	Vaginal discharge; vaginal burning and itching; vaginal bleeding after intercourse, between periods, or after bowel movements.
	Disseminated intravascular coagulation *Bleeding disorder marked by excessive and inappropriate blood coagulation*	Abnormal bleeding possibly at several sites at once; vomiting blood; bloody or black stools; abnormal vaginal bleeding; blood in the urine; severe abdominal or back pain; possibly, convulsions, or coma.
	Endometriosis *The migration of the uterine lining to other reproductive or abdominal organs*	Pain in the lower abdomen, vagina, and lower back beginning just prior to menses and intensifying after blood flow has ceased; heavy bleeding during periods; pain during intercourse; diarrhea; constipation; pain during bowel movements; bleeding from the rectum; bloody urine during menses; nausea and vomiting prior to menses; infertility.
	Fibroids, uterine *Benign growths of the muscular wall of the uterus*	Heavier or prolonged bleeding during menses; abdominal discomfort; lower back pain; pressure on the bladder and frequent urination; constipation. Possible, sharp, sudden, lower abdominal pain.
	Gallbladder disorders	Moderate to severe pain in the upper right side of the abdomen, chest, upper back, or right shoulder. Pain often follows the ingestion of high-fat foods and is episodic, lasting 20 minutes to several hours. Nausea and vomiting; low-grade fever; belching; heartburn; gas; possibly, jaundice, pale stools, and itchy skin.

Back pain *continued*

Associated Symptoms	Possible Diagnosis	Distinguishing Features
with abdominal pain/discomfort *continued*	Kidney cancer	Blood in the urine; abdominal and lower back pain; low-grade fever; fatigue; nausea and vomiting; loss of weight and appetite.
	Kidney cysts	Pain or tenderness in the lower back or abdomen; blood in the urine. In infants, symmetrical, protruding masses visible in the flanks.
	Pancreatitis *Inflammation of the pancreas*	Sudden, extreme abdominal pain; nausea and vomiting; weakness; fever; clammy skin; abdominal bloating and tenderness.
	Prostate cancer	Difficulty urinating; frequent urination with decreased urine output; pain in the pelvic area and lower back; painful ejaculation or bowel movements.
	Renal calculi *Kidney stones*	Intermittent spasms of pain in the back and flanks, radiating through the lower abdomen towards the groin; nausea and vomiting; blood in the urine; urge to urinate but only small amounts of urine are passed.
	Testicular cancer	Firm, usually painless mass, usually in one testicle. In later stages, a dull ache in the groin or lower abdomen may occur. Possibly, male breast development. In advanced cases, swollen lymph glands; abdominal or back pain; weight loss; breathing difficulty.
	Uterine prolapse	Often asymptomatic. Possibly, difficulty passing urine or stools, pain during intercourse, backache that intensifies when lifting, sensation of heaviness or dragging within the pelvis, painful or heavy menstrual periods, or bleeding between periods. In severe cases, uterus visibly protrudes outside of vagina.
without abdominal pain/discomfort	Ankylosing spondylitis *Inflammation of the joints between the spine and the pelvis*	Initially, pain and stiffness in the lower back and hips that becomes worse after resting; neck or chest pain; fatigue; possible pain in the hip, knee, and ankle joints; pain in the heel of the foot; eye pain; blurred vision.
	Fibromyalgia	Muscle aches, pains, and stiffness; specific points on the body that feel sore when pressed. Fatigue, headaches, and possible insomnia. Feeling unrefreshed upon awakening in the morning.
	Hyperparathyroidism *Overactivity of the parathyroid glands*	Increased susceptibility to bone fractures; depression; indigestion; increased thirst and urine output; fatigue, lethargy; somnolence; muscle weakness; nausea and vomiting; loss of appetite.

Back pain *continued*

Associated Symptoms	Possible Diagnosis	Distinguishing Features
	Intervertebral disk, herniated	Severe lower back or neck pain that is exacerbated by movement or lifting heavy objects, sneezing, coughing, straining at stool. Pain, tingling, or numbness in a leg or an arm, usually on one side.
	Kidney infection *Pyelonephritis*	Sudden fever and shaking chills; severe fatigue; burning and frequent urination; cloudy or bloody urine; lower back pain, sometimes severe; nausea and vomiting.
	Multiple myeloma *Production of malignant plasma cells in the bone marrow*	Bone pain, especially progressive, constant back pain that intensifies with movement; unexplained bone fractures; fatigue; pallor; shortness of breath; increased bleeding, such as bleeding gums or nosebleeds; easily bruised skin; increased susceptibility to infection; headache; vision disturbances; loss of height.
	Obesity	Excess storage of body fat resulting in a body weight 20% or greater than recommended.
	Osteoarthritis *Degeneration of the cartilage that lines the joints*	Pain, swelling, and stiffness in one or more joints; enlargement and distortion of affected joints.
	Osteomalacia and Rickets *Softening and weakening of the bones, usually due to poor calcification*	Bone pain, especially in the neck, legs, hips and ribs. Muscle weakness, numbness, or spasms in the hands, feet, and throat; increased susceptibility to bone fractures.
	Osteomyelitis *Infection of bone and bone marrow*	Fever; severe pain in the affected bone; inflammation and swelling of the skin over the affected area; deformity. In children, arrested growth of the affected bone.
	Osteoporosis *Loss of bone mass due to calcium depletion*	Backache; easily fractured bones, especially in the wrists, hips, and spine; gradual loss of height; stooped or hunched posture.
	Paget's disease *A weakening, thickening, and deformity of the bones*	Often asymptomatic. Possibly, bone pain or deformity, especially bowing of the legs, bent spine, and facial deformity; unexplained bone fractures; joint pain or stiffness; hearing loss; headaches; ringing in ears.
	Pelvic inflammatory disease	Initially, lower pelvic pain; pain during intercourse; irregular menstrual bleeding; vaginal discharge with abnormal color or odor; low-grade fever; chills; frequent urination; fatigue; loss of appetite; later, severe abdominal pain and high fever.
	Scoliosis	Gradual bending of the spine to one side or into an S-shape; shoulders and hips may appear uneven; possible back pain.

Back pain *continued*

Associated Symptoms	Possible Diagnosis	Distinguishing Features
	Spinal cord trauma	Severe pain and swelling in the affected area; loss of sensation, muscle weakness, or paralysis below the site of the injury; urinary or fecal incontinence or retention; impotence; breathing difficulty; shock.
	Spinal stenosis *Narrowing of the spinal canal due to bony overgrowth*	Numbness, pain, and weakness in the legs and back that is exacerbated by walking and alleviated by sitting.
	Spinal tumor	Progressive numbness, tingling, and muscle weakness; fecal or urinary incontinence; persistent back pain.
	Sprains and strains	Swelling, pain or tenderness in the affected joints; impaired joint function.

Bad breath Halitosis

Associated Symptoms	Possible Diagnosis	Distinguishing Features
with mouth pain	Gingivitis	Red-purple gums that are swollen, shiny, and bleed easily; bad breath.
	Impacted teeth	Gum pain; unpleasant taste in mouth, especially when biting down; red, swollen gums around the affected tooth; headache or jaw ache; possibly, bad breath.
	Periodontitis *Inflammation of the tissues supporting the teeth.*	Red, swollen, painful gums that bleed easily; loose teeth; bad breath; possible pus discharge.
	Sinusitis *Inflammation of the mucus membranes lining the sinuses*	Throbbing pain above or below one or both eyes that intensifies when bending the head forward or coughing; nasal congestion; loss of sense of smell; often, pus-like nasal discharge; possible dental pain in the upper jaw; fever.
	Sjögren's syndrome	Dry, itching, burning eyes; sensation of a foreign body under the eyelids; dry mouth; difficulty swallowing; vaginal dryness; dry skin; frequent dental cavities; joint pain; swelling of glands (parotids) in front of the ears; Raynaud's phenomenon.
	Tongue disorders	Symptoms vary depending on the specific disorder and include: dark or bright red, black, or dark brown tongue; sore, swollen, or smooth tongue; hair-like growths on the tongue; adjacent areas of the mouth may be inflamed; ulcers or raised, white patches on the tongue; excessive salivation; swallowing difficulty; bad breath.
	Tooth abscess	Persistent tooth pain; pain when biting or chewing; swollen glands in the neck; earache; fever; possibly, foul taste in the mouth or bad breath.
	Tooth decay	Tooth pain, especially after eating sweet or sour foods; tooth sensitivity to hot and cold; bad breath; unpleasant taste in the mouth.
	Trench mouth	Grayish film on the gums; red, swollen, painful, bleeding gums; bad breath; bad taste in the mouth; pain on swallowing or speaking; excessive salivation.
without mouth pain	Bronchiectasis *Lung condition that stretches and distorts the walls of the bronchial tubes*	Cough that produces dark green sputum; bad breath; possibly, shortness of breath; loss of appetite and weight; clubbed fingers.

Bad breath Halitosis *continued*

Associated Symptoms	Possible Diagnosis	Distinguishing Features
	Diverticular disorders *Swellings in the wall of the colon*	Usually no symptoms unless diverticulae become inflamed. Tenderness or pain in the lower left abdomen relieved by passing stools or gas; constipation or diarrhea; blood in the stool; severe, spasmodic abdominal pain that becomes constant; possibly, fever and nausea.
	Esophageal cancer	Swallowing difficulty and pain; weight loss; drooling; possibly, vomiting or coughing up of bloody mucus, regurgitation of food; chest pain; repeated respiratory infections.
	Intestinal obstruction	Abdominal pain and cramps; nausea; vomiting; weakness; gas; abdominal bloating; possible diarrhea; progressive constipation culminating in inability to pass stools or gas.
	Lung abscess	Cough producing foul-smelling sputum; bad breath; fever; chills; weight loss; possible chest pain.
	Pharyngitis *Inflammation of the pharynx, the part of the throat between the mouth and the esophagus*	Sore or red throat; speaking and swallowing difficulties; sensitive, swollen glands in the neck; fever; headache; possible earache.
	Renal failure, chronic *Persistent, mild kidney failure*	Asymptomatic in early stages. Possibly, mental confusion; shortness of breath; abdominal pain; decreased sex drive; fatigue; muscle and bone pain; numbness in the legs and feet; headache; impaired mental acuity; bad breath.

Behavior abnormalities/changes

Associated Symptoms	Possible Diagnosis	Distinguishing Features
	Adrenal insufficiency *Inadequate production of steroid hormones by the adrenal glands*	Loss of weight and appetite; fatigue; weakness; darkening of the skin; abdominal pain; diarrhea; indigestion; nausea and vomiting; constipation; lack of sex drive; dizziness when rising from sitting or lying position.
	AIDS *Acquired immunodeficiency syndrome*	Recurrent infections affecting the skin and respiratory system; cough; shortness of breath; loss of appetite; weight loss; fatigue; diarrhea; fever; dementia; malignant skin lesions; swollen lymph glands throughout the body; purplish skin nodules; memory loss; confusion; personality changes.
	Alzheimer's disease	Symptoms vary greatly in different individuals. Initially, minor forgetfulness gradually developing into severe, short-term memory loss, disorientation, an inability to concentrate, and sudden mood and personality changes. In later stages, severe confusion, possible hallucinations or paranoid delusions, loss of social and sexual inhibitions, impaired judgment, anxiety, depression, agitation and combativeness, wandering and getting lost, inability to write, urinary and fecal incontinence.
	Anemia, pernicious	Fatigue; inability to concentrate; sore, red tongue; weakness; dizziness; pallor; shortness of breath on exertion; palpitations; numbness and tingling in extremities; incoordination; headache; loss of weight and appetite; possibly, jaundice.
	Anxiety states	Sudden attacks of unreasonable fear and panic; rapid heartbeat or palpitations; perspiration; dry mouth; irritability; muscle tension; trembling; palpitations; shortness of breath; restlessness; poor concentration; insomnia; fatigue; weakness.
	Brain tumors	Headaches that become more severe when reclining; nausea and vomiting; memory loss; double vision; muscle weakness; numbness, tingling, or partial paralysis; vision loss; speech disturbances; seizures; drowsiness.
	Cushing's syndrome	Red, oval-shaped face; humped upper back and obese trunk; acne; purple stretch marks on the abdomen, thighs, and breasts; thin and easily bruised skin; easily fractured bones; depression or euphoria; insomnia; fatigue; muscle weakness; hirsutism (in women).
	Hydrocephalus *Overaccumulation of cerebrospinal fluid, the liquid surrounding the brain*	In infants, an enlarged head, rigidity of the legs, irritability, projectile vomiting, drowsiness, seizures, and lethargy. In older persons, headache, vomiting, loss of coordination, deterioration of mental faculties, speech difficulty, and loss of appetite.

Behavior abnormalities/changes *continued*

Associated Symptoms	Possible Diagnosis	Distinguishing Features
	Hyperparathyroidism *Overactivity of the parathyroid glands*	Increased susceptibility to bone fractures; depression; indigestion; increased thirst and urine output; fatigue, lethargy; somnolence; muscle weakness; nausea and vomiting; loss of appetite.
	Hypoglycemia *Low blood sugar*	Anxiety; hunger; trembling; headache; palpitations; perspiration; confusion; irritability; loss of coordination; possibly, double vision, seizures, or coma.
	Hypopituitarism *Underactivity of the pituitary gland*	Intolerance to cold; chronic headaches; decreased sex drive; fatigue; fine wrinkles around the eyes and mouth; dry skin; extreme thirst and excessive urination; loss of appetite; vaginal dryness; absence of milk production in new mothers; in men, reduced muscular strength, shrinking of the testes, and loss of body hair; growth retardation in children and adolescents
	Renal failure, acute *Severe kidney failure*	Initially, decreased urine output, weight gain and swelling due to edema, loss of appetite, nausea and vomiting, fatigue. If untreated, confusion, seizures, and drowsiness.
	Stroke	Symptoms vary with the location of brain injury. Sudden onset of weakness, paralysis, or loss of sensation, usually on one side of the body; a sudden heaviness in a limb; speech abnormalities; headache; vision disturbances; dizziness; confusion; coma; urinary and fecal incontinence.
	Syphilis	Initially, painless, ulcerated, red sore on the genitals, mouth, or rectum; swollen glands in the neck, armpit, or groin; rash with small, red, scaly bumps; fever; headache. If left untreated, damage to heart valves leading to congestive heart failure; mental deterioration; loss of balance; seizures; dementia; personality changes.
	Systemic lupus erythematosus *Inflammation of connective tissues throughout the body*	Red, blotchy, butterfly-shaped rash on the cheeks and bridge of the nose; fatigue; fever; loss of appetite and weight; nausea; joint and abdominal pain; headaches; blurred vision; increased sensitivity to sun exposure; depression; psychosis; mental confusion.
	Wilson's disease *An accumulation of copper in the liver, brain, and other tissues*	Anemia; fluid accumulation in the abdomen; vomiting blood; progressive intellectual impairment; tremor; weakness; walking difficulty; rigidity of limbs; personality changes; speech difficulties; dementia.

Belching/burping Eructation

Associated Symptoms	Possible Diagnosis	Distinguishing Features
	Colorectal cancer *A growth of malignant cells in the colon or rectum*	Change in bowel habits; diarrhea; constipation; narrow stools; bloody or dark stools; lower abdominal pain; bloating; cramps; gas; loss of weight and appetite; fatigue and heart palpitations due to anemia.
	Esophageal cancer	Swallowing difficulty and pain; weight loss; drooling; possibly, vomiting or coughing up of bloody mucus, regurgitation of food; chest pain; repeated respiratory infections.
	Esophageal stricture *Narrowing of the esophagus, the passageway from the mouth to the stomach*	Sudden or gradual decrease in the ability to swallow solid food or liquids; chest pain after eating; regurgitation of food and liquids; increased salivation; weight loss. Aspiration into lungs can cause cough, wheezing, shortness of breath.
	Gallbladder disorders	Moderate to severe pain in the upper right side of the abdomen, chest, upper back, or right shoulder. Pain often follows the ingestion of high-fat foods and is episodic, lasting 20 minutes to several hours. Nausea and vomiting; low-grade fever; belching; heartburn; gas; possibly, jaundice, pale stools, and itchy skin.
	Gastroesophageal reflux *Heartburn*	Burning sensation in the middle of the chest; pain and difficulty swallowing; slight regurgitation of stomach's contents into the mouth, especially when reclining or bending forward; mild abdominal pain.
	Hiatal hernia *Protrusion of a portion of the stomach through the diaphragm, into the chest cavity*	Often asymptomatic. Possibly, heartburn after meals or when bending forward or reclining. Belching, regurgitation.
	Peptic ulcer	Intermittent, burning or gnawing pain in the upper abdomen or lower chest; indigestion; loss of appetite and weight. Pain may be relieved by eating or antacids. Possible nausea and vomiting. Black, tarry stools, vomiting blood.

Bleeding gums

Associated Symptoms	Possible Diagnosis	Distinguishing Features
	Anemia, aplastic	Fatigue and weakness; shortness of breath; heart palpitations; pallor; bleeding gums; nosebleeds; tendency to bruise easily; small red dots under the skin (petechiae). Increased susceptibility to infection.
	Cirrhosis *Chronic damage to the cells of the liver*	No symptoms in early stages; loss of weight and appetite; nausea; swollen legs, ankles and abdomen; itching; jaundice; black stools; vomiting blood; fatigue; impotence; memory loss; confusion.
	Gingivitis	Red-purple gums that are swollen, shiny, and bleed easily; bad breath.
	Hemophilia	Profuse bleeding from minor injuries and tooth extractions; internal bleeding that may cause blood in the urine; bleeding into joints; symptoms of stroke due to intracerebral bleeding; possibly, extensive bruising.
	Leukemias	Symptoms vary depending on the type of leukemia and may include: loss of appetite and weight; increased bruising and bleeding; bone pain, especially in the legs; abdominal pain and distention; nausea; heart palpitations; severe fatigue; pallor; breathing difficulty; fever; night sweats; headache; enlarged lymph nodes; joint pains (due to gout).
	Multiple myeloma *Production of malignant plasma cells in the bone marrow*	Bone pain, especially progressive, constant back pain that intensifies with movement; unexplained bone fractures; fatigue; pallor; shortness of breath; increased bleeding, such as bleeding gums or nosebleeds; easily bruised skin; increased susceptibility to infection; headache; vision disturbances; loss of height.
	Periodontitis *Inflammation of the tissues supporting the teeth.*	Red, swollen, painful gums that bleed easily; loose teeth; bad breath; possible pus discharge.
	Platelet function disorders	Minor bleeding in the mouth or just beneath the surface of the skin, often appearing as clusters of small, pinpoint-sized red specks; frequent nosebleeds; easy bruising; prolonged menstrual periods; fatigue; pallor; dark-colored stools.
	Trench mouth	Grayish film on the gums; red, swollen, painful, bleeding gums; bad breath; bad taste in the mouth; pain on swallowing or speaking; excessive salivation.
	Von Willebrand's disease *Chronic bleeding disorder*	Frequent nosebleeds; excessive bleeding from cuts; bleeding gums; easy bruising; abnormal or excessive menstrual bleeding; blood in the stool.

Blemishes/skin discolorations

Associated Symptoms	Possible Diagnosis	Distinguishing Features
	Acne	Blackheads, whiteheads, pimples, pustules, or cysts usually on the face, chest, back, shoulders, and neck. May result in pockmarks and scarring.
	Adrenal insufficiency *Inadequate production of steroid hormones by the adrenal glands*	Loss of weight and appetite; fatigue; weakness; darkening of the skin; abdominal pain; diarrhea; indigestion; nausea and vomiting; constipation; lack of sex drive; dizziness when rising from sitting or lying position.
	AIDS *Acquired immunodeficiency syndrome*	Recurrent infections affecting the skin and respiratory system; cough; shortness of breath; loss of appetite; weight loss; fatigue; diarrhea; fever; dementia; malignant skin lesions; swollen lymph glands throughout the body; purplish skin nodules; memory loss; confusion; personality changes.
	Dermatomyositis *Inflammation of the muscles and skin*	Red rash on the cheeks and bridge of the nose; purple discoloration and swelling of the eyelids; areas of thickened skin; muscle weakness and stiffness, usually in the shoulders and pelvis; cold hands and feet; speaking or swallowing difficulty; fever; weight loss.
	Hemochromatosis *An excess accumulation of iron in the liver, pancreas, heart, testes, skin, and other organs*	A bronze or slate-grey tone to skin that is normally fair; chronic abdominal pain; heart palpitations; joint pain; drowsiness; confusion. In men, a decrease in the size of the testes, loss of sexual desire, and impotence.
	Hepatitis, chronic	Fatigue; nausea; vomiting; loss of appetite; jaundice; dark urine; clay-colored stools; depression; pain or discomfort in the upper right abdomen; abdominal swelling; fever; in women, cessation of menstruation, acne, and the appearance of male pattern facial hair.
	Polycythemia vera *An overproduction of red and white blood cells and platelets*	Headache; blurred vision; flushed skin; itching; dizziness; fatigue; night sweats; shortness of breath; weight loss.
	Scleroderma	Shiny, tight, and hardened skin, especially on the fingers, arms, and face; hands or feet may successively turn blue, white, and red upon exposure to cold (Raynaud's phenomenon); swallowing difficulty; bloating after eating; weight loss; shortness of breath on exertion; high blood pressure; symptoms of renal failure. Possibly, heartburn, muscle aches and weakness, joint pain, fever, or fatigue.
	Vitiligo *Loss of skin pigmentation*	White or abnormally pale patches of skin, usually on the face, hands, armpits, and groin.

Blood in the urine

Associated Symptoms	Possible Diagnosis	Distinguishing Features
with urinary difficulty or incontinence	Appendicitis, acute	Pain near the navel, spreading to the lower right abdomen; nausea and vomiting; constipation; possibly diarrhea; low-grade fever; loss of appetite.
	Bladder cancer	Blood in the urine; painful and frequent urination; pelvic pain; feeling of pressure in the back; persistent fever; urinary incontinence.
	Bladder infection *Cystitis*	Burning during urination; frequent and urgent urination with only small amounts of urine passed; blood in the urine; lower abdominal pain; low-grade fever; pain during sexual intercourse and, in men, during ejaculation.
	Bladder stones	Interruption of urine stream; inability to urinate except in certain positions; frequent and urgent urination with only small amounts of urine passed; blood in the urine; pain in the genitals, lower back, or abdomen; low-grade fever.
	Glomerulonephritis, acute *Sudden or intense inflammation of the glomeruli, tiny structures that filter blood in the kidneys*	Blood in the urine; passing only small amounts of urine; swelling of the ankles or the tissues around the eyes; shortness of breath; possibly, fatigue, nausea and vomiting, loss of appetite, itching, headaches, fever, impaired vision.
	Glomerulonephritis, chronic *Persistent inflammation of the glomeruli, tiny structures that filter blood in the kidneys*	Blood in the urine; passing only small amounts of urine; swelling of the ankles or the tissues around the eyes; shortness of breath; possibly, fatigue, nausea and vomiting, loss of appetite, itching, headaches, fever, impaired vision.
	Kidney cysts	Pain or tenderness in the lower back or abdomen; blood in the urine. In infants, symmetrical, protruding masses visible in the flanks.
	Kidney infection *Pyelonephritis*	Sudden fever and shaking chills; severe fatigue; burning and frequent urination; cloudy or bloody urine; lower back pain, sometimes severe; nausea and vomiting.
	Penile cancer	Sore, ulcer, or wart-like lump on the penis, usually near the head, possibly painful; bleeding or unusual discharge from the penis. Possibly, pain during urination, or enlarged lymph nodes in the groin.
	Prostatic hyperplasia, benign *Prostate enlargement*	Slow or delayed urination; dribbling urine; the need to urinate several times during the night; possibly, pain during urination; blood in the urine.

Blood in the urine *continued*

Associated Symptoms	Possible Diagnosis	Distinguishing Features
with urinary difficulty or incontinence *continued*	Prostatitis *Inflammation of the prostate gland*	Burning during urination; urgent and frequent urination; fever and chills; discharge from the penis; lower abdominal and back pain; blood in the urine.
	Renal calculi *Kidney stones*	Intermittent spasms of pain in the back and flanks, radiating through the lower abdomen towards the groin; nausea and vomiting; blood in the urine; urge to urinate but only small amounts of urine are passed.
	Urethritis *Infection of the urethra, the passageway that drains urine from the bladder*	Frequent and painful urination; blood in the urine; yellow, pus-filled discharge; possible difficulty passing urine; urinary urgency; pain during intercourse; in men, painful ejaculation.
without urinary difficulty or incontinence	Disseminated intravascular coagulation *Bleeding disorder marked by excessive and inappropriate blood coagulation*	Abnormal bleeding possibly at several sites at once; vomiting blood; bloody or black stools; abnormal vaginal bleeding; blood in the urine; severe abdominal or back pain; possibly, convulsions, or coma.
	Endometriosis *The migration of the uterine lining to other reproductive or abdominal organs*	Pain in the lower abdomen, vagina, and lower back beginning just prior to menses and intensifying after blood flow has ceased; heavy bleeding during periods; pain during intercourse; diarrhea; constipation; pain during bowel movements; bleeding from the rectum; bloody urine during menses; nausea and vomiting prior to menses; infertility.
	Hemophilia	Profuse bleeding from minor injuries and tooth extractions; internal bleeding that may cause blood in the urine; bleeding into joints; symptoms of stroke due to intracerebral bleeding; possibly, extensive bruising.
	Kidney cancer	Blood in the urine; abdominal and lower back pain; low-grade fever; fatigue; nausea and vomiting; loss of weight and appetite.
	Renal vein thrombosis *Blood clot in the vein leaving the kidney*	Severe lower back and flank pain, swelling of legs and face from edema.
	Systemic lupus erythematosus *Inflammation of connective tissues throughout the body*	Red, blotchy, butterfly-shaped rash on the cheeks and bridge of the nose; fatigue; fever; loss of appetite and weight; nausea; joint and abdominal pain; headaches; blurred vision; increased sensitivity to sun exposure; depression; psychosis; mental confusion.

Bloody sputum

Associated Symptoms	Possible Diagnosis	Distinguishing Features
with fever	Bronchitis, acute	Shortness of breath; persistent cough producing yellow or green sputum; possibly, chest pain; wheezing; fever.
	Legionnaire's disease	Dry cough progressing to one with blood-streaked sputum; high fever; chills; breathing difficulty; chest pain; headache; muscle aches; diarrhea; nausea; vomiting; mental confusion and disorientation.
	Lung abscess	Cough producing foul-smelling sputum; bad breath; fever; chills; weight loss; possible chest pain.
	Pneumonia	High fever; shortness of breath; cough with sputum; chest pain; fatigue.
	Systemic lupus erythematosus *Inflammation of connective tissues throughout the body*	Red, blotchy, butterfly-shaped rash on the cheeks and bridge of the nose; fatigue; fever; loss of appetite and weight; nausea; joint and abdominal pain; headaches; blurred vision; increased sensitivity to sun exposure; depression; psychosis; mental confusion.
	Tuberculosis	Often, asymptomatic. Possibly, low-grade fever; excessive perspiration; cough producing sputum or blood; weight loss; chronic fatigue; chest pain; shortness of breath; night sweats.
without fever	Aortic aneurysm *A sac-like ballooning at a weak spot in the wall of the aorta, the body's primary artery*	Usually asymptomatic; occasionally, severe abdominal and back pain; chest pain; swallowing difficulty; dizziness and fainting; hoarseness; cough.
	Bronchiectasis *Lung condition that stretches and distorts the walls of the bronchial tubes*	Cough that produces dark green sputum; bad breath; possibly, shortness of breath; loss of appetite and weight; clubbed fingers.
	Chronic obstructive pulmonary disease	Shortness of breath; wheezing; persistent, mucus-producing cough, especially in the morning; possibly, chest pain, swollen legs and ankles.
	Congestive heart failure	Shortness of breath; fatigue; need to sleep on several pillows; weakness; cough; heart palpitations; swelling in the legs, ankles, and abdomen; frequent urination at night; indigestion; nausea and vomiting; loss of appetite.
	Esophageal cancer	Swallowing difficulty and pain; weight loss; drooling; possibly, vomiting or coughing up of bloody mucus, regurgitation of food; chest pain; repeated respiratory infections.

Bloody sputum *continued*

Associated Symptoms	Possible Diagnosis	Distinguishing Features
	Lung cancer	Persistent cough; wheezing; shortness of breath; chest pain; fatigue; loss of appetite and weight loss.
	Pulmonary edema *An accumulation of fluid in the lungs*	Severe shortness of breath; rapid breathing; pallor; excessive perspiration; bluish nails and lips; cough with frothy sputum; wheezing; anxiety and restlessness.
	Pulmonary embolism *A blood clot travelling from legs or heart that lodges in an artery supplying the lungs*	Sudden shortness of breath and severe breathing difficulty; chest pain worse on inspiration; rapid heartbeat; cough, possibly with bloody sputum; wheezing; excessive perspiration.

Bluish skin/lips Cyanosis

Associated Symptoms	Possible Diagnosis	Distinguishing Features
	Anaphylaxis	Itching and hives; swelling of the eyes, lips, and tongue; weakness or faintness; tightening in the chest or throat; wheezing; shortness of breath; profuse sweating; palpitations; sudden, intense distress; feelings of impending doom; stomach cramps; nausea, vomiting, or diarrhea; bluish tinge (cyanosis) to the skin, lips, and nailbeds due to oxygen insufficiency.
	Atelectasis *Partial or complete collapse of a lung due to obstruction of a bronchus (an air passage through the lung)*	Breathing difficulty, mild or severe chest pain, and dry cough.
	Chronic obstructive pulmonary disease	Shortness of breath; wheezing; persistent, mucus-producing cough, especially in the morning; possibly, chest pain, swollen legs and ankles.
	Congestive heart failure	Shortness of breath; fatigue; need to sleep on several pillows; weakness; cough; heart palpitations; swelling in the legs, ankles, and abdomen; frequent urination at night; indigestion; nausea and vomiting; loss of appetite.
	Hypothermia *Low body temperature (below 94°)*	Shivering; pallor; puffy face; fatigue and confusion; slow, shallow breathing; muscle stiffness; normally warm areas of the body are cold; loss of consciousness.
	Pneumonia	High fever; shortness of breath; cough with sputum; chest pain; fatigue.
	Pneumothorax *Accumulation of air between the two membranes lining the lungs and the chest cavity*	Chest pain that may radiate into the abdomen or shoulder; shortness of breath; dry cough.
	Pulmonary edema *An accumulation of fluid in the lungs*	Severe shortness of breath; rapid breathing; pallor; excessive perspiration; bluish nails and lips; cough with frothy sputum; wheezing; anxiety and restlessness.
	Septic shock *Severe drop in blood pressure due to the presence of microorganisms or their toxins in the bloodstream*	Nausea and vomiting; prostration; diarrhea; sudden high fever; chills; rapid breathing; headache; mental confusion or agitation; decreased urine output; possible jaundice or skin rash; hands and feet may be unusually cold.

Blurred or double vision

Associated Symptoms	Possible Diagnosis	Distinguishing Features
with eye pain	Conjunctivitis *Pinkeye*	Itching and redness in the affected eye; discharge from the eye, clear or pus-filled; excessive tearing; aversion to bright lights; possibly, swollen eyelids.
	Corneal ulcers and infections	Severe eye pain; blurred vision; increased tear production; aversion to light.
	Eye cancers	Often initially asymptomatic. In later stages, gradual blurring and loss of vision, bulging eyes. Possibly, crossed eyes, change in eye color, or a tumor visible through the pupil. Painful red eye.
	Glaucoma	Often initially asymptomatic. In later stages, the symptoms of closed angle glaucoma include: the appearance of halos and rainbows around lights; dilated pupil in the affected eye; severe headache and eye pain; possibly, nausea and vomiting. Open angle glaucoma symptoms include: blurred vision and a gradual loss of peripheral vision.
	Hyphema *Blood within the eye*	Visible bleeding within the front portion of the eye in and around the iris; impaired vision.
	Optic neuritis	Sudden, partial loss of vision, usually in the central portion of the field of vision; blurred vision; pain in affected eye.
	Uveitis and iritis *Inflammation of the uvea, a group of structures in the eye including the iris*	Moderate to severe eye pain; aversion to light; redness in the eye; excessive tearing; blurred vision; spots in the field of vision.
without eye pain	Cataracts	Painless, increasingly blurred vision; appearance of halos around lights; changes in color perception; increased sensitivity to light and glare.
	Macular degeneration	Gradual loss of vision in the central portion of the field of vision, interfering with reading or any close work requiring keen near-vision; blurred vision.
	Retinal detachment	Possibly, bright flashes of light in the peripheral vision, blurred vision, shadows or blindness in part of the field of vision.
	Retinal vessel occlusion *Blockage of the retinal arteries and veins*	Sudden blurring or loss of vision in all or a portion of the field of vision in one eye, bleeding in the eye.
with speech difficulty	Botulism	Difficulty swallowing and speaking; nausea; vomiting; blurred or double vision.

Blurred or double vision *continued*

Associated Symptoms	Possible Diagnosis	Distinguishing Features
with speech difficulty *continued*	Brain tumors	Headaches that become more severe when reclining; nausea and vomiting; memory loss; double vision; muscle weakness; numbness, tingling, or partial paralysis; vision loss; speech disturbances; seizures; drowsiness.
	Encephalitis *Inflammation of the brain*	Initially, headache and fever followed by confusion, hallucinations, and paralysis on one side of the body; memory loss; difficulty with speech and eye movements; drowsiness; possible coma or epileptic seizures; loss of hearing; sensitivity to light; stiff neck.
	Multiple sclerosis *Gradual degeneration of the protective sheaths surrounding the nerves within the brain and spinal cord*	Symptoms may appear suddenly and then disappear; persistent symptoms may take years to develop and include numbness or tingling in any part of the body, weakness in the extremities, an unsteady walk, slurred speech, urinary incontinence, fatigue, depression, temporary loss of vision, double or blurred vision, mental confusion, and memory loss.
	Myasthenia gravis *Nerve degeneration causing gradual loss of voluntary muscle control*	Drooping eyelids; double or blurred vision; muscle weakness especially in the face, throat, and neck; chewing and swallowing difficulties; possible breathing difficulty. Slurred, nasal-sounding speech.
with headache	Brain hemorrhage	Sudden loss of consciousness; sudden, severe headache; paralysis on one side of the face or body; weakness and dizziness; loss of speech; blurred or double vision; dilated pupils; back and leg pain; fever; mental confusion; stiff neck.
	Concussion	Brief loss of consciousness following a blow to the head. Occasionally causes nausea and vomiting.
	Headache, migraine	Throbbing pain in the temple which spreads to the side of the head; nausea; vomiting. Pain may be preceded by blurred or impaired vision with bright spots and zig-zag patterns.
	Sarcoidosis *Accumulation of inflammatory cells in the lymph nodes and other tissues throughout the body*	Often no symptoms. Swollen lymph nodes in the neck or armpits; muscle aches; fever; breathing difficulty; possibly, purple rash on the face; reddish skin; bumps on the legs; numbness; joint pain or stiffness; a painful, red eye; blurred vision; loss of appetite and weight.
	Systemic lupus erythematosus *Inflammation of connective tissues throughout the body*	Red, blotchy, butterfly-shaped rash on the cheeks and bridge of the nose; fatigue; fever; loss of appetite and weight; nausea; joint and abdominal pain; headaches; blurred vision; increased sensitivity to sun exposure; depression; psychosis; mental confusion.

Bone pain

Associated Symptoms	Possible Diagnosis	Distinguishing Features
	Bone cancer	Pain, tenderness, and swelling in the affected bones and joints, often intensifying at night; a noticeable tumor or mass; increased susceptibility to bone fractures.
	Bone fractures	Pain in the affected bone which intensifies with movement or the application of pressure; swelling, bruising, or bleeding around the site of an injury; in a compound fracture, protrusion of bone through skin; possible loss of function or feeling in the injured area; local deformity.
	Fibrous dysplasia *Abnormal growth of bone tissue*	Often asymptomatic; possibly, bone pain, especially in the lower part of the leg, walking difficulty, bone fractures and deformities, irregular patches of increased pigmentation, precocious puberty.
	Infectious arthritis	Pain, swelling, stiffness, and redness, usually in one joint. Fever. Severity varies from a mild ache to severe, debilitating pain and eventual joint deformity.
	Multiple myeloma *Production of malignant plasma cells in the bone marrow*	Bone pain, especially progressive, constant back pain that intensifies with movement; unexplained bone fractures; fatigue; pallor; shortness of breath; increased bleeding, such as bleeding gums or nosebleeds; easily bruised skin; increased susceptibility to infection; headache; vision disturbances; loss of height.
	Myelofibrosis *An increase of fibrous scar tissue within the bone marrow*	Weakness and fatigue; abdominal fullness; a tendency to bleed easily; bone pain; pallor; shortness of breath during physical exertion; increased susceptibility to bruising and infections; jaundice; weight loss.
	Osteomalacia and Rickets *Softening and weakening of the bones, usually due to poor calcification*	Bone pain, especially in the neck, legs, hips and ribs. Muscle weakness, numbness, or spasms in the hands, feet, and throat; increased susceptibility to bone fractures.
	Osteomyelitis *Infection of bone and bone marrow*	Fever; severe pain in the affected bone; inflammation and swelling of the skin over the affected area; deformity. In children, arrested growth of the affected bone.
	Osteoporosis *Loss of bone mass due to calcium depletion*	Backache; easily fractured bones, especially in the wrists, hips, and spine; gradual loss of height; stooped or hunched posture.
	Paget's disease *A weakening, thickening, and deformity of the bones*	Often asymptomatic. Possibly, bone pain or deformity, especially bowing of the legs, bent spine, and facial deformity; unexplained bone fractures; joint pain or stiffness; hearing loss; headaches; ringing in ears.

Bones, frequent or easy breakage

Associated Symptoms	Possible Diagnosis	Distinguishing Features
	Bone cancer	Pain, tenderness, and swelling in the affected bones and joints, often intensifying at night; a noticeable tumor or mass; increased susceptibility to bone fractures.
	Cushing's syndrome	Red, oval-shaped face; humped upper back and obese trunk; acne; purple stretch marks on the abdomen, thighs, and breasts; thin and easily bruised skin; easily fractured bones; depression or euphoria; insomnia; fatigue; muscle weakness; hirsutism (in women).
	Fibrous dysplasia *Abnormal growth of bone tissue*	Often asymptomatic; possibly, bone pain, especially in the lower part of the leg, walking difficulty, bone fractures and deformities, irregular patches of increased pigmentation, precocious puberty.
	Hyperparathyroidism *Overactivity of the parathyroid glands*	Increased susceptibility to bone fractures; depression; indigestion; increased thirst and urine output; fatigue, lethargy; somnolence; muscle weakness; nausea and vomiting; loss of appetite.
	Multiple myeloma *Production of malignant plasma cells in the bone marrow*	Bone pain, especially progressive, constant back pain that intensifies with movement; unexplained bone fractures; fatigue; pallor; shortness of breath; increased bleeding, such as bleeding gums or nosebleeds; easily bruised skin; increased susceptibility to infection; headache; vision disturbances; loss of height.
	Osteomalacia and Rickets *Softening and weakening of the bones, usually due to poor calcification*	Bone pain, especially in the neck, legs, hips and ribs. Muscle weakness, numbness, or spasms in the hands, feet, and throat; increased susceptibility to bone fractures.
	Osteoporosis *Loss of bone mass due to calcium depletion*	Backache; easily fractured bones, especially in the wrists, hips, and spine; gradual loss of height; stooped or hunched posture.
	Paget's disease *A weakening, thickening, and deformity of the bones*	Often asymptomatic. Possibly, bone pain or deformity, especially bowing of the legs, bent spine, and facial deformity; unexplained bone fractures; joint pain or stiffness; hearing loss; headaches; ringing in ears.
	Rheumatoid arthritis	Fatigue and weakness; joint pain, stiffness, and inflammation, especially in the hands, feet, and arms; joint deformity; dry mouth; dry, painful eyes. Morning stiffness.

Breathing difficulty

Associated Symptoms	Possible Diagnosis	Distinguishing Features
with chest pain	Atelectasis *Partial or complete collapse of a lung due to obstruction of a bronchus (an air passage through the lung)*	Breathing difficulty, mild or severe chest pain, and dry cough.
	Cardiomyopathy *Disease of the heart muscle causing a reduction in the force of heart contractions*	Fatigue; chest pain and palpitations; shortness of breath; swelling of the legs; wheezing; cough.
	Chronic obstructive pulmonary disease	Shortness of breath; wheezing; persistent, mucus-producing cough, especially in the morning; possibly, chest pain, swollen legs and ankles.
	Empyema *Collection of pus in any body cavity, usually between the membranes covering the lungs*	Chest pain exacerbated by deep inhalation; shortness of breath; dry cough; fever and chills; exhaustion; weight loss; night sweats; abdominal pain and jaundice.
	Esophageal rupture *A tear in the esophagus, the passageway from the mouth to the stomach*	Chest pain; rapid, shallow breathing; excessive perspiration; vomiting with blood present.
	Legionnaire's disease	Dry cough progressing to one with blood-streaked sputum; high fever; chills; breathing difficulty; chest pain; headache; muscle aches; diarrhea; nausea; vomiting; mental confusion and disorientation.
	Lung cancer	Persistent cough; wheezing; shortness of breath; chest pain; fatigue; loss of appetite and weight loss.
	Myocardial infarction *Heart attack*	Sudden chest pain or pressure that may spread to the arm, shoulder and jaw; excessive perspiration; shortness of breath. Possible nausea and vomiting.
	Pericarditis *Inflammation of the membrane surrounding the heart*	Sharp chest pain that may spread to the neck and shoulders; pain may be relieved by sitting up and leaning forward; swollen legs and abdomen; breathing difficulty; chills; fever; fatigue.
	Pleurisy *Inflammation of the membranes lining the lungs and chest cavity.*	Sudden chest pain worse on inspiration that may also radiate into the shoulder or abdomen; rapid breathing; coughing; sneezing; possibly, fever.
	Pneumonia	High fever; shortness of breath; cough with sputum; chest pain; fatigue.

Breathing difficulty *continued*

Associated Symptoms	Possible Diagnosis	Distinguishing Features
with chest pain *continued*	Pneumothorax *Accumulation of air between the two membranes lining the lungs and the chest cavity*	Chest pain that may radiate into the abdomen or shoulder; shortness of breath; dry cough.
	Pulmonary embolism *A blood clot travelling from legs or heart that lodges in an artery supplying the lungs*	Sudden shortness of breath and severe breathing difficulty; chest pain worse on inspiration; rapid heart-beat; cough, possibly with bloody sputum; wheezing; excessive perspiration.
	Tuberculosis	Often, asymptomatic. Possibly, low-grade fever; excessive perspiration; cough producing sputum or blood; weight loss; chronic fatigue; chest pain; shortness of breath; night sweats.
without chest pain	Amyloidosis *Accumulation of amyloid, a starchy protein, in tissues and organs*	Symptoms vary greatly depending on the body parts affected and may include heart palpitations; shortness of breath; swelling of the legs; diarrhea; abdominal pain; raised spots on the armpits, groin, face, and neck; fatigue and weakness; numbness of the hands or feet; dizziness on standing; joint pains.
	Amyotrophic lateral sclerosis *Progressive degeneration of nerve cells of the central nervous system*	Progressive loss of strength and coordination in the limbs; muscle twitching and cramps that begin in the hands and spread to the arms, shoulders, and legs; stiff, clumsy gait; swallowing, breathing, or speaking difficulty; weight loss; drooling; involuntary laughing or crying.
	Anaphylaxis	Itching and hives; swelling of the eyes, lips, and tongue; weakness or faintness; tightening in the chest or throat; wheezing; shortness of breath; profuse sweating; palpitations; sudden, intense distress; feelings of impending doom; stomach cramps; nausea, vomiting, or diarrhea; bluish tinge (cyanosis) to the skin, lips, and nailbeds due to oxygen insufficiency.
	Asthma	Shortness of breath; wheezing; dry cough; tightness in the chest; possibly, excessive perspiration or rapid heartbeat.
	Botulism	Difficulty swallowing and speaking; nausea; vomiting; blurred or double vision.
	Congestive heart failure	Shortness of breath; fatigue; need to sleep on several pillows; weakness; cough; heart palpitations; swelling in the legs, ankles, and abdomen; frequent urination at night; indigestion; nausea and vomiting; loss of appetite.

Breathing difficulty *continued*

Associated Symptoms	Possible Diagnosis	Distinguishing Features
	Croup *Inflammation of the air passages in children*	Barking cough; hoarseness; wheezing; possibly, breathing difficulty; chest discomfort.
	Diphtheria *Bacterial throat infection*	Initially, swollen lymph glands in the neck and sore throat; difficulty swallowing; breathing difficulty; shortness of breath; rapid pulse; headache. In severe cases, paralysis of limbs or facial muscles; drooling.
	Epiglottitis *Inflammation of the epiglottis, the flap of tissue lying behind the tongue*	Sore throat; sudden fever; breathing difficulty which may become severe within hours of onset; pain or difficulty swallowing; muffled speech; hoarseness; drooling.
	Goiter *A swelling of the thyroid gland*	A swelling in the neck that can vary from a small lump to a huge growth. Possible breathing or swallowing difficulties. Can be associated with symptoms of hyper- or hypothyroidism.
	Jaw dislocation or fracture	Inability to close the jaw normally; painful, swollen, or numb jaw; misalignment of teeth; speaking difficulty; possible breathing difficulty.
	Leukemias	Symptoms vary depending on the type of leukemia and may include: loss of appetite and weight; increased bruising and bleeding; bone pain, especially in the legs; abdominal pain and distention; nausea; heart palpitations; severe fatigue; pallor; breathing difficulty; fever; night sweats; headache; enlarged lymph nodes; joint pains (due to gout).
	Liver tumors	Pain or discomfort in the upper right portion of the abdomen; abdominal swelling; loss of weight and appetite; nausea and vomiting; fever; excessive perspiration; jaundice; pallor; severe fatigue.
	Myasthenia gravis *Nerve degeneration causing gradual loss of voluntary muscle control*	Drooping eyelids; double or blurred vision; muscle weakness especially in the face, throat, and neck; chewing and swallowing difficulties; possible breathing difficulty. Slurred, nasal-sounding speech.
	Nephrotic syndrome *Damage to the filtering units of the kidneys*	Swelling in the ankles and around the eyes; weight gain, due to fluid retention throughout the body; shortness of breath; passing only small amounts of urine that has an unusually foamy appearance; fatigue; diarrhea; loss of appetite.
	Obesity	Excess storage of body fat resulting in a body weight 20% or greater than recommended.

Breathing difficulty *continued*

Associated Symptoms	Possible Diagnosis	Distinguishing Features
	Peripheral neuropathies *Degeneration of the nerves that supply the extremities*	Tingling or numbness commonly beginning in the hands and feet and gradually spreading toward the center of the body; sensitive skin; muscle weakness; possibly, pain in the hands and feet; lack of coordination; shooting pains exacerbated by touch or changes in temperature; breathing difficulty; urinary or fecal incontinence.
	Poliomyelitis *Polio*	Low fever; sore throat; headache; nausea and vomiting. In severe cases, paralysis without loss of sensation; stiff neck and back; twitching; swallowing and breathing difficulty; drooling.
	Pulmonary edema *An accumulation of fluid in the lungs*	Severe shortness of breath; rapid breathing; pallor; excessive perspiration; bluish nails and lips; cough with frothy sputum; wheezing; anxiety and restlessness.
	Renal failure, acute *Severe kidney failure*	Initially, decreased urine output, weight gain and swelling due to edema, loss of appetite, nausea and vomiting, fatigue. If untreated, confusion, seizures, and drowsiness.
	Sarcoidosis *Accumulation of inflammatory cells in the lymph nodes and other tissues throughout the body*	Often no symptoms. Swollen lymph nodes in the neck or armpits; muscle aches; fever; breathing difficulty; possibly, purple rash on the face; reddish skin; bumps on the legs; numbness; joint pain or stiffness; a painful, red eye; blurred vision; loss of appetite and weight.
	Thyroid cancer	Painless lump in the front of the neck; possibly, swallowing or breathing difficulty; hoarseness or loss of voice; enlarged lymph nodes in the neck.
	Thyroid nodules	Usually painless lump in the front of the neck; possibly, breathing or swallowing difficulty.

Bruising, easy or frequent

Associated Symptoms	Possible Diagnosis	Distinguishing Features
	Anemia, aplastic	Fatigue and weakness; shortness of breath; heart palpitations; pallor; bleeding gums; nosebleeds; tendency to bruise easily; small red dots under the skin (petechiae). Increased susceptibility to infection.
	Anemia, iron deficiency	Fatigue and weakness; pallor; shortness of breath and heart palpitations on exertion; irritability or inability to concentrate; sore tongue or tiny cracks at the corners of the mouth; black, tarry or bloody stools; unusual craving for dirt, paint, or ice.
	Cirrhosis *Chronic damage to the cells of the liver*	No symptoms in early stages; loss of weight and appetite; nausea; swollen legs, ankles and abdomen; itching; jaundice; black stools; vomiting blood; fatigue; impotence; memory loss; confusion.
	Cushing's syndrome	Red, oval-shaped face; humped upper back and obese trunk; acne; purple stretch marks on the abdomen, thighs, and breasts; thin and easily bruised skin; easily fractured bones; depression or euphoria; insomnia; fatigue; muscle weakness; hirsutism (in women).
	Hemophilia	Profuse bleeding from minor injuries and tooth extractions; internal bleeding that may cause blood in the urine; bleeding into joints; symptoms of stroke due to intracerebral bleeding; possibly, extensive bruising.
	Hepatitis, acute viral	Fever; fatigue; loss of appetite; aching muscles and joints; abdominal pain or discomfort; jaundice; dark urine and pale stools.
	Hepatitis, chronic	Fatigue; nausea; vomiting; loss of appetite; jaundice; dark urine; clay-colored stools; depression; pain or discomfort in the upper right abdomen; abdominal swelling; fever; in women, cessation of menstruation, acne, and the appearance of male pattern facial hair.
	Leukemias	Symptoms vary depending on the type of leukemia and may include: loss of appetite and weight; increased bruising and bleeding; bone pain, especially in the legs; abdominal pain and distention; nausea; heart palpitations; severe fatigue; pallor; breathing difficulty; fever; night sweats; headache; enlarged lymph nodes; joint pains (due to gout).
	Liver tumors	Pain or discomfort in the upper right portion of the abdomen; abdominal swelling; loss of weight and appetite; nausea and vomiting; fever; excessive perspiration; jaundice; pallor; severe fatigue.

Bruising, easy or frequent *continued*

Associated Symptoms	Possible Diagnosis	Distinguishing Features
	Lymphoma, Hodgkin's *Cancer of the lymph nodes and lymphoid tissue*	Painless swelling of the lymph nodes usually in the neck or armpits; loss of appetite; night sweats.
	Lymphoma, non–Hodgkin's *Cancer of the lymph nodes and lymphoid tissue*	Painless swelling of lymph nodes in the neck or groin; possible abdominal pain, vomiting of blood, headache.
	Multiple myeloma *Production of malignant plasma cells in the bone marrow*	Bone pain, especially progressive, constant back pain that intensifies with movement; unexplained bone fractures; fatigue; pallor; shortness of breath; increased bleeding, such as bleeding gums or nosebleeds; easily bruised skin; increased susceptibility to infection; headache; vision disturbances; loss of height.
	Myelofibrosis *An increase of fibrous scar tissue within the bone marrow*	Weakness and fatigue; abdominal fullness; a tendency to bleed easily; bone pain; pallor; shortness of breath during physical exertion; increased susceptibility to bruising and infections; jaundice; weight loss.
	Platelet function disorders	Minor bleeding in the mouth or just beneath the surface of the skin, often appearing as clusters of small, pinpoint-sized red specks; frequent nosebleeds; easy bruising; prolonged menstrual periods; fatigue; pallor; dark-colored stools.
	Polycythemia vera *An overproduction of red and white blood cells and platelets*	Headache; blurred vision; flushed skin; itching; dizziness; fatigue; night sweats; shortness of breath; weight loss.
	Systemic lupus erythematosus *Inflammation of connective tissues throughout the body*	Red, blotchy, butterfly-shaped rash on the cheeks and bridge of the nose; fatigue; fever; loss of appetite and weight; nausea; joint and abdominal pain; headaches; blurred vision; increased sensitivity to sun exposure; depression; psychosis; mental confusion.
	Typhoid fever	Headache; fever, loss of appetite; abdominal pain and tenderness; extreme weakness; constipation followed by diarrhea; drowsiness, stupor, or coma; raised, pink skin eruptions on the chest and abdomen; joint aches; sore throat.
	Von Willebrand's disease *Chronic bleeding disorder*	Frequent nosebleeds; excessive bleeding from cuts; bleeding gums; easy bruising; abnormal or excessive menstrual bleeding; blood in the stool.
	Wilson's disease *An accumulation of copper in the liver, brain, and other tissues*	Anemia; fluid accumulation in the abdomen; vomiting blood; progressive intellectual impairment; tremor; weakness; walking difficulty; rigidity of limbs; personality changes; speech difficulties; dementia.

Bumps on the skin

Associated Symptoms	Possible Diagnosis	Distinguishing Features
	Acne	Blackheads, whiteheads, pimples, pustules, or cysts usually on the face, chest, back, shoulders, and neck. May result in pockmarks and scarring.
	Herpes zoster *Shingles*	A sensitive band of skin on one side of the body that becomes severely painful and develops slightly raised red spots that blister, dry and crust over. Pain may persist for months or years after skin has healed.
	Lyme disease	A small red bump, surrounded by a concentric bulls-eye-like red rash with a pale center. Over the following month: fever and chills; extreme fatigue; headaches. Symptoms may progress over several months or years and may include: palpitations; joint or muscle pain; and chronic joint inflammation, especially in the knees.
	Sarcoidosis *Accumulation of inflammatory cells in the lymph nodes and other tissues throughout the body*	Often no symptoms. Swollen lymph nodes in the neck or armpits; muscle aches; fever; breathing difficulty; possibly, purple rash on the face; reddish skin; bumps on the legs; numbness; joint pain or stiffness; a painful, red eye; blurred vision; loss of appetite and weight.
	Syphilis	Initially, painless, ulcerated, red sore on the genitals, mouth, or rectum; swollen glands in the neck, armpit, or groin; rash with small, red, scaly bumps; fever; headache. If left untreated, damage to heart valves leading to congestive heart failure; mental deterioration; loss of balance; seizures; dementia; personality changes.

Chest pain

Associated Symptoms	Possible Diagnosis	Distinguishing Features
with shortness of breath	Asthma	Shortness of breath; wheezing; dry cough; tightness in the chest; possibly, excessive perspiration or rapid heartbeat.
	Atelectasis *Partial or complete collapse of a lung due to obstruction of a bronchus (an air passage through the lung)*	Breathing difficulty, mild or severe chest pain, and dry cough.
	Bronchitis, acute	Shortness of breath; persistent cough producing yellow or green sputum; possibly, chest pain; wheezing; fever.
	Cardiomyopathy *Disease of the heart muscle causing a reduction in the force of heart contractions*	Fatigue; chest pain and palpitations; shortness of breath; swelling of the legs; wheezing; cough.
	Chronic obstructive pulmonary disease	Shortness of breath; wheezing; persistent, mucus-producing cough, especially in the morning; possibly, chest pain, swollen legs and ankles.
	Coronary artery disease *Blockage in the arteries supplying blood to the heart muscle*	Initially, asymptomatic. In later stages, dull chest pain that may spread to the neck or the arms usually exacerbated by physical exertion and alleviated with rest; heart palpitations; shortness of breath.
	Empyema *Collection of pus in any body cavity, usually between the membranes covering the lungs*	Chest pain exacerbated by deep inhalation; shortness of breath; dry cough; fever and chills; exhaustion; weight loss; night sweats; abdominal pain and jaundice.
	Esophageal rupture *A tear in the esophagus, the passageway from the mouth to the stomach*	Chest pain; rapid, shallow breathing; excessive perspiration; vomiting with blood present.
	Esophageal stricture *Narrowing of the esophagus, the passageway from the mouth to the stomach*	Sudden or gradual decrease in the ability to swallow solid food or liquids; chest pain after eating; regurgitation of food and liquids; increased salivation; weight loss. Aspiration into lungs can cause cough, wheezing, shortness of breath.
	Legionnaire's disease	Dry cough progressing to one with blood-streaked sputum; high fever; chills; breathing difficulty; chest pain; headache; muscle aches; diarrhea; nausea; vomiting; mental confusion and disorientation.
	Lung cancer	Persistent cough; wheezing; shortness of breath; chest pain; fatigue; loss of appetite and weight loss.

Chest pain *continued*

Associated Symptoms	Possible Diagnosis	Distinguishing Features
with shortness of breath *continued*	Myocardial infarction *Heart attack*	Sudden chest pain or pressure that may spread to the arm, shoulder and jaw; excessive perspiration; shortness of breath. Possible nausea and vomiting.
	Pericarditis *Inflammation of the membrane surrounding the heart*	Sharp chest pain that may spread to the neck and shoulders; pain may be relieved by sitting up and leaning forward; swollen legs and abdomen; breathing difficulty; chills; fever; fatigue.
	Pleurisy *Inflammation of the membranes lining the lungs and chest cavity.*	Sudden chest pain worse on inspiration that may also radiate into the shoulder or abdomen; rapid breathing; coughing; sneezing; possibly, fever.
	Pneumonia	High fever; shortness of breath; cough with sputum; chest pain; fatigue.
	Pneumothorax *Accumulation of air between the two membranes lining the lungs and the chest cavity*	Chest pain that may radiate into the abdomen or shoulder; shortness of breath; dry cough.
	Pulmonary embolism *A blood clot travelling from legs or heart that lodges in an artery supplying the lungs*	Sudden shortness of breath and severe breathing difficulty; chest pain worse on inspiration; rapid heart-beat; cough, possibly with bloody sputum; wheezing; excessive perspiration.
	Valvular heart disease	Depends on which heart valve is affected. Often asymptomatic. Possibly, fatigue and weakness; dizziness; chest pain; shortness of breath; heart palpitations; fainting; edema; stroke from embolism to the brain.
without shortness of breath	Ankylosing spondylitis *Inflammation of the joints between the spine and the pelvis*	Initially, pain and stiffness in the lower back and hips that becomes worse after resting; neck or chest pain; fatigue; possible pain in the hip, knee, and ankle joints; pain in the heel of the foot; eye pain; blurred vision.
	Aortic aneurysm *A sac-like ballooning at a weak spot in the wall of the aorta, the body's primary artery*	Usually asymptomatic; occasionally, severe abdominal and back pain; chest pain; swallowing difficulty; dizziness and fainting; hoarseness; cough.
	Costochondritis *Inflammation of the cartilage of the rib cage.*	Pain in the chest, sometimes severe, aggravated by motion of the rib cage; possible swelling around the rib cage.
	Gastroesophageal reflux *Heartburn*	Burning sensation in the middle of the chest; pain and difficulty swallowing; slight regurgitation of stomach's contents into the mouth, especially when reclining or bending forward; mild abdominal pain.

Chest pain *continued*

Associated Symptoms	Possible Diagnosis	Distinguishing Features
	Hiatal hernia *Protrusion of a portion of the stomach through the diaphragm, into the chest cavity*	Often asymptomatic. Possibly, heartburn after meals or when bending forward or reclining. Belching, regurgitation.
	Influenza *Flu*	Chills, muscle aches, and loss of appetite followed by a cough, sore throat, nasal congestion, and fever; possible chest pain.
	Lung abscess	Cough producing foul-smelling sputum; bad breath; fever; chills; weight loss; possible chest pain.
	Pancreatitis *Inflammation of the pancreas*	Sudden, extreme abdominal pain; nausea and vomiting; weakness; fever; clammy skin; abdominal bloating and tenderness.
	Peptic ulcer	Intermittent, burning or gnawing pain in the upper abdomen or lower chest; indigestion; loss of appetite and weight. Pain may be relieved by eating or antacids. Possible nausea and vomiting. Black, tarry stools, vomiting blood.
	Pheochromocytoma *Tumor in central part of the adrenal, the glands above the kidneys*	Headaches, sometimes severe; rapid heartbeat or heart palpitations; excessive perspiration; faintness, especially when standing up; chest pain; abdominal pain; constipation; weight loss; nervousness, irritability, or anxiety; mental confusion or psychosis.
	Tuberculosis	Often, asymptomatic. Possibly, low-grade fever; excessive perspiration; cough producing sputum or blood; weight loss; chronic fatigue; chest pain; shortness of breath; night sweats.

Chewing difficulty

Associated Symptoms	Possible Diagnosis	Distinguishing Features
	Amyotrophic lateral sclerosis *Progressive degeneration of nerve cells of the central nervous system*	Progressive loss of strength and coordination in the limbs; muscle twitching and cramps that begin in the hands and spread to the arms, shoulders, and legs; stiff, clumsy gait; swallowing, breathing, or speaking difficulty; weight loss; drooling; involuntary laughing or crying.
	Dry mouth	Dry or burning sensation in the mouth; difficulty chewing, swallowing, and speaking; possibly, cracked lips, changes in the tongue's surface, mouth ulcers, changes in taste perception, or tooth decay.
	Jaw dislocation or fracture	Inability to close the jaw normally; painful, swollen, or numb jaw; misalignment of teeth; speaking difficulty; possible breathing difficulty.
	Mumps	Pain in the ear, below the ear, and in the jaw; swollen glands in the neck; headache; pain on swallowing and chewing. Testicular swelling and tenderness in adults.
	Myasthenia gravis *Nerve degeneration causing gradual loss of voluntary muscle control*	Drooping eyelids; double or blurred vision; muscle weakness especially in the face, throat, and neck; chewing and swallowing difficulties; possible breathing difficulty. Slurred, nasal-sounding speech.
	Oral cancers	Sore in the mouth that bleeds and does not heal; lump in the cheek; white or red patch on the gums; swallowing and chewing difficulties; numbness of the tongue; swelling of the jaw.
	Osteoarthritis *Degeneration of the cartilage that lines the joints*	Pain, swelling, and stiffness in one or more joints; enlargement and distortion of affected joints.
	Osteomyelitis *Infection of bone and bone marrow*	Fever; severe pain in the affected bone; inflammation and swelling of the skin over the affected area; deformity. In children, arrested growth of the affected bone.
	Peritonsillar abscess *A collection of pus between the tonsils and surrounding tissue due to infection*	Sore throat; severe pain when swallowing; fever; headache; impaired speech; drooling; swollen glands in the neck.
	Rheumatoid arthritis	Fatigue and weakness; joint pain, stiffness, and inflammation, especially in the hands, feet, and arms; joint deformity; dry mouth; dry, painful eyes. Morning stiffness.

Chewing difficulty *continued*

Associated Symptoms	Possible Diagnosis	Distinguishing Features
	Temporomandibular joint syndrome *TMJ*	Pain in the joints connecting the jaw to the skull; headache; tender jaw muscles; dull facial pain; clicking noise when opening or closing the mouth; pain when yawning and chewing. Jaw may temporarily lock in position.
	Tetanus	Often, lockjaw; stiffness and, later, muscle spasms in the neck and face; drooling; abdominal and back pain; extreme perspiration; swallowing difficulty; possible convulsions; fever.
	Tooth abscess	Persistent tooth pain; pain when biting or chewing; swollen glands in the neck; earache; fever; possibly, foul taste in the mouth or bad breath.

Chills

Associated Symptoms	Possible Diagnosis	Distinguishing Features
with cough	AIDS *Acquired immunodeficiency syndrome*	Recurrent infections affecting the skin and respiratory system; cough; shortness of breath; loss of appetite; weight loss; fatigue; diarrhea; fever; dementia; malignant skin lesions; swollen lymph glands throughout the body; purplish skin nodules; memory loss; confusion; personality changes.
	Common cold	Nasal congestion; watery eyes; sneezing; sore throat; cough; muscle aches; mild headache; listlessness; possibly, low-grade fever.
	Diphtheria *Bacterial throat infection*	Initially, swollen lymph glands in the neck and sore throat; difficulty swallowing; breathing difficulty; shortness of breath; rapid pulse; headache. In severe cases, paralysis of limbs or facial muscles; drooling.
	Empyema *Collection of pus in any body cavity, usually between the membranes covering the lungs*	Chest pain exacerbated by deep inhalation; shortness of breath; dry cough; fever and chills; exhaustion; weight loss; night sweats; abdominal pain and jaundice.
	Influenza *Flu*	Chills, muscle aches, and loss of appetite followed by a cough, sore throat, nasal congestion, and fever; possible chest pain.
	Legionnaire's disease	Dry cough progressing to one with blood-streaked sputum; high fever; chills; breathing difficulty; chest pain; headache; muscle aches; diarrhea; nausea; vomiting; mental confusion and disorientation.
	Lung abscess	Cough producing foul-smelling sputum; bad breath; fever; chills; weight loss; possible chest pain.
	Pneumonia	High fever; shortness of breath; cough with sputum; chest pain; fatigue.
	Rocky Mountain spotted fever	Within a week after exposure, high fever, loss of appetite, headache, muscle aches, nausea and vomiting; dry cough; sensitivity to light. Within six days, the appearance of small pink spots on wrists and ankles, eventually spreading over the entire body, where they then grow, darken in color, and bleed.
without cough	Anemia, hemolytic	Fatigue and weakness; shortness of breath on exertion; pallor; heart palpitations; jaundice and dark urine.
	Appendicitis, acute	Pain near the navel, spreading to the lower right abdomen; nausea and vomiting; constipation; possibly diarrhea; low-grade fever; loss of appetite.

Chills *continued*

Associated Symptoms	Possible Diagnosis	Distinguishing Features
	Ear infection, middle *Inflammation of the middle ear*	Earache; deafness; ringing in the ear; possibly, a discharge of pus from the ear; fever; dizziness.
	Hypothermia *Low body temperature (below 94°)*	Shivering; pallor; puffy face; fatigue and confusion; slow, shallow breathing; muscle stiffness; normally warm areas of the body are cold; loss of consciousness.
	Kidney infection *Pyelonephritis*	Sudden fever and shaking chills; severe fatigue; burning and frequent urination; cloudy or bloody urine; lower back pain, sometimes severe; nausea and vomiting.
	Laryngitis	Hoarseness that often progresses to loss of the voice; throat pain; dry cough; possible fever.
	Lyme disease	A small red bump, surrounded by a concentric bulls-eye-like red rash with a pale center. Over the following month: fever and chills; extreme fatigue; headaches. Symptoms may progress over several months or years and may include: palpitations; joint or muscle pain; and chronic joint inflammation, especially in the knees.
	Lymphoma, Hodgkin's *Cancer of the lymph nodes and lymphoid tissue*	Painless swelling of the lymph nodes usually in the neck or armpits; loss of appetite; night sweats.
	Malaria	Initially, severe chills and shivering. In later stages, extremely high fever followed by a period of profuse perspiration as fever subsides; headache, sometimes severe; vomiting.
	Pelvic inflammatory disease	Initially, lower pelvic pain; pain during intercourse; irregular menstrual bleeding; vaginal discharge with abnormal color or odor; low-grade fever; chills; frequent urination; fatigue; loss of appetite; later, severe abdominal pain and high fever.
	Pericarditis *Inflammation of the membrane surrounding the heart*	Sharp chest pain that may spread to the neck and shoulders; pain may be relieved by sitting up and leaning forward; swollen legs and abdomen; breathing difficulty; chills; fever; fatigue.
	Peritonitis *Inflammation of the abdominal membrane*	Sudden abdominal pain, rigidity, and swelling; chills and fever; weakness; rapid heartbeat; nausea and vomiting; extreme thirst; low urine output.
	Prostatitis *Inflammation of the prostate gland*	Burning during urination; urgent and frequent urination; fever and chills; discharge from the penis; lower abdominal and back pain; blood in the urine.

Chills *continued*

Associated Symptoms	Possible Diagnosis	Distinguishing Features
	Septic shock *Severe drop in blood pressure due to the presence of microorganisms or their toxins in the bloodstream*	Nausea and vomiting; prostration; diarrhea; sudden high fever; chills; rapid breathing; headache; mental confusion or agitation; decreased urine output; possible jaundice or skin rash; hands and feet may be unusually cold.
	Sinusitis *Inflammation of the mucus membranes lining the sinuses*	Throbbing pain above or below one or both eyes that intensifies when bending the head forward or coughing; nasal congestion; loss of sense of smell; often, pus-like nasal discharge; possible dental pain in the upper jaw; fever.
	Typhoid fever	Headache; fever, loss of appetite; abdominal pain and tenderness; extreme weakness; constipation followed by diarrhea; drowsiness, stupor, or coma; raised, pink skin eruptions on the chest and abdomen; joint aches; sore throat.

Confusion

Associated Symptoms	Possible Diagnosis	Distinguishing Features
	AIDS *Acquired immunodeficiency syndrome*	Recurrent infections affecting the skin and respiratory system; cough; shortness of breath; loss of appetite; weight loss; fatigue; diarrhea; fever; dementia; malignant skin lesions; swollen lymph glands throughout the body; purplish skin nodules; memory loss; confusion; personality changes.
	Alzheimer's disease	Symptoms vary greatly in different individuals. Initially, minor forgetfulness gradually developing into severe, short-term memory loss, disorientation, an inability to concentrate, and sudden mood and personality changes. In later stages, severe confusion, possible hallucinations or paranoid delusions, loss of social and sexual inhibitions, impaired judgment, anxiety, depression, agitation and combativeness, wandering and getting lost, inability to write, urinary and fecal incontinence.
	Anemia, pernicious	Fatigue; inability to concentrate; sore, red tongue; weakness; dizziness; pallor; shortness of breath on exertion; palpitations; numbness and tingling in extremities; incoordination; headache; loss of weight and appetite; possibly, jaundice.
	Cirrhosis *Chronic damage to the cells of the liver*	No symptoms in early stages; loss of weight and appetite; nausea; swollen legs, ankles and abdomen; itching; jaundice; black stools; vomiting blood; fatigue; impotence; memory loss; confusion.
	Diabetes mellitus *Insufficiency of or resistance to insulin*	Fatigue; excessive thirst; frequent urination; weight loss despite increased appetite; blurred vision; numbness and tingling of feet and hands; impotence.
	Hemochromatosis *An excess accumulation of iron in the liver, pancreas, heart, testes, skin, and other organs*	A bronze or slate-grey tone to skin that is normally fair; chronic abdominal pain; heart palpitations; joint pain; drowsiness; confusion. In men, a decrease in the size of the testes, loss of sexual desire, and impotence.
	Hyperparathyroidism *Overactivity of the parathyroid glands*	Increased susceptibility to bone fractures; depression; indigestion; increased thirst and urine output; fatigue, lethargy; somnolence; muscle weakness; nausea and vomiting; loss of appetite.
	Hypothermia *Low body temperature (below 94°)*	Shivering; pallor; puffy face; fatigue and confusion; slow, shallow breathing; muscle stiffness; normally warm areas of the body are cold; loss of consciousness.

Confusion *continued*

Associated Symptoms	Possible Diagnosis	Distinguishing Features
	Hypothyroidism *Underactivity of the thyroid gland*	Unexplained weight gain; fatigue; muscle weakness; cramps; dry skin; hair loss; deepening of the voice; intolerance for cold; constipation; chest pain; insomnia; puffiness around eyes; loss of sex drive; depression; menstrual abnormalities; possible swelling in the neck (goiter).
	Multiple sclerosis *Gradual degeneration of the protective sheaths surrounding the nerves within the brain and spinal cord*	Symptoms may appear suddenly and then disappear; persistent symptoms may take years to develop and include numbness or tingling in any part of the body, weakness in the extremities, an unsteady walk, slurred speech, urinary incontinence, fatigue, depression, temporary loss of vision, double or blurred vision, mental confusion, and memory loss.
	Renal failure, acute *Severe kidney failure*	Initially, decreased urine output, weight gain and swelling due to edema, loss of appetite, nausea and vomiting, fatigue. If untreated, confusion, seizures, and drowsiness.
	Reye's syndrome *Childhood disease marked by brain and liver damage*	Following recovery from an upper respiratory infection, nausea and vomiting; memory loss; confusion or delirium; possible seizures; drowsiness; lethargy.
	Seizures	Involuntary twitching or jerking; muscle rigidity; loss of consciousness; confusion; drooling; hallucinations.
with headache	Brain abscess	Headaches; drowsiness; nausea and vomiting; fever; seizures; possible partial paralysis; confusion; speaking difficulty.
	Brain hemorrhage	Sudden loss of consciousness; sudden, severe headache; paralysis on one side of the face or body; weakness and dizziness; loss of speech; blurred or double vision; dilated pupils; back and leg pain; fever; mental confusion; stiff neck.
	Brain tumors	Headaches that become more severe when reclining; nausea and vomiting; memory loss; double vision; muscle weakness; numbness, tingling, or partial paralysis; vision loss; speech disturbances; seizures; drowsiness.
	Chronic fatigue syndrome	Severe fatigue made worse by exercise; recurrent flu-like symptoms; persistent sore throat; low-grade fever; muscle and joint aches; headache; painful, swollen lymph nodes; depression and mental confusion; memory loss; sleep difficulties.

Confusion *continued*

Associated Symptoms	Possible Diagnosis	Distinguishing Features
with headache *continued*	Concussion	Brief loss of consciousness following a blow to the head. Occasionally causes nausea and vomiting.
	Encephalitis *Inflammation of the brain*	Initially, headache and fever followed by confusion, hallucinations, and paralysis on one side of the body; memory loss; difficulty with speech and eye movements; drowsiness; possible coma or epileptic seizures; loss of hearing; sensitivity to light; stiff neck.
	Heatstroke	Sudden dizziness; weakness; headache; hot, dry, red skin which later turns grey; high body temperature; muscle cramps; confusion; seizures; loss of consciousness.
	Hydrocephalus *Overaccumulation of cerebrospinal fluid, the liquid surrounding the brain*	In infants, an enlarged head, rigidity of the legs, irritability, projectile vomiting, drowsiness, seizures, and lethargy. In older persons, headache, vomiting, loss of coordination, deterioration of mental faculties, speech difficulty, and loss of appetite.
	Hypertension	Usually asymptomatic except in severe cases. Possibly, headache, easy fatigability, palpitations, chest pain, blurred vision, dizziness, nose bleeds, and confusion.
	Hypoglycemia *Low blood sugar*	Anxiety; hunger; trembling; headache; palpitations; perspiration; confusion; irritability; loss of coordination; possibly, double vision, seizures, or coma.
	Legionnaire's disease	Dry cough progressing to one with blood-streaked sputum; high fever; chills; breathing difficulty; chest pain; headache; muscle aches; diarrhea; nausea; vomiting; mental confusion and disorientation.
	Meningitis *Inflammation of the membranes covering the brain and spinal cord*	Severe headache; nausea and vomiting; sensitivity to light; stiffness in the neck; possible red skin rash; fever; mental confusion; drowsiness; loss of consciousness; seizures.
	Pheochromocytoma *Tumor in central part of the adrenal, the glands above the kidneys*	Headaches, sometimes severe; rapid heartbeat or heart palpitations; excessive perspiration; faintness, especially when standing up; chest pain; abdominal pain; constipation; weight loss; nervousness, irritability, or anxiety; mental confusion or psychosis.
	Rabies	Low-grade fever; headache; loss of appetite; tingling at site of animal bite; intense thirst exacerbated by the inability to drink without violent, painful throat spasms; paralysis of facial muscles; drooling. Agitation and violent behavior, confusion, convulsions, coma.

Confusion *continued*

Associated Symptoms	Possible Diagnosis	Distinguishing Features
	Renal failure, acute *Severe kidney failure*	Initially, decreased urine output, weight gain and swelling due to edema, loss of appetite, nausea and vomiting, fatigue. If untreated, confusion, seizures, and drowsiness.
	Septic shock *Severe drop in blood pressure due to the presence of microorganisms or their toxins in the bloodstream*	Nausea and vomiting; prostration; diarrhea; sudden high fever; chills; rapid breathing; headache; mental confusion or agitation; decreased urine output; possible jaundice or skin rash; hands and feet may be unusually cold.
	Stroke	Symptoms vary with the location of brain injury. Sudden onset of weakness, paralysis, or loss of sensation, usually on one side of the body; a sudden heaviness in a limb; speech abnormalities; headache; vision disturbances; dizziness; confusion; coma; urinary and fecal incontinence.
	Systemic lupus erythematosus *Inflammation of connective tissues throughout the body*	Red, blotchy, butterfly-shaped rash on the cheeks and bridge of the nose; fatigue; fever; loss of appetite and weight; nausea; joint and abdominal pain; headaches; blurred vision; increased sensitivity to sun exposure; depression; psychosis; mental confusion.
	Toxic shock syndrome	Lethargy; conjunctivitis; confusion; sudden high fever accompanied by nausea, watery diarrhea, sore throat, and headache. Red rash on the palms and soles of the feet, which, after a week or two, begins to peel.
	Transient ischemic attack *Temporary blockage in an artery supplying the brain*	Weakness or numbness in a limb; slurred speech; short-lived, temporary partial blindness; numbness and tingling; speech difficulties; confusion; dizziness.
	Typhoid fever	Headache; fever, loss of appetite; abdominal pain and tenderness; extreme weakness; constipation followed by diarrhea; drowsiness, stupor, or coma; raised, pink skin eruptions on the chest and abdomen; joint aches; sore throat.

Constipation

Associated Symptoms	Possible Diagnosis	Distinguishing Features
	Adrenal insufficiency *Inadequate production of steroid hormones by the adrenal gland*	Loss of weight and appetite; fatigue; weakness; darkening of the skin; abdominal pain; diarrhea; indigestion; nausea and vomiting; constipation; lack of sex drive; dizziness when rising from sitting or lying position.
	Anal fissure	Rectal pain during and immediately after bowel movements; blood in the stool or on toilet paper; rectal itching.
	Appendicitis, acute	Pain near the navel, spreading to the lower right abdomen; nausea and vomiting; constipation; possibly, diarrhea; low-grade fever; loss of appetite.
	Colorectal cancer *A growth of malignant cells in the colon or rectum*	Change in bowel habits; diarrhea; constipation; narrow stools; bloody or dark stools; lower abdominal pain; bloating; cramps; gas; loss of weight and appetite; fatigue and heart palpitations due to anemia.
	Constipation, chronic	Infrequent and possibly painful bowel movements; straining during bowel movements; hard, dry stool; abdominal swelling; continued sensation of fullness after evacuating bowels.
	Diverticular disorders *Swellings in the wall of the colon*	Usually no symptoms unless diverticulae become inflamed. Tenderness or pain in the lower left abdomen relieved by passing stools or gas; constipation or diarrhea; blood in the stool; severe, spasmodic abdominal pain that becomes constant; possibly, fever and nausea.
	Endometriosis *The migration of the uterine lining to other reproductive or abdominal organs*	Pain in the lower abdomen, vagina, and lower back beginning just prior to menses and intensifying after blood flow has ceased; heavy bleeding during periods; pain during intercourse; diarrhea; constipation; pain during bowel movements; bleeding from the rectum; bloody urine during menses; nausea and vomiting prior to menses; infertility.
	Fibroids, uterine *Benign growths of the muscular wall of the uterus*	Heavier or prolonged bleeding during menses; abdominal discomfort; lower back pain; pressure on the bladder and frequent urination; constipation. Possible, sharp, sudden, lower abdominal pain.
	Hemorrhoids	Pain during defecation; anal itching; mucus discharge from the anus. Bright, red blood on toilet paper, stool, or in toilet bowl after a bowel movement.
	Hyperparathyroidism *Overactivity of the parathyroid glands*	Increased susceptibility to bone fractures; depression; indigestion; increased thirst and urine output; fatigue, lethargy; somnolence; muscle weakness; nausea and vomiting; loss of appetite.

Constipation *continued*

Associated Symptoms	Possible Diagnosis	Distinguishing Features
	Hypothyroidism *Underactivity of the thyroid gland*	Unexplained weight gain; fatigue; muscle weakness; cramps; dry skin; hair loss; deepening of the voice; intolerance for cold; constipation; chest pain; insomnia; puffiness around eyes; loss of sex drive; depression; menstrual abnormalities; possible swelling in the neck (goiter).
	Intestinal obstruction	Abdominal pain and cramps; nausea; vomiting; weakness; gas; bloating; possible diarrhea; progressive constipation culminating in inability to pass stools or gas.
	Irritable bowel syndrome	Cramps in the middle or to one side of the lower abdomen that are usually relieved with bowel movements; nausea; bloating; gas; alternating diarrhea and constipation.
	Megacolon *Distention of the colon*	Severe constipation; abdominal bloating; loss of weight and appetite; possible diarrhea; in newborns, failure to pass a stool within 48 hours after birth; in children, slow growth from infancy to age five.
	Mesenteric ischemia *A blood clot blocking blood flow to the intestine*	Severe abdominal cramping, usually around the navel, that is exacerbated by eating and alleviated by fasting. Possibly, bloody stools.
	Multiple sclerosis *Gradual degeneration of the protective sheaths surrounding the nerves within the brain and spinal cord*	Symptoms may appear suddenly and then disappear; persistent symptoms may take years to develop and include numbness or tingling in any part of the body, weakness in the extremities, an unsteady walk, slurred speech, urinary incontinence, fatigue, depression, temporary loss of vision, double or blurred vision, mental confusion, and memory loss.
	Pheochromocytoma *Tumor in central part of the adrenal, the glands above the kidneys*	Headaches, sometimes severe; rapid heartbeat or heart palpitations; excessive perspiration; faintness, especially when standing up; chest pain; abdominal pain; constipation; weight loss; nervousness, irritability, or anxiety; mental confusion or psychosis.
	Proctitis *Inflammation of the rectum.*	Soreness in the rectal area; mucus discharge from the anus; constipation; painful bowel movements; possibly, rectal bleeding.
	Typhoid fever	Headache; fever, loss of appetite; abdominal pain and tenderness; extreme weakness; constipation followed by diarrhea; drowsiness, stupor, or coma; raised, pink skin eruptions on the chest and abdomen; joint aches; sore throat.

Convulsions

Associated Symptoms	Possible Diagnosis	Distinguishing Features
	Brain abscess	Headaches; drowsiness; nausea and vomiting; fever; seizures; possible partial paralysis; confusion; speaking difficulty.
	Brain tumors	Headaches that become more severe when reclining; nausea and vomiting; memory loss; double vision; muscle weakness; numbness, tingling, or partial paralysis; vision loss; speech disturbances; seizures; drowsiness.
	Diabetes mellitus *Insufficiency of or resistance to insulin*	Fatigue; excessive thirst; frequent urination; weight loss despite increased appetite; blurred vision; numbness and tingling of feet and hands; impotence.
	Disseminated intravascular coagulation *Bleeding disorder marked by excessive and inappropriate blood coagulation*	Abnormal bleeding possibly at several sites at once; vomiting blood; bloody or black stools; abnormal vaginal bleeding; blood in the urine; severe abdominal or back pain; possibly, convulsions, or coma.
	Encephalitis *Inflammation of the brain*	Initially, headache and fever followed by confusion, hallucinations, and paralysis on one side of the body; memory loss; difficulty with speech and eye movements; drowsiness; possible coma or epileptic seizures; loss of hearing; sensitivity to light; stiff neck.
	Heatstroke	Sudden dizziness; weakness; headache; hot, dry, red skin which later turns grey; high body temperature; muscle cramps; confusion; seizures; loss of consciousness.
	Hydrocephalus *Overaccumulation of cerebrospinal fluid, the liquid surrounding the brain*	In infants, an enlarged head, rigidity of the legs, irritability, projectile vomiting, drowsiness, seizures, and lethargy. In older persons, headache, vomiting, loss of coordination, deterioration of mental faculties, speech difficulty, and loss of appetite.
	Hypoglycemia *Low blood sugar*	Anxiety; hunger; trembling; headache; palpitations; perspiration; confusion; irritability; loss of coordination; possibly, double vision, seizures, or coma.
	Hypoparathyroidism *Underactivity of the parathyroid glands*	Numbness and tingling and painful, cramp-like spasms of the face, hands, arms, and feet; cataracts; possible seizures.
	Leukemias	Symptoms vary depending on the type of leukemia and may include: loss of appetite and weight; increased bruising and bleeding; bone pain, especially in the legs; abdominal pain and distention; nausea; heart palpitations; severe fatigue; pallor; breathing difficulty; fever; night sweats; headache; enlarged lymph nodes; joint pains (due to gout).

Convulsions *continued*

Associated Symptoms	Possible Diagnosis	Distinguishing Features
	Meningitis *Inflammation of the membranes covering the brain and spinal cord*	Severe headache; nausea and vomiting; sensitivity to light; stiffness in the neck; possible red skin rash; fever; mental confusion; drowsiness; loss of consciousness; seizures.
	Multiple sclerosis *Gradual degeneration of the protective sheaths surrounding the nerves within the brain and spinal cord*	Symptoms may appear suddenly and then disappear; persistent symptoms may take years to develop and include numbness or tingling in any part of the body, weakness in the extremities, an unsteady walk, slurred speech, urinary incontinence, fatigue, depression, temporary loss of vision, double or blurred vision, mental confusion, and memory loss.
	Renal failure, acute *Severe kidney failure*	Initially, decreased urine output, weight gain and swelling due to edema, loss of appetite, nausea and vomiting, fatigue. If untreated, confusion, seizures, and drowsiness.
	Renal failure, chronic *Persistent, mild kidney failure*	Asymptomatic in early stages. Possibly, mental confusion; shortness of breath; abdominal pain; decreased sex drive; fatigue; muscle and bone pain; numbness in the legs and feet; headache; impaired mental acuity; bad breath.
	Reye's syndrome *Childhood disease marked by brain and liver damage*	Following recovery from an upper respiratory infection, nausea and vomiting; memory loss; confusion or delirium; possible seizures; drowsiness; lethargy.
	Sarcoidosis *Accumulation of inflammatory cells in the lymph nodes and other tissues throughout the body*	Often no symptoms. Swollen lymph nodes in the neck or armpits; muscle aches; fever; breathing difficulty; possibly, purple rash on the face; reddish skin; bumps on the legs; numbness; joint pain or stiffness; a painful, red eye; blurred vision; loss of appetite and weight.
	Seizures	Involuntary twitching or jerking; muscle rigidity; loss of consciousness; confusion; drooling; hallucinations.
	Tetanus	Often, lockjaw; stiffness and, later, muscle spasms in the neck and face; drooling; abdominal and back pain; extreme perspiration; swallowing difficulty; possible convulsions; fever.

Cough, dry

Associated Symptoms	Possible Diagnosis	Distinguishing Features
with fever	Atelectasis *Partial or complete collapse of a lung due to obstruction of a bronchus (an air passage through the lung)*	Breathing difficulty, mild or severe chest pain, and dry cough.
	Chlamydia *Contagious, infectious disease caused by chlamydia, a group of microorganisms*	Usually asymptomatic; possibly, pain or burning during urination, watery discharge from the penis or vagina, painless pimple or blister on the penis or outer lips of the vagina, swelling of the testicles, breathing difficulty, cough, high fever, inflammation of the inner lining of the eyelids and the membrane covering the whites of the eyes.
	Common cold	Nasal congestion; watery eyes; sneezing; sore throat; cough; muscle aches; mild headache; listlessness; possibly, low-grade fever.
	Congestive heart failure	Shortness of breath; fatigue; need to sleep on several pillows; weakness; cough; heart palpitations; swelling in the legs, ankles, and abdomen; frequent urination at night; indigestion; nausea and vomiting; loss of appetite.
	Croup *Inflammation of the air passages in children*	Barking cough; hoarseness; wheezing; possibly, breathing difficulty; chest discomfort.
	Empyema *Collection of pus in any body cavity, usually between the membranes covering the lungs*	Chest pain exacerbated by deep inhalation; shortness of breath; dry cough; fever and chills; exhaustion; weight loss; night sweats; abdominal pain and jaundice.
	Laryngitis	Hoarseness that often progresses to loss of the voice; throat pain; dry cough; possible fever.
	Legionnaire's disease	Dry cough progressing to one with blood-streaked sputum; high fever; chills; breathing difficulty; chest pain; headache; muscle aches; diarrhea; nausea; vomiting; mental confusion and disorientation.
	Lung cancer	Persistent cough; wheezing; shortness of breath; chest pain; fatigue; loss of appetite and weight loss.
	Measles	Cough; fever; watery nasal discharge; loss of appetite; red, watering eyes; sore throat; body aches; red, slightly itchy rash that gradually spreads all over the body.
	Pleurisy *Inflammation of the membranes lining the lungs and chest cavity.*	Sudden chest pain worse on inspiration that may also radiate into the shoulder or abdomen; rapid breathing; coughing; sneezing; possibly, fever.

Cough, dry *continued*

Associated Symptoms	Possible Diagnosis	Distinguishing Features
with fever *continued*	Pneumonia	High fever; shortness of breath; cough with sputum; chest pain; fatigue.
	Rocky Mountain spotted fever	Within a week after exposure, high fever, loss of appetite, headache, muscle aches, nausea and vomiting; dry cough; sensitivity to light. Within six days, the appearance of small pink spots on wrists and ankles, eventually spreading over the entire body, where they then grow, darken in color, and bleed.
	Sarcoidosis *Accumulation of inflammatory cells in the lymph nodes and other tissues throughout the body*	Often no symptoms. Swollen lymph nodes in the neck or armpits; muscle aches; fever; breathing difficulty; possibly, purple rash on the face; reddish skin; bumps on the legs; numbness; joint pain or stiffness; a painful, red eye; blurred vision; loss of appetite and weight.
	Systemic lupus erythematosus *Inflammation of connective tissues throughout the body*	Red, blotchy, butterfly-shaped rash on the cheeks and bridge of the nose; fatigue; fever; loss of appetite and weight; nausea; joint and abdominal pain; headaches; blurred vision; increased sensitivity to sun exposure; depression; psychosis; mental confusion.
	Tuberculosis	Often, asymptomatic. Possibly, low-grade fever; excessive perspiration; cough producing sputum or blood; weight loss; chronic fatigue; chest pain; shortness of breath; night sweats.
	Whooping cough	Initially, mild cough, sneezing, nasal congestion, and irritated eyes. Within approximately two weeks, cough becomes severe and persistent, and is accompanied by characteristic high-pitched "whooping" sound during inhalation; loss of appetite; listlessness; vomiting or choking spells. Most common among young children.
without fever	Anaphylaxis	Itching and hives; swelling of the eyes, lips, and tongue; weakness or faintness; tightening in the chest or throat; wheezing; shortness of breath; profuse sweating; palpitations; sudden, intense distress; feelings of impending doom; stomach cramps; nausea, vomiting, or diarrhea; bluish tinge (cyanosis) to the skin, lips, and nailbeds due to oxygen insufficiency.
	Aortic aneurysm *A sac-like ballooning at a weak spot in the wall of the aorta, the body's primary artery*	Usually asymptomatic; occasionally, severe abdominal and back pain; chest pain; swallowing difficulty; dizziness and fainting; hoarseness; cough.

Cough, dry *continued*

Associated Symptoms	Possible Diagnosis	Distinguishing Features
	Asthma	Shortness of breath; wheezing; dry cough; tightness in the chest; possibly, excessive perspiration or rapid heartbeat.
	Cardiomyopathy *Disease of the heart muscle causing a reduction in the force of heart contractions*	Fatigue; chest pain and palpitations; shortness of breath; swelling of the legs; wheezing; cough.
	Esophageal stricture *Narrowing of the esophagus, the passageway from the mouth to the stomach*	Sudden or gradual decrease in the ability to swallow solid food or liquids; chest pain after eating; regurgitation of food and liquids; increased salivation; weight loss. Aspiration into lungs can cause cough, wheezing, shortness of breath.
	Pneumothorax *Accumulation of air between the two membranes lining the lungs and the chest cavity*	Chest pain that may radiate into the abdomen or shoulder; shortness of breath; dry cough.

Cough, wet

Associated Symptoms	Possible Diagnosis	Distinguishing Features
	Allergic rhinitis *Hay fever*	Nasal congestion; frequent sneezing; itchy eyes, nose, and throat.
	Asthma	Shortness of breath; wheezing; dry cough; tightness in the chest; possibly, excessive perspiration or rapid heartbeat.
	Bronchiectasis *Lung condition that stretches and distorts the walls of the bronchial tubes*	Cough that produces dark green sputum; bad breath; possibly, shortness of breath; loss of appetite and weight; clubbed fingers.
	Chronic obstructive pulmonary disease	Shortness of breath; wheezing; persistent, mucus-producing cough, especially in the morning; possibly, chest pain, swollen legs and ankles.
	Congestive heart failure	Shortness of breath; fatigue; need to sleep on several pillows; weakness; cough; heart palpitations; swelling in the legs, ankles, and abdomen; frequent urination at night; indigestion; nausea and vomiting; loss of appetite.
	Esophageal cancer	Swallowing difficulty and pain; weight loss; drooling; possibly, vomiting or coughing up of bloody mucus, regurgitation of food; chest pain; repeated respiratory infections.
	Lung cancer	Persistent cough; wheezing; shortness of breath; chest pain; fatigue; loss of appetite and weight loss.
	Pulmonary edema *An accumulation of fluid in the lungs*	Severe shortness of breath; rapid breathing; pallor; excessive perspiration; bluish nails and lips; cough with frothy sputum; wheezing; anxiety and restlessness.
	Pulmonary embolism *A blood clot travelling from legs or heart that lodges in an artery supplying the lungs*	Sudden shortness of breath and severe breathing difficulty; chest pain worse on inspiration; rapid heartbeat; cough, possibly with bloody sputum; wheezing; excessive perspiration.
with fever	AIDS *Acquired immunodeficiency syndrome*	Recurrent infections affecting the skin and respiratory system; cough; shortness of breath; loss of appetite; weight loss; fatigue; diarrhea; fever; dementia; malignant skin lesions; swollen lymph glands throughout the body; purplish skin nodules; memory loss; confusion; personality changes.
	Bronchitis, acute	Shortness of breath; persistent cough producing yellow or green sputum; possibly, chest pain; wheezing; fever.

Cough, wet *continued*

Associated Symptoms	Possible Diagnosis	Distinguishing Features
with fever *continued*	Common cold	Nasal congestion; watery eyes; sneezing; sore throat; cough; muscle aches; mild headache; listlessness; possibly, low-grade fever.
	Influenza *Flu*	Chills, muscle aches, and loss of appetite followed by a cough, sore throat, nasal congestion, and fever; possible chest pain.
	Legionnaire's disease	Dry cough progressing to one with blood-streaked sputum; high fever; chills; breathing difficulty; chest pain; headache; muscle aches; diarrhea; nausea; vomiting; mental confusion and disorientation.
	Lung abscess	Cough producing foul-smelling sputum; bad breath; fever; chills; weight loss; possible chest pain.
	Measles	Cough; fever; watery nasal discharge; loss of appetite; red, watering eyes; sore throat; body aches; red, slightly itchy rash that gradually spreads all over the body.
	Pneumonia	High fever; shortness of breath; cough with sputum; chest pain; fatigue.
	Tuberculosis	Often, asymptomatic. Possibly, low-grade fever; excessive perspiration; cough producing sputum or blood; weight loss; chronic fatigue; chest pain; shortness of breath; night sweats.
	Whooping cough	Initially, mild cough, sneezing, nasal congestion, and irritated eyes. Within approximately two weeks, cough becomes severe and persistent, and is accompanied by characteristic high-pitched "whooping" sound during inhalation; loss of appetite; listlessness; vomiting or choking spells. Most common among young children.

Depression

Associated Symptoms	Possible Diagnosis	Distinguishing Features
	Alzheimer's disease	Symptoms vary greatly in different individuals. Initially, minor forgetfulness gradually developing into severe, short-term memory loss, disorientation, an inability to concentrate, and sudden mood and personality changes. In later stages, severe confusion, possible hallucinations or paranoid delusions, loss of social and sexual inhibitions, impaired judgment, anxiety, depression, agitation and combativeness, wandering and getting lost, inability to write, urinary and fecal incontinence.
	Congestive heart failure	Shortness of breath; fatigue; need to sleep on several pillows; weakness; cough; heart palpitations; swelling in the legs, ankles, and abdomen; frequent urination at night; indigestion; nausea and vomiting; loss of appetite.
	Diabetes mellitus *Insufficiency of or resistance to insulin*	Fatigue; excessive thirst; frequent urination; weight loss despite increased appetite; blurred vision; numbness and tingling of feet and hands; impotence.
	Encephalitis *Inflammation of the brain*	Initially, headache and fever followed by confusion, hallucinations, and paralysis on one side of the body; memory loss; difficulty with speech and eye movements; drowsiness; possible coma or epileptic seizures; loss of hearing; sensitivity to light; stiff neck.
	Hepatitis, acute viral	Fever; fatigue; loss of appetite; aching muscles and joints; abdominal pain or discomfort; jaundice; dark urine and pale stools.
	Hepatitis, chronic	Fatigue; nausea; vomiting; loss of appetite; jaundice; dark urine; clay-colored stools; depression; pain or discomfort in the upper right abdomen; abdominal swelling; fever; in women, cessation of menstruation, acne, and the appearance of male pattern facial hair.
	Hyperthyroidism *Overactivity of the thyroid gland*	Protruding eyes; weight loss despite increased appetite; intolerance to heat; excessive perspiration; nervousness or restlessness; possibly, swelling in the neck (goiter); palpitations; tremor; diarrhea.
	Hypothyroidism *Underactivity of the thyroid gland*	Unexplained weight gain; fatigue; muscle weakness; cramps; dry skin; hair loss; deepening of the voice; intolerance for cold; constipation; chest pain; insomnia; puffiness around eyes; loss of sex drive; depression; menstrual abnormalities; possible swelling in the neck (goiter).

Depression *continued*

Associated Symptoms	Possible Diagnosis	Distinguishing Features
	Multiple sclerosis *Gradual degeneration of the protective sheaths surrounding the nerves within the brain and spinal cord*	Symptoms may appear suddenly and then disappear; persistent symptoms may take years to develop and include numbness or tingling in any part of the body, weakness in the extremities, an unsteady walk, slurred speech, urinary incontinence, fatigue, depression, temporary loss of vision, double or blurred vision, mental confusion, and memory loss.
	Pancreatic cancer	Often, no symptoms until far advanced. Upper abdominal pain which spreads to the back; loss of weight and appetite; jaundice; nausea, vomiting, and indigestion; diarrhea; fatigue; depression.
	Parkinson's disease *Degeneration of the basal ganglia, a cluster of nerve cells in the brain*	Tremors in the hands; stiffness and weakness; impaired voluntary movement; shuffling gait; stooped posture; unblinking, fixed expression; possibly, slow, hesitant speech; difficulty swallowing; drooling; depression. Tremors occur at rest (not with voluntary movements) and disappear during sleep.

Diarrhea

Associated Symptoms	Possible Diagnosis	Distinguishing Features
with nausea/vomiting	Adrenal insufficiency *Inadequate production of steroid hormones by the adrenal glands*	Loss of weight and appetite; fatigue; weakness; darkening of the skin; abdominal pain; diarrhea; indigestion; nausea and vomiting; constipation; lack of sex drive; dizziness when rising from sitting or lying position.
	Appendicitis, acute	Pain near the navel, spreading to the lower right abdomen; nausea and vomiting; constipation; possibly diarrhea; low-grade fever; loss of appetite.
	Crohn's disease *Inflammation of the lining of the small intestine*	Episodes of abdominal pain or cramps in lower abdomen; nausea; diarrhea; loss of weight and appetite; possibly, fever; rectal bleeding or blood in stools; fatigue; anal fissures; joint pains; inflammation of the eyes.
	Dysentery, bacillary	Watery diarrhea that may contain pus or blood; abdominal pain; rapid dehydration and weight loss; nausea and vomiting.
	Endometriosis *The migration of the uterine lining to other reproductive or abdominal organs*	Pain in the lower abdomen, vagina, and lower back beginning just prior to menses and intensifying after blood flow has ceased; heavy bleeding during periods; pain during intercourse; diarrhea; constipation; pain during bowel movements; bleeding from the rectum; bloody urine during menses; nausea and vomiting prior to menses; infertility.
	Intestinal obstruction	Abdominal pain and cramps; nausea; vomiting; weakness; gas; abdominal bloating; possible diarrhea; progressive constipation culminating in inability to pass stools or gas.
	Irritable bowel syndrome	Cramps in the middle or to one side of the lower abdomen that are usually relieved with bowel movements; nausea; bloating; gas; alternating diarrhea and constipation.
	Lactose intolerance *Difficulty digesting milk and dairy products*	Abdominal cramps; diarrhea; nausea; bloating; flatulence.
	Legionnaire's disease	Dry cough progressing to one with blood-streaked sputum; high fever; chills; breathing difficulty; chest pain; headache; muscle aches; diarrhea; nausea; vomiting; mental confusion and disorientation.
	Toxic shock syndrome	Lethargy; conjunctivitis; confusion; sudden high fever accompanied by nausea, watery diarrhea, sore throat, and headache. Red rash on the palms and soles of the feet, which, after a week or two, begins to peel.

Diarrhea *continued*

Associated Symptoms	Possible Diagnosis	Distinguishing Features
with nausea/vomiting *continued*	Trichinosis *Parasitic infestation*	Initially, crampy abdominal pain, diarrhea, vomiting, and fever, followed within one to two weeks by swelling around the eyes, muscle aches and tenderness, fever, and weakness. Possibly, coughing up of bloody phlegm; delirium; coma; heart failure symptoms.
without nausea/ vomiting	Colorectal cancer *A growth of malignant cells in the colon or rectum*	Change in bowel habits; diarrhea; constipation; narrow stools; bloody or dark stools; lower abdominal pain; bloating; cramps; gas; loss of weight and appetite; fatigue and heart palpitations due to anemia.
	Diarrhea, acute	Loose, watery stools; increased frequency of bowel movements; abdominal cramping and pain. In infants, possibly drowsiness, slack skin, dry, sticky mouth and tongue, or persistent crying.
	Malabsorption, digestive *A failure of the small intestine to absorb nutrients in the diet*	Diarrhea; weight loss; yellowish, foul-smelling stools; abdominal cramps, gas, and bloating; weakness and lethargy.
	Megacolon *Distention of the colon*	Severe constipation; abdominal bloating; loss of weight and appetite; possible diarrhea; in newborns, failure to pass a stool within 48 hours after birth; in children, slow growth from infancy to age five.
	Tapeworm infestation	Often asymptomatic. Unexplained weight loss; presence of white eggs or ribbon-like segments of worm in the stool, bedding, or clothing; symptoms of pernicious anemia.
	Typhoid fever	Headache; fever, loss of appetite; abdominal pain and tenderness; extreme weakness; constipation followed by diarrhea; drowsiness, stupor, or coma; raised, pink skin eruptions on the chest and abdomen; joint aches; sore throat.
may or may not cause nausea/vomiting	AIDS *Acquired immunodeficiency syndrome*	Recurrent infections affecting the skin and respiratory system; cough; shortness of breath; loss of appetite; weight loss; fatigue; diarrhea; fever; dementia; malignant skin lesions; swollen lymph glands throughout the body; purplish skin nodules; memory loss; confusion; personality changes.
	Amebiasis *Parasitic infection*	Usually asymptomatic; possibly, diarrhea; loose stools may contain mucus and blood; abdominal cramps; fatigue; weight loss; gas and flatulence. In severe cases, large amount of bloody stools daily; fever, nausea and vomiting, and abdominal tenderness.

Diarrhea *continued*

Associated Symptoms	Possible Diagnosis	Distinguishing Features
may or may not cause nausea/vomiting *continued*	Amyloidosis *Accumulation of amyloid, a starchy protein, in tissues and organs*	Symptoms vary greatly depending on the body parts affected and may include heart palpitations; shortness of breath; swelling of the legs; diarrhea; abdominal pain; raised spots on the armpits, groin, face, and neck; fatigue and weakness; numbness of the hands or feet; dizziness on standing; joint pains.
	Anemia, folic acid deficiency	Fatigue and weakness; pallor; shortness of breath, heart palpitations, or noticeably rapid heartbeat on exertion; sore, red, and glazed looking tongue; loss of weight and appetite; nausea and diarrhea; abdominal distention.
	Carcinoid tumors and carcinoid syndrome	May be asymptomatic; flushing or redness of the face and neck; gas and profuse diarrhea; abdominal cramping; watery, swollen eyes; shortness of breath or wheezing.
	Colitis, ulcerative *Inflammation of the lining of the colon*	Pain on the left side of the abdomen that lessens after bowel movements; bloody diarrhea; pain in the rectal area; possibly, fever, rapid heartbeat, nausea and vomiting, loss of appetite, dehydration with severe attacks.
	Diverticular disorders *Swellings in the wall of the colon*	Usually no symptoms unless diverticulae become inflamed. Tenderness or pain in the lower left abdomen relieved by passing stools or gas; constipation or diarrhea; blood in the stool; severe, spasmodic abdominal pain that becomes constant; possibly, fever and nausea.
	Food poisoning	Symptoms vary greatly depending on the type and extent of poisoning and may include nausea, vomiting, diarrhea, bloody stools, abdominal pain, and collapse.
	Pancreatic cancer	Often, no symptoms until far advanced. Upper abdominal pain which spreads to the back; loss of weight and appetite; jaundice; nausea, vomiting, and indigestion; diarrhea; fatigue; depression.

Dizziness

Associated Symptoms	Possible Diagnosis	Distinguishing Features
	Acoustic neuroma *A benign tumor in the cells covering the auditory nerve*	Gradual hearing loss; ringing in the ear; headache; numbness in the face; unsteady walk. In later stages, swallowing and speaking difficulties; possibly, slight paralysis.
	Amyloidosis *Accumulation of amyloid, a starchy protein, in tissues and organs*	Symptoms vary greatly depending on the body parts affected and may include heart palpitations; shortness of breath; swelling of the legs; diarrhea; abdominal pain; raised spots on the armpits, groin, face, and neck; fatigue and weakness; numbness of the hands or feet; dizziness on standing; joint pains.
	Anemia, aplastic	Fatigue and weakness; shortness of breath; heart palpitations; pallor; bleeding gums; nosebleeds; tendency to bruise easily; small red dots under the skin (petechiae). Increased susceptibility to infection.
	Anemia, folic acid deficiency	Fatigue and weakness; pallor; shortness of breath, heart palpitations, or noticeably rapid heartbeat on exertion; sore, red, and glazed-looking tongue; loss of weight and appetite; nausea and diarrhea; abdominal distention.
	Anemia, hemolytic	Fatigue and weakness; shortness of breath on exertion; pallor; heart palpitations; jaundice and dark urine.
	Anemia, iron deficiency	Fatigue and weakness; pallor; shortness of breath and heart palpitations on exertion; irritability or inability to concentrate; sore tongue or tiny cracks at the corners of the mouth; black, tarry or bloody stools; unusual craving for dirt, paint, or ice.
	Anemia, pernicious	Fatigue; inability to concentrate; sore, red tongue; weakness; dizziness; pallor; shortness of breath on exertion; palpitations; numbness and tingling in extremities; incoordination; headache; loss of weight and appetite; possibly, jaundice.
	Atelectasis *Partial or complete collapse of a lung due to obstruction of a bronchus (an air passage through the lung)*	Breathing difficulty, mild or severe chest pain, and dry cough.
	Barotrauma *Eardrum strain or damage due to changes in the atmospheric pressure*	Pain in the cheekbones, ear, or forehead; temporary hearing loss; sensation that the ears are plugged; dizziness; ringing in the ears.
	Cardiac arrhythmias *Irregularities in the heartbeat*	Frequently, asymptomatic; possibly; heart palpitations; light-headedness; shortness of breath; sudden weakness; loss of consciousness.

Dizziness *continued*

Associated Symptoms	Possible Diagnosis	Distinguishing Features
	Cardiomyopathy *Disease of the heart muscle causing a reduction in the force of heart contractions*	Fatigue; chest pain and palpitations; shortness of breath; swelling of the legs; wheezing; cough.
	Cervical acceleration/ deceleration injuries *Whiplash*	Pain and stiffness in the neck that usually intensifies 24 hours after a head injury or neck sprain.
	Cholesteatoma *Infected cyst in the eardrum or middle ear*	Hearing loss; discharge of pus from ear; headaches and earaches; weakness of facial muscles; dizziness.
	Concussion	Brief loss of consciousness following a blow to the head. Occasionally causes nausea and vomiting.
	Ear infection, middle *Inflammation of the middle ear*	Earache; deafness; ringing in the ear; possibly, a discharge of pus from the ear; fever; dizziness.
	Hypertension	Usually asymptomatic except in severe cases. Possibly, headache, easy fatigability, palpitations, chest pain, blurred vision, dizziness, nose bleeds, and confusion.
	Hypoglycemia *Low blood sugar*	Anxiety; hunger; trembling; headache; palpitations; perspiration; confusion; irritability; loss of coordination; possibly, double vision, seizures, or coma.
	Otosclerosis *An overgrowth of bone in the middle ear*	Progressive hearing loss; ringing in the ears; dizziness. Hearing is more distinct when background noise is present.
	Paget's disease *A weakening, thickening, and deformity of the bones*	Often asymptomatic. Possibly, bone pain or deformity, especially bowing of the legs, bent spine, and facial deformity; unexplained bone fractures; joint pain or stiffness; hearing loss; headaches; ringing in ears.
	Polycythemia vera *An overproduction of red and white blood cells and platelets*	Headache; blurred vision; flushed skin; itching; dizziness; fatigue; night sweats; shortness of breath; weight loss.
	Toxic shock syndrome	Lethargy; conjunctivitis; confusion; sudden high fever accompanied by nausea, watery diarrhea, sore throat, and headache. Red rash on the palms and soles of the feet, which, after a week or two, begins to peel.
	Transient ischemic attack *Temporary blockage in an artery supplying the brain*	Weakness or numbness in a limb; slurred speech; short-lived, temporary partial blindness; numbness and tingling; speech difficulties; confusion; dizziness.

Dizziness *continued*

Associated Symptoms	Possible Diagnosis	Distinguishing Features
with nausea/vomiting	Adrenal insufficiency *Inadequate production of steroid hormones by the adrenal gland*	Loss of weight and appetite; fatigue; weakness; darkening of the skin; abdominal pain; diarrhea; indigestion; nausea and vomiting; constipation; lack of sex drive; dizziness when rising from sitting or lying position.
	Benign paroxysmal positional vertigo	Sudden sensation of spinning that occurs after changing the position of the head; loss of balance; nausea and vomiting.
	Brain tumors	Headaches that become more severe when reclining; nausea and vomiting; memory loss; double vision; muscle weakness; numbness, tingling, or partial paralysis; vision loss; speech disturbances; seizures; drowsiness.
	Headache, migraine	Throbbing pain in the temple which spreads to the side of the head; nausea; vomiting. Pain may be preceded by blurred or impaired vision with bright spots and zig-zag patterns.
	Labyrinthitis *Inflammation of the semicircular canals of the inner ear*	Severe dizziness, loss of balance, jerky movements of the eyes; nausea and vomiting; ringing in the ears. In later stages, possible hearing loss.
	Meniere's disease *Dysfunction of structures in the inner ear*	Sudden attack of severe vertigo; nausea and vomiting; impaired sense of balance; ringing in the ears; hearing loss in the affected ear. Jerky movements of the eyes.

Drooling

Associated Symptoms	Possible Diagnosis	Distinguishing Features
with twitching, convulsions, or tremors	Parkinson's disease *Degeneration of the basal ganglia, a cluster of nerve cells in the brain*	Tremors in the hands; stiffness and weakness; impaired voluntary movement; shuffling gait; stooped posture; unblinking, fixed expression; possibly, slow, hesitant speech; difficulty swallowing; drooling; depression. Tremors occur at rest (not with voluntary movements) and disappear during sleep.
	Poliomyelitis *Polio*	Low fever; sore throat; headache; nausea and vomiting. In severe cases, paralysis without loss of sensation; stiff neck and back; twitching; swallowing and breathing difficulty; drooling.
	Rabies	Low-grade fever; headache; loss of appetite; tingling at site of animal bite; intense thirst exacerbated by the inability to drink without violent, painful throat spasms; paralysis of facial muscles; drooling. Agitation and violent behavior, confusion, convulsions, coma.
	Seizures	Involuntary twitching or jerking; muscle rigidity; loss of consciousness; confusion; drooling; hallucinations.
	Tetanus	Often, lockjaw; stiffness and, later, muscle spasms in the neck and face; drooling; abdominal and back pain; extreme perspiration; swallowing difficulty; possible convulsions; fever.
without twitching, convulsions, or tremors	Amyotrophic lateral sclerosis *Progressive degeneration of nerve cells of the central nervous system*	Progressive loss of strength and coordination in the limbs; muscle twitching and cramps that begin in the hands and spread to the arms, shoulders, and legs; stiff, clumsy gait; swallowing, breathing, or speaking difficulty; weight loss; drooling; involuntary laughing or crying.
	Bell's palsy *Paralysis of muscles on one side of the face*	Drooping muscles and weakness on one side of the face resulting in a distorted smile or an expressionless look; drooping eyelid, tearing and an inability to close the affected eye; drooling; possibly, ear pain on the affected side of the face; possibly, changes in taste perception; increased sensitivity to noise.
	Esophageal cancer	Swallowing difficulty and pain; weight loss; drooling; possibly, vomiting or coughing up of bloody mucus, regurgitation of food; chest pain; repeated respiratory infections.
	Myasthenia gravis *Nerve degeneration causing gradual loss of voluntary muscle control*	Drooping eyelids; double or blurred vision; muscle weakness especially in the face, throat, and neck; chewing and swallowing difficulties; possible breathing difficulty. Slurred, nasal-sounding speech.

Drooling *continued*

Associated Symptoms	Possible Diagnosis	Distinguishing Features
	Peritonsillar abscess *A collection of pus between the tonsils and surrounding tissue due to infection*	Sore throat; severe pain when swallowing; fever; headache; impaired speech; drooling; swollen glands in the neck.
	Salivary gland disorders	Swollen, painful glands behind the ear or under the tongue; soft, painful, swollen glands in the neck; bitter taste in the mouth; fever; dry mouth; increased number of dental cavities; difficulty swallowing.
	Tongue disorders	Symptoms vary depending on the specific disorder and include: dark or bright red, black, or dark brown tongue; sore, swollen, or smooth tongue; hair-like growths on the tongue; adjacent areas of the mouth may be inflamed; ulcers or raised, white patches on the tongue; excessive salivation; swallowing difficulty; bad breath.

Drowsiness

Associated Symptoms	Possible Diagnosis	Distinguishing Features
	Brain abscess	Headaches; drowsiness; nausea and vomiting; fever; seizures; possible partial paralysis; confusion; speaking difficulty.
	Encephalitis *Inflammation of the brain*	Initially, headache and fever followed by confusion, hallucinations, and paralysis on one side of the body; memory loss; difficulty with speech and eye movements; drowsiness; possible coma or epileptic seizures; loss of hearing; sensitivity to light; stiff neck.
	Hemochromatosis *An excess accumulation of iron in the liver, pancreas, heart, testes, skin, and other organs*	A bronze or slate-gray tone to skin that is normally fair; chronic abdominal pain; heart palpitations; joint pain; drowsiness; confusion. In men, a decrease in the size of the testes, loss of sexual desire, and impotence.
	Hydrocephalus *Overaccumulation of cerebrospinal fluid, the liquid surrounding the brain*	In infants, an enlarged head, rigidity of the legs, irritability, projectile vomiting, drowsiness, seizures, and lethargy. In older persons, headache, vomiting, loss of coordination, deterioration of mental faculties, speech difficulty, and loss of appetite.
	Insomnia	Difficulty falling asleep or staying asleep; daytime fatigue; irritability.
	Renal failure, acute *Severe kidney failure*	Initially, decreased urine output, weight gain and swelling due to edema, loss of appetite, nausea and vomiting, fatigue. If untreated, confusion, seizures, and drowsiness.
	Sleep apnea *Recurrent episodes of breathing cessation during sleep*	Loud snoring; morning fatigue and headache; sleep disturbances; daytime sleepiness; difficulty concentrating; memory loss. Most common among overweight men.
	Typhoid fever	Headache; fever, loss of appetite; abdominal pain and tenderness; extreme weakness; constipation followed by diarrhea; drowsiness, stupor, or coma; raised, pink skin eruptions on the chest and abdomen; joint aches; sore throat.

Ear, ringing or buzzing   Tinnitus

Associated Symptoms	Possible Diagnosis	Distinguishing Features
with dizziness	Anemia, aplastic	Fatigue and weakness; shortness of breath; heart palpitations; pallor; bleeding gums; nosebleeds; tendency to bruise easily; small red dots under the skin (petechiae). Increased susceptibility to infection.
	Anemia, folic acid deficiency	Fatigue and weakness; pallor; shortness of breath, heart palpitations, or noticeably rapid heartbeat on exertion; sore, red, and glazed-looking tongue; loss of weight and appetite; nausea and diarrhea; abdominal distention.
	Anemia, hemolytic	Fatigue and weakness; shortness of breath on exertion; pallor; heart palpitations; jaundice and dark urine.
	Anemia, iron deficiency	Fatigue and weakness; pallor; shortness of breath and heart palpitations on exertion; irritability or inability to concentrate; sore tongue or tiny cracks at the corners of the mouth; black, tarry or bloody stools; unusual craving for dirt, paint, or ice.
	Anemia, pernicious	Fatigue; inability to concentrate; sore, red tongue; weakness; dizziness; pallor; shortness of breath on exertion; palpitations; numbness and tingling in extremities; incoordination; headache; loss of weight and appetite; possibly, jaundice.
	Barotrauma *Eardrum strain or damage due to changes in the atmospheric pressure*	Pain in the cheekbones, ear, or forehead; temporary hearing loss; sensation that the ears are plugged; dizziness; ringing in the ears.
	Concussion	Brief loss of consciousness following a blow to the head. Occasionally causes nausea and vomiting.
	Ear infection, middle *Inflammation of the middle ear*	Earache; deafness; ringing in the ear; possibly, a discharge of pus from the ear; fever; dizziness.
	Hypertension	Usually asymptomatic except in severe cases. Possibly, headache, easy fatigability, palpitations, chest pain, blurred vision, dizziness, nose bleeds, and confusion.
	Labyrinthitis *Inflammation of the semicircular canals of the inner ear*	Severe dizziness, loss of balance, jerky movements of the eyes; nausea and vomiting; ringing in the ears. In later stages, possible hearing loss.
	Meniere's disease *Dysfunction of structures in the inner ear*	Sudden attack of severe vertigo; nausea and vomiting; impaired sense of balance; ringing in the ears; hearing loss in the affected ear. Jerky movements of the eyes.
	Otosclerosis *An overgrowth of bone in the middle ear*	Progressive hearing loss; ringing in the ears; dizziness. Hearing is more distinct when background noise is present.

Ear, ringing or buzzing *continued*

Associated Symptoms	Possible Diagnosis	Distinguishing Features
with dizziness *continued*	Paget's disease *A weakening, thickening, and deformity of the bones*	Often asymptomatic. Possibly, bone pain or deformity, especially bowing of the legs, bent spine, and facial deformity; unexplained bone fractures; joint pain or stiffness; hearing loss; headaches; ringing in ears.
	Transient ischemic attack *Temporary blockage in an artery supplying the brain*	Weakness or numbness in a limb; slurred speech; short–lived, temporary partial blindness; numbness and tingling; speech difficulties; confusion; dizziness.
without dizziness	Acoustic neuroma *A benign tumor in the cells covering the auditory nerve*	Gradual hearing loss; ringing in the ear; headache; numbness in the face; unsteady walk. In later stages, swallowing and speaking difficulties; possibly, slight paralysis.
	Acoustic trauma *Hearing loss due to exposure to loud noise*	Partial deafness; ringing in the ears; sensation that ears are plugged.
	Ear drum, perforated	Earache or sudden pain in the ear; partial hearing loss; slight bleeding or discharge from the ear; ringing or buzzing in the affected ear.
	Presbycusis *Loss of hearing due to age*	Progressive inability to hear well in the presence of background noise; difficulty understanding speech.
	Tinnitus *Ringing in one or both ears*	Ringing, buzzing, humming, or hissing sound in the ear, which may be continuous or episodic; possible hearing loss.

Earache

Associated Symptoms	Possible Diagnosis	Distinguishing Features
with hearing loss	Acoustic neuroma *A benign tumor in the cells covering the auditory nerve*	Gradual hearing loss; ringing in the ear; headache; numbness in the face; unsteady walk. In later stages, swallowing and speaking difficulties; possibly, slight paralysis.
	Barotrauma *Eardrum strain or damage due to changes in the atmospheric pressure*	Pain in the cheekbones, ear, or forehead; temporary hearing loss; sensation that the ears are plugged; dizziness; ringing in the ears.
	Cholesteatoma *Infected cyst in the eardrum or middle ear*	Hearing loss; discharge of pus from ear; headaches and earaches; weakness of facial muscles; dizziness.
	Ear drum, perforated	Earache or sudden pain in the ear; partial hearing loss; slight bleeding or discharge from the ear; ringing or buzzing in the affected ear.
	Ear infection, middle *Inflammation of the middle ear*	Earache; deafness; ringing in the ear; possibly, a discharge of pus from the ear; fever; dizziness.
	Ear infection, outer	Redness and itching of the ear canal; discharge from the ear; ear pain; possibly, temporary loss of hearing.
	Mastoiditis, acute *Inflammation of the mastoid, a bone behind the ear*	Severe pain and swelling behind and within the ear; fever; discharge from the ear; progressive hearing loss.
without hearing loss	Laryngitis	Hoarseness that often progresses to loss of the voice; throat pain; dry cough; possible fever.
	Neuralgia *Pain due to nerve damage or irritation*	Symptoms vary depending on the area affected and include: recurring episodes of sharp pain on one side of the lips, gums, cheek, or chin; radiating pain around the eyes; a burning pain along the path of a nerve encircling the torso. Pain may last from a few seconds to several minutes and always affects the same location. Attacks may occur several times a day for weeks with asymptomatic periods of weeks or months in between and may be triggered by touching or blowing on the affected area. Mouth pain may be exacerbated by talking, eating, or swallowing.
	Pharyngitis *Inflammation of the pharynx, the part of the throat between the mouth and the esophagus*	Sore or red throat; speaking and swallowing difficulties; sensitive, swollen glands in the neck; fever; headache; possible earache.

Earache *continued*

Associated Symptoms	Possible Diagnosis	Distinguishing Features
	Sinusitis *Inflammation of the mucus membranes lining the sinuses*	Throbbing pain above or below one or both eyes that intensifies when bending the head forward or coughing; nasal congestion; loss of sense of smell; often, pus-like nasal discharge; possible dental pain in the upper jaw; fever.
	Temporomandibular joint syndrome *TMJ*	Pain in the joints connecting the jaw to the skull; headache; tender jaw muscles; dull facial pain; clicking noise when opening or closing the mouth; pain when yawning and chewing. Jaw may temporarily lock in position.
	Tonsillitis	Sore, inflamed throat; swallowing difficulty; headache; swollen glands in the neck; fever; loss of voice. In children, nausea, vomiting, and abdominal pain.
	Tooth abscess	Persistent tooth pain; pain when biting or chewing; swollen glands in the neck; earache; fever; possibly, foul taste in the mouth or bad breath.
	Tooth decay	Tooth pain, especially after eating sweet or sour foods; tooth sensitivity to hot and cold; bad breath; unpleasant taste in the mouth.

Ejaculation, painful

Associated Symptoms	Possible Diagnosis	Distinguishing Features
	Bladder cancer	Blood in the urine; painful and frequent urination; pelvic pain; feeling of pressure in the back; persistent fever; urinary incontinence.
	Bladder infection *Cystitis*	Burning during urination; frequent and urgent urination with only small amounts of urine passed; blood in the urine; lower abdominal pain; low-grade fever; pain during sexual intercourse and, in men, during ejaculation.
	Candidiasis *Fungal infection of the mouth, genitals, or mucus membranes*	Thick, white discharge from the vagina; itching and irritation in the vaginal area; pain while urinating or during intercourse; in men, inflammation of the head of the penis; possibly, yellow raised patches in the mouth.
	Chlamydia *Contagious, infectious disease caused by chlamydia, a group of microorganisms*	Usually asymptomatic; possibly, pain or burning during urination, watery discharge from the penis or vagina, painless pimple or blister on the penis or outer lips of the vagina, swelling of the testicles, breathing difficulty, cough, high fever, inflammation of the inner lining of the eyelids and the membrane covering the whites of the eyes.
	Epididymitis *Inflammation of the coiled sperm conduit that rests on each testicle*	Severe pain and swelling at the back of a testicle; possibly, redness and swelling of the scrotum; burning on urination.
	Neurogenic bladder condition *Inability to control passage of urine due to damage to nerves to the bladder.*	Inability to control urine flow which may involuntarily release in large volumes or in a continuous dribbling. Bed-wetting during sleep; feeling the need to urinate though no urine is passed; pain or burning during urination.
	Orchitis *Inflammation of a testicle*	Swelling and severe pain in the affected testicle; possible bloody discharge in the semen; pain during intercourse; fever.
	Prostate cancer	Difficulty urinating; frequent urination with decreased urine output; pain in the pelvic area and lower back; painful ejaculation or bowel movements.
	Prostatitis *Inflammation of the prostate gland*	Burning during urination; urgent and frequent urination; fever and chills; discharge from the penis; lower abdominal and back pain; blood in the urine.
	Testicular torsion *Twisting of the spermatic cord*	Severe pain and swelling on one side of the scrotum; skin on the scrotum may appear red or purple; light-headedness or fainting; possibly, abdominal pain, nausea and vomiting.

Ejaculation, painful *continued*

Associated Symptoms	Possible Diagnosis	Distinguishing Features
	Urethritis *Infection of the urethra,* *the passageway that drains* *urine from the bladder*	Frequent and painful urination; blood in the urine; yellow, pus-filled discharge; possible difficulty passing urine; urinary urgency; pain during intercourse; in men, painful ejaculation.
	Varicocele *Varicose veins in the scrotum*	Visibly enlarged, twisted veins in the scrotum; swelling around the testicles, usually on the left side, that may subside when reclining; sensation of heaviness or dragging in the groin; possibly, scrotal pain or discomfort.

Elbow pain

Associated Symptoms	Possible Diagnosis	Distinguishing Features
	Bone cancer	Pain, tenderness, and swelling in the affected bones and joints, often intensifying at night; a noticeable tumor or mass; increased susceptibility to bone fractures.
	Bone fractures	Pain in the affected bone which intensifies with movement or the application of pressure; swelling, bruising, or bleeding around the site of an injury; in a compound fracture, protrusion of bone through skin; possible loss of function or feeling in the injured area; local deformity.
	Bursitis *Inflammation of the bursas, the lubricant-filled sacs in and around the joints*	Pain and swelling around a joint, usually the elbow, knee, or shoulder; painful movement in the affected joint; possibly, fever.
	Dislocations/subluxations	Deformity of the affected joint; joint pain and tenderness; difficulty moving a joint; swelling and stiffness within 30 minutes after joint injury.
	Infectious arthritis	Pain, swelling, stiffness, and redness, usually in one joint. Fever. Severity varies from a mild ache to severe, debilitating pain and eventual joint deformity.
	Osteoarthritis *Degeneration of the cartilage that lines the joints*	Pain, swelling, and stiffness in one or more joints; enlargement and distortion of affected joints.
	Osteomyelitis *Infection of bone and bone marrow*	Fever; severe pain in the affected bone; inflammation and swelling of the skin over the affected area; deformity. In children, arrested growth of the affected bone.
	Rheumatoid arthritis	Fatigue and weakness; joint pain, stiffness, and inflammation, especially in the hands, feet, and arms; joint deformity; dry mouth; dry, painful eyes. Morning stiffness.
	Rheumatoid arthritis, juvenile	Fever; rash; abdominal pain; weight loss; swelling, stiffness, and pain in the affected joints; enlarged lymph glands; fatigue; pallor; red, painful eyes; morning stiffness.
	Sprains and strains	Swelling, pain or tenderness in the affected joints; impaired joint function.
	Tendinitis *Inflammation of a tendon*	Pain and tenderness over a tendon anywhere in the body; if involved tendon is near or part of a joint, restricted movement of the joint.

Erectile dysfunction Impotence

Associated Symptoms	Possible Diagnosis	Distinguishing Features
	Adrenal insufficiency *Inadequate production of steroid hormones by the adrenal glands*	Loss of weight and appetite; fatigue; weakness; darkening of the skin; abdominal pain; diarrhea; indigestion; nausea and vomiting; constipation; lack of sex drive; dizziness when rising from sitting or lying position.
	Amyotrophic lateral sclerosis *Progressive degeneration of nerve cells of the central nervous system*	Progressive loss of strength and coordination in the limbs; muscle twitching and cramps that begin in the hands and spread to the arms, shoulders, and legs; stiff, clumsy gait; swallowing, breathing, or speaking difficulty; weight loss; drooling; involuntary laughing or crying.
	Cirrhosis *Chronic damage to the cells of the liver*	No symptoms in early stages; loss of weight and appetite; nausea; swollen legs, ankles and abdomen; itching; jaundice; black stools; vomiting blood; fatigue; impotence; memory loss; confusion.
	Coronary artery disease *Blockage in the arteries supplying blood to the heart muscle*	Initially, asymptomatic. In later stages, dull chest pain that may spread to the neck or the arms usually exacerbated by physical exertion and alleviated with rest; heart palpitations; shortness of breath.
	Cushing's syndrome	Red, oval-shaped face; humped upper back and obese trunk; acne; purple stretch marks on the abdomen, thighs, and breasts; thin and easily bruised skin; easily fractured bones; depression or euphoria; insomnia; fatigue; muscle weakness; hirsutism (in women).
	Diabetes mellitus *Insufficiency of or resistance to insulin*	Fatigue; excessive thirst; frequent urination; weight loss despite increased appetite; blurred vision; numbness and tingling of feet and hands; impotence.
	Erectile dysfunction	Inability to achieve or maintain an erection, despite sexual desire.
	Hemochromatosis *An excess accumulation of iron in the liver, pancreas, heart, testes, skin, and other organs*	A bronze or slate-gray tone to skin that is normally fair; chronic abdominal pain; heart palpitations; joint pain; drowsiness; confusion. In men, a decrease in the size of the testes, loss of sexual desire, and impotence.
	Hyperpituitarism *Overactivity of the pituitary gland*	In adults (in which the disease is called acromegaly): Gradual thickening of the bones of the face, jaw, and the extremities in adults; oily skin; severe headache; excessive hair growth; excessive perspiration; joint pains. In children (in which the disease is called gigantism): Rapid growth and unusual height; possibly, blindness.

Erectile dysfunction Impotence *continued*

Associated Symptoms	Possible Diagnosis	Distinguishing Features
	Hypopituitarism *Underactivity of the pituitary gland*	Intolerance to cold; chronic headaches; decreased sex drive; fatigue; fine wrinkles around the eyes and mouth; dry skin; extreme thirst and excessive urination; loss of appetite; vaginal dryness; absence of milk production in new mothers; in men, reduced muscular strength, shrinking of the testes, and loss of body hair; growth retardation in children and adolescents
	Hypothyroidism *Underactivity of the thyroid gland*	Unexplained weight gain; fatigue; muscle weakness; cramps; dry skin; hair loss; deepening of the voice; intolerance for cold; constipation; chest pain; insomnia; puffiness around eyes; loss of sex drive; depression; menstrual abnormalities; possible swelling in the neck (goiter).
	Multiple sclerosis *Gradual degeneration of the protective sheaths surrounding the nerves within the brain and spinal cord*	Symptoms may appear suddenly and then disappear; persistent symptoms may take years to develop and include numbness or tingling in any part of the body, weakness in the extremities, an unsteady walk, slurred speech, urinary incontinence, fatigue, depression, temporary loss of vision, double or blurred vision, mental confusion, and memory loss.
	Peripheral neuropathies *Degeneration of the nerves that supply the extremities*	Tingling or numbness commonly beginning in the hands and feet and gradually spreading toward the center of the body; sensitive skin; muscle weakness; possibly, pain in the hands and feet; lack of coordination; shooting pains exacerbated by touch or changes in temperature; breathing difficulty; urinary or fecal incontinence.
	Peripheral vascular disease *Narrowing of blood vessels in the legs or arms*	Muscle pain on one or both legs that occurs with exercise and subsides with rest; possible pain in the fingers, arms, buttocks, lower back, or the arch of the foot; impotence. Severe symptoms include: muscle pain at rest that intensifies at night; discolored or blue toes; cold or numb feet; open sores; heightened sensitivity to cold; weak or absent pulse in the affected limb; scaly or hairless skin over the affected area.
	Prostatitis *Inflammation of the prostate gland*	Burning during urination; urgent and frequent urination; fever and chills; discharge from the penis; lower abdominal and back pain; blood in the urine.
	Renal failure, chronic *Persistent, mild kidney failure*	Asymptomatic in early stages. Possibly, mental confusion; shortness of breath; abdominal pain; decreased sex drive; fatigue; muscle and bone pain; numbness in the legs and feet; headache; impaired mental acuity; bad breath.

Erectile dysfunction Impotence *continued*

Associated Symptoms	Possible Diagnosis	Distinguishing Features
	Spinal cord trauma	Severe pain and swelling in the affected area; loss of sensation, muscle weakness, or paralysis below the site of the injury; urinary or fecal incontinence or retention; impotence; breathing difficulty; shock.
	Spinal tumor	Progressive numbness, tingling, and muscle weakness; fecal or urinary incontinence; persistent back pain.
	Syphilis	Initially, painless, ulcerated, red sore on the genitals, mouth, or rectum; swollen glands in the neck, armpit, or groin; rash with small, red, scaly bumps; fever; headache. If left untreated, damage to heart valves leading to congestive heart failure; mental deterioration; loss of balance; seizures; dementia; personality changes.

Eye discharge

Associated Symptoms	Possible Diagnosis	Distinguishing Features
	Anaphylaxis	Itching and hives; swelling of the eyes, lips, and tongue; weakness or faintness; tightening in the chest or throat; wheezing; shortness of breath; profuse sweating; palpitations; sudden, intense distress; feelings of impending doom; stomach cramps; nausea, vomiting, or diarrhea; bluish tinge (cyanosis) to the skin, lips, and nailbeds due to oxygen insufficiency.
	Bell's palsy *Paralysis of muscles on one side of the face*	Drooping muscles and weakness on one side of the face resulting in a distorted smile or an expressionless look; drooping eyelid, tearing and an inability to close the affected eye; drooling; possibly, ear pain on the affected side of the face; possibly, changes in taste perception; increased sensitivity to noise.
	Blepharitis *Inflammation of the eyelids*	Red, irritated, scaly eyelids; burning sensation and feeling of grittiness in the eye. Crusted lids in the morning.
	Carcinoid tumors and carcinoid syndrome	May be asymptomatic; flushing or redness of the face and neck; gas and profuse diarrhea; abdominal cramping; watery, swollen eyes; shortness of breath or wheezing.
	Common cold	Nasal congestion; watery eyes; sneezing; sore throat; cough; muscle aches; mild headache; listlessness; possibly, low-grade fever.
	Conjunctivitis *Pinkeye*	Itching and redness in the affected eye; discharge from the eye, clear or pus-filled; excessive tearing; aversion to bright lights; possibly, swollen eyelids.
	Corneal ulcers and infections	Severe eye pain; blurred vision; increased tear production; aversion to light.
	Headache, cluster	Persistent pain in or around one eye; redness and tearing of one eye; nasal congestion on the same side of the face as the affected eye.
	Herpes zoster *Shingles*	A sensitive band of skin on one side of the body that becomes severely painful and develops slightly raised red spots that blister, dry and crust over. Pain may persist for months or years after skin has healed.
	Measles	Cough; fever; watery nasal discharge; loss of appetite; red, watering eyes; sore throat; body aches; red, slightly itchy rash that gradually spreads all over the body.
	Pemphigus *Disorder characterized by blistering of skin and mucus membranes*	Recurrent episodes of painful blisters on the skin and mouth; blisters may ooze or crust over; skin may peel or shed easily.

Eye discharge *continued*

Associated Symptoms	Possible Diagnosis	Distinguishing Features
	Scleritis and episcleritis *Inflammation of the sclera, the white of the eye*	Dull eye pain; redness in the white of the eye; possibly, blurred vision; aversion to light; copious tearing.
	Styes	Small, possibly painful, pus-filled abscess on the eyelid; watering of the eye; feeling of something in the eye.
	Uveitis and iritis *Inflammation of the uvea, a group of structures in the eye including the iris*	Moderate to severe eye pain; aversion to light; redness in the eye; excessive tearing; blurred vision; spots in the field of vision.

Eye pain

Associated Symptoms	Possible Diagnosis	Distinguishing Features
with eye discharge or copious tearing	Blepharitis *Inflammation of the eyelids*	Red, irritated, scaly eyelids; burning sensation and feeling of grittiness in the eye. Crusted lids in the morning.
	Conjunctivitis *Pinkeye*	Itching and redness in the affected eye; discharge from the eye, clear or pus-filled; excessive tearing; aversion to bright lights; possibly, swollen eyelids.
	Corneal ulcers and infections	Severe eye pain; blurred vision; increased tear production; aversion to light.
	Headache, cluster	Persistent pain in or around one eye; redness and tearing of one eye; nasal congestion on the same side of the face as the affected eye.
	Herpes zoster *Shingles*	A sensitive band of skin on one side of the body that becomes severely painful and develops slightly raised red spots that blister, dry and crust over. Pain may persist for months or years after skin has healed.
	Measles	Cough; fever; watery nasal discharge; loss of appetite; red, watering eyes; sore throat; body aches; red, slightly itchy rash that gradually spreads all over the body.
	Scleritis and episcleritis *Inflammation of the sclera, the white of the eye*	Dull eye pain; redness in the white of the eye; possibly, blurred vision; aversion to light; copious tearing.
	Uveitis and iritis *Inflammation of the uvea, a group of structures in the eye including the iris*	Moderate to severe eye pain; aversion to light; redness in the eye; excessive tearing; blurred vision; spots in the field of vision.
without eye discharge or copious tearing	Chlamydia *Contagious, infectious disease caused by chlamydia, a group of microorganisms*	Usually asymptomatic; possibly, pain or burning during urination, watery discharge from the penis or vagina, painless pimple or blister on the penis or outer lips of the vagina, swelling of the testicles, breathing difficulty, cough, high fever, inflammation of the inner lining of the eyelids and the membrane covering the whites of the eyes.
	Eye cancers	Often initially asymptomatic. In later stages, gradual blurring and loss of vision, bulging eyes. Possibly, crossed eyes, change in eye color, or a tumor visible through the pupil. Painful red eye.

Eye pain *continued*

Associated Symptoms	Possible Diagnosis	Distinguishing Features
	Glaucoma	Often initially asymptomatic. In later stages, the symptoms of closed angle glaucoma include: the appearance of halos and rainbows around lights; dilated pupil in the affected eye; severe headache and eye pain; possibly, nausea and vomiting. Open angle glaucoma symptoms include: blurred vision and a gradual loss of peripheral vision.
	Headache, migraine	Throbbing pain in the temple which spreads to the side of the head; nausea; vomiting. Pain may be preceded by blurred or impaired vision with bright spots and zig-zag patterns.
	Hyphema *Blood within the eye*	Visible bleeding within the front portion of the eye in and around the iris; impaired vision.
	Neuralgia *Pain due to nerve damage* *or irritation*	Symptoms vary depending on the area affected and include: recurring episodes of sharp pain on one side of the lips, gums, cheek, or chin; radiating pain around the eyes; a burning pain along the path of a nerve encircling the torso. Pain may last from a few seconds to several minutes and always affects the same location. Attacks may occur several times a day for weeks with asymptomatic periods of weeks or months in between and may be triggered by touching or blowing on the affected area. Mouth pain may be exacerbated by talking, eating, or swallowing.
	Optic neuritis	Sudden, partial loss of vision, usually in the central portion of the field of vision; blurred vision; pain in affected eye.
	Sinusitis *Inflammation of the mucus* *membranes lining the sinuses*	Throbbing pain above or below one or both eyes that intensifies when bending the head forward or coughing; nasal congestion; loss of sense of smell; often, pus-like nasal discharge; possible dental pain in the upper jaw; fever.
	Sjögren's syndrome	Dry, itching, burning eyes; sensation of a foreign body under the eyelids; dry mouth; difficulty swallowing; vaginal dryness; dry skin; frequent dental cavities; joint pain; swelling of glands (parotids) in front of the ears; Raynaud's phenomenon.
	Styes	Small, possibly painful, pus-filled abscess on the eyelid; watering of the eye; feeling of something in the eye.

Eye redness

Associated Symptoms	Possible Diagnosis	Distinguishing Features
	Allergic rhinitis *Hay fever*	Nasal congestion; frequent sneezing; itchy eyes, nose, and throat.
	Anaphylaxis	Itching and hives; swelling of the eyes, lips, and tongue; weakness or faintness; tightening in the chest or throat; wheezing; shortness of breath; profuse sweating; palpitations; sudden, intense distress; feelings of impending doom; stomach cramps; nausea, vomiting, or diarrhea; bluish tinge (cyanosis) to the skin, lips, and nailbeds due to oxygen insufficiency.
	Conjunctivitis *Pinkeye*	Itching and redness in the affected eye; discharge from the eye, clear or pus-filled; excessive tearing; aversion to bright lights; possibly, swollen eyelids.
	Corneal ulcers and infections	Severe eye pain; blurred vision; increased tear production; aversion to light.
	Crohn's disease *Inflammation of the lining of the small intestine*	Episodes of abdominal pain or cramps in lower abdomen; nausea; diarrhea; loss of weight and appetite; possibly, fever; rectal bleeding or blood in stools; fatigue; anal fissures; joint pains; inflammation of the eyes.
	Glaucoma	Often initially asymptomatic. In later stages, the symptoms of closed angle glaucoma include: the appearance of halos and rainbows around lights; dilated pupil in the affected eye; severe headache and eye pain; possibly, nausea and vomiting. Open angle glaucoma symptoms include: blurred vision and a gradual loss of peripheral vision.
	Headache, cluster	Persistent pain in or around one eye; redness and tearing of one eye; nasal congestion on the same side of the face as the affected eye.
	Hyphema *Blood within the eye*	Visible bleeding within the front portion of the eye in and around the iris; impaired vision.
	Meningitis *Inflammation of the membranes covering the brain and spinal cord*	Severe headache; nausea and vomiting; sensitivity to light; stiffness in the neck; possible red skin rash; fever; mental confusion; drowsiness; loss of consciousness; seizures.
	Sarcoidosis *Accumulation of inflammatory cells in the lymph nodes and other tissues throughout the body*	Often no symptoms. Swollen lymph nodes in the neck or armpits; muscle aches; fever; breathing difficulty; possibly, purple rash on the face; reddish skin; bumps on the legs; numbness; joint pain or stiffness; a painful, red eye; blurred vision; loss of appetite and weight.

Eye redness *continued*

Associated Symptoms	Possible Diagnosis	Distinguishing Features
	Scleritis and episcleritis *Inflammation of the sclera, the white of the eye*	Dull eye pain; redness in the white of the eye; possibly, blurred vision; aversion to light; copious tearing.
	Uveitis and iritis *Inflammation of the uvea, a group of structures in the eye including the iris*	Moderate to severe eye pain; aversion to light; redness in the eye; excessive tearing; blurred vision; spots in the field of vision.
	Whooping cough	Initially, mild cough, sneezing, nasal congestion, and irritated eyes. Within approximately two weeks, cough becomes severe and persistent, and is accompanied by characteristic high-pitched "whooping" sound during inhalation; loss of appetite; listlessness; vomiting or choking spells. Most common among young children.

Eyeballs bulging/protruding

Associated Symptoms	Possible Diagnosis	Distinguishing Features
	Anaphylaxis	Itching and hives; swelling of the eyes, lips, and tongue; weakness or faintness; tightening in the chest or throat; wheezing; shortness of breath; profuse sweating; palpitations; sudden, intense distress; feelings of impending doom; stomach cramps; nausea, vomiting, or diarrhea; bluish tinge (cyanosis) to the skin, lips, and nailbeds due to oxygen insufficiency.
	Carcinoid tumors and carcinoid syndrome	May be asymptomatic; flushing or redness of the face and neck; gas and profuse diarrhea; abdominal cramping; watery, swollen eyes; shortness of breath or wheezing.
	Eye cancers	Often initially asymptomatic. In later stages, gradual blurring and loss of vision, bulging eyes. Possibly, crossed eyes, change in eye color, or a tumor visible through the pupil. Painful red eye.
	Hyperthyroidism *Overactivity of the thyroid gland*	Protruding eyes; weight loss despite increased appetite; intolerance to heat; excessive perspiration; nervousness or restlessness; possibly, swelling in the neck (goiter); palpitations; tremor; diarrhea.
	Scleritis and episcleritis *Inflammation of the sclera, the white of the eye*	Dull eye pain; redness in the white of the eye; possibly, blurred vision; aversion to light; copious tearing.

Eyelid drooping

Associated Symptoms	Possible Diagnosis	Distinguishing Features
	Bell's palsy *Paralysis of muscles on one side of the face*	Drooping muscles and weakness on one side of the face resulting in a distorted smile or an expressionless look; drooping eyelid, tearing and an inability to close the affected eye; drooling; possibly, ear pain on the affected side of the face; possibly, changes in taste perception; increased sensitivity to noise.
	Botulism	Difficulty swallowing and speaking; nausea; vomiting; blurred or double vision.
	Myasthenia gravis *Nerve degeneration causing gradual loss of voluntary muscle control*	Drooping eyelids; double or blurred vision; muscle weakness especially in the face, throat, and neck; chewing and swallowing difficulties; possible breathing difficulty. Slurred, nasal-sounding speech.
	Hypothyroidism *Underactivity of the thyroid gland*	Unexplained weight gain; fatigue; muscle weakness; cramps; dry skin; hair loss; deepening of the voice; intolerance for cold; constipation; chest pain; insomnia; puffiness around eyes; loss of sex drive; depression; menstrual abnormalities; possible swelling in the neck (goiter).

Eyes, dry

Associated Symptoms	Possible Diagnosis	Distinguishing Features
	Corneal ulcers and infections	Severe eye pain; blurred vision; increased tear production; aversion to light.
	Rheumatoid arthritis	Fatigue and weakness; joint pain, stiffness, and inflammation, especially in the hands, feet, and arms; joint deformity; dry mouth; dry, painful eyes. Morning stiffness.
	Sjögren's syndrome	Dry, itching, burning eyes; sensation of a foreign body under the eyelids; dry mouth; difficulty swallowing; vaginal dryness; dry skin; frequent dental cavities; joint pain; swelling of glands (parotids) in front of the ears; Raynaud's phenomenon.

Eyes, tearing or watering also see Eye discharge

Associated Symptoms	Possible Diagnosis	Distinguishing Features
	Bell's palsy *Paralysis of muscles on one side of the face*	Drooping muscles and weakness on one side of the face resulting in a distorted smile or an expressionless look; drooping eyelid, tearing and an inability to close the affected eye; drooling; possibly, ear pain on the affected side of the face; possibly, changes in taste perception; increased sensitivity to noise.
	Common cold	Nasal congestion; watery eyes; sneezing; sore throat; cough; muscle aches; mild headache; listlessness; possibly, low-grade fever.
	Conjunctivitis *Pinkeye*	Itching and redness in the affected eye; discharge from the eye, clear or pus-filled; excessive tearing; aversion to bright lights; possibly, swollen eyelids.
	Corneal ulcers and infections	Severe eye pain; blurred vision; increased tear production; aversion to light.
	Headache, cluster	Persistent pain in or around one eye; redness and tearing of one eye; nasal congestion on the same side of the face as the affected eye.
	Measles	Cough; fever; watery nasal discharge; loss of appetite; red, watering eyes; sore throat; body aches; red, slightly itchy rash that gradually spreads all over the body.
	Scleritis and episcleritis *Inflammation of the sclera, the white of the eye*	Dull eye pain; redness in the white of the eye; possibly, blurred vision; aversion to light; copious tearing.
	Uveitis and iritis *Inflammation of the uvea, a group of structures in the eye including the iris*	Moderate to severe eye pain; aversion to light; redness in the eye; excessive tearing; blurred vision; spots in the field of vision.

Facial pain

Associated Symptoms	Possible Diagnosis	Distinguishing Features
	Impacted teeth	Gum pain; unpleasant taste in mouth, especially when biting down; red, swollen gums around the affected tooth; headache or jaw ache; possibly, bad breath.
	Jaw dislocation or fracture	Inability to close the jaw normally; painful, swollen, or numb jaw; misalignment of teeth; speaking difficulty; possible breathing difficulty.
	Multiple sclerosis *Gradual degeneration of the protective sheaths surrounding the nerves within the brain and spinal cord*	Symptoms may appear suddenly and then disappear; persistent symptoms may take years to develop and include numbness or tingling in any part of the body, weakness in the extremities, an unsteady walk, slurred speech, urinary incontinence, fatigue, depression, temporary loss of vision, double or blurred vision, mental confusion, and memory loss.
	Neuralgia *Pain due to nerve damage or irritation*	Symptoms vary depending on the area affected and include: recurring episodes of sharp pain on one side of the lips, gums, cheek, or chin; radiating pain around the eyes; a burning pain along the path of a nerve encircling the torso. Pain may last from a few seconds to several minutes and always affects the same location. Attacks may occur several times a day for weeks with asymptomatic periods of weeks or months in between and may be triggered by touching or blowing on the affected area. Mouth pain may be exacerbated by talking, eating, or swallowing.
	Sinusitis *Inflammation of the mucus membranes lining the sinuses*	Throbbing pain above or below one or both eyes that intensifies when bending the head forward or coughing; nasal congestion; loss of sense of smell; often, pus-like nasal discharge; possible dental pain in the upper jaw; fever.
	Temporomandibular joint syndrome *TMJ*	Pain in the joints connecting the jaw to the skull; headache; tender jaw muscles; dull facial pain; clicking noise when opening or closing the mouth; pain when yawning and chewing. Jaw may temporarily lock in position.
	Tooth abscess	Persistent tooth pain; pain when biting or chewing; swollen glands in the neck; earache; fever; possibly, foul taste in the mouth or bad breath.

Faintness or fainting

Associated Symptoms	Possible Diagnosis	Distinguishing Features
with shortness of breath	Anaphylaxis	Itching and hives; swelling of the eyes, lips, and tongue; weakness or faintness; tightening in the chest or throat; wheezing; shortness of breath; profuse sweating; palpitations; sudden, intense distress; feelings of impending doom; stomach cramps; nausea, vomiting, or diarrhea; bluish tinge (cyanosis) to the skin, lips, and nailbeds due to oxygen insufficiency.
	Anemia, aplastic	Fatigue and weakness; shortness of breath; heart palpitations; pallor; bleeding gums; nosebleeds; tendency to bruise easily; small red dots under the skin (petechiae). Increased susceptibility to infection.
	Anemia, folic acid deficiency	Fatigue and weakness; pallor; shortness of breath, heart palpitations, or noticeably rapid heartbeat on exertion; sore, red, and glazed-looking tongue; loss of weight and appetite; nausea and diarrhea; abdominal distention.
	Anemia, hemolytic	Fatigue and weakness; shortness of breath on exertion; pallor; heart palpitations; jaundice and dark urine.
	Anemia, iron deficiency	Fatigue and weakness; pallor; shortness of breath and heart palpitations on exertion; irritability or inability to concentrate; sore tongue or tiny cracks at the corners of the mouth; black, tarry or bloody stools; unusual craving for dirt, paint, or ice.
	Anemia, pernicious	Fatigue; inability to concentrate; sore, red tongue; weakness; dizziness; pallor; shortness of breath on exertion; palpitations; numbness and tingling in extremities; incoordination; headache; loss of weight and appetite; possibly, jaundice.
	Cardiac arrhythmias *Irregularities in the heartbeat*	Frequently, asymptomatic; possibly; heart palpitations; lightheadedness; shortness of breath; sudden weakness; loss of consciousness.
	Cardiomyopathy *Disease of the heart muscle causing a reduction in the force of heart contractions*	Fatigue; chest pain and palpitations; shortness of breath; swelling of the legs; wheezing; cough.
	Chronic obstructive pulmonary disease	Shortness of breath; wheezing; persistent, mucus-producing cough, especially in the morning; possibly, chest pain, swollen legs and ankles.
	Congestive heart failure	Shortness of breath; fatigue; need to sleep on several pillows; weakness; cough; heart palpitations; swelling in the legs, ankles, and abdomen; frequent urination at night; indigestion; nausea and vomiting; loss of appetite.

Faintness or fainting *continued*

Associated Symptoms	Possible Diagnosis	Distinguishing Features
with shortness of breath *continued*	Mitral valve prolapse *A deformity in the heart's mitral valve possibly causing it to leak*	Usually asymptomatic. Possible palpitations, shortness of breath, dizziness, fainting, or fatigue.
	Valvular heart disease	Depends on which heart valve is affected. Often asymptomatic. Possibly, fatigue and weakness; dizziness; chest pain; shortness of breath; heart palpitations; fainting; edema; stroke from embolism to the brain.
without shortness of breath	Adrenal insufficiency *Inadequate production of steroid hormones by the adrenal glands*	Loss of weight and appetite; fatigue; weakness; darkening of the skin; abdominal pain; diarrhea; indigestion; nausea and vomiting; constipation; lack of sex drive; dizziness when rising from sitting or lying position.
	Aortic aneurysm *A sac-like ballooning at a weak spot in the wall of the aorta, the body's primary artery*	Usually asymptomatic; occasionally, severe abdominal and back pain; chest pain; swallowing difficulty; dizziness and fainting; hoarseness; cough.
	Brain hemorrhage	Sudden loss of consciousness; sudden, severe headache; paralysis on one side of the face or body; weakness and dizziness; loss of speech; blurred or double vision; dilated pupils; back and leg pain; fever; mental confusion; stiff neck.
	Concussion	Brief loss of consciousness following a blow to the head. Occasionally causes nausea and vomiting.
	Heatstroke	Sudden dizziness; weakness; headache; hot, dry, red skin which later turns grey; high body temperature; muscle cramps; confusion; seizures; loss of consciousness.
	Hemochromatosis *An excess accumulation of iron in the liver, pancreas, heart, testes, skin, and other organs*	A bronze or slate-grey tone to skin that is normally fair; chronic abdominal pain; heart palpitations; joint pain; drowsiness; confusion. In men, a decrease in the size of the testes, loss of sexual desire, and impotence.
	Hypoglycemia *Low blood sugar*	Anxiety; hunger; trembling; headache; palpitations; perspiration; confusion; irritability; loss of coordination; possibly, double vision, seizures, or coma.
	Hypothermia *Low body temperature (below 94°)*	Shivering; pallor; puffy face; fatigue and confusion; slow, shallow breathing; muscle stiffness; normally warm areas of the body are cold; loss of consciousness.
	Inguinal hernia *Displaced loop of intestine in the inguinal canal, a tubular passage through the abdominal wall*	A swelling in the groin area that may recede when lying down; pain at the site of the swelling, especially when lifting a heavy object; swelling of the scrotum. Nausea, vomiting, loss of appetite, and abdominal pain if intestine becomes obstructed.

Faintness or fainting *continued*

Associated Symptoms	Possible Diagnosis	Distinguishing Features
	Meningitis *Inflammation of the membranes covering the brain and spinal cord*	Severe headache; nausea and vomiting; sensitivity to light; stiffness in the neck; possible red skin rash; fever; mental confusion; drowsiness; loss of consciousness; seizures.
	Seizures	Involuntary twitching or jerking; muscle rigidity; loss of consciousness; confusion; drooling; hallucinations.
	Testicular torsion *Twisting of the spermatic cord*	Severe pain and swelling on one side of the scrotum; skin on the scrotum may appear red or purple; light-headedness or fainting; possibly, abdominal pain, nausea and vomiting.
	Transient ischemic attack *Temporary blockage in an artery supplying the brain*	Weakness or numbness in a limb; slurred speech; short-lived, temporary partial blindness; numbness and tingling; speech difficulties; confusion; dizziness.

Fatigue

Associated Symptoms	Possible Diagnosis	Distinguishing Features
	Adrenal insufficiency *Inadequate production of steroid hormones by the adrenal gland*	Loss of weight and appetite; fatigue; weakness; darkening of the skin; abdominal pain; diarrhea; indigestion; nausea and vomiting; constipation; lack of sex drive; dizziness when rising from sitting or lying position.
	Ankylosing spondylitis *Inflammation of the joints between the spine and the pelvis*	Initially, pain and stiffness in the lower back and hips that becomes worse after resting; neck or chest pain; fatigue; possible pain in the hip, knee, and ankle joints; pain in the heel of the foot; eye pain; blurred vision.
	Cirrhosis *Chronic damage to the cells of the liver*	No symptoms in early stages; loss of weight and appetite; nausea; swollen legs, ankles and abdomen; itching; jaundice; black stools; vomiting blood; fatigue; impotence; memory loss; confusion.
	Colorectal cancer *A growth of malignant cells in the colon or rectum*	Change in bowel habits; diarrhea; constipation; narrow stools; bloody or dark stools; lower abdominal pain; bloating; cramps; gas; loss of weight and appetite; fatigue and heart palpitations due to anemia.
	Cushing's syndrome	Red, oval-shaped face; humped upper back and obese trunk; acne; purple stretch marks on the abdomen, thighs, and breasts; thin and easily bruised skin; easily fractured bones; depression or euphoria; insomnia; fatigue; muscle weakness; hirsutism (in women).
	Diabetes mellitus *Insufficiency of or resistance to insulin*	Fatigue; excessive thirst; frequent urination; weight loss despite increased appetite; blurred vision; numbness and tingling of feet and hands; impotence.
	Fibromyalgia	Muscle aches, pains, and stiffness; specific points on the body that feel sore when pressed. Fatigue, headaches, and possible insomnia. Feeling unrefreshed upon awakening in the morning.
	Hyperpituitarism *Overactivity of the pituitary gland*	In adults (in which the disease is called acromegaly): Gradual thickening of the bones of the face, jaw, and the extremities in adults; oily skin; severe headache; excessive hair growth; excessive perspiration; joint pains. In children (in which the disease is called gigantism) : Rapid growth and unusual height; possibly, blindness.
	Hyperthyroidism *Overactivity of the thyroid gland*	Protruding eyes; weight loss despite increased appetite; intolerance to heat; excessive perspiration; nervousness or restlessness; possibly, swelling in the neck (goiter); palpitations; tremor; diarrhea.

Fatigue *continued*

Associated Symptoms	Possible Diagnosis	Distinguishing Features
	Hypopituitarism *Underactivity of the pituitary gland*	Intolerance to cold; chronic headaches; decreased sex drive; fatigue; fine wrinkles around the eyes and mouth; dry skin; extreme thirst and excessive urination; loss of appetite; vaginal dryness; absence of milk production in new mothers; in men, reduced muscular strength, shrinking of the testes, and loss of body hair; growth retardation in children and adolescents.
	Hypothyroidism *Underactivity of the thyroid gland*	Unexplained weight gain; fatigue; muscle weakness; cramps; dry skin; hair loss; deepening of the voice; intolerance for cold; constipation; chest pain; insomnia; puffiness around eyes; loss of sex drive; depression; menstrual abnormalities; possible swelling in the neck (goiter).
	Insomnia	Difficulty falling asleep or staying asleep; daytime fatigue; irritability.
	Malabsorption, digestive *A failure of the small intestine to absorb nutrients in the diet*	Diarrhea; weight loss; yellowish, foul-smelling stools; abdominal cramps, gas, and bloating; weakness and lethargy.
	Multiple sclerosis *Gradual degeneration of the protective sheaths surrounding the nerves within the brain and spinal cord*	Symptoms may appear suddenly and then disappear; persistent symptoms may take years to develop and include numbness or tingling in any part of the body, weakness in the extremities, an unsteady walk, slurred speech, urinary incontinence, fatigue, depression, temporary loss of vision, double or blurred vision, mental confusion, and memory loss.
	Pancreatic cancer	Often, no symptoms until far advanced. Upper abdominal pain which spreads to the back; loss of weight and appetite; jaundice; nausea, vomiting, and indigestion; diarrhea; fatigue; depression.
	Renal failure, acute *Severe kidney failure*	Initially, decreased urine output, weight gain and swelling due to edema, loss of appetite, nausea and vomiting, fatigue. If untreated, confusion, seizures, and drowsiness.
	Rheumatoid arthritis	Fatigue and weakness; joint pain, stiffness, and inflammation, especially in the hands, feet, and arms; joint deformity; dry mouth; dry, painful eyes. Morning stiffness.

Fatigue *continued*

Associated Symptoms	Possible Diagnosis	Distinguishing Features
	Scleroderma	Shiny, tight, and hardened skin, especially on the fingers, arms, and face; hands or feet may successively turn blue, white, and red upon exposure to cold (Raynaud's phenomenon); swallowing difficulty; bloating after eating; weight loss; shortness of breath on exertion; high blood pressure; symptoms of renal failure. Possibly, heartburn, muscle aches and weakness, joint pain, fever, or fatigue.
	Sjögren's syndrome	Dry, itching, burning eyes; sensation of a foreign body under the eyelids; dry mouth; difficulty swallowing; vaginal dryness; dry skin; frequent dental cavities; joint pain; swelling of glands (parotids) in front of the ears; Raynaud's phenomenon.
	Sleep apnea *Recurrent episodes of breathing cessation during sleep*	Loud snoring; morning fatigue and headache; sleep disturbances; daytime sleepiness; difficulty concentrating; memory loss. Most common among overweight men.
with fever	AIDS *Acquired immunodeficiency syndrome*	Recurrent infections affecting the skin and respiratory system; cough; shortness of breath; loss of appetite; weight loss; fatigue; diarrhea; fever; dementia; malignant skin lesions; swollen lymph glands throughout the body; purplish skin nodules; memory loss; confusion; personality changes.
	Chronic fatigue syndrome	Severe fatigue made worse by exercise; recurrent flu-like symptoms; persistent sore throat; low-grade fever; muscle and joint aches; headache; painful, swollen lymph nodes; depression and mental confusion; memory loss; sleep difficulties.
	Crohn's disease *Inflammation of the lining of the small intestine*	Episodes of abdominal pain or cramps in lower abdomen; nausea; diarrhea; loss of weight and appetite; possibly, fever; rectal bleeding or blood in stools; fatigue; anal fissures; joint pains; inflammation of the eyes.
	Encephalitis *Inflammation of the brain*	Initially, headache and fever followed by confusion, hallucinations, and paralysis on one side of the body; memory loss; difficulty with speech and eye movements; drowsiness; possible coma or epileptic seizures; loss of hearing; sensitivity to light; stiff neck.
	Hepatitis, acute viral	Fever; fatigue; loss of appetite; aching muscles and joints; abdominal pain or discomfort; jaundice; dark urine and pale stools.

Fatigue *continued*

Associated Symptoms	Possible Diagnosis	Distinguishing Features
with fever *continued*	Hepatitis, chronic	Fatigue; nausea; vomiting; loss of appetite; jaundice; dark urine; clay-colored stools; depression; pain or discomfort in the upper right abdomen; abdominal swelling; fever; in women, cessation of menstruation, acne, and the appearance of male pattern facial hair.
	Infectious arthritis	Pain, swelling, stiffness, and redness, usually in one joint. Fever. Severity varies from a mild ache to severe, debilitating pain and eventual joint deformity.
	Kidney cancer	Blood in the urine; abdominal and lower back pain; low-grade fever; fatigue; nausea and vomiting; loss of weight and appetite.
	Kidney infection *Pyelonephritis*	Sudden fever and shaking chills; severe fatigue; burning and frequent urination; cloudy or bloody urine; lower back pain, sometimes severe; nausea and vomiting.
	Leukemias	Symptoms vary depending on the type of leukemia and may include: loss of appetite and weight; increased bruising and bleeding; bone pain, especially in the legs; abdominal pain and distention; nausea; heart palpitations; severe fatigue; pallor; breathing difficulty; fever; night sweats; headache; enlarged lymph nodes; joint pains (due to gout).
	Liver tumors	Pain or discomfort in the upper right portion of the abdomen; abdominal swelling; loss of weight and appetite; nausea and vomiting; fever; excessive perspiration; jaundice; pallor; severe fatigue.
	Lyme disease	A small red bump, surrounded by a concentric bulls-eye-like red rash with a pale center. Over the following month: fever and chills; extreme fatigue; headaches. Symptoms may progress over several months or years and may include: palpitations; joint or muscle pain; and chronic joint inflammation, especially in the knees.
	Pneumonia	High fever; shortness of breath; cough with sputum; chest pain; fatigue.
	Rheumatoid arthritis, juvenile	Fever; rash; abdominal pain; weight loss; swelling, stiffness, and pain in the affected joints; enlarged lymph glands; fatigue; pallor; red, painful eyes; morning stiffness.

Fatigue *continued*

Associated Symptoms	Possible Diagnosis	Distinguishing Features
with fever *continued*	Systemic lupus erythematosus *Inflammation of connective tissues throughout the body*	Red, blotchy, butterfly-shaped rash on the cheeks and bridge of the nose; fatigue; fever; loss of appetite and weight; nausea; joint and abdominal pain; headaches; blurred vision; increased sensitivity to sun exposure; depression; psychosis; mental confusion.
	Tuberculosis	Often, asymptomatic. Possibly, low-grade fever; excessive perspiration; cough producing sputum or blood; weight loss; chronic fatigue; chest pain; shortness of breath; night sweats.
with breathing difficulty/shortness of breath	Amyloidosis *Accumulation of amyloid, a starchy protein, in tissues and organs*	Symptoms vary greatly depending on the body parts affected and may include heart palpitations; shortness of breath; swelling of the legs; diarrhea; abdominal pain; raised spots on the armpits, groin, face, and neck; fatigue and weakness; numbness of the hands or feet; dizziness on standing; joint pains.
	Anemia, aplastic	Fatigue and weakness; shortness of breath; heart palpitations; pallor; bleeding gums; nosebleeds; tendency to bruise easily; small red dots under the skin (petechiae). Increased susceptibility to infection.
	Anemia, folic acid deficiency	Fatigue and weakness; pallor; shortness of breath, heart palpitations, or noticeably rapid heartbeat on exertion; sore, red, and glazed-looking tongue; loss of weight and appetite; nausea and diarrhea; abdominal distention.
	Anemia, hemolytic	Fatigue and weakness; shortness of breath on exertion; pallor; heart palpitations; jaundice and dark urine.
	Anemia, iron deficiency	Fatigue and weakness; pallor; shortness of breath and heart palpitations on exertion; irritability or inability to concentrate; sore tongue or tiny cracks at the corners of the mouth; black, tarry or bloody stools; unusual craving for dirt, paint, or ice.
	Anemia, pernicious	Fatigue; inability to concentrate; sore, red tongue; weakness; dizziness; pallor; shortness of breath on exertion; palpitations; numbness and tingling in extremities; incoordination; headache; loss of weight and appetite; possibly, jaundice.
	Cardiomyopathy *Disease of the heart muscle causing a reduction in the force of heart contractions*	Fatigue; chest pain and palpitations; shortness of breath; swelling of the legs; wheezing; cough.

Fatigue *continued*

Associated Symptoms	Possible Diagnosis	Distinguishing Features
with breathing difficulty/shortness of breath *continued*	Chronic obstructive pulmonary disease	Shortness of breath; wheezing; persistent, mucus-producing cough, especially in the morning; possibly, chest pain, swollen legs and ankles.
	Congestive heart failure	Shortness of breath; fatigue; need to sleep on several pillows; weakness; cough; heart palpitations; swelling in the legs, ankles, and abdomen; frequent urination at night; indigestion; nausea and vomiting; loss of appetite.
	Hypothermia *Low body temperature (below 94°)*	Shivering; pallor; puffy face; fatigue and confusion; slow, shallow breathing; muscle stiffness; normally warm areas of the body are cold; loss of consciousness.
	Lung cancer	Persistent cough; wheezing; shortness of breath; chest pain; fatigue; loss of appetite and weight loss.
	Mitral valve prolapse *A deformity in the heart's mitral valve possibly causing it to leak*	Usually asymptomatic. Possible palpitations, shortness of breath, dizziness, fainting, or fatigue.
	Multiple myeloma *Production of malignant plasma cells in the bone marrow*	Bone pain, especially progressive, constant back pain that intensifies with movement; unexplained bone fractures; fatigue; pallor; shortness of breath; increased bleeding, such as bleeding gums or nosebleeds; easily bruised skin; increased susceptibility to infection; headache; vision disturbances; loss of height.
	Myasthenia gravis *Nerve degeneration causing gradual loss of voluntary muscle control*	Drooping eyelids; double or blurred vision; muscle weakness especially in the face, throat, and neck; chewing and swallowing difficulties; possible breathing difficulty. Slurred, nasal-sounding speech.
	Myelofibrosis *An increase of fibrous scar tissue within the bone marrow*	Weakness and fatigue; abdominal fullness; a tendency to bleed easily; bone pain; pallor; shortness of breath during physical exertion; increased susceptibility to bruising and infections; jaundice; weight loss.
	Myocarditis *Inflammation of the heart muscle*	Fatigue; shortness of breath; heart palpitations; fever; edema; rarely, continuous pressure or vague pain in the chest.
	Nephrotic syndrome *Damage to the filtering units of the kidneys*	Swelling in the ankles and around the eyes; weight gain, due to fluid retention throughout the body; shortness of breath; passing only small amounts of urine that has an unusually foamy appearance; fatigue; diarrhea; loss of appetite.

Fatigue *continued*

Associated Symptoms	Possible Diagnosis	Distinguishing Features
with breathing difficulty/shortness of breath *continued*	Pericarditis *Inflammation of the membrane surrounding the heart*	Sharp chest pain that may spread to the neck and shoulders; pain may be relieved by sitting up and leaning forward; swollen legs and abdomen; breathing difficulty; chills; fever; fatigue.
	Polycythemia vera *An overproduction of red and white blood cells and platelets*	Headache; blurred vision; flushed skin; itching; dizziness; fatigue; night sweats; shortness of breath; weight loss.
	Renal failure, chronic *Persistent, mild kidney failure*	Asymptomatic in early stages. Possibly, mental confusion; shortness of breath; abdominal pain; decreased sex drive; fatigue; muscle and bone pain; numbness in the legs and feet; headache; impaired mental acuity; bad breath.
	Sarcoidosis *Accumulation of inflammatory cells in the lymph nodes and other tissues throughout the body*	Often no symptoms. Swollen lymph nodes in the neck or armpits; muscle aches; fever; breathing difficulty; possibly, purple rash on the face; reddish skin; bumps on the legs; numbness; joint pain or stiffness; a painful, red eye; blurred vision; loss of appetite and weight.
	Valvular heart disease	Depends on which heart valve is affected. Often asymptomatic. Possibly, fatigue and weakness; dizziness; chest pain; shortness of breath; heart palpitations; fainting; edema; stroke from embolism to the brain.

Fever

Associated Symptoms	Possible Diagnosis	Distinguishing Features
with swollen lymph nodes/glands	AIDS *Acquired immunodeficiency syndrome*	Recurrent infections affecting the skin and respiratory system; cough; shortness of breath; loss of appetite; weight loss; fatigue; diarrhea; fever; dementia; malignant skin lesions; swollen lymph glands throughout the body; purplish skin nodules; memory loss; confusion; personality changes.
	Chronic fatigue syndrome	Severe fatigue made worse by exercise; recurrent flu-like symptoms; persistent sore throat; low-grade fever; muscle and joint aches; headache; painful, swollen lymph nodes; depression and mental confusion; memory loss; sleep difficulties.
	Diphtheria *Bacterial throat infection*	Initially, swollen lymph glands in the neck and sore throat; difficulty swallowing; breathing difficulty; shortness of breath; rapid pulse; headache. In severe cases, paralysis of limbs or facial muscles; drooling.
	Leukemias	Symptoms vary depending on the type of leukemia and may include: loss of appetite and weight; increased bruising and bleeding; bone pain, especially in the legs; abdominal pain and distention; nausea; heart palpitations; severe fatigue; pallor; breathing difficulty; fever; night sweats; headache; enlarged lymph nodes; joint pains (due to gout).
	Lymphoma, Hodgkin's *Cancer of the lymph nodes and lymphoid tissue*	Painless swelling of the lymph nodes usually in the neck or armpits; loss of appetite; night sweats.
	Lymphoma, non-Hodgkin's *Cancer of the lymph nodes and lymphoid tissue*	Painless swelling of lymph nodes in the neck or groin; possible abdominal pain, vomiting of blood, headache.
	Mononucleosis, infectious	Headache; high fever; swollen glands in the neck, groin, and armpits; severe sore throat; swallowing difficulty.
	Mumps	Pain in the ear, below the ear, and in the jaw; swollen glands in the neck; headache; pain on swallowing and chewing. Testicular swelling and tenderness in adults.
	Peritonsillar abscess *A collection of pus between the tonsils and surrounding tissue due to infection*	Sore throat; severe pain when swallowing; fever; headache; impaired speech; drooling; swollen glands in the neck.
	Pharyngitis *Inflammation of the pharynx, the part of the throat between the mouth and the esophagus*	Sore or red throat; speaking and swallowing difficulties; sensitive, swollen glands in the neck; fever; headache; possible earache.

Fever *continued*

Associated Symptoms	Possible Diagnosis	Distinguishing Features
with swollen lymph nodes/glands *continued*	Sarcoidosis *Accumulation of inflammatory cells in the lymph nodes and other tissues throughout the body*	Often no symptoms. Swollen lymph nodes in the neck or armpits; muscle aches; fever; breathing difficulty; possibly, purple rash on the face; reddish skin; bumps on the legs; numbness; joint pain or stiffness; a painful, red eye; blurred vision; loss of appetite and weight.
	Thyroiditis, subacute *Inflammation of the thyroid gland*	Pain in the front of the neck and, often, the ear; possibly fever, weight loss, and fatigue; general feeling of being unwell (malaise); discomfort on swallowing.
	Tonsillitis	Sore, inflamed throat; swallowing difficulty; headache; swollen glands in the neck; fever; loss of voice. In children, nausea, vomiting, and abdominal pain.
	Tooth abscess	Persistent tooth pain; pain when biting or chewing; swollen glands in the neck; earache; fever; possibly, foul taste in the mouth or bad breath.
with cough/breathing difficulty	Atelectasis *Partial or complete collapse of a lung due to obstruction of a bronchus (an air passage through the lung)*	Breathing difficulty, mild or severe chest pain, and dry cough.
	Bronchitis, acute	Shortness of breath; persistent cough producing yellow or green sputum; possibly, chest pain; wheezing; fever.
	Empyema *Collection of pus in any body cavity, usually between the membranes covering the lungs*	Chest pain exacerbated by deep inhalation; shortness of breath; dry cough; fever and chills; exhaustion; weight loss; night sweats; abdominal pain and jaundice.
	Epiglottitis *Inflammation of the epiglottis, the flap of tissue lying behind the tongue*	Sore throat; sudden fever; breathing difficulty which may become severe within hours of onset; pain or difficulty swallowing; muffled speech; hoarseness; drooling.
	Influenza *Flu*	Chills, muscle aches, and loss of appetite followed by a cough, sore throat, nasal congestion, and fever; possible chest pain.
	Legionnaire's disease	Dry cough progressing to one with blood-streaked sputum; high fever; chills; breathing difficulty; chest pain; headache; muscle aches; diarrhea; nausea; vomiting; mental confusion and disorientation.
	Lung abscess	Cough producing foul-smelling sputum; bad breath; fever; chills; weight loss; possible chest pain.

Fever *continued*

Associated Symptoms	Possible Diagnosis	Distinguishing Features
with cough/breathing difficulty *continued*	Pericarditis *Inflammation of the membrane surrounding the heart*	Sharp chest pain that may spread to the neck and shoulders; pain may be relieved by sitting up and leaning forward; swollen legs and abdomen; breathing difficulty; chills; fever; fatigue.
	Pleurisy *Inflammation of the membranes lining the lungs and chest cavity.*	Sudden chest pain worse on inspiration that may also radiate into the shoulder or abdomen; rapid breathing; coughing; sneezing; possibly, fever.
	Pneumonia	High fever; shortness of breath; cough with sputum; chest pain; fatigue.
	Septic shock *Severe drop in blood pressure due to the presence of microorganisms or their toxins in the bloodstream*	Nausea and vomiting; prostration; diarrhea; sudden high fever; chills; rapid breathing; headache; mental confusion or agitation; decreased urine output; possible jaundice or skin rash; hands and feet may be unusually cold.
	Tuberculosis	Often, asymptomatic. Possibly, low-grade fever; excessive perspiration; cough producing sputum or blood; weight loss; chronic fatigue; chest pain; shortness of breath; night sweats.
	Whooping cough	Initially, mild cough, sneezing, nasal congestion, and irritated eyes. Within approximately two weeks, cough becomes severe and persistent, and is accompanied by characteristic high-pitched "whooping" sound during inhalation; loss of appetite; listlessness; vomiting or choking spells. Most common among young children.
with nausea/vomiting	Brain abscess	Headaches; drowsiness; nausea and vomiting; fever; seizures; possible partial paralysis; confusion; speaking difficulty.
	Brain hemorrhage	Sudden loss of consciousness; sudden, severe headache; paralysis on one side of the face or body; weakness and dizziness; loss of speech; blurred or double vision; dilated pupils; back and leg pain; fever; mental confusion; stiff neck.
	Dermatomyositis *Inflammation of the muscles and skin*	Red rash on the cheeks and bridge of the nose; purple discoloration and swelling of the eyelids; areas of thickened skin; muscle weakness and stiffness, usually in the shoulders and pelvis; cold hands and feet; speaking or swallowing difficulty; fever; weight loss.
	Encephalitis *Inflammation of the brain*	Initially, headache and fever followed by confusion, hallucinations, and paralysis on one side of the body; memory loss; difficulty with speech and eye movements; drowsiness; possible coma or epileptic seizures; loss of hearing; sensitivity to light; stiff neck.

Fever *continued*

Associated Symptoms	Possible Diagnosis	Distinguishing Features
with nausea/vomiting *continued*	Food poisoning	Symptoms vary greatly depending on the type and extent of poisoning and may include nausea, vomiting, diarrhea, bloody stools, abdominal pain, and collapse.
	Hepatitis, acute viral	Fever; fatigue; loss of appetite; aching muscles and joints; abdominal pain or discomfort; jaundice; dark urine and pale stools.
	Liver tumors	Pain or discomfort in the upper right portion of the abdomen; abdominal swelling; loss of weight and appetite; nausea and vomiting; fever; excessive perspiration; jaundice; pallor; severe fatigue.
	Meningitis *Inflammation of the membranes covering the brain and spinal cord*	Severe headache; nausea; vomiting; sensitivity to light; stiffness in the neck; possible red skin rash; fever; mental confusion; drowsiness; loss of consciousness; seizures.
	Mesenteric ischemia *A blood clot blocking blood flow to the intestine*	Severe abdominal cramping, usually around the navel, that is exacerbated by eating and alleviated by fasting. Possibly, bloody stools.
	Peritonitis *Inflammation of the abdominal membrane.*	Sudden abdominal pain, rigidity, and swelling; chills and fever; weakness; rapid heartbeat; nausea and vomiting; extreme thirst; low urine output.
	Trichinosis *Parasitic infestation*	Initially, crampy abdominal pain, diarrhea, vomiting, and fever, followed within one to two weeks by swelling around the eyes, muscle aches and tenderness, fever, and weakness. Possibly, coughing up of bloody phlegm; delirium; coma; heart failure symptoms.
with rash/spots	Infectious arthritis	Pain, swelling, stiffness, and redness, usually in one joint. Fever. Severity varies from a mild ache to severe, debilitating pain and eventual joint deformity.
	Lyme disease	A small red bump, surrounded by a concentric bulls-eye-like red rash with a pale center. Over the following month: fever and chills; extreme fatigue; headaches. Symptoms may progress over several months or years and may include: palpitations; joint or muscle pain; and chronic joint inflammation, especially in the knees.
	Measles	Cough; fever; watery nasal discharge; loss of appetite; red, watering eyes; sore throat; body aches; red, slightly itchy rash that gradually spreads all over the body.
	Rheumatic fever	Initially, a sore throat that gets better followed, one to six weeks later, by lethargy and fever. Possibly, swollen joints, rash, abdominal pain, involuntary jerky movements, emotional instability.

Fever *continued*

Associated Symptoms	Possible Diagnosis	Distinguishing Features
with rash/spots *continued*	Rocky Mountain spotted fever	Within a week after exposure, high fever, loss of appetite, headache, muscle aches, nausea and vomiting; dry cough; sensitivity to light. Within six days, the appearance of small pink spots on wrists and ankles, eventually spreading over the entire body, where they then grow, darken in color, and bleed.
	Roseola *Infectious disease primarily affecting children*	Abrupt onset of high fever that usually subsides within four to five days, at which time a rash appears on the torso, and spreads to the limbs, neck, and face. Sore throat; swollen lymph nodes in neck.
	Rubella *German Measles*	Rash on the face that spreads to the torso and limbs; enlargement of lymph nodes in neck; usually preceded by headache, fever, and runny nose.
	Toxic shock syndrome	Lethargy; conjunctivitis; confusion; sudden high fever accompanied by nausea, watery diarrhea, sore throat, and headache. Red rash on the palms and soles of the feet, which, after a week or two, begins to peel.
	Typhoid fever	Headache; fever, loss of appetite; abdominal pain and tenderness; extreme weakness; constipation followed by diarrhea; drowsiness, stupor, or coma; raised, pink skin eruptions on the chest and abdomen; joint aches; sore throat.
with violent, shaking chills	Malaria	Initially, severe chills and shivering. In later stages, extremely high fever followed by a period of profuse perspiration as fever subsides; headache, sometimes severe; vomiting.
without sweating	Heatstroke	Sudden dizziness; weakness; headache; hot, dry, red skin which later turns grey; high body temperature; muscle cramps; confusion; seizures; loss of consciousness.
with dizziness	Ear infection, middle *Inflammation of the middle ear*	Earache; deafness; ringing in the ear; possibly, a discharge of pus from the ear; fever; dizziness.
	Ear infection, outer	Redness and itching of the ear canal; discharge from the ear; ear pain; possibly, temporary loss of hearing.
with diarrhea	Amebiasis *Parasitic infection*	Usually asymptomatic; possibly, diarrhea; loose stools may contain mucus and blood; abdominal cramps; fatigue; weight loss; gas and flatulence. In severe cases, large amount of bloody stools daily; fever, nausea and vomiting, and abdominal tenderness.

Fever *continued*

Associated Symptoms	Possible Diagnosis	Distinguishing Features
with diarrhea *continued*	Crohn's disease *Inflammation of the lining of the small intestine*	Episodes of abdominal pain or cramps in lower abdomen; nausea; diarrhea; loss of weight and appetite; possibly, fever; rectal bleeding or blood in stools; fatigue; anal fissures; joint pains; inflammation of the eyes.
	Dysentery, bacillary	Watery diarrhea that may contain pus or blood; abdominal pain; rapid dehydration and weight loss; nausea and vomiting.
	Megacolon *Distention of the colon*	Severe constipation; abdominal bloating; loss of weight and appetite; possible diarrhea; in newborns, failure to pass a stool within 48 hours after birth; in children, slow growth from infancy to age five.
with genitourinary symptoms	Bladder cancer	Blood in the urine; painful and frequent urination; pelvic pain; feeling of pressure in the back; persistent fever; urinary incontinence.
	Epididymitis *Inflammation of the coiled sperm conduit that rests on each testicle*	Severe pain and swelling at the back of a testicle; possibly, redness and swelling of the scrotum; burning on urination.
	Kidney infection *Pyelonephritis*	Sudden fever and shaking chills; severe fatigue; burning and frequent urination; cloudy or bloody urine; lower back pain, sometimes severe; nausea and vomiting.
	Orchitis *Inflammation of a testicle*	Swelling and severe pain in the affected testicle; possible bloody discharge in the semen; pain during intercourse; fever.
	Prostatitis *Inflammation of the prostate gland*	Burning during urination; urgent and frequent urination; fever and chills; discharge from the penis; lower abdominal and back pain; blood in the urine.
	Urethritis *Infection of the urethra, the passageway that drains urine from the bladder*	Frequent and painful urination; blood in the urine; yellow, pus-filled discharge; possible difficulty passing urine; urinary urgency; pain during intercourse; in men, painful ejaculation.
low-grade fever	Appendicitis, acute	Pain near the navel, spreading to the lower right abdomen; nausea and vomiting; constipation; possibly, diarrhea; low-grade fever; loss of appetite.
	Common cold	Nasal congestion; watery eyes; sneezing; sore throat; cough; muscle aches; mild headache; listlessness; possibly, low-grade fever.

Fever *continued*

Associated Symptoms	Possible Diagnosis	Distinguishing Features
low-grade fever *continued*	Intestinal obstruction	Abdominal pain and cramps; nausea; vomiting; weakness; gas; abdominal bloating; possible diarrhea; progressive constipation culminating in inability to pass stools or gas.
	Pancreatitis *Inflammation of the pancreas*	Sudden, extreme abdominal pain; nausea and vomiting; weakness; fever; clammy skin; abdominal bloating and tenderness.
	Pelvic inflammatory disease	Initially, lower pelvic pain; pain during intercourse; irregular menstrual bleeding; vaginal discharge with abnormal color or odor; low-grade fever; chills; frequent urination; fatigue; loss of appetite; later, severe abdominal pain and high fever.
	Scleroderma	Shiny, tight, and hardened skin, especially on the fingers, arms, and face; hands or feet may successively turn blue, white, and red upon exposure to cold (Raynaud's phenomenon); swallowing difficulty; bloating after eating; weight loss; shortness of breath on exertion; high blood pressure; symptoms of renal failure. Possibly, heartburn, muscle aches and weakness, joint pain, fever, or fatigue.
	Sinusitis *Inflammation of the mucus membranes lining the sinuses*	Throbbing pain above or below one or both eyes that intensifies when bending the head forward or coughing; nasal congestion; loss of sense of smell; often, pus-like nasal discharge; possible dental pain in the upper jaw; fever.
	Tetanus	Often, lockjaw; stiffness and, later, muscle spasms in the neck and face; drooling; abdominal and back pain; extreme perspiration; swallowing difficulty; possible convulsions; fever.

Fingernail abnormalities

Associated Symptoms	Possible Diagnosis	Distinguishing Features
	Chronic obstructive pulmonary disease	Shortness of breath; wheezing; persistent, mucus-producing cough, especially in the morning; possibly, chest pain, swollen legs and ankles.
	Congestive heart failure	Shortness of breath; fatigue; need to sleep on several pillows; weakness; cough; heart palpitations; swelling in the legs, ankles, and abdomen; frequent urination at night; indigestion; nausea and vomiting; loss of appetite.
	Eczema *Inflammation of the skin*	Itching skin; thickened patches of skin; possibly, with oozing and crusting; in infants, rash on the face, inner elbows, or behind the knees that turns scaly and develops small red pimples that leak; swollen legs (stasis dermatitis).
	Lung cancer	Persistent cough; wheezing; shortness of breath; chest pain; fatigue; loss of appetite and weight loss.
	Pleurisy and pleural effusion *Inflammation of the membranes lining the lungs and chest cavity*	Sudden chest pain worse on inspiration that may also radiate into the shoulder or abdomen; rapid breathing; coughing; sneezing; possibly, fever.
	Psoriasis	Slightly raised patches of skin with red borders and white-silver scales; joint pain and stiffness; itching; pitted nails.
	Pulmonary edema *An accumulation of fluid in the lungs*	Severe shortness of breath; rapid breathing; pallor; excessive perspiration; bluish nails and lips; cough with frothy sputum; wheezing; anxiety and restlessness.

Flatulence

Associated Symptoms	Possible Diagnosis	Distinguishing Features
	Amebiasis *Parasitic infection*	Usually asymptomatic; possibly, diarrhea; loose stools may contain mucus and blood; abdominal cramps; fatigue; weight loss; gas and flatulence. In severe cases, large amount of bloody stools daily; fever, nausea and vomiting, and abdominal tenderness.
	Carcinoid tumors and carcinoid syndrome	May be asymptomatic; flushing or redness of the face and neck; gas and profuse diarrhea; abdominal cramping; watery, swollen eyes; shortness of breath or wheezing.
	Cirrhosis *Chronic damage to the cells of the liver*	No symptoms in early stages; loss of weight and appetite; nausea; swollen legs, ankles and abdomen; itching; jaundice; black stools; vomiting blood; fatigue; impotence; memory loss; confusion.
	Colorectal cancer *A growth of malignant cells in the colon or rectum*	Change in bowel habits; diarrhea; constipation; narrow stools; bloody or dark stools; lower abdominal pain; bloating; cramps; gas; loss of weight and appetite; fatigue and heart palpitations due to anemia.
	Crohn's disease *Inflammation of the lining of the small intestine*	Episodes of abdominal pain or cramps in lower abdomen; nausea; diarrhea; loss of weight and appetite; possibly, fever; rectal bleeding or blood in stools; fatigue; anal fissures; joint pains; inflammation of the eyes.
	Gallbladder disorders	Moderate to severe pain in the upper right side of the abdomen, chest, upper back, or right shoulder. Pain often follows the ingestion of high-fat foods and is episodic, lasting 20 minutes to several hours. Nausea and vomiting; low-grade fever; belching; heartburn; gas; possibly, jaundice, pale stools, and itchy skin.
	Intestinal obstruction	Abdominal pain and cramps; nausea; vomiting; weakness; gas; abdominal bloating; possible diarrhea; progressive constipation culminating in inability to pass stools or gas.
	Irritable bowel syndrome	Cramps in the middle or to one side of the lower abdomen that are usually relieved with bowel movements; nausea; bloating; gas; alternating diarrhea and constipation.
	Lactose intolerance *Difficulty digesting dairy products*	Abdominal cramps; diarrhea; nausea; bloating; flatulence.
	Malabsorption, digestive *A failure of the small intestine to absorb nutrients in the diet*	Diarrhea; weight loss; yellowish, foul-smelling stools; abdominal cramps, gas, and bloating; weakness and lethargy.

Foot pain

Associated Symptoms	Possible Diagnosis	Distinguishing Features
	Ankylosing spondylitis *Inflammation of the joints between the spine and the pelvis*	Initially, pain and stiffness in the lower back and hips that becomes worse after resting; neck or chest pain; fatigue; possible pain in the hip, knee, and ankle joints; pain in the heel of the foot; eye pain; blurred vision.
	Bone fractures	Pain in the affected bone which intensifies with movement or the application of pressure; swelling, bruising, or bleeding around the site of an injury; in a compound fracture, protrusion of bone through skin; possible loss of function or feeling in the injured area; local deformity.
	Bunions	Painful, bony lump at the side of the base of the big toe; foot pain and stiffness; redness and swelling at the base of the big toe.
	Bursitis *Inflammation of the bursas, the lubricant-filled sacs in and around the joints*	Pain and swelling around a joint, usually the elbow, knee, or shoulder; painful movement in the affected joint; possibly, fever.
	Corns and calluses	Area of thickened skin on the foot; pain in the affected area.
	Dislocations/subluxations	Deformity of the affected joint; joint pain and tenderness; difficulty moving a joint; swelling and stiffness within 30 minutes after joint injury.
	Gout	Most commonly affects the joints of the big toe. Affected joints are red, swollen, hot, and severely painful. In late stages, joint deformity. Kidney stones.
	Hammer toe and mallet toe	A toe, usually the second digit, next to the big toe, that is clenched into a painful, claw-like position, or a toe with an end joint that curls under itself. A painful corn on top of the bent joint or at the tip of the affected toe.
	Infectious arthritis	Pain, swelling, stiffness, and redness, usually in one joint. Fever. Severity varies from a mild ache to severe, debilitating pain and eventual joint deformity.
	Osteoarthritis *Degeneration of the cartilage that lines the joints*	Pain, swelling, and stiffness in one or more joints; enlargement and distortion of affected joints.
	Osteomalacia and Rickets *Softening and weakening of the bones, usually due to poor calcification*	Bone pain, especially in the neck, legs, hips and ribs. Muscle weakness, numbness, or spasms in the hands, feet, and throat; increased susceptibility to bone fractures.

Foot pain *continued*

Associated Symptoms	Possible Diagnosis	Distinguishing Features
	Osteomyelitis *Infection of bone and bone marrow*	Fever; severe pain in the affected bone; inflammation and swelling of the skin over the affected area; deformity. In children, arrested growth of the affected bone.
	Peripheral neuropathies *Degeneration of the nerves that supply the extremities*	Tingling or numbness commonly beginning in the hands and feet and gradually spreading toward the center of the body; sensitive skin; muscle weakness; possibly, pain in the hands and feet; lack of coordination; shooting pains exacerbated by touch or changes in temperature; breathing difficulty; urinary or fecal incontinence.
	Peripheral vascular disease *Narrowing of blood vessels in the legs or arms*	Muscle pain on one or both legs that occurs with exercise and subsides with rest; possible pain in the fingers, arms, buttocks, lower back, or the arch of the foot; impotence. Severe symptoms include: muscle pain at rest that intensifies at night; discolored or blue toes; cold or numb feet; open sores; heightened sensitivity to cold; weak or absent pulse in the affected limb; scaly or hairless skin over the affected area.
	Plantar fasciitis *Inflammation of the ligament between the front of the heel bone and base of the toes*	Heel pain, especially when running or walking; possibly, tenderness and swelling in the heel.
	Plantar warts *Hard, rough-surfaced growth on the foot occurring singularly or in groups*	Body weight causes wart to grow into skin surface rather than being raised, giving it the appearance of a callous. Pain when putting weight on the foot.
	Rheumatoid arthritis	Fatigue and weakness; joint pain, stiffness, and inflammation, especially in the hands, feet, and arms; joint deformity; dry mouth; dry, painful eyes. Morning stiffness.
	Rheumatoid arthritis, juvenile	Fever; rash; abdominal pain; weight loss; swelling, stiffness, and pain in the affected joints; enlarged lymph glands; fatigue; pallor; red, painful eyes; morning stiffness.
	Sprains and strains	Swelling, pain or tenderness in the affected joints; impaired joint function.
	Tendinitis *Inflammation of a tendon*	Pain and tenderness over a tendon anywhere in the body; if involved tendon is near or part of a joint, restricted movement of the joint.
	Varicose veins	Blue or purplish, knotted veins, usually in the legs; itching or discomfort in the affected area; swollen feet and ankles. Possible scaly skin, muscle cramps, or skin ulcers.

Gait abnormalities

Associated Symptoms	Possible Diagnosis	Distinguishing Features
	Acoustic neuroma *A benign tumor in the cells covering the auditory nerve*	Gradual hearing loss; ringing in the ear; headache; numbness in the face; unsteady walk. In later stages, swallowing and speaking difficulties; possibly, slight paralysis.
	Amyotrophic lateral sclerosis *Progressive degeneration of nerve cells of the central nervous system*	Progressive loss of strength and coordination in the limbs; muscle twitching and cramps that begin in the hands and spread to the arms, shoulders, and legs; stiff, clumsy gait; swallowing, breathing, or speaking difficulty; weight loss; drooling; involuntary laughing or crying.
	Multiple sclerosis *Gradual degeneration of the protective sheaths surrounding the nerves within the brain and spinal cord*	Symptoms may appear suddenly and then disappear; persistent symptoms may take years to develop and include numbness or tingling in any part of the body, weakness in the extremities, an unsteady walk, slurred speech, urinary incontinence, fatigue, depression, temporary loss of vision, double or blurred vision, mental confusion, and memory loss.
	Muscular dystrophy	Symptoms depend on type of muscular dystrophy and may include: Progressive muscle wasting, weakness, and loss of mobility; lack of coordination; muscular and skeletal deformities including backward curvature of the spine with protruding abdomen; waddling gait; cataracts; frontal baldness; gonadal atrophy.
	Osteoarthritis *Degeneration of the cartilage that lines the joints*	Pain, swelling, and stiffness in one or more joints; enlargement and distortion of affected joints.
	Parkinson's disease *Degeneration of the basal ganglia, a cluster of nerve cells in the brain*	Tremors in the hands; stiffness and weakness; impaired voluntary movement; shuffling gait; stooped posture; unblinking, fixed expression; possibly, slow, hesitant speech; difficulty swallowing; drooling; depression. Tremors occur at rest (not with voluntary movements) and disappear during sleep.
	Poliomyelitis *Polio*	Low fever; sore throat; headache; nausea and vomiting. In severe cases, paralysis without loss of sensation; stiff neck and back; twitching; swallowing and breathing difficulty; drooling.
	Rheumatic fever	Initially, a sore throat that gets better followed, one to six weeks later, by lethargy and fever. Possibly, swollen joints, rash, abdominal pain, involuntary jerky movements, emotional instability.

Gait abnormalities *continued*

Associated Symptoms	Possible Diagnosis	Distinguishing Features
	Rheumatoid arthritis	Fatigue and weakness; joint pain, stiffness, and inflammation, especially in the hands, feet, and arms; joint deformity; dry mouth; dry, painful eyes. Morning stiffness.
	Spinal cord trauma	Severe pain and swelling in the affected area; loss of sensation, muscle weakness, or paralysis below the site of the injury; urinary or fecal incontinence or retention; impotence; breathing difficulty; shock.
	Spinal tumor	Progressive numbness, tingling, and muscle weakness; fecal or urinary incontinence; persistent back pain.
	Spondylosis, cervical *Arthritis of the vertebral disks in the neck*	Neck pain and stiffness that spreads to the shoulders, upper arms, hands, or back of the head; numbness or tingling in the arms, hands, and fingers; weakness in the arms and legs; unsteady gait; possible loss of bladder control.

Gas

Associated Symptoms	Possible Diagnosis	Distinguishing Features
	Amebiasis *Parasitic infection*	Usually asymptomatic; possibly, diarrhea; loose stools may contain mucus and blood; abdominal cramps; fatigue; weight loss; gas and flatulence. In severe cases, large amount of bloody stools daily; fever, nausea and vomiting, and abdominal tenderness.
	Carcinoid tumors and carcinoid syndrome	May be asymptomatic; flushing or redness of the face and neck; gas and profuse diarrhea; abdominal cramping; watery, swollen eyes; shortness of breath or wheezing.
	Cirrhosis *Chronic damage to the cells of the liver*	No symptoms in early stages; loss of weight and appetite; nausea; swollen legs, ankles and abdomen; itching; jaundice; black stools; vomiting blood; fatigue; impotence; memory loss; confusion.
	Colorectal cancer *A growth of malignant cells in the colon or rectum*	Change in bowel habits; diarrhea; constipation; narrow stools; bloody or dark stools; lower abdominal pain; bloating; cramps; gas; loss of weight and appetite; fatigue and heart palpitations due to anemia.
	Crohn's disease *Inflammation of the lining of the small intestine*	Episodes of abdominal pain or cramps in lower abdomen; nausea; diarrhea; loss of weight and appetite; possibly, fever; rectal bleeding or blood in stools; fatigue; anal fissures; joint pains; inflammation of the eyes.
	Gallbladder disorders	Moderate to severe pain in the upper right side of the abdomen, chest, upper back, or right shoulder. Pain often follows the ingestion of high-fat foods and is episodic, lasting 20 minutes to several hours. Nausea and vomiting; low-grade fever; belching; heartburn; gas; possibly, jaundice, pale stools, and itchy skin.
	Intestinal obstruction	Abdominal pain and cramps; nausea; vomiting; weakness; gas; abdominal bloating; possible diarrhea; progressive constipation culminating in inability to pass stools or gas.
	Irritable bowel syndrome	Cramps in the middle or to one side of the lower abdomen that are usually relieved with bowel movements; nausea; bloating; gas; alternating diarrhea and constipation.
	Lactose intolerance *Difficulty digesting dairy products*	Abdominal cramps; diarrhea; nausea; bloating; flatulence.
	Malabsorption, digestive *A failure of the small intestine to absorb nutrients in the diet*	Diarrhea; weight loss; yellowish, foul-smelling stools; abdominal cramps, gas, and bloating; weakness and lethargy.

Genital lesions

Associated Symptoms	Possible Diagnosis	Distinguishing Features
	Candidiasis *Fungal infection of the mouth, genitals, or mucus membranes*	Thick, white discharge from the vagina; itching and irritation in the vaginal area; pain while urinating or during intercourse; in men, inflammation of the head of the penis; possibly, yellow raised patches in the mouth.
	Genital herpes	Approximately one week after infection, itching, burning, soreness, and small blisters in the genital area. Blisters later burst, leaving painful ulcers which heal 10 to 20 days later. Possibly, enlarged, painful lymph nodes in the groin; fever, headache, and cold sores around the mouth. In women, pain during urination.
	Genital warts	Small, red, round or flat, itchy bumps on or around the vagina, anus, penis, or perineum (area between the anus and genitals) developing between eight and 18 months after infection. Several warts may grow together into a cauliflower shape.
	Penile cancer	Sore, ulcer, or wart-like lump on the penis, usually near the head, possibly painful; bleeding or unusual discharge from the penis. Possibly, pain during urination, or enlarged lymph nodes in the groin.
	Ringworm *Fungal skin infection*	A rash with distinct, advancing borders and clear centers; affected areas may have abnormally dark pigmentation; itching; scaly patches of skin; bald patches on scalp; Athlete's foot; red, swollen finger- and toenails.
	Scabies	Tiny, grey, scaly blisters—usually on the wrists, genitals, armpits, or between the fingers—that rupture easily when scratched; severe itching; red lumps or rashes may develop.
	Syphilis	Initially, painless, ulcerated, red sore on the genitals, mouth, or rectum; swollen glands in the neck, armpit, or groin; rash with small, red, scaly bumps; fever; headache. If left untreated, damage to heart valves leading to congestive heart failure; mental deterioration; loss of balance; seizures; dementia; personality changes.
	Vaginal cancer	Vaginal itching; bleeding after intercourse or between menstrual periods; abnormal vaginal discharge; lesions with thick, raised edges; possibly rectal bleeding; discomfort when urinating or defecating; pain during intercourse; urinary frequency and urgency.

Genital pain

Associated Symptoms	Possible Diagnosis	Distinguishing Features
	Candidiasis *Fungal infection of the mouth, genitals, or mucus membrane*	Thick, white discharge from the vagina; itching and irritation in the vaginal area; pain while urinating or during intercourse; in men, inflammation of the head of the penis; possibly, yellow raised patches in the mouth.
	Cervical disorders, non-malignant	Vaginal discharge; vaginal burning and itching; vaginal bleeding after intercourse, between periods, or after bowel movements.
	Endometriosis *The migration of the uterine lining to other reproductive or abdominal organs*	Pain in the lower abdomen, vagina, and lower back beginning just prior to menses and intensifying after blood flow has ceased; heavy bleeding during periods; pain during intercourse; diarrhea; constipation; pain during bowel movements; bleeding from the rectum; bloody urine during menses; nausea and vomiting prior to menses; infertility.
	Epididymitis *Inflammation of the coiled sperm conduit that rests on each testicle*	Severe pain and swelling at the back of a testicle; possibly, redness and swelling of the scrotum; burning on urination.
	Gonorrhea	Burning pain during urination; yellowish, pus-like discharge from the penis or vagina; redness or swelling at the infection site; abnormal vaginal bleeding.
	Orchitis *Inflammation of a testicle*	Swelling and severe pain in the affected testicle; possible bloody discharge in the semen; pain during intercourse; fever.
	Pelvic inflammatory disease	Initially, lower pelvic pain; pain during intercourse; irregular menstrual bleeding; vaginal discharge with abnormal color or odor; low-grade fever; chills; frequent urination; fatigue; loss of appetite; later, severe abdominal pain and high fever.
	Prostatitis *Inflammation of the prostate gland*	Burning during urination; urgent and frequent urination; fever and chills; discharge from the penis; lower abdominal and back pain; blood in the urine.
	Testicular torsion *Twisting of the spermatic cord*	Severe pain and swelling on one side of the scrotum; skin on the scrotum may appear red or purple; light-headedness or fainting; possibly, abdominal pain, nausea and vomiting.
	Vaginitis *Inflammation of the vagina*	Vaginal irritation, itching, and discharge; painful intercourse and minor postcoital bleeding. In later stages, vaginal pain.

Growth/sore that does not heal

Associated Symptoms	Possible Diagnosis	Distinguishing Features
	Basal cell carcinoma *Skin cancer*	Small, flat, waxy bump, usually on the face, ears, or neck; darkened or flesh-colored lump on the back of torso; skin blemish that grows steadily over a period of weeks without healing, developing into a shallow ulcer with a moist center and raised edges that doesn't heal.
	Hemophilia	Profuse bleeding from minor injuries and tooth extractions; internal bleeding that may cause blood in the urine; bleeding into joints; symptoms of stroke due to intracerebral bleeding; possibly, extensive bruising.
	Melanoma *Skin cancer*	Change in the appearance of an existing mole including enlargement, bleeding, change in color, development of a black edge. Itching.
	Oral cancers	Sore in the mouth that bleeds and does not heal; lump in the cheek; white or red patch on the gums; swallowing and chewing difficulties; numbness of the tongue; swelling of the jaw.
	Peripheral vascular disease *Narrowing of blood vessels in the legs or arms*	Muscle pain on one or both legs that occurs with exercise and subsides with rest; possible pain in the fingers, arms, buttocks, lower back, or the arch of the foot; impotence. Severe symptoms include: muscle pain at rest that intensifies at night; discolored or blue toes; cold or numb feet; open sores; heightened sensitivity to cold; weak or absent pulse in the affected limb; scaly or hairless skin over the affected area.
	Sinusitis *Inflammation of the mucus membranes lining the sinuses*	Throbbing pain above or below one or both eyes that intensifies when bending the head forward or coughing; nasal congestion; loss of sense of smell; often, pus-like nasal discharge; possible dental pain in the upper jaw; fever.
	Varicose veins	Blue or purplish, knotted veins, usually in the legs; itching or discomfort in the affected area; swollen feet and ankles. Possible scaly skin, muscle cramps, or skin ulcers.

Gum swelling

Associated Symptoms	Possible Diagnosis	Distinguishing Features
	Gingivitis	Red-purple gums that are swollen, shiny, and bleed easily; bad breath.
	Impacted teeth	Gum pain; unpleasant taste in mouth, especially when biting down; red, swollen gums around the affected tooth; headache or jaw ache; possibly, bad breath.
	Oral cancers	Sore in the mouth that bleeds and does not heal; lump in the cheek; white or red patch on the gums; swallowing and chewing difficulties; numbness of the tongue; swelling of the jaw.
	Periodontitis *Inflammation of the tissues supporting the teeth.*	Red, swollen, painful gums that bleed easily; loose teeth; bad breath; possible pus discharge.
	Tooth abscess	Persistent tooth pain; pain when biting or chewing; swollen glands in the neck; earache; fever; possibly, foul taste in the mouth or bad breath.
	Tooth decay	Tooth pain, especially after eating sweet or sour foods; tooth sensitivity to hot and cold; bad breath; unpleasant taste in the mouth.
	Tongue disorders	Symptoms vary depending on the specific disorder and include: dark or bright red, black, or dark brown tongue; sore, swollen, or smooth tongue; hair-like growths on the tongue; adjacent areas of the mouth may be inflamed; ulcers or raised, white patches on the tongue; excessive salivation; swallowing difficulty; bad breath.
	Trench mouth	Grayish film on the gums; red, swollen, painful, bleeding gums; bad breath; bad taste in the mouth; pain on swallowing or speaking; excessive salivation.

Hair growth in women, unusual

Associated Symptoms	Possible Diagnosis	Distinguishing Features
	Hepatitis, chronic	Fatigue; nausea; vomiting; loss of appetite; jaundice; dark urine; clay-colored stools; depression; pain or discomfort in the upper right abdomen; abdominal swelling; fever; in women, cessation of menstruation, acne, and the appearance of male pattern facial hair.
	Ovarian cancer	Often asymptomatic until widespread. Possibly, abdominal swelling or discomfort, nausea, and vomiting. In advanced stages, excessive hair growth, unexplained weight loss, abnormal menstrual bleeding or post-menopausal bleeding; urinary frequency.
	Ovarian cysts	In many cases, no symptoms. Painless swelling in the lower abdomen; possibly, pain during intercourse; brown vaginal discharge; lack of or heavier than usual menstrual periods; vomiting; unusual hair growth on face or body.
	Polycystic ovaries	Absent or unpredictable menstrual periods; infertility; excessive hair growth with a male pattern of distribution; obesity; acne.

Hair loss

Associated Symptoms	Possible Diagnosis	Distinguishing Features
	Alopecia *Hair loss*	Gradual loss of hair from the head or any other hair-bearing area of the body.
	Hypopituitarism *Underactivity of the pituitary gland*	Intolerance to cold; chronic headaches; decreased sex drive; fatigue; fine wrinkles around the eyes and mouth; dry skin; extreme thirst and excessive urination; loss of appetite; vaginal dryness; absence of milk production in new mothers; in men, reduced muscular strength, shrinking of the testes, and loss of body hair; growth retardation in children and adolescents
	Hypothyroidism *Underactivity of the thyroid gland*	Unexplained weight gain; fatigue; muscle weakness; cramps; dry skin; hair loss; deepening of the voice; intolerance for cold; constipation; chest pain; insomnia; puffiness around eyes; loss of sex drive; depression; menstrual abnormalities; possible swelling in the neck (goiter).
	Ringworm *Fungal skin infection*	A rash with distinct, advancing borders and clear centers; affected areas may have abnormally dark pigmentation; itching; scaly patches of skin; bald patches on scalp; Athlete's foot; red, swollen finger- and toenails.
	Systemic lupus erythematosus *Inflammation of connective tissues throughout the body*	Red, blotchy, butterfly-shaped rash on the cheeks and bridge of the nose; fatigue; fever; loss of appetite and weight; nausea; joint and abdominal pain; headaches; blurred vision; increased sensitivity to sun exposure; depression; psychosis; mental confusion.

Hallucinations

Associated Symptoms	Possible Diagnosis	Distinguishing Features
	Alzheimer's disease	Symptoms vary greatly in different individuals. Initially, minor forgetfulness gradually developing into severe, short-term memory loss, disorientation, an inability to concentrate, and sudden mood and personality changes. In later stages, severe confusion, possible hallucinations or paranoid delusions, loss of social and sexual inhibitions, impaired judgment, anxiety, depression, agitation and combativeness, wandering and getting lost, inability to write, urinary and fecal incontinence.
	Encephalitis *Inflammation of the brain*	Initially, headache and fever followed by confusion, hallucinations, and paralysis on one side of the body; memory loss; difficulty with speech and eye movements; drowsiness; possible coma or epileptic seizures; loss of hearing; sensitivity to light; stiff neck.
	Heatstroke	Sudden dizziness; weakness; headache; hot, dry, red skin which later turns grey; high body temperature; muscle cramps; confusion; seizures; loss of consciousness.
	Seizures	Involuntary twitching or jerking; muscle rigidity; loss of consciousness; confusion; drooling; hallucinations.

Hand pain

Associated Symptoms	Possible Diagnosis	Distinguishing Features
	Bone cancer	Pain, tenderness, and swelling in the affected bones and joints, often intensifying at night; a noticeable tumor or mass; increased susceptibility to bone fractures.
	Bone fractures	Pain in the affected bone which intensifies with movement or the application of pressure; swelling, bruising, or bleeding around the site of an injury; in a compound fracture, protrusion of bone through skin; possible loss of function or feeling in the injured area; local deformity.
	Carpal tunnel syndrome	Numbness, tingling, and pain in the hand and wrist, often intensifying at night; weakness of the fingers and hand.
	Dislocations/subluxations	Deformity of the affected joint; joint pain and tenderness; difficulty moving a joint; swelling and stiffness within 30 minutes after joint injury.
	Dupuytren's contracture	Inability to straighten one or more fingers or toes, usually the ring and little fingers; hard nodule on the palm of the hand; puckering of the skin on the hand.
	Ganglion	A round swelling or cyst under the skin, usually on the wrist, which may feel soft and rubbery or hard and solid. Possible pain or tenderness in the lump, especially when the wrist is extended or flexed.
	Osteoarthritis *Degeneration of the cartilage that lines the joints*	Pain, swelling, and stiffness in one or more joints; enlargement and distortion of affected joints.
	Osteomalacia and Rickets *Softening and weakening of the bones, usually due to poor calcification*	Bone pain, especially in the neck, legs, hips and ribs. Muscle weakness, numbness, or spasms in the hands, feet, and throat; increased susceptibility to bone fractures.
	Osteomyelitis *Infection of bone and bone marrow*	Fever; severe pain in the affected bone; inflammation and swelling of the skin over the affected area; deformity. In children, arrested growth of the affected bone.
	Osteoporosis *Loss of bone mass due to calcium depletion*	Backache; easily fractured bones, especially in the wrists, hips, and spine; gradual loss of height; stooped or hunched posture.
	Rheumatoid arthritis	Fatigue and weakness; joint pain, stiffness, and inflammation, especially in the hands, feet, and arms; joint deformity; dry mouth; dry, painful eyes. Morning stiffness.

Hand pain *continued*

Associated Symptoms	Possible Diagnosis	Distinguishing Features
	Rheumatoid arthritis, juvenile	Fever; rash; abdominal pain; weight loss; swelling, stiffness, and pain in the affected joints; enlarged lymph glands; fatigue; pallor; red, painful eyes; morning stiffness.
	Sprains and strains	Swelling, pain or tenderness in the affected joints; impaired joint function.
	Tendinitis *Inflammation of a tendon*	Pain and tenderness over a tendon anywhere in the body; if involved tendon is near or part of a joint, restricted movement of the joint.

Headache

Associated Symptoms	Possible Diagnosis	Distinguishing Features
	Acoustic neuroma *A benign tumor in the cells covering the auditory nerve*	Gradual hearing loss; ringing in the ear; headache; numbness in the face; unsteady walk. In later stages, swallowing and speaking difficulties; possibly, slight paralysis.
	Anemia, aplastic	Fatigue and weakness; shortness of breath; heart palpitations; pallor; bleeding gums; nosebleeds; tendency to bruise easily; small red dots under the skin (petechiae). Increased susceptibility to infection.
	Anemia, folic acid deficiency	Fatigue and weakness; pallor; shortness of breath, heart palpitations, or noticeably rapid heartbeat on exertion; sore, red, and glazed-looking tongue; loss of weight and appetite; nausea and diarrhea; abdominal distention.
	Anemia, hemolytic	Fatigue and weakness; shortness of breath on exertion; pallor; heart palpitations; jaundice and dark urine.
	Anemia, iron deficiency	Fatigue and weakness; pallor; shortness of breath and heart palpitations on exertion; irritability or inability to concentrate; sore tongue or tiny cracks at the corners of the mouth; black, tarry or bloody stools; unusual craving for dirt, paint, or ice.
	Anemia, pernicious	Fatigue; inability to concentrate; sore, red tongue; weakness; dizziness; pallor; shortness of breath on exertion; palpitations; numbness and tingling in extremities; incoordination; headache; loss of weight and appetite; possibly, jaundice.
	Brain tumors	Headaches that become more severe when reclining; nausea and vomiting; memory loss; double vision; muscle weakness; numbness, tingling, or partial paralysis; vision loss; speech disturbances; seizures; drowsiness.
	Cholesteatoma *Infected cyst in the eardrum or middle ear*	Hearing loss; discharge of pus from ear; headaches and earaches; weakness of facial muscles; dizziness.
	Fibromyalgia	Muscle aches, pains, and stiffness; specific points on the body that feel sore when pressed. Fatigue, headaches, and possible insomnia. Feeling unrefreshed upon awakening in the morning.
	Glaucoma	Often initially asymptomatic. In later stages, the symptoms of closed angle glaucoma include: the appearance of halos and rainbows around lights; dilated pupil in the affected eye; severe headache and eye pain; possibly, nausea and vomiting. Open angle glaucoma symptoms include: blurred vision and a gradual loss of peripheral vision.

Headache *continued*

Associated Symptoms	Possible Diagnosis	Distinguishing Features
	Headache, cluster	Persistent pain in or around one eye; redness and tearing of one eye; nasal congestion on the same side of the face as the affected eye.
	Headache, migraine	Throbbing pain in the temple which spreads to the side of the head; nausea; vomiting. Pain may be preceded by blurred or impaired vision with bright spots and zig-zag patterns.
	Headache, tension	Dull, persistent pain in the forehead, temples, or back of the neck. Sensation of constricting band encircling the head.
	Hydrocephalus *Overaccumulation of cerebrospinal fluid, the liquid surrounding the brain*	In infants, an enlarged head, rigidity of the legs, irritability, projectile vomiting, drowsiness, seizures, and lethargy. In older persons, headache, vomiting, loss of coordination, deterioration of mental faculties, speech difficulty, and loss of appetite.
	Hyperpituitarism *Overactivity of the pituitary gland*	In adults (in which the disease is called acromegaly): Gradual thickening of the bones of the face, jaw, and the extremities in adults; oily skin; severe headache; excessive hair growth; excessive perspiration; joint pains. In children (in which the disease is called gigantism): Rapid growth and unusual height; possibly, blindness.
	Hypertension	Usually asymptomatic except in severe cases. Possibly, headache, easy fatigability, palpitations, chest pain, blurred vision, dizziness, nose bleeds, and confusion.
	Hypoglycemia *Low blood sugar*	Anxiety; hunger; trembling; headache; palpitations; perspiration; confusion; irritability; loss of coordination; possibly, double vision, seizures, or coma.
	Hypopituitarism *Underactivity of the pituitary gland*	Intolerance to cold; chronic headaches; decreased sex drive; fatigue; fine wrinkles around the eyes and mouth; dry skin; extreme thirst and excessive urination; loss of appetite; vaginal dryness; absence of milk production in new mothers; in men, reduced muscular strength, shrinking of the testes, and loss of body hair; growth retardation in children and adolescents.
	Impacted teeth	Gum pain; unpleasant taste in mouth, especially when biting down; red, swollen gums around the affected tooth; headache or jaw ache; possibly, bad breath.
	Lymphoma, non-Hodgkin's *Cancer of the lymph nodes and lymphoid tissue*	Painless swelling of lymph nodes in the neck or groin; possible abdominal pain, vomiting of blood, headache.

Headache *continued*

Associated Symptoms	Possible Diagnosis	Distinguishing Features
	Multiple myeloma *Production of malignant plasma cells in the bone marrow*	Bone pain, especially progressive, constant back pain that intensifies with movement; unexplained bone fractures; fatigue; pallor; shortness of breath; increased bleeding, such as bleeding gums or nosebleeds; easily bruised skin; increased susceptibility to infection; headache; vision disturbances; loss of height.
	Mumps	Pain in the ear, below the ear, and in the jaw; swollen glands in the neck; headache; pain on swallowing and chewing. Testicular swelling and tenderness in adults.
	Nasal polyps	Impaired sense of smell; a feeling of fullness in the face; possible nasal discharge, facial pain, or headaches.
	Paget's disease *A weakening, thickening, and deformity of the bones*	Often asymptomatic. Possibly, bone pain or deformity, especially bowing of the legs, bent spine, and facial deformity; unexplained bone fractures; joint pain or stiffness; hearing loss; headaches; ringing in ears.
	Pheochromocytoma *Tumor in central part of the adrenal, the glands above the kidneys*	Headaches, sometimes severe; rapid heartbeat or heart palpitations; excessive perspiration; faintness, especially when standing up; chest pain; abdominal pain; constipation; weight loss; nervousness, irritability, or anxiety; mental confusion or psychosis.
	Polycythemia vera *An overproduction of red and white blood cells and platelets*	Headache; blurred vision; flushed skin; itching; dizziness; fatigue; night sweats; shortness of breath; weight loss.
	Presbyopia *Loss of elasticity of lens of the eye*	Progressive decrease in the ability to focus on objects at close range; eye strain; possibly headache.
	Refractive disorders	Depending on the specific disorder, blurred vision or an inability to clearly see objects that are either near or far.
	Renal failure, acute *Severe kidney failure*	Initially, decreased urine output, weight gain and swelling due to edema, loss of appetite, nausea and vomiting, fatigue. If untreated, confusion, seizures, and drowsiness.
	Sleep apnea *Recurrent episodes of breathing cessation during sleep*	Loud snoring; morning fatigue and headache; sleep disturbances; daytime sleepiness; difficulty concentrating; memory loss. Most common among overweight men.
	Spondylosis, cervical *Arthritis of the vertebral disks in the neck*	Neck pain and stiffness that spreads to the shoulders, upper arms, hands, or back of the head; numbness or tingling in the arms, hands, and fingers; weakness in the arms and legs; unsteady gait; possible loss of bladder control.

Headache *continued*

Associated Symptoms	Possible Diagnosis	Distinguishing Features
	Stroke	Symptoms vary with the location of brain injury. Sudden onset of weakness, paralysis, or loss of sensation, usually on one side of the body; a sudden heaviness in a limb; speech abnormalities; headache; vision disturbances; dizziness; confusion; coma; urinary and fecal incontinence.
	Temporomandibular joint syndrome *TMJ*	Pain in the joints connecting the jaw to the skull; headache; tender jaw muscles; dull facial pain; clicking noise when opening or closing the mouth; pain when yawning and chewing. Jaw may temporarily lock in position.
with fever	Brain hemorrhage	Sudden loss of consciousness; sudden, severe headache; paralysis on one side of the face or body; weakness and dizziness; loss of speech; blurred or double vision; dilated pupils; back and leg pain; fever; mental confusion; stiff neck.
	Chronic fatigue syndrome	Severe fatigue made worse by exercise; recurrent flu-like symptoms; persistent sore throat; low-grade fever; muscle and joint aches; headache; painful, swollen lymph nodes; depression and mental confusion; memory loss; sleep difficulties.
	Common cold	Nasal congestion; watery eyes; sneezing; sore throat; cough; muscle aches; mild headache; listlessness; possibly, low-grade fever.
	Encephalitis *Inflammation of the brain*	Initially, headache and fever followed by confusion, hallucinations, and paralysis on one side of the body; memory loss; difficulty with speech and eye movements; drowsiness; possible coma or epileptic seizures; loss of hearing; sensitivity to light; stiff neck.
	Genital herpes	Approximately one week after infection, itching, burning, soreness, and small blisters in the genital area. Blisters later burst, leaving painful ulcers which heal 10 to 20 days later. Possibly, enlarged, painful lymph nodes in the groin; fever, headache, and cold sores around the mouth. In women, pain during urination.
	Heatstroke	Sudden dizziness; weakness; headache; hot, dry, red skin which later turns grey; high body temperature; muscle cramps; confusion; seizures; loss of consciousness.
	Influenza *Flu*	Chills, muscle aches, and loss of appetite followed by a cough, sore throat, nasal congestion, and fever; possible chest pain.

Headache *continued*

Associated Symptoms	Possible Diagnosis	Distinguishing Features
with fever *continued*	Lyme disease	A small red bump, surrounded by a concentric bulls-eye-like red rash with a pale center. Over the following month: fever and chills; extreme fatigue; headaches. Symptoms may progress over several months or years and may include: palpitations; joint or muscle pain; and chronic joint inflammation, especially in the knees.
	Mastoiditis, acute *Inflammation of the mastoid, a bone behind the ear*	Severe pain and swelling behind and within the ear; fever; discharge from the ear; progressive hearing loss.
	Mononucleosis, infectious	Headache; high fever; swollen glands in the neck, groin, and armpits; severe sore throat; swallowing difficulty.
	Peritonsillar abscess *A collection of pus between the tonsils and surrounding tissue due to infection*	Sore throat; severe pain when swallowing; fever; headache; impaired speech; drooling; swollen glands in the neck.
	Pharyngitis *Inflammation of the pharynx, the part of the throat between the mouth and the esophagus*	Sore or red throat; speaking and swallowing difficulties; sensitive, swollen glands in the neck; fever; headache; possible earache.
	Rabies	Low-grade fever; headache; loss of appetite; tingling at site of animal bite; intense thirst exacerbated by the inability to drink without violent, painful throat spasms; paralysis of facial muscles; drooling. Agitation and violent behavior, confusion, convulsions, coma.
	Rubella *German Measles*	Rash on the face that spreads to the torso and limbs; enlargement of lymph nodes in neck; usually preceded by headache, fever, and runny nose.
	Septic shock *Severe drop in blood pressure due to the presence of microorganisms or their toxins in the bloodstream*	Nausea and vomiting; prostration; diarrhea; sudden high fever; chills; rapid breathing; headache; mental confusion or agitation; decreased urine output; possible jaundice or skin rash; hands and feet may be unusually cold.
	Sinusitis *Inflammation of the mucus membranes lining the sinuses*	Throbbing pain above or below one or both eyes that intensifies when bending the head forward or coughing; nasal congestion; loss of sense of smell; pus-like nasal discharge; possible dental pain in the upper jaw; fever.
	Syphilis	Initially, painless, ulcerated, red sore on the genitals, mouth, or rectum; swollen glands in the neck, armpit, or groin; rash with small, red, scaly bumps; fever; headache. If left untreated, damage to heart valves leading to congestive heart failure; mental deterioration; loss of balance; seizures; dementia; personality changes.

Headache *continued*

Associated Symptoms	Possible Diagnosis	Distinguishing Features
with fever *continued*	Tonsillitis	Sore, inflamed throat; swallowing difficulty; headache; swollen glands in the neck; fever; loss of voice. In children, nausea, vomiting, and abdominal pain.
	Typhoid fever	Headache; fever, loss of appetite; abdominal pain and tenderness; extreme weakness; constipation followed by diarrhea; drowsiness, stupor, or coma; raised, pink skin eruptions on the chest and abdomen; joint aches; sore throat.
with fever and nausea	Brain abscess	Headaches; drowsiness; nausea and vomiting; fever; seizures; possible partial paralysis; confusion; speaking difficulty.
	Glomerulonephritis, acute *Sudden or intense inflammation of the glomeruli, tiny structures that filter blood in the kidneys*	Blood in the urine; passing only small amounts of urine; swelling of the ankles or the tissues around the eyes; shortness of breath; possibly, fatigue, nausea and vomiting, loss of appetite, itching, headaches, fever, impaired vision.
	Glomerulonephritis, chronic *Persistent inflammation of the glomeruli, tiny structures that filter blood in the kidneys*	Blood in the urine; passing only small amounts of urine; swelling of the ankles or the tissues around the eyes; shortness of breath; possibly, fatigue, nausea and vomiting, loss of appetite, itching, headaches, fever, impaired vision.
	Legionnaire's disease	Dry cough progressing to one with blood-streaked sputum; high fever; chills; breathing difficulty; chest pain; headache; muscle aches; diarrhea; nausea; vomiting; mental confusion and disorientation.
	Leukemias	Symptoms vary depending on the type of leukemia and may include: loss of appetite and weight; increased bruising and bleeding; bone pain, especially in the legs; abdominal pain and distention; nausea; heart palpitations; severe fatigue; pallor; breathing difficulty; fever; night sweats; headache; enlarged lymph nodes; joint pains (due to gout).
	Malaria	Initially, severe chills and shivering. In later stages, extremely high fever followed by a period of profuse perspiration as fever subsides; headache, sometimes severe; vomiting.
	Meningitis *Inflammation of the membranes covering the brain and spinal cord*	Severe headache; nausea and vomiting; sensitivity to light; stiffness in the neck; possible red skin rash; fever; mental confusion; drowsiness; loss of consciousness; seizures.

Headache *continued*

Associated Symptoms	Possible Diagnosis	Distinguishing Features
with fever and nausea *continued*	Poliomyelitis *Polio*	Low fever; sore throat; headache; nausea and vomiting. In severe cases, paralysis without loss of sensation; stiff neck and back; twitching; swallowing and breathing difficulty; drooling.
	Rocky Mountain spotted fever	Within a week after exposure, high fever, loss of appetite, headache, muscle aches, nausea and vomiting; dry cough; sensitivity to light. Within six days, the appearance of small pink spots on wrists and ankles, eventually spreading over the entire body, where they then grow, darken in color, and bleed.
	Systemic lupus erythematosus *Inflammation of connective tissues throughout the body*	Red, blotchy, butterfly-shaped rash on the cheeks and bridge of the nose; fatigue; fever; loss of appetite and weight; nausea; joint and abdominal pain; headaches; blurred vision; increased sensitivity to sun exposure; depression; psychosis; mental confusion.
	Toxic shock syndrome	Lethargy; conjunctivitis; confusion; sudden high fever accompanied by nausea, watery diarrhea, sore throat, and headache. Red rash on the palms and soles of the feet, which, after a week or two, begins to peel.

Hearing loss

Associated Symptoms	Possible Diagnosis	Distinguishing Features
with ear pain	Barotrauma *Eardrum strain or damage due to changes in the atmospheric pressure*	Pain in the cheekbones, ear, or forehead; temporary hearing loss; sensation that the ears are plugged; dizziness; ringing in the ears.
	Cholesteatoma *Infected cyst in the eardrum or middle ear*	Hearing loss; discharge of pus from ear; headaches and earaches; weakness of facial muscles; dizziness.
	Ear drum, perforated	Earache or sudden pain in the ear; partial hearing loss; slight bleeding or discharge from the ear; ringing or buzzing in the affected ear.
	Ear infection, middle *Inflammation of the middle ear*	Earache; deafness; ringing in the ear; possibly, a discharge of pus from the ear; fever; dizziness.
	Ear infection, outer	Redness and itching of the ear canal; discharge from the ear; ear pain; possibly, temporary loss of hearing.
	Mastoiditis, acute *Inflammation of the mastoid, a bone behind the ear*	Severe pain and swelling behind and within the ear; fever; discharge from the ear; progressive hearing loss.
without ear pain	Acoustic neuroma *A benign tumor in the cells covering the auditory nerve*	Gradual hearing loss; ringing in the ear; headache; numbness in the face; unsteady walk. In later stages, swallowing and speaking difficulties; possibly, slight paralysis.
	Acoustic trauma *Hearing loss due to exposure to loud noise*	Partial deafness; ringing in the ears; sensation that ears are plugged.
	Labyrinthitis *Inflammation of the semicircular canals of the inner ear*	Severe dizziness, loss of balance, jerky movements of the eyes; nausea and vomiting; ringing in the ears. In later stages, possible hearing loss.
	Meniere's disease *Dysfunction of structures in the inner ear*	Sudden attack of severe vertigo; nausea and vomiting; impaired sense of balance; ringing in the ears; hearing loss in the affected ear. Jerky movements of the eyes.
	Otosclerosis *An overgrowth of bone in the middle ear*	Progressive hearing loss; ringing in the ears; dizziness. Hearing is more distinct when background noise is present.
	Paget's disease *A weakening, thickening, and deformity of the bones*	Often asymptomatic. Possibly, bone pain or deformity, especially bowing of the legs, bent spine, and facial deformity; unexplained bone fractures; joint pain or stiffness; hearing loss; headaches; ringing in ears.
	Presbycusis *Loss of hearing due to age*	Progressive inability to hear well in the presence of background noise; difficulty understanding speech.

Heartburn

Associated Symptoms	Possible Diagnosis	Distinguishing Features
	Cirrhosis *Chronic damage to the cells of the liver*	No symptoms in early stages; loss of weight and appetite; nausea; swollen legs, ankles and abdomen; itching; jaundice; black stools; vomiting blood; fatigue; impotence; memory loss; confusion.
	Esophageal cancer	Swallowing difficulty and pain; weight loss; drooling; possibly, vomiting or coughing up of bloody mucus, regurgitation of food; chest pain; repeated respiratory infections.
	Esophageal stricture *Narrowing of the esophagus, the passageway from the mouth to the stomach*	Sudden or gradual decrease in the ability to swallow solid food or liquids; chest pain after eating; regurgitation of food and liquids; increased salivation; weight loss. Aspiration into lungs can cause cough, wheezing, shortness of breath.
	Gallbladder disorders	Moderate to severe pain in the upper right side of the abdomen, chest, upper back, or right shoulder. Pain often follows the ingestion of high-fat foods and is episodic, lasting 20 minutes to several hours. Nausea and vomiting; low-grade fever; belching; heartburn; gas; possibly, jaundice, pale stools, and itchy skin.
	Gastroesophageal reflux *Heartburn*	Burning sensation in the middle of the chest; pain and difficulty swallowing; slight regurgitation of stomach's contents into the mouth, especially when reclining or bending forward; mild abdominal pain.
	Hiatal hernia *Protrusion of a portion of the stomach through the diaphragm, into the chest cavity*	Often asymptomatic. Possibly, heartburn after meals or when bending forward or reclining. Belching, regurgitation.
	Peptic ulcer	Intermittent, burning or gnawing pain in the upper abdomen or lower chest; indigestion; loss of appetite and weight. Pain may be relieved by eating or antacids. Possible nausea and vomiting. Black, tarry stools, vomiting blood.
	Scleroderma	Shiny, tight, and hardened skin, especially on the fingers, arms, and face; hands or feet may successively turn blue, white, and red upon exposure to cold (Raynaud's phenomenon); swallowing difficulty; bloating after eating; weight loss; shortness of breath on exertion; high blood pressure; symptoms of renal failure. Possibly, heartburn, muscle aches and weakness, joint pain, fever, or fatigue.

Hip pain

Associated Symptoms	Possible Diagnosis	Distinguishing Features
	Bone cancer	Pain, tenderness, and swelling in the affected bones and joints, often intensifying at night; a noticeable tumor or mass; increased susceptibility to bone fractures.
	Bone fractures	Pain in the affected bone which intensifies with movement or the application of pressure; swelling, bruising, or bleeding around the site of an injury; in a compound fracture, protrusion of bone through skin; possible loss of function or feeling in the injured area; local deformity.
	Bursitis *Inflammation of the bursas, the lubricant-filled sacs in and around the joints*	Pain and swelling around a joint, usually the elbow, knee, or shoulder; painful movement in the affected joint; possibly, fever.
	Dislocations/subluxations	Deformity of the affected joint; joint pain and tenderness; difficulty moving a joint; swelling and stiffness within 30 minutes after joint injury.
	Infectious arthritis	Pain, swelling, stiffness, and redness, usually in one joint. Fever. Severity varies from a mild ache to severe, debilitating pain and eventual joint deformity.
	Osteoarthritis *Degeneration of the cartilage that lines the joints*	Pain, swelling, and stiffness in one or more joints; enlargement and distortion of affected joints.
	Osteomalacia and Rickets *Softening and weakening of the bones, usually due to poor calcification*	Bone pain, especially in the neck, legs, hips and ribs. Muscle weakness, numbness, or spasms in the hands, feet, and throat; increased susceptibility to bone fractures.
	Osteomyelitis *Infection of bone and bone marrow*	Fever; severe pain in the affected bone; inflammation and swelling of the skin over the affected area; deformity. In children, arrested growth of the affected bone.
	Osteoporosis *Loss of bone mass due to calcium depletion*	Backache; easily fractured bones, especially in the wrists, hips, and spine; gradual loss of height; stooped or hunched posture.
	Rheumatoid arthritis	Fatigue and weakness; joint pain, stiffness, and inflammation, especially in the hands, feet, and arms; joint deformity; dry mouth; dry, painful eyes. Morning stiffness.
	Rheumatoid arthritis, juvenile	Fever; rash; abdominal pain; weight loss; swelling, stiffness, and pain in the affected joints; enlarged lymph glands; fatigue; pallor; red, painful eyes; morning stiffness.

Hip pain *continued*

Associated Symptoms	Possible Diagnosis	Distinguishing Features
	Sprains and strains	Swelling, pain or tenderness in the affected joints; impaired joint function.
	Tendinitis *Inflammation of a tendon*	Pain and tenderness over a tendon anywhere in the body; if involved tendon is near or part of a joint, restricted movement of the joint.
	Thrombophlebitis *Inflammation associated with a blood clot*	Redness, swelling, pain, and tenderness in the affected area; most often occurs in the leg; swelling of the affected leg; prominent superficial veins around affected area; possibly, fever.

Hoarseness

Associated Symptoms	Possible Diagnosis	Distinguishing Features
	Hypothyroidism *Underactivity of the thyroid gland*	Unexplained weight gain; fatigue; muscle weakness; cramps; dry skin; hair loss; deepening of the voice; intolerance for cold; constipation; chest pain; insomnia; puffiness around eyes; loss of sex drive; depression; menstrual abnormalities; possible swelling in the neck (goiter).
	Laryngeal cancer	Initially, hoarseness, sore throat, and swallowing difficulty; later, pain when swallowing; swelling in the neck.
	Laryngitis	Hoarseness that often progresses to loss of the voice; throat pain; dry cough; possible fever.
	Pharyngitis *Inflammation of the pharynx, the part of the throat between the mouth and the esophagus*	Sore or red throat; speaking and swallowing difficulties; sensitive, swollen glands in the neck; fever; headache; possible earache.
	Rheumatoid arthritis, juvenile	Fever; rash; abdominal pain; weight loss; swelling, stiffness, and pain in the affected joints; enlarged lymph glands; fatigue; pallor; red, painful eyes; morning stiffness.
	Sjögren's syndrome	Dry, itching, burning eyes; sensation of a foreign body under the eyelids; dry mouth; difficulty swallowing; vaginal dryness; dry skin; frequent dental cavities; joint pain; swelling of glands (parotids) in front of the ears; Raynaud's phenomenon.
	Tuberculosis	Often, asymptomatic. Possibly, low-grade fever; excessive perspiration; cough producing sputum or blood; weight loss; chronic fatigue; chest pain; shortness of breath; night sweats.

Hunger, unusual Polyphagia

Associated Symptoms	Possible Diagnosis	Distinguishing Features
	Anemia, iron deficiency	Fatigue and weakness; pallor; shortness of breath and heart palpitations on exertion; irritability or inability to concentrate; sore tongue or tiny cracks at the corners of the mouth; black, tarry or bloody stools; unusual craving for dirt, paint, or ice.
	Diabetes mellitus *Insufficiency of or resistance to insulin*	Fatigue; excessive thirst; frequent urination; weight loss despite increased appetite; blurred vision; numbness and tingling of feet and hands; impotence.
	Hyperthyroidism *Overactivity of the thyroid gland*	Protruding eyes; weight loss despite increased appetite; intolerance to heat; excessive perspiration; nervousness or restlessness; possibly, swelling in the neck (goiter); palpitations; tremor; diarrhea.
	Hypoglycemia *Low blood sugar*	Anxiety; hunger; trembling; headache; palpitations; perspiration; confusion; irritability; loss of coordination; possibly, double vision, seizures, or coma.
	Tapeworm infestation	Often asymptomatic. Unexplained weight loss; presence of white eggs or ribbon-like segments of worm in the stool, bedding, or clothing; symptoms of pernicious anemia.

Incontinence, fecal

Associated Symptoms	Possible Diagnosis	Distinguishing Features
	Alzheimer's disease	Symptoms vary greatly in different individuals. Initially, minor forgetfulness gradually developing into severe, short-term memory loss, disorientation, an inability to concentrate, and sudden mood and personality changes. In later stages, severe confusion, possible hallucinations or paranoid delusions, loss of social and sexual inhibitions, impaired judgment, anxiety, depression, agitation and combativeness, wandering and getting lost, inability to write, urinary and fecal incontinence.
	Brain tumors	Headaches that become more severe when reclining; nausea and vomiting; memory loss; double vision; muscle weakness; numbness, tingling, or partial paralysis; vision loss; speech disturbances; seizures; drowsiness.
	Colitis, ulcerative *Inflammation of the lining of the colon*	Pain on the left side of the abdomen that lessens after bowel movements; bloody diarrhea; pain in the rectal area; possibly, fever, rapid heartbeat, nausea and vomiting, loss of appetite, dehydration with severe attacks.
	Multiple sclerosis *Gradual degeneration of the protective sheaths surrounding the nerves within the brain and spinal cord*	Symptoms may appear suddenly and then disappear; persistent symptoms may take years to develop and include numbness or tingling in any part of the body, weakness in the extremities, an unsteady walk, slurred speech, urinary incontinence, fatigue, depression, temporary loss of vision, double or blurred vision, mental confusion, and memory loss.
	Peripheral neuropathies *Degeneration of the nerves that supply the extremities*	Tingling or numbness commonly beginning in the hands and feet and gradually spreading toward the center of the body; sensitive skin; muscle weakness; possibly, pain in the hands and feet; lack of coordination; shooting pains exacerbated by touch or changes in temperature; breathing difficulty; urinary or fecal incontinence.
	Spinal cord trauma	Severe pain and swelling in the affected area; loss of sensation, muscle weakness, or paralysis below the site of the injury; urinary or fecal incontinence or retention; impotence; breathing difficulty; shock.
	Spinal tumor	Progressive numbness, tingling, and muscle weakness; fecal or urinary incontinence; persistent back pain.
	Stroke	Symptoms vary with the location of brain injury. Sudden onset of weakness, paralysis, or loss of sensation, usually on one side of the body; a sudden heaviness in a limb; speech abnormalities; headache; vision disturbances; dizziness; confusion; coma; urinary and fecal incontinence.

Incontinence, urinary

Associated Symptoms	Possible Diagnosis	Distinguishing Features
	Alzheimer's disease	Symptoms vary greatly in different individuals. Initially, minor forgetfulness gradually developing into severe, short-term memory loss, disorientation, an inability to concentrate, and sudden mood and personality changes. In later stages, severe confusion, possible hallucinations or paranoid delusions, loss of social and sexual inhibitions, impaired judgment, anxiety, depression, agitation and combativeness, wandering and getting lost, inability to write, urinary and fecal incontinence.
	Irritable bladder	Sudden, urgent need to urinate; frequent urination.
	Multiple sclerosis *Gradual degeneration of the protective sheaths surrounding the nerves within the brain and spinal cord*	Symptoms may appear suddenly and then disappear; persistent symptoms may take years to develop and include numbness or tingling in any part of the body, weakness in the extremities, an unsteady walk, slurred speech, urinary incontinence, fatigue, depression, temporary loss of vision, double or blurred vision, mental confusion, and memory loss.
	Neurogenic bladder *Inability to control passage of urine due to damage to nerves to the bladder.*	Inability to control urine flow which may involuntarily release in large volumes or in a continuous dribbling. Bed-wetting during sleep; feeling the need to urinate though no urine is passed; pain or burning during urination.
	Peripheral neuropathies *Degeneration of the nerves that supply the extremities*	Tingling or numbness commonly beginning in the hands and feet and gradually spreading toward the center of the body; sensitive skin; muscle weakness; possibly, pain in the hands and feet; lack of coordination; shooting pains exacerbated by touch or changes in temperature; breathing difficulty; urinary or fecal incontinence.
	Prostate cancer	Difficulty urinating; frequent urination with decreased urine output; pain in the pelvic area and lower back; painful ejaculation or bowel movements.
	Seizures	Involuntary twitching or jerking; muscle rigidity; loss of consciousness; confusion; drooling; hallucinations.
	Spinal cord trauma	Severe pain and swelling in the affected area; loss of sensation, muscle weakness, or paralysis below the site of the injury; urinary or fecal incontinence or retention; impotence; breathing difficulty; shock.
	Spinal tumor	Progressive numbness, tingling, and muscle weakness; fecal or urinary incontinence; persistent back pain.

Incontinence, urinary *continued*

Associated Symptoms	Possible Diagnosis	Distinguishing Features
	Stroke	Symptoms vary with the location of brain injury. Sudden onset of weakness, paralysis, or loss of sensation, usually on one side of the body; a sudden heaviness in a limb; speech abnormalities; headache; vision disturbances; dizziness; confusion; coma; urinary and fecal incontinence.
	Urinary incontinence	Uncontrollable, involuntary release of urine, either in large volumes or a continuous dribble. May be increased by coughing, sneezing, laughing, or with any activity involving contraction of the abdominal muscles.
with blood in the urine	Bladder cancer	Blood in the urine; painful and frequent urination; pelvic pain; feeling of pressure in the back; persistent fever; urinary incontinence.
	Bladder infection *Cystitis*	Burning during urination; frequent and urgent urination with only small amounts of urine passed; blood in the urine; lower abdominal pain; low-grade fever; pain during sexual intercourse and, in men, during ejaculation.
	Kidney infection *Pyelonephritis*	Sudden fever and shaking chills; severe fatigue; burning and frequent urination; cloudy or bloody urine; lower back pain, sometimes severe; nausea and vomiting.

Indigestion

Associated Symptoms	Possible Diagnosis	Distinguishing Features
	Adrenal insufficiency *Inadequate production of steroid hormones by the adrenal glands*	Loss of weight and appetite; fatigue; weakness; darkening of the skin; abdominal pain; diarrhea; indigestion; nausea and vomiting; constipation; lack of sex drive; dizziness when rising from sitting or lying position.
	Carcinoid tumors and carcinoid syndrome	May be asymptomatic; flushing or redness of the face and neck; gas and profuse diarrhea; abdominal cramping; watery, swollen eyes; shortness of breath or wheezing.
	Cirrhosis *Chronic damage to the cells of the liver*	No symptoms in early stages; loss of weight and appetite; nausea; swollen legs, ankles and abdomen; itching; jaundice; black stools; vomiting blood; fatigue; impotence; memory loss; confusion.
	Colitis, ulcerative *Inflammation of the lining of the colon*	Pain on the left side of the abdomen that lessens after bowel movements; bloody diarrhea; pain in the rectal area; possibly, fever, rapid heartbeat, nausea and vomiting, loss of appetite, dehydration with severe attacks.
	Congestive heart failure	Shortness of breath; fatigue; need to sleep on several pillows; weakness; cough; heart palpitations; swelling in the legs, ankles, and abdomen; frequent urination at night; indigestion; nausea and vomiting; loss of appetite.
	Crohn's disease *Inflammation of the lining of the small intestine*	Episodes of abdominal pain or cramps in lower abdomen; nausea; diarrhea; loss of weight and appetite; possibly, fever; rectal bleeding or blood in stools; fatigue; anal fissures; joint pains; inflammation of the eyes.
	Gastroesophageal reflux *Heartburn*	Burning sensation in the middle of the chest; pain and difficulty swallowing; slight regurgitation of stomach's contents into the mouth, especially when reclining or bending forward; mild abdominal pain.
	Hepatitis, acute viral	Fever; fatigue; loss of appetite; aching muscles and joints; abdominal pain or discomfort; jaundice; dark urine and pale stools.
	Hepatitis, chronic	Fatigue; nausea; vomiting; loss of appetite; jaundice; dark urine; clay-colored stools; depression; pain or discomfort in the upper right abdomen; abdominal swelling; fever; in women, cessation of menstruation, acne, and the appearance of male pattern facial hair.
	Hyperparathyroidism *Overactivity of the parathyroid glands*	Increased susceptibility to bone fractures; depression; indigestion; increased thirst and urine output; fatigue, lethargy; somnolence; muscle weakness; nausea and vomiting; loss of appetite.

Indigestion *continued*

Associated Symptoms	Possible Diagnosis	Distinguishing Features
	Intestinal obstruction	Abdominal pain and cramps; nausea; vomiting; weakness; gas; abdominal bloating; possible diarrhea; progressive constipation culminating in inability to pass stools or gas.
	Lactose intolerance *Difficulty digesting milk and dairy products*	Abdominal cramps; diarrhea; nausea; bloating; flatulence.
	Malabsorption, digestive *A failure of the small intestine to absorb nutrients in the diet*	Diarrhea; weight loss; yellowish, foul-smelling stools; abdominal cramps, gas, and bloating; weakness and lethargy.
	Pancreatic cancer	Often, no symptoms until far advanced. Upper abdominal pain which spreads to the back; loss of weight and appetite; jaundice; nausea, vomiting, and indigestion; diarrhea; fatigue; depression.
	Pancreatitis *Inflammation of the pancreas*	Sudden, extreme abdominal pain; nausea and vomiting; weakness; fever; clammy skin; abdominal bloating and tenderness.
	Peptic ulcer	Intermittent, burning or gnawing pain in the upper abdomen or lower chest; indigestion; loss of appetite and weight. Pain may be relieved by eating or antacids. Possible nausea and vomiting. Black, tarry stools, vomiting blood.

Insomnia

Associated Symptoms	Possible Diagnosis	Distinguishing Features
	Anxiety states	Sudden attacks of unreasonable fear and panic; rapid heartbeat or palpitations; perspiration; dry mouth; irritability; muscle tension; trembling; palpitations; shortness of breath; restlessness; poor concentration; insomnia; fatigue; weakness.
	Chronic fatigue syndrome	Severe fatigue made worse by exercise; recurrent flu-like symptoms; persistent sore throat; low-grade fever; muscle and joint aches; headache; painful, swollen lymph nodes; depression and mental confusion; memory loss; sleep difficulties.
	Cushing's syndrome	Red, oval-shaped face; humped upper back and obese trunk; acne; purple stretch marks on the abdomen, thighs, and breasts; thin and easily bruised skin; easily fractured bones; depression or euphoria; insomnia; fatigue; muscle weakness; hirsutism (in women).
	Fibromyalgia	Muscle aches, pains, and stiffness; specific points on the body that feel sore when pressed. Fatigue, headaches, and possible insomnia. Feeling unrefreshed upon awakening in the morning.
	Hyperthyroidism *Overactivity of the thyroid gland*	Protruding eyes; weight loss despite increased appetite; intolerance to heat; excessive perspiration; nervousness or restlessness; possibly, swelling in the neck (goiter); palpitations; tremor; diarrhea.
	Hypothyroidism *Underactivity of the thyroid gland*	Unexplained weight gain; fatigue; muscle weakness; cramps; dry skin; hair loss; deepening of the voice; intolerance for cold; constipation; chest pain; insomnia; puffiness around eyes; loss of sex drive; depression; menstrual abnormalities; possible swelling in the neck (goiter).
	Insomnia	Difficulty falling asleep or staying asleep; daytime fatigue; irritability.

Itching skin/scalp

Associated Symptoms	Possible Diagnosis	Distinguishing Features
with rash/red skin/ marks on skin	Breast cancer	Lump or swelling, usually painless, in the breast or under the armpit; flattening, dimpling, indentation, redness, or scaliness of the breast; itching sensation in the nipple; change in size or symmetry of the breasts; breast pain.
	Chiggers *Parasitic infestation*	Itchy patches of red skin. Itching may persist for weeks.
	Dermatomyositis *Inflammation of the muscles and skin*	Red rash on the cheeks and bridge of the nose; purple discoloration and swelling of the eyelids; areas of thickened skin; muscle weakness and stiffness, usually in the shoulders and pelvis; cold hands and feet; speaking or swallowing difficulty; fever; weight loss.
	Eczema *Inflammation of the skin*	Itching skin; thickened patches of skin; possibly, with oozing and crusting; in infants, rash on the face, inner elbows, or behind the knees that turns scaly and develops small red pimples that leak; swollen legs (stasis dermatitis).
	Herpes zoster *Shingles*	A sensitive band of skin on one side of the body that becomes severely painful and develops slightly raised red spots that blister, dry and crust over. Pain may persist for months or years after skin has healed.
	Lice	Intense itching, usually on hair-covered areas; visible nits (eggs) on hair shafts; red bite marks; visible lice on clothing.
	Melanoma *Skin cancer*	Change in the appearance of an existing mole including enlargement, bleeding, change in color, development of a black edge. Itching.
	Polycythemia vera *An overproduction of red and white blood cells and platelets*	Headache; blurred vision; flushed skin; itching; dizziness; fatigue; night sweats; shortness of breath; weight loss.
	Psoriasis	Slightly raised patches of skin with red borders and white-silver scales; joint pain and stiffness; itching; pitted nails.
	Ringworm *Fungal skin infection*	A rash with distinct, advancing borders and clear centers; affected areas may have abnormally dark pigmentation; itching; scaly patches of skin; bald patches on scalp; Athlete's foot; red, swollen finger- and toenails.
	Scabies	Tiny, gray, scaly blisters—usually on the wrists, genitals, armpits, or between the fingers—that rupture easily when scratched; severe itching; red lumps or rashes may develop.

Itching skin/scalp *continued*

Associated Symptoms	Possible Diagnosis	Distinguishing Features
without rash/ red skin/ marks on skin	Anaphylaxis	Itching and hives; swelling of the eyes, lips, and tongue; weakness or faintness; tightening in the chest or throat; wheezing; shortness of breath; profuse sweating; palpitations; sudden, intense distress; feelings of impending doom; stomach cramps; nausea, vomiting, or diarrhea; bluish tinge (cyanosis) to the skin, lips, and nailbeds due to oxygen insufficiency.
	Anemia, aplastic	Fatigue and weakness; shortness of breath; heart palpitations; pallor; bleeding gums; nosebleeds; tendency to bruise easily; small red dots under the skin (petechiae). Increased susceptibility to infection.
	Anemia, folic acid deficiency	Fatigue and weakness; pallor; shortness of breath, heart palpitations, or noticeably rapid heartbeat on exertion; sore, red, and glazed-looking tongue; loss of weight and appetite; nausea and diarrhea; abdominal distention.
	Anemia, hemolytic	Fatigue and weakness; shortness of breath on exertion; pallor; heart palpitations; jaundice and dark urine.
	Anemia, iron deficiency	Fatigue and weakness; pallor; shortness of breath and heart palpitations on exertion; irritability or inability to concentrate; sore tongue or tiny cracks at the corners of the mouth; black, tarry or bloody stools; unusual craving for dirt, paint, or ice.
	Anemia, pernicious	Fatigue; inability to concentrate; sore, red tongue; weakness; dizziness; pallor; shortness of breath on exertion; palpitations; numbness and tingling in extremities; incoordination; headache; loss of weight and appetite; possibly, jaundice.
	Cirrhosis *Chronic damage to the cells of the liver*	No symptoms in early stages; loss of weight and appetite; nausea; swollen legs, ankles and abdomen; itching; jaundice; black stools; vomiting blood; fatigue; impotence; memory loss; confusion.
	Glomerulonephritis, acute *Sudden or intense inflammation of the glomeruli, tiny structures that filter blood in the kidneys*	Blood in the urine; passing only small amounts of urine; swelling of the ankles or the tissues around the eyes; shortness of breath; possibly, fatigue, nausea and vomiting, loss of appetite, itching, headaches, fever, impaired vision.
	Glomerulonephritis, chronic *Persistent inflammation of the glomeruli, tiny structures that filter blood in the kidneys*	Blood in the urine; passing only small amounts of urine; swelling of the ankles or the tissues around the eyes; shortness of breath; possibly, fatigue, nausea and vomiting, loss of appetite, itching, headaches, fever, impaired vision.

Itching skin/scalp *continued*

Associated Symptoms	Possible Diagnosis	Distinguishing Features
	Leukemias	Symptoms vary depending on the type of leukemia and may include: loss of appetite and weight; increased bruising and bleeding; bone pain, especially in the legs; abdominal pain and distention; nausea; heart palpitations; severe fatigue; pallor; breathing difficulty; fever; night sweats; headache; enlarged lymph nodes; joint pains (due to gout).
	Lymphoma, Hodgkin's *Cancer of the lymph nodes and lymphoid tissue*	Painless swelling of the lymph nodes usually in the neck or armpits; loss of appetite; night sweats.
	Renal failure, chronic *Persistent, mild kidney failure*	Asymptomatic in early stages. Possibly, mental confusion; shortness of breath; abdominal pain; decreased sex drive; fatigue; muscle and bone pain; numbness in the legs and feet; headache; impaired mental acuity; bad breath.
	Sjögren's syndrome	Dry, itching, burning eyes; sensation of a foreign body under the eyelids; dry mouth; difficulty swallowing; vaginal dryness; dry skin; frequent dental cavities; joint pain; swelling of glands (parotids) in front of the ears; Raynaud's phenomenon.
	Varicose veins	Blue or purplish, knotted veins, usually in the legs; itching or discomfort in the affected area; swollen feet and ankles. Possible scaly skin, muscle cramps, or skin ulcers.

Jaundice, skin/eyes

Associated Symptoms	Possible Diagnosis	Distinguishing Features
	Anemia, pernicious	Fatigue; inability to concentrate; sore, red tongue; weakness; dizziness; pallor; shortness of breath on exertion; palpitations; numbness and tingling in extremities; incoordination; headache; loss of weight and appetite; possibly, jaundice.
	Cirrhosis *Chronic damage to the cells of the liver*	No symptoms in early stages; loss of weight and appetite; nausea; swollen legs, ankles and abdomen; itching; jaundice; black stools; vomiting blood; fatigue; impotence; memory loss; confusion.
	Empyema *Collection of pus in any body cavity, usually between the membranes covering the lungs*	Chest pain exacerbated by deep inhalation; shortness of breath; dry cough; fever and chills; exhaustion; weight loss; night sweats; abdominal pain and jaundice.
	Gallbladder disorders	Moderate to severe pain in the upper right side of the abdomen, chest, upper back, or right shoulder. Pain often follows the ingestion of high-fat foods and is episodic, lasting 20 minutes to several hours. Nausea and vomiting; low-grade fever; belching; heartburn; gas; possibly, jaundice, pale stools, and itchy skin.
	Hepatitis, acute viral	Fever; fatigue; loss of appetite; aching muscles and joints; abdominal pain or discomfort; jaundice; dark urine and pale stools.
	Hepatitis, chronic	Fatigue; nausea; vomiting; loss of appetite; jaundice; dark urine; clay-colored stools; depression; pain or discomfort in the upper right abdomen; abdominal swelling; fever; in women, cessation of menstruation, acne, and the appearance of male pattern facial hair.
	Liver tumors	Pain or discomfort in the upper right portion of the abdomen; abdominal swelling; loss of weight and appetite; nausea and vomiting; fever; excessive perspiration; jaundice; pallor; severe fatigue.
	Myelofibrosis *An increase of fibrous scar tissue within the bone marrow*	Weakness and fatigue; abdominal fullness; a tendency to bleed easily; bone pain; pallor; shortness of breath during physical exertion; increased susceptibility to bruising and infections; jaundice; weight loss.
	Pancreatic cancer	Often, no symptoms until far advanced. Upper abdominal pain which spreads to the back; loss of weight and appetite; jaundice; nausea, vomiting, and indigestion; diarrhea; fatigue; depression.

Jaundice, skin/eyes *continued*

Associated Symptoms	Possible Diagnosis	Distinguishing Features
	Pancreatitis *Inflammation of the pancreas*	Sudden, extreme abdominal pain; nausea and vomiting; weakness; fever; clammy skin; abdominal bloating and tenderness.
	Reye's syndrome *Childhood disease marked by brain and liver damage*	Following recovery from an upper respiratory infection, nausea and vomiting; memory loss; confusion or delirium; possible seizures; drowsiness; lethargy.
	Septic shock *Severe drop in blood pressure due to the presence of microorganisms or their toxins in the bloodstream*	Nausea and vomiting; prostration; diarrhea; sudden high fever; chills; rapid breathing; headache; mental confusion or agitation; decreased urine output; possible jaundice or skin rash; hands and feet may be unusually cold.

Jaw pain

Associated Symptoms	Possible Diagnosis	Distinguishing Features
	Impacted teeth	Gum pain; unpleasant taste in mouth, especially when biting down; red, swollen gums around the affected tooth; headache or jaw ache; possibly, bad breath.
	Jaw dislocation or fracture	Inability to close the jaw normally; painful, swollen, or numb jaw; misalignment of teeth; speaking difficulty; possible breathing difficulty.
	Mumps	Pain in the ear, below the ear, and in the jaw; swollen glands in the neck; headache; pain on swallowing and chewing. Testicular swelling and tenderness in adults.
	Myocardial infarction *Heart attack*	Sudden chest pain or pressure that may spread to the arm, shoulder and jaw; excessive perspiration; shortness of breath. Possible nausea and vomiting.
	Neuralgia *Pain due to nerve damage or irritation*	Symptoms vary depending on the area affected and include: recurring episodes of sharp pain on one side of the lips, gums, cheek, or chin; radiating pain around the eyes; a burning pain along the path of a nerve encircling the torso. Pain may last from a few seconds to several minutes and always affects the same location. Attacks may occur several times a day for weeks with asymptomatic periods of weeks or months in between and may be triggered by touching or blowing on the affected area. Mouth pain may be exacerbated by talking, eating, or swallowing.
	Oral cancers	Sore in the mouth that bleeds and does not heal; lump in the cheek; white or red patch on the gums; swallowing and chewing difficulties; numbness of the tongue; swelling of the jaw.
	Osteomyelitis *Infection of bone and bone marrow*	Fever; severe pain in the affected bone; inflammation and swelling of the skin over the affected area; deformity. In children, arrested growth of the affected bone.
	Rheumatoid arthritis	Fatigue and weakness; joint pain, stiffness, and inflammation, especially in the hands, feet, and arms; joint deformity; dry mouth; dry, painful eyes. Morning stiffness.
	Sinusitis *Inflammation of the mucus membranes lining the sinuses*	Throbbing pain above or below one or both eyes that intensifies when bending the head forward or coughing; nasal congestion; loss of sense of smell; often, pus-like nasal discharge; possible dental pain in the upper jaw; fever.

Jaw pain *continued*

Associated Symptoms	Possible Diagnosis	Distinguishing Features
	Temporomandibular joint syndrome *TMJ*	Pain in the joints connecting the jaw to the skull; headache; tender jaw muscles; dull facial pain; clicking noise when opening or closing the mouth; pain when yawning and chewing. Jaw may temporarily lock in position.
	Tetanus	Often, lockjaw; stiffness and, later, muscle spasms in the neck and face; drooling; abdominal and back pain; extreme perspiration; swallowing difficulty; possible convulsions; fever.
	Thyroiditis *Inflammation of the thyroid gland*	Pain in the front of the neck and, often, the ear; possibly fever, weight loss, and fatigue; general feeling of being unwell (malaise); discomfort on swallowing.
	Tooth abscess	Persistent tooth pain; pain when biting or chewing; swollen glands in the neck; earache; fever; possibly, foul taste in the mouth or bad breath.
	Tooth decay	Tooth pain, especially after eating sweet or sour foods; tooth sensitivity to hot and cold; bad breath; unpleasant taste in the mouth.

Joint pain

Associated Symptoms	Possible Diagnosis	Distinguishing Features
with fever	Gout	Most commonly affects the joints of the big toe. Affected joints are red, swollen, hot, and severely painful. In late stages, joint deformity. Kidney stones.
	Hepatitis, acute viral	Fever; fatigue; loss of appetite; aching muscles and joints; abdominal pain or discomfort; jaundice; dark urine and pale stools.
	Infectious arthritis	Pain, swelling, stiffness, and redness, usually in one joint. Fever. Severity varies from a mild ache to severe, debilitating pain and eventual joint deformity.
	Influenza *Flu*	Chills, muscle aches, and loss of appetite followed by a cough, sore throat, nasal congestion, and fever; possible chest pain.
	Lyme disease	A small red bump, surrounded by a concentric bulls-eye-like red rash with a pale center. Over the following month: fever and chills; extreme fatigue; headaches. Symptoms may progress over several months or years and may include: palpitations; joint or muscle pain; and chronic joint inflammation, especially in the knees.
	Osteomyelitis *Infection of bone and bone marrow*	Fever; severe pain in the affected bone; inflammation and swelling of the skin over the affected area; deformity. In children, arrested growth of the affected bone.
	Rheumatic fever	Initially, a sore throat that gets better followed, one to six weeks later, by lethargy and fever. Possibly, swollen joints, rash, abdominal pain, involuntary jerky movements, emotional instability.
	Rheumatoid arthritis	Fatigue and weakness; joint pain, stiffness, and inflammation, especially in the hands, feet, and arms; joint deformity; dry mouth; dry, painful eyes. Morning stiffness.
	Rheumatoid arthritis, juvenile	Fever; rash; abdominal pain; weight loss; swelling, stiffness, and pain in the affected joints; enlarged lymph glands; fatigue; pallor; red, painful eyes; morning stiffness.
	Sarcoidosis *Accumulation of inflammatory cells in the lymph nodes and other tissues throughout the body*	Often no symptoms. Swollen lymph nodes in the neck or armpits; muscle aches; fever; breathing difficulty; possibly, purple rash on the face; reddish skin; bumps on the legs; numbness; joint pain or stiffness; a painful, red eye; blurred vision; loss of appetite and weight.

Joint pain *continued*

Associated Symptoms	Possible Diagnosis	Distinguishing Features
with fever *continued*	Scleroderma	Shiny, tight, and hardened skin, especially on the fingers, arms, and face; hands or feet may successively turn blue, white, and red upon exposure to cold (Raynaud's phenomenon); swallowing difficulty; bloating after eating; weight loss; shortness of breath on exertion; high blood pressure; symptoms of renal failure. Possibly, heartburn, muscle aches and weakness, joint pain, fever, or fatigue.
	Syphilis	Initially, painless, ulcerated, red sore on the genitals, mouth, or rectum; swollen glands in the neck, armpit, or groin; rash with small, red, scaly bumps; fever; headache. If left untreated, damage to heart valves leading to congestive heart failure; mental deterioration; loss of balance; seizures; dementia; personality changes.
	Systemic lupus erythematosus *Inflammation of connective tissues throughout the body*	Red, blotchy, butterfly-shaped rash on the cheeks and bridge of the nose; fatigue; fever; loss of appetite and weight; nausea; joint and abdominal pain; headaches; blurred vision; increased sensitivity to sun exposure; depression; psychosis; mental confusion.
	Tendinitis *Inflammation of a tendon*	Pain and tenderness over a tendon anywhere in the body; if involved tendon is near or part of a joint, restricted movement of the joint.
without fever	Ankylosing spondylitis *Inflammation of the joints between the spine and the pelvis*	Initially, pain and stiffness in the lower back and hips that becomes worse after resting; neck or chest pain; fatigue; possible pain in the hip, knee, and ankle joints; pain in the heel of the foot; eye pain; blurred vision.
	Bone cancer	Pain, tenderness, and swelling in the affected bones and joints, often intensifying at night; a noticeable tumor or mass; increased susceptibility to bone fractures.
	Bursitis *Inflammation of the bursa, the lubricant-filled sacs in and around the joints*	Pain and swelling around a joint, usually the elbow, knee, or shoulder; painful movement in the affected joint; possibly, fever.
	Dislocations/subluxations	Deformity of the affected joint; joint pain and tenderness; difficulty moving a joint; swelling and stiffness within 30 minutes after joint injury.
	Hemochromatosis *An excess accumulation of iron in the liver, pancreas, heart, testes, skin, and other organs*	A bronze or slate-grey tone to skin that is normally fair; chronic abdominal pain; heart palpitations; joint pain; drowsiness; confusion. In men, a decrease in the size of the testes, loss of sexual desire, and impotence.

Joint pain *continued*

Associated Symptoms	Possible Diagnosis	Distinguishing Features
	Hemophilia	Profuse bleeding from minor injuries and tooth extractions; internal bleeding that may cause blood in the urine; bleeding into joints; symptoms of stroke due to intracerebral bleeding; possibly, extensive bruising.
	Hyperparathyroidism *Overactivity of the parathyroid glands*	Increased susceptibility to bone fractures; depression; indigestion; increased thirst and urine output; fatigue, lethargy; somnolence; muscle weakness; nausea and vomiting; loss of appetite.
	Hyperpituitarism *Overactivity of the pituitary gland*	In adults (in which the disease is called acromegaly): Gradual thickening of the bones of the face, jaw, and the extremities in adults; oily skin; severe headache; excessive hair growth; excessive perspiration; joint pains. In children (in which the disease is called gigantism): Rapid growth and unusual height; possibly, blindness.
	Osteoarthritis *Degeneration of the cartilage that lines the joints*	Pain, swelling, and stiffness in one or more joints; enlargement and distortion of affected joints.
	Paget's disease *A weakening, thickening, and deformity of the bones*	Often asymptomatic. Possibly, bone pain or deformity, especially bowing of the legs, bent spine, and facial deformity; unexplained bone fractures; joint pain or stiffness; hearing loss; headaches; ringing in ears.
	Psoriasis	Slightly raised patches of skin with red borders and white-silver scales; joint pain and stiffness; itching; pitted nails.
	Sjögren's syndrome	Dry, itching, burning eyes; sensation of a foreign body under the eyelids; dry mouth; difficulty swallowing; vaginal dryness; dry skin; frequent dental cavities; joint pain; swelling of glands (parotids) in front of the ears; Raynaud's phenomenon.
	Sprains and strains	Swelling, pain or tenderness in the affected joints; impaired joint function.
	Temporomandibular joint syndrome *TMJ*	Pain in the joints connecting the jaw to the skull; headache; tender jaw muscles; dull facial pain; clicking noise when opening or closing the mouth; pain when yawning and chewing. Jaw may temporarily lock in position.

Knee pain

Associated Symptoms	Possible Diagnosis	Distinguishing Features
	Bone cancer	Pain, tenderness, and swelling in the affected bones and joints, often intensifying at night; a noticeable tumor or mass; increased susceptibility to bone fractures.
	Bone fractures	Pain in the affected bone which intensifies with movement or the application of pressure; swelling, bruising, or bleeding around the site of an injury; in a compound fracture, protrusion of bone through skin; possible loss of function or feeling in the injured area; local deformity.
	Bursitis *Inflammation of the bursas, the lubricant-filled sacs in and around the joints*	Pain and swelling around a joint, usually the elbow, knee, or shoulder; painful movement in the affected joint; possibly, fever.
	Dislocations/subluxations	Deformity of the affected joint; joint pain and tenderness; difficulty moving a joint; swelling and stiffness within 30 minutes after joint injury.
	Infectious arthritis	Pain, swelling, stiffness, and redness, usually in one joint. Fever. Severity varies from a mild ache to severe, debilitating pain and eventual joint deformity.
	Osteoarthritis *Degeneration of the cartilage that lines the joints*	Pain, swelling, and stiffness in one or more joints; enlargement and distortion of affected joints.
	Osteomalacia and Rickets *Softening and weakening of the bones, usually due to poor calcification*	Bone pain, especially in the neck, legs, hips and ribs. Muscle weakness, numbness, or spasms in the hands, feet, and throat; increased susceptibility to bone fractures.
	Osteomyelitis *Infection of bone and bone marrow*	Fever; severe pain in the affected bone; inflammation and swelling of the skin over the affected area; deformity. In children, arrested growth of the affected bone.
	Rheumatoid arthritis	Fatigue and weakness; joint pain, stiffness, and inflammation, especially in the hands, feet, and arms; joint deformity; dry mouth; dry, painful eyes. Morning stiffness.
	Rheumatoid arthritis, juvenile	Fever; rash; abdominal pain; weight loss; swelling, stiffness, and pain in the affected joints; enlarged lymph glands; fatigue; pallor; red, painful eyes; morning stiffness.
	Sprains and strains	Swelling, pain or tenderness in the affected joints; impaired joint function.

Knee pain *continued*

Associated Symptoms	Possible Diagnosis	Distinguishing Features
	Tendinitis *Inflammation of a tendon*	Pain and tenderness over a tendon anywhere in the body; if involved tendon is near or part of a joint, restricted movement of the joint.
	Thrombophlebitis *Inflammation associated with a blood clot*	Redness, swelling, pain, and tenderness in the affected area; most often occurs in the leg; swelling of the affected leg; prominent superficial veins around affected area; possibly, fever.
	Varicose veins	Blue or purplish, knotted veins, usually in the legs; itching or discomfort in the affected area; swollen feet and ankles. Possible scaly skin, muscle cramps, or skin ulcers.

Leg pain

Associated Symptoms	Possible Diagnosis	Distinguishing Features
	Bone cancer	Pain, tenderness, and swelling in the affected bones and joints, often intensifying at night; a noticeable tumor or mass; increased susceptibility to bone fractures.
	Bone fractures	Pain in the affected bone which intensifies with movement or the application of pressure; swelling, bruising, or bleeding around the site of an injury; in a compound fracture, protrusion of bone through skin; possible loss of function or feeling in the injured area; local deformity.
	Bursitis _Inflammation of the bursas, the lubricant-filled sacs in and around the joints_	Pain and swelling around a joint, usually the elbow, knee, or shoulder; painful movement in the affected joint; possibly, fever.
	Fibrous dysplasia _Abnormal growth of bone tissue_	Often asymptomatic; possibly, bone pain, especially in the lower part of the leg, walking difficulty, bone fractures and deformities, irregular patches of increased pigmentation, precocious puberty.
	Infectious arthritis	Pain, swelling, stiffness, and redness, usually in one joint. Fever. Severity varies from a mild ache to severe, debilitating pain and eventual joint deformity.
	Lyme disease	A small red bump, surrounded by a concentric bulls-eye-like red rash with a pale center. Over the following month: fever and chills; extreme fatigue; headaches. Symptoms may progress over several months or years and may include: palpitations; joint or muscle pain; and chronic joint inflammation, especially in the knees.
	Osteoarthritis _Degeneration of the cartilage that lines the joints_	Pain, swelling, and stiffness in one or more joints; enlargement and distortion of affected joints.
	Osteomalacia and Rickets _Softening and weakening of the bones, usually due to poor calcification_	Bone pain, especially in the neck, legs, hips and ribs. Muscle weakness, numbness, or spasms in the hands, feet, and throat; increased susceptibility to bone fractures.
	Osteomyelitis _Infection of bone and bone marrow_	Fever; severe pain in the affected bone; inflammation and swelling of the skin over the affected area; deformity. In children, arrested growth of the affected bone.
	Osteoporosis _Loss of bone mass due to calcium depletion_	Backache; easily fractured bones, especially in the wrists, hips, and spine; gradual loss of height; stooped or hunched posture.

Leg pain *continued*

Associated Symptoms	Possible Diagnosis	Distinguishing Features
	Paget's disease *A weakening, thickening, and deformity of the bones*	Often asymptomatic. Possibly, bone pain or deformity, especially bowing of the legs, bent spine, and facial deformity; unexplained bone fractures; joint pain or stiffness; hearing loss; headaches; ringing in ears.
	Peripheral vascular disease *Narrowing of blood vessels in the legs or arms*	Muscle pain on one or both legs that occurs with exercise and subsides with rest; possible pain in the fingers, arms, buttocks, lower back, or the arch of the foot; impotence. Severe symptoms include: muscle pain at rest that intensifies at night; discolored or blue toes; cold or numb feet; open sores; heightened sensitivity to cold; weak or absent pulse in the affected limb; scaly or hairless skin over the affected area.
	Rheumatoid arthritis	Fatigue and weakness; joint pain, stiffness, and inflammation, especially in the hands, feet, and arms; joint deformity; dry mouth; dry, painful eyes. Morning stiffness.
	Rheumatoid arthritis, juvenile	Fever; rash; abdominal pain; weight loss; swelling, stiffness, and pain in the affected joints; enlarged lymph glands; fatigue; pallor; red, painful eyes; morning stiffness.
	Shin splints	Pain in the front of the calf that may intensify during walking or running.
	Sprains and strains	Swelling, pain or tenderness in the affected joints; impaired joint function.
	Tendinitis *Inflammation of a tendon*	Pain and tenderness over a tendon anywhere in the body; if involved tendon is near or part of a joint, restricted movement of the joint.
	Thrombophlebitis *Inflammation associated with a blood clot*	Redness, swelling, pain, and tenderness in the affected area; most often occurs in the leg; swelling of the affected leg; prominent superficial veins around affected area; possibly, fever.
	Varicose veins	Blue or purplish, knotted veins, usually in the legs; itching or discomfort in the affected area; swollen feet and ankles. Possible scaly skin, muscle cramps, or skin ulcers.

Lethargy

Associated Symptoms	Possible Diagnosis	Distinguishing Features
	Adrenal insufficiency *Inadequate production of steroid hormones by the adrenal glands*	Loss of weight and appetite; fatigue; weakness; darkening of the skin; abdominal pain; diarrhea; indigestion; nausea and vomiting; constipation; lack of sex drive; dizziness when rising from sitting or lying position.
	Anemia, aplastic	Fatigue and weakness; shortness of breath; heart palpitations; pallor; bleeding gums; nosebleeds; tendency to bruise easily; small red dots under the skin (petechiae). Increased susceptibility to infection.
	Anemia, folic acid deficiency	Fatigue and weakness; pallor; shortness of breath, heart palpitations, or noticeably rapid heartbeat on exertion; sore, red, and glazed-looking tongue; loss of weight and appetite; nausea and diarrhea; abdominal distention.
	Anemia, hemolytic	Fatigue and weakness; shortness of breath on exertion; pallor; heart palpitations; jaundice and dark urine.
	Anemia, iron deficiency	Fatigue and weakness; pallor; shortness of breath and heart palpitations on exertion; irritability or inability to concentrate; sore tongue or tiny cracks at the corners of the mouth; black, tarry or bloody stools; unusual craving for dirt, paint, or ice.
	Anemia, pernicious	Fatigue; inability to concentrate; sore, red tongue; weakness; dizziness; pallor; shortness of breath on exertion; palpitations; numbness and tingling in extremities; incoordination; headache; loss of weight and appetite; possibly, jaundice.
	Anxiety states	Sudden attacks of unreasonable fear and panic; rapid heartbeat or palpitations; perspiration; dry mouth; irritability; muscle tension; trembling; palpitations; shortness of breath; restlessness; poor concentration; insomnia; fatigue; weakness.
	Congestive heart failure	Shortness of breath; fatigue; need to sleep on several pillows; weakness; cough; heart palpitations; swelling in the legs, ankles, and abdomen; frequent urination at night; indigestion; nausea and vomiting; loss of appetite.
	Diabetes mellitus *Insufficiency of or resistance to insulin*	Fatigue; excessive thirst; frequent urination; weight loss despite increased appetite; blurred vision; numbness and tingling of feet and hands; impotence.
	Hyperparathyroidism *Overactivity of the parathyroid glands*	Increased susceptibility to bone fractures; depression; indigestion; increased thirst and urine output; fatigue, lethargy; somnolence; muscle weakness; nausea and vomiting; loss of appetite.

Lethargy *continued*

Associated Symptoms	Possible Diagnosis	Distinguishing Features
	Hyperpituitarism *Overactivity of the pituitary gland*	In adults (in which the disease is called acromegaly): Gradual thickening of the bones of the face, jaw, and the extremities in adults; oily skin; severe headache; excessive hair growth; excessive perspiration; joint pains. In children (in which the disease is called gigantism): Rapid growth and unusual height; possibly, blindness.
	Hypothyroidism *Underactivity of the thyroid gland*	Unexplained weight gain; fatigue; muscle weakness; cramps; dry skin; hair loss; deepening of the voice; intolerance for cold; constipation; chest pain; insomnia; puffiness around eyes; loss of sex drive; depression; menstrual abnormalities; possible swelling in the neck (goiter).
	Malabsorption, digestive *A failure of the small intestine to absorb nutrients in the diet*	Diarrhea; weight loss; yellowish, foul-smelling stools; abdominal cramps, gas, and bloating; weakness and lethargy.
	Mononucleosis, infectious	Headache; high fever; swollen glands in the neck, groin, and armpits; severe sore throat; swallowing difficulty.
	Reye's syndrome *Childhood disease marked by brain and liver damage*	Following recovery from an upper respiratory infection, nausea and vomiting; memory loss; confusion or delirium; possible seizures; drowsiness; lethargy.
	Rheumatoid arthritis, juvenile	Fever; rash; abdominal pain; weight loss; swelling, stiffness, and pain in the affected joints; enlarged lymph glands; fatigue; pallor; red, painful eyes; morning stiffness.
	Toxic shock syndrome	Lethargy; conjunctivitis; confusion; sudden high fever accompanied by nausea, watery diarrhea, sore throat, and headache. Red rash on the palms and soles of the feet, which, after a week or two, begins to peel.

Loss of coordination

Associated Symptoms	Possible Diagnosis	Distinguishing Features
	Acoustic neuroma *A benign tumor in the cells covering the auditory nerve*	Gradual hearing loss; ringing in the ear; headache; numbness in the face; unsteady walk. In later stages, swallowing and speaking difficulties; possibly, slight paralysis.
	Amyotrophic lateral sclerosis *Progressive degeneration of nerve cells of the central nervous system*	Progressive loss of strength and coordination in the limbs; muscle twitching and cramps that begin in the hands and spread to the arms, shoulders, and legs; stiff, clumsy gait; swallowing, breathing, or speaking difficulty; weight loss; drooling; involuntary laughing or crying.
	Diphtheria *Bacterial throat infection*	Initially, swollen lymph glands in the neck and sore throat; difficulty swallowing; breathing difficulty; shortness of breath; rapid pulse; headache. In severe cases, paralysis of limbs or facial muscles; drooling.
	Hydrocephalus *Overaccumulation of cerebrospinal fluid, the liquid surrounding the brain*	In infants, an enlarged head, rigidity of the legs, irritability, projectile vomiting, drowsiness, seizures, and lethargy. In older persons, headache, vomiting, loss of coordination, deterioration of mental faculties, speech difficulty, and loss of appetite.
	Hypoglycemia *Low blood sugar*	Anxiety; hunger; trembling; headache; palpitations; perspiration; confusion; irritability; loss of coordination; possibly, double vision, seizures, or coma.
	Muscular dystrophy	Symptoms depend on type of muscular dystrophy and may include: Progressive muscle wasting, weakness, and loss of mobility; lack of coordination; muscular and skeletal deformities including backward curvature of the spine with protruding abdomen; waddling gait; cataracts; frontal baldness; gonadal atrophy.
	Myasthenia gravis *Nerve degeneration causing gradual loss of voluntary muscle control*	Drooping eyelids; double or blurred vision; muscle weakness especially in the face, throat, and neck; chewing and swallowing difficulties; possible breathing difficulty. Slurred, nasal-sounding speech.
	Osteoarthritis *Degeneration of the cartilage that lines the joints*	Pain, swelling, and stiffness in one or more joints; enlargement and distortion of affected joints.
	Parkinson's disease *Degeneration of the basal ganglia, a cluster of nerve cells in the brain*	Tremors in the hands; stiffness and weakness; impaired voluntary movement; shuffling gait; stooped posture; unblinking, fixed expression; possibly, slow, hesitant speech; difficulty swallowing; drooling; depression. Tremors occur at rest (not with voluntary movements) and disappear during sleep.

Loss of coordination *continued*

Associated Symptoms	Possible Diagnosis	Distinguishing Features
	Peripheral neuropathies *Degeneration of the nerves that supply the extremities*	Tingling or numbness commonly beginning in the hands and feet and gradually spreading toward the center of the body; sensitive skin; muscle weakness; possibly, pain in the hands and feet; lack of coordination; shooting pains exacerbated by touch or changes in temperature; breathing difficulty; urinary or fecal incontinence.
	Poliomyelitis *Polio*	Low fever; sore throat; headache; nausea and vomiting. In severe cases, paralysis without loss of sensation; stiff neck and back; twitching; swallowing and breathing difficulty; drooling.
	Rheumatic fever	Initially, a sore throat that gets better followed, one to six weeks later, by lethargy and fever. Possibly, swollen joints, rash, abdominal pain, involuntary jerky movements, emotional instability.
	Rheumatoid arthritis	Fatigue and weakness; joint pain, stiffness, and inflammation, especially in the hands, feet, and arms; joint deformity; dry mouth; dry, painful eyes. Morning stiffness.
	Seizures	Involuntary twitching or jerking; muscle rigidity; loss of consciousness; confusion; drooling; hallucinations.
	Stroke	Symptoms vary with the location of brain injury. Sudden onset of weakness, paralysis, or loss of sensation, usually on one side of the body; a sudden heaviness in a limb; speech abnormalities; headache; vision disturbances; dizziness; confusion; coma; urinary and fecal incontinence.

Loss of smell

Associated Symptoms	Possible Diagnosis	Distinguishing Features
	Anemia, pernicious	Fatigue; inability to concentrate; sore, red tongue; weakness; dizziness; pallor; shortness of breath on exertion; palpitations; numbness and tingling in extremities; incoordination; headache; loss of weight and appetite; possibly, jaundice.
	Brain tumors	Headaches that become more severe when reclining; nausea and vomiting; memory loss; double vision; muscle weakness; numbness, tingling, or partial paralysis; vision loss; speech disturbances; seizures; drowsiness.
	Diabetes mellitus *Insufficiency of or resistance to insulin*	Fatigue; excessive thirst; frequent urination; weight loss despite increased appetite; blurred vision; numbness and tingling of feet and hands; impotence.
	Nasal polyps	Impaired sense of smell; a feeling of fullness in the face; possible nasal discharge, facial pain, or headaches.

Loss of taste

Associated Symptoms	Possible Diagnosis	Distinguishing Features
	Bell's palsy *Paralysis of muscles on one side of the face*	Drooping muscles and weakness on one side of the face resulting in a distorted smile or an expressionless look; drooping eyelid, tearing and an inability to close the affected eye; drooling; possibly, ear pain on the affected side of the face; possibly, changes in taste perception; increased sensitivity to noise.
	Brain tumors	Headaches that become more severe when reclining; nausea and vomiting; memory loss; double vision; muscle weakness; numbness, tingling, or partial paralysis; vision loss; speech disturbances; seizures; drowsiness.
	Dry mouth	Dry or burning sensation in the mouth; difficulty chewing, swallowing, and speaking; possibly, cracked lips, changes in the tongue's surface, mouth ulcers, changes in taste perception, or tooth decay.
	Headache, migraine	Throbbing pain in the temple which spreads to the side of the head; nausea; vomiting. Pain may be preceded by blurred or impaired vision with bright spots and zig-zag patterns.
	Oral cancers	Sore in the mouth that bleeds and does not heal; lump in the cheek; white or red patch on the gums; swallowing and chewing difficulties; numbness of the tongue; swelling of the jaw.
	Salivary gland disorders	Swollen, painful glands behind the ear or under the tongue; soft, painful, swollen glands in the neck; bitter taste in the mouth; fever; dry mouth; increased number of dental cavities; difficulty swallowing.
	Sjögren's syndrome	Dry, itching, burning eyes; sensation of a foreign body under the eyelids; dry mouth; difficulty swallowing; vaginal dryness; dry skin; frequent dental cavities; joint pain; swelling of glands (parotids) in front of the ears; Raynaud's phenomenon.
	Tongue disorders	Symptoms vary depending on the specific disorder and include: dark or bright red, black, or dark brown tongue; sore, swollen, or smooth tongue; hair-like growths on the tongue; adjacent areas of the mouth may be inflamed; ulcers or raised, white patches on the tongue; excessive salivation; swallowing difficulty; bad breath.

Loss of vision

Associated Symptoms	Possible Diagnosis	Distinguishing Features
	Cataracts	Painless, increasingly blurred vision; appearance of halos around lights; changes in color perception; increased sensitivity to light and glare.
	Eye cancers	Often initially asymptomatic. In later stages, gradual blurring and loss of vision, bulging eyes. Possibly, crossed eyes, change in eye color, or a tumor visible through the pupil. Painful red eye.
	Glaucoma	Often initially asymptomatic. In later stages, the symptoms of closed angle glaucoma include: the appearance of halos and rainbows around lights; dilated pupil in the affected eye; severe headache and eye pain; possibly, nausea and vomiting. Open angle glaucoma symptoms include: blurred vision and a gradual loss of peripheral vision.
	Macular degeneration	Gradual loss of vision in the central portion of the field of vision, interfering with reading or any close work requiring keen near-vision; blurred vision.
	Optic neuritis	Sudden, partial loss of vision, usually in the central portion of the field of vision; blurred vision; pain in affected eye.
	Retinal detachment	Possibly, bright flashes of light in the peripheral vision, blurred vision, shadows or blindness in part of the field of vision.
	Retinal vessel occlusion *Blockage of the retinal arteries and veins*	Sudden blurring or loss of vision in all or a portion of the field of vision in one eye, bleeding in the eye.
	Strabismus *Crossed or misaligned eyes*	Double vision; possible vision loss in one eye associated with loss of depth perception; crossed eyes.
	Uveitis and iritis *Inflammation of the uvea, a group of structures in the eye including the iris*	Moderate to severe eye pain; aversion to light; redness in the eye; excessive tearing; blurred vision; spots in the field of vision.

Loss of voice

Associated Symptoms	Possible Diagnosis	Distinguishing Features
	Amyotrophic lateral sclerosis *Progressive degeneration of nerve cells of the central nervous system*	Progressive loss of strength and coordination in the limbs; muscle twitching and cramps that begin in the hands and spread to the arms, shoulders, and legs; stiff, clumsy gait; swallowing, breathing, or speaking difficulty; weight loss; drooling; involuntary laughing or crying.
	Botulism	Difficulty swallowing and speaking; nausea; vomiting; blurred or double vision.
	Laryngitis	Hoarseness that often progresses to loss of the voice; throat pain; dry cough; possible fever.
	Multiple sclerosis *Gradual degeneration of the protective sheaths surrounding the nerves within the brain and spinal cord*	Symptoms may appear suddenly and then disappear; persistent symptoms may take years to develop and include numbness or tingling in any part of the body, weakness in the extremities, an unsteady walk, slurred speech, urinary incontinence, fatigue, depression, temporary loss of vision, double or blurred vision, mental confusion, and memory loss.
	Myasthenia gravis *Nerve degeneration causing gradual loss of voluntary muscle control*	Drooping eyelids; double or blurred vision; muscle weakness especially in the face, throat, and neck; chewing and swallowing difficulties; possible breathing difficulty. Slurred, nasal-sounding speech.
	Parkinson's disease *Degeneration of the basal ganglia, a cluster of nerve cells in the brain*	Tremors in the hands; stiffness and weakness; impaired voluntary movement; shuffling gait; stooped posture; unblinking, fixed expression; possibly, slow, hesitant speech; difficulty swallowing; drooling; depression. Tremors occur at rest (not with voluntary movements) and disappear during sleep.
	Pharyngitis *Inflammation of the pharynx, the part of the throat between the mouth and the esophagus*	Sore or red throat; speaking and swallowing difficulties; sensitive, swollen glands in the neck; fever; headache; possible earache.
	Stroke	Symptoms vary with the location of brain injury. Sudden onset of weakness, paralysis, or loss of sensation, usually on one side of the body; a sudden heaviness in a limb; speech abnormalities; headache; vision disturbances; dizziness; confusion; coma; urinary and fecal incontinence.

Lump(s) or thickening in the breast

Associated Symptoms	Possible Diagnosis	Distinguishing Features
	Breast cancer	Lump or swelling, usually painless, in the breast or under the armpit; flattening, dimpling, indentation, redness, or scaliness of the breast; itching sensation in the nipple; change in size or symmetry of the breasts; breast pain.
	Fibrocystic breast disease *Benign lumps in the breast*	A lump or swelling, usually painless, anywhere in the breast or underarm, typically located in the upper and outer part of the breast. Pain around the lump, usually more apparent during the week prior to menses. Changes in the size or symmetry of the breasts.

Memory problems

Associated Symptoms	Possible Diagnosis	Distinguishing Features
	AIDS *Acquired immunodeficiency syndrome*	Recurrent infections affecting the skin and respiratory system; cough; shortness of breath; loss of appetite; weight loss; fatigue; diarrhea; fever; dementia; malignant skin lesions; swollen lymph glands throughout the body; purplish skin nodules; memory loss; confusion; personality changes.
	Alzheimer's disease	Symptoms vary greatly in different individuals. Initially, minor forgetfulness gradually developing into severe, short-term memory loss, disorientation, an inability to concentrate, and sudden mood and personality changes. In later stages, severe confusion, possible hallucinations or paranoid delusions, loss of social and sexual inhibitions, impaired judgment, anxiety, depression, agitation and combativeness, wandering and getting lost, inability to write, urinary and fecal incontinence.
	Brain tumors	Headaches that become more severe when reclining; nausea and vomiting; memory loss; double vision; muscle weakness; numbness, tingling, or partial paralysis; vision loss; speech disturbances; seizures; drowsiness.
	Chronic fatigue syndrome	Severe fatigue made worse by exercise; recurrent flu-like symptoms; persistent sore throat; low-grade fever; muscle and joint aches; headache; painful, swollen lymph nodes; depression and mental confusion; memory loss; sleep difficulties.
	Cirrhosis *Chronic damage to the cells of the liver*	No symptoms in early stages; loss of weight and appetite; nausea; swollen legs, ankles and abdomen; itching; jaundice; black stools; vomiting blood; fatigue; impotence; memory loss; confusion.
	Encephalitis *Inflammation of the brain*	Initially, headache and fever followed by confusion, hallucinations, and paralysis on one side of the body; memory loss; difficulty with speech and eye movements; drowsiness; possible coma or epileptic seizures; loss of hearing; sensitivity to light; stiff neck.
	Hemochromatosis *An excess accumulation of iron in the liver, pancreas, heart, testes, skin, and other organs*	A bronze or slate-gray tone to skin that is normally fair; chronic abdominal pain; heart palpitations; joint pain; drowsiness; confusion. In men, a decrease in the size of the testes, loss of sexual desire, and impotence.
	Hypothermia *Low body temperature (below 94°)*	Shivering; pallor; puffy face; fatigue and confusion; slow, shallow breathing; muscle stiffness; normally warm areas of the body are cold; loss of consciousness.

Memory problems *continued*

Associated Symptoms	Possible Diagnosis	Distinguishing Features
	Multiple sclerosis *Gradual degeneration of the protective sheaths surrounding the nerves within the brain and spinal cord*	Symptoms may appear suddenly and then disappear; persistent symptoms may take years to develop and include numbness or tingling in any part of the body, weakness in the extremities, an unsteady walk, slurred speech, urinary incontinence, fatigue, depression, temporary loss of vision, double or blurred vision, mental confusion, and memory loss.
	Reye's syndrome *Childhood disease marked by brain and liver damage*	Following recovery from an upper respiratory infection, nausea and vomiting; memory loss; confusion or delirium; possible seizures; drowsiness; lethargy.
	Seizures	Involuntary twitching or jerking; muscle rigidity; loss of consciousness; confusion; drooling; hallucinations.
	Stroke	Symptoms vary with the location of brain injury. Sudden onset of weakness, paralysis, or loss of sensation, usually on one side of the body; a sudden heaviness in a limb; speech abnormalities; headache; vision disturbances; dizziness; confusion; coma; urinary and fecal incontinence.
	Systemic lupus erythematosus *Inflammation of connective tissues throughout the body*	Red, blotchy, butterfly-shaped rash on the cheeks and bridge of the nose; fatigue; fever; loss of appetite and weight; nausea; joint and abdominal pain; headaches; blurred vision; increased sensitivity to sun exposure; depression; psychosis; mental confusion.

Menstrual pain

Associated Symptoms	Possible Diagnosis	Distinguishing Features
	Cervical disorders, non–malignant	Vaginal discharge; vaginal burning and itching; vaginal bleeding after intercourse, between periods, or after bowel movements.
	Endometrial polyps *Growths on the lining of the uterus*	Often no symptoms; light bleeding between periods, especially following sexual intercourse; abnormally heavy or prolonged bleeding during menses; pelvic cramps; foul-smelling vaginal discharge.
	Endometriosis *The migration of the uterine lining to other reproductive or abdominal organs*	Pain in the lower abdomen, vagina, and lower back beginning just prior to menses and intensifying after blood flow has ceased; heavy bleeding during periods; pain during intercourse; diarrhea; constipation; pain during bowel movements; bleeding from the rectum; bloody urine during menses; nausea and vomiting prior to menses; infertility.
	Fibroids, uterine *Benign growths of the muscular wall of the uterus*	Heavier or prolonged bleeding during menses; abdominal discomfort; lower back pain; pressure on the bladder and frequent urination; constipation. Possible, sharp, sudden, lower abdominal pain.
	Pelvic inflammatory disease	Initially, lower pelvic pain; pain during intercourse; irregular menstrual bleeding; vaginal discharge with abnormal color or odor; low-grade fever; chills; frequent urination; fatigue; loss of appetite; later, severe abdominal pain and high fever.
	Uterine prolapse	Often asymptomatic. Possibly, difficulty passing urine or stools, pain during intercourse, backache that intensifies when lifting, sensation of heaviness or dragging within the pelvis, painful or heavy menstrual periods, or bleeding between periods. In severe cases, uterus visibly protrudes outside of vagina.

Mouth, dry

Associated Symptoms	Possible Diagnosis	Distinguishing Features
	Anxiety states	Sudden attacks of unreasonable fear and panic; rapid heartbeat or palpitations; perspiration; dry mouth; irritability; muscle tension; trembling; palpitations; shortness of breath; restlessness; poor concentration; insomnia; fatigue; weakness.
	Diarrhea, acute	Loose, watery stools; increased frequency of bowel movements; abdominal cramping and pain. In infants, possibly drowsiness, slack skin, dry, sticky mouth and tongue, or persistent crying.
	Dry mouth	Dry or burning sensation in the mouth; difficulty chewing, swallowing, and speaking; possibly, cracked lips, changes in the tongue's surface, mouth ulcers, changes in taste perception, or tooth decay.
	Rheumatoid arthritis	Fatigue and weakness; joint pain, stiffness, and inflammation, especially in the hands, feet, and arms; joint deformity; dry mouth; dry, painful eyes. Morning stiffness.
	Salivary gland disorders	Swollen, painful glands behind the ear or under the tongue; soft, painful, swollen glands in the neck; bitter taste in the mouth; fever; dry mouth; increased number of dental cavities; difficulty swallowing.
	Sjögren's syndrome	Dry, itching, burning eyes; sensation of a foreign body under the eyelids; dry mouth; difficulty swallowing; vaginal dryness; dry skin; frequent dental cavities; joint pain; swelling of glands (parotids) in front of the ears; Raynaud's phenomenon.

Mouth, sore

Associated Symptoms	Possible Diagnosis	Distinguishing Features
	Anaphylaxis	Itching and hives; swelling of the eyes, lips, and tongue; weakness or faintness; tightening in the chest or throat; wheezing; shortness of breath; profuse sweating; palpitations; sudden, intense distress; feelings of impending doom; stomach cramps; nausea, vomiting, or diarrhea; bluish tinge (cyanosis) to the skin, lips, and nailbeds due to oxygen insufficiency.
	Anemia, pernicious	Fatigue; inability to concentrate; sore, red tongue; weakness; dizziness; pallor; shortness of breath on exertion; palpitations; numbness and tingling in extremities; incoordination; headache; loss of weight and appetite; possibly, jaundice.
	Candidiasis *Fungal infection of the mouth, genitals, or mucus membrane*	Thick, white discharge from the vagina; itching and irritation in the vaginal area; pain while urinating or during intercourse; in men, inflammation of the head of the penis; possibly, yellow raised patches in the mouth.
	Canker sores	Small, painful, white or gray, crater-like, red-rimmed ulcers in the gums, tongue, or lips; burning sensation preceding the development of ulcers; possibly, fever, swollen glands.
	Dry mouth	Dry or burning sensation in the mouth; difficulty chewing, swallowing, and speaking; possibly, cracked lips, changes in the tongue's surface, mouth ulcers, changes in taste perception, or tooth decay.
	Gingivitis	Red-purple gums that are swollen, shiny, and bleed easily; bad breath.
	Impacted teeth	Gum pain; unpleasant taste in mouth, especially when biting down; red, swollen gums around the affected tooth; headache or jaw ache; possibly, bad breath.
	Neuralgia *Pain due to nerve damage or irritation*	Symptoms vary depending on the area affected and include: recurring episodes of sharp pain on one side of the lips, gums, cheek, or chin; radiating pain around the eyes; a burning pain along the path of a nerve encircling the torso. Pain may last from a few seconds to several minutes and always affects the same location. Attacks may occur several times a day for weeks with asymptomatic periods of weeks or months in between and may be triggered by touching or blowing on the affected area. Mouth pain may be exacerbated by talking, eating, or swallowing.

Mouth, sore *continued*

Associated Symptoms	Possible Diagnosis	Distinguishing Features
	Oral cancers	Sore in the mouth that bleeds and does not heal; lump in the cheek; white or red patch on the gums; swallowing and chewing difficulties; numbness of the tongue; swelling of the jaw.
	Pemphigus *Skin disorder characterized by blistering of skin and mucus membranes*	Recurrent episodes of painful blisters on the skin and mouth; blisters may ooze or crust over; skin may peel or shed easily
	Salivary gland disorders	Swollen, painful glands behind the ear or under the tongue; soft, painful, swollen glands in the neck; bitter taste in the mouth; fever; dry mouth; increased number of dental cavities; difficulty swallowing.
	Temporomandibular joint syndrome *TMJ*	Pain in the joints connecting the jaw to the skull; headache; tender jaw muscles; dull facial pain; clicking noise when opening or closing the mouth; pain when yawning and chewing. Jaw may temporarily lock in position.
	Tongue disorders	Symptoms vary depending on the specific disorder and include: dark or bright red, black, or dark brown tongue; sore, swollen, or smooth tongue; hair-like growths on the tongue; adjacent areas of the mouth may be inflamed; ulcers or raised, white patches on the tongue; excessive salivation; swallowing difficulty; bad breath.
	Trench mouth	Grayish film on the gums; red, swollen, painful, bleeding gums; bad breath; bad taste in the mouth; pain on swallowing or speaking; excessive salivation.

Movement, slowed

Associated Symptoms	Possible Diagnosis	Distinguishing Features
	Amyotrophic lateral sclerosis *Progressive degeneration of nerve cells of the central nervous system*	Progressive loss of strength and coordination in the limbs; muscle twitching and cramps that begin in the hands and spread to the arms, shoulders, and legs; stiff, clumsy gait; swallowing, breathing, or speaking difficulty; weight loss; drooling; involuntary laughing or crying.
	Botulism	Difficulty swallowing and speaking; nausea; vomiting; blurred or double vision.
	Cardiomyopathy *Disease of the heart muscle causing a reduction in the force of heart contractions*	Fatigue; chest pain and palpitations; shortness of breath; swelling of the legs; wheezing; cough.
	Congestive heart failure	Shortness of breath; fatigue; need to sleep on several pillows; weakness; cough; heart palpitations; swelling in the legs, ankles, and abdomen; frequent urination at night; indigestion; nausea and vomiting; loss of appetite.
	Dermatomyositis *Inflammation of the muscles and skin*	Red rash on the cheeks and bridge of the nose; purple discoloration and swelling of the eyelids; areas of thickened skin; muscle weakness and stiffness, usually in the shoulders and pelvis; cold hands and feet; speaking or swallowing difficulty; fever; weight loss.
	Dislocations/subluxations	Deformity of the affected joint; joint pain and tenderness; difficulty moving a joint; swelling and stiffness within 30 minutes after joint injury.
	Hypothyroidism *Underactivity of the thyroid gland*	Unexplained weight gain; fatigue; muscle weakness; cramps; dry skin; hair loss; deepening of the voice; intolerance for cold; constipation; chest pain; insomnia; puffiness around eyes; loss of sex drive; depression; menstrual abnormalities; possible swelling in the neck (goiter).
	Multiple sclerosis *Gradual degeneration of the protective sheaths surrounding the nerves within the brain and spinal cord*	Symptoms may appear suddenly and then disappear; persistent symptoms may take years to develop and include numbness or tingling in any part of the body, weakness in the extremities, an unsteady walk, slurred speech, urinary incontinence, fatigue, depression, temporary loss of vision, double or blurred vision, mental confusion, and memory loss.
	Muscular dystrophy	Symptoms depend on type of muscular dystrophy and may include: Progressive muscle wasting, weakness, and loss of mobility; lack of coordination; muscular and skeletal deformities including backward curvature of the spine with protruding abdomen; waddling gait; cataracts; frontal baldness; gonadal atrophy.

Movement, slowed *continued*

Associated Symptoms	Possible Diagnosis	Distinguishing Features
	Myasthenia gravis *Nerve degeneration causing gradual loss of voluntary muscle control*	Drooping eyelids; double or blurred vision; muscle weakness especially in the face, throat, and neck; chewing and swallowing difficulties; possible breathing difficulty. Slurred, nasal-sounding speech.
	Osteoarthritis *Degeneration of the cartilage that lines the joints*	Pain, swelling, and stiffness in one or more joints; enlargement and distortion of affected joints.
	Parkinson's disease *Degeneration of the basal ganglia, a cluster of nerve cells in the brain*	Tremors in the hands; stiffness and weakness; impaired voluntary movement; shuffling gait; stooped posture; unblinking, fixed expression; possibly, slow, hesitant speech; difficulty swallowing; drooling; depression. Tremors occur at rest (not with voluntary movements) and disappear during sleep.
	Rheumatoid arthritis	Fatigue and weakness; joint pain, stiffness, and inflammation, especially in the hands, feet, and arms; joint deformity; dry mouth; dry, painful eyes. Morning stiffness.
	Valvular heart disease	Depends on which heart valve is affected. Often asymptomatic. Possibly, fatigue and weakness; dizziness; chest pain; shortness of breath; heart palpitations; fainting; edema; stroke from embolism to the brain.

Mucus production, excessive

Associated Symptoms	Possible Diagnosis	Distinguishing Features
	Anaphylaxis	Itching and hives; swelling of the eyes, lips, and tongue; weakness or faintness; tightening in the chest or throat; wheezing; shortness of breath; profuse sweating; palpitations; sudden, intense distress; feelings of impending doom; stomach cramps; nausea, vomiting, or diarrhea; bluish tinge (cyanosis) to the skin, lips, and nailbeds due to oxygen insufficiency.
	Asthma	Shortness of breath; wheezing; dry cough; tightness in the chest; possibly, excessive perspiration or rapid heartbeat.
	Bronchiectasis *Lung condition that stretches and distorts the walls of the bronchial tubes*	Cough that produces dark green sputum; bad breath; possibly, shortness of breath; loss of appetite and weight; clubbed fingers.
	Bronchitis, acute	Shortness of breath; persistent cough producing yellow or green sputum; possibly, chest pain; wheezing; fever.
	Chronic obstructive pulmonary disease	Shortness of breath; wheezing; persistent, mucus-producing cough, especially in the morning; possibly, chest pain, swollen legs and ankles.
	Esophageal cancer	Swallowing difficulty and pain; weight loss; drooling; possibly, vomiting or coughing up of bloody mucus, regurgitation of food; chest pain; repeated respiratory infections.
	Influenza *Flu*	Chills, muscle aches, and loss of appetite followed by a cough, sore throat, nasal congestion, and fever; possible chest pain.
	Nasal polyps	Impaired sense of smell; a feeling of fullness in the face; possible nasal discharge, facial pain, or headaches.
	Sinusitis *Inflammation of the mucus membranes lining the sinuses*	Throbbing pain above or below one or both eyes that intensifies when bending the head forward or coughing; nasal congestion; loss of sense of smell; often, pus–like nasal discharge; possible dental pain in the upper jaw; fever.
	Strep infection	Symptoms depend on the location and nature of the specific infection, but may include fever, headaches, swollen lymph glands, fatigue, loss of appetite, nasal discharge, red skin rash.
	Tuberculosis	Often, asymptomatic. Possibly, low-grade fever; excessive perspiration; cough producing sputum or blood; weight loss; chronic fatigue; chest pain; shortness of breath; night sweats.

Muscle aches/pains

Associated Symptoms	Possible Diagnosis	Distinguishing Features
	Carpal tunnel syndrome	Numbness, tingling, and pain in the hand and wrist, often intensifying at night; weakness of the fingers and hand.
	Fibromyalgia	Muscle aches, pains, and stiffness; specific points on the body that feel sore when pressed. Fatigue, headaches, and possible insomnia. Feeling unrefreshed upon awakening in the morning.
	Heatstroke	Sudden dizziness; weakness; headache; hot, dry, red skin which later turns grey; high body temperature; muscle cramps; confusion; seizures; loss of consciousness.
	Hyperparathyroidism *Overactivity of the parathyroid glands*	Increased susceptibility to bone fractures; depression; indigestion; increased thirst and urine output; fatigue, lethargy; somnolence; muscle weakness; nausea and vomiting; loss of appetite.
	Hypoparathyroidism *Underactivity of the parathyroid glands*	Numbness and tingling and painful, cramp-like spasms of the face, hands, arms, and feet; cataracts; possible seizures.
	Hypothermia *Low body temperature (below 94°)*	Shivering; pallor; puffy face; fatigue and confusion; slow, shallow breathing; muscle stiffness; normally warm areas of the body are cold; loss of consciousness.
	Multiple myeloma *Production of malignant plasma cells in the bone marrow*	Bone pain, especially progressive, constant back pain that intensifies with movement; unexplained bone fractures; fatigue; pallor; shortness of breath; increased bleeding, such as bleeding gums or nosebleeds; easily bruised skin; increased susceptibility to infection; headache; vision disturbances; loss of height.
	Peripheral neuropathies *Degeneration of the nerves that supply the extremities*	Tingling or numbness commonly beginning in the hands and feet and gradually spreading toward the center of the body; sensitive skin; muscle weakness; possibly, pain in the hands and feet; lack of coordination; shooting pains exacerbated by touch or changes in temperature; breathing difficulty; urinary or fecal incontinence.
	Peripheral vascular disease *Narrowing of blood vessels in the legs or arms*	Muscle pain on one or both legs that occurs with exercise and subsides with rest; possible pain in the fingers, arms, buttocks, lower back, or the arch of the foot; impotence. Severe symptoms include: muscle pain at rest that intensifies at night; discolored or blue toes; cold or numb feet; open sores; heightened sensitivity to cold; weak or absent pulse in the affected limb; scaly or hairless skin over the affected area.

Muscle aches/pains *continued*

Associated Symptoms	Possible Diagnosis	Distinguishing Features
	Renal failure, chronic *Persistent, mild kidney failure*	Asymptomatic in early stages. Possibly, mental confusion; shortness of breath; abdominal pain; decreased sex drive; fatigue; muscle and bone pain; numbness in the legs and feet; headache; impaired mental acuity; bad breath.
	Rotator cuff injury	Pain in the shoulder; difficulty raising and lowering the arm; recurring dull ache in the shoulder; pain after sleeping on the shoulder; shoulder weakness.
	Shin splints	Pain in the front of the calf that may intensify during walking or running.
	Sprains and strains	Swelling, pain or tenderness in the affected joints; impaired joint function.
	Tetanus	Often, lockjaw; stiffness and, later, muscle spasms in the neck and face; drooling; abdominal and back pain; extreme perspiration; swallowing difficulty; possible convulsions; fever.
with fever	Chronic fatigue syndrome	Severe fatigue made worse by exercise; recurrent flu-like symptoms; persistent sore throat; low-grade fever; muscle and joint aches; headache; painful, swollen lymph nodes; depression and mental confusion; memory loss; sleep difficulties.
	Common cold	Nasal congestion; watery eyes; sneezing; sore throat; cough; muscle aches; mild headache; listlessness; possibly, low-grade fever.
	Dermatomyositis *Inflammation of the muscles and skin*	Red rash on the cheeks and bridge of the nose; purple discoloration and swelling of the eyelids; areas of thickened skin; muscle weakness and stiffness, usually in the shoulders and pelvis; cold hands and feet; speaking or swallowing difficulty; fever; weight loss.
	Encephalitis *Inflammation of the brain*	Initially, headache and fever followed by confusion, hallucinations, and paralysis on one side of the body; memory loss; difficulty with speech and eye movements; drowsiness; possible coma or epileptic seizures; loss of hearing; sensitivity to light; stiff neck.
	Hepatitis, acute viral	Fever; fatigue; loss of appetite; aching muscles and joints; abdominal pain or discomfort; jaundice; dark urine and pale stools.
	Influenza *Flu*	Chills, muscle aches, and loss of appetite followed by a cough, sore throat, nasal congestion, and fever; possible chest pain.

Muscle aches/pains *continued*

Associated Symptoms	Possible Diagnosis	Distinguishing Features
with fever *continued*	Legionnaire's disease	Dry cough progressing to one with blood-streaked sputum; high fever; chills; breathing difficulty; chest pain; headache; muscle aches; diarrhea; nausea; vomiting; mental confusion and disorientation.
	Lyme disease	A small red bump, surrounded by a concentric bulls-eye-like red rash with a pale center. Over the following month: fever and chills; extreme fatigue; headaches. Symptoms may progress over several months or years and may include: palpitations; joint or muscle pain; and chronic joint inflammation, especially in the knees.
	Malaria	Initially, severe chills and shivering. In later stages, extremely high fever followed by a period of profuse perspiration as fever subsides; headache, sometimes severe; vomiting.
	Measles	Cough; fever; watery nasal discharge; loss of appetite; red, watering eyes; sore throat; body aches; red, slightly itchy rash that gradually spreads all over the body.
	Mumps	Pain in the ear, below the ear, and in the jaw; swollen glands in the neck; headache; pain on swallowing and chewing. Testicular swelling and tenderness in adults.
	Poliomyelitis *Polio*	Low fever; sore throat; headache; nausea and vomiting. In severe cases, paralysis without loss of sensation; stiff neck and back; twitching; swallowing and breathing difficulty; drooling.
	Pneumonia	High fever; shortness of breath; cough with sputum; chest pain; fatigue.
	Pancreatitis *Inflammation of the pancreas*	Sudden, extreme abdominal pain; nausea and vomiting; weakness; fever; clammy skin; abdominal bloating and tenderness.
	Prostatitis *Inflammation of the prostate gland*	Burning during urination; urgent and frequent urination; fever and chills; discharge from the penis; lower abdominal and back pain; blood in the urine.
	Rocky Mountain spotted fever	Within a week after exposure, high fever, loss of appetite, headache, muscle aches, nausea and vomiting; dry cough; sensitivity to light. Within six days, the appearance of small pink spots on wrists and ankles, eventually spreading over the entire body, where they then grow, darken in color, and bleed.

Muscle aches/pains *continued*

Associated Symptoms	Possible Diagnosis	Distinguishing Features
with fever *continued*	Sarcoidosis *Accumulation of inflammatory cells in the lymph nodes and other tissues throughout the body*	Often no symptoms. Swollen lymph nodes in the neck or armpits; muscle aches; fever; breathing difficulty; possibly, purple rash on the face; reddish skin; bumps on the legs; numbness; joint pain or stiffness; a painful, red eye; blurred vision; loss of appetite and weight.
	Scleroderma	Shiny, tight, and hardened skin, especially on the fingers, arms, and face; hands or feet may successively turn blue, white, and red upon exposure to cold (Raynaud's phenomenon); swallowing difficulty; bloating after eating; weight loss; shortness of breath on exertion; high blood pressure; symptoms of renal failure. Possibly, heartburn, muscle aches and weakness, joint pain, fever, or fatigue.
	Toxic shock syndrome	Lethargy; conjunctivitis; confusion; sudden high fever accompanied by nausea, watery diarrhea, sore throat, and headache. Red rash on the palms and soles of the feet, which, after a week or two, begins to peel.
	Trichinosis *Parasitic infestation*	Initially, crampy abdominal pain, diarrhea, vomiting, and fever, followed within one to two weeks by swelling around the eyes, muscle aches and tenderness, fever, and weakness. Possibly, coughing up of bloody phlegm; delirium; coma; heart failure symptoms.

Muscle cramps

Associated Symptoms	Possible Diagnosis	Distinguishing Features
	Amyotrophic lateral sclerosis *Progressive degeneration of nerve cells of the central nervous system*	Progressive loss of strength and coordination in the limbs; muscle twitching and cramps that begin in the hands and spread to the arms, shoulders, and legs; stiff, clumsy gait; swallowing, breathing, or speaking difficulty; weight loss; drooling; involuntary laughing or crying.
	Dermatomyositis *Inflammation of the muscles and skin*	Red rash on the cheeks and bridge of the nose; purple discoloration and swelling of the eyelids; areas of thickened skin; muscle weakness and stiffness, usually in the shoulders and pelvis; cold hands and feet; speaking or swallowing difficulty; fever; weight loss.
	Fibromyalgia	Muscle aches, pains, and stiffness; specific points on the body that feel sore when pressed. Fatigue, headaches, and possible insomnia. Feeling unrefreshed upon awakening in the morning.
	Heatstroke	Sudden dizziness; weakness; headache; hot, dry, red skin which later turns grey; high body temperature; muscle cramps; confusion; seizures; loss of consciousness.
	Hypothyroidism *Underactivity of the thyroid gland*	Unexplained weight gain; fatigue; muscle weakness; cramps; dry skin; hair loss; deepening of the voice; intolerance for cold; constipation; chest pain; insomnia; puffiness around eyes; loss of sex drive; depression; menstrual abnormalities; possible swelling in the neck (goiter).
	Tetanus	Often, lockjaw; stiffness and, later, muscle spasms in the neck and face; drooling; abdominal and back pain; extreme perspiration; swallowing difficulty; possible convulsions; fever.
	Varicose veins	Blue or purplish, knotted veins, usually in the legs; itching or discomfort in the affected area; swollen feet and ankles. Possible scaly skin, muscle cramps, or skin ulcers.

Muscle spasms

Associated Symptoms	Possible Diagnosis	Distinguishing Features
	Amyotrophic lateral sclerosis *Progressive degeneration of nerve cells of the central nervous system*	Progressive loss of strength and coordination in the limbs; muscle twitching and cramps that begin in the hands and spread to the arms, shoulders, and legs; stiff, clumsy gait; swallowing, breathing, or speaking difficulty; weight loss; drooling; involuntary laughing or crying.
	Hypothyroidism *Underactivity of the thyroid gland*	Unexplained weight gain; fatigue; muscle weakness; cramps; dry skin; hair loss; deepening of the voice; intolerance for cold; constipation; chest pain; insomnia; puffiness around eyes; loss of sex drive; depression; menstrual abnormalities; possible swelling in the neck (goiter).
	Osteomalacia and Rickets *Softening and weakening of the bones, usually due to poor calcification*	Bone pain, especially in the neck, legs, hips and ribs. Muscle weakness, numbness, or spasms in the hands, feet, and throat; increased susceptibility to bone fractures.
	Parkinson's disease *Degeneration of the basal ganglia, a cluster of nerve cells in the brain*	Tremors in the hands; stiffness and weakness; impaired voluntary movement; shuffling gait; stooped posture; unblinking, fixed expression; possibly, slow, hesitant speech; difficulty swallowing; drooling; depression. Tremors occur at rest (not with voluntary movements) and disappear during sleep.
	Poliomyelitis *Polio*	Low fever; sore throat; headache; nausea and vomiting. In severe cases, paralysis without loss of sensation; stiff neck and back; twitching; swallowing and breathing difficulty; drooling.
	Rabies	Low-grade fever; headache; loss of appetite; tingling at site of animal bite; intense thirst exacerbated by the inability to drink without violent, painful throat spasms; paralysis of facial muscles; drooling. Agitation and violent behavior, confusion, convulsions, coma.
	Seizures	Involuntary twitching or jerking; muscle rigidity; loss of consciousness; confusion; drooling; hallucinations.
	Spinal cord trauma	Severe pain and swelling in the affected area; loss of sensation, muscle weakness, or paralysis below the site of the injury; urinary or fecal incontinence or retention; impotence; breathing difficulty; shock.
	Tetanus	Often, lockjaw; stiffness and, later, muscle spasms in the neck and face; drooling; abdominal and back pain; extreme perspiration; swallowing difficulty; possible convulsions; fever.

Muscle spasticity

Associated Symptoms	Possible Diagnosis	Distinguishing Features
	Amyotrophic lateral sclerosis *Progressive degeneration of nerve cells of the central nervous system*	Progressive loss of strength and coordination in the limbs; muscle twitching and cramps that begin in the hands and spread to the arms, shoulders, and legs; stiff, clumsy gait; swallowing, breathing, or speaking difficulty; weight loss; drooling; involuntary laughing or crying.
	Hypoparathyroidism *Underactivity of the parathyroid glands*	Numbness and tingling and painful, cramp-like spasms of the face, hands, arms, and feet; cataracts; possible seizures.
	Multiple sclerosis *Gradual degeneration of the protective sheaths surrounding the nerves within the brain and spinal cord*	Symptoms may appear suddenly and then disappear; persistent symptoms may take years to develop and include numbness or tingling in any part of the body, weakness in the extremities, an unsteady walk, slurred speech, urinary incontinence, fatigue, depression, temporary loss of vision, double or blurred vision, mental confusion, and memory loss.
	Parkinson's disease *Degeneration of the basal ganglia, a cluster of nerve cells in the brain*	Tremors in the hands; stiffness and weakness; impaired voluntary movement; shuffling gait; stooped posture; unblinking, fixed expression; possibly, slow, hesitant speech; difficulty swallowing; drooling; depression. Tremors occur at rest (not with voluntary movements) and disappear during sleep.
	Rabies	Low-grade fever; headache; loss of appetite; tingling at site of animal bite; intense thirst exacerbated by the inability to drink without violent, painful throat spasms; paralysis of facial muscles; drooling. Agitation and violent behavior, confusion, convulsions, coma.
	Seizures	Involuntary twitching or jerking; muscle rigidity; loss of consciousness; confusion; drooling; hallucinations.
	Spinal cord trauma	Severe pain and swelling in the affected area; loss of sensation, muscle weakness, or paralysis below the site of the injury; urinary or fecal incontinence or retention; impotence; breathing difficulty; shock.
	Tetanus	Often, lockjaw; stiffness and, later, muscle spasms in the neck and face; drooling; abdominal and back pain; extreme perspiration; swallowing difficulty; possible convulsions; fever.
	Tics	Recurring, involuntary twitch, usually in the face, shoulders, or arms.

Muscle wasting

Associated Symptoms	Possible Diagnosis	Distinguishing Features
	AIDS *Acquired immunodeficiency syndrome*	Recurrent infections affecting the skin and respiratory system; cough; shortness of breath; loss of appetite; weight loss; fatigue; diarrhea; fever; dementia; malignant skin lesions; swollen lymph glands throughout the body; purplish skin nodules; memory loss; confusion; personality changes.
	Amyotrophic lateral sclerosis *Progressive degeneration of nerve cells of the central nervous system*	Progressive loss of strength and coordination in the limbs; muscle twitching and cramps that begin in the hands and spread to the arms, shoulders, and legs; stiff, clumsy gait; swallowing, breathing, or speaking difficulty; weight loss; drooling; involuntary laughing or crying.
	Hypothyroidism *Underactivity of the thyroid gland*	Unexplained weight gain; fatigue; muscle weakness; cramps; dry skin; hair loss; deepening of the voice; intolerance for cold; constipation; chest pain; insomnia; puffiness around eyes; loss of sex drive; depression; menstrual abnormalities; possible swelling in the neck (goiter).
	Multiple sclerosis *Gradual degeneration of the protective sheaths surrounding the nerves within the brain and spinal cord*	Symptoms may appear suddenly and then disappear; persistent symptoms may take years to develop and include numbness or tingling in any part of the body, weakness in the extremities, an unsteady walk, slurred speech, urinary incontinence, fatigue, depression, temporary loss of vision, double or blurred vision, mental confusion, and memory loss.
	Muscular dystrophy	Symptoms depend on type of muscular dystrophy and may include: Progressive muscle wasting, weakness, and loss of mobility; lack of coordination; muscular and skeletal deformities including backward curvature of the spine with protruding abdomen; waddling gait; cataracts; frontal baldness; gonadal atrophy.
	Osteoarthritis *Degeneration of the cartilage that lines the joints*	Pain, swelling, and stiffness in one or more joints; enlargement and distortion of affected joints.
	Parkinson's disease *Degeneration of the basal ganglia, a cluster of nerve cells in the brain*	Tremors in the hands; stiffness and weakness; impaired voluntary movement; shuffling gait; stooped posture; unblinking, fixed expression; possibly, slow, hesitant speech; difficulty swallowing; drooling; depression. Tremors occur at rest (not with voluntary movements) and disappear during sleep.

Muscle wasting *continued*

Associated Symptoms	Possible Diagnosis	Distinguishing Features
	Peripheral neuropathies *Degeneration of the nerves that supply the extremities*	Tingling or numbness commonly beginning in the hands and feet and gradually spreading toward the center of the body; sensitive skin; muscle weakness; possibly, pain in the hands and feet; lack of coordination; shooting pains exacerbated by touch or changes in temperature; breathing difficulty; urinary or fecal incontinence.
	Poliomyelitis *Polio*	Low fever; sore throat; headache; nausea and vomiting. In severe cases, paralysis without loss of sensation; stiff neck and back; twitching; swallowing and breathing difficulty; drooling.
	Rheumatoid arthritis	Fatigue and weakness; joint pain, stiffness, and inflammation, especially in the hands, feet, and arms; joint deformity; dry mouth; dry, painful eyes. Morning stiffness.
	Spinal cord trauma	Severe pain and swelling in the affected area; loss of sensation, muscle weakness, or paralysis below the site of the injury; urinary or fecal incontinence or retention; impotence; breathing difficulty; shock.
	Spinal tumor	Progressive numbness, tingling, and muscle weakness; fecal or urinary incontinence; persistent back pain.

Muscle weakness

Associated Symptoms	Possible Diagnosis	Distinguishing Features
	Cushing's syndrome	Red, oval-shaped face; humped upper back and obese trunk; acne; purple stretch marks on the abdomen, thighs, and breasts; thin and easily bruised skin; easily fractured bones; depression or euphoria; insomnia; fatigue; muscle weakness; hirsutism (in women).
	Dermatomyositis *Inflammation of the muscles and skin*	Red rash on the cheeks and bridge of the nose; purple discoloration and swelling of the eyelids; areas of thickened skin; muscle weakness and stiffness, usually in the shoulders and pelvis; cold hands and feet; speaking or swallowing difficulty; fever; weight loss.
	Hyperparathyroidism *Overactivity of the parathyroid glands*	Increased susceptibility to bone fractures; depression; indigestion; increased thirst and urine output; fatigue, lethargy; somnolence; muscle weakness; nausea and vomiting; loss of appetite.
	Muscular dystrophy	Symptoms depend on type of muscular dystrophy and may include: Progressive muscle wasting, weakness, and loss of mobility; lack of coordination; muscular and skeletal deformities including backward curvature of the spine with protruding abdomen; waddling gait; cataracts; frontal baldness; gonadal atrophy.
	Myasthenia gravis *Nerve degeneration causing gradual loss of voluntary muscle control*	Drooping eyelids; double or blurred vision; muscle weakness especially in the face, throat, and neck; chewing and swallowing difficulties; possible breathing difficulty. Slurred, nasal-sounding speech.
	Trichinosis *Parasitic infestation*	Initially, crampy abdominal pain, diarrhea, vomiting, and fever, followed within one to two weeks by swelling around the eyes, muscle aches and tenderness, fever, and weakness. Possibly, coughing up of bloody phlegm; delirium; coma; heart failure symptoms.
with tingling or loss of sensation	Brain tumors	Headaches that become more severe when reclining; nausea and vomiting; memory loss; double vision; muscle weakness; numbness, tingling, or partial paralysis; vision loss; speech disturbances; seizures; drowsiness.
	Multiple sclerosis *Gradual degeneration of the protective sheaths surrounding the nerves within the brain and spinal cord*	Symptoms may appear suddenly and then disappear; persistent symptoms may take years to develop and include numbness or tingling in any part of the body, weakness in the extremities, an unsteady walk, slurred speech, urinary incontinence, fatigue, depression, temporary loss of vision, double or blurred vision, mental confusion, and memory loss.

Muscle weakness *continued*

Associated Symptoms	Possible Diagnosis	Distinguishing Features
with tingling or loss of sensation *continued*	Peripheral neuropathies *Degeneration of the nerves that supply the extremities*	Tingling or numbness commonly beginning in the hands and feet and gradually spreading toward the center of the body; sensitive skin; muscle weakness; possibly, pain in the hands and feet; lack of coordination; shooting pains exacerbated by touch or changes in temperature; breathing difficulty; urinary or fecal incontinence.
	Spinal cord trauma	Severe pain and swelling in the affected area; loss of sensation, muscle weakness, or paralysis below the site of the injury; urinary or fecal incontinence or retention; impotence; breathing difficulty; shock.
	Spinal tumor	Progressive numbness, tingling, and muscle weakness; fecal or urinary incontinence; persistent back pain.
	Spondylosis, cervical *Arthritis of the vertebral disks in the neck*	Neck pain and stiffness that spreads to the shoulders, upper arms, hands, or back of the head; numbness or tingling in the arms, hands, and fingers; weakness in the arms and legs; unsteady gait; possible loss of bladder control.
with twitching or muscle spasms	Amyotrophic lateral sclerosis *Progressive degeneration of nerve cells of the central nervous system*	Progressive loss of strength and coordination in the limbs; muscle twitching and cramps that begin in the hands and spread to the arms, shoulders, and legs; stiff, clumsy gait; swallowing, breathing, or speaking difficulty; weight loss; drooling; involuntary laughing or crying.
	Hypothyroidism *Underactivity of the thyroid gland*	Unexplained weight gain; fatigue; muscle weakness; cramps; dry skin; hair loss; deepening of the voice; intolerance for cold; constipation; chest pain; insomnia; puffiness around eyes; loss of sex drive; depression; menstrual abnormalities; possible swelling in the neck (goiter).
	Parkinson's disease *Degeneration of the basal ganglia, a cluster of nerve cells in the brain*	Tremors in the hands; stiffness and weakness; impaired voluntary movement; shuffling gait; stooped posture; unblinking, fixed expression; possibly, slow, hesitant speech; difficulty swallowing; drooling; depression. Tremors occur at rest (not with voluntary movements) and disappear during sleep.
	Poliomyelitis *Polio*	Low fever; sore throat; headache; nausea and vomiting. In severe cases, paralysis without loss of sensation; stiff neck and back; twitching; swallowing and breathing difficulty; drooling.

Nasal congestion

Associated Symptoms	Possible Diagnosis	Distinguishing Features
	Allergic rhinitis *Hay fever*	Nasal congestion; frequent sneezing; itchy eyes, nose, and throat.
	Common cold	Nasal congestion; watery eyes; sneezing; sore throat; cough; muscle aches; mild headache; listlessness; possibly, low-grade fever.
	Headache, cluster	Persistent pain in or around one eye; redness and tearing of one eye; nasal congestion on the same side of the face as the affected eye.
	Influenza *Flu*	Chills, muscle aches, and loss of appetite followed by a cough, sore throat, nasal congestion, and fever; possible chest pain.
	Pneumonia	High fever; shortness of breath; cough with sputum; chest pain; fatigue.
	Sinusitis *Inflammation of the mucus membranes lining the sinuses*	Throbbing pain above or below one or both eyes that intensifies when bending the head forward or coughing; nasal congestion; loss of sense of smell; often, pus-like nasal discharge; possible dental pain in the upper jaw; fever.
	Whooping cough	Initially, mild cough, sneezing, nasal congestion, and irritated eyes. Within approximately two weeks, cough becomes severe and persistent, and is accompanied by characteristic high-pitched "whooping" sound during inhalation; loss of appetite; listlessness; vomiting or choking spells. Most common among young children.

Nasal discharge, excessive

Associated Symptoms	Possible Diagnosis	Distinguishing Features
	Allergic rhinitis *Hay fever*	Nasal congestion; frequent sneezing; itchy eyes, nose, and throat.
	Common cold	Nasal congestion; watery eyes; sneezing; sore throat; cough; muscle aches; mild headache; listlessness; possibly, low-grade fever.
	Diphtheria *Bacterial throat infection*	Initially, swollen lymph glands in the neck and sore throat; difficulty swallowing; breathing difficulty; shortness of breath; rapid pulse; headache. In severe cases, paralysis of limbs or facial muscles; drooling.
	Influenza *Flu*	Chills, muscle aches, and loss of appetite followed by a cough, sore throat, nasal congestion, and fever; possible chest pain.
	Measles	Cough; fever; watery nasal discharge; loss of appetite; red, watering eyes; sore throat; body aches; red, slightly itchy rash that gradually spreads all over the body.
	Nasal polyps	Impaired sense of smell; a feeling of fullness in the face; possible nasal discharge, facial pain, or headaches.
	Pneumonia	High fever; shortness of breath; cough with sputum; chest pain; fatigue.
	Rubella *German Measles*	Rash on the face that spreads to the torso and limbs; enlargement of lymph nodes in neck; usually preceded by headache, fever, and runny nose.
	Sinusitis *Inflammation of the mucus membranes lining the sinuses*	Throbbing pain above or below one or both eyes that intensifies when bending the head forward or coughing; nasal congestion; loss of sense of smell; often, pus-like nasal discharge; possible dental pain in the upper jaw; fever.
	Strep infection	Symptoms depend on the location and nature of the specific infection, but may include fever, headaches, swollen lymph glands, fatigue, loss of appetite, nasal discharge, red skin rash.

Nausea and/or vomiting

Associated Symptoms	Possible Diagnosis	Distinguishing Features
	Adrenal insufficiency *Inadequate production of steroid hormones by the adrenal glands*	Loss of weight and appetite; fatigue; weakness; darkening of the skin; abdominal pain; diarrhea; indigestion; nausea and vomiting; constipation; lack of sex drive; dizziness when rising from sitting or lying position.
	Anaphylaxis	Itching and hives; swelling of the eyes, lips, and tongue; weakness or faintness; tightening in the chest or throat; wheezing; shortness of breath; profuse sweating; palpitations; sudden, intense distress; feelings of impending doom; stomach cramps; nausea, vomiting, or diarrhea; bluish tinge (cyanosis) to the skin, lips, and nailbeds due to oxygen insufficiency.
	Anemia, folic acid deficiency	Fatigue and weakness; pallor; shortness of breath, heart palpitations, or noticeably rapid heartbeat on exertion; sore, red, and glazed-looking tongue; loss of weight and appetite; nausea and diarrhea; abdominal distention.
	Anemia, pernicious	Fatigue; inability to concentrate; sore, red tongue; weakness; dizziness; pallor; shortness of breath on exertion; palpitations; numbness and tingling in extremities; incoordination; headache; loss of weight and appetite; possibly, jaundice.
	Benign paroxysmal positional vertigo	Sudden sensation of spinning that occurs after changing the position of the head; loss of balance; nausea and vomiting.
	Botulism	Difficulty swallowing and speaking; nausea; vomiting; blurred or double vision.
	Cirrhosis *Chronic damage to the cells of the liver*	No symptoms in early stages; loss of weight and appetite; nausea; swollen legs, ankles and abdomen; itching; jaundice; black stools; vomiting blood; fatigue; impotence; memory loss; confusion.
	Congestive heart failure	Shortness of breath; fatigue; need to sleep on several pillows; weakness; cough; heart palpitations; swelling in the legs, ankles, and abdomen; frequent urination at night; indigestion; nausea and vomiting; loss of appetite.
	Coronary artery disease *Blockage in the arteries supplying blood to the heart muscle*	Initially, asymptomatic. In later stages, dull chest pain that may spread to the neck or the arms usually exacerbated by physical exertion and alleviated with rest; heart palpitations; shortness of breath.
	Esophageal cancer	Swallowing difficulty and pain; weight loss; drooling; possibly, vomiting or coughing up of bloody mucus, regurgitation of food; chest pain; repeated respiratory infections.

Nausea and/or vomiting *continued*

Associated Symptoms	Possible Diagnosis	Distinguishing Features
	Esophageal rupture *A tear in the esophagus, the passageway from the mouth to the stomach*	Chest pain; rapid, shallow breathing; excessive perspiration; vomiting with blood present.
	Hyperparathyroidism *Overactivity of the parathyroid glands*	Increased susceptibility to bone fractures; depression; indigestion; increased thirst and urine output; fatigue, lethargy; somnolence; muscle weakness; nausea and vomiting; loss of appetite.
	Kidney infection *Pyelonephritis*	Sudden fever and shaking chills; severe fatigue; burning and frequent urination; cloudy or bloody urine; lower back pain, sometimes severe; nausea and vomiting.
	Labyrinthitis *Inflammation of the semicircular canals of the inner ear*	Severe dizziness, loss of balance, jerky movements of the eyes; nausea and vomiting; ringing in the ears. In later stages, possible hearing loss.
	Meniere's disease *Dysfunction of structures in the inner ear*	Sudden attack of severe vertigo; nausea and vomiting; impaired sense of balance; ringing in the ears; hearing loss in the affected ear. Jerky movements of the eyes.
	Myocardial infarction *Heart attack*	Sudden chest pain or pressure that may spread to the arm, shoulder and jaw; excessive perspiration; shortness of breath. Possible nausea and vomiting.
	Ovarian cysts	In many cases, no symptoms. Painless swelling in the lower abdomen; possibly, pain during intercourse; brown vaginal discharge; lack of or heavier than usual menstrual periods; vomiting; unusual hair growth on face or body.
	Poliomyelitis *Polio*	Low fever; sore throat; headache; nausea and vomiting. In severe cases, paralysis without loss of sensation; stiff neck and back; twitching; swallowing and breathing difficulty; drooling.
	Renal calculi *Kidney stones*	Intermittent spasms of pain in the back and flanks, radiating through the lower abdomen towards the groin; nausea and vomiting; blood in the urine; urge to urinate but only small amounts of urine are passed.
	Renal failure, acute *Severe kidney failure*	Initially, decreased urine output, weight gain and swelling due to edema, loss of appetite, nausea and vomiting, fatigue. If untreated, confusion, seizures, and drowsiness.
	Reye's syndrome *Childhood disease marked by brain and liver damage*	Following recovery from an upper respiratory infection, nausea and vomiting; memory loss; confusion or delirium; possible seizures; drowsiness; lethargy.

Nausea and/or vomiting *continued*

Associated Symptoms	Possible Diagnosis	Distinguishing Features
	Trichinosis *Parasitic infestation*	Initially, crampy abdominal pain, diarrhea, vomiting, and fever, followed within one to two weeks by swelling around the eyes, muscle aches and tenderness, fever, and weakness. Possibly, coughing up of bloody phlegm; delirium; coma; heart failure symptoms.
with abdominal pain	Adrenal insufficiency *Inadequate production of steroid hormones by the adrenal gland*	Loss of weight and appetite; fatigue; weakness; darkening of the skin; abdominal pain; diarrhea; indigestion; nausea and vomiting; constipation; lack of sex drive; dizziness when rising from sitting or lying position.
	Amebiasis *Parasitic infection*	Usually asymptomatic; possibly, diarrhea; loose stools may contain mucus and blood; abdominal cramps; fatigue; weight loss; gas and flatulence. In severe cases, large amount of bloody stools daily; fever, nausea and vomiting, and abdominal tenderness.
	Disseminated intravascular coagulation *Bleeding disorder marked by excessive and inappropriate blood coagulation*	Abnormal bleeding possibly at several sites at once; vomiting blood; bloody or black stools; abnormal vaginal bleeding; blood in the urine; severe abdominal or back pain; possibly, convulsions, or coma.
	Diverticular disorders *Swellings in the wall of the colon*	Usually no symptoms unless diverticulae become inflamed. Tenderness or pain in the lower left abdomen relieved by passing stools or gas; constipation or diarrhea; blood in the stool; severe, spasmodic abdominal pain that becomes constant; possibly, fever and nausea.
	Dysentery, bacillary	Watery diarrhea that may contain pus or blood; abdominal pain; rapid dehydration and weight loss; nausea and vomiting.
	Endometriosis *The migration of the uterine lining to other reproductive or abdominal organs*	Pain in the lower abdomen, vagina, and lower back beginning just prior to menses and intensifying after blood flow has ceased; heavy bleeding during periods; pain during intercourse; diarrhea; constipation; pain during bowel movements; bleeding from the rectum; bloody urine during menses; nausea and vomiting prior to menses; infertility.
	Gallbladder disorders	Moderate to severe pain in the upper right side of the abdomen, chest, upper back, or right shoulder. Pain often follows the ingestion of high-fat foods and is episodic, lasting 20 minutes to several hours. Nausea and vomiting; low-grade fever; belching; heartburn; gas; possibly, jaundice, pale stools, and itchy skin.

Nausea and/or vomiting *continued*

Associated Symptoms	Possible Diagnosis	Distinguishing Features
with abdominal pain *continued*	Hepatitis, chronic	Fatigue; nausea; vomiting; loss of appetite; jaundice; dark urine; clay-colored stools; depression; pain or discomfort in the upper right abdomen; abdominal swelling; fever; in women, cessation of menstruation, acne, and the appearance of male pattern facial hair.
	Inguinal hernia *Displaced loop of intestine in the inguinal canal, a tubular passage through the abdominal wall*	A swelling in the groin area that may recede when lying down; pain at the site of the swelling, especially when lifting a heavy object; swelling of the scrotum. Nausea, vomiting, loss of appetite, and abdominal pain if intestine becomes obstructed.
	Intestinal obstruction	Abdominal pain and cramps; nausea; vomiting; weakness; gas; abdominal bloating; possible diarrhea; progressive constipation culminating in inability to pass stools or gas.
	Irritable bowel syndrome	Cramps in the middle or to one side of the lower abdomen that are usually relieved with bowel movements; nausea; bloating; gas; alternating diarrhea and constipation.
	Kidney cancer	Blood in the urine; abdominal and lower back pain; low-grade fever; fatigue; nausea and vomiting; loss of weight and appetite.
	Lactose intolerance *Difficulty digesting milk and dairy products*	Abdominal cramps; diarrhea; nausea; bloating; flatulence.
	Liver tumors	Pain or discomfort in the upper right portion of the abdomen; abdominal swelling; loss of weight and appetite; nausea and vomiting; fever; excessive perspiration; jaundice; pallor; severe fatigue.
	Mesenteric ischemia *A blood clot blocking blood flow to the intestine*	Severe abdominal cramping, usually around the navel, that is exacerbated by eating and alleviated by fasting. Possibly, bloody stools.
	Ovarian cancer	Often asymptomatic until widespread. Possibly, abdominal swelling or discomfort, nausea, and vomiting. In advanced stages, excessive hair growth, unexplained weight loss, abnormal menstrual bleeding or postmenopausal bleeding; urinary frequency.
	Pancreatic cancer	Often, no symptoms until far advanced. Upper abdominal pain which spreads to the back; loss of weight and appetite; jaundice; nausea, vomiting, and indigestion; diarrhea; fatigue; depression.

Nausea and/or vomiting *continued*

Associated Symptoms	Possible Diagnosis	Distinguishing Features
with abdominal pain *continued*	Pancreatitis *Inflammation of the pancreas*	Sudden, extreme abdominal pain; nausea and vomiting; weakness; fever; clammy skin; abdominal bloating and tenderness.
	Peptic ulcer	Intermittent, burning or gnawing pain in the upper abdomen or lower chest; indigestion; loss of appetite and weight. Pain may be relieved by eating or antacids. Possible nausea and vomiting. Black, tarry stools, vomiting blood.
	Peritonitis *Inflammation of the abdominal membrane.*	Sudden abdominal pain, rigidity, and swelling; chills and fever; weakness; rapid heartbeat; nausea and vomiting; extreme thirst; low urine output.
	Stomach cancer	Discomfort in the upper abdomen; black, tarry stools; vomiting of blood; loss of appetite and weight; vomiting after meals.
	Testicular torsion *Twisting of the spermatic cord*	Severe pain and swelling on one side of the scrotum; skin on the scrotum may appear red or purple; light-headedness or fainting; possibly, abdominal pain, nausea and vomiting.
with headache	Brain abscess	Headaches; drowsiness; nausea and vomiting; fever; seizures; possible partial paralysis; confusion; speaking difficulty.
	Brain tumors	Headaches that become more severe when reclining; nausea and vomiting; memory loss; double vision; muscle weakness; numbness, tingling, or partial paralysis; vision loss; speech disturbances; seizures; drowsiness.
	Concussion	Brief loss of consciousness following a blow to the head. Occasionally causes nausea and vomiting.
	Glaucoma	Often initially asymptomatic. In later stages, the symptoms of closed angle glaucoma include: the appearance of halos and rainbows around lights; dilated pupil in the affected eye; severe headache and eye pain; possibly, nausea and vomiting. Open angle glaucoma symptoms include: blurred vision and a gradual loss of peripheral vision.
	Glomerulonephritis, acute *Sudden or intense inflammation of the glomeruli, tiny structures that filter blood in the kidneys*	Blood in the urine; passing only small amounts of urine; swelling of the ankles or the tissues around the eyes; shortness of breath; possibly, fatigue, nausea and vomiting, loss of appetite, itching, headaches, fever, impaired vision.

Nausea and/or vomiting *continued*

Associated Symptoms	Possible Diagnosis	Distinguishing Features
with headache *continued*	Glomerulonephritis, chronic *Persistent inflammation of the glomeruli, tiny structures that filter blood in the kidneys*	Blood in the urine; passing only small amounts of urine; swelling of the ankles or the tissues around the eyes; shortness of breath; possibly, fatigue, nausea and vomiting, loss of appetite, itching, headaches, fever, impaired vision.
	Headache, migraine	Throbbing pain in the temple which spreads to the side of the head; nausea; vomiting. Pain may be preceded by blurred or impaired vision with bright spots and zig-zag patterns.
	Hydrocephalus *Overaccumulation of cerebrospinal fluid, the liquid surrounding the brain*	In infants, an enlarged head, rigidity of the legs, irritability, projectile vomiting, drowsiness, seizures, and lethargy. In older persons, headache, vomiting, loss of coordination, deterioration of mental faculties, speech difficulty, and loss of appetite.
	Legionnaire's disease	Dry cough progressing to one with blood-streaked sputum; high fever; chills; breathing difficulty; chest pain; headache; muscle aches; diarrhea; nausea; vomiting; mental confusion and disorientation.
	Malaria	Initially, severe chills and shivering. In later stages, extremely high fever followed by a period of profuse perspiration as fever subsides; headache, sometimes severe; vomiting.
	Meningitis *Inflammation of the membranes covering the brain and spinal cord*	Severe headache; nausea and vomiting; sensitivity to light; stiffness in the neck; possible red skin rash; fever; mental confusion; drowsiness; loss of consciousness; seizures.
	Rocky Mountain spotted fever	Within a week after exposure, high fever, loss of appetite, headache, muscle aches, nausea and vomiting; dry cough; sensitivity to light. Within six days, the appearance of small pink spots on wrists and ankles, eventually spreading over the entire body, where they then grow, darken in color, and bleed.
	Toxic shock syndrome	Lethargy; conjunctivitis; confusion; sudden high fever accompanied by nausea, watery diarrhea, sore throat, and headache. Red rash on the palms and soles of the feet, which, after a week or two, begins to peel.
with abdominal pain and headache	Food poisoning	Symptoms vary greatly depending on the type and extent of poisoning and may include nausea, vomiting, diarrhea, bloody stools, abdominal pain, and collapse.

Nausea and/or vomiting *continued*

Associated Symptoms	Possible Diagnosis	Distinguishing Features
with abdominal pain and headache *continued*	Leukemias	Symptoms vary depending on the type of leukemia and may include: loss of appetite and weight; increased bruising and bleeding; bone pain, especially in the legs; abdominal pain and distention; nausea; heart palpitations; severe fatigue; pallor; breathing difficulty; fever; night sweats; headache; enlarged lymph nodes; joint pains (due to gout).
	Systemic lupus erythematosus *Inflammation of connective tissues throughout the body*	Red, blotchy, butterfly-shaped rash on the cheeks and bridge of the nose; fatigue; fever; loss of appetite and weight; nausea; joint and abdominal pain; headaches; blurred vision; increased sensitivity to sun exposure; depression; psychosis; mental confusion.

Neck pain

Associated Symptoms	Possible Diagnosis	Distinguishing Features
	Ankylosing spondylitis *Inflammation of the joints between the spine and the pelvis*	Initially, pain and stiffness in the lower back and hips that becomes worse after resting; neck or chest pain; fatigue; possible pain in the hip, knee, and ankle joints; pain in the heel of the foot; eye pain; blurred vision.
	Cervical acceleration/deceleration injuries *Whiplash*	Pain and stiffness in the neck that usually intensifies 24 hours after a head injury or neck sprain.
	Meningitis *Inflammation of the membranes covering the brain and spinal cord*	Severe headache; nausea and vomiting; sensitivity to light; stiffness in the neck; possible red skin rash; fever; mental confusion; drowsiness; loss of consciousness; seizures.
	Osteoarthritis *Degeneration of the cartilage that lines the joints*	Pain, swelling, and stiffness in one or more joints; enlargement and distortion of affected joints.
	Osteomalacia and Rickets *Softening and weakening of the bones, usually due to poor calcification*	Bone pain, especially in the neck, legs, hips and ribs. Muscle weakness, numbness, or spasms in the hands, feet, and throat; increased susceptibility to bone fractures.
	Osteomyelitis *Infection of bone and bone marrow*	Fever; severe pain in the affected bone; inflammation and swelling of the skin over the affected area; deformity. In children, arrested growth of the affected bone.
	Osteoporosis *Loss of bone mass due to calcium depletion*	Backache; easily fractured bones, especially in the wrists, hips, and spine; gradual loss of height; stooped or hunched posture.
	Paget's disease *A weakening, thickening, and deformity of the bones*	Often asymptomatic. Possibly, bone pain or deformity, especially bowing of the legs, bent spine, and facial deformity; unexplained bone fractures; joint pain or stiffness; hearing loss; headaches; ringing in ears.
	Rheumatoid arthritis	Fatigue and weakness; joint pain, stiffness, and inflammation, especially in the hands, feet, and arms; joint deformity; dry mouth; dry, painful eyes. Morning stiffness.
	Rheumatoid arthritis, juvenile	Fever; rash; abdominal pain; weight loss; swelling, stiffness, and pain in the affected joints; enlarged lymph glands; fatigue; pallor; red, painful eyes; morning stiffness.
	Spinal cord trauma	Severe pain and swelling in the affected area; loss of sensation, muscle weakness, or paralysis below the site of the injury; urinary or fecal incontinence or retention; impotence; breathing difficulty; shock.

Neck pain *continued*

Associated Symptoms	Possible Diagnosis	Distinguishing Features
	Spinal stenosis *Narrowing of the spinal canal due to bony overgrowth*	Numbness, pain, and weakness in the legs and back that is exacerbated by walking and alleviated by sitting.
	Spinal tumor	Progressive numbness, tingling, and muscle weakness; fecal or urinary incontinence; persistent back pain.
	Spondylosis, cervical *Arthritis of the vertebral disks in the neck*	Neck pain and stiffness that spreads to the shoulders, upper arms, hands, or back of the head; numbness or tingling in the arms, hands, and fingers; weakness in the arms and legs; unsteady gait; possible loss of bladder control.
	Sprains and strains	Swelling, pain or tenderness in the affected joints; impaired joint function.

Night blindness

Associated Symptoms	Possible Diagnosis	Distinguishing Features
	Cataracts	Painless, increasingly blurred vision; appearance of halos around lights; changes in color perception; increased sensitivity to light and glare.
	Glaucoma	Often initially asymptomatic. In later stages, the symptoms of closed angle glaucoma include: the appearance of halos and rainbows around lights; dilated pupil in the affected eye; severe headache and eye pain; possibly, nausea and vomiting. Open angle glaucoma symptoms include: blurred vision and a gradual loss of peripheral vision.
	Malabsorption, digestive *A failure of the small intestine to absorb nutrients in the diet*	Diarrhea; weight loss; yellowish, foul-smelling stools; abdominal cramps, gas, and bloating; weakness and lethargy.

Night sweats

Associated Symptoms	Possible Diagnosis	Distinguishing Features
	AIDS *Acquired immunodeficiency syndrome*	Recurrent infections affecting the skin and respiratory system; cough; shortness of breath; loss of appetite; weight loss; fatigue; diarrhea; fever; dementia; malignant skin lesions; swollen lymph glands throughout the body; purplish skin nodules; memory loss; confusion; personality changes.
	Empyema *Collection of pus in any body cavity, usually between the membranes covering the lungs*	Chest pain exacerbated by deep inhalation; shortness of breath; dry cough; fever and chills; exhaustion; weight loss; night sweats; abdominal pain and jaundice.
	Leukemias	Symptoms vary depending on the type of leukemia and may include: loss of appetite and weight; increased bruising and bleeding; bone pain, especially in the legs; abdominal pain and distention; nausea; heart palpitations; severe fatigue; pallor; breathing difficulty; fever; night sweats; headache; enlarged lymph nodes; joint pains (due to gout).
	Lymphoma, Hodgkin's *Cancer of the lymph nodes and lymphoid tissue*	Painless swelling of the lymph nodes usually in the neck or armpits; loss of appetite; night sweats.
	Lymphoma, non–Hodgkin's *Cancer of the lymph nodes and lymphoid tissue*	Painless swelling of lymph nodes in the neck or groin; possible abdominal pain, vomiting of blood, headache.
	Polycythemia vera *An overproduction of red and white blood cells and platelets*	Headache; blurred vision; flushed skin; itching; dizziness; fatigue; night sweats; shortness of breath; weight loss.
	Tuberculosis	Often, asymptomatic. Possibly, low-grade fever; excessive perspiration; cough producing sputum or blood; weight loss; chronic fatigue; chest pain; shortness of breath; night sweats.

Nipple discharge

Associated Symptoms	Possible Diagnosis	Distinguishing Features
	Breast cancer	Lump or swelling, usually painless, in the breast or under the armpit; flattening, dimpling, indentation, redness, or scaliness of the breast; itching sensation in the nipple; change in size or symmetry of the breasts; breast pain.
	Fibrocystic breast disease *Benign lumps in the breast*	A lump or swelling, usually painless, anywhere in the breast or underarm, typically located in the upper and outer part of the breast. Pain around the lump, usually more apparent during the week prior to menses. Changes in the size or symmetry of the breasts.
	Hypothyroidism *Underactivity of the thyroid gland*	Unexplained weight gain; fatigue; muscle weakness; cramps; dry skin; hair loss; deepening of the voice; intolerance for cold; constipation; chest pain; insomnia; puffiness around eyes; loss of sex drive; depression; menstrual abnormalities; possible swelling in the neck (goiter).

Nosebleeds

Associated Symptoms	Possible Diagnosis	Distinguishing Features
	Cirrhosis *Chronic damage to the cells of the liver*	No symptoms in early stages; loss of weight and appetite; nausea; swollen legs, ankles and abdomen; itching; jaundice; black stools; vomiting blood; fatigue; impotence; memory loss; confusion.
	Hemophilia	Profuse bleeding from minor injuries and tooth extractions; internal bleeding that may cause blood in the urine; bleeding into joints; symptoms of stroke due to intracerebral bleeding; possibly, extensive bruising.
	Hypertension	Usually asymptomatic except in severe cases. Possibly, headache, easy fatigability, palpitations, chest pain, blurred vision, dizziness, nose bleeds, and confusion.
	Leukemias	Symptoms vary depending on the type of leukemia and may include: loss of appetite and weight; increased bruising and bleeding; bone pain, especially in the legs; abdominal pain and distention; nausea; heart palpitations; severe fatigue; pallor; breathing difficulty; fever; night sweats; headache; enlarged lymph nodes; joint pains (due to gout).
	Platelet function disorders	Minor bleeding in the mouth or just beneath the surface of the skin, often appearing as clusters of small, pinpoint-sized red specks; frequent nosebleeds; easy bruising; prolonged menstrual periods; fatigue; pallor; dark-colored stools.
	Polycythemia vera *An overproduction of red and white blood cells and platelets*	Headache; blurred vision; flushed skin; itching; dizziness; fatigue; night sweats; shortness of breath; weight loss.
	Sinusitis *Inflammation of the mucus membranes lining the sinuses*	Throbbing pain above or below one or both eyes that intensifies when bending the head forward or coughing; nasal congestion; loss of sense of smell; often, pus-like nasal discharge; possible dental pain in the upper jaw; fever.

Numbness or tingling sensation Paresthesia

Associated Symptoms	Possible Diagnosis	Distinguishing Features
	Anemia, pernicious	Fatigue; inability to concentrate; sore, red tongue; weakness; dizziness; pallor; shortness of breath on exertion; palpitations; numbness and tingling in extremities; incoordination; headache; loss of weight and appetite; possibly, jaundice.
	Brain tumors	Headaches that become more severe when reclining; nausea and vomiting; memory loss; double vision; muscle weakness; numbness, tingling, or partial paralysis; vision loss; speech disturbances; seizures; drowsiness.
	Carpal tunnel syndrome	Numbness, tingling, and pain in the hand and wrist, often intensifying at night; weakness of the fingers and hand.
	Cervical acceleration/ deceleration injuries *Whiplash*	Pain and stiffness in the neck that usually intensifies 24 hours after a head injury or neck sprain.
	Diabetes mellitus *Insufficiency of or resistance to insulin*	Fatigue; excessive thirst; frequent urination; weight loss despite increased appetite; blurred vision; numbness and tingling of feet and hands; impotence.
	Herpes zoster *Shingles*	A sensitive band of skin on one side of the body that becomes severely painful and develops slightly raised red spots that blister, dry and crust over. Pain may persist for months or years after skin has healed.
	Intervertebral disk, herniated	Severe lower back or neck pain that is exacerbated by movement or lifting heavy objects, sneezing, coughing, straining at stool. Pain, tingling, or numbness in a leg or an arm, usually on one side.
	Multiple sclerosis *Gradual degeneration of the protective sheaths surrounding the nerves within the brain and spinal cord*	Symptoms may appear suddenly and then disappear; persistent symptoms may take years to develop and include numbness or tingling in any part of the body, weakness in the extremities, an unsteady walk, slurred speech, urinary incontinence, fatigue, depression, temporary loss of vision, double or blurred vision, mental confusion, and memory loss.
	Peripheral neuropathies *Degeneration of the nerves that supply the extremities*	Tingling or numbness commonly beginning in the hands and feet and gradually spreading toward the center of the body; sensitive skin; muscle weakness; possibly, pain in the hands and feet; lack of coordination; shooting pains exacerbated by touch or changes in temperature; breathing difficulty; urinary or fecal incontinence.

Numbness or tingling sensation Paresthesia *continued*

Associated Symptoms	Possible Diagnosis	Distinguishing Features
	Rabies	Low-grade fever; headache; loss of appetite; tingling at site of animal bite; intense thirst exacerbated by the inability to drink without violent, painful throat spasms; paralysis of facial muscles; drooling. Agitation and violent behavior, confusion, convulsions, coma.
	Renal failure, chronic *Persistent, mild kidney failure*	Asymptomatic in early stages. Possibly, mental confusion; shortness of breath; abdominal pain; decreased sex drive; fatigue; muscle and bone pain; numbness in the legs and feet; headache; impaired mental acuity; bad breath.
	Sarcoidosis *Accumulation of inflammatory cells in the lymph nodes and other tissues throughout the body*	Often no symptoms. Swollen lymph nodes in the neck or armpits; muscle aches; fever; breathing difficulty; possibly, purple rash on the face; reddish skin; bumps on the legs; numbness; joint pain or stiffness; a painful, red eye; blurred vision; loss of appetite and weight.
	Spondylosis, cervical *Arthritis of the vertebral disks in the neck*	Neck pain and stiffness that spreads to the shoulders, upper arms, hands, or back of the head; numbness or tingling in the arms, hands, and fingers; weakness in the arms and legs; unsteady gait; possible loss of bladder control.
	Spinal cord trauma	Severe pain and swelling in the affected area; loss of sensation, muscle weakness, or paralysis below the site of the injury; urinary or fecal incontinence or retention; impotence; breathing difficulty; shock.
	Spinal stenosis *Narrowing of the spinal canal due to bony overgrowth*	Numbness, pain, and weakness in the legs and back that is exacerbated by walking and alleviated by sitting.
	Spinal tumor	Progressive numbness, tingling, and muscle weakness; fecal or urinary incontinence; persistent back pain.
	Transient ischemic attack *Temporary blockage in an artery supplying the brain*	Weakness or numbness in a limb; slurred speech; short-lived, temporary partial blindness; numbness and tingling; speech difficulties; confusion; dizziness.

Painful urination

Associated Symptoms	Possible Diagnosis	Distinguishing Features
	Bladder cancer	Blood in the urine; painful and frequent urination; pelvic pain; feeling of pressure in the back; persistent fever; urinary incontinence.
	Bladder infection *Cystitis*	Burning during urination; frequent and urgent urination with only small amounts of urine passed; blood in the urine; lower abdominal pain; low-grade fever; pain during sexual intercourse and, in men, during ejaculation.
	Bladder stones	Interruption of urine stream; inability to urinate except in certain positions; frequent and urgent urination with only small amounts of urine passed; blood in the urine; pain in the genitals, lower back, or abdomen; low-grade fever.
	Candidiasis *Fungal infection of the mouth, genitals, or mucus membranes*	Thick, white discharge from the vagina; itching and irritation in the vaginal area; pain while urinating or during intercourse; in men, inflammation of the head of the penis; possibly, yellow raised patches in the mouth.
	Epididymitis *Inflammation of the coiled sperm conduit that rests on each testicle*	Severe pain and swelling at the back of a testicle; possibly, redness and swelling of the scrotum; burning on urination.
	Genital herpes	Approximately one week after infection, itching, burning, soreness, and small blisters in the genital area. Blisters later burst, leaving painful ulcers which heal 10 to 20 days later. Possibly, enlarged, painful lymph nodes in the groin; fever, headache, and cold sores around the mouth. In women, pain during urination.
	Gonorrhea	Burning pain during urination; yellowish, pus-like discharge from the penis or vagina; redness or swelling at the infection site; abnormal vaginal bleeding.
	Kidney cysts	Pain or tenderness in the lower back or abdomen; blood in the urine. In infants, symmetrical, protruding masses visible in the flanks.
	Kidney infection *Pyelonephritis*	Sudden fever and shaking chills; severe fatigue; burning and frequent urination; cloudy or bloody urine; lower back pain, sometimes severe; nausea and vomiting.
	Pelvic inflammatory disease	Initially, lower pelvic pain; pain during intercourse; irregular menstrual bleeding; vaginal discharge with abnormal color or odor; low-grade fever; chills; frequent urination; fatigue; loss of appetite; later, severe abdominal pain and high fever.

Painful urination *continued*

Associated Symptoms	Possible Diagnosis	Distinguishing Features
	Prostate cancer	Difficulty urinating; frequent urination with decreased urine output; pain in the pelvic area and lower back; painful ejaculation or bowel movements.
	Prostatic hyperplasia, benign *Prostate enlargement*	Slow or delayed urination; dribbling urine; the need to urinate several times during the night; possibly, pain during urination; blood in the urine.
	Prostatitis *Inflammation of the prostate gland*	Burning during urination; urgent and frequent urination; fever and chills; discharge from the penis; lower abdominal and back pain; blood in the urine.
	Renal calculi *Kidney stones*	Intermittent spasms of pain in the back and flanks, radiating through the lower abdomen towards the groin; nausea and vomiting; blood in the urine; urge to urinate but only small amounts of urine are passed.
	Urethritis *Infection of the urethra, the passageway that drains urine from the bladder*	Frequent and painful urination; blood in the urine; yellow, pus-filled discharge; possible difficulty passing urine; urinary urgency; pain during intercourse; in men, painful ejaculation.
	Vaginitis *Inflammation of the vagina*	Vaginal irritation, itching, and discharge; painful intercourse and minor postcoital bleeding. In later stages, vaginal pain.

Pallor Paleness

Associated Symptoms	Possible Diagnosis	Distinguishing Features
	Anemia, aplastic	Fatigue and weakness; shortness of breath; heart palpitations; pallor; bleeding gums; nosebleeds; tendency to bruise easily; small red dots under the skin (petechiae). Increased susceptibility to infection.
	Anemia, folic acid deficiency	Fatigue and weakness; pallor; shortness of breath, heart palpitations, or noticeably rapid heartbeat on exertion; sore, red, and glazed-looking tongue; loss of weight and appetite; nausea and diarrhea; abdominal distention.
	Anemia, hemolytic	Fatigue and weakness; shortness of breath on exertion; pallor; heart palpitations; jaundice and dark urine.
	Anemia, iron deficiency	Fatigue and weakness; pallor; shortness of breath and heart palpitations on exertion; irritability or inability to concentrate; sore tongue or tiny cracks at the corners of the mouth; black, tarry or bloody stools; unusual craving for dirt, paint, or ice.
	Anemia, pernicious	Fatigue; inability to concentrate; sore, red tongue; weakness; dizziness; pallor; shortness of breath on exertion; palpitations; numbness and tingling in extremities; incoordination; headache; loss of weight and appetite; possibly, jaundice.
	Hypothermia *Low body temperature (below 94°)*	Shivering; pallor; puffy face; fatigue and confusion; slow, shallow breathing; muscle stiffness; normally warm areas of the body are cold; loss of consciousness.
	Leukemias	Symptoms vary depending on the type of leukemia and may include: loss of appetite and weight; increased bruising and bleeding; bone pain, especially in the legs; abdominal pain and distention; nausea; heart palpitations; severe fatigue; pallor; breathing difficulty; fever; night sweats; headache; enlarged lymph nodes; joint pains (due to gout).
	Liver tumors	Pain or discomfort in the upper right portion of the abdomen; abdominal swelling; loss of weight and appetite; nausea and vomiting; fever; excessive perspiration; jaundice; pallor; severe fatigue.
	Malabsorption, digestive *A failure of the small intestine to absorb nutrients in the diet*	Diarrhea; weight loss; yellowish, foul-smelling stools; abdominal cramps, gas, and bloating; weakness and lethargy.

Pallor Paleness *continued*

Associated Symptoms	Possible Diagnosis	Distinguishing Features
	Multiple myeloma *Production of malignant plasma cells in the bone marrow*	Bone pain, especially progressive, constant back pain that intensifies with movement; unexplained bone fractures; fatigue; pallor; shortness of breath; increased bleeding, such as bleeding gums or nosebleeds; easily bruised skin; increased susceptibility to infection; headache; vision disturbances; loss of height.
	Myelofibrosis *An increase of fibrous scar tissue within the bone marrow*	Weakness and fatigue; abdominal fullness; a tendency to bleed easily; bone pain; pallor; shortness of breath during physical exertion; increased susceptibility to bruising and infections; jaundice; weight loss.
	Platelet function disorders	Minor bleeding in the mouth or just beneath the surface of the skin, often appearing as clusters of small, pinpoint-sized red specks; frequent nosebleeds; easy bruising; prolonged menstrual periods; fatigue; pallor; dark-colored stools.
	Pulmonary edema *An accumulation of fluid in the lungs*	Severe shortness of breath; rapid breathing; pallor; excessive perspiration; bluish nails and lips; cough with frothy sputum; wheezing; anxiety and restlessness.
	Rheumatoid arthritis, juvenile	Fever; rash; abdominal pain; weight loss; swelling, stiffness, and pain in the affected joints; enlarged lymph glands; fatigue; pallor; red, painful eyes; morning stiffness.

Palpitations

Associated Symptoms	Possible Diagnosis	Distinguishing Features
with shortness of breath	Amyloidosis *Accumulation of amyloid, a starchy protein, in tissues and organs*	Symptoms vary greatly depending on the body parts affected and may include heart palpitations; shortness of breath; swelling of the legs; diarrhea; abdominal pain; raised spots on the armpits, groin, face, and neck; fatigue and weakness; numbness of the hands or feet; dizziness on standing; joint pains.
	Anemia, aplastic	Fatigue and weakness; shortness of breath; heart palpitations; pallor; bleeding gums; nosebleeds; tendency to bruise easily; small red dots under the skin (petechiae). Increased susceptibility to infection.
	Anemia, folic acid deficiency	Fatigue and weakness; pallor; shortness of breath, heart palpitations, or noticeably rapid heartbeat on exertion; sore, red, and glazed-looking tongue; loss of weight and appetite; nausea and diarrhea; abdominal distention.
	Anemia, hemolytic	Fatigue and weakness; shortness of breath on exertion; pallor; heart palpitations; jaundice and dark urine.
	Anemia, iron deficiency	Fatigue and weakness; pallor; shortness of breath and heart palpitations on exertion; irritability or inability to concentrate; sore tongue or tiny cracks at the corners of the mouth; black, tarry or bloody stools; unusual craving for dirt, paint, or ice.
	Anemia, pernicious	Fatigue; inability to concentrate; sore, red tongue; weakness; dizziness; pallor; shortness of breath on exertion; palpitations; numbness and tingling in extremities; incoordination; headache; loss of weight and appetite; possibly, jaundice.
	Anxiety states	Sudden attacks of unreasonable fear and panic; rapid heartbeat or palpitations; perspiration; dry mouth; irritability; muscle tension; trembling; palpitations; shortness of breath; restlessness; poor concentration; insomnia; fatigue; weakness.
	Cardiac arrhythmias *Irregularities in the heartbeat*	Frequently, asymptomatic; possibly; heart palpitations; lightheadedness; shortness of breath; sudden weakness; loss of consciousness.
	Cardiomyopathy *Disease of the heart muscle causing a reduction in the force of heart contractions*	Fatigue; chest pain and palpitations; shortness of breath; swelling of the legs; wheezing; cough.

Palpitations *continued*

Associated Symptoms	Possible Diagnosis	Distinguishing Features
with shortness of breath *continued*	Congestive heart failure	Shortness of breath; fatigue; need to sleep on several pillows; weakness; cough; heart palpitations; swelling in the legs, ankles, and abdomen; frequent urination at night; indigestion; nausea and vomiting; loss of appetite.
	Leukemias	Symptoms vary depending on the type of leukemia and may include: loss of appetite and weight; increased bruising and bleeding; bone pain, especially in the legs; abdominal pain and distention; nausea; heart palpitations; severe fatigue; pallor; breathing difficulty; fever; night sweats; headache; enlarged lymph nodes; joint pains (due to gout).
	Mitral valve prolapse *A deformity in the heart's mitral valve possibly causing it to leak*	Usually asymptomatic. Possible palpitations, shortness of breath, dizziness, fainting, or fatigue.
	Myocarditis *Inflammation of the heart muscle*	Fatigue; shortness of breath; heart palpitations; fever; edema; rarely, continuous pressure or vague pain in the chest.
	Valvular heart disease	Depends on which heart valve is affected. Often asymptomatic. Possibly, fatigue and weakness; dizziness; chest pain; shortness of breath; heart palpitations; fainting; edema; stroke from embolism to the brain.
without shortness of breath	Colorectal cancer *A growth of malignant cells in the colon or rectum*	Change in bowel habits; diarrhea; constipation; narrow stools; bloody or dark stools; lower abdominal pain; bloating; cramps; gas; loss of weight and appetite; fatigue and heart palpitations due to anemia.
	Hemochromatosis *An excess accumulation of iron in the liver, pancreas, heart, testes, skin, and other organs*	A bronze or slate-gray tone to skin that is normally fair; chronic abdominal pain; heart palpitations; joint pain; drowsiness; confusion. In men, a decrease in the size of the testes, loss of sexual desire, and impotence.
	Hypertension	Usually asymptomatic except in severe cases. Possibly, headache, easy fatigability, palpitations, chest pain, blurred vision, dizziness, nose bleeds, and confusion.
	Hyperthyroidism *Overactivity of the thyroid gland*	Protruding eyes; weight loss despite increased appetite; intolerance to heat; excessive perspiration; nervousness or restlessness; possibly, swelling in the neck (goiter); palpitations; tremor; diarrhea.
	Hypoglycemia *Low blood sugar*	Anxiety; hunger; trembling; headache; palpitations; perspiration; confusion; irritability; loss of coordination; possibly, double vision, seizures, or coma.

Palpitations *continued*

Associated Symptoms	Possible Diagnosis	Distinguishing Features
	Lyme disease	A small red bump, surrounded by a concentric bulls-eye-like red rash with a pale center. Over the following month: fever and chills; extreme fatigue; headaches. Symptoms may progress over several months or years and may include: palpitations; joint or muscle pain; and chronic joint inflammation, especially in the knees.
	Pheochromocytoma *Tumor in central part of the adrenal, the glands above the kidneys*	Headaches, sometimes severe; rapid heartbeat or heart palpitations; excessive perspiration; faintness, especially when standing up; chest pain; abdominal pain; constipation; weight loss; nervousness, irritability, or anxiety; mental confusion or psychosis.

Paralysis

Associated Symptoms	Possible Diagnosis	Distinguishing Features
with headache	Brain abscess	Headaches; drowsiness; nausea and vomiting; fever; seizures; possible partial paralysis; confusion; speaking difficulty.
	Brain hemorrhage	Sudden loss of consciousness; sudden, severe headache; paralysis on one side of the face or body; weakness and dizziness; loss of speech; blurred or double vision; dilated pupils; back and leg pain; fever; mental confusion; stiff neck.
	Brain tumors	Headaches that become more severe when reclining; nausea and vomiting; memory loss; double vision; muscle weakness; numbness, tingling, or partial paralysis; vision loss; speech disturbances; seizures; drowsiness.
	Diphtheria *Bacterial throat infection*	Initially, swollen lymph glands in the neck and sore throat; difficulty swallowing; breathing difficulty; shortness of breath; rapid pulse; headache. In severe cases, paralysis of limbs or facial muscles; drooling.
	Encephalitis *Inflammation of the brain*	Initially, headache and fever followed by confusion, hallucinations, and paralysis on one side of the body; memory loss; difficulty with speech and eye movements; drowsiness; possible coma or epileptic seizures; loss of hearing; sensitivity to light; stiff neck.
	Multiple sclerosis *Gradual degeneration of the protective sheaths surrounding the nerves within the brain and spinal cord*	Symptoms may appear suddenly and then disappear; persistent symptoms may take years to develop and include numbness or tingling in any part of the body, weakness in the extremities, an unsteady walk, slurred speech, urinary incontinence, fatigue, depression, temporary loss of vision, double or blurred vision, mental confusion, and memory loss.
	Poliomyelitis *Polio*	Low fever; sore throat; headache; nausea and vomiting. In severe cases, paralysis without loss of sensation; stiff neck and back; twitching; swallowing and breathing difficulty; drooling.
	Rabies	Low-grade fever; headache; loss of appetite; tingling at site of animal bite; intense thirst exacerbated by the inability to drink without violent, painful throat spasms; paralysis of facial muscles; drooling. Agitation and violent behavior, confusion, convulsions, coma.

Paralysis *continued*

Associated Symptoms	Possible Diagnosis	Distinguishing Features
with headache *continued*	Stroke	Symptoms vary with the location of brain injury. Sudden onset of weakness, paralysis, or loss of sensation, usually on one side of the body; a sudden heaviness in a limb; speech abnormalities; headache; vision disturbances; dizziness; confusion; coma; urinary and fecal incontinence.
	Transient ischemic attack *Temporary blockage in an artery supplying the brain*	Weakness or numbness in a limb; slurred speech; short-lived, temporary partial blindness; numbness and tingling; speech difficulties; confusion; dizziness.
without headache	Amyotrophic lateral sclerosis *Progressive degeneration of nerve cells of the central nervous system*	Progressive loss of strength and coordination in the limbs; muscle twitching and cramps that begin in the hands and spread to the arms, shoulders, and legs; stiff, clumsy gait; swallowing, breathing, or speaking difficulty; weight loss; drooling; involuntary laughing or crying.
	Bell's palsy *Paralysis of muscles on one side of the face*	Drooping muscles and weakness on one side of the face resulting in a distorted smile or an expressionless look; drooping eyelid, tearing and an inability to close the affected eye; drooling; possibly, ear pain on the affected side of the face; possibly, changes in taste perception; increased sensitivity to noise.
	Botulism	Difficulty swallowing and speaking; nausea; vomiting; blurred or double vision.
	Myasthenia gravis *Nerve degeneration causing gradual loss of voluntary muscle control*	Drooping eyelids; double or blurred vision; muscle weakness especially in the face, throat, and neck; chewing and swallowing difficulties; possible breathing difficulty. Slurred, nasal-sounding speech.
	Parkinson's disease *Degeneration of the basal ganglia, a cluster of nerve cells in the brain*	Tremors in the hands; stiffness and weakness; impaired voluntary movement; shuffling gait; stooped posture; unblinking, fixed expression; possibly, slow, hesitant speech; difficulty swallowing; drooling; depression. Tremors occur at rest (not with voluntary movements) and disappear during sleep.
	Peripheral neuropathies *Degeneration of the nerves that supply the extremities*	Tingling or numbness commonly beginning in the hands and feet and gradually spreading toward the center of the body; sensitive skin; muscle weakness; possibly, pain in the hands and feet; lack of coordination; shooting pains exacerbated by touch or changes in temperature; breathing difficulty; urinary or fecal incontinence.
	Seizures	Involuntary twitching or jerking; muscle rigidity; loss of consciousness; confusion; drooling; hallucinations.

Paralysis *continued*

Associated Symptoms	Possible Diagnosis	Distinguishing Features
	Spinal cord trauma	Severe pain and swelling in the affected area; loss of sensation, muscle weakness, or paralysis below the site of the injury; urinary or fecal incontinence or retention; impotence; breathing difficulty; shock.
	Spinal tumor	Progressive numbness, tingling, and muscle weakness; fecal or urinary incontinence; persistent back pain.
	Syphilis	Initially, painless, ulcerated, red sore on the genitals, mouth, or rectum; swollen glands in the neck, armpit, or groin; rash with small, red, scaly bumps; fever; headache. If left untreated, damage to heart valves leading to congestive heart failure; mental deterioration; loss of balance; seizures; dementia; personality changes.

Postnasal drip

Associated Symptoms	Possible Diagnosis	Distinguishing Features
	Allergic rhinitis *Hay fever*	Nasal congestion; frequent sneezing; itchy eyes, nose, and throat.
	Common cold	Nasal congestion; watery eyes; sneezing; sore throat; cough; muscle aches; mild headache; listlessness; possibly, low-grade fever.
	Sinusitis *Inflammation of the mucus membranes lining the sinuses*	Throbbing pain above or below one or both eyes that intensifies when bending the head forward or coughing; nasal congestion; loss of sense of smell; often, pus-like nasal discharge; possible dental pain in the upper jaw; fever.
	Strep infection	Symptoms depend on the location and nature of the specific infection, but may include fever, headaches, swollen lymph glands, fatigue, loss of appetite, nasal discharge, red skin rash.

Posture or height changes

Associated Symptoms	Possible Diagnosis	Distinguishing Features
	Amyotrophic lateral sclerosis *Progressive degeneration of nerve cells of the central nervous system*	Progressive loss of strength and coordination in the limbs; muscle twitching and cramps that begin in the hands and spread to the arms, shoulders, and legs; stiff, clumsy gait; swallowing, breathing, or speaking difficulty; weight loss; drooling; involuntary laughing or crying.
	Ankylosing spondylitis *Inflammation of the joints between the spine and the pelvis*	Initially, pain and stiffness in the lower back and hips that becomes worse after resting; neck or chest pain; fatigue; possible pain in the hip, knee, and ankle joints; pain in the heel of the foot; eye pain; blurred vision.
	Bone cancer	Pain, tenderness, and swelling in the affected bones and joints, often intensifying at night; a noticeable tumor or mass; increased susceptibility to bone fractures.
	Bursitis *Inflammation of the bursas, the lubricant-filled sacs in and around the joints*	Pain and swelling around a joint, usually the elbow, knee, or shoulder; painful movement in the affected joint; possibly, fever.
	Hyperpituitarism *Overactivity of the pituitary gland*	In adults (in which the disease is called acromegaly): Gradual thickening of the bones of the face, jaw, and the extremities in adults; oily skin; severe headache; excessive hair growth; excessive perspiration; joint pains. In children (in which the disease is called gigantism): Rapid growth and unusual height; possibly, blindness.
	Multiple myeloma *Production of malignant plasma cells in the bone marrow*	Bone pain, especially progressive, constant back pain that intensifies with movement; unexplained bone fractures; fatigue; pallor; shortness of breath; increased bleeding, such as bleeding gums or nosebleeds; easily bruised skin; increased susceptibility to infection; headache; vision disturbances; loss of height.
	Muscular dystrophy	Symptoms depend on type of muscular dystrophy and may include: Progressive muscle wasting, weakness, and loss of mobility; lack of coordination; muscular and skeletal deformities including backward curvature of the spine with protruding abdomen; waddling gait; cataracts; frontal baldness; gonadal atrophy.
	Osteoporosis *Loss of bone mass due to calcium depletion*	Backache; easily fractured bones, especially in the wrists, hips, and spine; gradual loss of height; stooped or hunched posture.
	Scoliosis	Gradual bending of the spine to one side or into an S-shape; shoulders and hips may appear uneven; possible back pain.

Pupils, constricted

Associated Symptoms	Possible Diagnosis	Distinguishing Features
	Corneal ulcers and infections	Severe eye pain; blurred vision; increased tear production; aversion to light.
	Headache, cluster	Persistent pain in or around one eye; redness and tearing of one eye; nasal congestion on the same side of the face as the affected eye.
	Uveitis and iritis *Inflammation of the uvea, a group of structures in the eye including the iris*	Moderate to severe eye pain; aversion to light; redness in the eye; excessive tearing; blurred vision; spots in the field of vision.

Pupils, dilated

Associated Symptoms	Possible Diagnosis	Distinguishing Features
	Anxiety states	Sudden attacks of unreasonable fear and panic; rapid heartbeat or palpitations; perspiration; dry mouth; irritability; muscle tension; trembling; palpitations; shortness of breath; restlessness; poor concentration; insomnia; fatigue; weakness.
	Botulism	Difficulty swallowing and speaking; nausea; vomiting; blurred or double vision.
	Glaucoma	Often initially asymptomatic. In later stages, the symptoms of closed angle glaucoma include: the appearance of halos and rainbows around lights; dilated pupil in the affected eye; severe headache and eye pain; possibly, nausea and vomiting. Open angle glaucoma symptoms include: blurred vision and a gradual loss of peripheral vision.
	Heatstroke	Sudden dizziness; weakness; headache; hot, dry, red skin which later turns grey; high body temperature; muscle cramps; confusion; seizures; loss of consciousness.

Rash

Associated Symptoms	Possible Diagnosis	Distinguishing Features
	Anaphylaxis	Itching and hives; swelling of the eyes, lips, and tongue; weakness or faintness; tightening in the chest or throat; wheezing; shortness of breath; profuse sweating; palpitations; sudden, intense distress; feelings of impending doom; stomach cramps; nausea, vomiting, or diarrhea; bluish tinge (cyanosis) to the skin, lips, and nailbeds due to oxygen insufficiency.
	Eczema *Inflammation of the skin*	Itching skin; thickened patches of skin; possibly, with oozing and crusting; in infants, rash on the face, inner elbows, or behind the knees that turns scaly and develops small red pimples that leak; swollen legs (stasis dermatitis).
	Psoriasis	Slightly raised patches of skin with red borders and white-silver scales; joint pain and stiffness; itching; pitted nails.
	Ringworm *Fungal skin infection*	A rash with distinct, advancing borders and clear centers; affected areas may have abnormally dark pigmentation; itching; scaly patches of skin; bald patches on scalp; Athlete's foot; red, swollen finger- and toenails.
	Scabies	Tiny, gray, scaly blisters—usually on the wrists, genitals, armpits, or between the fingers—that rupture easily when scratched; severe itching; red lumps or rashes may develop.
with fever	Dermatomyositis *Inflammation of the muscles and skin*	Red rash on the cheeks and bridge of the nose; purple discoloration and swelling of the eyelids; areas of thickened skin; muscle weakness and stiffness, usually in the shoulders and pelvis; cold hands and feet; speaking or swallowing difficulty; fever; weight loss.
	Herpes zoster *Shingles*	A sensitive band of skin on one side of the body that becomes severely painful and develops slightly raised red spots that blister, dry and crust over. Pain may persist for months or years after skin has healed.
	Lyme disease	A small red bump, surrounded by a concentric bulls-eye-like red rash with a pale center. Over the following month: fever and chills; extreme fatigue; headaches. Symptoms may progress over several months or years and may include: palpitations; joint or muscle pain; and chronic joint inflammation, especially in the knees.
	Measles	Cough; fever; watery nasal discharge; loss of appetite; red, watering eyes; sore throat; body aches; red, slightly itchy rash that gradually spreads all over the body.

Rash *continued*

Associated Symptoms	Possible Diagnosis	Distinguishing Features
with fever *continued*	Meningitis *Inflammation of the membranes covering the brain and spinal cord*	Severe headache; nausea and vomiting; sensitivity to light; stiffness in the neck; possible red skin rash; fever; mental confusion; drowsiness; loss of consciousness; seizures.
	Rheumatic fever	Initially, a sore throat that gets better followed, one to six weeks later, by lethargy and fever. Possibly, swollen joints, rash, abdominal pain, involuntary jerky movements, emotional instability.
	Rheumatoid arthritis, juvenile	Fever; rash; abdominal pain; weight loss; swelling, stiffness, and pain in the affected joints; enlarged lymph glands; fatigue; pallor; red, painful eyes; morning stiffness.
	Rocky Mountain spotted fever	Within a week after exposure, high fever, loss of appetite, headache, muscle aches, nausea and vomiting; dry cough; sensitivity to light. Within six days, the appearance of small pink spots on wrists and ankles, eventually spreading over the entire body, where they then grow, darken in color, and bleed.
	Roseola *Infectious disease primarily affecting children*	Abrupt onset of high fever that usually subsides within four to five days, at which time a rash appears on the torso, and spreads to the limbs, neck, and face. Sore throat; swollen lymph nodes in neck.
	Rubella *German Measles*	Rash on the face that spreads to the torso and limbs; enlargement of lymph nodes in neck; usually preceded by headache, fever, and runny nose.
	Sarcoidosis *Accumulation of inflammatory cells in the lymph nodes and other tissues throughout the body*	Often no symptoms. Swollen lymph nodes in the neck or armpits; muscle aches; fever; breathing difficulty; possibly, purple rash on the face; reddish skin; bumps on the legs; numbness; joint pain or stiffness; a painful, red eye; blurred vision; loss of appetite and weight.
	Syphilis	Initially, painless, ulcerated, red sore on the genitals, mouth, or rectum; swollen glands in the neck, armpit, or groin; rash with small, red, scaly bumps; fever; headache. If left untreated, damage to heart valves leading to congestive heart failure; mental deterioration; loss of balance; seizures; dementia; personality changes.
	Systemic lupus erythematosus *Inflammation of connective tissues throughout the body*	Red, blotchy, butterfly-shaped rash on the cheeks and bridge of the nose; fatigue; fever; loss of appetite and weight; nausea; joint and abdominal pain; headaches; blurred vision; increased sensitivity to sun exposure; depression; psychosis; mental confusion.

Rash *continued*

Associated Symptoms	Possible Diagnosis	Distinguishing Features
with fever *continued*	Toxic shock syndrome	Lethargy; conjunctivitis; confusion; sudden high fever accompanied by nausea, watery diarrhea, sore throat, and headache. Red rash on the palms and soles of the feet, which, after a week or two, begins to peel.
	Typhoid fever	Headache; fever, loss of appetite; abdominal pain and tenderness; extreme weakness; constipation followed by diarrhea; drowsiness, stupor, or coma; raised, pink skin eruptions on the chest and abdomen; joint aches; sore throat.

Rectal bleeding

Associated Symptoms	Possible Diagnosis	Distinguishing Features
	Amebiasis *Parasitic infection*	Usually asymptomatic; possibly, diarrhea; loose stools may contain mucus and blood; abdominal cramps; fatigue; weight loss; gas and flatulence. In severe cases, large amount of bloody stools daily; fever, nausea and vomiting, and abdominal tenderness.
	Amyloidosis *Accumulation of amyloid, a starchy protein, in tissues and organs*	Symptoms vary greatly depending on the body parts affected and may include heart palpitations; shortness of breath; swelling of the legs; diarrhea; abdominal pain; raised spots on the armpits, groin, face, and neck; fatigue and weakness; numbness of the hands or feet; dizziness on standing; joint pains.
	Anal fissure	Rectal pain during and immediately after bowel movements; blood in the stool or on toilet paper; rectal itching.
	Colitis, ulcerative *Inflammation of the lining of the colon*	Pain on the left side of the abdomen that lessens after bowel movements; bloody diarrhea; pain in the rectal area; possibly, fever, rapid heartbeat, nausea and vomiting, loss of appetite, dehydration with severe attacks.
	Colon Polyps	Rectal bleeding; blood in the stool; abdominal pain; change in bowel habits.
	Colorectal cancer *A growth of malignant cells in the colon or rectum*	Change in bowel habits; diarrhea; constipation; narrow stools; bloody or dark stools; lower abdominal pain; bloating; cramps; gas; loss of weight and appetite; fatigue and heart palpitations due to anemia.
	Crohn's disease *Inflammation of the lining of the small intestine*	Episodes of abdominal pain or cramps in lower abdomen; nausea; diarrhea; loss of weight and appetite; possibly, fever; rectal bleeding or blood in stools; fatigue; anal fissures; joint pains; inflammation of the eyes.
	Diverticular disorders *Swellings in the wall of the colon*	Usually no symptoms unless diverticulae become inflamed. Tenderness or pain in the lower left abdomen relieved by passing stools or gas; constipation or diarrhea; blood in the stool; severe, spasmodic abdominal pain that becomes constant; possibly, fever and nausea.
	Dysentery, bacillary	Watery diarrhea that may contain pus or blood; abdominal pain; rapid dehydration and weight loss; nausea and vomiting.
	Food poisoning	Symptoms vary greatly depending on the type and extent of poisoning and may include nausea, vomiting, diarrhea, bloody stools, abdominal pain, and collapse.

Rectal bleeding *continued*

Associated Symptoms	Possible Diagnosis	Distinguishing Features
	Hemophilia	Profuse bleeding from minor injuries and tooth extractions; internal bleeding that may cause blood in the urine; bleeding into joints; symptoms of stroke due to intracerebral bleeding; possibly, extensive bruising.
	Hemorrhoids	Pain during defecation; anal itching; mucus discharge from the anus. Bright, red blood on toilet paper, stool, or in toilet bowl after a bowel movement.
	Mesenteric ischemia *A blood clot blocking blood flow to the intestine*	Severe abdominal cramping, usually around the navel, that is exacerbated by eating and alleviated by fasting. Possibly, bloody stools.
	Proctitis *Inflammation of the rectum*	Soreness in the rectal area; mucus discharge from the anus; constipation; painful bowel movements; possibly, rectal bleeding.
	Vaginal cancer	Vaginal itching; bleeding after intercourse or between menstrual periods; abnormal vaginal discharge; lesions with thick, raised edges; possibly rectal bleeding; discomfort when urinating or defecating; pain during intercourse; urinary frequency and urgency.
	Von Willebrand's disease *Chronic bleeding disorder*	Frequent nosebleeds; excessive bleeding from cuts; bleeding gums; easy bruising; abnormal or excessive menstrual bleeding; blood in the stool.

Rectal itching

Associated Symptoms	Possible Diagnosis	Distinguishing Features
	Anal fissure	Rectal pain during and immediately after bowel movements; blood in the stool or on toilet paper; rectal itching.
	Candidiasis *Fungal infection of the mouth, genitals, or mucus membranes*	Thick, white discharge from the vagina; itching and irritation in the vaginal area; pain while urinating or during intercourse; in men, inflammation of the head of the penis; possibly, yellow raised patches in the mouth.
	Hemorrhoids	Pain during defecation; anal itching; mucus discharge from the anus. Bright, red blood on toilet paper, stool, or in toilet bowl after a bowel movement.
	Pinworm	Anal itching, often at night; irritability; fidgetiness; restless sleep.
	Proctitis *Inflammation of the rectum*	Soreness in the rectal area; mucus discharge from the anus; constipation; painful bowel movements; possibly, rectal bleeding.

Rectal pain

Associated Symptoms	Possible Diagnosis	Distinguishing Features
	Anal fissure	Rectal pain during and immediately after bowel movements; blood in the stool or on toilet paper; rectal itching.
	Colitis, ulcerative *Inflammation of the lining of the colon*	Pain on the left side of the abdomen that lessens after bowel movements; bloody diarrhea; pain in the rectal area; possibly, fever, rapid heartbeat, nausea and vomiting, loss of appetite, dehydration with severe attacks.
	Constipation, chronic	Infrequent and possibly painful bowel movements; straining during bowel movements; hard, dry stool; abdominal swelling; continued sensation of fullness after evacuating bowels.
	Crohn's disease *Inflammation of the lining of the small intestine*	Episodes of abdominal pain or cramps in lower abdomen; nausea; diarrhea; loss of weight and appetite; possibly, fever; rectal bleeding or blood in stools; fatigue; anal fissures; joint pains; inflammation of the eyes.
	Hemorrhoids	Pain during defecation; anal itching; mucus discharge from the anus. Bright, red blood on toilet paper, stool, or in toilet bowl after a bowel movement.
	Proctitis *Inflammation of the rectum*	Soreness in the rectal area; mucus discharge from the anus; constipation; painful bowel movements; possibly, rectal bleeding.
	Prostate cancer	Difficulty urinating; frequent urination with decreased urine output; pain in the pelvic area and lower back; painful ejaculation or bowel movements.
	Prostatitis *Inflammation of the prostate gland*	Burning during urination; urgent and frequent urination; fever and chills; discharge from the penis; lower abdominal and back pain; blood in the urine.

Seizures

Associated Symptoms	Possible Diagnosis	Distinguishing Features
	Brain abscess	Headaches; drowsiness; nausea and vomiting; fever; seizures; possible partial paralysis; confusion; speaking difficulty.
	Brain tumors	Headaches that become more severe when reclining; nausea and vomiting; memory loss; double vision; muscle weakness; numbness, tingling, or partial paralysis; vision loss; speech disturbances; seizures; drowsiness.
	Diabetes mellitus *Insufficiency of or resistance to insulin*	Fatigue; excessive thirst; frequent urination; weight loss despite increased appetite; blurred vision; numbness and tingling of feet and hands; impotence.
	Disseminated intravascular coagulation *Bleeding disorder marked by excessive and inappropriate blood coagulation*	Abnormal bleeding possibly at several sites at once; vomiting blood; bloody or black stools; abnormal vaginal bleeding; blood in the urine; severe abdominal or back pain; possibly, convulsions, or coma.
	Encephalitis *Inflammation of the brain*	Initially, headache and fever followed by confusion, hallucinations, and paralysis on one side of the body; memory loss; difficulty with speech and eye movements; drowsiness; possible coma or epileptic seizures; loss of hearing; sensitivity to light; stiff neck.
	Heatstroke	Sudden dizziness; weakness; headache; hot, dry, red skin which later turns grey; high body temperature; muscle cramps; confusion; seizures; loss of consciousness.
	Hydrocephalus *Overaccumulation of cerebrospinal fluid, the liquid surrounding the brain*	In infants, an enlarged head, rigidity of the legs, irritability, projectile vomiting, drowsiness, seizures, and lethargy. In older persons, headache, vomiting, loss of coordination, deterioration of mental faculties, speech difficulty, and loss of appetite.
	Hypoglycemia *Low blood sugar*	Anxiety; hunger; trembling; headache; palpitations; perspiration; confusion; irritability; loss of coordination; possibly, double vision, seizures, or coma.
	Hypoparathyroidism *Underactivity of the parathyroid glands*	Numbness and tingling and painful, cramp-like spasms of the face, hands, arms, and feet; cataracts; possible seizures.
	Leukemias	Symptoms vary depending on the type of leukemia and may include: loss of appetite and weight; increased bruising and bleeding; bone pain, especially in the legs; abdominal pain and distention; nausea; heart palpitations; severe fatigue; pallor; breathing difficulty; fever; night sweats; headache; enlarged lymph nodes; joint pains (due to gout).

Seizures *continued*

Associated Symptoms	Possible Diagnosis	Distinguishing Features
	Meningitis *Inflammation of the membranes covering the brain and spinal cord*	Severe headache; nausea and vomiting; sensitivity to light; stiffness in the neck; possible red skin rash; fever; mental confusion; drowsiness; loss of consciousness; seizures.
	Multiple sclerosis *Gradual degeneration of the protective sheaths surrounding the nerves within the brain and spinal cord*	Symptoms may appear suddenly and then disappear; persistent symptoms may take years to develop and include numbness or tingling in any part of the body, weakness in the extremities, an unsteady walk, slurred speech, urinary incontinence, fatigue, depression, temporary loss of vision, double or blurred vision, mental confusion, and memory loss.
	Renal failure, acute *Severe kidney failure*	Initially, decreased urine output, weight gain and swelling due to edema, loss of appetite, nausea and vomiting, fatigue. If untreated, confusion, seizures, and drowsiness.
	Renal failure, chronic *Persistent, mild kidney failure*	Asymptomatic in early stages. Possibly, mental confusion; shortness of breath; abdominal pain; decreased sex drive; fatigue; muscle and bone pain; numbness in the legs and feet; headache; impaired mental acuity; bad breath.
	Reye's syndrome *Childhood disease marked by brain and liver damage*	Following recovery from an upper respiratory infection, nausea and vomiting; memory loss; confusion or delirium; possible seizures; drowsiness; lethargy.
	Sarcoidosis *Accumulation of inflammatory cells in the lymph nodes and other tissues throughout the body*	Often no symptoms. Swollen lymph nodes in the neck or armpits; muscle aches; fever; breathing difficulty; possibly, purple rash on the face; reddish skin; bumps on the legs; numbness; joint pain or stiffness; a painful, red eye; blurred vision; loss of appetite and weight.
	Seizures	Involuntary twitching or jerking; muscle rigidity; loss of consciousness; confusion; drooling; hallucinations.
	Tetanus	Often, lockjaw; stiffness and, later, muscle spasms in the neck and face; drooling; abdominal and back pain; extreme perspiration; swallowing difficulty; possible convulsions; fever.

Sensitivity to light, increased

Associated Symptoms	Possible Diagnosis	Distinguishing Features
	Cataracts	Painless, increasingly blurred vision; appearance of halos around lights; changes in color perception; increased sensitivity to light and glare.
	Conjunctivitis *Pinkeye*	Itching and redness in the affected eye; discharge from the eye, clear or pus-filled; excessive tearing; aversion to bright lights; possibly, swollen eyelids.
	Corneal ulcers and infections	Severe eye pain; blurred vision; increased tear production; aversion to light.
	Headache, migraine	Throbbing pain in the temple which spreads to the side of the head; nausea; vomiting. Pain may be preceded by blurred or impaired vision with bright spots and zig-zag patterns.
	Meningitis *Inflammation of the membranes covering the brain and spinal cord*	Severe headache; nausea and vomiting; sensitivity to light; stiffness in the neck; possible red skin rash; fever; mental confusion; drowsiness; loss of consciousness; seizures.
	Scleritis and episcleritis *Inflammation of the sclera, the white of the eye*	Dull eye pain; redness in the white of the eye; possibly, blurred vision; aversion to light; copious tearing.
	Uveitis and iritis *Inflammation of the uvea, a group of structures in the eye including the iris*	Moderate to severe eye pain; aversion to light; redness in the eye; excessive tearing; blurred vision; spots in the field of vision.

Sexual intercourse, painful Dyspareunia

Associated Symptoms	Possible Diagnosis	Distinguishing Features
	Bladder infection *Cystitis*	Burning during urination; frequent and urgent urination with only small amounts of urine passed; blood in the urine; lower abdominal pain; low-grade fever; pain during sexual intercourse and, in men, during ejaculation.
	Candidiasis *Fungal infection of the mouth, genitals, or mucus membrane*	Thick, white discharge from the vagina; itching and irritation in the vaginal area; pain while urinating or during intercourse; in men, inflammation of the head of the penis; possibly, yellow raised patches in the mouth.
	Dyspareunia *Pain during sexual intercourse*	Pain occurs primarily during sexual activity. May include any type of discomfort from a burning sensation in the genitals to lower back pain.
	Epididymitis *Inflammation of the coiled sperm conduit that rests on each testicle*	Severe pain and swelling at the back of a testicle; possibly, redness and swelling of the scrotum; burning on urination.
	Genital herpes	Approximately one week after infection, itching, burning, soreness, and small blisters in the genital area. Blisters later burst, leaving painful ulcers which heal 10 to 20 days later. Possibly, enlarged, painful lymph nodes in the groin; fever, headache, and cold sores around the mouth. In women, pain during urination.
	Gonorrhea	Burning pain during urination; yellowish, pus-like discharge from the penis or vagina; redness or swelling at the infection site; abnormal vaginal bleeding.
	Orchitis *Inflammation of a testicle*	Swelling and severe pain in the affected testicle; possible bloody discharge in the semen; pain during intercourse; fever.
	Penile cancer	Sore, ulcer, or wart-like lump on the penis, usually near the head, possibly painful; bleeding or unusual discharge from the penis. Possibly, pain during urination, or enlarged lymph nodes in the groin.
	Prostatitis *Inflammation of the prostate gland*	Burning during urination; urgent and frequent urination; fever and chills; discharge from the penis; lower abdominal and back pain; blood in the urine.
	Urethritis *Infection of the urethra, the passageway that drains urine from the bladder*	Frequent and painful urination; blood in the urine; yellow, pus-filled discharge; possible difficulty passing urine; urinary urgency; pain during intercourse; in men, painful ejaculation.

Sexual intercourse, painful Dyspareunia *continued*

Associated Symptoms	Possible Diagnosis	Distinguishing Features
	Endometriosis *The migration of the uterine lining to other reproductive or abdominal organs*	Pain in the lower abdomen, vagina, and lower back beginning just prior to menses and intensifying after blood flow has ceased; heavy bleeding during periods; pain during intercourse; diarrhea; constipation; pain during bowel movements; bleeding from the rectum; bloody urine during menses; nausea and vomiting prior to menses; infertility.
	Ovarian cysts	In many cases, no symptoms. Painless swelling in the lower abdomen; possibly, pain during intercourse; brown vaginal discharge; lack of or heavier than usual menstrual periods; vomiting; unusual hair growth on face or body.
	Pelvic inflammatory disease	Initially, lower pelvic pain; pain during intercourse; irregular menstrual bleeding; vaginal discharge with abnormal color or odor; low-grade fever; chills; frequent urination; fatigue; loss of appetite; later, severe abdominal pain and high fever.
	Uterine prolapse	Often asymptomatic. Possibly, difficulty passing urine or stools, pain during intercourse, backache that intensifies when lifting, sensation of heaviness or dragging within the pelvis, painful or heavy menstrual periods, or bleeding between periods. In severe cases, uterus visibly protrudes outside of vagina.
	Vaginitis *Inflammation of the vagina*	Vaginal irritation, itching, and discharge; painful intercourse and minor postcoital bleeding. In later stages, vaginal pain.

Shakiness

Associated Symptoms	Possible Diagnosis	Distinguishing Features
	Brain tumors	Headaches that become more severe when reclining; nausea and vomiting; memory loss; double vision; muscle weakness; numbness, tingling, or partial paralysis; vision loss; speech disturbances; seizures; drowsiness.
	Essential tremor	Involuntary rhythmic shaking of the hands and arms and, less frequently, the head, tongue, larynx, eyelids, or other parts of the body. Tremors intensify during emotional stress and voluntary movements, and cease during periods of rest or sleep. Shaky handwriting; quavering voice.
	Hyperthyroidism *Overactivity of the thyroid gland*	Protruding eyes; weight loss despite increased appetite; intolerance to heat; excessive perspiration; nervousness or restlessness; possibly, swelling in the neck (goiter); palpitations; tremor; diarrhea.
	Hypoglycemia *Low blood sugar*	Anxiety; hunger; trembling; headache; palpitations; perspiration; confusion; irritability; loss of coordination; possibly, double vision, seizures, or coma.
	Parkinson's disease *Degeneration of the basal ganglia, a cluster of nerve cells in the brain*	Tremors in the hands; stiffness and weakness; impaired voluntary movement; shuffling gait; stooped posture; unblinking, fixed expression; possibly, slow, hesitant speech; difficulty swallowing; drooling; depression. Tremors occur at rest (not with voluntary movements) and disappear during sleep.

Shoulder pain

Associated Symptoms	Possible Diagnosis	Distinguishing Features
	Bone cancer	Pain, tenderness, and swelling in the affected bones and joints, often intensifying at night; a noticeable tumor or mass; increased susceptibility to bone fractures.
	Bone fractures	Pain in the affected bone which intensifies with movement or the application of pressure; swelling, bruising, or bleeding around the site of an injury; in a compound fracture, protrusion of bone through skin; possible loss of function or feeling in the injured area; local deformity.
	Bursitis *Inflammation of the bursas, the lubricant-filled sacs in and around the joints*	Pain and swelling around a joint, usually the elbow, knee, or shoulder; painful movement in the affected joint; possibly, fever.
	Dislocations/subluxations	Deformity of the affected joint; joint pain and tenderness; difficulty moving a joint; swelling and stiffness within 30 minutes after joint injury.
	Infectious arthritis	Pain, swelling, stiffness, and redness, usually in one joint. Fever. Severity varies from a mild ache to severe, debilitating pain and eventual joint deformity.
	Myocardial infarction Heart attack	Sudden chest pain or pressure that may spread to the arm, shoulder and jaw; excessive perspiration; shortness of breath. Possible nausea and vomiting.
	Osteoarthritis *Degeneration of the cartilage that lines the joints*	Pain, swelling, and stiffness in one or more joints; enlargement and distortion of affected joints.
	Osteomyelitis *Infection of bone and bone marrow*	Fever; severe pain in the affected bone; inflammation and swelling of the skin over the affected area; deformity. In children, arrested growth of the affected bone.
	Pneumothorax *Accumulation of air between the two membranes lining the lungs and the chest cavity*	Chest pain that may radiate into the abdomen or shoulder; shortness of breath; dry cough.
	Rheumatoid arthritis	Fatigue and weakness; joint pain, stiffness, and inflammation, especially in the hands, feet, and arms; joint deformity; dry mouth; dry, painful eyes. Morning stiffness.
	Rheumatoid arthritis, juvenile	Fever; rash; abdominal pain; weight loss; swelling, stiffness, and pain in the affected joints; enlarged lymph glands; fatigue; pallor; red, painful eyes; morning stiffness.

Shoulder pain *continued*

Associated Symptoms	Possible Diagnosis	Distinguishing Features
	Rotator cuff injury	Pain in the shoulder; difficulty raising and lowering the arm; recurring dull ache in the shoulder; pain after sleeping on the shoulder; shoulder weakness.
	Spondylosis, cervical *Arthritis of the vertebral disks in the neck*	Neck pain and stiffness that spreads to the shoulders, upper arms, hands, or back of the head; numbness or tingling in the arms, hands, and fingers; weakness in the arms and legs; unsteady gait; possible loss of bladder control.
	Tendinitis *Inflammation of a tendon*	Pain and tenderness over a tendon anywhere in the body; if involved tendon is near or part of a joint, restricted movement of the joint.

Skin, clammy

Associated Symptoms	Possible Diagnosis	Distinguishing Features
	Anxiety states	Sudden attacks of unreasonable fear and panic; rapid heartbeat or palpitations; perspiration; dry mouth; irritability; muscle tension; trembling; palpitations; shortness of breath; restlessness; poor concentration; insomnia; fatigue; weakness.
	Hypoglycemia *Low blood sugar*	Anxiety; hunger; trembling; headache; palpitations; perspiration; confusion; irritability; loss of coordination; possibly, double vision, seizures, or coma.
	Peripheral vascular disease *Narrowing of blood vessels in the legs or arms*	Muscle pain on one or both legs that occurs with exercise and subsides with rest; possible pain in the fingers, arms, buttocks, lower back, or the arch of the foot; impotence. Severe symptoms include: muscle pain at rest that intensifies at night; discolored or blue toes; cold or numb feet; open sores; heightened sensitivity to cold; weak or absent pulse in the affected limb; scaly or hairless skin over the affected area.
	Septic shock *Severe drop in blood pressure due to the presence of microorganisms or their toxins in the bloodstream*	Nausea and vomiting; prostration; diarrhea; sudden high fever; chills; rapid breathing; headache; mental confusion or agitation; decreased urine output; possible jaundice or skin rash; hands and feet may be unusually cold.

Skin, dry

Associated Symptoms	Possible Diagnosis	Distinguishing Features
	Eczema *Inflammation of the skin*	Itching skin; thickened patches of skin; possibly, with oozing and crusting; in infants, rash on the face, inner elbows, or behind the knees that turns scaly and develops small red pimples that leak; swollen legs (stasis dermatitis).
	Heatstroke	Sudden dizziness; weakness; headache; hot, dry, red skin which later turns grey; high body temperature; muscle cramps; confusion; seizures; loss of consciousness.
	Hypopituitarism *Underactivity of the pituitary gland*	Intolerance to cold; chronic headaches; decreased sex drive; fatigue; fine wrinkles around the eyes and mouth; dry skin; extreme thirst and excessive urination; loss of appetite; vaginal dryness; absence of milk production in new mothers; in men, reduced muscular strength, shrinking of the testes, and loss of body hair; growth retardation in children and adolescents
	Hypothyroidism *Underactivity of the thyroid gland*	Unexplained weight gain; fatigue; muscle weakness; cramps; dry skin; hair loss; deepening of the voice; intolerance for cold; constipation; chest pain; insomnia; puffiness around eyes; loss of sex drive; depression; menstrual abnormalities; possible swelling in the neck (goiter).
	Psoriasis	Slightly raised patches of skin with red borders and white-silver scales; joint pain and stiffness; itching; pitted nails.
	Scleroderma	Shiny, tight, and hardened skin, especially on the fingers, arms, and face; hands or feet may successively turn blue, white, and red upon exposure to cold (Raynaud's phenomenon); swallowing difficulty; bloating after eating; weight loss; shortness of breath on exertion; high blood pressure; symptoms of renal failure. Possibly, heartburn, muscle aches and weakness, joint pain, fever, or fatigue.
	Sjögren's syndrome	Dry, itching, burning eyes; sensation of a foreign body under the eyelids; dry mouth; difficulty swallowing; vaginal dryness; dry skin; frequent dental cavities; joint pain; swelling of glands (parotids) in front of the ears; Raynaud's phenomenon.

Skin, mottled

Associated Symptoms	Possible Diagnosis	Distinguishing Features
	Melanoma *Skin cancer*	Change in the appearance of an existing mole including enlargement, bleeding, change in color, development of a black edge. Itching.
	Peripheral vascular disease *Narrowing of blood vessels in the legs or arms*	Muscle pain on one or both legs that occurs with exercise and subsides with rest; possible pain in the fingers, arms, buttocks, lower back, or the arch of the foot; impotence. Severe symptoms include: muscle pain at rest that intensifies at night; discolored or blue toes; cold or numb feet; open sores; heightened sensitivity to cold; weak or absent pulse in the affected limb; scaly or hairless skin over the affected area.
	Polycythemia vera *An overproduction of red and white blood cells and platelets*	Headache; blurred vision; flushed skin; itching; dizziness; fatigue; night sweats; shortness of breath; weight loss.
	Rheumatoid arthritis	Fatigue and weakness; joint pain, stiffness, and inflammation, especially in the hands, feet, and arms; joint deformity; dry mouth; dry, painful eyes. Morning stiffness.
	Rheumatoid arthritis, juvenile	Fever; rash; abdominal pain; weight loss; swelling, stiffness, and pain in the affected joints; enlarged lymph glands; fatigue; pallor; red, painful eyes; morning stiffness.
	Systemic lupus erythematosus *Inflammation of connective tissues throughout the body*	Red, blotchy, butterfly-shaped rash on the cheeks and bridge of the nose; fatigue; fever; loss of appetite and weight; nausea; joint and abdominal pain; headaches; blurred vision; increased sensitivity to sun exposure; depression; psychosis; mental confusion.
	Vitiligo *Loss of skin pigmentation*	White or abnormally pale patches of skin, usually on the face, hands, armpits, and groin.

Skin, red

Associated Symptoms	Possible Diagnosis	Distinguishing Features
	Anaphylaxis	Itching and hives; swelling of the eyes, lips, and tongue; weakness or faintness; tightening in the chest or throat; wheezing; shortness of breath; profuse sweating; palpitations; sudden, intense distress; feelings of impending doom; stomach cramps; nausea, vomiting, or diarrhea; bluish tinge (cyanosis) to the skin, lips, and nailbeds due to oxygen insufficiency.
	Candidiasis *Fungal infection of the mouth, genitals, or mucus membrane*	Thick, white discharge from the vagina; itching and irritation in the vaginal area; pain while urinating or during intercourse; in men, inflammation of the head of the penis; possibly, yellow raised patches in the mouth.
	Carcinoid tumors and carcinoid syndrome	May be asymptomatic; flushing or redness of the face and neck; gas and profuse diarrhea; abdominal cramping; watery, swollen eyes; shortness of breath or wheezing.
	Cirrhosis *Chronic damage to the cells of the liver*	No symptoms in early stages; loss of weight and appetite; nausea; swollen legs, ankles and abdomen; itching; jaundice; black stools; vomiting blood; fatigue; impotence; memory loss; confusion.
	Dermatomyositis *Inflammation of the muscles and skin*	Red rash on the cheeks and bridge of the nose; purple discoloration and swelling of the eyelids; areas of thickened skin; muscle weakness and stiffness, usually in the shoulders and pelvis; cold hands and feet; speaking or swallowing difficulty; fever; weight loss.
	Frostbite	Initially, prickling sensation or numbness in affected area. White or bluish-gray skin that is hard and numb. Thawed skin becomes red, swollen, painful, and blistered. In severe cases, shivering; slurred speech; memory loss.
	Heatstroke	Sudden dizziness; weakness; headache; hot, dry, red skin which later turns grey; high body temperature; muscle cramps; confusion; seizures; loss of consciousness.
	Psoriasis	Slightly raised patches of skin with red borders and white-silver scales; joint pain and stiffness; itching; pitted nails.
	Rheumatoid arthritis	Fatigue and weakness; joint pain, stiffness, and inflammation, especially in the hands, feet, and arms; joint deformity; dry mouth; dry, painful eyes. Morning stiffness.

Skin, red *continued*

Associated Symptoms	Possible Diagnosis	Distinguishing Features
	Ringworm *Fungal skin infection*	A rash with distinct, advancing borders and clear centers; affected areas may have abnormally dark pigmentation; itching; scaly patches of skin; bald patches on scalp; Athlete's foot; red, swollen finger- and toenails.
	Roseola *Infectious disease primarily affecting children*	Abrupt onset of high fever that usually subsides within four to five days, at which time a rash appears on the torso, and spreads to the limbs, neck, and face. Sore throat; swollen lymph nodes in neck.
	Rubella *German Measles*	Rash on the face that spreads to the torso and limbs; enlargement of lymph nodes in neck; usually preceded by headache, fever, and runny nose.
	Systemic lupus erythematosus *Inflammation of connective tissues throughout the body*	Red, blotchy, butterfly-shaped rash on the cheeks and bridge of the nose; fatigue; fever; loss of appetite and weight; nausea; joint and abdominal pain; headaches; blurred vision; increased sensitivity to sun exposure; depression; psychosis; mental confusion.
	Toxic shock syndrome	Lethargy; conjunctivitis; confusion; sudden high fever accompanied by nausea, watery diarrhea, sore throat, and headache. Red rash on the palms and soles of the feet, which, after a week or two, begins to peel.

Skin, scaly

Associated Symptoms	Possible Diagnosis	Distinguishing Features
	Eczema *Inflammation of the skin*	Itching skin; thickened patches of skin; possibly, with oozing and crusting; in infants, rash on the face, inner elbows, or behind the knees that turns scaly and develops small red pimples that leak; swollen legs (stasis dermatitis).
	Lymphoma, non-Hodgkin's *Cancer of the lymph nodes and lymphoid tissue*	Painless swelling of lymph nodes in the neck or groin; possible abdominal pain, vomiting of blood, headache.
	Peripheral vascular disease *Narrowing of blood vessels in the legs or arms*	Muscle pain on one or both legs that occurs with exercise and subsides with rest; possible pain in the fingers, arms, buttocks, lower back, or the arch of the foot; impotence. Severe symptoms include: muscle pain at rest that intensifies at night; discolored or blue toes; cold or numb feet; open sores; heightened sensitivity to cold; weak or absent pulse in the affected limb; scaly or hairless skin over the affected area.
	Psoriasis	Slightly raised patches of skin with red borders and white-silver scales; joint pain and stiffness; itching; pitted nails.
	Ringworm *Fungal skin infection*	A rash with distinct, advancing borders and clear centers; affected areas may have abnormally dark pigmentation; itching; scaly patches of skin; bald patches on scalp; Athlete's foot; red, swollen finger- and toenails.
	Scabies	Tiny, grey, scaly blisters—usually on the wrists, genitals, armpits, or between the fingers—that rupture easily when scratched; severe itching; red lumps or rashes may develop.
	Sjögren's syndrome	Dry, itching, burning eyes; sensation of a foreign body under the eyelids; dry mouth; difficulty swallowing; vaginal dryness; dry skin; frequent dental cavities; joint pain; swelling of glands (parotids) in front of the ears; Raynaud's phenomenon.
	Systemic lupus erythematosus *Inflammation of connective tissues throughout the body*	Red, blotchy, butterfly-shaped rash on the cheeks and bridge of the nose; fatigue; fever; loss of appetite and weight; nausea; joint and abdominal pain; headaches; blurred vision; increased sensitivity to sun exposure; depression; psychosis; mental confusion.
	Varicose veins	Blue or purplish, knotted veins, usually in the legs; itching or discomfort in the affected area; swollen feet and ankles. Possible scaly skin, muscle cramps, or skin ulcers.

Sneezing

Associated Symptoms	Possible Diagnosis	Distinguishing Features
	Allergic rhinitis *Hay fever*	Nasal congestion; frequent sneezing; itchy eyes, nose, and throat.
	Anaphylaxis	Itching and hives; swelling of the eyes, lips, and tongue; weakness or faintness; tightening in the chest or throat; wheezing; shortness of breath; profuse sweating; palpitations; sudden, intense distress; feelings of impending doom; stomach cramps; nausea, vomiting, or diarrhea; bluish tinge (cyanosis) to the skin, lips, and nailbeds due to oxygen insufficiency.
	Common cold	Nasal congestion; watery eyes; sneezing; sore throat; cough; muscle aches; mild headache; listlessness; possibly, low-grade fever.
	Pleurisy and Pleural effusion *Inflammation of the membranes lining the lungs and chest cavity.*	Sudden chest pain worse on inspiration that may also radiate into the shoulder or abdomen; rapid breathing; coughing; sneezing; possibly, fever.
	Whooping cough	Initially, mild cough, sneezing, nasal congestion, and irritated eyes. Within approximately two weeks, cough becomes severe and persistent, and is accompanied by characteristic high-pitched "whooping" sound during inhalation; loss of appetite; listlessness; vomiting or choking spells. Most common among young children.

Snoring, heavy

Associated Symptoms	Possible Diagnosis	Distinguishing Features
	Sleep apnea *Recurrent episodes of breathing cessation during sleep*	Loud snoring; morning fatigue and headache; sleep disturbances; daytime sleepiness; difficulty concentrating; memory loss. Most common among overweight men.
	Common cold	Nasal congestion; watery eyes; sneezing; sore throat; cough; muscle aches; mild headache; listlessness; possibly, low-grade fever.
	Obesity	Excess storage of body fat resulting in a body weight 20% or greater than recommended.
	Sinusitis *Inflammation of the mucus membranes lining the sinuses*	Throbbing pain above or below one or both eyes that intensifies when bending the head forward or coughing; nasal congestion; loss of sense of smell; often, pus-like nasal discharge; possible dental pain in the upper jaw; fever.

Sore throat

Associated Symptoms	Possible Diagnosis	Distinguishing Features
with cough	Chronic fatigue syndrome	Severe fatigue made worse by exercise; recurrent flu-like symptoms; persistent sore throat; low-grade fever; muscle and joint aches; headache; painful, swollen lymph nodes; depression and mental confusion; memory loss; sleep difficulties.
	Common cold	Nasal congestion; watery eyes; sneezing; sore throat; cough; muscle aches; mild headache; listlessness; possibly, low-grade fever.
	Diphtheria *Bacterial throat infection*	Initially, swollen lymph glands in the neck and sore throat; difficulty swallowing; breathing difficulty; shortness of breath; rapid pulse; headache. In severe cases, paralysis of limbs or facial muscles; drooling.
	Influenza *Flu*	Chills, muscle aches, and loss of appetite followed by a cough, sore throat, nasal congestion, and fever; possible chest pain.
	Laryngeal cancer	Initially, hoarseness, sore throat, and swallowing difficulty; later, pain when swallowing; swelling in the neck.
	Laryngitis	Hoarseness that often progresses to loss of the voice; throat pain; dry cough; possible fever.
	Measles	Cough; fever; watery nasal discharge; loss of appetite; red, watering eyes; sore throat; body aches; red, slightly itchy rash that gradually spreads all over the body.
without cough	Epiglottitis *Inflammation of the epiglottis, the flap of tissue lying behind the tongue*	Sore throat; sudden fever; breathing difficulty which may become severe within hours of onset; pain or difficulty swallowing; muffled speech; hoarseness; drooling.
	Gingivitis	Red-purple gums that are swollen, shiny, and bleed easily; bad breath.
	Mononucleosis, infectious	Headache; high fever; swollen glands in the neck, groin, and armpits; severe sore throat; swallowing difficulty.
	Peritonsillar abscess *A collection of pus between the tonsils and surrounding tissue due to infection*	Sore throat; severe pain when swallowing; fever; headache; impaired speech; drooling; swollen glands in the neck.
	Pharyngitis *Inflammation of the pharynx, the part of the throat between the mouth and the esophagus*	Sore or red throat; speaking and swallowing difficulties; sensitive, swollen glands in the neck; fever; headache; possible earache.

Sore throat *continued*

Associated Symptoms	Possible Diagnosis	Distinguishing Features
	Poliomyelitis *Polio*	Low fever; sore throat; headache; nausea and vomiting. In severe cases, paralysis without loss of sensation; stiff neck and back; twitching; swallowing and breathing difficulty; drooling.
	Roseola *Infectious disease primarily affecting children*	Abrupt onset of high fever that usually subsides within four to five days, at which time a rash appears on the torso, and spreads to the limbs, neck, and face. Sore throat; swollen lymph nodes in neck.
	Sinusitis *Inflammation of the mucus membranes lining the sinuses*	Throbbing pain above or below one or both eyes that intensifies when bending the head forward or coughing; nasal congestion; loss of sense of smell; often, pus-like nasal discharge; possible dental pain in the upper jaw; fever.
	Strep infection	Symptoms depend on the location and nature of the specific infection, but may include fever, headaches, swollen lymph glands, fatigue, loss of appetite, nasal discharge, red skin rash.
	Tonsillitis	Sore, inflamed throat; swallowing difficulty; headache; swollen glands in the neck; fever; loss of voice. In children, nausea, vomiting, and abdominal pain.

Sore tongue

Associated Symptoms	Possible Diagnosis	Distinguishing Features
	Anemia, folic acid deficiency	Fatigue and weakness; pallor; shortness of breath, heart palpitations, or noticeably rapid heartbeat on exertion; sore, red, and glazed-looking tongue; loss of weight and appetite; nausea and diarrhea; abdominal distention.
	Anemia, iron deficiency	Fatigue and weakness; pallor; shortness of breath and heart palpitations on exertion; irritability or inability to concentrate; sore tongue or tiny cracks at the corners of the mouth; black, tarry or bloody stools; unusual craving for dirt, paint, or ice.
	Anemia, pernicious	Fatigue; inability to concentrate; sore, red tongue; weakness; dizziness; pallor; shortness of breath on exertion; palpitations; numbness and tingling in extremities; incoordination; headache; loss of weight and appetite; possibly, jaundice.
	Canker sores	Small, painful, white or gray, crater-like, red-rimmed ulcers in the gums, tongue, or lips; burning sensation preceding the development of ulcers; possibly, fever, swollen glands.
	Dry mouth	Dry or burning sensation in the mouth; difficulty chewing, swallowing, and speaking; possibly, cracked lips, changes in the tongue's surface, mouth ulcers, changes in taste perception, or tooth decay.
	Salivary gland disorders	Swollen, painful glands behind the ear or under the tongue; soft, painful, swollen glands in the neck; bitter taste in the mouth; fever; dry mouth; increased number of dental cavities; difficulty swallowing.
	Tongue disorders	Symptoms vary depending on the specific disorder and include: dark or bright red, black, or dark brown tongue; sore, swollen, or smooth tongue; hair-like growths on the tongue; adjacent areas of the mouth may be inflamed; ulcers or raised, white patches on the tongue; excessive salivation; swallowing difficulty; bad breath.

Speaking difficulty

Associated Symptoms	Possible Diagnosis	Distinguishing Features
with numbness/ paralysis	Amyotrophic lateral sclerosis *Progressive degeneration of nerve cells of the central nervous system*	Progressive loss of strength and coordination in the limbs; muscle twitching and cramps that begin in the hands and spread to the arms, shoulders, and legs; stiff, clumsy gait; swallowing, breathing, or speaking difficulty; weight loss; drooling; involuntary laughing or crying.
	Brain abscess	Headaches; drowsiness; nausea and vomiting; fever; seizures; possible partial paralysis; confusion; speaking difficulty.
	Brain hemorrhage	Sudden loss of consciousness; sudden, severe headache; paralysis on one side of the face or body; weakness and dizziness; loss of speech; blurred or double vision; dilated pupils; back and leg pain; fever; mental confusion; stiff neck.
	Brain tumors	Headaches that become more severe when reclining; nausea and vomiting; memory loss; double vision; muscle weakness; numbness, tingling, or partial paralysis; vision loss; speech disturbances; seizures; drowsiness.
	Encephalitis *Inflammation of the brain*	Initially, headache and fever followed by confusion, hallucinations, and paralysis on one side of the body; memory loss; difficulty with speech and eye movements; drowsiness; possible coma or epileptic seizures; loss of hearing; sensitivity to light; stiff neck.
	Hypothermia *Low body temperature (below 94°)*	Shivering; pallor; puffy face; fatigue and confusion; slow, shallow breathing; muscle stiffness; normally warm areas of the body are cold; loss of consciousness.
	Multiple sclerosis *Gradual degeneration of the protective sheaths surrounding the nerves within the brain and spinal cord*	Symptoms may appear suddenly and then disappear; persistent symptoms may take years to develop and include numbness or tingling in any part of the body, weakness in the extremities, an unsteady walk, slurred speech, urinary incontinence, fatigue, depression, temporary loss of vision, double or blurred vision, mental confusion, and memory loss.
	Stroke	Symptoms vary with the location of brain injury. Sudden onset of weakness, paralysis, or loss of sensation, usually on one side of the body; a sudden heaviness in a limb; speech abnormalities; headache; vision disturbances; dizziness; confusion; coma; urinary and fecal incontinence.
	Transient ischemic attack *Temporary blockage in an artery supplying the brain*	Weakness or numbness in a limb; slurred speech; short-lived, temporary partial blindness; numbness and tingling; speech difficulties; confusion; dizziness.

Speaking difficulty *continued*

Associated Symptoms	Possible Diagnosis	Distinguishing Features
without numbness/ paralysis	Botulism	Difficulty swallowing and speaking; nausea; vomiting; blurred or double vision.
	Concussion	Brief loss of consciousness following a blow to the head. Occasionally causes nausea and vomiting.
	Dermatomyositis *Inflammation of the muscles and skin*	Red rash on the cheeks and bridge of the nose; purple discoloration and swelling of the eyelids; areas of thickened skin; muscle weakness and stiffness, usually in the shoulders and pelvis; cold hands and feet; speaking or swallowing difficulty; fever; weight loss.
	Dry mouth	Dry or burning sensation in the mouth; difficulty chewing, swallowing, and speaking; possibly, cracked lips, changes in the tongue's surface, mouth ulcers, changes in taste perception, or tooth decay.
	Epiglottitis *Inflammation of the epiglottis, the flap of tissue lying behind the tongue*	Sore throat; sudden fever; breathing difficulty which may become severe within hours of onset; pain or difficulty swallowing; muffled speech; hoarseness; drooling.
	Hydrocephalus *Overaccumulation of cerebrospinal fluid, the liquid surrounding the brain*	In infants, an enlarged head, rigidity of the legs, irritability, projectile vomiting, drowsiness, seizures, and lethargy. In older persons, headache, vomiting, loss of coordination, deterioration of mental faculties, speech difficulty, and loss of appetite.
	Jaw dislocation or fracture	Inability to close the jaw normally; painful, swollen, or numb jaw; misalignment of teeth; speaking difficulty; possible breathing difficulty.
	Myasthenia gravis *Nerve degeneration causing gradual loss of voluntary muscle control*	Drooping eyelids; double or blurred vision; muscle weakness especially in the face, throat, and neck; chewing and swallowing difficulties; possible breathing difficulty. Slurred, nasal-sounding speech.
	Parkinson's disease *Degeneration of the basal ganglia, a cluster of nerve cells in the brain*	Tremors in the hands; stiffness and weakness; impaired voluntary movement; shuffling gait; stooped posture; unblinking, fixed expression; possibly, slow, hesitant speech; difficulty swallowing; drooling; depression. Tremors occur at rest (not with voluntary movements) and disappear during sleep.
	Peritonsillar abscess *A collection of pus between the tonsils and surrounding tissue due to infection*	Sore throat; severe pain when swallowing; fever; headache; impaired speech; drooling; swollen glands in the neck.

Stool, abnormal appearance

Associated Symptoms	Possible Diagnosis	Distinguishing Features
	Amebiasis *Parasitic infection*	Usually asymptomatic; possibly, diarrhea; loose stools may contain mucus and blood; abdominal cramps; fatigue; weight loss; gas and flatulence. In severe cases, large amount of bloody stools daily; fever, nausea and vomiting, and abdominal tenderness.
	Anemia, iron deficiency	Fatigue and weakness; pallor; shortness of breath and heart palpitations on exertion; irritability or inability to concentrate; sore tongue or tiny cracks at the corners of the mouth; black, tarry or bloody stools; unusual craving for dirt, paint, or ice.
	Cirrhosis *Chronic damage to the cells of the liver*	No symptoms in early stages; loss of weight and appetite; nausea; swollen legs, ankles and abdomen; itching; jaundice; black stools; vomiting blood; fatigue; impotence; memory loss; confusion.
	Colorectal cancer *A growth of malignant cells in the colon or rectum*	Change in bowel habits; diarrhea; constipation; narrow stools; bloody or dark stools; lower abdominal pain; bloating; cramps; gas; loss of weight and appetite; fatigue and heart palpitations due to anemia.
	Constipation, chronic	Infrequent and possibly painful bowel movements; straining during bowel movements; hard, dry stool; abdominal swelling; continued sensation of fullness after evacuating bowels.
	Diarrhea, acute	Loose, watery stools; increased frequency of bowel movements; abdominal cramping and pain. In infants, possibly drowsiness, slack skin, dry, sticky mouth and tongue, or persistent crying.
	Disseminated intravascular coagulation *Bleeding disorder marked by excessive and inappropriate blood coagulation*	Abnormal bleeding possibly at several sites at once; vomiting blood; bloody or black stools; abnormal vaginal bleeding; blood in the urine; severe abdominal or back pain; possibly, convulsions, or coma.
	Gallbladder disorders	Moderate to severe pain in the upper right side of the abdomen, chest, upper back, or right shoulder. Pain often follows the ingestion of high-fat foods and is episodic, lasting 20 minutes to several hours. Nausea and vomiting; low-grade fever; belching; heartburn; gas; possibly, jaundice, pale stools, and itchy skin.
	Hepatitis, acute viral	Fever; fatigue; loss of appetite; aching muscles and joints; abdominal pain or discomfort; jaundice; dark urine and pale stools.

Stool, abnormal appearance *continued*

Associated Symptoms	Possible Diagnosis	Distinguishing Features
	Hepatitis, chronic	Fatigue; nausea; vomiting; loss of appetite; jaundice; dark urine; clay-colored stools; depression; pain or discomfort in the upper right abdomen; abdominal swelling; fever; in women, cessation of menstruation, acne, and the appearance of male pattern facial hair.
	Malabsorption, digestive *A failure of the small intestine to absorb nutrients in the diet*	Diarrhea; weight loss; yellowish, foul-smelling stools; abdominal cramps, gas, and bloating; weakness and lethargy.
	Peptic ulcer	Intermittent, burning or gnawing pain in the upper abdomen or lower chest; indigestion; loss of appetite and weight. Pain may be relieved by eating or antacids. Possible nausea and vomiting. Black, tarry stools, vomiting blood.
	Platelet function disorders	Minor bleeding in the mouth or just beneath the surface of the skin, often appearing as clusters of small, pinpoint-sized red specks; frequent nosebleeds; easy bruising; prolonged menstrual periods; fatigue; pallor; dark-colored stools.
	Stomach cancer	Discomfort in the upper abdomen; black, tarry stools; vomiting of blood; loss of appetite and weight; vomiting after meals.
	Tapeworm infestation	Often asymptomatic. Unexplained weight loss; presence of white eggs or ribbon-like segments of worm in the stool, bedding, or clothing; symptoms of pernicious anemia.

Swallowing difficulty

Associated Symptoms	Possible Diagnosis	Distinguishing Features
	Aortic aneurysm *A sac-like ballooning at a weak spot in the wall of the aorta, the body's primary artery*	Usually asymptomatic; occasionally, severe abdominal and back pain; chest pain; swallowing difficulty; dizziness and fainting; hoarseness; cough.
	Botulism	Difficulty swallowing and speaking; nausea; vomiting; blurred or double vision.
	Dermatomyositis *Inflammation of the muscles and skin*	Red rash on the cheeks and bridge of the nose; purple discoloration and swelling of the eyelids; areas of thickened skin; muscle weakness and stiffness, usually in the shoulders and pelvis; cold hands and feet; speaking or swallowing difficulty; fever; weight loss.
	Dry mouth	Dry or burning sensation in the mouth; difficulty chewing, swallowing, and speaking; possibly, cracked lips, changes in the tongue's surface, mouth ulcers, changes in taste perception, or tooth decay.
	Epiglottitis *Inflammation of the epiglottis, the flap of tissue lying behind the tongue*	Sore throat; sudden fever; breathing difficulty which may become severe within hours of onset; pain or difficulty swallowing; muffled speech; hoarseness; drooling.
	Esophageal cancer	Swallowing difficulty and pain; weight loss; drooling; possibly, vomiting or coughing up of bloody mucus, regurgitation of food; chest pain; repeated respiratory infections.
	Gastroesophageal reflux *Heartburn*	Burning sensation in the middle of the chest; pain and difficulty swallowing; slight regurgitation of stomach's contents into the mouth, especially when reclining or bending forward; mild abdominal pain.
	Goiter *A swelling of the thyroid gland*	A swelling in the neck that can vary from a small lump to a huge growth. Possible breathing or swallowing difficulties. Can be associated with symptoms of hyper- or hypothyroidism.
	Hiatal hernia *Protrusion of a portion of the stomach through the diaphragm, into the chest cavity*	Often asymptomatic. Possibly, heartburn after meals or when bending forward or reclining. Belching, regurgitation.
	Laryngeal cancer	Initially, hoarseness, sore throat, and swallowing difficulty; later, pain when swallowing; swelling in the neck.
	Laryngitis	Hoarseness that often progresses to loss of the voice; throat pain; dry cough; possible fever.

Swallowing difficulty *continued*

Associated Symptoms	Possible Diagnosis	Distinguishing Features
	Neuralgia *Pain due to nerve damage or irritation*	Symptoms vary depending on the area affected and include: recurring episodes of sharp pain on one side of the lips, gums, cheek, or chin; radiating pain around the eyes; a burning pain along the path of a nerve encircling the torso. Pain may last from a few seconds to several minutes and always affects the same location. Attacks may occur several times a day for weeks with asymptomatic periods of weeks or months in between and may be triggered by touching or blowing on the affected area. Mouth pain may be exacerbated by talking, eating, or swallowing.
	Oral cancers	Sore in the mouth that bleeds and does not heal; lump in the cheek; white or red patch on the gums; swallowing and chewing difficulties; numbness of the tongue; swelling of the jaw.
	Parkinson's disease *Degeneration of the basal ganglia, a cluster of nerve cells in the brain*	Tremors in the hands; stiffness and weakness; impaired voluntary movement; shuffling gait; stooped posture; unblinking, fixed expression; possibly, slow, hesitant speech; difficulty swallowing; drooling; depression. Tremors occur at rest (not with voluntary movements) and disappear during sleep.
	Sjögren's syndrome	Dry, itching, burning eyes; sensation of a foreign body under the eyelids; dry mouth; difficulty swallowing; vaginal dryness; dry skin; frequent dental cavities; joint pain; swelling of glands (parotids) in front of the ears; Raynaud's phenomenon.
	Stomach cancer	Discomfort in the upper abdomen; black, tarry stools; vomiting of blood; loss of appetite and weight; vomiting after meals.
	Tetanus	Often, lockjaw; stiffness and, later, muscle spasms in the neck and face; drooling; abdominal and back pain; extreme perspiration; swallowing difficulty; possible convulsions; fever.
	Thyroid cancer	Painless lump in the front of the neck; possibly, swallowing or breathing difficulty; hoarseness or loss of voice; enlarged lymph nodes in the neck.
	Thyroid nodules	Usually painless lump in the front of the neck; possibly, breathing or swallowing difficulty.
	Thyroiditis *Inflammation of the thyroid gland*	Pain in the front of the neck and, often, the ear; possibly fever, weight loss, and fatigue; general feeling of being unwell (malaise); discomfort on swallowing.

Swallowing difficulty *continued*

Associated Symptoms	Possible Diagnosis	Distinguishing Features
	Tongue disorders	Symptoms vary depending on the specific disorder and include: dark or bright red, black, or dark brown tongue; sore, swollen, or smooth tongue; hair-like growths on the tongue; adjacent areas of the mouth may be inflamed; ulcers or raised, white patches on the tongue; excessive salivation; swallowing difficulty; bad breath.
	Wilson's disease *An accumulation of copper in the liver, brain, and other tissues*	Anemia; fluid accumulation in the abdomen; vomiting blood; progressive intellectual impairment; tremor; weakness; walking difficulty; rigidity of limbs; personality changes; speech difficulties; dementia.
with shortness of breath	Amyotrophic lateral sclerosis *Progressive degeneration of nerve cells of the central nervous system*	Progressive loss of strength and coordination in the limbs; muscle twitching and cramps that begin in the hands and spread to the arms, shoulders, and legs; stiff, clumsy gait; swallowing, breathing, or speaking difficulty; weight loss; drooling; involuntary laughing or crying.
	Anaphylaxis	Itching and hives; swelling of the eyes, lips, and tongue; weakness or faintness; tightening in the chest or throat; wheezing; shortness of breath; profuse sweating; palpitations; sudden, intense distress; feelings of impending doom; stomach cramps; nausea, vomiting, or diarrhea; bluish tinge (cyanosis) to the skin, lips, and nailbeds due to oxygen insufficiency.
	Esophageal stricture *Narrowing of the esophagus, the passageway from the mouth to the stomach*	Sudden or gradual decrease in the ability to swallow solid food or liquids; chest pain after eating; regurgitation of food and liquids; increased salivation; weight loss. Aspiration into lungs can cause cough, wheezing, shortness of breath.
	Myasthenia gravis *Nerve degeneration causing gradual loss of voluntary muscle control*	Drooping eyelids; double or blurred vision; muscle weakness especially in the face, throat, and neck; chewing and swallowing difficulties; possible breathing difficulty. Slurred, nasal-sounding speech.
	Scleroderma	Shiny, tight, and hardened skin, especially on the fingers, arms, and face; hands or feet may successively turn blue, white, and red upon exposure to cold (Raynaud's phenomenon); swallowing difficulty; bloating after eating; weight loss; shortness of breath on exertion; high blood pressure; symptoms of renal failure. Possibly, heartburn, muscle aches and weakness, joint pain, fever, or fatigue.

Swallowing difficulty *continued*

Associated Symptoms	Possible Diagnosis	Distinguishing Features
with headache	Mononucleosis, infectious	Headache; high fever; swollen glands in the neck, groin, and armpits; severe sore throat; swallowing difficulty.
	Mumps	Pain in the ear, below the ear, and in the jaw; swollen glands in the neck; headache; pain on swallowing and chewing. Testicular swelling and tenderness in adults.
	Peritonsillar abscess *A collection of pus between the tonsils and surrounding tissue due to infection*	Sore throat; severe pain when swallowing; fever; headache; impaired speech; drooling; swollen glands in the neck.
	Pharyngitis *Inflammation of the pharynx, the part of the throat between the mouth and the esophagus*	Sore or red throat; speaking and swallowing difficulties; sensitive, swollen glands in the neck; fever; headache; possible earache.
	Poliomyelitis *Polio*	Low fever; sore throat; headache; nausea and vomiting. In severe cases, paralysis without loss of sensation; stiff neck and back; twitching; swallowing and breathing difficulty; drooling.
	Strep infection	Symptoms depend on the location and nature of the specific infection, but may include fever, headaches, swollen lymph glands, fatigue, loss of appetite, nasal discharge, red skin rash.
	Tonsillitis	Sore, inflamed throat; swallowing difficulty; headache; swollen glands in the neck; fever; loss of voice. In children, nausea, vomiting, and abdominal pain.

Sweating, profuse

Associated Symptoms	Possible Diagnosis	Distinguishing Features
with shortness of breath	Anxiety states	Sudden attacks of unreasonable fear and panic; rapid heartbeat or palpitations; perspiration; dry mouth; irritability; muscle tension; trembling; palpitations; shortness of breath; restlessness; poor concentration; insomnia; fatigue; weakness.
	Congestive heart failure	Shortness of breath; fatigue; need to sleep on several pillows; weakness; cough; heart palpitations; swelling in the legs, ankles, and abdomen; frequent urination at night; indigestion; nausea and vomiting; loss of appetite.
	Empyema *Collection of pus in any body cavity, usually between the membranes covering the lungs*	Chest pain exacerbated by deep inhalation; shortness of breath; dry cough; fever and chills; exhaustion; weight loss; night sweats; abdominal pain and jaundice.
	Lung abscess	Cough producing foul-smelling sputum; bad breath; fever; chills; weight loss; possible chest pain.
	Myocardial infarction *Heart attack*	Sudden chest pain or pressure that may spread to the arm, shoulder and jaw; excessive perspiration; shortness of breath. Possible nausea and vomiting.
	Pneumonia	High fever; shortness of breath; cough with sputum; chest pain; fatigue.
without shortness of breath	AIDS *Acquired immunodeficiency syndrome*	Recurrent infections affecting the skin and respiratory system; cough; shortness of breath; loss of appetite; weight loss; fatigue; diarrhea; fever; dementia; malignant skin lesions; swollen lymph glands throughout the body; purplish skin nodules; memory loss; confusion; personality changes.
	Hyperpituitarism *Overactivity of the pituitary gland*	In adults (in which the disease is called acromegaly): Gradual thickening of the bones of the face, jaw, and the extremities in adults; oily skin; severe headache; excessive hair growth; excessive perspiration; joint pains. In children (in which the disease is called gigantism): Rapid growth and unusual height; possibly, blindness.
	Hyperthyroidism *Overactivity of the thyroid gland*	Protruding eyes; weight loss despite increased appetite; intolerance to heat; excessive perspiration; nervousness or restlessness; possibly, swelling in the neck (goiter); palpitations; tremor; diarrhea.
	Hypoglycemia *Low blood sugar*	Anxiety; hunger; trembling; headache; palpitations; perspiration; confusion; irritability; loss of coordination; possibly, double vision, seizures, or coma.

Sweating, profuse *continued*

Associated Symptoms	Possible Diagnosis	Distinguishing Features
	Malaria	Initially, severe chills and shivering. In later stages, extremely high fever followed by a period of profuse perspiration as fever subsides; headache, sometimes severe; vomiting.
	Meniere's disease *Dysfunction of structures in the inner ear*	Sudden attack of severe vertigo; nausea and vomiting; impaired sense of balance; ringing in the ears; hearing loss in the affected ear. Jerky movements of the eyes.
	Pheochromocytoma *Tumor in central part of the adrenal, the glands above the kidneys*	Headaches, sometimes severe; rapid heartbeat or heart palpitations; excessive perspiration; faintness, especially when standing up; chest pain; abdominal pain; constipation; weight loss; nervousness, irritability, or anxiety; mental confusion or psychosis.
	Renal vein thrombosis *Blood clot in the vein leaving the kidney*	Severe lower back and flank pain, swelling of legs and face from edema.
	Tetanus	Often, lockjaw; stiffness and, later, muscle spasms in the neck and face; drooling; abdominal and back pain; extreme perspiration; swallowing difficulty; possible convulsions; fever.
	Tuberculosis	Often, asymptomatic. Possibly, low-grade fever; excessive perspiration; cough producing sputum or blood; weight loss; chronic fatigue; chest pain; shortness of breath; night sweats.

Swelling, face and neck

Associated Symptoms	Possible Diagnosis	Distinguishing Features
	Anaphylaxis	Itching and hives; swelling of the eyes, lips, and tongue; weakness or faintness; tightening in the chest or throat; wheezing; shortness of breath; profuse sweating; palpitations; sudden, intense distress; feelings of impending doom; stomach cramps; nausea, vomiting, or diarrhea; bluish tinge (cyanosis) to the skin, lips, and nailbeds due to oxygen insufficiency.
	Cushing's syndrome	Red, oval-shaped face; humped upper back and obese trunk; acne; purple stretch marks on the abdomen, thighs, and breasts; thin and easily bruised skin; easily fractured bones; depression or euphoria; insomnia; fatigue; muscle weakness; hirsutism (in women).
	Glomerulonephritis, acute *Sudden or intense inflammation of the glomeruli, tiny structures that filter blood in the kidneys*	Blood in the urine; passing only small amounts of urine; swelling of the ankles or the tissues around the eyes; shortness of breath; possibly, fatigue, nausea and vomiting, loss of appetite, itching, headaches, fever, impaired vision.
	Glomerulonephritis, chronic *Persistent inflammation of the glomeruli, tiny structures that filter blood in the kidneys*	Blood in the urine; passing only small amounts of urine; swelling of the ankles or the tissues around the eyes; shortness of breath; possibly, fatigue, nausea and vomiting, loss of appetite, itching, headaches, fever, impaired vision.
	Goiter *A swelling of the thyroid gland*	A swelling in the neck that can vary from a small lump to a huge growth. Possible breathing or swallowing difficulties. Can be associated with symptoms of hyper- or hypothyroidism.
	Hyperpituitarism *Overactivity of the pituitary gland*	In adults (in which the disease is called acromegaly): Gradual thickening of the bones of the face, jaw, and the extremities in adults; oily skin; severe headache; excessive hair growth; excessive perspiration; joint pains. In children (in which the disease is called gigantism): Rapid growth and unusual height; possibly, blindness.
	Hyperthyroidism *Overactivity of the thyroid gland*	Protruding eyes; weight loss despite increased appetite; intolerance to heat; excessive perspiration; nervousness or restlessness; possibly, swelling in the neck (goiter); palpitations; tremor; diarrhea.
	Hypothermia *Low body temperature (below 94°)*	Shivering; pallor; puffy face; fatigue and confusion; slow, shallow breathing; muscle stiffness; normally warm areas of the body are cold; loss of consciousness.

Swelling, face and neck *continued*

Associated Symptoms	Possible Diagnosis	Distinguishing Features
	Hypothyroidism *Underactivity of the thyroid gland*	Unexplained weight gain; fatigue; muscle weakness; cramps; dry skin; hair loss; deepening of the voice; intolerance for cold; constipation; chest pain; insomnia; puffiness around eyes; loss of sex drive; depression; menstrual abnormalities; possible swelling in the neck (goiter).
	Laryngeal cancer	Initially, hoarseness, sore throat, and swallowing difficulty; later, pain when swallowing; swelling in the neck.
	Mumps	Pain in the ear, below the ear, and in the jaw; swollen glands in the neck; headache; pain on swallowing and chewing. Testicular swelling and tenderness in adults.
	Nephrotic syndrome *Damage to the filtering units of the kidneys*	Swelling in the ankles and around the eyes; weight gain, due to fluid retention throughout the body; shortness of breath; passing only small amounts of urine that has an unusually foamy appearance; fatigue; diarrhea; loss of appetite.
	Renal vein thrombosis *Blood clot in the vein leaving the kidney*	Severe lower back and flank pain, swelling of legs and face from edema.
	Thyroid cancer	Painless lump in the front of the neck; possibly, swallowing or breathing difficulty; hoarseness or loss of voice; enlarged lymph nodes in the neck.
	Thyroid nodules	Usually painless lump in the front of the neck; possibly, breathing or swallowing difficulty.
	Trichinosis *Parasitic infestation*	Initially, crampy abdominal pain, diarrhea, vomiting, and fever, followed within one to two weeks by swelling around the eyes, muscle aches and tenderness, fever, and weakness. Possibly, coughing up of bloody phlegm; delirium; coma; heart failure symptoms.

Swelling, legs/ankles/feet

Associated Symptoms	Possible Diagnosis	Distinguishing Features
	Bone fractures	Pain in the affected bone which intensifies with movement or the application of pressure; swelling, bruising, or bleeding around the site of an injury; in a compound fracture, protrusion of bone through skin; possible loss of function or feeling in the injured area; local deformity.
	Cirrhosis *Chronic damage to the cells of the liver*	No symptoms in early stages; loss of weight and appetite; nausea; swollen legs, ankles and abdomen; itching; jaundice; black stools; vomiting blood; fatigue; impotence; memory loss; confusion.
	Eczema *Inflammation of the skin*	Itching skin; thickened patches of skin; possibly, with oozing and crusting; in infants, rash on the face, inner elbows, or behind the knees that turns scaly and develops small red pimples that leak; swollen legs (stasis dermatitis).
	Gout	Most commonly affects the joints of the big toe. Affected joints are red, swollen, hot, and severely painful. In late stages, joint deformity. Kidney stones.
	Renal failure, acute *Severe kidney failure*	Initially, decreased urine output, weight gain and swelling due to edema, loss of appetite, nausea and vomiting, fatigue. If untreated, confusion, seizures, and drowsiness.
	Renal failure, chronic *Persistent, mild kidney failure*	Asymptomatic in early stages. Possibly, mental confusion; shortness of breath; abdominal pain; decreased sex drive; fatigue; muscle and bone pain; numbness in the legs and feet; headache; impaired mental acuity; bad breath.
	Sprains and strains	Swelling, pain or tenderness in the affected joints; impaired joint function.
	Varicose veins	Blue or purplish, knotted veins, usually in the legs; itching or discomfort in the affected area; swollen feet and ankles. Possible scaly skin, muscle cramps, or skin ulcers.
with shortness of breath/breathing difficulty	Amyloidosis *Accumulation of amyloid, a starchy protein, in tissues and organs*	Symptoms vary greatly depending on the body parts affected and may include heart palpitations; shortness of breath; swelling of the legs; diarrhea; abdominal pain; raised spots on the armpits, groin, face, and neck; fatigue and weakness; numbness of the hands or feet; dizziness on standing; joint pains.
	Cardiomyopathy *Disease of the heart muscle causing a reduction in the force of heart contractions*	Fatigue; chest pain and palpitations; shortness of breath; swelling of the legs; wheezing; cough.

Swelling, legs/ankles/feet *continued*

Associated Symptoms	Possible Diagnosis	Distinguishing Features
with shortness of breath/breathing difficulty *continued*	Chronic obstructive pulmonary disease	Shortness of breath; wheezing; persistent, mucus-producing cough, especially in the morning; possibly, chest pain, swollen legs and ankles.
	Congestive heart failure	Shortness of breath; fatigue; need to sleep on several pillows; weakness; cough; heart palpitations; swelling in the legs, ankles, and abdomen; frequent urination at night; indigestion; nausea and vomiting; loss of appetite.
	Glomerulonephritis, acute *Sudden or intense inflammation of the glomeruli, tiny structures that filter blood in the kidneys*	Blood in the urine; passing only small amounts of urine; swelling of the ankles or the tissues around the eyes; shortness of breath; possibly, fatigue, nausea and vomiting, loss of appetite, itching, headaches, fever, impaired vision.
	Glomerulonephritis, chronic *Persistent inflammation of the glomeruli, tiny structures that filter blood in the kidneys*	Blood in the urine; passing only small amounts of urine; swelling of the ankles or the tissues around the eyes; shortness of breath; possibly, fatigue, nausea and vomiting, loss of appetite, itching, headaches, fever, impaired vision.
	Kidney cysts	Pain or tenderness in the lower back or abdomen; blood in the urine. In infants, symmetrical, protruding masses visible in the flanks.
	Nephrotic syndrome *Damage to the filtering units of the kidneys*	Swelling in the ankles and around the eyes; weight gain, due to fluid retention throughout the body; shortness of breath; passing only small amounts of urine that has an unusually foamy appearance; fatigue; diarrhea; loss of appetite.
	Pericarditis *Inflammation of the membrane surrounding the heart*	Sharp chest pain that may spread to the neck and shoulders; pain may be relieved by sitting up and leaning forward; swollen legs and abdomen; breathing difficulty; chills; fever; fatigue.
	Systemic lupus erythematosus *Inflammation of connective tissues throughout the body*	Red, blotchy, butterfly-shaped rash on the cheeks and bridge of the nose; fatigue; fever; loss of appetite and weight; nausea; joint and abdominal pain; headaches; blurred vision; increased sensitivity to sun exposure; depression; psychosis; mental confusion.
	Valvular heart disease	Depends on which heart valve is affected. Often asymptomatic. Possibly, fatigue and weakness; dizziness; chest pain; shortness of breath; heart palpitations; fainting; edema; stroke from embolism to the brain.

Swollen glands

Associated Symptoms	Possible Diagnosis	Distinguishing Features
	AIDS *Acquired immunodeficiency syndrome*	Recurrent infections affecting the skin and respiratory system; cough; shortness of breath; loss of appetite; weight loss; fatigue; diarrhea; fever; dementia; malignant skin lesions; swollen lymph glands throughout the body; purplish skin nodules; memory loss; confusion; personality changes.
	Canker sores	Small, painful, white or gray, crater-like, red-rimmed ulcers in the gums, tongue, or lips; burning sensation preceding the development of ulcers; possibly, fever, swollen glands.
	Chronic fatigue syndrome	Severe fatigue made worse by exercise; recurrent flu-like symptoms; persistent sore throat; low-grade fever; muscle and joint aches; headache; painful, swollen lymph nodes; depression and mental confusion; memory loss; sleep difficulties.
	Diphtheria *Bacterial throat infection*	Initially, swollen lymph glands in the neck and sore throat; difficulty swallowing; breathing difficulty; shortness of breath; rapid pulse; headache. In severe cases, paralysis of limbs or facial muscles; drooling.
	Leukemias	Symptoms vary depending on the type of leukemia and may include: loss of appetite and weight; increased bruising and bleeding; bone pain, especially in the legs; abdominal pain and distention; nausea; heart palpitations; severe fatigue; pallor; breathing difficulty; fever; night sweats; headache; enlarged lymph nodes; joint pains (due to gout).
	Lymphoma, Hodgkin's *Cancer of the lymph nodes and lymphoid tissue*	Painless swelling of the lymph nodes usually in the neck or armpits; loss of appetite; night sweats.
	Lymphoma, non-Hodgkin's *Cancer of the lymph nodes and lymphoid tissue*	Painless swelling of lymph nodes in the neck or groin; possible abdominal pain, vomiting of blood, headache.
	Mononucleosis, infectious	Headache; high fever; swollen glands in the neck, groin, and armpits; severe sore throat; swallowing difficulty.
	Mumps	Pain in the ear, below the ear, and in the jaw; swollen glands in the neck; headache; pain on swallowing and chewing. Testicular swelling and tenderness in adults.
	Peritonsillar abscess *A collection of pus between the tonsils and surrounding tissue due to infection*	Sore throat; severe pain when swallowing; fever; headache; impaired speech; drooling; swollen glands in the neck.

Swollen glands *continued*

Associated Symptoms	Possible Diagnosis	Distinguishing Features
	Pharyngitis *Inflammation of the pharynx, the part of the throat between the mouth and the esophagus*	Sore or red throat; speaking and swallowing difficulties; sensitive, swollen glands in the neck; fever; headache; possible earache.
	Rheumatoid arthritis, juvenile	Fever; rash; abdominal pain; weight loss; swelling, stiffness, and pain in the affected joints; enlarged lymph glands; fatigue; pallor; red, painful eyes; morning stiffness.
	Rubella German Measles	Rash on the face that spreads to the torso and limbs; enlargement of lymph nodes in neck; usually preceded by headache, fever, and runny nose.
	Salivary gland disorders	Swollen, painful glands behind the ear or under the tongue; soft, painful, swollen glands in the neck; bitter taste in the mouth; fever; dry mouth; increased number of dental cavities; difficulty swallowing.
	Strep infection	Symptoms depend on the location and nature of the specific infection, but may include fever, headaches, swollen lymph glands, fatigue, loss of appetite, nasal discharge, red skin rash.
	Syphilis	Initially, painless, ulcerated, red sore on the genitals, mouth, or rectum; swollen glands in the neck, armpit, or groin; rash with small, red, scaly bumps; fever; headache. If left untreated, damage to heart valves leading to congestive heart failure; mental deterioration; loss of balance; seizures; dementia; personality changes.
	Tonsillitis	Sore, inflamed throat; swallowing difficulty; headache; swollen glands in the neck; fever; loss of voice. In children, nausea, vomiting, and abdominal pain.
	Tooth abscess	Persistent tooth pain; pain when biting or chewing; swollen glands in the neck; earache; fever; possibly, foul taste in the mouth or bad breath.

Testicles, painful or swollen

Associated Symptoms	Possible Diagnosis	Distinguishing Features
	Epididymitis *Inflammation of the coiled sperm conduit that rests on each testicle*	Severe pain and swelling at the back of a testicle; possibly, redness and swelling of the scrotum; burning on urination.
	Mumps	Pain in the ear, below the ear, and in the jaw; swollen glands in the neck; headache; pain on swallowing and chewing. Testicular swelling and tenderness in adults.
	Orchitis *Inflammation of a testicle*	Swelling and severe pain in the affected testicle; possible bloody discharge in the semen; pain during intercourse; fever.
	Renal calculi *Kidney stones*	Intermittent spasms of pain in the back and flanks, radiating through the lower abdomen towards the groin; nausea and vomiting; blood in the urine; urge to urinate but only small amounts of urine are passed.
	Testicular cancer	Firm, usually painless mass, usually in one testicle. In later stages, a dull ache in the groin or lower abdomen may occur. Possibly, male breast development. In advanced cases, swollen lymph glands; abdominal or back pain; weight loss; breathing difficulty.
	Testicular torsion *Twisting of the spermatic cord*	Severe pain and swelling on one side of the scrotum; skin on the scrotum may appear red or purple; light-headedness or fainting; possibly, abdominal pain, nausea and vomiting.
	Varicocele *Varicose veins in the scrotum*	Visibly enlarged, twisted veins in the scrotum; swelling around the testicles, usually on the left side, that may subside when reclining; sensation of heaviness or dragging in the groin; possibly, scrotal pain or discomfort.

Thirst, excessive

Associated Symptoms	Possible Diagnosis	Distinguishing Features
	Diabetes insipidus *Insufficient amounts of antidiuretic hormone, leading to excessive urination and possible dehydration*	Extreme thirst; copious urination. When fluid intake is insufficient, confusion, stupor and coma.
	Diabetes mellitus *Insufficiency of or resistance to insulin*	Fatigue; excessive thirst; frequent urination; weight loss despite increased appetite; blurred vision; numbness and tingling of feet and hands; impotence.
	Hypopituitarism *Underactivity of the pituitary gland*	Intolerance to cold; chronic headaches; decreased sex drive; fatigue; fine wrinkles around the eyes and mouth; dry skin; extreme thirst and excessive urination; loss of appetite; vaginal dryness; absence of milk production in new mothers; in men, reduced muscular strength, shrinking of the testes, and loss of body hair; growth retardation in children and adolescents
	Peritonitis *Inflammation of the abdominal membrane.*	Sudden abdominal pain, rigidity, and swelling; chills and fever; weakness; rapid heartbeat; nausea and vomiting; extreme thirst; low urine output.
	Rabies	Low-grade fever; headache; loss of appetite; tingling at site of animal bite; intense thirst exacerbated by the inability to drink without violent, painful throat spasms; paralysis of facial muscles; drooling. Agitation and violent behavior, confusion, convulsions, coma.

Toothache

Associated Symptoms	Possible Diagnosis	Distinguishing Features
	Gingivitis	Red-purple gums that are swollen, shiny, and bleed easily; bad breath.
	Impacted teeth	Gum pain; unpleasant taste in mouth, especially when biting down; red, swollen gums around the affected tooth; headache or jaw ache; possibly, bad breath.
	Neuralgia Pain due to nerve damage or irritation	Symptoms vary depending on the area affected and include: recurring episodes of sharp pain on one side of the lips, gums, cheek, or chin; radiating pain around the eyes; a burning pain along the path of a nerve encircling the torso. Pain may last from a few seconds to several minutes and always affects the same location. Attacks may occur several times a day for weeks with asymptomatic periods of weeks or months in between and may be triggered by touching or blowing on the affected area. Mouth pain may be exacerbated by talking, eating, or swallowing.
	Salivary gland disorders	Swollen, painful glands behind the ear or under the tongue; soft, painful, swollen glands in the neck; bitter taste in the mouth; fever; dry mouth; increased number of dental cavities; difficulty swallowing.
	Sinusitis *Inflammation of the mucus membranes lining the sinuses*	Throbbing pain above or below one or both eyes that intensifies when bending the head forward or coughing; nasal congestion; loss of sense of smell; often, pus-like nasal discharge; possible dental pain in the upper jaw; fever.
	Sjögren's syndrome	Dry, itching, burning eyes; sensation of a foreign body under the eyelids; dry mouth; difficulty swallowing; vaginal dryness; dry skin; frequent dental cavities; joint pain; swelling of glands (parotids) in front of the ears; Raynaud's phenomenon.
	Tooth abscess	Persistent tooth pain; pain when biting or chewing; swollen glands in the neck; earache; fever; possibly, foul taste in the mouth or bad breath.
	Tooth decay	Tooth pain, especially after eating sweet or sour foods; tooth sensitivity to hot and cold; bad breath; unpleasant taste in the mouth.

Tremors

Associated Symptoms	Possible Diagnosis	Distinguishing Features
	Anxiety states	Sudden attacks of unreasonable fear and panic; rapid heartbeat or palpitations; perspiration; dry mouth; irritability; muscle tension; trembling; palpitations; shortness of breath; restlessness; poor concentration; insomnia; fatigue; weakness.
	Essential tremor	Involuntary rhythmic shaking of the hands and arms and, less frequently, the head, tongue, larynx, eyelids, or other parts of the body. Tremors intensify during emotional stress and voluntary movements, and cease during periods of rest or sleep. Shaky handwriting; quavering voice.
	Hyperthyroidism *Overactivity of the thyroid gland*	Protruding eyes; weight loss despite increased appetite; intolerance to heat; excessive perspiration; nervousness or restlessness; possibly, swelling in the neck (goiter); palpitations; tremor; diarrhea.
	Multiple sclerosis *Gradual degeneration of the protective sheaths surrounding the nerves within the brain and spinal cord*	Symptoms may appear suddenly and then disappear; persistent symptoms may take years to develop and include numbness or tingling in any part of the body, weakness in the extremities, an unsteady walk, slurred speech, urinary incontinence, fatigue, depression, temporary loss of vision, double or blurred vision, mental confusion, and memory loss.
	Parkinson's disease *Degeneration of the basal ganglia, a cluster of nerve cells in the brain*	Tremors in the hands; stiffness and weakness; impaired voluntary movement; shuffling gait; stooped posture; unblinking, fixed expression; possibly, slow, hesitant speech; difficulty swallowing; drooling; depression. Tremors occur at rest (not with voluntary movements) and disappear during sleep.

Twitching/tics

Associated Symptoms	Possible Diagnosis	Distinguishing Features
with confusion/ loss of memory	Brain abscess	Headaches; drowsiness; nausea and vomiting; fever; seizures; possible partial paralysis; confusion; speaking difficulty.
	Brain tumors	Headaches that become more severe when reclining; nausea and vomiting; memory loss; double vision; muscle weakness; numbness, tingling, or partial paralysis; vision loss; speech disturbances; seizures; drowsiness.
	Encephalitis *Inflammation of the brain*	Initially, headache and fever followed by confusion, hallucinations, and paralysis on one side of the body; memory loss; difficulty with speech and eye movements; drowsiness; possible coma or epileptic seizures; loss of hearing; sensitivity to light; stiff neck.
	Hydrocephalus *Overaccumulation of cerebrospinal fluid, the liquid surrounding the brain*	In infants, an enlarged head, rigidity of the legs, irritability, projectile vomiting, drowsiness, seizures, and lethargy. In older persons, headache, vomiting, loss of coordination, deterioration of mental faculties, speech difficulty, and loss of appetite.
	Renal failure, acute *Severe kidney failure*	Initially, decreased urine output, weight gain and swelling due to edema, loss of appetite, nausea and vomiting, fatigue. If untreated, confusion, seizures, and drowsiness.
	Reye's syndrome *Childhood disease marked by brain and liver damage*	Following recovery from an upper respiratory infection, nausea and vomiting; memory loss; confusion or delirium; possible seizures; drowsiness; lethargy.
	Seizures	Involuntary twitching or jerking; muscle rigidity; loss of consciousness; confusion; drooling; hallucinations.
without confusion/ memory loss	Amyotrophic lateral sclerosis *Progressive degeneration of nerve cells of the central nervous system*	Progressive loss of strength and coordination in the limbs; muscle twitching and cramps that begin in the hands and spread to the arms, shoulders, and legs; stiff, clumsy gait; swallowing, breathing, or speaking difficulty; weight loss; drooling; involuntary laughing or crying.
	Bone fractures	Pain in the affected bone which intensifies with movement or the application of pressure; swelling, bruising, or bleeding around the site of an injury; in a compound fracture, protrusion of bone through skin; possible loss of function or feeling in the injured area; local deformity.
	Hypoparathyroidism *Underactivity of the parathyroid glands*	Numbness and tingling and painful, cramp-like spasms of the face, hands, arms, and feet; cataracts; possible seizures.

Twitching/tics *continued*

Associated Symptoms	Possible Diagnosis	Distinguishing Features
	Hypothyroidism *Underactivity of the thyroid gland*	Unexplained weight gain; fatigue; muscle weakness; cramps; dry skin; hair loss; deepening of the voice; intolerance for cold; constipation; chest pain; insomnia; puffiness around eyes; loss of sex drive; depression; menstrual abnormalities; possible swelling in the neck (goiter).
	Leukemias	Symptoms vary depending on the type of leukemia and may include: loss of appetite and weight; increased bruising and bleeding; bone pain, especially in the legs; abdominal pain and distention; nausea; heart palpitations; severe fatigue; pallor; breathing difficulty; fever; night sweats; headache; enlarged lymph nodes; joint pains (due to gout).
	Neuralgia *Pain due to nerve damage or irritation*	Symptoms vary depending on the area affected and include: recurring episodes of sharp pain on one side of the lips, gums, cheek, or chin; radiating pain around the eyes; a burning pain along the path of a nerve encircling the torso. Pain may last from a few seconds to several minutes and always affects the same location. Attacks may occur several times a day for weeks with asymptomatic periods of weeks or months in between. Mouth pain may be exacerbated by talking, eating, or swallowing.
	Parkinson's disease *Degeneration of the basal ganglia, a cluster of nerve cells in the brain*	Tremors in the hands; stiffness and weakness; impaired voluntary movement; shuffling gait; stooped posture; unblinking, fixed expression; possibly, slow, hesitant speech; difficulty swallowing; drooling; depression. Tremors occur at rest (not with voluntary movements) and disappear during sleep.
	Poliomyelitis *Polio*	Low fever; sore throat; headache; nausea and vomiting. In severe cases, paralysis without loss of sensation; stiff neck and back; twitching; swallowing and breathing difficulty; drooling.
	Rheumatic fever	Initially, a sore throat that gets better followed, one to six weeks later, by lethargy and fever. Possibly, swollen joints, rash, abdominal pain, involuntary jerky movements, emotional instability.
	Tetanus	Often, lockjaw; stiffness and, later, muscle spasms in the neck and face; drooling; abdominal and back pain; extreme perspiration; swallowing difficulty; possible convulsions; fever.
	Tics	Recurring, involuntary twitch, usually in the face, shoulders, or arms.

Urinary frequency

Associated Symptoms	Possible Diagnosis	Distinguishing Features
	Bladder cancer	Blood in the urine; painful and frequent urination; pelvic pain; feeling of pressure in the back; persistent fever; urinary incontinence.
	Bladder infection *Cystitis*	Burning during urination; frequent and urgent urination with only small amounts of urine passed; blood in the urine; lower abdominal pain; low-grade fever; pain during sexual intercourse and, in men, during ejaculation.
	Congestive heart failure	Shortness of breath; fatigue; need to sleep on several pillows; weakness; cough; heart palpitations; swelling in the legs, ankles, and abdomen; frequent urination at night; indigestion; nausea and vomiting; loss of appetite.
	Diabetes insipidus *Insufficient amounts of antidiuretic hormone, leading to excessive urination and possible dehydration*	Extreme thirst; copious urination. When fluid intake is insufficient, confusion, stupor and coma.
	Diabetes mellitus *Insufficiency of or resistance to insulin*	Fatigue; excessive thirst; frequent urination; weight loss despite increased appetite; blurred vision; numbness and tingling of feet and hands; impotence.
	Fibroids, uterine *Benign growths of the muscular wall of the uterus*	Heavier or prolonged bleeding during menses; abdominal discomfort; lower back pain; pressure on the bladder and frequent urination; constipation. Possible, sharp, sudden, lower abdominal pain.
	Hypopituitarism *Underactivity of the pituitary gland*	Intolerance to cold; chronic headaches; decreased sex drive; fatigue; fine wrinkles around the eyes and mouth; dry skin; extreme thirst and excessive urination; loss of appetite; vaginal dryness; absence of milk production in new mothers; in men, reduced muscular strength, shrinking of the testes, and loss of body hair; growth retardation in children and adolescents.
	Irritable bladder	Sudden, urgent need to urinate; frequent urination.
	Kidney infection *Pyelonephritis*	Sudden fever and shaking chills; severe fatigue; burning and frequent urination; cloudy or bloody urine; lower back pain, sometimes severe; nausea and vomiting.
	Neurogenic bladder *Inability to control passage of urine due to damage to nerves to the bladder*	Inability to control urine flow which may involuntarily release in large volumes or in a continuous dribbling. Bed-wetting during sleep; feeling the need to urinate though no urine is passed; pain or burning during urination.

Urinary frequency *continued*

Associated Symptoms	Possible Diagnosis	Distinguishing Features
	Pelvic inflammatory disease	Initially, lower pelvic pain; pain during intercourse; irregular menstrual bleeding; vaginal discharge with abnormal color or odor; low-grade fever; chills; frequent urination; fatigue; loss of appetite; later, severe abdominal pain and high fever.
	Prostate cancer	Difficulty urinating; frequent urination with decreased urine output; pain in the pelvic area and lower back; painful ejaculation or bowel movements.
	Prostatitis *Inflammation of the prostate gland*	Burning during urination; urgent and frequent urination; fever and chills; discharge from the penis; lower abdominal and back pain; blood in the urine.
	Urethritis *Infection of the urethra, the passageway that drains urine from the bladder*	Frequent and painful urination; blood in the urine; yellow, pus-filled discharge; possible difficulty passing urine; urinary urgency; pain during intercourse; in men, painful ejaculation.
	Uterine prolapse	Often asymptomatic. Possibly, difficulty passing urine or stools, pain during intercourse, backache that intensifies when lifting, sensation of heaviness or dragging within the pelvis, painful or heavy menstrual periods, or bleeding between periods. In severe cases, uterus visibly protrudes outside of vagina.

Urinary pain

Associated Symptoms	Possible Diagnosis	Distinguishing Features
	Bladder cancer	Blood in the urine; painful and frequent urination; pelvic pain; feeling of pressure in the back; persistent fever; urinary incontinence.
	Bladder infection *Cystitis*	Burning during urination; frequent and urgent urination with only small amounts of urine passed; blood in the urine; lower abdominal pain; low-grade fever; pain during sexual intercourse and, in men, during ejaculation.
	Candidiasis *Fungal infection of the mouth, genitals, or mucus membrane*	Thick, white discharge from the vagina; itching and irritation in the vaginal area; pain while urinating or during intercourse; in men, inflammation of the head of the penis; possibly, yellow raised patches in the mouth.
	Chlamydia *Contagious, infectious disease caused by chlamydia, a group of microorganisms*	Usually asymptomatic; possibly, pain or burning during urination, watery discharge from the penis or vagina, painless pimple or blister on the penis or outer lips of the vagina, swelling of the testicles, breathing difficulty, cough, high fever, inflammation of the inner lining of the eyelids and membrane covering the whites of the eyes.
	Epididymitis *Inflammation of the coiled sperm conduit that rests on each testicle*	Severe pain and swelling at the back of a testicle; possibly, redness and swelling of the scrotum; burning on urination.
	Genital herpes	Approximately one week after infection, itching, burning, soreness, and small blisters in the genital area. Blisters later burst, leaving painful ulcers which heal 10 to 20 days later. Possibly, enlarged, painful lymph nodes in the groin; fever, headache, and cold sores around the mouth. In women, pain during urination.
	Gonorrhea	Burning pain during urination; yellowish, pus-like discharge from the penis or vagina; redness or swelling at the infection site; abnormal vaginal bleeding.
	Kidney infection *Pyelonephritis*	Sudden fever and shaking chills; severe fatigue; burning and frequent urination; cloudy or bloody urine; lower back pain, sometimes severe; nausea and vomiting.
	Neurogenic bladder *Inability to control passage of urine due to damage to nerves to the bladder*	Inability to control urine flow which may involuntarily release in large volumes or in a continuous dribbling. Bed-wetting during sleep; feeling the need to urinate though no urine is passed; pain or burning during urination.
	Penile cancer	Sore, ulcer, or wart-like lump on the penis, usually near the head, possibly painful; bleeding or unusual discharge from the penis. Possibly, pain during urination, or enlarged lymph nodes in the groin.

Urinary pain *continued*

Associated Symptoms	Possible Diagnosis	Distinguishing Features
	Prostatic hyperplasia, benign *Prostate enlargement*	Slow or delayed urination; dribbling urine; the need to urinate several times during the night; possibly, pain during urination; blood in the urine.
	Prostatitis *Inflammation of the prostate gland*	Burning during urination; urgent and frequent urination; fever and chills; discharge from the penis; lower abdominal and back pain; blood in the urine.
	Urethritis *Infection of the urethra, the passageway that drains urine from the bladder*	Frequent and painful urination; blood in the urine; yellow, pus-filled discharge; possible difficulty passing urine; urinary urgency; pain during intercourse; in men, painful ejaculation.
	Vaginal cancer	Vaginal itching; bleeding after intercourse or between menstrual periods; abnormal vaginal discharge; lesions with thick, raised edges; possibly rectal bleeding; discomfort when urinating or defecating; pain during intercourse; urinary frequency and urgency.
	Vaginitis *Inflammation of the vagina*	Vaginal irritation, itching, and discharge; painful intercourse and minor postcoital bleeding. In later stages, vaginal pain.

Urinary urgency

Associated Symptoms	Possible Diagnosis	Distinguishing Features
	Bladder cancer	Blood in the urine; painful and frequent urination; pelvic pain; feeling of pressure in the back; persistent fever; urinary incontinence.
	Bladder infection *Cystitis*	Burning during urination; frequent and urgent urination with only small amounts of urine passed; blood in the urine; lower abdominal pain; low-grade fever; pain during sexual intercourse and, in men, during ejaculation.
	Bladder stones	Interruption of urine stream; inability to urinate except in certain positions; frequent and urgent urination with only small amounts of urine passed; blood in the urine; pain in the genitals, lower back, or abdomen; low-grade fever.
	Fibroids, uterine *Benign growths of the muscular wall of the uterus*	Heavier or prolonged bleeding during menses; abdominal discomfort; lower back pain; pressure on the bladder and frequent urination; constipation. Possible, sharp, sudden, lower abdominal pain.
	Irritable bladder	Sudden, urgent need to urinate; frequent urination.
	Kidney infection *Pyelonephritis*	Sudden fever and shaking chills; severe fatigue; burning and frequent urination; cloudy or bloody urine; lower back pain, sometimes severe; nausea and vomiting.
	Neurogenic bladder *Inability to control passage of urine due to damage to nerves to the bladder*	Inability to control urine flow which may involuntarily release in large volumes or in a continuous dribbling. Bed-wetting during sleep; feeling the need to urinate though no urine is passed; pain or burning during urination.
	Pelvic inflammatory disease	Initially, lower pelvic pain; pain during intercourse; irregular menstrual bleeding; vaginal discharge with abnormal color or odor; low-grade fever; chills; frequent urination; fatigue; loss of appetite; later, severe abdominal pain and high fever.
	Prostate cancer	Difficulty urinating; frequent urination with decreased urine output; pain in the pelvic area and lower back; painful ejaculation or bowel movements.
	Prostatitis *Inflammation of the prostate gland*	Burning during urination; urgent and frequent urination; fever and chills; discharge from the penis; lower abdominal and back pain; blood in the urine.
	Urethritis *Infection of the urethra, the passageway that drains urine from the bladder*	Frequent and painful urination; blood in the urine; yellow, pus-filled discharge; possible difficulty passing urine; urinary urgency; pain during intercourse; in men, painful ejaculation.

Urine, abnormal appearance or smell

Associated Symptoms	Possible Diagnosis	Distinguishing Features
with pain during urination	Bladder cancer	Blood in the urine; painful and frequent urination; pelvic pain; feeling of pressure in the back; persistent fever; urinary incontinence.
	Bladder infection *Cystitis*	Burning during urination; frequent and urgent urination with only small amounts of urine passed; blood in the urine; lower abdominal pain; low-grade fever; pain during sexual intercourse and, in men, during ejaculation.
	Bladder stones	Interruption of urine stream; inability to urinate except in certain positions; frequent and urgent urination with only small amounts of urine passed; blood in the urine; pain in the genitals, lower back, or abdomen; low-grade fever.
	Kidney infection *Pyelonephritis*	Sudden fever and shaking chills; severe fatigue; burning and frequent urination; cloudy or bloody urine; lower back pain, sometimes severe; nausea and vomiting.
	Prostate cancer	Difficulty urinating; frequent urination with decreased urine output; pain in the pelvic area and lower back; painful ejaculation or bowel movements.
	Renal calculi *Kidney stones*	Intermittent spasms of pain in the back and flanks, radiating through the lower abdomen towards the groin; nausea and vomiting; blood in the urine; urge to urinate but only small amounts of urine are passed.
	Urethritis *Infection of the urethra, the passageway that drains urine from the bladder*	Frequent and painful urination; blood in the urine; yellow, pus-filled discharge; possible difficulty passing urine; urinary urgency; pain during intercourse; in men, painful ejaculation.
	Vaginitis *Inflammation of the vagina*	Vaginal irritation, itching, and discharge; painful intercourse and minor postcoital bleeding. In later stages, vaginal pain.
without pain during urination	Anemia, hemolytic	Fatigue and weakness; shortness of breath on exertion; pallor; heart palpitations; jaundice and dark urine.
	Appendicitis, acute	Pain near the navel, spreading to the lower right abdomen; nausea and vomiting; constipation; possibly, diarrhea; low-grade fever; loss of appetite.
	Cirrhosis *Chronic damage to the cells of the liver*	No symptoms in early stages; loss of weight and appetite; nausea; swollen legs, ankles and abdomen; itching; jaundice; black stools; vomiting blood; fatigue; impotence; memory loss; confusion.

Urine, abnormal appearance or smell *continued*

Associated Symptoms	Possible Diagnosis	Distinguishing Features
	Glomerulonephritis, acute *Sudden or intense inflammation of the glomeruli, tiny structures that filter blood in the kidneys*	Blood in the urine; passing only small amounts of urine; swelling of the ankles or the tissues around the eyes; shortness of breath; possibly, fatigue, nausea and vomiting, loss of appetite, itching, headaches, fever, impaired vision.
	Glomerulonephritis, chronic *Persistent inflammation of the glomeruli, tiny structures that filter blood in the kidneys*	Blood in the urine; passing only small amounts of urine; swelling of the ankles or the tissues around the eyes; shortness of breath; possibly, fatigue, nausea and vomiting, loss of appetite, itching, headaches, fever, impaired vision.
	Hepatitis, acute viral	Fever; fatigue; loss of appetite; aching muscles and joints; abdominal pain or discomfort; jaundice; dark urine and pale stools.
	Kidney cancer	Blood in the urine; abdominal and lower back pain; low-grade fever; fatigue; nausea and vomiting; loss of weight and appetite.
	Pancreatic cancer	Often, no symptoms until far advanced. Upper abdominal pain which spreads to the back; loss of weight and appetite; jaundice; nausea, vomiting, and indigestion; diarrhea; fatigue; depression.
	Systemic lupus erythematosus *Inflammation of connective tissues throughout the body*	Red, blotchy, butterfly-shaped rash on the cheeks and bridge of the nose; fatigue; fever; loss of appetite and weight; nausea; joint and abdominal pain; headaches; blurred vision; increased sensitivity to sun exposure; depression; psychosis; mental confusion.

Vaginal bleeding, abnormal

Associated Symptoms	Possible Diagnosis	Distinguishing Features
	Cushing's syndrome	Red, oval-shaped face; humped upper back and obese trunk; acne; purple stretch marks on the abdomen, thighs, and breasts; thin and easily bruised skin; easily fractured bones; depression or euphoria; insomnia; fatigue; muscle weakness; hirsutism (in women).
	Hyperpituitarism *Overactivity of the pituitary gland*	In adults (in which the disease is called acromegaly): Gradual thickening of the bones of the face, jaw, and the extremities in adults; oily skin; severe headache; excessive hair growth; excessive perspiration; joint pains. In children (in which the disease is called gigantism): Rapid growth and unusual height; possibly, blindness.
	Hyperthyroidism *Overactivity of the thyroid gland*	Protruding eyes; weight loss despite increased appetite; intolerance to heat; excessive perspiration; nervousness or restlessness; possibly, swelling in the neck (goiter); palpitations; tremor; diarrhea.
	Hypopituitarism *Underactivity of the pituitary gland*	Intolerance to cold; chronic headaches; decreased sex drive; fatigue; fine wrinkles around the eyes and mouth; dry skin; extreme thirst and excessive urination; loss of appetite; vaginal dryness; absence of milk production in new mothers; in men, reduced muscular strength, shrinking of the testes, and loss of body hair; growth retardation in children and adolescents.
	Hypothyroidism *Underactivity of the thyroid gland*	Unexplained weight gain; fatigue; muscle weakness; cramps; dry skin; hair loss; deepening of the voice; intolerance for cold; constipation; chest pain; insomnia; puffiness around eyes; loss of sex drive; depression; menstrual abnormalities; possible swelling in the neck (goiter).
	Ovarian cancer	Often asymptomatic until widespread. Possibly, abdominal swelling or discomfort, nausea, and vomiting. In advanced stages, excessive hair growth, unexplained weight loss, abnormal menstrual bleeding or post-menopausal bleeding; urinary frequency.
	Ovarian cysts	In many cases, no symptoms. Painless swelling in the lower abdomen; possibly, pain during intercourse; brown vaginal discharge; lack of or heavier than usual menstrual periods; vomiting; unusual hair growth on face or body.
	Platelet function disorders	Minor bleeding in the mouth or just beneath the surface of the skin, often appearing as clusters of small, pinpoint-sized red specks; frequent nosebleeds; easy bruising; prolonged menstrual periods; fatigue; pallor; dark-colored stools.

Vaginal bleeding, abnormal *continued*

Associated Symptoms	Possible Diagnosis	Distinguishing Features
	Polycystic ovaries	Absent or unpredictable menstrual periods; infertility; excessive hair growth with a male pattern of distribution; obesity; acne.
	Vaginal cancer	Vaginal itching; bleeding after intercourse or between menstrual periods; abnormal vaginal discharge; lesions with thick, raised edges; possibly rectal bleeding; discomfort when urinating or defecating; pain during intercourse; urinary frequency and urgency.
	Von Willebrand's disease *Chronic bleeding disorder*	Frequent nosebleeds; excessive bleeding from cuts; bleeding gums; easy bruising; abnormal or excessive menstrual bleeding; blood in the stool.
with abdominal, back, or vaginal pain	Cervical cancer	Initially, asymptomatic. In later stages, unexpected vaginal bleeding or discharge between periods, after intercourse, or after menopause. If untreated, pelvic pain.
	Cervical disorders, non-malignant	Vaginal discharge; vaginal burning and itching; vaginal bleeding after intercourse, between periods, or after bowel movements.
	Disseminated intravascular coagulation *Bleeding disorder marked by excessive and inappropriate blood coagulation*	Abnormal bleeding possibly at several sites at once; vomiting blood; bloody or black stools; abnormal vaginal bleeding; blood in the urine; severe abdominal or back pain; possibly, convulsions, or coma.
	Endometrial hyperplasia *Thickening of the uterine lining due to an overgrowth of cells*	Vaginal bleeding between menstrual periods; heavy or prolonged bleeding during menses; postmenstrual bleeding.
	Endometrial polyps *Growths on the lining of the uterus*	Often no symptoms; light bleeding between periods, especially following sexual intercourse; abnormally heavy or prolonged bleeding during menses; pelvic cramps; foul-smelling vaginal discharge.
	Endometriosis *The migration of the uterine lining to other reproductive or abdominal organs*	Pain in the lower abdomen, vagina, and lower back beginning just prior to menses and intensifying after blood flow has ceased; heavy bleeding during periods; pain during intercourse; diarrhea; constipation; pain during bowel movements; bleeding from the rectum; bloody urine during menses; nausea and vomiting prior to menses; infertility.
	Fibroids, uterine *Benign growths of the muscular wall of the uterus*	Heavier or prolonged bleeding during menses; abdominal discomfort; lower back pain; pressure on the bladder and frequent urination; constipation. Possible, sharp, sudden, lower abdominal pain.

Vaginal bleeding, abnormal *continued*

Associated Symptoms	Possible Diagnosis	Distinguishing Features
with abdominal, back, or vaginal pain *continued*	Gonorrhea	Burning pain during urination; yellowish, pus-like discharge from the penis or vagina; redness or swelling at the infection site; abnormal vaginal bleeding.
	Hepatitis, chronic	Fatigue; nausea; vomiting; loss of appetite; jaundice; dark urine; clay-colored stools; depression; pain or discomfort in the upper right abdomen; abdominal swelling; fever; in women, cessation of menstruation, acne, and the appearance of male pattern facial hair.
	Pelvic inflammatory disease	Initially, lower pelvic pain; pain during intercourse; irregular menstrual bleeding; vaginal discharge with abnormal color or odor; low-grade fever; chills; frequent urination; fatigue; loss of appetite; later, severe abdominal pain and high fever.
	Uterine cancer	Heavy bleeding during menses; bleeding between menses or after intercourse; postmenopausal bleeding; abnormal vaginal discharge usually watery and blood-streaked; weight loss.
	Uterine prolapse	Often asymptomatic. Possibly, difficulty passing urine or stools, pain during intercourse, backache that intensifies when lifting, sensation of heaviness or dragging within the pelvis, painful or heavy menstrual periods, or bleeding between periods. In severe cases, uterus visibly protrudes outside of vagina.
	Vaginitis *Inflammation of the vagina*	Vaginal irritation, itching, and discharge; painful intercourse and minor postcoital bleeding. In later stages, vaginal pain.

Vaginal discharge, abnormal

Associated Symptoms	Possible Diagnosis	Distinguishing Features
	Candidiasis *Fungal infection of the mouth, genitals, or mucus membrane*	Thick, white discharge from the vagina; itching and irritation in the vaginal area; pain while urinating or during intercourse; in men, inflammation of the head of the penis; possibly, yellow raised patches in the mouth.
	Cervical cancer	Initially, asymptomatic. In later stages, unexpected vaginal bleeding or discharge between periods, after intercourse, or after menopause. If untreated, pelvic pain.
	Cervical disorders, non-malignant	Vaginal discharge; vaginal burning and itching; vaginal bleeding after intercourse, between periods, or after bowel movements.
	Chlamydia *Contagious, infectious disease caused by chlamydia, a group of microorganisms*	Usually asymptomatic; possibly, pain or burning during urination, watery discharge from the penis or vagina, painless pimple or blister on the penis or outer lips of the vagina, swelling of the testicles, breathing difficulty, cough, high fever, inflammation of the inner lining of the eyelids and the membrane covering the whites of the eyes.
	Endometrial polyps *Growths on the lining of the uterus*	Often no symptoms; light bleeding between periods, especially following sexual intercourse; abnormally heavy or prolonged bleeding during menses; pelvic cramps; foul-smelling vaginal discharge.
	Gonorrhea	Burning pain during urination; yellowish, pus-like discharge from the penis or vagina; redness or swelling at the infection site; abnormal vaginal bleeding.
	Ovarian cysts	In many cases, no symptoms. Painless swelling in the lower abdomen; possibly, pain during intercourse; brown vaginal discharge; lack of or heavier than usual menstrual periods; vomiting; unusual hair growth on face or body.
	Pelvic inflammatory disease	Initially, lower pelvic pain; pain during intercourse; irregular menstrual bleeding; vaginal discharge with abnormal color or odor; low-grade fever; chills; frequent urination; fatigue; loss of appetite; later, severe abdominal pain and high fever.
	Urethritis *Infection of the urethra, the passageway that drains urine from the bladder*	Frequent and painful urination; blood in the urine; yellow, pus-filled discharge; possible difficulty passing urine; urinary urgency; pain during intercourse; in men, painful ejaculation.

Vaginal discharge, abnormal *continued*

Associated Symptoms	Possible Diagnosis	Distinguishing Features
	Uterine cancer	Heavy bleeding during menses; bleeding between menses or after intercourse; postmenopausal bleeding; abnormal vaginal discharge usually watery and blood-streaked; weight loss.
	Vaginal cancer	Vaginal itching; bleeding after intercourse or between menstrual periods; abnormal vaginal discharge; lesions with thick, raised edges; possibly rectal bleeding; discomfort when urinating or defecating; pain during intercourse; urinary frequency and urgency.
	Vaginitis *Inflammation of the vagina*	Vaginal irritation, itching, and discharge; painful intercourse and minor postcoital bleeding. In later stages, vaginal pain.

Vaginal itching

Associated Symptoms	Possible Diagnosis	Distinguishing Features
	Candidiasis *Fungal infection of the mouth, genitals, or mucus membrane*	Thick, white discharge from the vagina; itching and irritation in the vaginal area; pain while urinating or during intercourse; in men, inflammation of the head of the penis; possibly, yellow raised patches in the mouth.
	Genital herpes	Approximately one week after infection, itching, burning, soreness, and small blisters in the genital area. Blisters later burst, leaving painful ulcers which heal 10 to 20 days later. Possibly, enlarged, painful lymph nodes in the groin; fever, headache, and cold sores around the mouth. In women, pain during urination.
	Gonorrhea	Burning pain during urination; yellowish, pus-like discharge from the penis or vagina; redness or swelling at the infection site; abnormal vaginal bleeding.
	Lice	Intense itching, usually on hair-covered areas; visible nits (eggs) on hair shafts; red bite marks; visible lice on clothing.
	Pinworms	Anal itching, often at night; irritability; fidgetiness; restless sleep.
	Vaginal cancer	Vaginal itching; bleeding after intercourse or between menstrual periods; abnormal vaginal discharge; lesions with thick, raised edges; possibly rectal bleeding; discomfort when urinating or defecating; pain during intercourse; urinary frequency and urgency.
	Vaginitis *Inflammation of the vagina*	Vaginal irritation, itching, and discharge; painful intercourse and minor postcoital bleeding. In later stages, vaginal pain.

Visual Floaters

Associated Symptoms	Possible Diagnosis	Distinguishing Features
	Refractive disorders	Depending on the specific disorder, blurred vision or an inability to clearly see objects that are either near or far.
	Retinal detachment	Possibly, bright flashes of light in the peripheral vision, blurred vision, shadows or blindness in part of the field of vision.
	Uveitis and iritis *Inflammation of the uvea, a group of structures in the eye including the iris*	Moderate to severe eye pain; aversion to light; redness in the eye; excessive tearing; blurred vision; spots in the field of vision.

Weight gain, unintentional

Associated Symptoms	Possible Diagnosis	Distinguishing Features
	Congestive heart failure	Shortness of breath; fatigue; need to sleep on several pillows; weakness; cough; heart palpitations; swelling in the legs, ankles, and abdomen; frequent urination at night; indigestion; nausea and vomiting; loss of appetite.
	Hyperpituitarism *Overactivity of the pituitary gland*	In adults (in which the disease is called acromegaly): Gradual thickening of the bones of the face, jaw, and the extremities in adults; oily skin; severe headache; excessive hair growth; excessive perspiration; joint pains. In children (in which the disease is called gigantism): Rapid growth and unusual height; possibly, blindness.
	Hypothyroidism *Underactivity of the thyroid gland*	Unexplained weight gain; fatigue; muscle weakness; cramps; dry skin; hair loss; deepening of the voice; intolerance for cold; constipation; chest pain; insomnia; puffiness around eyes; loss of sex drive; depression; menstrual abnormalities; possible swelling in the neck (goiter).
	Nephrotic syndrome *Damage to the filtering units of the kidneys*	Swelling in the ankles and around the eyes; weight gain, due to fluid retention throughout the body; shortness of breath; passing only small amounts of urine that has an unusually foamy appearance; fatigue; diarrhea; loss of appetite.
	Obesity	Excess storage of body fat resulting in a body weight 20% or greater than recommended.
	Renal failure, acute *Severe kidney failure*	Initially, decreased urine output, weight gain and swelling due to edema, loss of appetite, nausea and vomiting, fatigue. If untreated, confusion, seizures, and drowsiness.

Weight loss, unintentional

Associated Symptoms	Possible Diagnosis	Distinguishing Features
	AIDS *Acquired immunodeficiency syndrome*	Recurrent infections affecting the skin and respiratory system; cough; shortness of breath; loss of appetite; weight loss; fatigue; diarrhea; fever; dementia; malignant skin lesions; swollen lymph glands throughout the body; purplish skin nodules; memory loss; confusion; personality changes.
	Amyotrophic lateral sclerosis *Progressive degeneration of nerve cells of the central nervous system*	Progressive loss of strength and coordination in the limbs; muscle twitching and cramps that begin in the hands and spread to the arms, shoulders, and legs; stiff, clumsy gait; swallowing, breathing, or speaking difficulty; weight loss; drooling; involuntary laughing or crying.
	Anemia, folic acid deficiency	Fatigue and weakness; pallor; shortness of breath, heart palpitations, or noticeably rapid heartbeat on exertion; sore, red, and glazed-looking tongue; loss of weight and appetite; nausea and diarrhea; abdominal distention.
	Anemia, pernicious	Fatigue; inability to concentrate; sore, red tongue; weakness; dizziness; pallor; shortness of breath on exertion; palpitations; numbness and tingling in extremities; incoordination; headache; loss of weight and appetite; possibly, jaundice.
	Cirrhosis *Chronic damage to the cells of the liver*	No symptoms in early stages; loss of weight and appetite; nausea; swollen legs, ankles and abdomen; itching; jaundice; black stools; vomiting blood; fatigue; impotence; memory loss; confusion.
	Dermatomyositis *Inflammation of the muscles and skin*	Red rash on the cheeks and bridge of the nose; purple discoloration and swelling of the eyelids; areas of thickened skin; muscle weakness and stiffness, usually in the shoulders and pelvis; cold hands and feet; speaking or swallowing difficulty; fever; weight loss.
	Diabetes mellitus *Insufficiency of or resistance to insulin*	Fatigue; excessive thirst; frequent urination; weight loss despite increased appetite; blurred vision; numbness and tingling of feet and hands; impotence.
	Esophageal cancer	Swallowing difficulty and pain; weight loss; drooling; possibly, vomiting or coughing up of bloody mucus, regurgitation of food; chest pain; repeated respiratory infections.
	Hyperthyroidism *Overactivity of the thyroid gland*	Protruding eyes; weight loss despite increased appetite; intolerance to heat; excessive perspiration; nervousness or restlessness; possibly, swelling in the neck (goiter); palpitations; tremor; diarrhea.

Weight loss, unintentional *continued*

Associated Symptoms	Possible Diagnosis	Distinguishing Features
	Hypothyroidism *Underactivity of the thyroid gland*	Unexplained weight gain; fatigue; muscle weakness; cramps; dry skin; hair loss; deepening of the voice; intolerance for cold; constipation; chest pain; insomnia; puffiness around eyes; loss of sex drive; depression; menstrual abnormalities; possible swelling in the neck (goiter).
	Lung abscess	Cough producing foul-smelling sputum; bad breath; fever; chills; weight loss; possible chest pain.
	Lung cancer	Persistent cough; wheezing; shortness of breath; chest pain; fatigue; loss of appetite and weight loss.
	Lymphoma, Hodgkin's *Cancer of the lymph nodes and lymphoid tissue*	Painless swelling of the lymph nodes usually in the neck or armpits; loss of appetite; night sweats.
	Lymphoma, non-Hodgkin's *Cancer of the lymph nodes and lymphoid tissue*	Painless swelling of lymph nodes in the neck or groin; possible abdominal pain, vomiting of blood, headache.
	Ovarian cancer	Often asymptomatic until widespread. Possibly, abdominal swelling or discomfort, nausea, and vomiting. In advanced stages, excessive hair growth, unexplained weight loss, abnormal menstrual bleeding or post-menopausal bleeding; urinary frequency.
	Peripheral neuropathies *Degeneration of the nerves that supply the extremities*	Tingling or numbness commonly beginning in the hands and feet and gradually spreading toward the center of the body; sensitive skin; muscle weakness; possibly, pain in the hands and feet; lack of coordination; shooting pains exacerbated by touch or changes in temperature; breathing difficulty; urinary or fecal incontinence.
	Polycythemia vera *An overproduction of red and white blood cells and platelets*	Headache; blurred vision; flushed skin; itching; dizziness; fatigue; night sweats; shortness of breath; weight loss.
	Rheumatoid arthritis, juvenile	Fever; rash; abdominal pain; weight loss; swelling, stiffness, and pain in the affected joints; enlarged lymph glands; fatigue; pallor; red, painful eyes; morning stiffness.
	Sarcoidosis *Accumulation of inflammatory cells in the lymph nodes and other tissues throughout the body*	Often no symptoms. Swollen lymph nodes in the neck or armpits; muscle aches; fever; breathing difficulty; possibly, purple rash on the face; reddish skin; bumps on the legs; numbness; joint pain or stiffness; a painful, red eye; blurred vision; loss of appetite and weight.

Weight loss, unintentional *continued*

Associated Symptoms	Possible Diagnosis	Distinguishing Features
	Scleroderma	Shiny, tight, and hardened skin, especially on the fingers, arms, and face; hands or feet may successively turn blue, white, and red upon exposure to cold (Raynaud's phenomenon); swallowing difficulty; bloating after eating; weight loss; shortness of breath on exertion; high blood pressure; symptoms of renal failure. Possibly, heartburn, muscle aches and weakness, joint pain, fever, or fatigue.
	Systemic lupus erythematosus *Inflammation of connective tissues throughout the body*	Red, blotchy, butterfly-shaped rash on the cheeks and bridge of the nose; fatigue; fever; loss of appetite and weight; nausea; joint and abdominal pain; headaches; blurred vision; increased sensitivity to sun exposure; depression; psychosis; mental confusion.
	Thyroiditis *Inflammation of the thyroid gland*	Pain in the front of the neck and, often, the ear; possibly fever, weight loss, and fatigue; general feeling of being unwell (malaise); discomfort on swallowing.
	Tuberculosis	Often, asymptomatic. Possibly, low-grade fever; excessive perspiration; cough producing sputum or blood; weight loss; chronic fatigue; chest pain; shortness of breath; night sweats.
with abdominal pain	Adrenal insufficiency *Inadequate production of steroid hormones by the adrenal gland*	Loss of weight and appetite; fatigue; weakness; darkening of the skin; abdominal pain; diarrhea; indigestion; nausea and vomiting; constipation; lack of sex drive; dizziness when rising from sitting or lying position.
	Amebiasis *Parasitic infection*	Usually asymptomatic; possibly, diarrhea; loose stools may contain mucus and blood; abdominal cramps; fatigue; weight loss; gas and flatulence. In severe cases, large amount of bloody stools daily; fever, nausea and vomiting, and abdominal tenderness.
	Colitis, ulcerative *Inflammation of the lining of the colon*	Pain on the left side of the abdomen that lessens after bowel movements; bloody diarrhea; pain in the rectal area; possibly, fever, rapid heartbeat, nausea and vomiting, loss of appetite, dehydration with severe attacks.
	Colorectal cancer *A growth of malignant cells in the colon or rectum*	Change in bowel habits; diarrhea; constipation; narrow stools; bloody or dark stools; lower abdominal pain; bloating; cramps; gas; loss of weight and appetite; fatigue and heart palpitations due to anemia.
	Crohn's disease *Inflammation of the lining of the small intestine*	Episodes of abdominal pain or cramps in lower abdomen; nausea; diarrhea; loss of weight and appetite; possibly, fever; rectal bleeding or blood in stools; fatigue; anal fissures; joint pains; inflammation of the eyes.

Weight loss, unintentional *continued*

Associated Symptoms	Possible Diagnosis	Distinguishing Features
with abdominal pain *continued*	Dysentery, bacillary	Watery diarrhea that may contain pus or blood; abdominal pain; rapid dehydration and weight loss; nausea and vomiting.
	Empyema *Collection of pus in any body cavity, usually between the membranes covering the lungs*	Chest pain exacerbated by deep inhalation; shortness of breath; dry cough; fever and chills; exhaustion; weight loss; night sweats; abdominal pain and jaundice.
	Kidney cancer	Blood in the urine; abdominal and lower back pain; low-grade fever; fatigue; nausea and vomiting; loss of weight and appetite.
	Leukemias	Symptoms vary depending on the type of leukemia and may include: loss of appetite and weight; increased bruising and bleeding; bone pain, especially in the legs; abdominal pain and distention; nausea; heart palpitations; severe fatigue; pallor; breathing difficulty; fever; night sweats; headache; enlarged lymph nodes; joint pains (due to gout).
	Liver tumors	Pain or discomfort in the upper right portion of the abdomen; abdominal swelling; loss of weight and appetite; nausea and vomiting; fever; excessive perspiration; jaundice; pallor; severe fatigue.
	Malabsorption, digestive *A failure of the small intestine to absorb nutrients in the diet*	Diarrhea; weight loss; yellowish, foul-smelling stools; abdominal cramps, gas, and bloating; weakness and lethargy.
	Pancreatic cancer	Often, no symptoms until far advanced. Upper abdominal pain which spreads to the back; loss of weight and appetite; jaundice; nausea, vomiting, and indigestion; diarrhea; fatigue; depression.
	Pancreatitis *Inflammation of the pancreas*	Sudden, extreme abdominal pain; nausea and vomiting; weakness; fever; clammy skin; abdominal bloating and tenderness.
	Peptic ulcer	Intermittent, burning or gnawing pain in the upper abdomen or lower chest; indigestion; loss of appetite and weight. Pain may be relieved by eating or antacids. Possible nausea and vomiting. Black, tarry stools, vomiting blood.
	Pheochromocytoma *Tumor in central part of the adrenal, the glands above the kidneys*	Headaches, sometimes severe; rapid heartbeat or heart palpitations; excessive perspiration; faintness, especially when standing up; chest pain; abdominal pain; constipation; weight loss; nervousness, irritability, or anxiety; mental confusion or psychosis.

Weight loss, unintentional *continued*

Associated Symptoms	Possible Diagnosis	Distinguishing Features
with abdominal pain *continued*	Stomach cancer	Discomfort in the upper abdomen; black, tarry stools; vomiting of blood; loss of appetite and weight; vomiting after meals.
	Tapeworm infestation	Often asymptomatic. Unexplained weight loss; presence of white eggs or ribbon–like segments of worm in the stool, bedding, or clothing; symptoms of pernicious anemia.
	Trichinosis *Parasitic infestation*	Initially, crampy abdominal pain, diarrhea, vomiting, and fever, followed within one to two weeks by swelling around the eyes, muscle aches and tenderness, fever, and weakness. Possibly, coughing up of bloody phlegm; delirium; coma; heart failure symptoms.
	Uterine cancer	Heavy bleeding during menses; bleeding between menses or after intercourse; postmenopausal bleeding; abnormal vaginal discharge, usually watery and blood–streaked; weight loss.

Wheezing

Associated Symptoms	Possible Diagnosis	Distinguishing Features
	Allergic rhinitis *Hay fever*	Nasal congestion; frequent sneezing; itchy eyes, nose, and throat.
	Anaphylaxis	Itching and hives; swelling of the eyes, lips, and tongue; weakness or faintness; tightening in the chest or throat; wheezing; shortness of breath; profuse sweating; palpitations; sudden, intense distress; feelings of impending doom; stomach cramps; nausea, vomiting, or diarrhea; bluish tinge (cyanosis) to the skin, lips, and nailbeds due to oxygen insufficiency.
	Asthma	Shortness of breath; wheezing; dry cough; tightness in the chest; possibly, excessive perspiration or rapid heartbeat.
	Bronchiectasis *Lung condition that stretches and distorts the walls of the bronchial tubes*	Cough that produces dark green sputum; bad breath; possibly, shortness of breath; loss of appetite and weight; clubbed fingers.
	Bronchitis, acute	Shortness of breath; persistent cough producing yellow or green sputum; possibly, chest pain; wheezing; fever.
	Carcinoid tumors and carcinoid syndrome	May be asymptomatic; flushing or redness of the face and neck; gas and profuse diarrhea; abdominal cramping; watery, swollen eyes; shortness of breath or wheezing.
	Cardiomyopathy *Disease of the heart muscle causing a reduction in the force of heart contractions*	Fatigue; chest pain and palpitations; shortness of breath; swelling of the legs; wheezing; cough.
	Chronic obstructive pulmonary disease	Shortness of breath; wheezing; persistent, mucus-producing cough, especially in the morning; possibly, chest pain, swollen legs and ankles.
	Croup *Inflammation of the air passages in children*	Barking cough; hoarseness; wheezing; possibly, breathing difficulty; chest discomfort.
	Esophageal stricture *Narrowing of the esophagus, the passageway from the mouth to the stomach*	Sudden or gradual decrease in the ability to swallow solid food or liquids; chest pain after eating; regurgitation of food and liquids; increased salivation; weight loss. Aspiration into lungs can cause cough, wheezing, shortness of breath.
	Gastroesophageal reflux *Heartburn*	Burning sensation in the middle of the chest; pain and difficulty swallowing; slight regurgitation of stomach's contents into the mouth, especially when reclining or bending forward; mild abdominal pain.

Wheezing *continued*

Associated Symptoms	Possible Diagnosis	Distinguishing Features
	Lung cancer	Persistent cough; wheezing; shortness of breath; chest pain; fatigue; loss of appetite and weight loss.
	Pneumonia	High fever; shortness of breath; cough with sputum; chest pain; fatigue.
	Pulmonary edema *An accumulation of fluid in the lungs*	Severe shortness of breath; rapid breathing; pallor; excessive perspiration; bluish nails and lips; cough with frothy sputum; wheezing; anxiety and restlessness.
	Pulmonary embolism *A blood clot travelling from legs or heart that lodges in an artery supplying the lungs*	Sudden shortness of breath and severe breathing difficulty; chest pain worse on inspiration; rapid heartbeat; cough, possibly with bloody sputum; wheezing; excessive perspiration.

DISORDERS

In this section, you will find an entry for each of the disorders listed in the "Possible Diagnosis" column of the Symptoms charts in the first half of the book. Each entry offers a brief definition of the disorder, a discussion of its causes and risk factors, a comprehensive list of the symptoms commonly associated with the disorder, prevention tips, diagnostic tests required, how the disorder should be remedied, and when to consult your doctor.

THE EDITORS

Acne

WHAT IS IT?

Acne is characterized by minor skin eruptions due to inflammation of the sebaceous glands. These tiny glands, located along hair shafts all over the body, produce sebum, a thick, oily substance that lubricates the skin. A hormonal imbalance—common during adolescence, menstrual periods, pregnancy, or when first using oral contraceptives—may trigger overactivity of the sebaceous glands. Male hormones (androgens) stimulate sebum production, and when sebum is secreted faster than it can exit through the pores, it may plug the hair follicle and produce a whitehead. If the follicle is not plugged completely, skin pigments may oxidize and darken, forming a blackhead. Bacteria normally found on the surface of the skin may then infect the whitehead or blackhead and produce pus

SYMPTOMS

- Pimples or skin eruptions (blackheads and whiteheads) most prominent on the face, but also found on the neck, shoulders, back, chest, buttocks, and, more rarely, the upper arms and thighs.
- Clusters of red, inflamed cysts in more severe cases (cystic acne).
- Thick, firm, painless lumps below the surface of the skin (sebaceous cysts).
- Pockmarks and scarring from chronic acne.

that causes pimples or, in more severe cases (known as cystic acne), boils. Except in cases that cause widespread skin infections and scarring, acne is generally harmless and responsive to treatment. It is most common during adolescence and can cause considerable psychological distress. Eruptions tend to wane by one's 20s, but may persist in some. Among women, acne may first appear in the 20s and 30s. Unexplained outbreaks of acne in older adults may be a sign of a more serious underlying problem.

WHAT CAUSES IT?

- Hormonal changes (especially excessive androgen secretion) resulting in increased sebum production.
- Hereditary factors.

- Certain drugs or compounds, including oral contraceptives, corticosteroids, or other hormones, as well as barbiturates, iodides, bromides, vitamin B_{12}, antiseizure drugs, and lithium.
- Grease, tar, heavy oils, cosmetics, tight clothing, or anything else that can physically block the pores.
- In adults, underlying medical conditions, including ovary or adrenal gland dysfunction, such as polycystic ovary disease and Cushing's syndrome.
- Other factors including climate changes, stress, and exposure to dioxin.

PREVENTION

- There is little evidence that dietary modifications (such as avoiding chocolate or greasy foods) will reduce the incidence of acne in those so predisposed, although good hygiene may reduce severity.
- Picking or squeezing acne lesions may increase the danger of infection and scarring.

DIAGNOSIS

- Diagnosis can be made upon visual inspection. Unless an underlying disorder of the ovaries or adrenals is suspected, further tests are unnecessary.

HOW TO TREAT IT

- Frequent washing of the face with unscented soap to remove excessive oil is recommended.
- Topical solutions that dry the skin and promote peeling may help to eliminate acne over time. Over-the-counter preparations may contain benzoyl peroxide (a potent antibacterial agent), sulfur, or resorcinol.
- In more severe cases, topical or oral antibiotics like tetracycline and erythromycin may be prescribed.
- A synthetic form of vitamin A (topical tretinoin)—administered either topically or orally—is useful against cystic acne (although it may cause birth defects when taken orally by pregnant women).
- Controlled exposure to sunlight or artificial ultraviolet light may help to heal acne.
- In extreme cases chemical peeling, surgical drainage, or removal of cysts may be warranted.

WHEN TO CALL A DOCTOR

- Consult a doctor or dermatologist to discuss optimal ways to treat acne.

Acoustic Neuroma

WHAT IS IT?

Acoustic neuromas are benign (noncancerous) tumors arising from abnormal growth in the cells of the protective sheath (myelin) that surrounds the eighth cranial nerve (or auditory nerve). These tumors tend to grow very slowly, eventually leading to partial or total hearing loss in the affected ear. If left untreated, the tumor may continue to expand and press on several other cranial nerves, causing dizziness and loss of balance, facial pain (see Neuralgias), or double vision. In some cases an acoustic neuroma grows large enough to involve the brain stem, leading to loss of muscle coordination (cerebellar ataxia) on the affected side of the body. However, most patients seek treatment before such complications occur. Prognosis depends on the size of the tumor but is generally quite favorable. While acoustic neuroma is the most common tumor of cranial nerves and represents about 5 percent of primary brain tumors, it is still a rather uncommon disorder. Incidence is highest among those between the ages of 30 and 50.

WHAT CAUSES IT?

• The cause of acoustic neuromas is unknown, except in the small fraction of cases that occur in association with a hereditary disorder known as neurofibromatosis, which is characterized by widespread abnormalities in the nervous system, skin, and bones. Neurofibromatosis can be associated with acoustic neuromas that affect both auditory nerves. (In almost all other cases, neuromas develop only in one auditory nerve.)

PREVENTION

• There is no known way to prevent acoustic neuromas.

DIAGNOSIS

• Patient history and hearing tests (audiography) are strongly suggestive of the diagnosis. Evaluation by an otolaryngologist (an ear, nose, and throat specialist) is essential for any signs of hearing loss.
• CT (computed tomography) or MRI (magnetic resonance imaging) scans can confirm the presence of even very small acoustic neuromas.

HOW TO TREAT IT

• The only effective treatment for acoustic neuromas is surgical removal of the tumor. Current microsurgery techniques often yield quite favorable results; it is possible to preserve hearing for many patients, especially those who had good hearing preoperatively. Occasionally, however, some degree of permanent hearing loss in the affected ear is inevitable, and sometimes the surgery itself can result in weakness in the facial muscles, numbness, or other neurological symptoms owing to unavoidable damage to surrounding nerves.

WHEN TO CALL A DOCTOR

• Consult a doctor regarding any signs of hearing loss. You will most likely be referred to an audiologist or an otolaryngologist for testing and examination.

SYMPTOMS

• Partial or complete hearing loss in one ear (or rarely, both).
• Persistent ringing or buzzing in the affected ear (tinnitus).
• Ear pain (in some cases).
• Symptoms that may appear if a tumor affects other nerves or the cerebellum: dizziness and vertigo; facial pain; double vision; loss of muscle coordination on the affected side of the body.

Acoustic Trauma

WHAT IS IT?

Acoustic trauma refers to hearing impairment caused by exposure to loud noise. Prolonged exposure to noisy environments may be even more likely than sudden bursts of intensely loud sound to result in permanent damage. Similar to age-related hearing loss (see Presbycusis), the ability to hear high frequency sounds tends to deteriorate first, followed later by difficulty in hearing lower-frequency sounds. Those whose occupations require prolonged exposure to noisy conditions (for example, factory workers, machinists, lumberjacks, airport employees, disk jockeys, or rock musicians) are at greatest risk for acoustic trauma (known as occupational hearing loss in such cases).

SYMPTOMS

- Partial hearing loss that may worsen over time.
- A sensation that the ears are plugged or submerged underwater.
- Ringing or buzzing in the ears (tinnitus).

WHAT CAUSES IT?

- Physical trauma to the ear, which can occur with a blow to the side of the head, an explosive burst of sound too near to the ear, or rapid changes in air pressure.
- Loud, electronically amplified music.
- Cumulative exposure to a noisy environment. Urban or industrial sounds such as traffic, sirens, portable stereos, jet engines, power tools, chain saws, jackhammers, hydraulic machinery, and so forth are common sources of potentially hazardous noise.

PREVENTION

- Carry earplugs to be worn in noisy environments. A variety of plugs are available, including those made of foam, plastic, rubber, or wax. Do not use wadded up tissue paper or cotton balls; these do not protect adequately against loud noise—especially the more dangerous high frequencies—and they may become lodged in the ear canal.
- Be cautious when using stereo headphones. If music is so loud that others can hear it plainly or you can't hear other sounds around you, the volume is too high.
- If your job requires spending lots of time in noisy conditions, special earmuffs are available that almost totally block out sound.
- Have your hearing checked every five years if you work in a noisy environment.

DIAGNOSIS

- In many cases acoustic trauma may be self-diagnosed, especially when it occurs suddenly.
- If hearing difficulty is suspected, your doctor may refer you to an audiologist or otolaryngologist (ear, nose, and throat specialist) for a complete series of hearing tests (audiometry). Such an evaluation will confirm diagnosis and determine the extent of hearing loss.

HOW TO TREAT IT

- Hearing loss due to nerve damage is irreversible; the only practical treatment is a hearing aid. It is important to stave off any further damage by following the preventive measures above.
- Learning skills such as lipreading may augment communication abilities.

WHEN TO CALL A DOCTOR

- See a doctor if a loud noise results in hearing loss that persists longer than two days.
- Hearing loss is often gradual, and may develop unnoticed. Have your hearing checked if you can't hear your watch ticking or a faucet dripping; you can't hear speech well with your eyes closed or you often have to ask people to repeat what they've said; or you can't understand a conversation while driving in traffic with a window open.

Adrenal Insufficiency

WHAT IS IT?

Adrenal insufficiency is a relatively rare disorder caused either by destruction of tissue in the portion of the adrenal glands known as the cortex, which normally secretes the corticosteroid hormones (Addison's disease), or by atrophy of the adrenal cortex resulting from a loss of stimulation from the pituitary gland (secondary adrenal failure). Addison's disease produces symptoms only after some 90 percent of the adrenal cortices have been destroyed. Insufficiency of corticosteroids can lead to a number of health problems, including an inability to recover from even a minor infection. Complications such as protracted weakness, shock, or death may result. Adrenal insufficiency may occur at any age and affects both sexes equally. Once invariably fatal, the disorder is now highly treatable since the advent of corticosteroid replacement therapy in the 1950s; thus, a patient's outlook is quite favorable. Steps must be taken, however, to avert adrenal crisis—a sudden, life-threatening steroid deficiency usually brought on by infection, injury, or stress—which requires immediate emergency treatment.

WHAT CAUSES IT?

• Addison's disease results from the destruction of the adrenal cortices. In the majority of cases, no under-

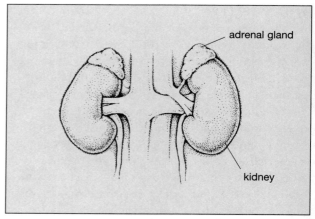

The powerful and crucial corticosteroid hormones are produced in the cortex of the adrenal glands, located atop either kidney.

lying cause for this can be pinpointed, although it often appears to involve an autoimmune disorder (an attack upon healthy tissue by the body's defenses against disease).
• A family history of autoimmune disorders is associated with a higher risk of Addison's disease.
• In a few cases Addison's may occur as a complication of certain infections, such as tuberculosis, histoplasmosis, or cytomegalovirus (in AIDS patients).
• Adrenal tissue may be destroyed by metastatic cancer or other disorders (see Amyloidosis and Sarcoidosis).
• Secondary adrenal insufficiency most often results from a pituitary tumor that destroys a part of the pituitary gland or from surgical removal of the pituitary.
• Long-term treatment with steroid hormones leads to atrophy of the adrenal cortex; recovery of adrenal function may take many months after steroid treatment is stopped.

PREVENTION

• There is no way to prevent Addison's disease.

DIAGNOSIS

• The diagnosis is suspected from patient history and physical evaluation.
• Blood and urine tests are taken to measure hormone levels.

SYMPTOMS

• Progressive fatigue and weakness.
• Nausea and vomiting.
• Decreased appetite and weight loss.
• Increased pigmentation of skin and mucus membranes (dark freckles, uneven patches of darkened skin, or unusually persistent tanning following sun exposure). Hyperpigmentation does not occur with secondary adrenal insufficiency.
• Abdominal pain.
• Diarrhea or constipation.
• Dizziness, especially when rising from a lying or sitting position.
• Personality changes, such as increased irritability or restlessness.
• Enhanced senses of smell, taste, or hearing.

Adrenal Insufficiency *continued*

HOW TO TREAT IT

• Lifelong hormone replacement is the key to treatment. Corticosteroids, such as cortisol, prednisone, and dexamethasone, are prescribed. Doses should be taken with meals, milk, or antacids, since the drugs promote increased secretion of stomach acid.

• A mineralocorticoid such as fludrocortisone is often needed to help control salt and mineral balance and thus prevent dehydration and hypotension (unusually low blood pressure) in those with Addison's disease.

• The dose of corticosteroids must be increased during stressful times, such as infections, gastrointestinal illness, dental extractions, or surgery.

• Patients should wear or carry medical alert identification.

• Adrenal crisis requires emergency medical treatment, which includes intravenous fluid and hydrocortisone infusions.

WHEN TO CALL A DOCTOR

• See a doctor for any persistent unexplained weakness, weight loss, or stomach upset.

• **EMERGENCY** If you have been diagnosed with Addison's disease and experience symptoms of severe lethargy, nausea, vomiting, dizziness, or dehydration, get immediate medical assistance—these may be indications of adrenal crisis.

AIDS Acquired Immunodeficiency Syndrome

WHAT IS IT?

AIDS is the deadly final phase of infection with the human immunodeficiency virus (HIV). The virus, which is carried in blood, semen, and other body fluids, invades and destroys a specific type of white blood cell—the T4 lymphocyte—a chief component of the body's immune system. After initial infection, the virus multiplies over a period of several months, sometimes producing fever, fatigue, sore throat, skin rash, and other symptoms resembling a common virus like mononucleosis. Such symptoms tend to last only one or two weeks. The infected patient may then exhibit no symptoms (but still be contagious) for one to five years or, in some cases, even 10 or more years. Eventually, however—as increasing numbers of T4 lymphocytes are destroyed by the virus—symptoms such as swollen glands, fever, night sweats, diarrhea, and weight loss appear. At this point the patient is said to have AIDS-related complex (ARC)—a collection of nonspecific symptoms common to AIDS but without the more serious life-threatening infections characteristic of AIDS. The

The outer envelope of the human immunodeficiency virus binds readily with protein receptors on the surface of the immune system's T cells. In this way, the virus's genetic material may enter the T cell and integrate with its genetic material, forever altering the infected cell's genetic code. From this point on, the host cell's protein synthesizing mechanism serves to produce new copies of the virus.

patient is designated as having full-blown AIDS only when the immune system becomes so impaired that opportunistic infections (those normally kept at bay by healthy immune defenses) or an unusual type of cancer (Kaposi's sarcoma) begins to occur. Outlook is not good at this point. Indeed, within one to three years after diagnosis of full-blown AIDS, the patient usually succumbs to pneumonia, cancer, or some other fatal complication. AIDS is now a major worldwide public health threat; there is no cure, but the disease is highly preventable. Homosexual and bisexual men and intravenous drug users are at especially high risk, but the virus can be transmitted through heterosexual sex too.

WHAT CAUSES IT?

• AIDS is caused by the human immunodeficiency virus (HIV), which is carried in the body fluids (blood, semen, female genital secretions, saliva, and breast milk) of infected patients. The virus progressively destroys the body's immune defenses, rendering the patient vulnerable to a multitude of potentially deadly secondary infections and cancers, especially Kaposi's sarcoma.

• HIV is transmitted by exchange of body fluids

SYMPTOMS

• Swollen lymph nodes.
• Persistent fatigue and general feeling of poor health.
• Recurring or prolonged fevers, chills, or night sweats.
• Sore throat.
• Increased susceptibility to colds, yeast infections (candidiasis), cold sores, fungal infections in the mouth (thrush), and other infections.
• Loss of appetite and unintentional weight loss.
• Cough and breathing problems.
• Changes in bowel habits, such as frequent diarrhea or constipation.
• Outbreaks of skin rashes or discolorations, especially purplish lesions (Kaposi's sarcoma).
• Tenderness or pain in the muscles and joints.
• Vision disturbances.
• Memory loss, confusion, and personality changes.

AIDS Acquired Immunodeficiency Syndrome *continued*

during sexual contact with an infected partner (particularly during anal sex, which establishes a path for the virus to enter the bloodstream via small tears in the mucus membranes lining the rectum), and by exposure to contaminated blood or blood products (as occurs among intravenous drug users who share needles, or hemophiliacs who must receive multiple transfusions; however, improved testing of blood has recently eliminated HIV risk during a transfusion). Pregnant women may also transmit the virus to their unborn children. HIV is, however, a very fragile virus and does not last long outside of the body. It is impossible to contract the virus by casual contact such as hugging, dry kissing, or drinking from the same glass as an infected person.

PREVENTION
• HIV infection is preventable by practicing safe sex behaviors, including using condoms (especially those treated with nonoxynol-9 spermicide), avoiding anal sex, and by limiting one's number of sexual partners over a lifetime (short of complete abstinence, an exclusive, mutually monogamous relationship is safest).
• Do not use intravenous drugs; if you do, do not share needles.
• Avoid contact with the blood of others.

DIAGNOSIS
• Patient history and physical examination.
• Blood tests. Presence of antibodies against HIV usually confirms the diagnosis; measurement of the T-cell count indicates the extent of immune system impairment.
• A diagnosis of full-blown AIDS is made when one or more opportunistic infections or Kaposi's sarcoma affects a patient meeting the above criteria for HIV infection.

HOW TO TREAT IT
• There is no cure for AIDS; treatment is aimed at easing discomfort and managing the various secondary infections that occur.
• The antiviral drugs zidovudine (AZT) and acyclovir may prolong the life of the patient by inhibiting the replication of HIV. Infection may be prevented by immediate treatment with AZT at the time of exposure to HIV.
• Vaccines and other preparations are available to prevent toxoplasmosis (a type of feline leukemia) and *Pneumocystis carinii* pneumonia, two potentially life-threatening diseases that frequently affect people with AIDS.
• Receiving a diagnosis of HIV infection is often emotionally devastating; psychological counseling, support groups, and outreach from friends and family are invaluable.

WHEN TO CALL A DOCTOR
• Call a doctor if you experience any of the symptoms of ARC or AIDS.
• Be tested if you have any reason to suspect that you may have been infected with HIV.

Allergic Rhinitis

WHAT IS IT?

Allergic rhinitis and related nasal or upper respiratory conditions involve inflammation of the mucus membranes in the nasal passages, caused by a hypersensitive response of the immune system to an airborne allergen or irritant. Sneezing, eye irritation, and runny nose are the characteristic symptoms, which may occur seasonally or persist throughout the year. The specific allergens that trigger rhinitis vary from person to person and may include pollen, mold, animal dander, or dust. Symptoms usually first appear between the ages of 10 and 20, and tend to diminish in the later decades of life. Allergic rhinitis is exceedingly common—as many as 25 percent of young adults are afflicted with it—but it is highly treatable.

SYMPTOMS
- Frequent sneezing.
- Profuse nasal discharge (usually clear and watery).
- Nasal congestion and itching.
- Red, watering, itching eyes.
- Puffiness and dark circles around the eyes.
- Possible cough or wheezing.
- Impaired sense of taste or smell.
- Itching in the back of the throat.

WHAT CAUSES IT?

- Airborne pollen from various seasonal plants, including grasses, flowers, trees, and ragweed. (Such allergies are commonly referred to as hay fever, although hay is not the cause and fever is not a symptom.)
- Mold spores.
- Animal dander (small scales composed of dead skin or dried saliva, shed from the hair of certain mammals).
- Household dust.
- Hereditary factors affecting immune sensitivity.
- Overuse of decongestant sprays.
- A hypersensitivity to medications, including aspirin and other nonsteroidal anti-inflammatory drugs.
- Hormonal disturbances that may occur with pregnancy, oral contraceptive use, or hypothyroidism (rare).

PREVENTION

- When seasonal allergies flare up, try to stay inside a climate-controlled environment as much as possible, or travel to pollen-free areas. Consider moving to such areas if symptoms are sufficiently severe.
- If necessary, avoid or isolate furred animals.
- To eliminate dust mites commonly found in bedding, use machine-washable polyester pillows, seal your mattress in a zippered cover, and launder bed linens frequently. Use air filters in bedrooms.

DIAGNOSIS

- Patient history and physical examination.
- Skin tests. The skin is scratched or pricked with a number of needles, each containing a small amount of an allergen; a specific allergen is implicated if the area becomes red or itchy, or a raised welt appears.
- Analysis of nasal secretions.
- Blood tests to reveal a heightened antibody count, indicating an allergic response.

HOW TO TREAT IT

- Antihistamines are the first line of treatment for allergic rhinitis. Many nonprescription varieties are available, although they may cause drowsiness or drying of the mucus membranes. New nonsedating antihistamines are available by prescription—including terfenadine (Seldane), astemizole (Hismanal), and loratadine (Claritin)—although these are expensive.
- Short-term use of decongestants (in the form of drops, sprays, or tablets) may be beneficial.
- Special eyedrops may be prescribed when eye symptoms persist despite other treatment.
- Inhaled or even oral corticosteroids may be prescribed to reduce extreme inflammatory symptoms.
- When all else fails, an allergist may gradually administer increasing amounts of the offending allergen (immunotherapy or allergy shots), which may eventually help to desensitize the patient to the allergen.

WHEN TO CALL A DOCTOR

- Call a doctor if allergic rhinitis interferes with normal activities. Also, if you take over-the-counter antihistamines for allergic rhinitis and they cause excessive drowsiness, your doctor can prescribe a nonsedating antihistamine.

Alopecia Hair Loss

WHAT IS IT?

Alopecia refers to hair loss of any sort—be it normal male-pattern baldness (MPB) that commonly occurs as men age, or abnormal hair loss associated with certain diseases, hormonal disturbances, or treatments such as chemotherapy. There are two general types of alopecia: scarring and nonscarring. In scarring alopecia, hair follicles are destroyed by the underlying condition, so that hair loss is irreversible. In nonscarring alopecia (which includes MPB), the hair shaft disappears, but the follicles are preserved, so that regrowth of lost hair remains a possibility. Alopecia has a variety of causes, some of which affect women as often as men. It is wise to consult a doctor whenever hair loss occurs unexpectedly, in case the cause is pathological in nature.

SYMPTOMS

- Male pattern baldness: receding hairline, especially at the temples; progressively widening bald spot on the crown of the head.
- Alopecia areata, a common type of hair loss believed to be caused by an autoimmune reaction that affects men and women equally: loss of hair in patches or clumps.
- Female pattern baldness: overall gradual thinning of hair throughout the scalp.

WHAT CAUSES IT?

- Hormonal changes that normally occur with age, the aftermath of pregnancy (the postpartum period), or use of oral contraceptives.
- Congenital and developmental defects or autoimmune activity.
- Bacterial, fungal, viral, and protozoal infections.
- Skin diseases such as dermatitis, pemphigus, psoriasis, sarcoidosis, and scleroderma (the most common causes of scarring alopecia).
- Reactions to certain drugs including anticoagulants, anticonvulsants, antidepressants, antihypertensives, antiparkinson agents, antithyroid agents, and especially chemotherapeutic agents used for cancer.
- Malnutrition, digestive malabsorption, anorexia nervosa, or crash diets.

- Physical or emotional stress.
- Various kinds of cancers, including basal cell carcinoma and lymphoma.
- Chemical and physical agents, such as acids, bleach, burns, freezing, or radiation (including x-rays and radiotherapy for cancer).
- Poisoning with toxic levels of arsenic, bismuth, boric acid, and vitamin A.

PREVENTION

- Handle hair gently, particularly if it is thinning. Don't overbrush or overcomb it.
- Minimize exposure to chlorinated pools and wear a hat when out in the sun.
- Use mild shampoos and avoid rough towel drying and blowdryers, as well as hot rollers and curling irons.

DIAGNOSIS

- Alopecia can usually be diagnosed by observation of characteristic patterns of hair loss.
- More extensive medical tests are warranted when a pathological condition is believed to cause hair loss.

HOW TO TREAT IT

- Any underlying medical condition causing alopecia must be diagnosed and treated.
- Hormone therapy is recommended in some cases.
- Treatment for nonpathologic alopecia (such as normal male-pattern baldness) is not necessary, although there are a number of ways to restore cosmetic appearance.
- Topical minoxidil often slows the loss of hair and may lead to regrowth of hair in a considerably smaller fraction of sufferers (a number of which only grow soft "peach fuzz"). The drug is expensive and all benefits are lost when minoxidil is discontinued.
- Wigs, hair transplants, or surgery to reposition existing portions of the scalp are other methods to consider.

WHEN TO CALL A DOCTOR

- Consult a physician or dermatologist if you notice unusual shedding of hair, in order to determine if hair loss is excessive and whether it is a symptom of an underlying pathological condition.

Alzheimer's Disease

WHAT IS IT?

Alzheimer's disease results from the gradual degeneration of crucial neurons in the part of the brain that handles cognitive functioning. The onset of symptoms is usually very slow. As symptoms progress, they tend to follow an irreversible course, beginning with minor forgetfulness that becomes more pronounced over time, and culminating in profound losses of memory, identity, intellectual faculties, and control over body functions. In the final stages, severe mental impairment leads to complete dependence upon caregivers. Most patients die within five to 10 years of diagnosis, frequently from complications such as urinary tract infections or pneumonia. Alzheimer's disease affects about 6 percent of people over the age of 65, more than 10 percent of those between 75 and 85, and by some estimates, upward of 20 percent of those over 85.

WHAT CAUSES IT?

• Good evidence indicates that a genetic component predisposes certain individuals to Alzheimer's disease, but the true cause is unknown. The mechanism of the disease is nonetheless distinctive and is characterized by the death of neurons in the cerebral cortex of the brain, leading to atrophy in the specific brain regions where integration of new information and retrieval of memory take place.

• In people with Down's syndrome, Alzheimer's disease occurs at an early age.

PREVENTION

• There is no way to prevent Alzheimer's disease.

DIAGNOSIS

• No tests are available to specifically identify Alzheimer's; diagnosis is based largely on patient history (including input from family members) and clinical examination, including a test of mental status. The primary criterion is progressive loss of memory and cognitive functioning. Other disorders that can cause dementia must be ruled out; this may be facilitated by imaging of the brain and various laboratory tests:

• MRI (magnetic resonance imaging) or CT (computed tomography) scans of the brain to rule out brain tumors, subdural hematomas, various neurologic abnormalities, or multiple small strokes due to vascular disease.

• Electroencephalogram to evaluate brain wave patterns.

• Blood tests to rule out vitamin deficiencies, hypothyroidism, syphilis, HIV, or heavy-metal poisoning.

HOW TO TREAT IT

• Tacrine hydrochloride (Cognex), an inhibitor of the enzyme acetylcholinesterase, provides some improvement in symptoms of patients with mild to

---

SYMPTOMS

• Increasing forgetfulness and short-term memory losses.
• Difficulty making decisions.
• Impaired judgment; difficulty making mathematical calculations or handling money.
• Decreased knowledge of current events.
• Anxiety, withdrawal, and depression as awareness of deficits become frightening and embarrassing.
• Language difficulties, including rambling speech, inability to name familiar objects, long pauses to find the right word, and repetition of the same words, phrases, or questions.
• Loss of the ability to write or understand written language.
• Complete loss of ability to communicate verbally.
• Delusions, hallucinations, paranoia, or irrational accusations of family members.
• Agitation and combativeness.
• Unusual quiet and serenity at times.
• Wandering and frequently getting lost.
• Urinary and fecal incontinence.
• Inappropriate social behavior; indifference to others; failure to recognize friends and family.
• Inability to dress, eat, bathe, or use a bathroom without assistance.
• Walking difficulty, leading to falls and bedsores.

Alzheimer's Disease *continued*

moderate Alzheimer's disease, but side effects of the drug are quite common.

• Insomnia, depression, aggression, and other psychological manifestations may be eased with drug therapy.

• Much of the responsibility to feed, clothe, medicate, and otherwise treat an Alzheimer's patient falls into the hands of the primary caregiver. Supportive counseling as well as day care, visiting nurses, and eventual inpatient nursing facilities may help to ease the caregiver's burden. Contact your local chapter of the Alzheimer's Association for further information.

WHEN TO CALL A DOCTOR

• Occasional incidences of forgetfulness such as misplacing the car keys are perfectly normal and rarely anything to worry about, but consult a doctor if you or a family member begins to show increasing signs of memory lapses, especially if accompanied by changes in personality.

Amebiasis

WHAT IS IT?

Amebiasis is an infection with the parasite *Entamoeba histolytica*. It initially involves the intestine, following consumption of contaminated food or water. Most often, the infected host experiences no symptoms and the infection clears within eight to 12 months. While dwelling in the intestine of the host, the amoebae multiply, living off of bacteria, food residues, blood cells, and other tissue. Some of the parasites form hard, acid-resistant shells or cysts around themselves. When excreted, these cysts can survive for lengthy periods and are highly resilient to hostile environments or water purification systems. If water or food become contaminated with cysts (common in countries where human waste is used as fertilizer),

---

SYMPTOMS

- Diarrhea, possibly containing blood or mucus.
- Severe abdominal cramping and tenderness.
- Excessive gas.
- Loss of weight.
- High fever.
- Nausea and vomiting (with liver abscess).

---

infection may spread. Although amebiasis is rare in the United States, as many as half of the inhabitants of some underdeveloped countries are infected. Amebiasis may cause symptoms ranging from chronic, mild diarrhea to acute amebic dysentery, marked by fever, abdominal pain, and severe diarrhea. Serious complications include the formation of a liver abscess that can rupture into the abdominal cavity (see Peritonitis), the pleural membranes covering the lungs (see Empyema), or the tissues surrounding the heart (see Pericarditis). In very rare cases, infection may spread via the bloodstream to the lungs or brain. But mostly, amebiasis responds quickly and completely to therapy; relapse and fatality are unlikely with proper treatment.

WHAT CAUSES IT?

- Infection with *Entamoeba histolytica* results from ingestion of the fecally excreted, acid-resistant, cystic form of the amoeba. Transmission of the infection commonly results from fecal contamination of water or food, which is most prevalent in regions with poor sanitary conditions. Another mode of transmission is oral sex preceded by anal sex.
- At highest risk for severe illness from amebiasis are those who are malnourished; under two years of age; receiving corticosteroid therapy; or pregnant; or who have compromised immune systems.

PREVENTION

- When visiting underdeveloped countries, drink only boiled or purified water (chlorine is ineffective against amebic cysts; however, water treated with iodine or globaline tablets is safe), and do not eat uncooked vegetables (especially leafy greens, which are often fertilized with human waste) or unpeeled fruit. Prophylactic immunization is not available.

DIAGNOSIS

- Patient history and physical examination are needed.
- Confirmation of the diagnosis requires identification of *E. histolytica* in stool or tissue samples. Three stool specimens are usually taken over a two-day period.
- Blood tests may be done to look for antibodies to the parasite.
- An abdominal ultrasound scan is done to check for a liver abscess.
- Sigmoidoscopy (use of a lighted rectal scope) and a barium enema (use of barium to create a clear x-ray image of the intestine) may be done to rule out other disorders that can mimic or occur in conjunction with amebiasis. Tissue biopsies from sigmoidoscopy are examined for amoebae.

HOW TO TREAT IT

- Replacement of fluids, electrolytes (mineral salts), and blood may be needed.
- Several drugs (including diloxanide furoate, chloroquine, iodoguinol, and metronidazole) can be used to eliminate the amoebae.
- A liver abscess may be treated with needle aspiration (removal of pus with a syringe) or, occasionally, surgical drainage.

WHEN TO CALL A DOCTOR

- Call a doctor for persistent or recurrent diarrhea.

Amyloidosis

WHAT IS IT?

Amyloidosis is a rare disorder resulting from the buildup of a starchlike protein known as amyloid in one or more organs. In most cases amyloidosis occurs as a complication of another underlying disorder (secondary amyloidosis); in other incidences it occurs for no apparent or identifiable reason (primary amyloidosis). The most common sites for amyloid deposition are the kidneys, heart, skin, gastrointestinal tract, and nervous system. Interference with function of the involved organs, symptoms, and prognosis depend upon the location and the amount of accumulated amyloid protein. In most cases, however, outlook is poor. Kidney failure, congestive heart failure, cardiac arrhythmias, and gastrointestinal bleeding are the major life-threatening complications of amyloidosis.

WHAT CAUSES IT?

• In the minority of cases, amyloidosis has no discernible cause (primary amyloidosis).

> ### SYMPTOMS
> • If the heart is affected: congestive heart failure with excessive accumulation of fluid in the tissues (edema); breathing difficulty; fatigue; heart rhythm disturbances with palpitations.
> • If the kidneys are affected: symptoms of kidney failure (see Renal Failure, Chronic).
> • If the skin is affected: slightly raised, waxy nodules clustered in the armpits, groin, face, neck, ears, or tongue; easy bleeding or bruising.
> • If the gastrointestinal tract is affected: diarrhea; abdominal pain; blood in stool.
> • If the nervous system is affected: dizziness upon standing; numbness; inability to sweat; hoarseness; urinary or fecal incontinence.
> • If the joints are affected: arthritic pain; morning stiffness.
> • If the respiratory system is affected: breathing difficulty.
> • Carpal tunnel syndrome and joint pains in amyloidosis resulting from chronic hemodialysis.

• Secondary amyloidosis is common in patients with multiple myeloma (a cancer of plasma cells in the bone marrow).
• Secondary amyloidosis may occur as a complication of a number of chronic inflammatory or infectious diseases, including rheumatoid arthritis and tuberculosis. The reason such diseases cause amyloidosis remains unknown.
• Some forms of amyloidosis are inherited.
• Long-term hemodialysis therapy may lead to amyloidosis.
• Risk increases with age.

PREVENTION

• There are no known ways to prevent most forms of amyloidosis.
• Effective treatment of infections such as tuberculosis can prevent chronic inflammation that causes secondary amyloidosis.

DIAGNOSIS

• Patient history and physical examination are necessary.
• Urine protein levels are measured.
• Biopsy (removal of a tissue sample for microscopic examination) of subcutaneous abdominal fat, rectum, lip, or a suspected site of amyloid accumulation is needed to confirm diagnosis.

HOW TO TREAT IT

• No specific treatment exists for amyloidosis, although certain medications are being used experimentally.
• The underlying disorder is treated in cases of secondary amyloidosis.
• Pain relievers and other drugs may be prescribed to reduce discomfort.
• Kidney transplant may be needed for patients with renal failure.

WHEN TO CALL A DOCTOR

• Amyloidosis can manifest itself in a myriad of ways; see a doctor for any unusual, persistent symptoms, especially serious ones such as breathing difficulty, decreased urine output, heart palpitations, or swelling in the ankles or elsewhere in the body.

Amyotrophic Lateral Sclerosis

WHAT IS IT?
• Amyotrophic lateral sclerosis (ALS), also known as Lou Gehrig's disease, is a slowly progressive degeneration of the nerve cells of the spinal cord and lower brain stem, resulting in gradual loss of voluntary muscle control. (Sensory nerves and mental function are unaffected.) The disease is eventually fatal as muscles governing breathing, swallowing, or other crucial body functions are affected. Patients live an average of three years after the onset of symptoms; most die from respiratory insufficiency or from lung infections that tend to occur when breathing is impaired for long periods of time. ALS generally strikes between the ages of 50 and 70, and affects men slightly more often than women.

WHAT CAUSES IT?
• The cause of ALS is unknown; however, about 10 percent of cases appear to be inherited.
• Incidence is highest among those whose occupations demand strenuous physical labor.
• Viral infections and physical trauma or exhaustion can accelerate deterioration in those already suffering from ALS.

SYMPTOMS
• Slow but relentlessly progressive muscle weakness and wasting (atrophy) in the limbs, trunk, breathing muscles, throat, and tongue. Weakness usually begins in the limbs.
• Muscle twitching, cramps, stiffness, and easy fatigability.
• Slowed, progressively unintelligible speech.
• Difficulty breathing and swallowing; choking.
• Weight loss, due to both atrophy and swallowing difficulty.
• Sudden involuntary bursts of laughter or crying.
• Changes in gait, progressing to inability to walk.

PREVENTION
• There is no known way to prevent ALS.

DIAGNOSIS
• There are no specific tests to confirm the diagnosis; patient history and physical examination are necessary. Diagnosis is based on clinical manifestations of the disease.
• Special neurological tests or MRI (magnetic resonance imaging) scans may be performed to rule out other possible causes of symptoms.

HOW TO TREAT IT
• There is no cure or specific treatment for ALS; therapy is aimed at making the patient as comfortable as possible.
• Mechanical aids, such as special utensils for eating, are available to facilitate various tasks.
• A cane or walker may be helpful for patients with gait impairment.
• Patients should carefully consider the option of using a mechanical respirator in the event that they become unable to breathe unassisted. Artificial ventilation can help some patients survive for years; however, many patients choose not to be kept alive in a state of total paralysis, unable to communicate except with eye movements. It is important to discuss this issue with doctors and family early on, so that decisions about emergency resuscitation may be made in the event of a respiratory crisis.
• Emotional support is crucial. Beyond the help that friends and family provide, a qualified counselor or psychotherapist can be a valuable asset. For assistance, contact the ALS Society of America (818-340-7500).

WHEN TO CALL A DOCTOR
• See your doctor at the earliest signs of unexplained muscle weakness or difficulty controlling movement, particularly if speaking, breathing, or swallowing seems to be affected.

Anal Fissures

WHAT IS IT?

• An anal fissure is a shallow ulceration or tear in the tissue along the anal canal. During bowel movements, irritation of the fissure can trigger a spasm in the anal sphincter, the muscle that surrounds the opening of the anus. Such spasms are often quite painful and may be accompanied by bleeding. This condition is more common among women.

SYMPTOMS

• Sharp rectal pain during and immediately after bowel movements, especially when the stool is hard or bulky.
• Bright red blood in stool or bloody streaks on toilet paper or underwear.
• Rectal itching.

WHAT CAUSES IT?

• Anal fissures are typically caused when large, hard stools tear the lining of the anal canal as they pass.
• Fissures may also occur as a secondary complication to anal surgery, proctitis (inflammation of the rectum), or other disorders.
• The risk of anal fissures increases with constipation, multiple pregnancies, and the use of rectal thermometers or enema nozzles. Also, older people may be more likely to develop anal fissures, owing to age-related changes in the skin as well as increased frequency of constipation.

PREVENTION

• Eat a high-fiber diet that includes lots of fresh fruits and legumes and whole-grain products.
• Drink plenty of liquids (at least eight glasses of water per day) to soften the feces and prevent constipation.
• Avoid straining during bowel movements.

DIAGNOSIS

• Patient history and physical exam are necessary.
• Examination with an anoscope or sigmoidoscope are required to rule out other causes of rectal bleeding.

HOW TO TREAT IT

• Most anal fissures heal naturally within a few days (although spasms of the sphincter may aggravate the condition and delay healing).
• A warm sitz bath after a difficult bowel movement may ease painful spasms of the anal sphincter. Apply a nonprescription topical cream, such as zinc oxide, after a sitz bath.
• Stool softeners may be advised; check with your doctor.
• Persistent or recurrent anal fissures may require surgical removal of the fissure or anal dilatation, a procedure to enlarge the anus. After such surgery, healing is usually rapid and the prospect of full recovery is very good.

WHEN TO CALL A DOCTOR

• If symptoms of an anal fissure persist, contact your doctor.
• Blood in the stool may be a warning sign of a more serious condition: a doctor's evaluation is warranted.

Anaphylaxis

WHAT IS IT?

Anaphylaxis is a severe, life-threatening allergic reaction that affects organ systems throughout the body. It occurs when the immune system becomes sensitized to an allergen (be it a food, drug, insect venom, or anything that elicits an allergic response) and then, upon exposure to the allergen, overreacts, releasing cascades of histamines and other substances that can cause contraction of the intestinal smooth muscles, skin reactions, constriction of the airways, and a precipitous drop in blood pressure that may lead to shock. Immediate medical attention is essential; severe cases may prove fatal even with treatment.

SYMPTOMS
- Itching and hives.
- Swelling of the eyes, lips, and tongue.
- Weakness or faintness.
- Tightening in the chest or throat; wheezing; shortness of breath.
- Profuse sweating.
- Palpitations.
- Sudden, intense distress; feelings of impending doom.
- Stomach cramps, nausea, vomiting, or diarrhea.
- Bluish tinge (cyanosis) to the skin, lips, and nail beds due to oxygen insufficiency.

WHAT CAUSES IT?
- Ingestion of a food or food additive.
- An insect bite.
- Injection of a drug, vaccine, or a chemical used in a diagnostic procedure. Penicillin is the most common cause of anaphylaxis.
- Previous severe allergic reactions are a risk factor for anaphylaxis, since the immune system tends to react with greater virulence with each successive exposure to an allergen to which it has become sensitized.

PREVENTION
- Avoid allergens that have caused an adverse reaction in the past.

- Those who have previously had a severe allergic reaction should wear a Medic-Alert bracelet and get a prescription for an emergency kit containing a syringe of epinephrine (adrenaline), which halts the allergic reaction. The kit should be carried at all times. Also available (and easier to use) is the Epi-pen, a spring-loaded device that automatically injects a dose of epinephrine when pressed against the skin (usually the leg). Such measures do not substitute for necessary medical treatment but do buy valuable time until help can be found.

DIAGNOSIS
- Diagnosis is indicated by sudden onset of characteristic symptoms, particularly when they appear following exposure to a suspected allergen. Since anaphylaxis is an emergency, immediate treatment supersedes the need for further confirmatory procedures. Tests for the specific allergen may be done after the patient has stabilized.

HOW TO TREAT IT
- Immediate medical treatment is necessary. An injection of the adrenal hormone epinephrine (adrenaline) is necessary to counteract the effect of histamines throughout the body. Doses may need to be repeated every 20 minutes until the reaction ceases.
- Inhalation of beta-sympathomimetic agents and intravenous aminophylline are used to halt asthmatic symptoms.
- If life-threatening breathing obstruction has occurred due to swelling of the larynx, a tube may be placed through the mouth or nose to aid in breathing; in very serious cases a tracheostomy (insertion of a breathing tube through a surgical opening in the throat) may be needed.
- Intravenous fluids are administered if shock occurs.
- Antihistamines (such as nonprescription diphenhydramine) may be used after the initial crisis has passed to ease symptoms of swelling, hives, and itching.

WHEN TO CALL A DOCTOR
- **EMERGENCY** An anaphylactic reaction requires immediate medical attention. Call an ambulance or get to an emergency room right away.

Anemia, Aplastic

WHAT IS IT?

Aplastic anemia occurs when the bone marrow fails to produce an adequate supply of all varieties of blood cells. The onset is usually gradual but may be sudden (acute). Low levels of red blood cells result in weakness, fatigue, pallor, and shortness of breath. Lack of white blood cells leaves the patient vulnerable to serious infection, while an inadequate amount of platelets increases the risk of uncontrolled bleeding. For these reasons, aplastic anemia is potentially life-threatening. In fact, severe aplastic anemia is fatal in more that 70 percent of patients. Recovery is most likely when the anemia is caused by an anticancer drug or other medication. Even then, recovery may take six to eight months. This relatively rare disorder is more common among men and often strikes people in their thirties.

WHAT CAUSES IT?

- About half of all cases are due to external causes including toxic agents (arsenic, benzene, various solvents, and other industrial chemicals), certain drugs (such as immunosuppressive and anticancer drugs), and exposure to radiation.
- Severe diseases such as hepatitis or the early stages of leukemia may cause aplastic anemia.
- Risk is increased among those with a family history of aplastic anemia or those who have had a recent severe illness.

SYMPTOMS
- Increased susceptibility to infections.
- Ulcers in the mouth, throat, and rectum.
- Unusual bruising or bleeding (including spontaneous unexplained bleeding from the nose, mouth, gums, rectum, or vagina).
- Small red dots (petechiae) under the skin, indicating bleeding.
- Pallor.
- Weakness, fatigue, and breathlessness.

PREVENTION

- There is no known way to prevent aplastic anemia, except by avoiding exposure to toxic chemicals, radiation, and drugs that have caused previous bouts of the disorder.

DIAGNOSIS

- Blood tests are needed to confirm the diagnosis.
- A bone marrow biopsy may be done to determine the cause of aplastic anemia.

HOW TO TREAT IT

- A doctor may order transfusions of whole blood or specific cell types (platelets or white cells, for example) until the bone marrow begins to function properly again.
- The patient should eliminate exposure to an identifiable cause of aplastic anemia. If a prescription drug is the suspected cause, a safer substitute may be available.
- Antibiotics are typically given (often intravenously) to ward off infection.
- Medications are available to treat aplastic anemia, but they are successful in only a small percentage of patients.
- Because of the risk of serious bleeding, the patient should avoid cuts and scratches. To this end, using items such as electric razors and soft toothbrushes is advised.
- Medicated mouthwash or diluted hydrogen peroxide is often used to ward off infections that originate in the mouth.
- A bone marrow transplant is the treatment of choice in people under 50 with severe cases, provided a compatible donor can be found. (A twin or other sibling is usually the best choice.) Immunosuppressive drugs are necessary to prevent rejection if a bone marrow transplant is performed.

WHEN TO CALL A DOCTOR

- The symptoms of aplastic anemia warrant a doctor's prompt attention.

Anemia, Folic Acid Deficiency

WHAT IS IT?

Folic acid deficiency causes anemia since folic acid is an essential vitamin for the production of red blood cells. A reduced number of red cells deprives body tissues of an adequate supply of oxygen, resulting in the classic symptoms of anemia (see below). The disorder is particularly common among infants, adolescents during a growth spurt, pregnant or lactating women, the elderly, smokers, alcoholics, and those on fad diets or who suffer from intestinal disorders. It is often accompanied by iron deficiency anemia.

WHAT CAUSES IT?

• Folic acid deficiency is due to either insufficient dietary intake of folic acid or an inability of the intestine to absorb folic acid properly (which is rarer and often harder to treat).
• Alcoholism interferes with the body's ability to absorb and use folic acid, and many alcoholics also have poor diets.
• Smoking depletes essential B vitamins including folic acid.
• Intestinal disorders, such as tropical sprue, celiac disease, or bowel resection, may impede folic acid absorption.
• Overcooking foods destroys their folic acid content.
• The body cannot store folic acid, and at certain times in the lifecycle (such as infancy, adolescence, and pregnancy) the body's demands for it outweigh dietary intake.
• Certain medications (such as anticonvulsants and anticancer drugs) can lead to folic acid deficiency.
• Parasites and certain bacteria within the intestine may compete with their hosts for folic acid.
• Risk of folic acid deficiency increases in association with certain skin diseases, including psoriasis, acne rosacea, and eczema.

PREVENTION

• Eat a balanced, sensible diet. Main sources of folic acid include meat, poultry, cheese, milk, eggs, liver, fresh green leafy vegetables, raw fruits, mushrooms, lima and kidney beans, and yeast.
• Avoid overcooking foods.
• Consume alcohol only in moderation.
• Don't smoke.

DIAGNOSIS

• Blood tests are necessary, including one test that requires injections of folic acid to determine if there is a true deficiency of the vitamin or if the body is having difficulty absorbing it.

HOW TO TREAT IT

• Proper diet is frequently all that's required to correct the problem.
• Folic acid tablets cure the anemia quickly. If intestinal disorders impede folic acid absorption, a supplement may be needed for a time; in rare instances, injections of folic acid are necessary.
• Elimination of causative factors (smoking and excessive drinking, for example) is essential.
• Treatment of an underlying intestinal disorder causing folic acid deficiency may serve as a cure.

WHEN TO CALL A DOCTOR

• Contact your doctor if you have anemia symptoms.
• If you're already being treated for folic acid deficiency and symptoms don't improve after two weeks, notify your doctor.
• All women who are considering pregnancy should discuss folic acid supplementation with their doctors. Increasing evidence indicates that such supplementation during the early weeks of pregnancy may decrease the incidence of neural defects in the fetus, as well as protect against cervical cancer in the mother.

SYMPTOMS

• Severe fatigue and weakness.
• Pallor.
• Shortness of breath.
• Heart palpitations or noticeably rapid heartbeat upon exertion.
• Sore, red, and glazed-looking tongue.
• Loss of appetite leading to weight loss.
• Abdominal distention.
• Nausea and diarrhea.

Anemia, Hemolytic

WHAT IS IT?

Hemolytic anemia occurs when red blood cells are destroyed prematurely and the bone marrow cannot produce new red cells fast enough to compensate for the loss (despite the fact that marrow is capable of producing red cells at up to six times the normal rate). The disorder is rarely life-threatening but may be difficult to treat.

WHAT CAUSES IT?

• Hemolytic anemia is either inherited or acquired. Inherited cases are due to a genetic abnormality in the red blood cells themselves, and anemia generally appears early in life. Hereditary forms include sickle cell anemia, thalassemia, and spherocytosis (a condition in which the red cells are spherical instead of the normal doughnutshape).

SYMPTOMS

• Fatigue and weakness.
• Pallor.
• Shortness of breath.
• Palpitations or other heartbeat irregularities.
• Jaundice and dark urine (caused by excessive formation of the bile pigment, bilirubin) as red cells are destroyed.

• In people with an inherited deficiency of the enzyme glucose-6-phosphate dehydrogenase (G6PD), certain medications may trigger hemolytic anemia. Such drugs include methyldopa (used in the treatment of hypertension), antibiotics, and anti-malarial drugs.
• Hemolytic anemia in one form of G6PD deficiency, common in the Greek isles, results from the ingestion of fava beans (or inhalation of pollen from the plant).
• Certain infectious diseases (like malaria) destroy red blood cells.
• Antibodies produced to battle infections may mistakenly attack red blood cells. Such an autoimmune disorder may be triggered by a blood transfusion with an incompatible blood type.
• Abnormalities in the lining of the blood vessels, artificial heart valves, or blood clots may cause mechanical damage that destroys red blood cells.

PREVENTION

• When hemolytic anemia is provoked by specific substances, avoiding them can prevent recurrence.

DIAGNOSIS

• Blood tests, including a complete blood count, are necessary.
• Bone marrow biopsies may be performed.
• A radioactive chromium test may be performed to assess red blood cell survival.

HOW TO TREAT IT

• Immunosuppressant drugs may be useful in cases where hemolytic anemia is caused by an auto-immune disorder.
• Corticosteroid drugs (such as prednisone) may help to prevent blood cell destruction.
• Anemia due to hereditary spherocytosis can be greatly improved by removal of the spleen (splenectomy), as the spleen is the primary site of red-blood-cell destruction.
• Blood transfusions are sometimes required as emergency treatment.

WHEN TO CALL A DOCTOR

• Anemia symptoms warrant a call to your doctor.

Anemia, Iron Deficiency

WHAT IS IT?

Iron deficiency anemia occurs when the body's usual stores of iron are so depleted that the bone marrow cannot produce enough hemoglobin, the iron-containing protein in red blood cells that carries oxygen in the bloodstream. Iron deficiency is the most common cause of anemia, is rarely serious, and is easily treated in most cases. In fact, in mild chronic cases, it often produces little or no symptoms and is generally discovered only when a doctor obtains a complete blood count (CBC). Of course, more severe anemia gradually leads to noticeable fatigue and other symptoms.

The shape of the red blood cell affords optimum surface area for the transport of oxygen molecules. All of the various types of anemia are characterized by a deficiency of healthy red blood cells.

SYMPTOMS
- Fatigue and weakness.
- Pallor (may be especially noticeable in the gums, eyelids, and nailbeds).
- Heart palpitations, rapid heartbeat, or breathing difficulty, especially upon exertion.
- Irritability or inability to concentrate.
- Smooth, sore tongue or tiny cracks at the corners of the mouth.
- Brittle nails.
- Black, tarry (or even bloody) stools (when anemia is due to substantial blood loss in the gastrointestinal tract).
- Unusual cravings (called pica) for clay, dirt, or ice.

WHAT CAUSES IT?

The most common cause of iron deficiency anemia is gradual, prolonged blood loss. For this reason, menstruating women are particularly prone to anemia. In men, the most common cause of iron deficiency is blood loss in the digestive tract, resulting from disorders such as peptic ulcers, diverticulitis, and stomach or colon cancer. Sometimes hemorrhoids bleed enough to result in anemia.
- Long-term use of aspirin (for heart attack prevention) or nonsteroidal anti-inflammatory drugs (such as ibuprofen and naproxen sodium, used for pain

relief) can irritate the lining of the stomach and cause bleeding, resulting in anemia.
- An uncommon cause of iron deficiency is a poor diet—specifically, one that lacks iron-rich foods such as shellfish, liver, meat, fish, poultry, beans, green leafy vegetables, potatoes, and rice.
- Poor absorption of iron may result from surgical removal of the stomach (gastrectomy) or from intestinal disorders that cause chronic diarrhea.

PREVENTION
- Eat a balanced, sensible diet.
- Pregnant and menstruating women should discuss iron supplementation with their doctors.
- If you must regularly take aspirin or nonsteroidal anti-inflammatory drugs, take them with food or an antacid (one containing magnesium and aluminum hydroxide is best).

DIAGNOSIS
- Blood tests are necessary
- X-rays of the gastrointestinal tract may be taken.

HOW TO TREAT IT
- First, it is essential for a doctor to determine the underlying cause of an iron deficiency, and each case

Anemia, Iron Deficiency *continued*

is treated based on the doctor's conclusions. Do not attempt to treat anemia yourself.

• If poor diet is the underlying cause, dietary changes are in order. Foods rich in iron include shellfish, liver, meat, fish, poultry, beans, green leafy vegetables, potatoes, and rice.

• Iron supplementation may be required—but only under a doctor's supervision. Taking too many iron supplements can lead to excessive storage of iron and serious health problems, including liver damage, arthritis, a rare type of diabetes, and heart failure. Also, if you are losing blood due to a disease such as colon cancer, supplements might mask the problem and delay the diagnosis.

• If iron supplements are prescribed, be sure to take them for the full term recommended by your doctor, even if you feel perfectly well again. After the anemia is cured, your body needs to replenish its reserve stores of iron, which may take three months or more.

• Iron absorption is enhanced by ascorbic acid (vitamin C) and decreased by milk and antacids.

• In very rare and severe cases anemia is treated with a transfusion of packed red blood cells.

WHEN TO CALL A DOCTOR

• Call your doctor if you experience the symptoms of anemia. Sometimes iron-deficiency anemia is an indication of a more serious underlying disorder, such as peptic ulcer or colon cancer. Certain tests may be needed to confirm or rule out such a possible diagnosis.

• Women who are pregnant or menstruate heavily should contact their doctors to discuss iron supplementation.

• Strict vegetarians and those on rapid weight loss programs should discuss their dietary needs for iron and other nutrients with a doctor or a qualified nutritionist.

Anemia, Pernicious

WHAT IS IT?

Pernicious anemia is a rare type of anemia (an inadequate number of red blood cells) that results from an insufficiency of vitamin B_{12} (cobalamin), an essential component in the manufacture of red blood cells. A dietary deficiency of B_{12} is very rare; rather, pernicious anemia usually occurs because the body cannot properly absorb the vitamin. The disorder, which comes on and progresses subtly, may at first produce the characteristic symptoms of anemia: weakness, fatigue, and pallor. Untreated, the disease may cause disturbances in the gastrointestinal and cardiovascular systems and especially the nervous system, since B_{12} is essential for proper nerve function. With treatment, prognosis is excellent, although any neurologic damage is usually permanent. Pernicious anemia most often affects those of northern European or African descent; incidence is highest in those over 60.

SYMPTOMS

- Fatigue and weakness.
- Lightheadedness or dizziness.
- Pallor (may be especially noticeable in the lips, gums, eyelids, and nail beds).
- Heart palpitations.
- Shortness of breath or chest pain on exertion.
- Sore, red, and glazed-looking tongue.
- Irritability or inability to concentrate.
- Mild jaundice of the eyes or skin.
- Ringing in the ears (tinnitus).
- Loss of appetite leading to weight loss.
- Nausea and diarrhea.
- Neurologic symptoms in advanced cases: numbness and tingling in the extremities; poor coordination; cognitive disturbances ranging from forgetfulness to dementia or psychosis.

WHAT CAUSES IT?

- Pernicious anemia almost always results from an impaired ability to absorb vitamin B_{12}. This occurs when cells in the lining of the stomach atrophy (probably as a result of an autoimmune reaction) and fail to produce normal amounts of digestive acids and a substance known as intrinsic factor, which is essential for the absorption of B_{12}.
- Incidence of pernicious anemia is higher in those with a history of other apparent autoimmune disorders, such as Graves' disease, vitiligo, and hypoparathyroidism.
- Risk increases with age.
- Partial or total surgical resection of the stomach or damage to the lining of the stomach (following ingestion of corrosive chemicals, for example) may prevent secretion of intrinsic factor.
- Disorders of the small intestine can interfere with B_{12} absorption and cause pernicious anemia.
- Rarely, a dietary lack of B_{12} causes the disorder.

PREVENTION

- There is no way to prevent pernicious anemia, except in the rare cases caused by a dietary B_{12} deficiency, which may affect strict vegetarians who avoid meat and dairy products entirely. Such people should take vitamin supplements to prevent pernicious anemia.

DIAGNOSIS

- Patient history and physical examination.
- Blood tests to measure levels of B_{12} and the number of red blood cells, as well as the size of red cells and the appearance of white cells.
- A Schilling test (using radioactive cobalamin to accurately measure the amount being absorbed into the bloodstream).

HOW TO TREAT IT

- Lifelong intramuscular injections of cobalamin (usually self-administered once a month) are necessary. Oral B_{12} is generally not used, since the problem lies in the body's inability to absorb the vitamin. However, massive oral doses of B_{12} are effective when injections are not feasible.
- Those with very severe anemia may need an initial blood transfusion.
- Pernicious anemia is associated with an increased risk of stomach cancer, so lifelong cancer screening is recommended.

WHEN TO CALL A DOCTOR

- Consult your doctor if you experience persistent fatigue, weakness, or pallor.

Ankylosing Spondylitis

WHAT IS IT?

Ankylosing spondylitis (AS) is an uncommon type of inflammatory arthritis that primarily affects the joints of the spinal column. Typically, AS originates in the sacroiliac joints, where the vertebrae of the spine meet the pelvis. The disease tends to progress from the lower back up to the vertebrae in the neck. (Peripheral joints are involved too in as many as 30 percent of cases, especially among women.) Cartilage and other tissue between the joints gradually deteriorate and are replaced by hard, fibrous tissue. Eventually the bones fuse together and joint flexibility is lost. Symptoms—primarily lower back pain and stiffness—often first appear in late adolescence or early adulthood; onset after age 40 is very rare. Early onset of the disease is associated with a worse prognosis. The most serious complication is spinal fracture that can result in quadriplegia; however, most patients suffer no serious disability despite the pain and are able to continue working. The disease may get progressively worse, stabilize, or go into remission at any point. About 20 percent of AS patients are affected by inflammation and scarring of structures within the eye (see Uveitis and Iritis), and a few patients may develop an abnormality of the aortic valve in the heart, or scarring of lung tissue. Ankylosing spondylitis is more common among Caucasians and is three times more prevalent in men than women.

SYMPTOMS
- Lower back pain that may be intermittent or persistent. Pain may be worse at night.
- Morning stiffness in the back or hips that improves with activity.
- Limited chest capacity due to pain and stiffness in the ribs.
- Neck or chest pain.
- Fatigue.
- Weight loss and poor appetite.
- Fever.
- Eye pain, blurred vision, watery eyes, and aversion to light (due to associated uveitis).
- Pain in the peripheral joints.

WHAT CAUSES IT?
- The cause of AS is unknown; hereditary factors appear to play a role. It is likely that autoimmune activity (where the body's defenses against disease attack healthy tissue) is involved in the mechanism of joint deterioration.

PREVENTION
- There is no known way to prevent AS.

DIAGNOSIS
- No definitive tests exist to distinguish AS from similar inflammatory diseases. Diagnosis is primarily based on patient history, physical examination, and x-ray findings.
- Blood tests may detect a specific antigen (HLA-B27) that, for unknown reasons, is highly correlated with the incidence of AS. The presence of this antigen does not confirm the diagnosis but does suggest a genetic predisposition to the disease.
- X-rays may reveal signs of joint deterioration in the spine, pelvis, or hips.

HOW TO TREAT IT
- There is no specific way to treat AS; therapy is aimed at relieving discomfort and maintaining joint function.
- Nonsteroidal anti-inflammatory drugs (NSAIDs), especially indomethacin, are commonly prescribed to ease pain and inflammation.
- Strength-training exercises and other forms of physical therapy may help improve flexibility.
- Braces and light-weight supports may help stave off deformity and maintain good posture.
- Occasionally, direct injections of corticosteroids may be beneficial in patients unresponsive to NSAIDs.
- Severe arthritis in the hips may warrant total hip replacement surgery (arthroplasty).
- If uveitis occurs, it can be treated with corticosteroids and medicated eyedrops.

WHEN TO CALL A DOCTOR
- Make an appointment with a doctor for any persistent back pain.

Anxiety States

WHAT IS IT?

Anxiety—as it provokes the primal "fight or flight" impulse—is a natural, often beneficial, reaction to stress or danger. However, a state of anxiety is unhealthy when it becomes excessive or unreasonable, persists in the absence of an obvious stressful situation, or interferes with normal daily functioning. Anxiety states may occur acutely, as in panic disorder, which is marked by repeated episodes of sudden, intense, and unwarranted bouts of terror. Panic attacks are accompanied by dread and fear of dying; symptoms are often mistaken for a heart attack. People with recurrent panic attacks often develop agoraphobia (fear of crowds, leading to a hesitancy to leave the house).

Chronic anxiety states, such as generalized anxiety disorder (GAD), a milder but persistent problem, can endure for months or years. Other chronic anxiety states include posttraumatic stress disorder—long-term psychological distress following a traumatic event such as a natural catastrophe, warfare, rape, child abuse, or surviving a plane or car crash. Obsessive-compulsive disorder is marked by unremitting disabling thoughts, such as harming a family member, or irrational behaviors or rituals, such as constant handwashing or repeatedly checking to see if a door is locked. Phobias—such as fear of being in a confined space (claustrophobia) or driving across a bridge—are marked by unreasonable fears. Anxiety states are exceedingly common (with a higher incidence in women) and are also among the most successfully treatable of all mental disorders. Untreated, those with anxiety disorders are at increased risk for hypertension, drug and alcohol abuse, and suicide.

WHAT CAUSES IT?

• The reason some people manage to cope with the stresses of life while others suffer debilitating anxiety is unclear. A genetic or biochemical predisposition appears to be part of the explanation, but certainly early childhood experiences and pivotal life events play a role.
• Various drugs or chemical substances can trigger anxiety. These include excessive doses of caffeine, high doses of nonprescription decongestants and cold remedies, thyroid hormone, and inhaled asthma drugs. Anxiety also accompanies withdrawal from caffeine, alcohol, tobacco, sedatives, narcotics, and other addictive drugs.

PREVENTION

• It is difficult to predict if and when a person will experience an anxiety state. Those who have suffered them in the past may prevent future ones by receiving proper therapy and counseling.

DIAGNOSIS

• A thorough patient history establishes a diagnosis.
• Certain tests, such as blood tests and CT (computed tomography) scans may be done to rule out an underlying cause of anxiety, such as hyperthyroidism.

HOW TO TREAT IT

• Psychotherapy is an important part of the treatment of any mental illness; results are often enhanced by drug therapy.

SYMPTOMS

• Heightened self-awareness and alertness to surroundings (hypervigilance).
• Intense worry and feelings of dread.
• Impaired concentration; fleeting attention.
• Restlessness and irritability.
• Insomnia.
• Profuse sweating.
• Muscle tension and trembling.
• Rapid, shallow breathing (hyperventilation) or breathlessness.
• Palpitations or chest pains.
• Dilated pupils.
• Dry mouth and a feeling of a lump in the throat.
• Hot flashes.
• Excessive fatigue or weakness.
• Fear of leaving the house (agoraphobia).
• Persistent maladaptive thoughts or behaviors (obsessive-compulsive disorder).
• Nightmares and upsetting flashbacks (posttraumatic stress disorder).

Anxiety States *continued*

• Short-term therapy with benzodiazepine tranquilizers (like alprazolam and diazepam) is the primary component of treatment for milder types of anxiety, such as GAD. These drugs carry the risk of abuse, and long-term use can lead to dependence, accompanied by withdrawal symptoms when the medication is discontinued.

• The tricyclic antidepressants (such as amitriptyline, desipramine, and doxepin) are effective for panic disorder and posttraumatic stress.

• New drugs known as serotonin reuptake inhibitors (which affect the action of neurotransmitter chemicals in the brain) are helpful against obsessive-compulsive disorder.

• Many patients benefit from learning relaxation techniques such as biofeedback, self-hypnosis, meditation, and yoga.

WHEN TO CALL A DOCTOR

• Consult a physician or psychotherapist if fears, anxieties, or panic attacks interfere with your normal quality of life.

Aortic Aneurysm

WHAT IS IT?

An aortic aneurysm is a weak spot in the wall of the aorta, the primary artery that carries blood from the heart to the head and extremities. There are three common types of aortic aneurysm. Saccular and fusiform aneurysms are balloonlike swellings of the arterial wall that can occur in the portion of the aorta within the chest or, more commonly, just below the kidney in the abdomen. A dissecting aneurysm is a longitudinal, blood-filled split in the lining of the artery, usually occurring in the aortic arch near the heart. As blood is pumped through the aorta, the weak spot in the elastic arterial wall bulges outward. The risk is that the aneurysm will eventually rupture, with great bleeding internally and complete collapse of circulation. Sudden severe pain, shock, and loss of consciousness usually occur within seconds, and death is imminent in more than 50 percent of cases, even with emergency surgery. Thus, the goal is to detect and treat an aortic aneurysm before it ruptures. Aortic aneurysms generally affect people over 60 and are more common among men.

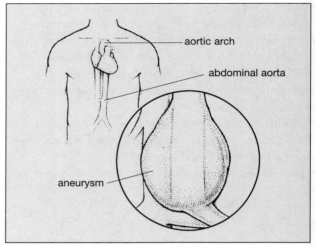

aortic arch

abdominal aorta

aneurysm

Just above the heart, the aorta branches upward to carry blood to the head and also arches downward to supply the lower extremities. An aneurysm may balloon outward anywhere along the aortic wall, but they are more common in the abdominal aorta.

SYMPTOMS

- In the majority of cases there are no warning symptoms. More likely, an aortic aneurysm is detected with an x-ray or during a routine physical examination.
- Hoarseness, difficulty in swallowing, or persistent cough may indicate a saccular or fusiform aneurysm in the chest area.
- A throbbing lump in the abdominal area, severe backache, leg pain or a feeling of coldness in the leg (due to an embolus from a clot formed in an abdominal aneurysm), or severe abdominal pain (due to the rupture of an abdominal aneurysm) may indicate a saccular or fusiform aneurysm in the abdominal area.
- Severe chest pain that may be mistaken for a heart attack may signal a dissecting aneurysm.

WHAT CAUSES IT?

- Approximately 95 percent of aortic aneurysms are caused by atherosclerosis, the narrowing of an artery due to the buildup of fatty plaque.
- The muscular middle layer of the artery may be congenitally weak and thus prone to a dissecting aneurysm.
- High blood pressure (hypertension) intensifies the force of blood on the walls of the arteries and contributes to the development of dissecting aneurysms.
- Syphilis may cause a saccular or fusiform aneurysm near the heart (now rare).
- The arterial wall may also be weakened as a result of trauma or complication of other diseases, possibly leading to saccular or fusiform aneurysms.

PREVENTION

- Eat a diet low in cholesterol and saturated fats to reduce the risk of atherosclerosis.
- Take steps to prevent, detect, or treat high blood pressure.

DIAGNOSIS

- Physical examination of your abdomen by the doctor may reveal a pulsing aneurysm.
- X-rays, CT scans, or ultrasound imaging may confirm the presence of an aneurysm.

Aortic Aneurysm *continued*

• Angiography (an injection of an opaque dye into an artery to produce a clear x-ray image of the aorta) may be performed.

HOW TO TREAT IT

• Have regular physical exams to detect an aortic aneurysm before it has a chance to rupture. Your doctor may recommend x-rays and angiography to determine the size and location of an aneurysm if one is suspected.
• If an aneurysm is detected, your doctor may recommend watching and waiting (especially if it is small), since aneurysms tend to grow very slowly.
• Periodic ultrasound examinations are used to follow the expansion of an aneurysm over time.

• Certain aneurysms require immediate treatment, often involving surgical removal of the affected portion of the artery and replacement with a synthetic arterial graft. Surgery may also be required if an aneurysm is causing pain, is larger than six centimeters, or is rapidly expanding. Surgery on an unruptured aneurysm has an 80 to 90 percent success rate.

WHEN TO CALL A DOCTOR

• Call a doctor if you experience symptoms of an aortic aneurysm.
• See your doctor regularly if you suffer from high blood pressure or high cholesterol, each a major risk factor for the different types of aneurysm.

Appendicitis, Acute

WHAT IS IT?

Acute appendicitis is inflammation of the appendix, the narrow, finger-shaped organ that branches off the first part of the large intestine on the right side of the abdomen. Although the appendix is a vestigial organ with no known function, it can become diseased. In fact, acute appendicitis is the most common reason for abdominal surgery in the world. If it is not treated promptly, there is the chance that the inflamed appendix will burst, spilling fecal material into the abdominal cavity. The usual result is a potentially life-threatening infection (peritonitis), but

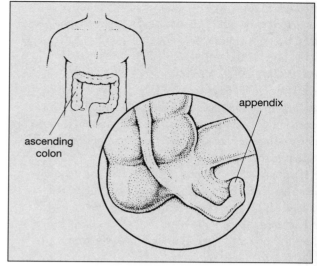

The appendix, about 3.5 inches long, extends from the bottom of the first or ascending portion of the colon. It serves no known function.

SYMPTOMS

- In very young children or people over 65, symptoms may be deceptively mild. Otherwise, symptoms can vary widely and may include the following:
- Vague discomfort near the navel (early in an attack), migrating throughout the right lower quadrant of the abdomen.
- Sharp, localized, persistent pain within a few hours.
- Pain that worsens with movement, deep breathing, coughing, sneezing, walking or being touched.
- In some people there may be little abdominal pain but severe pain upon rectal examination.
- Abdominal rigidity.
- Constipation and inability to pass gas, possibly alternating with diarrhea.
- Low fever (below 102°F). A high fever (possibly accompanied by chills) may indicate an abscessed appendix.
- Rapid heartbeat.
- Abdominal swelling (in late stages).
- Abrupt cessation of abdominal pain after other symptoms occur, indicating the appendix has burst—an emergency.
- Nausea and vomiting (in some cases).
- Loss of appetite.
- Coated tongue and bad breath.
- Painful urination.
- Blood in the urine.

the infection may become sealed off and form an abscess. Appendicitis is uncommon among older people, and symptoms are generally mild, so that diagnosis of the acute episode is often not made. Members of this age group are thus at greater risk for rupture with peritonitis or abscess formation.

WHAT CAUSES IT?

- Appendicitis is usually caused by a bacterial infection, although the reason the appendix becomes infected is unknown.
- The appendix may become obstructed by a lump of feces or pinworms, leading to inflammation and infection.

PREVENTION

- There are no specific preventive measures. Contrary to popular belief, swallowing seeds from fruit does not precipitate appendicitis.

DIAGNOSIS

- Physical examination is necessary to rule out other disorders that produce symptoms which may mimic those of appendicitis.
- A rectal examination may be performed.
- Blood and urine samples will be taken for analysis.
- An abdominal x-ray may be necessary.

Appendicitis, Acute *continued*

• A small incision in the abdomen (laparotomy) is sometimes required to confirm the diagnosis.

HOW TO TREAT IT
• Call your doctor immediately.
• The appendix must be removed, and surgery should not be delayed more than a few hours.
• If you are unsure of your symptoms, take your temperature every two hours and keep a record for your doctor.
• If you suspect appendicitis, avoid laxatives and enemas (they can cause an inflamed appendix to burst), and pain relievers (they may hinder an accurate diagnosis). Avoid eating or drinking (take small sips of water if you are thirsty), since anesthesia is safer on an empty stomach. Rest in a chair or bed. Do not apply a heating pad to the painful area, as it may cause the appendix to burst.
• If an abscess has formed, your doctor may drain it and prescribe large doses of antibiotics for days or weeks. Appendectomy may be scheduled for a later date.

WHEN TO CALL A DOCTOR
• Call a doctor immediately if you experience symptoms that may indicate appendicitis.

Asthma

WHAT IS IT?

Bronchial asthma is a condition caused by chroni-cally hyperreactive and inflamed airways, punctu-ated by acute episodes of reversible obstruction of the airways. For reasons not fully understood, those suffering from asthma are hyperresponsive to irri-tants such as dust, cold air, and viral infections. Such irritants may periodically cause a broncho-spasm, a contraction of the muscles within the bronchi (the airways between the trachea and the air sacs of the lungs), and provoke increased mucus production. These two reactions further narrow the

---

SYMPTOMS

- Typical symptoms include: sudden breathing difficulty, wheezing, rapid, shallow breathing eased by sitting up, and a sense of suffocation; painless tightness in the chest; coughing, pos-sibly with production of a thick, clear, or yellow sputum (symptoms in young children may in fact mimic those of a viral infection).
- More severe symptoms include: inability to speak more than a few words without gasping for breath; clenched or constricted neck muscles; rapid pulse; sweating; severe anxiety.
- Emergency symptoms include: bluish tinge in the face or lips; extremely labored breathing; mental confusion; profound feeling of exhaustion.

---

already inflamed airways and make it very difficult for the asthma sufferer to breathe. Attacks may be mild or severe and may last anywhere from a few minutes to a few days. Asthma may develop at any age, although 50 percent of children with asthma outgrow the condition as they get older and the bronchial passages widen.

WHAT CAUSES IT?

- While asthma is generally caused by sensitivity to some type of irritant or trigger, no extrinsic trigger can be found in some types of asthma. Irritants include, but are not limited to, pollen, food allergies, dust mites, feathers, animal dander, extremely cold or dry air, molds, smoke, air pollution, bronchitis and other lung infections, some drugs such as aspirin, vigorous exercise, emotional excitement, stress, and other allergic conditions such as eczema or hay fever.
- A predisposition to asthma may be hereditary.

PREVENTION

- Try to identify allergens in home and work envi-ronments, and eliminate them if possible.
- Don't smoke; try to avoid secondary smoke.
- Reduce the amount of dust in your home: vacuum regularly, encase mattresses with plastic to discourage dust-mite infestation, and eliminate carpets that are difficult to clean.
- Avoid foods (such as milk, nuts, chocolates, fish) and medicines (such as aspirin or ibuprofen) that have triggered asthma attacks in the past.
- Drink at least eight glasses of liquid per day to keep mucus secretions loose.
- Each morning, practice deep breathing by inhaling fully, bending over with arms crossed over abdomen, and coughing to loosen accumulated lung secretions.
- Take preventive medications regularly, as prescribed.
- There is no need to avoid exercise; however, your doctor may advise you to take preventive medicines before exercising.

DIAGNOSIS

- Your doctor will conduct a physical examination.
- Allergy skin tests will be performed. A small amount of a suspected allergen will be injected just under the skin. If the area turns red or itchy, or a lump appears, you may be allergic to that substance.
- Chest x-rays will be required.
- Blood samples will be taken.
- Pulmonary-function tests that measure the strength and efficiency of your lungs may be performed.
- Keep a diary of the occurrence and severity of asthma attacks.

HOW TO TREAT IT

- Regularly use an inhaler of prescribed cortico-steroids (anti-inflammatory drugs) to control the underlying inflammation.
- A bronchodilator inhaler should be kept on hand

Asthma *continued*

in the event it is needed to relieve a severe attack. However, it is not recommended for regular use as overreliance on it may be harmful.

• When possible, inhalers should be used with a spacer to help ensure that medicine reaches the lungs, rather than just being absorbed in the back of the throat.

• Your doctor may advise you to use a peak flow meter, a small, handheld device that measures airflow. Your peak airflow will go down hours, and sometimes even a day or two, before an attack, so the meter can serve as an early warning system.

• Corticosteroid pills may be prescribed briefly during severe attacks, which at times may require hospitalization.

• Your doctor may give you desensitizing injections to known irritants (antigens).

WHEN TO CALL A DOCTOR

EMERGENCY Call an ambulance if an attack does not respond after two doses of prescribed inhalant.

• Call a doctor if you notice that the frequency of attacks has increased significantly.

Atelectasis

WHAT IS IT?

Atelectasis is the partial—or sometimes complete—collapse of a lung, due to an obstruction in the small or large bronchial passages. The affected portion of the lung loses its elasticity and thus its ability to function properly. In adults, the other lung or the uncollapsed parts of the affected lung usually compensate for this loss, but in newborns, atelectasis can be fatal. Onset may be sudden or gradual.

WHAT CAUSES IT?

• The accumulation of excess mucus in the airways can create a blockage leading to partial or total collapse of the lung. Such mucus accumulation is most likely to occur in the aftermath of abdominal or chest surgery or the use of general anesthesia, or it may be precipitated by asthma, bronchitis, or other lung infections.
• A foreign body (a peanut or piece of hard candy, for instance) may accidentally be inhaled into the windpipe and obstruct the airway.
• A tumor in the lungs may obstruct an air passage.
• Enlarged lymph glands due to cancer, tuberculosis, or other lung infections may block air passages.
• Chest injury or fractured ribs may result in atelectasis.
• Risk is increased among smokers and people over 65.

PREVENTION

• Don't smoke, especially if you are undergoing surgery within a week.

SYMPTOMS

• With the gradual onset of atelectasis, you may suffer only a cough, mild shortness of breath, and fever.
• If a large part of a lung collapses suddenly, severe symptoms include the following:
• Breathing difficulty.
• Fever, possibly spiking to 102°F or higher.
• Severe hacking cough and chest pain on the affected side.
• Rapid heartbeat.
• Dizziness.
• Blue fingernails and lips.

• Risk of atelectasis increases significantly after general anesthesia for surgery, especially on the chest or abdomen, because coughing or taking a deep breath is painful. To reduce risk after an operation, take deep breaths and try to get up and walk around as soon as possible. Usually a device is prescribed to encourage forceful expiration.
• An inhalant may be temporarily prescribed after surgery to dilate air passages and help keep lungs clear.
• Avoid sedatives and other depressive drugs, including alcohol.
• Drink at least eight glasses of water a day if you have asthma, emphysema, or bronchitis.
• Practice postural drainage—various positions that lower your head below your torso and so drain mucus from your lungs—during bouts of bronchitis or following surgery.

DIAGNOSIS

• Your doctor will give you a physical examination, concentrating on the chest.
• Chest x-rays will be taken.
• Blood samples will be drawn for analysis.

HOW TO TREAT IT

• Treatment is aimed at clearing whatever is causing the blockage. A doctor can apply several techniques to help drain the lungs of excess mucus and clear the blockage. The collapsed lung will reexpand once the obstruction is removed.
• Antibiotics may be prescribed to cure an underlying infection.
• Pain relievers may be used.
• A foreign body or mucus plug can be removed by fiber-optic bronchoscopy (passage of a flexible tube into the lung).
• Surgery may be required to remove a tumor or other obstruction.

WHEN TO CALL A DOCTOR

• **EMERGENCY** Call a doctor or an ambulance if you have severe symptoms of lung collapse or if you notice sudden shortness of breath in a child.
• Call a doctor if you have gradual, progressive difficulty in breathing or a persistent cough.

Barotrauma Barotitis Media

WHAT IS IT?

Barotrauma is damage to the middle ear that occurs when the eustachian tube (the narrow passage between the ear and nose) or a sinus duct has become blocked, and external barometric pressure increases dramatically. The blockage prevents the equalization of pressure between the middle ear and outer ear. Consequently, the higher pressure on the outer ear pushes the eardrum inward. Tiny blood vessels in the middle ear may burst and bleed and, in more severe cases, the eardrum may rupture. Typically, however, barotrauma is easily treated and its effects are temporary.

SYMPTOMS

- Moderate to severe pain in the ear, cheek-bones, or forehead.
- Some degree of temporary hearing loss, usually mild.
- A sensation that the ears are plugged or submerged underwater.
- Dizziness.
- Ringing in the ears (tinnitus).

WHAT CAUSES IT?

- Blockage in the eustachian tube or a sinus duct is usually due to an upper respiratory infection (including the common cold) or an allergy.
- Dramatic changes in atmospheric pressure are most commonly experienced when aboard an airplane that is landing or while scuba diving.

PREVENTION

- Avoid flying or scuba diving when you have an allergy, cold, or throat infection.
- If you must fly, use a nonprescription decongestant spray or antihistamine (such as generic chlorpheniramine or diphenhydramine) an hour before takeoff and an hour before landing.
- Chew gum or suck on hard candy while ascending and descending.
- Take a moderate breath, hold your nose and mouth closed, and gently puff out the cheeks with air to force air into the eustachian tube.
- Infants should be breast- or bottle-fed during descent, since the sucking motion helps equalize air pressure in the ear.

DIAGNOSIS

- Barotrauma may be self-diagnosed.

HOW TO TREAT IT

- Barotrauma usually clears up on its own within a few hours.
- You may take nonprescription decongestants and pain relievers to ease discomfort.
- Use a cotton ball to absorb fluid draining out of the ear.
- Your doctor may prescribe antibiotics to ward off infection of the middle ear.
- Surgery to perforate the eardrum may be required to release fluid trapped inside. The eardrum generally heals completely in about two weeks.

WHEN TO CALL A DOCTOR

- Call a doctor if symptoms of barotrauma persist for more than a few hours.

Basal Cell Carcinoma

WHAT IS IT?

Basal cell carcinoma is by far the most common form of skin cancer in the United States. It is believed to occur when the basal cells at the deepest layer of the epidermis are damaged by ultraviolet radiation and turn cancerous. These cells then rise toward the skin's surface, appearing as a bump or lesion that may ulcerate. The most common site for basal cell carcinoma is the face (typically the nose or ears), although it may appear anywhere. It is a painless, slow-growing cancer and very rarely spreads to other parts of the body. Left untreated, however, it can slowly invade and destroy adjacent tissues, causing disfigurement. Fortunately, with early detection and treatment, basal cell carcinoma is curable in over 95 percent of cases.

WHAT CAUSES IT?

• Skin cells are damaged by cumulative exposure to ultraviolet radiation from the sun or from artificial sources (such as sunlamps). Risk of skin cancer therefore increases steadily with age.
• Those with fair skin, blue eyes, or red or blond hair are most at risk, since they have relatively little melanin, the substance that naturally protects the skin from ultraviolet radiation.
• Risk is greater in sunny climates and locales near the equator, where the sun's rays are most intense.
• The erosion of the atmosphere's protective ozone layer is allowing more ultraviolet radiation to reach the earth's surface.

PREVENTION

• Avoid exposure to direct sunlight between 10 AM and 2 PM, whenever possible.

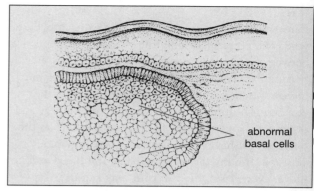

The basal cells—or those at the base of the epidermis—may be damaged by ultraviolet radiation and later rise upward to form skin cancer.

• Block the sun's rays with protective clothing such as hats and long sleeves.
• A half hour before you go out, apply a sunscreen lotion containing PABA (para-aminobenzoic acid) with a sun protection factor (SPF) of 15 or higher. Reapply often, especially after swimming or perspiring heavily.
• Avoid sunlamps and tanning booths.
• Perform regular skin self-examinations.
• Basal cell cancer does not recur at the same site very often (if properly treated), but people who have had one episode of basal cell cancer are likely to develop others in the future. For this reason, preventive measures are especially important after initial diagnosis.

DIAGNOSIS

• A biopsy to remove part or all of the suspicious growth will be performed, and the tissue will be analyzed.

HOW TO TREAT IT

• To remove cancerous cells, surgery, liquid nitrogen, or radiation therapy may be used.

WHEN TO CALL A DOCTOR

• Make an appointment with your doctor when you notice a change in the appearance of your skin. Most skin growths are harmless, but self-diagnosis is not possible, and a biopsy is required.
• Make follow-up appointments for regular checkups after an episode of basal cell carcinoma, owing to the increased likelihood of subsequent episodes.

SYMPTOMS

• A small, flat, waxy bump, most commonly appearing on the face, ears, or neck.
• A darkened or flesh-colored lump or lesion on the back or torso.
• An unusual skin blemish that grows steadily over a period of weeks. It may develop into a shallow ulcer with raised edges and a moist center. The ulcer may then bleed and form crusts and won't heal.

Bell's Palsy

WHAT IS IT?

Bell's palsy is paralysis of the muscles on one side of the face. It results from inflammation of the facial nerve, which runs through a tiny hole in the bone between the ear and the jaw. Inflammation of this nerve compresses it inside its bony channel, thus paralyzing the muscles between the forehead and mouth. Onset is usually sudden, typically occurring upon awakening, and most commonly strikes those between the ages of 30 and 60.

WHAT CAUSES IT?

• The cause is unknown in most cases.
• Viral infection (including herpes zoster, the same virus that causes chicken pox and shingles), physical trauma, heredity, and circulatory problems have been proposed as potential causative factors.

Bell's palsy is characterized by paralysis of the muscles on one side of the face, causing the affected eyelid, cheek, and mouth to droop.

SYMPTOMS

• Drooping muscles and weakness on one side of the face, resulting in a distorted smile or an expressionless look.
• Drooping eyelid, inability to close the eye, and tearing on the affected side.
• Possible pain in the ear and on the affected side of the face.
• Drooling.
• Possible changes in taste and increased sensitivity to noise.

PREVENTION

There is no way to prevent Bell's palsy at present.

DIAGNOSIS

• Physical examination is necessary. Other disorders, such as a stroke, will have to be ruled out.
• Electrical tests of the facial nerves (electromyography) may be performed to determine the extent of nerve damage.

HOW TO TREAT IT

• Spontaneous recovery occurs in 80 to 90 percent of cases (often beginning within three weeks), so many physicians believe treatment is unnecessary or ineffective. Outlook is most favorable when paralysis is incomplete and improvement begins soon after onset. Treatment is thus aimed at easing symptoms and preventing damage to the eye.
• Protect the eye if the eyelid cannot close. Wear goggles during the day and apply an eye patch at night to hold the eyelid shut. An artificial tear solution may also be recommended.
• For mild to moderate pain, use nonprescription pain relievers and apply a heating pad to the painful area for 15 minutes at a time.
• For more severe pain or for cases that fail to improve over time, corticosteroids (such as prednisone) may be prescribed—although the effectiveness of such therapy for Bell's palsy is a point of debate.
• As muscle strength returns, exercise the weak facial muscles and perform a facial massage for 15 to 20 minutes a day.
• Occasionally, surgery may be used to reduce pressure on the facial nerve.
• Plastic surgery may improve appearance and muscle function in the rare cases where facial paralysis persists.

WHEN TO CALL A DOCTOR

• Facial paralysis always warrants a doctor's attention. Although Bell's palsy is the most common cause and is not a medical emergency, more serious problems such as a stroke or tumor should be ruled out.

Benign Paroxysmal Positional Vertigo BPPV

WHAT IS IT?

Benign paroxysmal positional vertigo is dizziness that comes on abruptly upon changing the position of the head (for instance, while tilting the head to look upward, sitting up, or turning over in bed). Symptoms generally last less than a minute, but they can be extremely disconcerting and may be accompanied by loss of balance, nausea, and vomiting. Such episodes may recur several times a day. Contrary to popular belief, recurrent or chronic dizziness indicates a brain tumor less than 1 percent of the time.

SYMPTOMS

- Sudden, acute dizziness or a spinning sensation that occurs after changing the position of the head.
- Loss of balance.
- Nausea and vomiting.

WHAT CAUSES IT?

- Balance is maintained by otoliths, tiny calcium stones that press on hairlike fibers deep in the canals of the inner ear. When bent, these fibers send signals to the brain so it can calculate the head's position. As people age, minuscule amounts of debris may slough off and press on these fibers. This interferes with the sense of balance by sending false signals to the brain, resulting in BPPV.
- A prior head injury or viral infection may also contribute to the development of BPPV.

PREVENTION

- Until you receive successful treatment, try to avoid the positions that induce dizziness.
- Avoid sudden, rapid head movements.

DIAGNOSIS.

- Your doctor may order various tests to determine the exact cause of vertigo and to rule out a more serious underlying disorder.

HOW TO TREAT IT

- Lie down until dizziness and other symptoms go away.
- Certain medications—such as antihistamines (which can have an antinausea effect) and scopolamine (a motion-sickness drug) may be prescribed to ease dizziness.
- In one treatment technique, a doctor will induce dizziness by moving the patient's head rapidly or slowly to one side, holding the position for a few minutes, then repeat the procedure for the opposite side. Afterward, the patient sits up and must keep the head upright for 48 hours (even while sleeping). This treatment produces complete remission in 60 percent of BPPV cases and improvement in another 30 percent.
- The patient is instructed to move his or her head in a way that induces dizziness. He or she then performs this technique several times a day for a few weeks. This treatment has been shown to be effective in nearly all patients.

WHEN TO CALL A DOCTOR

- Make an appointment with your doctor if you experience episodes of severe dizziness.

Bladder Cancer

WHAT IS IT?

Bladder cancer is the growth of malignant cells in the lining of the bladder. Often, more than one tumor is present at a time, and the cancer may spread through the wall of the bladder to nearby organs. The most frequent symptom of bladder cancer is painless hematuria (blood in the urine), although commonly there are no symptoms at all. Therefore, when symptoms of a bladder disorder do arise, they are most often due to other, less serious, conditions such as infections, benign tumors, or bladder stones. Bladder cancer is rare before the age of 40 and is more common among men.

WHAT CAUSES IT?

• Smoking is associated with increased incidence of bladder cancer.
• Exposure to toxic chemicals (such as those used in the rubber industry as well as industrial dyes and solvents) is a potential risk factor.
• A family history of bladder cancer is associated with an increased risk.

SYMPTOMS

• Blood in the urine.
• Difficult, frequent, or painful urination.
• Pain in the pelvic region.
• Feeling of pressure in the back.
• Persistent fever.
• Urinary incontinence or dribbling.

PREVENTION

• Don't smoke cigarettes.
• Exercise caution if you work with industrial dyes or in the rubber industry.

• If you have a family history of the disease, get regular checkups.
• See your doctor regularly if you have had bladder cancer to screen for recurrences.

DIAGNOSIS

• Patient history and physical exam help to establish the presence of a bladder disorder.
• Cystoscopy (the use of a thin, lighted tube that allows a surgeon to see the bladder directly) and biopsy (removal and analysis of tissue samples) are required for a definitive diagnosis.
• Urinalysis may be used to detect cancer cells and blood in the urine.
• CT (computed tomography) scans provide a view of the bladder and surrounding tissues to reveal any structural abnormalities.

HOW TO TREAT IT

• Tumors in the early stages may be removed surgically through the cystoscope. Such tumors may recur, thus requiring fulguration (destruction of suspect tissue using electrical current) every three months for several years.
• Recurrences may also be treated with chemotherapy. Chemotherapeutic agents may be instilled directly into the bladder with a cystoscope or may be administered by mouth or intravenously. The latter two methods are especially likely to be used if evidence indicates that the cancer has spread.
• If the cancer is advanced, removal of the entire bladder is required in addition to radiation and chemotherapy.

WHEN TO CALL A DOCTOR

• Call a doctor if you have blood in the urine or you experience other symptoms of bladder cancer.

Bladder Infection Cystitis

WHAT IS IT?

Bladder infection, also known as cystitis, occurs when bacteria, generally from outside the body, enter the urinary tract and infect the urethra and the bladder. It is most common in women.

WHAT CAUSES IT?

• About 80 percent of urinary tract infections are caused by bacteria that normally inhabit the anal area with no ill effect; however, if these bacteria enter the urinary tract, infection may ensue. The relatively short urethra of women, as compared to that of men, provides less of a barrier to bacteria.
• Use of a urinary catheter may introduce bacteria to the bladder.
• Bacteria may migrate to the bladder from a kidney infection.
• Sexual activity may bruise the urethra in women, promoting infection.
• Obstruction of urine flow by a bladder tumor or, in men, an enlarged prostate may lead to bladder infection.

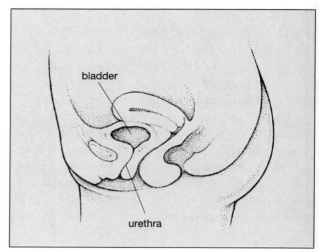

Bacteria may ascend the urethra to infect the bladder. Women are more prone to such infections, as the female urethra is relatively short.

SYMPTOMS

• Burning sensation during urination.
• Frequent urination with only small amounts of urine passed on each occasion.
• Urgent need to urinate; lack of urinary control.
• Blood in the urine.
• Pain in the lower abdomen or the lower back.
• Low-grade fever (under 102°F).
• Painful sexual intercourse.

PREVENTION

• Women should practice careful hygiene. After using the toilet, wipe from front to back to avoid spreading fecal bacteria to the urethra.
• Obtain prompt treatment of bacterial infections elsewhere in the body, especially kidney infections.
• Drink at least eight glasses of water a day.
• Urinate when you feel the urge: retaining a full bladder promotes infection.
• Do not douche unless instructed otherwise by a doctor. It may irritate the urinary tract.
• Women who have serious or recurrent bladder infections should take showers instead of baths. They should also drink a glass of water before intercourse and urinate within 15 minutes afterward. Such women are also advised to ask their doctor about taking preventive antibacterial medications.

DIAGNOSIS

• Diagnosis is based upon a culture of a urine sample for bacteria.

HOW TO TREAT IT

• Your doctor may prescribe antibiotics to fight the infection. Take them for the full term prescribed.
• You may also be given antispasmodics and analgesics to relieve the pain.
• Drink cranberry juice to increase the acidity of the urine, as some medicines are more effective with a more acidic urine.

WHEN TO CALL A DOCTOR

• Call your doctor if you experience symptoms of a bladder infection, especially if they are accompanied by a high fever or if symptoms recur or persist despite treatment.

Bladder Stones

WHAT IS IT?

Bladder stones form when substances (such as calcium oxalate) in the urine concentrate and coalesce into hard, solid lumps that lodge in the bladder. Often, several stones form at once. Normally, they are fairly small and are excreted in the urine without complications, but sometimes stones become trapped in the neck of the bladder and—as residues in the urine continue to accumulate—grow large enough to cause pain, urinary blockage, or infections, thus requiring surgical intervention. Bladder stones almost exclusively affect middle-aged and older men, but, for unknown reasons, are becoming increasingly rare.

WHAT CAUSES IT?

• Most commonly, stones occur when the neck of the bladder becomes obstructed due to prostate enlargement, a benign growth (adenoma) within the prostate, or abnormal contraction or stricture of the bladder neck. Stones often originate elsewhere in the urinary tract (such as in the kidneys), or in the bladder itself. Hereditary factors may be involved.
• Other causes include the long-term use of a urinary catheter, chronic urinary tract infections, or a nerve injury that impairs bladder function.
• Mild, chronic dehydration concentrates the urine, which may promote stone formation.
• A diet high in oxalic acid (found in rhubarb, spinach, leafy vegetables, and coffee), or low in phosphates or protein, may lead to bladder stones.

PREVENTION

• Drink at least eight glasses of water per day.
• Get prompt treatment for urinary tract infections.

SYMPTOMS

• Interruption of the urine stream, inability to urinate except in certain positions, frequent urge to urinate but with only small amounts of urine passed.
• Blood in the urine, often in the last few drops.
• Pain—sometimes severe—in the pelvic region, genitals, lower abdomen, or lower back.
• Low-grade fever (under 102°F).

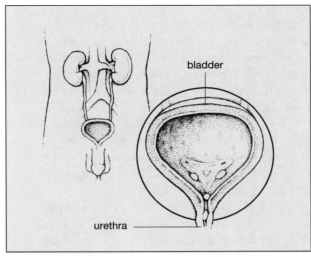

Bladder stones may grow large enough to lodge in the neck of the bladder and obstruct the outflow of urine through the urethra.

DIAGNOSIS

• A thorough medical history and physical exam (including a rectal exam) are necessary.
• Urine samples are taken and analyzed.
• Stones can be located with x-rays or ultrasound.
• Cystoscopy (inspection of the inside of the bladder using a scope) confirms the diagnosis.

HOW TO TREAT IT

• Your doctor may prescribe narcotic analgesics to relieve pain and antibiotics to treat an infection.
• Smaller stones can be removed through a cystoscope, a tube inserted through the urethra that allows the doctor to view the stones. The scope can also be outfitted with a device that crushes the stones, after which the fragments are washed away.
• Larger stones can be treated with extracorporeal shock-wave lithotripsy, which aims concentrated bursts of sound waves that pulverize the stones.
• On rare occasions, very large stones may require surgical removal (suprapubic lithotomy).
• The underlying problem (such as prostate enlargement) causing stones to be trapped in the bladder must be identified and treated to prevent recurrence.

WHEN TO CALL A DOCTOR

• Call a doctor for symptoms of bladder stones.

Blepharitis

WHAT IS IT?

Blepharitis is an inflammation of the edges of the eyelids, resulting in a persistent, unsightly redness and scaliness. The condition tends to recur, but it is generally not serious and rarely poses any threat to vision. Blepharitis often affects both eyes at once and is common among children.

WHAT CAUSES IT?

• Seborrheic dermatitis—characterized by greasy, red, scaly, itchy patches of skin—may migrate from the scalp to affect the eyelids.
• A bacterial infection may cause or complicate blepharitis due to seborrhea.
• Lice infestation of the eyelashes may cause blepharitis.

SYMPTOMS

• Red, sticky, and crusty eyelid edges.
• Itching, burning, continual blinking, and a sensation that something is in the eyes.
• A crust that requires the eyelids to be pried apart in the morning.
• Greasy scales (from seborrhea), dry scales (from a bacterial infection), or flakes of skin appearing on the eyelid edges. (Scales or flakes may fall into the eye and cause conjunctivitis.)
• Small ulcerations on the eyelid (in severe cases).
• Loss of eyelashes.
• Visible nits on the lashes, when blepharitis is caused by lice infestation.

• Mascara or eye shadow may result in contact dermatitis of the eyelids.

PREVENTION

• Control seborrhea of the scalp with medicated shampoos.
• Avoid locations where lice might be prevalent.

DIAGNOSIS

• Patient history and physical examination are necessary. The doctor may culture material from an ulcer on the eyelid for bacteria.

HOW TO TREAT IT

• Apply warm-water compresses on eyelids for 15 minutes to loosen scales. Then scrub scales away with a solution of water and sodium bicarbonate (baking soda) or baby shampoo.
• Your doctor may prescribe topical corticosteroid medications or antibiotics if a bacterial infection is present.
• For lice infestation, nits will be removed with forceps. An insecticide ointment will be prescribed for daily use.

WHEN TO CALL A DOCTOR

• If the condition does not respond to cleansing treatments within two weeks, call your doctor.
• Call your doctor if ulcers form on the eyelids. This suggests a bacterial infection.
• If you notice nits, make an appointment to see your doctor right away.

Bone Cancer

WHAT IS IT?

Bone cancer is the growth of malignant cells that gradually replace normal bone cells, leading to weakness and pain in the affected bone. Primary bone cancer, which arises directly in the bone (usually in the leg), is relatively rare and generally strikes people under the age of 20. Much more common is metastatic or secondary bone cancer, which originates in another organ and then spreads to the bone. Cancer may also develop in associated bone structures, including the marrow and the connective tissues. Some types of bone cancer may spread to other organs. With modern therapies, the outlook for many patients (especially those with primary bone cancer) has improved significantly.

SYMPTOMS
- Pain and tenderness in the affected bones. The pain is usually dull and localized and is often worse at night.
- Swelling or a noticeable tumor or mass around the site of a primary tumor. (Swelling generally does not occur with metastatic tumors.)
- Greater susceptibility to bone fractures (as healthy bone cells are replaced by malignant ones).

WHAT CAUSES IT?

- The cause of primary bone cancer is unknown, but hereditary factors, environmental factors, trauma, or excessive radiation therapy (to treat other types of cancer) may be involved.
- Metastatic bone cancer most often stems from cancers of the breast, lung, prostate, thyroid, or kidney.

- The incidence of bone cancer is higher in patients with Paget's disease, a degenerative bone disease that primarily affects older people (see Paget's disease for more).

PREVENTION

- Get regular checkups to detect cancers elsewhere in the body before they have a chance to spread.

DIAGNOSIS

- X-rays are taken.
- Diagnostic imaging techniques such as CT (computed tomography) scans or MRI (magnetic resonance imaging) are used to detect tumors and metastatic areas.
- A biopsy of the affected bone may be taken to confirm the presence of cancer (especially in the case of primary tumors, since cancer has usually already been diagnosed in the case of metastatic tumors).
- Blood tests may be performed.

HOW TO TREAT IT

- Bone(s) affected by primary tumors may need to be surgically removed. This may involve amputation, although in some cases only the tumor is removed and the remaining bone is reinforced with a metal prosthesis.
- Chemotherapy and radiation therapy may be required.
- Orthopedic surgery may be necessary to repair bone fractures.

WHEN TO CALL A DOCTOR

- Call a doctor if you feel persistent pain in one or more bones, if you develop weakness or paralysis in the limbs, or you begin to limp unexpectedly.

Bone Fractures

WHAT IS IT?

A bone fracture is simply a break in a bone. The different types of fractures are classified according to the degree of damage involved. In a simple fracture ends of the broken bone do not penetrate the skin. Bone fractures that break the skin are known as compound fractures. Comminuted or complex fractures describe bones broken into more than two pieces. An incomplete, or "greenstick," fracture is a crack—but not a complete break—in the bone. A tiny hairline crack in a bone is referred to as a stress fracture. Other fractures are classified according to the pattern of the break, such as displaced fractures, where the two broken ends are no longer aligned properly; impacted fractures, where the two ends have been pushed into each other; transverse fractures, where the bone breaks straight across; and oblique fractures, where the bone breaks along a diagonal plane.

WHAT CAUSES IT?

• Fractures usually occur as a result of an accident or trauma, when the bone is subjected to more physical force than it can withstand.
• Prolonged, excessive stress on a bone (as may occur with a repetitive, strenuous activity) may eventually result in a fracture.
• Pathologic fractures may occur with minimal stress or injury when bones are weakened by disorders such as osteoporosis or bone cancer.

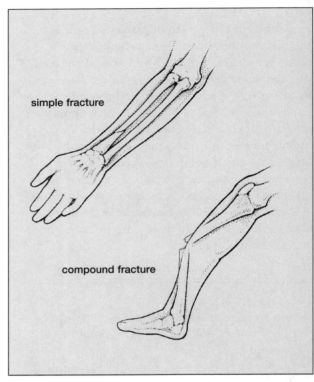

simple fracture

compound fracture

A simple fracture is characterized by a clean break; a compound fracture, in which the bone penetrates the skin, is far more serious.

SYMPTOMS

• Localized, intense pain which worsens with movement or the application of pressure.
• Swelling, bruising, or bleeding around the site of an injury.
• Protrusion of bone through the skin (in a compound fracture).
• Deformity.
• Loss of function or feeling in the injured area.
• Numbness and tingling, in addition to mottled, bluish, gray, or unusually cool skin at the end of an extremity.

PREVENTION

• Since bone fractures typically occur unexpectedly, they often cannot be prevented, apart from trying to avoid accidents in general. Don't drink and drive; wear protective gear when playing sports.
• Get enough calcium to reduce the risk of osteoporosis. Hormone replacement therapy may be recommended to postmenopausal women to prevent osteoporosis.

DIAGNOSIS

• Physical examination is necessary.
• X-rays of the affected area confirm the type and extent of the injury.
• CT scans may provide a detailed image of a fracture.

HOW TO TREAT IT

• Cover any open wounds with clean dressing.
• Apply ice or a cold pack to the affected area.

Bone Fractures *continued*

• Elevate the affected area, if possible, and immobilize the broken extremity with a splint. Move the patient as little as possible.

• Use over-the-counter pain relievers.

• Treatment for shock may be necessary for severe breaks.

• For most fractures, the bone must be reset by bringing the broken ends into alignment. Your doctor may do this with surgery (open reduction) or without it (closed reduction), depending upon the extent and location of the fracture.

• After the bone has been reset, it must be immobilized by a splint, a cast, or occasionally, traction. In some cases, a fractured bone might be held together internally with a metal screw, nail, or plate. Bones such as ribs are held together naturally by the surrounding muscles and don't require a cast. A fractured finger or toe may be taped to an adjacent finger or toe for support.

• Antibiotics may be prescribed to treat infections that may occur, especially as a complication of a compound fracture.

• As soon as possible, even while a cast is in place, the muscles and joints near the site of the fracture should be exercised to minimize swelling, stimulate blood flow, and combat weakness, atrophy, and stiffness.

• If the bone sets incorrectly, it may need to be rebroken and reset.

• Occasionally, a bone graft may be necessary if a fracture fails to mend.

• Stress fractures, a cause of "shin splints," may require rest only. Sports and other demanding physical activities should be avoided until the fracture mends.

WHEN TO CALL A DOCTOR

• Get to a doctor as soon as possible if you think you may have broken a bone. Bone tissue begins to repair itself immediately, so it is important that a doctor align the broken ends properly. Never attempt to reset the bone yourself.

Botulism

WHAT IS IT?

Botulism is a life-threatening form of bacterial food poisoning that, unlike common forms of food poisoning, affects the central nervous system. Symptoms usually appear approximately 18 to 36 hours after eating contaminated food, and currently the disease is fatal in about 10 percent of cases, most often because of respiratory failure. Patients who exhibit symptoms in less than 24 hours of infection tend to experience the most severe course of the disease and have the highest mortality rate; those that survive the first few days can usually expect full recovery. The most common form of the disease involves infants younger than six months old. Both the incidence of botulism and its mortality rate are declining.

SYMPTOMS

- Dry mouth and sore throat.
- Blurred and double vision.
- Fixed, dilated pupils.
- Breathing and swallowing difficulty.
- Slurred speech.
- Abdominal cramps, diarrhea, nausea, and vomiting.
- Weakness in arms and legs, leading to paralysis.
- Absence of fever and no disturbance of mental faculties.

WHAT CAUSES IT?

- Botulism is caused by consumption of food contaminated with the bacterium *Clostridium botulinum*, which produces a deadly toxin that suppresses the central nervous system. Foods that are undercooked or that have a low acid content are the most likely to transmit botulism.
- The disease may also occur, although more rarely so, when spores of the bacterium infect an open wound.

PREVENTION

- Never eat even a minuscule amount of food from a can that is bulging (a sign of bacterial activity) or that has an unusual odor or color.

- Do not feed honey to children less than a year old (contaminated honey is a common cause of infant botulism).
- Be cautious with the following foods, which are most likely to be contaminated: home-canned fruits and vegetables (green beans in particular), fish, undercooked sausage and other pork products, smoked meats, red meat, and milk products.
- Cook foods thoroughly (preferably 20 minutes or longer) at temperatures greater than the boiling point (212°F or 100°C).

DIAGNOSIS

- Patient history and physical examination are needed.
- Blood, stool, or stomach contents and the suspected food may be tested for the presence of botulinum toxin and the bacterium.
- An electromyogram (EMG), which tests the conduction of electrical impulses along the nerves, may be done to rule out other disorders.

HOW TO TREAT IT

- Call an ambulance immediately; emergency care and hospitalization are necessary.
- If only a few hours have passed since eating contaminated food, induce vomiting.
- If possible, try to refrigerate some of the suspected contaminated food for analysis.
- Doctors will administer a botulism antitoxin, which can save life but can have pronounced unpleasant side effects. When botulism is strongly suspected, the antitoxin is given before laboratory confirmation of the diagnosis.
- Enemas and drugs that induce bowel evacuation may be given to help rid the body of the toxin.
- Mechanical respiration may be needed in the case of severe breathing difficulty.

WHEN TO CALL A DOCTOR

- **EMERGENCY** Get immediate medical help if you develop any of the characteristic symptoms of botulism.

Brain Abscess

WHAT IS IT?

A brain abscess is an accumulation of pus (due to infection) inside the brain. These abscesses produce symptoms by raising pressure inside the rigid skull or by destroying or irritating surrounding brain tissue. Brain abscesses are most common in the frontal and temporal lobes of the cerebrum—the portion of the brain that controls higher functions, including speech and thinking. Prompt medical treatment usually ensures full recovery; however, approximately 10 percent of cases are fatal, while others result in some permanent neurological disorder such as epilepsy. Brain abscesses are becoming increasingly rare due to the widespread use of antibiotics to treat underlying infections before they can cause such complications.

SYMPTOMS

- Headaches—often severe.
- Nausea and vomiting.
- Drowsiness.
- Partial paralysis, weakness, or loss of sensation on one side of the body or in the legs; or, progressive speech difficulty (depending on the location of the abscess).
- Epileptic seizures.
- Fever.
- Discharge of pus from the nose or ear.

WHAT CAUSES IT?

- Most brain abscesses result from the spread of an infection from another (typically adjacent) part of the body to the brain. Indeed, about one-third of all cases originate as an infection in the middle ear or the sinuses.
- Blood-borne infections may also spread to the brain and result in an abscess or—more commonly in such cases—multiple abscesses. Patients with bacterial endocarditis (an infection of a heart valve) or immune deficiencies are prone to brain abscesses from infectious organisms carried in the blood.
- A head wound that penetrates the skull can lead to brain infection and thus an abscess.

PREVENTION

- Receive prompt medical treatment for any infections elsewhere in the body—especially those occurring in the middle ear or the sinuses.
- Wear protective headgear when engaging in any activity where risk of head injury is possible.

DIAGNOSIS

- Diagnosis is strongly suspected from CT (computed tomography) or MRI (magnetic resonance imaging) brain scans.
- A culture of organisms taken from the pus confirms the diagnosis and is required to select appropriate antibiotic treatment.

HOW TO TREAT IT

- Large doses of antibiotics are given to attack the underlying infection.
- Some type of surgical procedure is often necessary as well. Frequently, a hole is drilled into the skull so that the abscess can be drained or completely removed. This procedure also allows doctors to identify the precise underlying organism in order to determine the appropriate antibiotic treatment. After such surgery, antibiotics will usually be prescribed for one or two months.
- Anticonvulsant drugs may be prescribed if the abscess has caused epileptic seizures.

WHEN TO CALL A DOCTOR

- **EMERGENCY** See a doctor immediately if you have any signs of serious infection or symptoms such as speech difficulty, seizures, or partial paralysis.

Brain Hemorrhage Intracranial Bleeds

WHAT IS IT?

A brain hemorrhage (one of the three main types of strokes) results when a ruptured artery causes bleeding into the brain (intracerebral bleed) or into the space between the membranes surrounding the brain (subarachnoid hemorrhage). Damage occurs two ways. First, blood supply is cut off to the parts of the brain beyond the site of the rupture in the artery. Second—and posing the greatest danger—the escaped blood forms a mass that increases pressure on the surrounding brain tissue. Blood continues to flow until it coagulates or until it simply has no place left to go. Intracerebral bleeds usually occur in the cerebrum, the part of the brain that controls higher functions such as speaking and reasoning. Subarachnoid hemorrhages usually occur at the base of the brain. Massive hemorrhages are usually fatal; indeed, only about 25 percent of patients survive.

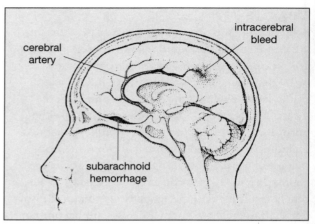

A ruptured artery may release blood into the tissues of the cerebrum or into the space between the brain and the subarachnoid membrane.

SYMPTOMS

- Paralysis on one side of the face or body.
- Speech difficulty or loss of ability to speak.
- Blurred or double vision, dilated pupils, crossed eyes, or inability to move the eye.
- Back and leg pain.
- Fever.
- Stiff neck.
- Sudden, excruciating headache.
- Nausea and vomiting.
- Mental confusion.
- Sudden loss of consciousness with no warning.

WHAT CAUSES IT?

- Hypertension is the main cause of intracerebral bleeds.
- Atherosclerosis (the buildup of fatty plaque in the arteries) weakens arterial walls, further increasing the risk of bleeds due to hypertension.
- Bleeding disorders (such as hemophilia and leukemia) or the use of anticoagulant or thrombolytic drugs increases the risk of intracerebral bleeding.
- Aneurysms (weak spots in the wall of an artery that may burst) are a major cause of subarachnoid hemorrhage. Aneurysms are often due to congenital defects.
- A head injury may rupture arteries in the brain.

PREVENTION

- Keep blood pressure and weight under control.
- Often, people with aneurysms will have minor bleeds initially. If the cause of these can be identified, arteriography (diagnostic imaging of the arteries) may reveal a surgically treatable aneurysm.

DIAGNOSIS

- Arteriography may be used to detect cerebral aneurysms before they rupture.
- A lumbar puncture (spinal tap) may be used to test for blood in the cerebrospinal fluid and to check for increased pressure within the skull.
- X-rays or CT (computed tomography) scans of the head may be taken to identify and assess the amount of blood spillage in the brain.

HOW TO TREAT IT

- Call an ambulance immediately.
- Physicians will take emergency measures to drastically reduce blood pressure in order to minimize flow of blood from the ruptured artery.
- Life support may be necessary.
- Surgical repair, if attempted at all, is usually delayed for one to two weeks after the incident, although a newer approach calls for more rapid surgical intervention in some cases.

WHEN TO CALL A DOCTOR

- **EMERGENCY** Call an ambulance immediately.

Brain Tumors

WHAT IS IT?

A brain tumor is an abnormal growth of cells in the brain or the membranes surrounding the brain (a tumor known as a meningioma). The tumor increases pressure inside the skull and so exerts pressure on the entire brain: this phenomenon is responsible for many of the symptoms of brain tumors regardless of whether they are benign or malignant. Primary brain tumors originate in the brain but are much less common than secondary, or metastatic, tumors, which spread to the brain from cancers elsewhere in the body. Symptoms tend to appear gradually and vary according to the area of the brain affected. Primary malignant brain tumors are uncommon, accounting for less than 2 percent of all cancers.

SYMPTOMS
- Frequent headaches that are more painful when lying down.
- Vomiting, with or without nausea.
- Blurred or double vision.
- Seizures.
- Impaired thinking, mental confusion, or even coma.
- Other symptoms depend on the location of the tumor within the brain and may include weakness or unsteadiness, paralysis on one side of the body, dizziness, speech difficulty, memory loss, loss of the sense of smell or hearing, or personality change.

WHAT CAUSES IT?
- The cause of primary brain tumors is unknown.
- Metastatic tumors may spread from cancers of the lungs, liver, intestines, breast, skin, and other parts of the body.

PREVENTION
- Get regular checkups to detect cancers elsewhere in the body before they have a chance to spread.

DIAGNOSIS
- A thorough patient history and physical examination are necessary.
- CT (computed tomography) scans or an MRI (magnetic resonance imaging) may be necessary to locate the tumor.
- A spinal tap or lumbar puncture (the use of a needle to remove and analyze a sample from the cerebrospinal fluid surrounding the spinal cord) is often performed. (However, spinal taps should not be performed if other diagnostic imaging techniques reveal evidence of a mass. Under such circumstances a spinal tap is dangerous.)
- A biopsy of the tumor will most likely be necessary to confirm the diagnosis.
- Electroencephalography may be used to measure and assess electrical activity in the brain.
- Cerebral arteriography may be used in preparation for surgery to outline the arteries supplying blood to the tumor.

HOW TO TREAT IT
- Tumors near the surface of the brain may be surgically removed. In many cases, however, it is only possible to remove a portion of a tumor, since taking it all out would cause unacceptable amounts of brain damage. Still, removing even part of it may afford a period of improvement by relieving pressure within the cranium.
- Tumors deep within the brain may be treated with microsurgery, laser surgery, or ultrasound.
- For malignant primary tumors, surgery may be followed with radiation or chemotherapy. Surgery may also be preceded by radiation.
- Your doctor may prescribe corticosteroids to reduce swelling of brain tissue, anticonvulsant drugs to control seizures, and pain relievers.

WHEN TO CALL A DOCTOR
- Call a doctor if you ever have a seizure.
- Call a doctor if you experience a severe, persistent headache—especially one that is worse in the mornings or when lying down.
- Call a doctor if you experience double vision or if you notice weakness, numbness, or loss of sensation in the limbs.

Breast Cancer

WHAT IS IT?

Breast cancer, the growth of malignant cells in the breast, is the most common cancer among women. (It is rare among men.) Breast cancer usually originates in the milk-carrying ducts, although it may arise in the milk-producing lobes or, even more rarely, in the dense connective tissue of the breast. A breast tumor is not in itself life-threatening, but there is a high risk that the cancer will spread to other organs via the lymph nodes or the bloodstream, so early detection is imperative. In 90 percent of cases, only one breast is affected, although those who have had cancer in one breast are at increased risk of eventually developing it in the other. In all cases, early detection and treatment improve the outlook significantly.

WHAT CAUSES IT?

• The precise cause is unknown, but the following factors correlate with a higher incidence of breast cancer.
• Age. The risk of breast cancer increases progressively after age 50.
• Family history. Women whose immediate or near-immediate family members have had breast cancer are at greater risk, especially if the cancer occurred at an early age.
• Having had children late in life or not at all. Women

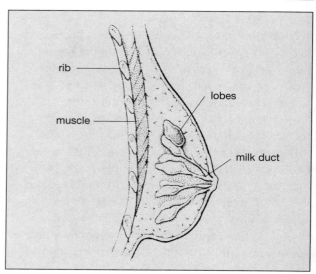

The breast contains 15 to 20 lobes, each containing dozens of milk-producing glands. Breast cancer originates in these glands.

who have no children, have their first child in their 30s, or have never breast fed may be more susceptible to breast cancer.
• Early onset of menstruation (that is, before age 11).
• Late menopause (that is, not having reached menopause by one's early 50s).
• Nonmalignant cysts and tumors in the breasts.
• A diet high in animal fat .
• Environmental toxins (possibly).

PREVENTION

• Mammograms can detect tumors too small to feel. Women over 50 should have annual mammograms, and those between ages 40 and 50 should discuss their individual risk factors with their doctors to determine when to begin mammography. The exam should be performed by a radiologist specializing in mammography or by a mammography center accredited by the American College of Radiology. A list of accredited centers is available from the National Cancer Institute at 1-800-4-CANCER.
• Women should have a yearly breast exam performed by a doctor or other trained specialist.
• Women should perform monthly breast exams (the best time is two or three days after menstruation ends). Breast tissue is normally somewhat lumpy and uneven, so it is important to become familiar with

SYMPTOMS

• A lump or swelling, usually painless, anywhere in the breast or underarm (but most commonly in the upper and outer region of the breast).
• Changes in the appearance of the breast's skin, including flattening, indentation, dimpling, creasing, redness, or scaliness.
• Changes in the nipple, including indentation, an itching or burning sensation, or dark or bloody discharge.
• Changes in the size or symmetry of the breasts.
• Discomfort or pain in the breast in advanced cases.

Breast Cancer *continued*

the normal contour and texture of the breasts. Changes in texture and appearance will then become more easily detectable. Follow these steps:
• Stand before a mirror and check both breasts for anything unusual. Look for puckering, dimpling, or scaling of the skin or a discharge from the nipples.
• Changes in position may reveal unusual lumps or indentations. Clasp your hands behind your head and press your hands forward. Look for any changes in the breasts' appearance.
• Next, press your hands firmly on your hips and bow slightly toward the mirror, pulling your shoulders and elbows forward (again, checking for anything unusual).
• Raise your left arm. Moving in tiny, gentle, circular motions with three or four fingers of your right hand, feel all around the left breast. Start at the outer part of the breast and work gradually toward the nipple in concentric circles. Pay special attention to the underarm area. Feel for any unusual lump or mass beneath the skin. Gently squeeze the nipple and look for any discharge.
• Repeat the previous step for the right breast.
• Repeat the last two steps while lying flat on your back, with a small pillow or folded towel placed under your shoulder.

DIAGNOSIS

• Breast examination or mammography may reveal the presence of a lump in the breast.
• A biopsy of the lump is necessary to determine whether cancerous cells are present. Tissue or fluid may be drawn out of the lump with a needle, or a sample of tissue may be removed during minor surgery.
• Ultrasound, thermography, or CT (computed tomography) scans may be recommended.

HOW TO TREAT IT

• Surgery is necessary to remove the tumor. The patient will be given the choice of having any necessary surgery performed at the time of the biopsy or later, in a subsequent operation. Depending upon how far the cancer has spread, surgery may involve removing only the mass or lump (lumpectomy) or the entire breast (mastectomy), either of which may include removal of the neighboring lymph nodes. If a tumor has invaded the muscle tissue under the breast, the removal of the breast and the underlying muscle tissue (radical mastectomy) may be advised.
• Radiation therapy may be required after surgery to prevent further spread of the cancer, especially if the lymph nodes were affected.
• Chemotherapy may be required before and after surgery to prevent further spread of the cancer. Such treatment generally lasts from six months to a year.
• Hormone therapy may be prescribed after surgery for estrogen-receptor-positive tumors. The estrogen-blocking drug tamoxifen may be continued indefinitely.
• Reconstructive plastic surgery is available for women who have had part or all of the breast removed. Women may have reconstructive surgery at the same time as surgery to remove the tumor, or at a later date.

WHEN TO CALL A DOCTOR

• Make an appointment with a doctor if you notice a lump anywhere in the breast or under the arm. Most lumps are not cancerous, but a biopsy is necessary to diagnose breast cancer with certainty.
• Make an appointment with a doctor if you notice any change in the size, shape, or appearance of the breast or if you experience any discharge from the nipple.

Bronchiectasis

WHAT IS IT?

Bronchiectasis is now a rare chronic lung condition resulting from persistent inflammation that ultimately stretches and distorts the walls of the bronchial tubes. The impaired ability to expel mucus—which may then accumulate and stagnate—leads to further inflammation and infection. Eventually (usually over a period of years), the affected air passages may be completely destroyed. Inflammation of the bronchial walls may be isolated to one area or may be distributed throughout the lungs. Bronchiectasis is mainly a childhood disease; it is now rare, thanks to vaccines to prevent whooping cough and antibiotics to control bacterial infections that often complicate measles or whooping cough (two diseases that were once among the most common causes of bronchiectasis).

SYMPTOMS

- A persistent cough that produces large amounts of thick, foul-smelling gray-green sputum, possibly flecked with blood.
- Shortness of breath.
- Bad breath.
- Fits of coughing brought on by a change in posture, such as lying down.
- Frequent respiratory infections.
- Appetite loss, weight loss, clubbed fingers, fever, and anemia in more advanced cases.

WHAT CAUSES IT?

- Currently, cystic fibrosis causes one-half of all cases of bronchiectasis.
- Other diseases that affect the lungs (like pneumonia, chronic bronchitis, emphysema, measles, silicosis, or tuberculosis) may result in bronchiectasis.
- A congenital bronchial defect may distort or weaken the walls of the bronchial tubes.
- Inhalation of foreign objects (such as a peanut) or of vomit during surgery may irritate and inflame bronchial walls, thus initiating a cycle of infection that may lead to bronchiectasis.
- Lung cancer or a lung abscess may cause bronchiectasis.

PREVENTION

- Be sure children have been properly vaccinated against childhood diseases.

DIAGNOSIS

- A patient history and physical exam are necessary.
- Sputum samples will be analyzed.
- Chest x-rays or a CT (computed tomography) scan are often used to confirm the diagnosis.

HOW TO TREAT IT

- Don't smoke; avoid dust- and smoke-filled rooms.
- Drink plenty of fluids to dilute and loosen mucus secretions in the lungs.
- Your doctor may prescribe antibiotics to treat an infection. Take antibiotics for the full term prescribed.
- Your doctor may instruct you in how to expel mucus from your lungs by assuming various positions that lower your head below your torso (a technique known as postural drainage).
- Surgery may be required in advanced cases to remove affected portions of the lungs.

WHEN TO CALL A DOCTOR

- Call a doctor if you have a persistent cough, especially one that yields heavy sputum or mucus, or if you have recurrent respiratory infections.

Bronchitis, Acute

WHAT IS IT?

Acute bronchitis occurs when an irritant or infection causes inflammation and swelling of the lining of the bronchial tubes, which narrows the air passages. When the cells lining the airways are irritated beyond a certain point, the tiny cilia (hairs) that normally trap and eliminate foreign matter cease to function properly. The buildup of irritants leads to the production of excess mucus, which clogs air passages further and produces the characteristic heavy cough of bronchitis. Attacks of acute bronchitis are common but usually not a major health threat, and symptoms generally disappear spontaneously in a few days. However, such attacks may be a major threat to people with chronic lung diseases like emphysema or asthma.

WHAT CAUSES IT?

• Viral infections (including the common cold and flu) and bacterial infections may lead to bronchitis.
• Irritants including chemical fumes, dust, smoke, or other air pollutants may provoke an attack.
• Smoking, asthma, poor nutrition, cold weather, congestive heart failure, and chronic pulmonary disorders may increase the risk of an attack of acute bronchitis.
• The elderly and the very young are most vulnerable to severe consequences.

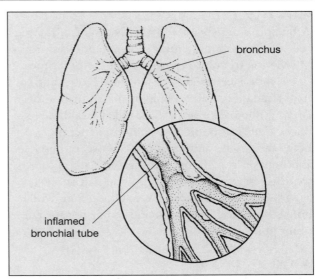

Inflammation of the bronchi and bronchial tubes results in swelling and narrowing of the air passages, and stimulates excess mucus production.

SYMPTOMS

• Deep, persistent cough that may produce gray, green, or yellowish sputum.
• Shortness of breath and wheezing.
• Fever.
• Chest pain, exacerbated by cough.

PREVENTION

• Don't smoke; try to avoid second-hand smoke.
• People at increased risk for bronchitis should avoid long outings, strenuous outdoor work, and exercise on poor air-quality days.

DIAGNOSIS

• Patient history and physical exam are necessary.
• Occasionally, chest x-rays, sputum samples, or blood tests may be taken to rule out other lung disorders.

HOW TO TREAT IT

• Take aspirin or ibuprofen to reduce fever and pain.
• Take an over-the-counter cough suppressant containing dextromethorphan if you have a persistent dry cough that disrupts sleep or normal activities. However, if you are coughing up sputum, suppressing the cough may encourage mucus accumulation in the lungs, potentially leading to serious complications.
• Stay in a warm room. Inhale steam, use a humidifier, or take frequent hot showers to loosen phlegm in the lungs.
• Drink at least eight glasses of water a day to help thin mucus and make it easier to expel.
• Antibiotics are prescribed for bacterial infections.
• Smokers should abstain from cigarettes during convalescence.

WHEN TO CALL A DOCTOR

• Call a doctor if symptoms do not ease within 36 to 48 hours, or if episodes of acute bronchitis recur.
• Call a doctor if you suffer from a lung disease or congestive heart failure and you experience symptoms of acute bronchitis.
• Call a doctor if during an attack of bronchitis you cough up blood, become short of breath, or have a fever above 102°F.

Bunions

WHAT IS IT?

A bunion is a deformity of the first joint of the big toe. The bones in the joint protrude outward, forcing the toe to point inward toward the other toes. Shoes may exert pressure against the protruding joint, leading to painful bursitis (inflammation of a bursa, one of the small, fluid-filled sacs that produces a lubricating fluid to minimize friction between muscles and tendons or between muscles and bones). In addition, the skin over a bunion may become irritated owing to constant rubbing against the shoe. Bunions are common and, while not serious, may be painful and limit the toe's range of motion.

WHAT CAUSES IT?

• Wearing shoes with pointed toes and high heels is the most common cause of painful bunions.
• A hereditary trait known as hallux valgus may cause weakness in the joints of the toes and lead to the formation of bunions.

Inflammation of the joint at the base of the big toe may be further aggravated as shoes rub against the protruding bunion.

SYMPTOMS

• A painful, bony lump at the side of the base of the big toe.
• A big toe that points inward and possibly overlaps one or two toes.
• Foot pain and stiffness that may interfere with walking and other activities.
• Redness and swelling at the base of the big toe.

PREVENTION

• Avoid high-heeled shoes whenever possible. Choose shoes with low heels and plenty of room for the toes.

DIAGNOSIS

• Physical examination and x-rays of the affected toe confirm the diagnosis.

HOW TO TREAT IT

• Avoid wearing high-heeled shoes, especially those with pointed toes.
• Commercially available felt pads or cushions may ease pressure from the shoe on the bunion and the other toes. Around the house it may be helpful to wear an old shoe with a hole cut out above the bunion.
• Arch supports, or an orthotic shoe insert prescribed by your doctor, may help to redistribute weight on the foot.
• Surgery to realign the joint and remove the bunion may be recommended in severe cases.

WHEN TO CALL A DOCTOR

• Make an appointment if you experience continuing pain due to a bunion or if the bunion is interfering with walking or other activities.

Bursitis

WHAT IS IT?

Bursitis is inflammation of a bursa—one of the small, fluid-filled sacs located in or near joints throughout the body. The bursas act as cushions between muscles and tendons or between muscles and bones. They produce a lubricating fluid to minimize friction at these sites, thus facilitating joint movement. Irritation, overuse, or injury to a joint can inflame a bursa, resulting in painful bursitis. The shoulders, elbows, wrists, hands, hips, knees, heels, and the base of the big toe are among the sites most often affected. Bursitis is so common that it has acquired a number of familiar names, including tennis elbow, trigger finger, student's elbow, and housemaid's knee. Bursitis is not serious and usually subsides on its own within one or two weeks; however, it does have a tendency to recur.

SYMPTOMS
- Pain and swelling in or around a joint.
- Restricted and painful movement in the affected joint.
- Pain spreading into the neck, arms, or fingertips due to bursitis in the shoulder.
- Fever (when associated with an infection).

WHAT CAUSES IT?
- Activities that put constant pressure on a joint (like resting the elbow on a desk or kneeling).
- Repetitive and vigorous joint movement (such as swinging a tennis racquet or hammering).
- A blow or other injury to a joint.
- Arthritis, gout, and certain infections.
- Calcium deposits in, or degeneration of, a nearby tendon is sometimes associated with bursitis.

PREVENTION
- Wear protective gear when playing sports. Check with a coach, trainer, or pro to be sure that you are using proper techniques.
- Avoid overly strenuous or repetitive physical activities if possible.
- If you must work in a kneeling position, use knee pads or cushions, change positions often, and take frequent breaks.
- To prevent bursitis in the feet, wear high heels only when you must; buy new running shoes when old ones wear out.

DIAGNOSIS
- Patient history and physical examination are necessary.
- X-rays of the affected area may rule out other disorders.

HOW TO TREAT IT
- Rest and avoid putting pressure on the affected area. Your doctor may prescribe splints, braces, or slings to keep the joint still.
- Take an over-the-counter pain reliever as needed.
- Use ice packs for the first 48 hours to relieve pain, swelling, and inflammation. Then, if desired, switch to heat packs, which stimulate blood flow and ease pain.
- Your doctor may administer injections of corticosteroids and a local anesthetic to reduce swelling and ease pain.
- To reduce swelling, your doctor may draw excess fluid from the bursa with a syringe and then tightly bandage the joint.
- Gradually resume using the affected joint to prevent stiffening and muscle atrophy, although naturally you should temporarily avoid any activities that aggravate the condition.
- Surgery to remove the bursa may be necessary in severe, persistent cases.

WHEN TO CALL A DOCTOR
- Make an appointment with a doctor if joint pain or swelling persists for more than two weeks despite treatment.

Candidiasis

WHAT IS IT?

Candidiasis (also known as moniliasis) is a fungal infection that may affect the mouth, vagina, gastro-intestinal tract, skin, nails, or mucus membranes throughout the body. The infection can spread from the genitals or mouth to other moist regions of the body. Normally, the body harbors a small amount of the fungus *Candida albicans*, in addition to some harmless bacteria that compete with this fungus and thus keep it under control. If the number of such bacteria diminish for any reason (the use of anti-biotics, for example), the fungus may grow without restriction and begin to cause symptoms. Candidiasis occurring in the vagina—better known as a yeast infection—is very common and tends to recur, but it is not serious. However, among drug addicts and immunosuppressed or other seriously ill people, the *Candida* fungus may enter the bloodstream and invade the kidneys, lungs, or brain, although this is rare.

SYMPTOMS

- Vaginal itching, discomfort, and redness, in addition to a thick, white, odorless discharge. Vaginal infections may also cause discomfort during urination and sexual intercourse.
- Oral infections (thrush) produce a cream-colored or bluish-white discharge on the tongue or mouth, with sore, creamy yellow, raised patches in the mouth.
- Skin infections produce an itchy, red rash with flaky white patches. In infants, skin infections may accompany diaper rash.
- Male genital infections produce inflammation of the head of the penis (balanitis).
- Serious, widespread infections may produce chills, fever, and severe malaise.

WHAT CAUSES IT?

- The use of antibiotics may kill the bacteria that normally keep the fungus in check.
- Birth control pills or pregnancy may disrupt the normal acidity and moisture of the vagina, thus pro-moting a yeast infection.

- Patients with diabetes mellitus are at greater risk.
- A weakened immune system may encourage the growth of the fungus. Those taking immunosuppres-sant drugs or undergoing chemotherapy and people with AIDS or other immune disorders are especially susceptible.

PREVENTION

- Women should wear cotton undergarments. Nylon fibers, which do not "breathe," create a warm, moist environment that may encourage fun-gal growth.
- Douche or use feminine hygiene sprays only when so advised by your doctor.
- Avoid sexual intercourse with a partner infected with *Candida albicans* until the infection is cured.
- Women prone to candidiasis and using oral contra-ceptives should consider another birth control method.
- Pregnant women in the third trimester should be examined for candidiasis to avoid spreading an infec-tion to the baby.
- Those prone to *Candida* infections of the skin should keep their skin as dry as possible.

DIAGNOSIS

- Analysis of skin scrapings, vaginal discharge, pus, or sputum is necessary to confirm the diagnosis.
- Blood or tissue cultures may be required.

HOW TO TREAT IT

- For candidiasis of the vagina, penis, mouth, or throat, your doctor may prescribe antifungal creams, suppositories, or tablets. Preparations for vaginal yeast infections are also available over the counter but should not be used without seeing a doctor initially.
- Your doctor may advise using a gentle mouthwash to loosen hardened secretions in the mouth.
- Intravenous antifungal drugs may be prescribed in severe cases of candidiasis of the mouth, throat, and digestive system.

WHEN TO CALL A DOCTOR

- Call a doctor if you experience symptoms of candidiasis.

Canker Sores

WHAT IS IT?

Canker sores (also called aphthous ulcers) are small, painful, craterlike ulcers in the lining of the mouth. They often occur two or three at a time, but it's not unusual for 15 or more to appear at once. Similar to cold sores (which are caused by the herpes simplex virus), canker sores may sometimes be contagious, although their precise cause is not known. They are very common, occurring predominantly among those between the ages of 10 and 40, especially women. Canker sores usually heal within two weeks, although they may recur. While they pose no serious health threat, severe canker sores can make eating and talking unpleasant.

SYMPTOMS

- Small, painful, white or gray, craterlike, red-rimmed ulcers located anywhere inside the mouth, including the gums, tongue, and lips. Ulcers may appear singularly or in groups.
- Sometimes, a tingling or burning sensation preceding the appearance of ulcers.
- Fever, fatigue, and swollen glands in severe cases.

WHAT CAUSES IT?

- While the precise cause of canker sores is unknown, there are several things that may trigger them.
- Injuries due to rough dentures, toothbrushes, chipped or jagged teeth, dental work, or burns from hot food or liquids may lead to mouth ulcers.
- Canker sores are more likely to appear during periods of emotional stress or physical exhaustion.
- Viral or bacterial infections may induce canker sores; thus, close contact (including sharing utensils) with others who have canker sores may be a risk.
- Irritation from certain foods, including citrus fruits, pineapple, vinegar, or highly salted foods, may cause mouth ulcers.

- Food allergies, allergic rhinitis, and certain vitamin deficiencies are associated with canker sores.
- Recurrences may be triggered by sun exposure or hormonal changes that occur during the menstrual cycle.

PREVENTION

- Practice proper oral hygiene; brush and floss regularly.
- Try to determine if certain foods seem to trigger canker sores and then avoid those foods.
- Avoid intimate contact with someone who has canker sores (since they may be contagious).

DIAGNOSIS

- In severe or persistent cases, a biopsy of the ulcers may be taken to test for the presence of the herpes simplex virus or for secondary bacterial infections.
- A blood sample may also be required.

HOW TO TREAT IT

- Apply an ice cube to the affected area to relieve pain.
- Rinse the mouth several times a day with warm salt water.
- Avoid spicy or acidic foods that irritate the ulcers.
- For recurrent or more severe ulcers, your doctor may recommend using an antiseptic mouthwash. In addition, a doctor may prescribe topical anesthetics, antihistamines, antibiotics, or corticosteroids to speed healing.
- A waterproof ointment may be used to cover the ulcer as it heals.

WHEN TO CALL A DOCTOR

- Call your doctor if, in addition to canker sores, you develop a high fever or swollen glands.
- Call your doctor if you experience severe pain from the ulcers.
- Call your doctor if the ulcers persist for longer than two weeks despite treatment.

Carcinoid Tumors and Carcinoid Syndrome

WHAT IS IT?

A carcinoid tumor is a growth composed of cells with properties of both endocrine and neural tissues. By far the most common site for carcinoid tumors is the wall of the intestines, but they may occur in other organs such as the lungs or pancreas. This rare type of tumor can be benign or malignant. Even when malignant, the tumor grows very slowly and thus may never produce any symptoms or affect general health in any way, although occasionally a tumor may cause abdominal pain or intestinal bleeding or grow large enough to cause intestinal obstruction. In about 10 percent of cases, however, the cells of a malignant carcinoid tumor get into the bloodstream and spread to other organs, especially the liver, where they multiply. Carcinoid tumors secrete a number of powerful substances (serotonin, histamine, prostaglandins, and several hormones). Consequently, tumors that have spread to the liver produce unpleasant symptoms that characterize what is known as carcinoid syndrome (see Symptoms below). Although carcinoid tumors can be life-threatening, the patient may live 10 or 20 years after the initial diagnosis, since the tumors grow so slowly. On the other hand, if they are detected before spreading, surgical treatment may allow for full recovery.

WHAT CAUSES IT?

• The cause of carcinoid tumors is unknown.
• Risk factors may include obesity, smoking, and excessive alcohol consumption.

PREVENTION

• There is currently no known way to prevent carcinoid tumors.

DIAGNOSIS

• A urine sample is analyzed for the presence of a product of the breakdown of serotonin, the major substance secreted by carcinoid tumors.
• Abdominal x-rays will be performed. A CT (computed tomography) scan of the abdomen may be required as well.
• Endoscopy or sigmoidoscopy (examination of the bowel using a small, flexible, illuminated scope) is often performed. A biopsy of any suspicious tissue in the colon may be taken during these procedures.

HOW TO TREAT IT

• If carcinoid tumors are detected before they have spread or in the early stages after spreading, surgery will be performed in an attempt to remove them. Carcinoid tumors may be detected during abdominal surgery for another, unrelated disorder.
• Chemotherapy may be used to slow the progress of the cancer.
• If the cancer has invaded the liver, treatment is aimed at relieving the symptoms of carcinoid syndrome. Medical treatments may include serotonin-blocking drugs and bronchodilators (to relieve wheezing and shortness of breath). Also, niacin supplements may be given, since the chemical activity of the tumors results in a niacin deficiency that, in fact, causes a number of the symptoms associated with carcinoid syndrome.

WHEN TO CALL A DOCTOR

• Obviously, the symptoms of carcinoid syndrome are disturbing and warrant a doctor's attention.

SYMPTOMS

• Carcinoid tumors may cause no symptoms, but they can possibly cause abdominal pain, gastrointestinal bleeding, or intestinal obstruction. Carcinoid syndrome, however, may produce a number of the following symptoms:
• Flushing or redness of the face and neck lasting up to several hours owing to the secretion of excess hormones and other substances. Such symptoms may be triggered by exercise, alcohol consumption, stress, or certain foods.
• Gas and profuse diarrhea with possible abdominal cramping and vomiting.
• Wheezing or breathlessness.
• Watery, swollen eyes.
• Palpitations.
• Symptoms of congestive heart failure (CHF), as the abundance of serotonin may damage heart valves.

Cardiac Arrhythmias

WHAT IS IT?

Cardiac arrhythmias are disturbances in the normal rhythm of the heartbeat. The patient suffers episodes in which the heart may beat too rapidly (tachycardia) or too slowly (bradycardia), or irregularly—although some patients experience no symptoms. An occasional palpitation or fluttering is usually not serious, but a persistent arrhythmia may be life-threatening. Atrial arrhythmias interfere with the heart's ability to pump blood properly from its upper chambers (atria). The atria do not always empty completely, and blood remaining there too long may stagnate and potentially clot. Such clots may travel to other parts of the body, where they may cause blockages in the blood supply to the limbs, brain, or heart. In ventricular fibrillation, the lower chambers of the heart (ventricles) quiver feebly instead of contracting powerfully. This is the most severe type of arrhythmia, causing death in minutes unless medical assistance is obtained immediately.

SYMPTOMS
• Palpitations or irregular-feeling heartbeats.
• Shortness of breath.
• Chest pain.
• Dizziness, lightheadedness, and fainting spells.
• Mental confusion.
• Loss of consciousness.

WHAT CAUSES IT?
• Disorders that damage the heart or its valves, including endocarditis, myocarditis, and rheumatic fever.
• Injury to the heart due to a heart attack.
• Disorders of the thyroid gland.
• Chest or heart-surgery patients may develop an arrhythmia immediately after an operation.
• Some drugs, including digitalis, stimulants, and diuretics, as well as overdoses of cocaine, marijuana, or antidepressants may provoke an arrhythmia.
• Dehydration, or depletion of potassium or other electrolytes, may trigger an arrhythmia.
• Risk increases with smoking, excess consumption of caffeine or alcohol, hypertension, kidney disease, stress, fatigue, and overwork.

PREVENTION
• Engage in regular aerobic exercise. Avoid cigarettes, illegal drugs, and excessive amounts of alcohol and caffeine. Try to reduce emotional stress.
• Carefully follow instructions for prescription drugs.

DIAGNOSIS
• Electrocardiography (ECG or EKG), to monitor the electrical impulses that control heartbeat. May require Holter monitoring (portable ECG) for a brief period (usually 24 hours).
• Blood pressure and blood tests.
• Exercise (treadmill) stress test.
• Chest x-rays and angiography (injection of a contrast material into an artery to produce a clear x-ray image of the blood vessels).
• Echocardiogram (use of ultrasound to map the heart's movements and structure).

HOW TO TREAT IT
• Antiarrhythmic drugs (such as a beta-blocker or procainamide) may be prescribed.
• Anticoagulants (such as aspirin or warfarin) may be prescribed to prevent the formation of blood clots.
• Digitalis (a drug that slows ventricular response to the rapid impulses coming from the atrium) is often prescribed for those with atrial fibrillation.
• Defibrillation—a jolt of electricity applied to the chest by an emergency medical team—may restore normal heart rhythm if administered within a few minutes of the onset of ventricular fibrillation. An electric shock (cardioversion) may also be administered under nonemergency conditions to correct atrial arrhythmias.
• A pacemaker may be implanted in the chest to regulate the heartbeat.
• Surgery may be done to interrupt an abnormal electrical pathway in the heart, replace a damaged heart valve, or bypass blocked coronary arteries.

WHEN TO CALL A DOCTOR
• **EMERGENCY** Call an ambulance if you experience severe chest pain, shortness of breath, or palpitations.
• **EMERGENCY** Call an ambulance if someone loses consciousness. If heartbeat or breathing has stopped, perform cardiopulmonary resuscitation (CPR).

Cardiomyopathy

WHAT IS IT?

Cardiomyopathy is the term for any disease of the heart muscle that interferes with the heart's ability to pump blood with sufficient force. There are several forms of it: Dilated (or congestive) cardiomyopathy is weakness in the walls of the heart that causes them to balloon out, which compromises the heart's efficiency and increases the risk of congestive heart failure, arrhythmias, and the formation of blood clots (which may cause heart attacks or strokes). Hypertrophic cardiomyopathy, overgrowth or thickening of heart muscle, may compromise blood flow through the heart. Restrictive cardiomyopathy involves loss of elasticity of the heart walls that prevents the heart from adequately filling with blood prior to contracting. Except when caused by viral infections, cardiomyopathy develops slowly and may produce no symptoms until the later stages. The disorder is relatively rare, accounting for only 1 percent of heart disease fatalities in the United States, although it is one of the relatively more common causes of serious heart disease in younger people.

SYMPTOMS
- Often, there are no symptoms until the disease's very advanced stages. These may include the following:
- Shortness of breath, especially during exertion.
- Swelling of the feet, ankles, or hands (edema).
- Fatigue.
- Palpitations.
- Dizziness or fainting.
- Wheezing and a dry cough, or a cough producing foamy, bloody phlegm.
- Chest pain (may be mild).
- Stroke or painful and cold extremity due to a blood clot blocking a blood vessel.

WHAT CAUSES IT?

- In many cases of cardiomyopathy, the cause is unknown.
- Hypertrophic cardiomyopathy appears to run in families.
- Viral infections of the heart cause inflammation of the heart muscle (myocarditis) and may result in permanent damage to the muscle.
- Excess consumption of alcohol may be toxic to the heart muscle over time.
- Nutritional deficiencies (such as lack of vitamin B_1 or potassium) and hormone imbalances may damage and weaken the heart muscle.
- Amyloidosis, a disorder in which the walls of the heart are infiltrated by a starchlike protein, may cause restrictive cardiomyopathy.
- The risk of developing cardiomyopathy increases with smoking, obesity, chronic diarrhea, or the long-term use of diuretic drugs.
- Advanced coronary artery disease may be a cause.

PREVENTION

- To reduce the risk of heart disease in general, eat a well-balanced low-fat diet, exercise regularly, and lose weight if you are more than 20 percent overweight. Limit yourself to no more than two alcoholic beverages per day, and don't smoke.

DIAGNOSIS

- An electrocardiogram (ECG or EKG) monitors the electrical impulses that control the heartbeat. You may be asked to wear a portable electrocardiogram device, known as a Holter monitor, for 24 hours.
- Chest x-rays may be taken.
- Your doctor may perform an echocardiogram, which uses ultrasonic waves to image the structure and the movements of the heart.
- A biopsy of heart muscle may be taken.

HOW TO TREAT IT

- Your doctor may prescribe medications to reduce heart muscle exertion, improve the heart's pumping ability, regulate the heartbeat, and ease symptoms.
- Avoid strenuous physical activity.
- Abstinence from alcohol may be necessary.
- A heart transplant may be advised if the heart muscle has been badly damaged.

WHEN TO CALL A DOCTOR

- Symptoms of cardiomyopathy indicate late-stage disease, warranting prompt attention from a doctor.

Carpal Tunnel Syndrome

WHAT IS IT?

Carpal tunnel syndrome results when the median nerve, which passes through a narrow tunnel of wrist bones (carpals) and a ligament at the base of the hand, is compressed by surrounding tissue or excess fluid. Symptoms, including numbness and pain in the hand and wrist, may appear suddenly or gradually and often affect both hands. The disorder occurs most often among women between the ages of 30 and 60.

WHAT CAUSES IT?

• Activities that require prolonged bending of the wrist or constant repeated hand motions may lead to carpal tunnel syndrome. Such activities include typing, assembly-line work, knitting, sewing, golf, tennis, and canoeing.
• Dislocation or sprain in the wrist may damage the median nerve.
• Hormonal changes due to pregnancy, birth control pills, or menopause may cause fluid accumulation in the carpal tunnel.
• Diseases such as rheumatoid arthritis, diabetes mellitus, hypothyroidism, Raynaud's syndrome, and acromegaly may promote carpal tunnel syndrome.
• A tumor on the median nerve may compress the nerve (although this is extremely rare).

Repetitive hand motion can narrow the carpal tunnel, which may exert pressure on the median nerve and cause pain, numbness, or tingling.

PREVENTION

• Take frequent breaks when engaged in strenuous work or activities requiring repetitive hand motions, and try to vary activities so that wrists are not constantly bent.
• Use a wrist-support pad while typing.

DIAGNOSIS

• Physical exam and patient history are necessary.
• The hands and wrists may be x-rayed.
• An electromyogram may be used to monitor the electrical impulses along the median nerve to determine if it is compressed.

HOW TO TREAT IT

• Take over-the-counter pain relievers.
• A wrist splint may be prescribed, especially for nighttime use.
• Diuretics may be prescribed to reduce fluid accumulation in swollen tissue.
• Corticosteroids may be injected in more severe cases to reduce inflammation.
• If symptoms persist despite treatment, surgery may be recommended to relieve pressure on the median nerve.

WHEN TO CALL A DOCTOR

• Call a doctor if symptoms of carpal tunnel syndrome become sufficiently troublesome or begin to interfere with normal daily activity.

SYMPTOMS

• Numbness, tingling, and eventually pain in the thumb and first three fingers (and perhaps half of the fourth finger).
• Pain, often worse at night, possibly severe enough to awaken you.
• Possible pain in the entire hand, forearm, or shoulder.
• Weakness in the hands and fingers that may make it difficult to pick up or hold onto objects.
• A sensation of swelling in the fingers (without any visible swelling).
• Atrophy of the muscles of the thumb (occurs in 50 percent of cases).

Cataracts

WHAT IS IT?

A cataract is a loss of transparency in the normally clear lens of the eye. At first, a small, hazy spot may appear in the field of vision. Gradually (often over a period of years), as the lens grows more opaque, vision becomes more blurry, especially at night or in very bright light. In the United States about 75 percent of all people over age 60 show some signs of cataracts. Advanced cases are easily treated with surgery, although most patients can postpone this for years.

WHAT CAUSES IT?

• Aging is the single greatest risk factor for cataracts, as cumulative exposure to the sun's ultraviolet rays over a lifetime appears to be a primary cause.
• Exposure to radiation, including x-rays and microwaves, may promote cataracts.
• Physical injury to or inflammation of the eye (for example, uveitis or iritis) may lead to cataracts.
• Long-term use of corticosteroid drugs may be a contributing factor.
• Hereditary factors and birth defects may be involved.
• Cataracts may occur at a younger age in those with diabetes mellitus.

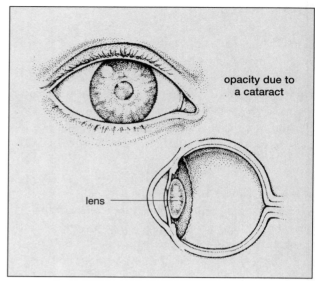

opacity due to a cataract

lens

The eye's lens is normally perfectly clear, but when a cataract forms, light is absorbed and diffused by the opacity, resulting in blurred vision.

SYMPTOMS

• Gradual, painless, increasingly blurred or double vision.
• Halos or blurriness around lights. Vision may actually be better in dim light, since bright light causes the pupil to constrict, restricting the passage of light to the part of the lens often most affected by a cataract.
• Increased sensitivity to light and glare.
• Dulled color perception.
• Temporary improvement in near vision (patient may no longer need reading glasses for a brief period).
• Frequent changes in eyeglass or contact lens prescriptions.
• Yellowish or milky white appearance of the lens in advanced cases.

PREVENTION

• Wear sunglasses marked "general purpose" or "special purpose," or those that indicate they block at least 95 percent of ultraviolet-B (UVB) rays.

DIAGNOSIS

• Eye examination by an ophthalmologist.

HOW TO TREAT IT

• To minimize glare outdoors, wear a wide-brimmed hat and yellow-tinted sunglasses.
• Indoors, use floor or desk lamps with incandescent bulbs instead of ceiling or fluorescent lights. Avoid pinpoint halogen lights, since they cause the pupils to constrict. Installing dimmer controls is advised.
• Try large-print books and newspapers.
• Surgery is the only true cure for cataracts. It can often be postponed indefinitely but is advised when cataracts interfere with normal activities. During the operation the lens is removed and replaced with a plastic intraocular lens implant. (Special contact lenses or eyeglasses may be used when an implant is ruled out.) Cataract surgery has a 95 percent success rate.

WHEN TO CALL A DOCTOR

• See an ophthalmologist for any vision problems.

Cervical Acceleration/Deceleration Injuries Whiplash

WHAT IS IT?

Whiplash is a neck injury sustained when the head is thrown backward and then forward (or vice versa) violently. Such trauma may damage the muscles, ligaments, tendons, and cartilaginous disks in the neck and may even result in fractures of the cervical (neck) vertebrae. Typically, pain and stiffness are much worse a day or two following the injury; fortunately, full recovery is likely.

WHAT CAUSES IT?

• Car accidents (especially rear-end collisions) are the most common cause of whiplash.
• Whiplash may occur during recreational activities like high-impact sports, dancing, or waterskiing.
• Osteoarthritis of the spine may stiffen the spine and increase vulnerability to neck injuries.

PREVENTION

• Use properly adjusted headrests in the car and always use lap and shoulder belts. Drive defensively.

SYMPTOMS

• Neck pain or stiffness, appearing within 24 hours of an injury. Often, pain in the front of the neck diminishes over several days, while pain in the back of the neck intensifies.
• Dizziness and headache.
• Nausea and vomiting.
• Numbness or stiffness in the arms.
• Gait instability.

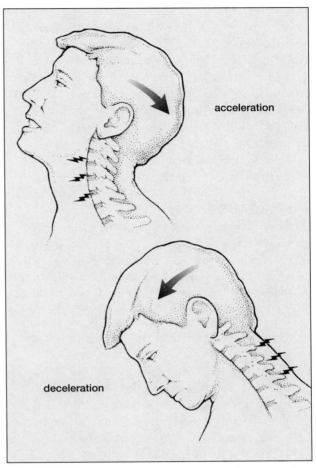

Sudden forward acceleration causes the head to be thrown back; the head is then thrown forward as the force of rear impact is absorbed.

DIAGNOSIS

• X-rays of the neck and spine may be taken.
• Your doctor will perform a physical examination to detect changes in motor ability and sensation.

HOW TO TREAT IT

• Apply ice packs for the first 24 hours after the injury to reduce pain and swelling.
• Take nonprescription pain relievers.
• Sleep without a pillow. Instead, place a rolled towel (less than two inches in diameter) behind your neck, or sleep wearing a neck brace.

• After 24 hours, use either heat or ice packs as desired. Try hot showers or warm compresses.
• Your doctor may recommend a padded neck brace or collar to immobilize the injured region for several days or weeks as pain subsides. In more severe cases, short-term traction may be recommended.
• Muscle relaxants or narcotics may be prescribed in more severe cases. (Avoid alcohol with such drugs.)
• During recuperation, don't lift heavy objects, and be especially cautious when driving.

WHEN TO CALL A DOCTOR

• Call a doctor if you suffer a painful neck injury or if you develop severe pain, numbness, or weakness in the arm or face.

Cervical Cancer

WHAT IS IT?

Cervical cancer is the growth of malignant cells in the cervix, the narrow opening of the uterus. Cervical cancer develops slowly from a distinct precancerous stage (dysplasia). Cancer confined to the surface of the cervix is classified as preinvasive, while cancer that has spread into deeper layers or to other organs is classified as invasive. Symptoms may not appear until the cancer reaches the more dangerous invasive phase; however, with early diagnosis and treatment, long-term prognosis is extremely favorable.

WHAT CAUSES IT?

• The cause is unknown, but risk factors include sexual activity at an early age, multiple sexual partners, multiple pregnancies, a history of herpes, genital warts or other venereal infections, and smoking. Women whose mothers took the synthetic hormone DES during pregnancy may also be at greater risk.

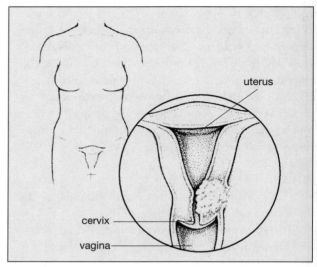

The cervix, located at the end of the vaginal canal, marks the entrance to the uterus. It is the most common site of gynecological cancer.

SYMPTOMS
• No symptoms during early stages.
• Abnormal vaginal bleeding between periods, after intercourse, or after menopause; heavier and lengthier monthly periods (in later stages).
• Persistent, unusual vaginal discharge.
• Back and abdominal pain.
• General malaise and loss of weight and appetite after cancer has spread.
• Leakage of urine and feces through the vagina (in very late stages).

PREVENTION

• Women should have a Pap smear (microscopic examination of a small sample of cells scraped from the cervix and upper vagina) regularly once they reach age 18 or become sexually active. A Pap smear can detect dysplasia before cancer develops.
• Women whose mothers took the drug DES during pregnancy should have Pap smears at least once a year.

DIAGNOSIS

• Pap smear.
• Colposcopy (inspection of the vagina and cervix with a special scope) to identify suspicious growths.
• Conization (a biopsy of a cone-shaped section of the cervix) to detect and remove abnormal cells.
• Dilatation and curettage (D&C), in which the cervix is dilated to obtain tissue samples for analysis.
• Blood and urine samples.

HOW TO TREAT IT

• Preinvasive cervical cancer may be destroyed by cauterization (use of heat to burn away cancerous cells), cryosurgery (use of liquid nitrogen to freeze and destroy cancerous cells), or laser surgery. Larger cancers may require conization or, rarely, a hysterectomy (removal of the cervix and uterus).
• Surgery for invasive cervical cancer may warrant radical hysterectomy (removal of all of the reproductive organs and neighboring lymph nodes); very severe cases may also require removal of the bladder and rectum (very rare).
• Radiation and chemotherapy may be used if cancer has spread throughout the uterus or to other organs.

WHEN TO CALL A DOCTOR

• Women 18 or older should schedule regular Pap smears.
• Call your doctor if you experience abnormal vaginal bleeding or any other symptoms of cervical cancer.

Cervical Disorders, Nonmalignant

WHAT IS IT?

Nonmalignant disorders of the cervix (the narrow opening at the mouth of the uterus) include cervicitis, cervical eversion, cervical polyps, and cervical dysplasia. Cervicitis is a broad term for an inflammation or infection of the cervix. Cervical eversion (often mistakenly termed cervical erosion) is the migration of cells from the lining of the uterus to the cervix and vagina. The cells from the uterine lining are more delicate than the cells in the vaginal lining and thus more susceptible to infection. (Actual erosion of cervical tissue is quite rare but may occur following certain medical procedures, sexual intercourse, or the use of an IUD.) Cervical polyps are grapelike growths in the lining of the cervix. They may occur singly or in groups, and in some women, large polyps may interfere with conception by creating a barrier to sperm. In very rare cases, polyps are an early precursor of cervical cancer. Cervical dysplasia is the presence of abnormal cells on the surface of the cervix and may be classified as mild, moderate, or severe, depending upon the extent of the cellular abnormality. Although dysplasia (at any stage) is not cancerous and may go away on its own, it may be the first step in the eventual development of cervical cancer and thus warrants prompt treatment.

WHAT CAUSES IT?

• Cervicitis may be caused by vaginal infections, sexually transmitted diseases, and pelvic inflammatory disease (see this disorder for more). Tears or lacerations in the cervix occurring during childbirth or abortion may lead to infections resulting in cervicitis.
• The cause of cervical eversion is not known. The condition is normal in early puberty, and some women are born with it. Pregnancy and long-term use of birth control pills may increase risk.
• The growth of cervical polyps may be triggered by injury to the cervix, vaginal infections, or hormonal changes that occur during pregnancy. Women with diabetes mellitus are at increased risk for developing polyps.
• The cause of cervical dysplasia is not known, although it may be associated with cervical eversion and sexually transmitted diseases. Women who have had many sexual partners are at greater risk (see Cervical Cancer for more).

PREVENTION

• Women should have regular Pap smears for early detection of any irregularities in the cervix.
• Obtain prompt treatment for any vaginal infection or sexually transmitted disease.
• Women should wear cotton undergarments. Nylon fibers, which cannot "breathe," create a warm, moist environment that may encourage infections.

DIAGNOSIS

• A Pap smear (microscopic examination of a small sample of cells scraped from the cervix and upper vagina) is necessary.
• A sample of vaginal discharge, if any is present, may be taken for analysis.
• Colposcopy (inspection of the vagina and cervix with a special microscope) can identify abnormalities.
• A biopsy of cervical tissue may be performed.

SYMPTOMS

• Cervicitis: clear, gray, or yellow vaginal discharge; vaginal bleeding after intercourse or between periods; burning and itching of external genitalia. (Simultaneously occurring infections of adjacent organs may produce additional symptoms of frequent and urgent need to urinate, painful urination, and lower abdominal or back pain.)
• Cervical eversion: white or slightly bloody vaginal discharge, often appearing one week prior to a period; vaginal bleeding after intercourse or between periods.
• Cervical polyps: heavy, watery, and bloody vaginal discharge; vaginal bleeding after intercourse, between periods, or after a bowel movement; heavy bleeding during periods; pelvic cramps.
• Cervical dysplasia: no symptoms. A Pap smear is necessary to detect it.

Cervical Disorders, Nonmalignant *continued*

HOW TO TREAT IT

• Cervicitis: Your doctor may prescribe antibiotics, or antifungal or antiviral agents. If symptoms persist, the affected area of the cervix may be painlessly destroyed by heat (cauterization), the use of liquid nitrogen (cryosurgery), or laser surgery. If the infection has penetrated deeply into the cervical tissue, the affected tissue may be surgically removed in a conical section (conization). A hysterectomy may be recommended in cases of severe, chronic cervicitis—although this is quite rare.

• Cervical eversion: The affected tissues may be destroyed by cauterization, cryosurgery, or laser surgery. Treatment is unnecessary if the condition produces no symptoms.

• Cervical polyps: Polyps are removed surgically. Single growths may be removed under a local anesthetic in the doctor's office. Removal of groups of larger polyps may require brief hospitalization.

• Cervical dysplasia: Mild cervical dysplasia may disappear without treatment. Surgery for persistent cervical dysplasia may include laser surgery, cryosurgery, cauterization, or conization. In severe cases a hysterectomy may be advised (see Cervical Cancer).

WHEN TO CALL A DOCTOR

• Make an appointment with a gynecologist if you experience symptoms of any cervical disorders.

• See your gynecologist for regularly scheduled Pap smears.

Chiggers

WHAT IS IT?

Chiggers are the larvae of the harvest mite or red bug. The tiny larvae, measuring only about a third of a millimeter in length, inhabit grasses, weeds, shrubs, and brush, primarily in the southern United States (although they may be found as far north as Canada). They most often attach themselves to human hosts at the ankles and legs, since these are the parts of the body most commonly exposed to the low-lying vegetation where chiggers dwell. However, chiggers generally prefer warm, moist places and so may lodge in the groin area, the armpits, the crook of the elbow, beneath the waistband of clothing, or any region where clothing is

SYMPTOMS

- Extremely itchy, red bumps about one-half inch in diameter. Chiggers may be visible in the center of unscratched bumps. Itching may persist for weeks.
- Hives, blisters, swelling, or large red patches at the site of the bite(s).

tight. Chiggers release an enzyme that dissolves the skin; then they insert a feeding tube into their victim's bloodstream. They feast on their host's blood for up to four days, until they become engorged and drop off. Skin at the site of the chigger bite may react in a variety of ways. An allergic reaction is common, producing extremely itchy red patches. Blisters and swelling may also appear. While serious diseases due to chigger bites are not a threat in the United States, minor secondary infections may ensue, especially if the sufferer scratches itchy skin

until it bleeds. While itching and discomfort may persist for weeks, chigger bites cause no permanent ill effects.

WHAT CAUSES IT?

- Spending time in the woods or fields during the summer increases the risk of chigger bites.

PREVENTION

- Use an insect repellent during outdoor summer activities.
- When walking in the woods or fields, cover your legs completely by wearing long pants and tucking them into your socks or boots.

DIAGNOSIS

- Diagnosis is determined by visual observation and generally does not require a doctor.

HOW TO TREAT IT

- Try not to scratch chigger bites, since scratching increases the risk of infection.
- Calamine lotion may soothe itching.
- Take an antihistamine, such as pseudoephedrine or diphenhydramine, to relieve allergic reaction and itching.
- Over-the-counter corticosteroid creams (hydrocortisone) may alleviate itching. More potent hydrocortisone creams are available by prescription.
- Your doctor may prescribe antibiotics to treat a secondary infection. Antibiotics should be taken for the full term prescribed.

WHEN TO CALL A DOCTOR

- Call a doctor if you suffer an allergic reaction (such as hives) to chigger bites or if over-the-counter treatments fail to relieve severe itching.

Chlamydia

WHAT IS IT?

Chlamydia is any of a group of highly contagious microorganisms that can infect various sites in the body, including the genitals, eyes, lymph nodes, and respiratory tract. In developed countries, it most commonly appears as a sexually transmitted genital infection, characterized by nonspecific urethritis (inflammation of the urethra). Diagnosis of genital chlamydia may be difficult, since the infection may cause no symptoms, especially among women. However, without treatment, it may involve the vagina, cervix (cervicitis), and fallopian tubes (salpingitis), creating disorders also known as pelvic inflammatory disease. Untreated chlamydia may also result in sterility. Prompt treatment with antibiotics offers a favorable prognosis. In underdeveloped countries, chlamydia infection of the eyes (trachoma) is the leading cause of blindness.

SYMPTOMS

- Painful or burning urination; possible redness and itching in and around the urethra.
- Watery mucus discharge from the penis or vagina.
- A painless pimple or blister on the penis or outer lips of the vagina.
- Painful swelling of the scrotum.
- Inflamed, painful lymph nodes in the groin area.
- Inflammation of the inner lining of the eyelids and the membrane covering the whites of the eyes (conjunctivitis), leading to blindness if untreated.
- In newborns, difficulty in breathing and a staccato cough, indicating a respiratory chlamydial infection.
- High fever (103°F to 106°F), a symptom of psittacosis pneumonia. Other symptoms range from those of a mild flu to those of severe pneumonia.

WHAT CAUSES IT?

- Chlamydial infections may be transmitted by vaginal or anal intercourse and by oral-genital contact.
- Chlamydial infection of the cervix in pregnant women may cause eye and respiratory infections in newborns.
- Touching the eyes with contaminated hands may transfer the infection to them. (In developing countries, chlamydial infections of the eyes are commonly spread by flies.)
- A respiratory chlamydial infection spread via the droppings and feathers of infected birds (including parrots, parakeets, and live poultry) may lead to a rare type of pneumonia called psittacosis.

DIAGNOSIS

- A culture of urethral or vaginal discharge is taken.

PREVENTION

- Avoid intimate contact with infected people until the infection is cured.
- A monogamous sexual relationship or complete abstinence will protect against genital infection; otherwise, use condoms to help reduce risk.
- To prevent psittacosis, make sure that any imported or exotic pet bird has been quarantined for 30 days before you buy it. Also be sure that birds of the parrot family have been treated with the necessary antibiotics.

HOW TO TREAT IT

- To treat all chlamydial infections, your doctor will prescribe antibiotics such as tetracycline, which should be taken for the full term prescribed. Antibiotics will be administered to both sexual partners for genital chlamydia. Only one partner may exhibit symptoms, but both must be treated. Since chlamydia is so contagious, it is very likely that the symptomless partner is also infected.

WHEN TO CALL A DOCTOR

- Make an appointment with a doctor if you or your partner experience symptoms of genital chlamydia, if the inner eyelids become inflamed, or if you develop a high fever (over 102°F).

Cholesteatoma

WHAT IS IT?

A cholesteatoma is a benign, cyst-like tumor in the eardrum or middle ear. Most commonly, a cholesteatoma develops when the eustachian tube (the passage between the ear and nose) becomes blocked. Gradually, the air trapped in the middle ear is absorbed by surrounding tissue, resulting in greater air pressure outside the eardrum than inside. This pressure imbalance pushes the weakest part of the eardrum inward, creating a pocket. Old skin cells normally shed by the eardrum collect into a ball inside this pocket and form a cyst. If the eardrum is perforated, a cyst may form directly in the middle ear. The most common problem associated with cholesteatoma is permanent, mild-to-moderate hearing loss due to damage to the delicate bones in the middle ear. If left untreated, the cyst may also eventually begin to erode the eardrum, the facial nerve, the bones lining the ear canal, or even the skull. In such advanced cases, complications can include epidural abscess and meningitis, two types of potentially life-threatening infections of the tissues surrounding the brain.

SYMPTOMS

- Hearing loss, ranging from mild to severe.
- Pus leaking from the ear.
- Headaches and earaches.
- Weakness of facial muscles.
- Dizziness.

WHAT CAUSES IT?

- Repeated middle ear infections may lead to blockage in the eustachian tube, creating the conditions conducive to the development of a cholesteatoma.
- A congenital defect may prevent the eustachian tube from opening as it normally should during infancy.

- Risk of cholesteatoma is higher among those with a childhood history of ear problems.

PREVENTION

- There is no known way to prevent cholesteatoma.

DIAGNOSIS

- Patient history and physical exam are necessary. Your doctor will examine your ear with an otoscope, a device that permits a clear view of the entire ear canal.
- If your doctor suspects a cholesteatoma, a thorough examination by an otolaryngologist (ear, nose, and throat specialist) will be required.
- An MRI (magnetic resonance imaging) scan may be used to confirm the diagnosis.

HOW TO TREAT IT

- Surgery is the sole cure for cholesteatoma. Removal of small cysts usually requires only a minor operation. To minimize the risk of recurrence, great care must be taken during the procedure to remove all traces of the cholesteatoma.
- In more advanced cases, several operations may be necessary to rebuild the bones of the ear. Additional operations may be required to remove cysts that have grown back.
- If the infection spreads to the mastoid process (a honeycomb-like bone behind the ear) and cannot be cured by antibiotics, a mastoidectomy (removal of the mastoid process) may be necessary. This procedure is generally used only as a last resort in very advanced cases and will not restore lost hearing.
- A hearing aid may be prescribed if normal hearing cannot be restored.

WHEN TO CALL A DOCTOR

- Call a doctor if you experience hearing loss or any of the symptoms of cholesteatoma.

Chronic Fatigue Syndrome

WHAT IS IT?

The term *chronic fatigue syndrome* is used to designate a group of symptoms that includes, among other things, extreme and persistent weakness and exhaustion. Several criteria must be met to establish a diagnosis of chronic fatigue syndrome. For one, symptoms must interfere with the patient's ability to work and function normally for a period of at least six months. All other disorders (including psychiatric illnesses) must be ruled out. The causes of chronic fatigue are extremely elusive, and thus the disorder is fertile ground for unproven theories and quack remedies. No true cure exists; however, in most cases, symptoms are at their worst early on and gradually diminish on their own.

SYMPTOMS

- Severe, debilitating fatigue, usually made worse by exercise.
- Recurrent flu-like symptoms, including a chronic sore throat.
- Aches and pains in the muscles and joints.
- Painful lymph nodes in the armpits and neck.
- Headaches.
- Low-grade fever (99.5°F to 100.5° F) and chills.
- Depression.
- Mental confusion, irritability, and memory loss.
- Sleep difficulties.

WHAT CAUSES IT?

- The cause of chronic fatigue is unknown. For a time, it was believed that the Epstein-Barr virus was the cause, since tests showed that most chronic fatigue sufferers had been exposed to it. However, almost 90 percent of healthy people have also been exposed to the virus with no ill effects, and not everyone with chronic fatigue symptoms has been exposed. Thus, there is no evidence that chronic fatigue is caused by any virus or that it is in any way contagious.

- Another proposed theory is that chronic fatigue is an autoimmune disorder, meaning that the immune system overcompensates in response to a perceived threat (such as a virus) and ultimately attacks otherwise healthy body tissues.
- A new (and as yet unconfirmed) theory suggests that people with chronic fatigue symptoms have lower levels of specific hormones (cortisol and corticotropin-releasing hormone) involved with mood and energy levels.
- Psychological and emotional factors appear to play a contributory role.

PREVENTION

- Chronic fatigue syndrome cannot be prevented. Contrary to popular opinion, you cannot "catch it" from someone else.

DIAGNOSIS

- Patient history and physical exam are necessary.
- The patient must exhibit all of the aforementioned symptoms, and tests will need to be conducted to rule out anemia, infection, diabetes, heart disease, cancer, and other ailments that may produce persistent weakness and exhaustion.

HOW TO TREAT IT

- Over-the-counter pain relievers may be used for muscle and joint pain and headaches.
- Don't exceed your physical limits, since exercise and exertion can exacerbate symptoms. Do try to stay active and even gradually increase your tolerance for exercise.
- Get plenty of rest and eat a healthy, balanced diet.
- Low-dose antidepressants may improve sleep disturbances and decrease fatigue and muscle pain.
- Psychological counseling may be helpful—not because chronic fatigue is a psychosomatic disorder but because it is often accompanied by depression. Treating the depression may make the overall illness less debilitating.

WHEN TO CALL A DOCTOR

- Make an appointment with your doctor if you experience symptoms of chronic fatigue syndrome.

Chronic Obstructive Pulmonary Disease COPD

WHAT IS IT?

Chronic obstructive pulmonary disease (COPD) is an umbrella term for conditions that obstruct the air passages (bronchi) or damage the small air sacs (alveoli) in the lungs, resulting in progressively impaired breathing. The two primary disorders that constitute COPD are emphysema and chronic bronchitis; many COPD patients exhibit some combination of both.

Chronic bronchitis is a persistent inflammation of the bronchial tubes in the lungs, producing a recurrent cough with large amounts of mucus. When the cells lining the airways are irritated beyond a certain point, the tiny cilia (hairs) that normally trap and eliminate foreign matter cease to function properly. The buildup of irritants leads to the production of excess mucus, which clogs air passages and produces the characteristic heavy cough of bronchitis. Bronchitis is classified as chronic when the patient coughs up sputum most of the days of a three-month period, two consecutive years in a row.

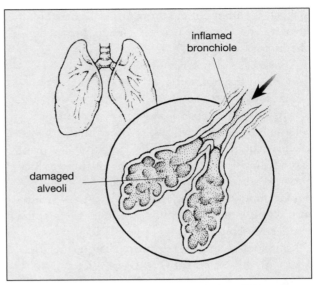

As the alveoli (the tiny air sacs at the ends of the bronchial trees) are damaged by emphysema, the lungs are able to transfer less and less oxygen to the bloodstream, causing shortness of breath. Also, chronic inflammation of the airways may inhibit the entry of air into the alveoli.

SYMPTOMS

- Shortness of breath and wheezing.
- A persistent, mucus-producing cough, especially in the morning (a symptom of chronic bronchitis).
- A persistent, dry cough (a symptom of emphysema).
- In severe cases, symptoms of COPD may include coughing up blood, persistent chest pain, and blue-purple complexion.
- Swollen legs and ankles from right-sided heart failure (cor pulmonale).
- Difficulty in exhaling.

Emphysema is progressive damage to the lungs, resulting from loss of elasticity in the alveoli, where oxygen enters and carbon dioxide exits the bloodstream. If the lungs are damaged by the chemicals in cigarette smoke or by the persistent inflammation and coughing of chronic bronchitis, the delicate walls of the alveoli may burst and fuse with other alveoli, becoming enlarged, inelastic, and far less

functional. The loss of elasticity, often combined with narrowing of the small airways in the lungs (sometimes to the point of collapse), traps stale air instead of allowing it to be exhaled. The affected air sacs are thus unable to deliver oxygen to the bloodstream or to remove carbon dioxide—producing the characteristic shortness of breath of emphysema. Lung damage may progress until breathing is severely impaired, at which time the condition is potentially life-threatening. Low blood-oxygen levels can increase the pressure in the pulmonary arteries (pulmonary hypertension), which in turn may lead to right-sided heart failure (cor pulmonale).

Onset of COPD is very gradual. It develops over a number of years, and symptoms may not appear until the disease has already progressed quite far. Lung damage is permanent, but it is preventable in many cases by avoiding smoking. COPD is two to three times more common in men as women.

WHAT CAUSES IT?

- Smoking is the most common cause of COPD.
- Air pollution may be a contributing factor.
- Industrial or chemical fumes can damage the airways.
- Repeated viral or bacterial lung infections may

Chronic Obstructive Pulmonary Disease COPD *continued*

thicken the lining of the bronchial walls, narrow the airways, and stimulate excessive mucus production in the lungs.

• A hereditary deficiency of the enzyme alpha1-antitrypsin may cause the walls of the air sacs to break down.

• People with occupations that require constant exposure to dust, chemicals, or other lung irritants or that require heavy use of the lungs, such as glass-blowing or playing a wind musical instrument, may be more susceptible to emphysema.

• The labored breathing resulting from the narrowed airways of chronic bronchitis may strain the air sacs and lead to emphysema.

• Asthma or recurrent respiratory allergies are associated with greater risk of COPD.

• Young children living with heavy smokers are more susceptible to chronic respiratory inflammation.

PREVENTION

• Don't smoke, since smoking is the primary cause of COPD.

• Avoid spending long periods outside on days when the air quality is poor.

DIAGNOSIS

• Patient history and exam are necessary.

• A sputum sample may be taken for analysis.

• Blood samples will be taken from both an artery (to measure oxygen and carbon dioxide levels) and a vein.

• A chest x-ray will be performed.

• Spirometry and various other pulmonary-function tests that measure breathing capacity and efficiency will be done.

• Tests that measure the strength and efficiency of the heart muscle may be ordered.

HOW TO TREAT IT

• Don't smoke; avoid smoke-filled rooms.

• Drink plenty of fluids to loosen mucus secretions. Avoid caffeine and alcohol, however, since they have a diuretic effect and may lead to dehydration.

• A bronchodilator may be prescribed to widen the bronchial passages. Oxygen may be administered in more severe cases.

• When indoors, moisten the air with a cool-mist humidifier.

• Try to avoid going outside on cold days or days when the air quality is poor, and avoid exposure to cold, wet weather. If bronchitis is advanced and unrelenting, you may want to consider moving to a warmer and drier climate.

• A cold virus may trigger a flare-up in those suffering from COPD, so try to avoid catching one (wash hands regularly with warm, soapy water). Get vaccinated for influenza (annually) and pneumonia (a one-time inoculation).

• Don't use cough suppressants. Coughing is necessary to clear accumulated mucus from the lungs, and suppressing it may potentially lead to serious complications.

• Your doctor may prescribe antibiotics to treat or to prevent bacterial lung infections, since patients with COPD are more susceptible to these. Antibiotics should be taken for the full term prescribed.

• Your doctor may instruct you on how to drain mucus from your lungs by assuming various positions that lower your head below your torso (a technique known as postural drainage).

• Breathing exercises (as instructed by your doctor) may prove beneficial.

• In very severe cases of emphysema with extensive lung damage, a lung transplant may be advised (heart-and-lung transplants are advised if progressive lung disease has weakened the heart). Heart-and-lung transplant has a 50 percent survival rate after four years, and single lung transplant has a 65 percent survival rate after one year.

WHEN TO CALL A DOCTOR

• **EMERGENCY** Get medical assistance immediately if your complexion turns bluish or purplish.

• Call a doctor if symptoms of COPD become more severe, for example, if shortness of breath or chest pain becomes more intense, your cough worsens or you cough up blood, you develop a fever, you begin to vomit, or your legs and ankles swell more than usual.

• Make an appointment with a doctor if you have experienced a recurrent, persistent, mucus-producing cough for the last two winters or if you experience persistent shortness of breath.

Cirrhosis

WHAT IS IT?

Cirrhosis is characterized by progressive destruction of liver cells and the deposition of fibrous scar tissue and fatty deposits. The loss of liver cells interferes with the organ's ability to process nutrients, hormones, and drugs and slows the production of proteins and other important substances manufactured in the liver. Eventually, liver failure may result. The scar tissue interferes with blood flow from the intestine through the liver via the portal vein. Pressure in the portal vein increases (portal hypertension), the spleen becomes enlarged, and blood is shunted around the liver through enlarged, fragile veins (varices) in the stomach and esophagus. Toxic substances formed in the intestine, and normally cleared in the liver, bypass the liver and are carried to the brain, where they can interfere with its function (hepatic encephalopathy). Those with cirrhosis may exhibit no symptoms until the damage—which is irreversible—is quite extensive. Cirrhosis is twice as common among men as women, and some forms of it are associated with increased risk of liver cancer.

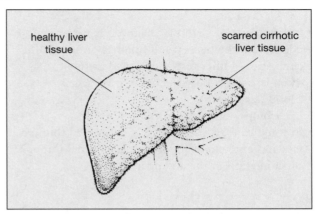

In the cirrhotic liver, healthy cells die and are replaced by scar tissue. Initially, the liver enlarges; in end-stage cirrhosis, the organ shrivels.

SYMPTOMS

- No symptoms in early stages.
- Loss of appetite; weight loss; nausea; diarrhea.
- Fatigue, weakness, and exhaustion.
- Jaundice; small, red, spidery veins (spider nevi) appearing on the skin, along with a tendency to bruise or bleed easily; severe itching.
- Swelling in the legs and ankles (edema) or abdomen (ascites).
- Darkened urine.
- Impotence, testicular atrophy, and enlarged breasts in men; cessation of menstruation (amenorrhea) in women.
- Black or bloody stools; vomiting of blood.
- Inability to concentrate, impaired memory, and irritability; mental confusion; trembling hands.

WHAT CAUSES IT?

- Alcoholism is the primary cause of cirrhosis, owing to a combination of the alcoholic's poor diet and the direct toxic effects of alcohol.
- Chronic viral hepatitis (types B, C, and D) or chronic active hepatitis may lead to cirrhosis.
- Some hereditary diseases, such as cystic fibrosis, hemochromatosis (iron accumulation), and Wilson's disease (deposition of copper), may injure the liver.
- Bile ducts, through which bile is released to the intestines to aid in digestion, may become blocked, inflamed, or scarred, resulting in a type of cirrhosis called biliary cirrhosis. Bile ducts may also be injured during gallbladder surgery.
- Prolonged exposure to toxic chemicals, like insecticides, herbicides, cleaning solvents, and engine exhaust, may harm the liver.
- Severe malnutrition alone may cause cirrhosis.
- Congestive heart failure may eventually lead to cirrhosis.

PREVENTION

- Consume no more than two drinks per day. If you suspect that you may have a drinking problem, seek help immediately. You will need to avoid alcohol completely in order to halt the progress of cirrhosis, and a doctor or support group may help you achieve this goal.
- Eat a healthy, balanced diet.

Cirrhosis *continued*

DIAGNOSIS

• In late stages of cirrhosis, diagnosis is very often evident from the history and findings on physical examination. Other tests mentioned are confirmatory in late stages but essential in early stages.

• Blood tests.

• Liver biopsy or scan.

• In some cases, the liver may be examined through a viewing instrument (laparoscope) inserted through a small incision in the abdomen.

HOW TO TREAT IT

• Stop drinking alcohol completely. Even if cirrhosis is not alcohol-induced, the liver may be further damaged by alcohol.

• Eat a low-salt diet to reduce fluid retention. Diuretics may be prescribed for this purpose as well.

• Antibiotics may be prescribed if excess fluid retained in the ankles or abdomen has become infected.

• Cholestyramine may be prescribed to relieve severe itching by binding bile salts in the small intestine.

• Antihypertensive drugs, such as beta-blockers, may be prescribed to lower blood pressure within the portal vein and thus reduce the risk of bleeding from esophageal varices.

• Surgical procedures to bypass or close off esophageal varices may be warranted.

• Restriction of dietary protein may ease or prevent neurological changes (hepatic encephalopathy).

• Laxatives (such as lactulose) may be used to speed the passage of toxins through the intestine.

• In advanced cases, a liver transplant may be recommended.

WHEN TO CALL A DOCTOR

• **EMERGENCY** If you begin to vomit blood, call an ambulance.

• Make an appointment with a doctor if you develop symptoms of cirrhosis.

• Seek help from a health professional or a support group if you are worried that you or someone close to you has a drinking problem.

Colitis, Ulcerative

WHAT IS IT?

Ulcerative colitis is a persistent inflammation of the lining of the colon; small ulcers form and eventually develop into abscesses. Episodes of painful, bloody diarrhea and other symptoms may vary in intensity and alternate with symptomless periods of normal bowel function. The condition may develop gradually over a period of years or appear without warning in a sudden, severe attack. In very severe episodes, the patient is at risk for potentially life-threatening blood poisoning (due to toxins found in infected abscesses) and excessive blood loss (due to bloody diarrhea). Other serious complications include massive dilatation of the colon (toxic megacolon) and perforation of the colon wall, allowing intestinal contents to spill into and infect the abdominal cavity (peritonitis). Those who have had ulcerative colitis for 10 years or more are at increased risk of colorectal cancer. The disorder most often affects young adults, especially women.

SYMPTOMS

- Recurrent episodes of bloody, pus- and mucus-filled diarrhea.
- Pain on the left side of the abdomen that lessens after a bowel movement.
- Painful bowel movements.
- Rectal pain and cramps.
- Weight loss.
- Symptoms in remote sites of the body, including arthritis and inflammation of the eyes.
- Symptoms of a severe attack: nausea and vomiting, dehydration, profuse sweating, loss of appetite, abdominal bloating, high fever (104°F), and heart palpitations.

WHAT CAUSES IT?

- The precise cause of ulcerative colitis is unknown, but several factors are correlated with increased risk.
- Hereditary factors may predispose people to ulcerative colitis. Those whose family members have had the disorder are at greater risk.
- Stress, anxiety, or depression may intensify symptoms in those who already have ulcerative colitis.
- Sensitivity to certain foods may also exacerbate symptoms in those so predisposed.

PREVENTION

- Ulcerative colitis cannot be prevented at present.

DIAGNOSIS

- Blood and stool samples are taken.
- Sigmoidoscopy (use of a lighted viewing tube) is employed to inspect the lower large intestine, or colonoscopy is used to view the entire large intestine.
- A biopsy of the colon lining is often taken during the sigmoidoscopy or colonoscopy.
- A barium enema may be performed. The barium creates a sharp x-ray image of the colon.
- Periodic screening for early colon cancer (with colonoscopy) is recommended for those who have had ulcerative colitis for more than 10 years.

HOW TO TREAT IT

- A hot water bottle or a heating pad may be applied to the abdomen to relieve cramps.
- Guard against irritating the colon during a flare-up by avoiding milk and milk products.
- Bed rest may be necessary during severe attacks.
- Anti-inflammatory drugs, such as sulfasalazine or corticosteroids, may be prescribed.
- Enemas containing corticosteroids or aspirin-like drugs may be used to treat internal inflammation.
- Nutritional supplements may be recommended for malnutrition and anemia, which are likely to occur.
- When diarrhea is severe, patients are hospitalized and fed intravenously to provide needed calories and nutrients and to allow the bowel to rest.
- Surgical removal of part or all of the colon may be required if the inflammation does not respond to medication. Results of such surgery are often very favorable. Some physicians recommend removal of the colon to prevent colon cancer in those who have had ulcerative colitis for 10 to 20 years.

WHEN TO CALL A DOCTOR

- Call a doctor if you experience painful diarrhea that contains blood or mucus.
- Call a doctor immediately if abdominal pain becomes severe, especially if you develop a high fever.

Colon Polyps

WHAT IS IT?

Colon polyps are nodular growths on the lining of the colon. Generally, they produce no symptoms and are only discovered when a colonoscopy (use of a flexible, lighted tube called a colonoscope to examine the colon) is performed. Polyps are common; two out of every three people over 60 have them. However, 90 percent of colorectal cancers arise from initially benign polyps, and the larger the polyp, the more likely it is to become cancerous. Thus, early detection and treatment are imperative (see Colorectal Cancer for recommendations on early detection screening procedures).

WHAT CAUSES IT?

• The cause of most colon polyps is unknown.
• Chronic inflammation of the colon due to ulcerative colitis may lead to the development of polyps.
• A diet high in fat (especially from red meat) and low in fiber may contribute to polyp formation.
• Hereditary factors may be involved. One disorder, known as familial colonic polyposis, is characterized by the growth of a large number of polyps (as many as 1,000 or more) in the colon. Gardner's syndrome, another hereditary disorder, produces multiple colonic and intestinal polyps as well as nonmalignant tumors in the bones and skin.
• People who have had colon polyps in the past are at increased risk of future polyps.

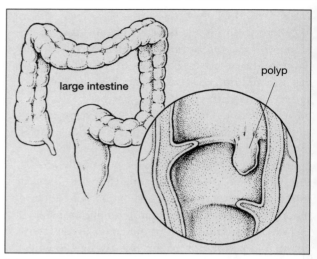

Polyps may form anywhere along the wall of the large intestine. Most are benign, although almost all colon cancers originate as polyps.

DIAGNOSIS

• A small, lighted viewing tube will be passed through the anus to the lower large intestine (sigmoidoscopy) or to the entire large intestine (colonoscopy) to allow the doctor to examine the colon.
• A barium enema may be necessary. Barium provides a clear outline of the colon when an x-ray is taken.
• Blood and stool samples may be taken. Stool samples are examined for occult blood (amounts too small to be seen) with a chemical test (stool guaiac).

HOW TO TREAT IT

• Generally, polyps are surgically removed upon detection, which often may be done during the diagnostic colonoscopy. In a few cases, a small incision (laparotomy) may be made in the abdomen to gain access to a portion of the colon. Surgery may involve removing the polyp and possibly a section of the colon and neighboring lymph nodes.

SYMPTOMS
• Rectal bleeding.
• Blood and mucus in the stool.
• Change in bowel movements.
• Abdominal pain.

PREVENTION

• Eat a diet low in animal fats and red meat but high in fiber.
• Get regular checkups if you have had colon polyps. Regular checkups are also advised if members of your family have had polyps.

WHEN TO CALL A DOCTOR

• Make an appointment with a doctor if you experience symptoms of colon polyps.
• Children in families with a hereditary predisposition toward colon polyps should be screened for colon disorders by age 12.

Colorectal Cancer

WHAT IS IT?

Colorectal cancer—one of the most common types of cancer—is the growth of malignant cells in the colon or rectum. Tumors in the colon are slow-growing but may eventually become large enough to obstruct the digestive tract. The cancer may spread to the liver, the lymph nodes, or other parts of the body, and symptoms may not appear until the cancer is quite advanced. However, if detected and treated early, the outlook is optimistic.

WHAT CAUSES IT?

• A diet high in animal fats (especially from red meat) and low in fiber is associated with a higher incidence of colorectal cancer.
• A personal or family history of colon polyps or ulcerative colitis increases the likelihood of colorectal cancer. A family history of colorectal, breast, or endometrial cancers is also a risk factor.
• The risk of colorectal cancer increases after age 40.

SYMPTOMS

• Often, there are no symptoms in early stages.
• Change in bowel habits (constipation, diarrhea, or extremely narrow stools) lasting for more than 10 days.
• Bloody or black, tarry stools.
• Pain or tenderness in the lower abdomen.
• Bloating, cramps, gas pains, and a protracted feeling of fullness.
• Loss of appetite and loss of weight.
• Fatigue, paleness, and heart palpitations (due to anemia that often occurs in conjunction with colorectal cancer).
• Inability to pass stools (a sign of intestinal obstruction, an emergency situation).

PREVENTION

• Eat a diet low in animal fats and high in fiber.
• Get regular checkups if you have a personal or family history of colon or digestive tract disease.
• The American Cancer Society recommends that people over 40 have an annual digital rectal exam, since 50 percent of colorectal cancers occur in the rectum.

• People over 50 should have an annual stool guaiac (Hemocult) test and a sigmoidoscopy (in which a lighted viewing tube is used to examine the colon) every three to five years (provided that two successive examinations prove negative).

DIAGNOSIS

• Blood and stool samples are taken.
• A digital rectal exam (wherein the doctor examines the rectum with a gloved finger) is performed.
• A barium enema may be necessary. The barium creates a sharp x-ray image of the colon.
• Sigmoidoscopy or colonoscopy is used to view the bowel, during which a biopsy may be taken.
• Colon cancer should always be suspected (and proper tests conducted) in older men and post-menopausal women with iron deficiency anemia.

HOW TO TREAT IT

• Surgery is necessary to remove the tumor. If the cancer is detected early, the surgery may be limited to a bowel resection (partial colectomy), in which the cancerous part of the colon is removed and the healthy parts are rejoined. Neighboring lymph nodes are also removed.
• If the tumor is blocking the colon, the cancerous part of the colon is removed, and the end of the remaining upper portion of the colon is brought through an opening created in the abdominal wall for wastes to pass through, into a bag. This procedure (colostomy) may be temporary, to allow the colon to heal after the operation, or permanent, when cancer is extensive (about 15 percent of cases).
• Radiation therapy may be used before surgery to reduce the size of the tumor or after surgery to destroy remaining cancer cells; chemotherapy may be used to halt the spread of the cancer.

WHEN TO CALL A DOCTOR

• Call a doctor if you experience changes in your bowel movements that persist for 10 days or more.
• Make an appointment with a doctor if you have a personal or family history of colon disease.
• **EMERGENCY** Get immediate medical attention if you experience a total inability to pass stools (intestinal obstruction).

Common Cold

WHAT IS IT?

The common cold is a general term for a group of minor, highly contagious viral infections that cause inflammation of the mucus linings of the nose and throat. Symptoms generally develop one to two days after exposure to the virus, and the cold is contagious for the first two to three days of symptoms. No cure exists, but spontaneous recovery generally occurs within a week to 10 days. Colds tend to be more frequent in the winter than in the summer and more common among children than adults, since immunity to many cold viruses develops with age. Colds may, however, cause serious complications in patients suffering from chronic respiratory disorders.

SYMPTOMS
- Nasal and sinus congestion.
- Nasal discharge and watering eyes.
- Sneezing.
- Dry cough, or a cough that produces little sputum.
- Sore throat.
- Headache.
- Mild fever (under 102°F) with chills.
- Fatigue.
- Cold sores on the mouth (due to the cold virus reactivating a dormant herpes simplex infection).
- General muscle and joint aches.

WHAT CAUSES IT?
- Over 200 different strains of viruses (predominantly rhinoviruses and coronaviruses) cause colds.
- Infected persons may spread cold viruses by direct contact, such as shaking hands or kissing, or through the air, by coughing or sneezing. The virus may also spread via contaminated objects, such as drinking glasses or playing cards.
- Contrary to popular belief, colds are not caused by fatigue, cold air, or wet hair or clothes.

PREVENTION
- Wash hands frequently with soap and warm water, especially after visiting public places.
- Avoid touching the face with unwashed hands.
- Don't share towels or drinking glasses.
- Try to limit exposure to people with colds.
- Contrary to popular belief, taking large doses of vitamin C has not been shown to prevent colds.

DIAGNOSIS
- Diagnosis is by observation of symptoms and does not require a doctor.

HOW TO TREAT IT
- Take aspirin or acetaminophen to relieve headaches and muscle aches and to reduce fever. Acetaminophen is recommended for children under 12.
- Use cold medications sparingly. Avoid "shotgun" remedies that claim to treat all cold symptoms—they are often ineffectual. Nasal decongestant sprays and drops should not be used for more than a few days, as they may actually aggravate congestion with extensive use. If you are coughing up mucus, avoid cough suppressants, since they will permit mucus to accumulate in the lungs.
- Drink plenty of fluids to help loosen mucus secretions in the lungs.
- Gargle with warm, salty water several times a day to soothe a sore throat. Sucking on hard candy will help keep the throat lubricated.
- Rest at home (in bed if you feel like it) for the first day or two to aid recovery and to prevent spreading the cold to others.
- Antibiotics do not help treat a cold, but they may be prescribed if you develop a secondary bacterial infection.

WHEN TO CALL A DOCTOR
- Call a doctor if cold symptoms persist for more than two weeks, especially if they increase in severity.
- Call a doctor if you suffer from a chronic respiratory disorder and you catch a cold.

Concussion

WHAT IS IT?

A concussion is characterized by a brief loss of consciousness following an injury or blow to the head. The blow is forceful enough to cause the brain to bump against the skull and temporarily disturb the normal electrical activity in the brain, but it is not traumatic enough to result in more-severe injuries, such as cerebral lacerations or bruises. Indeed, concussion is the mildest form of brain-skull impact, and full recovery generally occurs within 24 to 48 hours; however, repeated concussions may eventually cause permanent brain damage.

WHAT CAUSES IT?

• Automobile crashes, industrial accidents, and falls are the most common causes of head injury.
• Blows to the head sustained due to boxing, sports injuries, or physical assault may cause a concussion.

SYMPTOMS

• Brief loss of consciousness.
• Headache, dizziness, and blurred vision.
• Occasional nausea and vomiting.
• Inability to remember events immediately prior to the injury.
• Drowsiness.
• Mental confusion.
• Persistent insomnia, headaches, dizziness, irritability, moodiness, and depression. This combination of symptoms is known as postconcussive syndrome and may continue for several weeks.
• Slow thinking, impaired concentration, and slurred speech—known as punch-drunk syndrome—as a result of repeated concussions (an occupational hazard for boxers).

PREVENTION

• Wear seat belts in the car and drive defensively. Wear a helmet if you ride a motorcycle or bicycle.
• Wear protective head gear when playing sports.

DIAGNOSIS

• Your doctor will request a thorough description of the accident or event that resulted in the concussion.
• An observation period of 24 to 48 hours will be recommended to monitor your mental state, level of alertness, and any symptoms.
• X-rays or CT (computed tomography) scans of the skull may be necessary.

HOW TO TREAT IT

• Call a doctor immediately after any loss of consciousness following a head injury. The doctor will recommend 24 hours of bed rest under observation.
• Avoid driving a car until the doctor has ruled out any complications.
• Acetaminophen or ibuprofen may be recommended to relieve pain. However, avoid aspirin, because it may provoke internal bleeding.

WHEN TO CALL A DOCTOR

• See a doctor immediately if you or someone you know has sustained a concussion. The doctor will run tests to determine whether more-severe head injuries have occurred in addition to the concussion.
• Call a doctor if the initial symptoms do not diminish within a few days after the first examination.
• **EMERGENCY** After the preliminary examination, call the doctor back immediately if any of the following symptoms occur: the patient cannot awaken or is incoherent upon awakening; convulsions; severe headaches; repeated vomiting; visual disturbances; persistent drowsiness; shortness of breath; speech difficulty; or a staggering gait.

Congestive Heart Failure

WHAT IS IT?

Congestive heart failure (CHF) is a serious condition marked by the inability of the heart to pump enough blood to meet the body's oxygen demands. Heart failure can result from either a reduced ability of the heart muscle to contract or from a mechanical problem that limits the ability of the heart's chambers to fill with blood. When weakened, the heart is unable to keep up with the demands placed upon it; blood returns to the heart faster than it can be pumped out so that it gets backed up or congested—hence the name of the disorder. The heart attempts to compensate in a number of ways. It beats faster and expands somewhat more than usual as it fills with blood, so that when it contracts, more blood is forced out to the body. In addition, the decreased volume of blood reaching the kidneys causes them to stimulate a hormonal cascade (renin-angiotensin system), which results in the retention of sodium and water. These efforts help meet the body's demands in the short term, but they ultimately have deleterious long-term effects. Faster beating allows less time for the heart to refill after contraction, so that less blood ends up being circulated. Also, the extra effort increases the heart muscle's demand for oxygen; if this need is not met adequately, heart rhythm can become dangerously erratic (see Cardiac Arrhythmias) and ultimately fatal.

Failure of the left side of the heart (left-sided failure) is more common. It leads to increased pressure in the pulmonary veins in the lungs, which forces fluid into the surrounding microscopic air sacs, or alveoli, that transfer oxygen to the bloodstream. As the alveoli fill with fluid, they no longer function properly, which drastically limits the amount of oxygen available to the body (see Pulmonary Edema for more information) and produces the most characteristic symptoms of congestive heart failure: fatigue and shortness of breath. In right-sided failure, the increased pressure in the veins returning blood from the rest of the body combined with the compensatory retention of sodium and water leads to fluid accumulation and swelling in the abdomen, liver, and legs. Often, both left- and right-sided heart failure occur together.

Congestive heart failure should not be confused with a heart attack, which involves sudden tissue death of the heart muscle. Although heart failure may occur suddenly in some cases, gradual loss of function is more common. Fatigue, shortness of breath on exertion, and increased frequency of nighttime urination develop and worsen over time. Shortness of breath is often worse when lying down—a condition known as orthopnea—as fluid from the legs pools in the lungs. Elevating the head with pillows eases chest congestion, but in advanced stages the patient may be unable to recline at all without severe breathlessness, and may need to sleep upright in a chair. CHF occurs most frequently in those over 60 and is the leading cause of hospitalization and death in that age group. In over 50 percent of cases, sudden death occurs due to a cardiac arrhythmia, or irregular heartbeat (see Cardiac

SYMPTOMS

- Severe fatigue and weakness.
- Irregular or rapid heartbeat.
- Shortness of breath and wheezing after limited physical exertion. In advanced cases shortness of breath occurs even at rest, and attacks of severe breathlessness disturb sleep (left-sided failure).
- Dry cough or cough that produces frothy or bloody sputum (left-sided failure).
- Frequent urination at night (right-sided failure).
- Swelling of the ankles and feet, or swelling in the lower back if the patient is bedridden (right-sided failure).
- Rapid weight gain due to fluid retention (right-sided failure).
- Abdominal pain and fullness (right-sided failure).
- Swollen neck veins (right-sided failure).
- Loss of appetite (anorexia), nausea, and vomiting.
- General feeling of poor health.
- Anxiety. In severe cases irritability, restlessness, and mental confusion may occur.

Congestive Heart Failure *continued*

Arrhythmias for more information). Unfortunately, antiarrhythmic medications may not be effective in controlling arrhythmias caused by CHF.

There is no cure for heart failure, although measures are taken to treat the underlying cause, if possible. Rest, restricted salt intake, and medication are used to ease the strain on the heart and to relieve symptoms. CHF is a serious health risk; for many patients the outlook is uncertain and depends on the extent of the disease and the patient's response to therapy. However, with proper treatment it is possible for many patients to live with CHF and to manage many symptoms effectively. It is important that patients adhere to prescribed treatment regimens; noncompliance with a doctor's recommendations regarding diet, rest, or medication essentially guarantees that the disease will worsen.

WHAT CAUSES IT?

• Coronary artery disease (obstruction of the coronary arteries by atherosclerotic plaque so that heart muscle is starved of oxygen) leading to damaged heart muscle due to heart attacks is the most common cause of CHF (see Coronary Artery Disease and Myocardial Infarction for more information).
• Heart-muscle injury due to viral infection (see Myocarditis) or long-term drug or alcohol use (see Cardiomyopathy) may result in CHF.
• Conditions that overwork the heart may lead to CHF. Such conditions include: heart valve defects, high blood pressure, increased levels of thyroid hormones (thyrotoxicosis), and anemia.
• Infiltration of the heart muscle by other tissue, as occurs with amyloidosis (accumulation of a starch-like protein) for instance, may cause CHF.
• Triggers for CHF to develop in a weakened heart include pulmonary embolism, severe bacterial or viral infections, pregnancy or childbirth, sudden, severe blood loss (hypovolemic shock), and physical overexertion.
• Right-sided heart failure commonly results from left-sided heart failure.
• CHF may result from restricted entry of blood into the heart due to thickening of the tissue surrounding the heart (pericardium), or to accumulation of excessive fibrous tissue in the heart muscle.

PREVENTION

• Don't smoke.
• Consume no more than two alcoholic beverages per day.
• Eat a healthy, balanced diet low in salt and fat, exercise regularly, and lose weight if you are more than 20 percent overweight.
• Adhere to a prescribed treatment program for other forms of heart disease.

DIAGNOSIS

• Patient history and physical examination.
• Chest x-rays.
• Blood and urine tests.
• An electrocardiogram (ECG or EKG) may be performed to measure the electrical activity of the heart. ECG abnormalities can indicate rhythm disturbances, heart-muscle damage, inadequate blood flow to segments of the heart, and enlargement of the heart muscle. You may be given a portable ECG device, known as a Holter monitor, to measure the heart's electrical activity over a 24-hour period.
• Exercise stress testing. Blood pressure, heart rate, ECG, and oxygen consumption rates are measured while you walk on a treadmill.
• An echocardiogram, which uses sound waves to produce images of the heart, may be performed.
• A coronary angiography may be performed to evaluate narrowings of the coronary arteries. In this procedure a tiny catheter is inserted into an artery in a leg or arm and threaded up to the coronary arteries. A contrast material is then injected, which provides a clear x-ray image of the blood vessels.

HOW TO TREAT IT

• Your doctor will advise you to decrease activity and get more rest. (This may include more sleep per night, and planned naps or rest periods during the day.) However, limited physical activity should be resumed if at all possible to prevent wasting of muscle tissue. Physical therapy may be recommended in advanced cases.
• Your doctor will advise you to reduce your salt intake, since salt contributes to fluid retention and swelling. Eat smaller, more frequent meals, since less effort is required to digest smaller portions.

Congestive Heart Failure *continued*

• Avoid caffeine, which may exacerbate heartbeat irregularities.

• Vasodilators, such as captopril, enalapril, or hydralazine, may be prescribed to expand blood vessels, thus reducing blood pressure and easing blood flow.

• Various types of diuretics, such as hydrochlorothiazide, metolazone, furosemide, or bumetanide, will be prescribed to help eliminate excess fluid from body tissues.

• Digitalis glycosides may be prescribed to strengthen contractions of the heart muscle (in the United States digoxin is the most commonly prescribed type of digitalis).

• Various other medications, including anticoagulants such as heparin, calcium channel blockers such as nifedipine, bronchodilators such as aminophylline, and tranquilizers such as diazepam, may be prescribed to improve blood flow, ease breathing, and relieve anxiety.

• Special elastic support stockings that reduce swelling in the legs may be prescribed.

• In severe cases it may be necessary to administer oxygen through a nasal tube. Mechanical devices for administration of oxygen are available for home use after the condition has stabilized in the hospital.

• Surgery may be required to repair or replace heart valves or bypass blocked coronary arteries.

• Percutaneous transluminal angioplasty (insertion and then inflation of a small balloon in an obstructed coronary artery via a catheter) may be performed to widen the artery and improve blood flow.

• A heart transplant may be advised if the heart muscle has been badly damaged. The survival rate for this surgery is 80 percent after one year and over 60 percent after four years.

WHEN TO CALL A DOCTOR

• Make an appointment with a doctor if you regularly experience fatigue and shortness of breath after mild physical activity.

• **EMERGENCY** Call an ambulance immediately if you experience severe breathlessness.

• **EMERGENCY** Call an ambulance if you experience crushing chest pain, with or without nausea, vomiting, profuse sweating, breathlessness, weakness, or intense feelings of dread. Such symptoms may indicate a heart attack.

• Call a doctor if you experience any of the following during treatment for congestive heart failure: fever, rapid or irregular heartbeat, wheezing, severe shortness of breath, or any worsening of the other symptoms of congestive heart failure.

Conjunctivitis

WHAT IS IT?

Conjunctivitis is an inflammation of the mucus membranes (conjunctiva) that line the inner surface of the eyelids and the whites of the eyes. It may be triggered either by an infection or an allergic reaction. Known as pinkeye because the blood vessels in the whites of the eyes dilate and redden, conjunctivitis is highly contagious when caused by an infection. It is usually not serious, although it should be treated promptly to prevent possible complications and transmission to others. With proper treatment, conjunctivitis generally disappears within two or three weeks.

WHAT CAUSES IT?

• Bacterial or viral infections are the most common causes of conjunctivitis.
• Allergies (to such things as pollen, cosmetics, and contact lens cleaning solution) are a possible cause.
• Air pollution or chemical irritants may lead to conjunctivitis.
• Cervical infections (chlamydia, genital herpes, or gonorrhea) in a pregnant woman may result in potentially blinding conjunctivitis in the baby.
• A partially blocked tear duct is a possible cause.

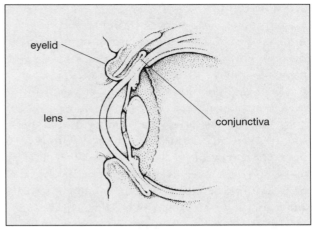

Inflammation of the conjunctiva produces characteristic redness and irritation in the eyes but seldom affects vision.

SYMPTOMS

• Redness of the white of the eye.
• Itching and a gritty sensation in the eye.
• Oozing discharge from the eyes.
• Copious tearing.
• Dried crusts that form during sleep, which may bind the eyelids together.
• Swollen eyelids.
• Aversion to bright lights (photophobia).

PREVENTION

• Try never to touch the eyes, for example, when handling contact lenses.
• Wash your hands often with soap and warm water.
• Change towels and pillowcases often.
• Do not share towels.
• Do not share eye makeup; replace cosmetics every four to six months.
• Avoid substances that trigger eye irritation.

DIAGNOSIS

• The diagnosis can generally be made by the typical findings on physical examination.
• Swab samples may be taken and cultured to identify the type of bacterial infection involved.

HOW TO TREAT IT

• First, consult a doctor or ophthalmologist to confirm the diagnosis. It's important to determine whether infectious conjunctivitis is bacterial or viral in origin. Bacterial conjunctivitis is the more serious of the two and requires treatment; viral conjunctivitis typically resolves on its own, without complication.
• Your doctor may prescribe antibiotic or steroid eyedrops or ointments. Use as directed and be careful not to allow the tip of the eyedrop bottle to touch the eyes.
• For infectious conjunctivitis, soak a clean cloth in warm water, wring it dry, and apply it to the eye.
• For allergic conjunctivitis, apply cool compresses to the eye. Antihistamines may be recommended.

WHEN TO CALL A DOCTOR

• Call a doctor if conjunctivitis symptoms do not improve after three or four days of treatment, especially if fever, increased pain, or changes in vision develop. In the case of bacterial conjunctivitis, prompt treatment will avert complications.

Constipation

WHAT IS IT?
Constipation is characterized by infrequent and sometimes painful bowel movements. Intestinal contractions slow down, allowing more time for the bowels to remove water from food wastes. This results in hard stools that are difficult to pass. However, it should be noted that normal frequency of bowel movements varies greatly from person to person. It is perfectly normal for some people to have three bowel movements per day, while others have as few as three per week; true constipation involves the passage of hard stools less than three times in a week and is usually accompanied by bloating and discomfort. (Note: Any change in a person's usual frequency of bowel movements may be a sign of a more serious underlying disorder.)

SYMPTOMS
- Infrequent, difficult, and possibly painful bowel movements.
- Straining during bowel movements.
- Continued sensation of fullness after bowel movements.
- Hard, dry stool.
- Abdominal swelling.

WHAT CAUSES IT?
- Lack of fiber in the diet or inadequate fluid intake.
- Prolonged inactivity or severe depression.
- Irregular or abnormal contractions of the bowel muscles owing to lack of exercise or to disorders such as irritable bowel syndrome, diabetes mellitus, hypercalcemia, hypothyroidism, or colorectal cancer.
- Failure to go to the bathroom when the urge strikes may lead to the formation of hard, impacted stools.
- Overuse of laxatives, aspirin, or aluminum- or calcium-based antacids may impair normal bowel function.
- Constipation may occur as a side effect of certain medications, including antihypertensive drugs (calcium channel blockers and beta-blockers), tricyclic antidepressants, narcotics, and atropine.

PREVENTION
- Eat high fiber, low fat. Try to get at least five servings per day of fiber-rich foods, including raw fruits and vegetables, whole-grain breads and cereals, bran, dried peas and beans, and potato skins.
- Drink at least eight glasses of water per day.
- Exercise regularly.
- Go to the bathroom as soon as the urge strikes.

DIAGNOSIS
- Evaluation will include medical history (with emphasis on bowel habits) and a physical exam.
- Blood and stool samples may be obtained.
- Rarely, a sigmoidoscopy (use of a long, flexible, lighted scope to view the lower large intestine) may be performed.
- A barium enema may be necessary. The barium dye creates a sharp x-ray image of the colon.

HOW TO TREAT IT
- Follow prevention tips above.
- Drink a cup of hot liquid (like coffee or tea), especially first thing in the morning, since it may activate what is known as the gastrocolic reflex, which induces a bowel movement by stimulating the colon.
- Use laxatives only as a last resort, on your doctor's advice. Bulk-forming agents, including bran, psyllium (Metamucil, Konsyl), and methyl cellulose (Citrucel, Cologel), are usually the best choice. Never use mineral oil as a laxative.
- Do not use enemas unless otherwise instructed by your doctor, as they may damage the bowel.

WHEN TO CALL A DOCTOR
- Make an appointment with a doctor if constipation persists for two weeks or more, and increased fiber intake and exercise have failed to help.
- Call a doctor if fever or severe abdominal pain occurs with constipation, if abdominal bloating, cramping, or other discomfort disrupts your routine, or if you notice blood in the stool.
- Call a doctor if you experience constipation shortly after beginning a new medication. The prescription may need to be adjusted.
- Call your doctor if you notice any major change in normal bowel habits.

Corneal Ulcers

WHAT IS IT?

A corneal ulcer is an open sore on the cornea—the tough, transparent membrane that covers and protects the pupil and iris (colored portion) of the eye. Corneal ulcers are typically very painful, especially when caused by a bacterial infection, and feel as if something is intractably lodged in the eye even if no foreign object is visible upon close inspection. A simple abrasion on the surface of the cornea produces the same sort of pain, but this usually subsides within 48 hours. If pain persists longer, chances are great that some type of infection has set in, causing an ulceration, which requires immediate treatment. If neglected, corneal ulcers may permanently scar the cornea, resulting in permanent vision impairment. In rare cases the infection may penetrate the cornea to involve other structures of the eye, requiring emergency surgery.

SYMPTOMS

- Severe eye pain; feeling that something is lodged in the eye.
- Redness in the eyes.
- Heightened sensitivity to light; aversion to bright light.
- Excessive tearing.
- Blurred vision.
- Eyelid spasms.
- Visible white, gray, or yellow ulceration on the cornea.

WHAT CAUSES IT?

- Corneal ulcers most often originate as a corneal abrasion (due to a scratch from an insect or a tiny fleck of steel, glass, dirt, or dust) that then becomes infected with bacteria, viruses, fungus, or protozoans like amoebae. Viral corneal ulcers are most often due to infection with the herpes simplex virus.
- Contact lens wearers are particularly prone to corneal ulcers.
- Eye surgery or preexisting corneal disease may increase the likelihood of corneal ulceration.
- Hyperthyroidism (Graves' disease) often causes the eyelids to retract, preventing the eyes from being bathed in tears, thus promoting corneal ulcers.
- Chemical irritation may be a cause.

PREVENTION

- If you wear contact lenses, remove and clean them daily (or as recommended by the manufacturer or your ophthalmologist).
- Avoid smoke and other airborne irritants.
- Wear protective goggles when warranted (at a workbench, for example); wear sunglasses outdoors on windy days.
- Wash hands frequently and keep your fingers away from your eyes if you have cold sores.

DIAGNOSIS

- Physical examination by an ophthalmologist is usually all that is required to diagnose a corneal ulcer. A special dye (fluorescein) that provides a clear view of the corneal surface when blue light is shined upon it may be used to aid in diagnosis.
- A swab culture of the ulcer or, if necessary, a biopsy (tissue sample) will be obtained to identify the infectious organism.

HOW TO TREAT IT

- Corneal ulcers caused by bacterial infections are treated with antibiotic eyedrops or ointments, and sometimes oral antibiotics. In severe cases antibiotics may be injected locally near the eye for faster absorption.
- Viral ulcers may be treated with antiviral drops. While these may help to ease the ulcer, further ulcers may occur in cases where the infection is persistent, such as those caused by the herpes simplex virus.
- Fungal or amebic corneal ulcers are treated with an appropriate drug.
- Topical corticosteroid drops may be prescribed in some cases to reduce inflammation.
- Severe cases that result in corneal scarring may warrant corneal transplant.
- Any underlying eye disorder is also treated.

WHEN TO CALL A DOCTOR

- See an ophthalmologist right away for any eye pain that persists more than 48 hours.

Corns and Calluses

WHAT IS IT?

A callus is a patch of rough, thickened skin that forms on the feet, hands, or other sites where constant pressure or irritation provokes the skin cells in the affected area to grow at an accelerated rate. The callus itself is generally painless (and in fact forms to protect the skin below), although the underlying skin may be tender. A corn is a small, round callus on or between the toes. Corns and calluses are common, minor problems and usually respond promptly to treatment. However, corns and calluses put people with diabetes mellitus at greater risk of foot infection and other complications.

SYMPTOMS

- For calluses: a thickened, hard, rough, sometimes yellowish patch of skin.
- For corns: a small bump of thickened skin on the side or top of a toe joint or between the toes. The skin surrounding it may be tender.

WHAT CAUSES IT?

- Constant pressure from ill-fitting shoes is the most common cause of corns and calluses on the feet.
- Activities such as tennis, carpentry, dancing, writing, or playing the violin or guitar may cause calluses by putting repeated pressure and friction on the hands, fingers, or other parts of the body.

PREVENTION

- Wear comfortable shoes that fit well.
- Wear work gloves when performing manual labor.

DIAGNOSIS

- Diagnosis is based on visual examination of the affected area and does not require a doctor.

HOW TO TREAT IT

- Some calluses, such as those formed by dancing or playing the guitar, protect the skin from abrasion and need not be treated.
- Corns and calluses on the feet often disappear on their own if ill-fitting shoes are replaced with good, comfortable footwear.
- Doughnut-shaped felt pads (available in drugstores) may ease pressure from shoes around the corn or callus.
- Soak the affected area in warm water daily for at least five minutes, then use a pumice stone, rough towel, or callus file to rub away the upper layers of the thickened skin. (However, abrading a callus in this manner is not recommended for those with diabetes or poor circulation.)
- Do not use salicylic acid–containing ointment (such as wart medications) on a corn or callus.
- The doctor may inject cortisone into the corn or callus to prevent inflammation and pain.
- The doctor may use surgery or chemical peels to remove a corn or callus that is resistant to treatment.

WHEN TO CALL A DOCTOR

- People with diabetes mellitus should see a doctor if corns or calluses develop on the feet, since sensation and circulation may be diminished.
- Make an appointment with a podiatrist if the corn or callus persists despite treatment and it is interfering with your normal daily activities.
- Make an appointment with a podiatrist if the area around the corn or callus becomes red, painful, swollen, hot, or ulcerated—signs of inflammation, possibly due to infection.

Coronary Artery Disease

WHAT IS IT?

Coronary artery disease (CAD), the leading cause of death in the United States, is a narrowing of the coronary arteries, the vessels that supply blood to the heart muscle. Physical activity increases the oxygen needs of the body, and the heart responds to the greater demand by pumping blood more vigorously, which in turn increases the oxygen needs of the heart muscle. In CAD, narrowed coronary arteries limit the supply of blood to the heart muscle. If narrowing is not extensive, difficulties may occur only during physical exertion, when the narrowed arteries are unable to meet the increased oxygen requirements of the heart; however, as the disease worsens, the narrowed arteries may starve heart muscle of oxygen during periods of normal activity, or even at rest. Coronary artery disease is generally due to the buildup of plaques in the arterial walls, a process known as atherosclerosis. Plaques are composed of cholesterol-rich fatty deposits, collagen, other proteins, and excess smooth muscle cells. Atherosclerosis, which usually progresses very gradually over a

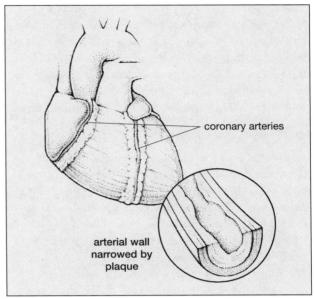

coronary arteries

arterial wall
narrowed by
plaque

The coronary arteries supply the heart muscle with freshly oxygenated blood. A buildup of atherosclerotic plaque in these arteries may deprive the heart of a sufficient amount of oxygen (causing chest pain) and, if the artery becomes totally blocked, result in a heart attack.

lifetime, thickens and narrows the arterial walls, impeding the flow of blood. Blood clots form more easily on arterial walls roughened by plaque deposits. If the clots grow, they may block the narrowed coronary artery completely and cause a heart attack (see Myocardial Infarction for more information). Arteries may also narrow suddenly as a result of an arterial spasm. (Spasms are most commonly triggered by smoking.) Symptoms of coronary artery disease usually develop insidiously. In the early stages of the disease, there are generally no symptoms. As the disease progresses, chest pain (angina pectoris) may develop during periods of physical activity or emotional stress, because the narrowed arteries cannot supply the heart with the increased amount of blood and oxygen necessary at those times. Angina usually subsides quickly with rest, but over time, symptoms arise with less exertion, and CAD may eventually lead to a full-blown heart attack. However, in a third of CAD cases, angina never develops, and a heart attack can occur suddenly with no prior warning. Although CAD can be a life-threatening condition, the outcome of the disease is in many ways up to the

SYMPTOMS

- No symptoms in the early stages of coronary artery disease.
- Chest pain (angina), or milder pressure, tightness, squeezing, burning, aching, or heaviness in the chest, lasting between 30 seconds to five minutes. The pain or discomfort is usually located in the center of the chest just under the breastbone, and may radiate down the arm (usually the left), up into the neck, or along the jaw line. The pain is generally brought on by exertion or stress and stops with rest. The amount of exertion required to produce angina is reproducible and predictable.
- Shortness of breath, dizziness, or a choking sensation, accompanying chest pain.
- A sudden increase in the severity of angina, or angina at rest, is a sign of unstable angina that requires immediate medical attention because a heart attack may shortly occur.

Coronary Artery Disease *continued*

patient. Damage to the arteries can be slowed or halted with lifestyle changes, including smoking cessation, dietary modifications, and regular exercise, or by medications to lower blood pressure and cholesterol levels. Additional goals of treatment, which may involve medication and sometimes surgery, are to relieve symptoms, ease circulation, and prolong life.

WHAT CAUSES IT?

• Smoking promotes the development of plaque in the arteries. Also, by increasing the amount of carbon monoxide in the bloodstream and decreasing the amount of oxygen available to the heart, smoking increases the likelihood of angina pectoris.

• High blood cholesterol levels lead to coronary artery disease. LDL (low-density lipoprotein) enters the lining of the arterial walls where, after being chemically altered, its cholesterol can be incorporated into plaque (see Hypercholesterolemia for more information).

• High blood pressure predisposes to CAD.

• People with diabetes mellitus are at greater risk for atherosclerosis.

• Obesity may promote atherosclerosis.

• Lack of exercise (sedentary lifestyle) may encourage atherosclerosis.

• Men are at greater risk than women for coronary artery disease, although the risk for postmenopausal women approaches that of men as estrogen production decreases with the menopause. This risk may be partly offset, however, by estrogen replacement therapy.

• Women over age 35 who take birth control pills and smoke cigarettes have a higher risk of atherosclerosis.

• A family history of premature heart attacks is associated with greater CAD risk.

• A spasm of the muscular layer of the arterial walls may cause an artery to contract and produce angina. Spasms may be induced by smoking, extreme emotional stress, or exposure to cold air.

PREVENTION

• Don't smoke.

• Eat a diet low in saturated fat, cholesterol, and salt.

• Pursue a program of moderate, regular exercise. People over age 50 who have led a sedentary lifestyle should check with a doctor before beginning an exercise program.

• Lose weight if you are more than 20 percent overweight.

• Your doctor may advise you to take a low dose of aspirin every day if you are at high risk for CAD. Aspirin reduces the tendency for the blood to clot, thereby decreasing the risk of heart attack. However, such a regimen should only be initiated under a doctor's expressed recommendation.

• Women at or approaching menopause may want to discuss the cardioprotective benefits of postmenopausal estrogen replacement therapy with their doctors.

DIAGNOSIS

• Patient history and physical exam. If you suffer a heart attack, diagnosis will often be made immediately upon examination by a doctor or emergency rescue technician.

• An electrocardiogram (ECG or EKG) may be performed to measure changes in the electrical activity of the heart resulting from abnormalities in the flow of blood or a prior heart attack. In some cases your doctor may provide you with a portable ECG device, known as a Holter monitor, in order to record the electrical activity of the heart over a 24-hour period.

• Chest x-rays.

• Blood tests.

• Exercise testing. Blood pressure, heartbeat, and breathing rates are measured by ECG while you walk on a treadmill.

• An injection of the radioisotope thallium may be given after an exercise test to determine the flow of blood to the heart muscle. Images are recorded with a special detector and camera.

• An echocardiogram, which uses ultrasound waves to create moving images of the heart, may be performed.

• A coronary angiography is performed to determine the presence of narrowings in the coronary arteries. In this procedure a tiny catheter is inserted into an artery of a leg or arm and threaded up into the coronary arteries. A contrast material is then injected from the end of the catheter into the coronary arteries, and x-rays are taken.

Coronary Artery Disease *continued*

HOW TO TREAT IT

• Emergency treatment and immediate hospitalization is necessary if a heart attack occurs—commonly signaled by crushing, persistent chest pain (see Myocardial Infarction).

• Follow prevention tips for a heart-healthy lifestyle, including a low-fat diet and regular physical exercise. Avoid excessive alcohol consumption, nasal decongestants, and diet pills, all of which may raise blood pressure.

• Rapidly acting nitrates, such as nitroglycerin, or longer-acting nitrates like isosorbide dinitrate may be prescribed to dilate blood vessels and relieve or prevent symptoms of angina. A nitroglycerin tablet placed under your tongue (sublingually) at the onset of an angina attack usually relieves the pain within minutes. Sublingual nitroglycerin may also be taken just prior to activities that commonly provoke angina. However, for a given angina attack, you should not take more than three nitroglycerin tablets at five-minute intervals—pain lasting longer than this may signal a heart attack. Intravenous nitrates may be administered in patients with unstable angina. Nitrates may also be prescribed in the form of patches or ointments for continuous protection.

• Beta-blockers, such as propranolol or metoprolol, are prescribed to reduce the heart's oxygen demand by slowing the heart rate and lowering blood pressure.

• ACE inhibitors, such as enalapril, may be prescribed to reduce blood pressure and dilate blood vessels.

• Calcium channel blockers, such as verapamil, diltiazem, or nifedipine, may be prescribed to reduce the heart's oxygen demands and to increase coronary blood flow.

• Anticoagulants such as heparin will be administered to reduce the risk of blood clots in patients with unstable angina.

• Vasodilators, such as captopril, enalapril, or hydralazine, may be prescribed to expand blood vessels, thus reducing blood pressure and easing blood flow.

• An obstructed coronary may be opened with percutaneous transluminal coronary angioplasty, or PTCA. In this procedure a small balloon is inserted into the circulatory system via a catheter and guided to the site of an arterial blockage. The balloon is then inflated to compress the plaque, widening the passageway and thereby improving blood flow. PTCA usually requires a hospital stay of only a few days.

• Coronary bypass surgery may be performed to improve blood flow to the heart. A mammary artery or a vein taken from the leg is grafted onto the damaged coronary artery to circumvent a narrowed or blocked portion.

• A heart transplant may be advised in severe cases where the heart muscle has been badly damaged. The survival rate for heart transplant is 80 percent after one year and 63 percent after four years.

WHEN TO CALL A DOCTOR

• **EMERGENCY** Call an ambulance if you experience crushing chest pain, with or without nausea, vomiting, profuse sweating, shortness of breath, weakness, or intense feelings of dread.

• **EMERGENCY** Call an ambulance if chest pain from previously diagnosed angina does not subside after 10 to 15 minutes.

• **EMERGENCY** Call an ambulance the first time you experience intense chest pain.

• Call a doctor if attacks of previously diagnosed angina become more frequent or severe or occur at rest.

Costochondritis

WHAT IS IT?

Costochondritis is an inflammation of the cartilage of the rib cage. Commonly, it involves the second and third ribs, near the top of the breastbone. Also known as Tietze's syndrome (after the German physician who identified it), this condition generally affects young adults and occurs in both sexes with equal frequency. The symptoms of chest pain and tenderness, which can come on gradually or suddenly, may be either moderate or intense. The pain is often aggravated by body movement and may radiate to the shoulder or arm. Even though costochondritis is not a serious disorder, it may cause great anxiety, since the intense chest pain can be mistaken for that of a heart attack. The condition may last for a week, or up to several years. While some patients experience recurrent episodes, spontaneous and permanent remission is the norm.

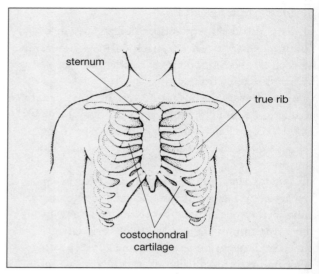

The rib cage is not comprised entirely of bone; a significant portion of it is cartilage that connects the true ribs to the sternum (breastbone).

SYMPTOMS

- Chest pain, usually in the front of the rib cage. The pain is exacerbated by movements that change the position of the ribs or by the direct application of pressure on the affected region.
- Hard swelling of the tissues around the breast bone.
- Anxiety and hyperventilation during acute episodes of pain.

WHAT CAUSES IT?

- The cause of costochondritis is unknown in the majority of cases.
- Costochondritis may result from an injury or blow to the chest or even from an episode of especially vigorous coughing.
- Costochondritis may be one feature of polyarthritis (widespread inflammation of cartilage).

PREVENTION

- Wear seat belts and drive defensively.
- Wear protective gear when playing sports.

DIAGNOSIS

- Physical examination and patient history are necessary.
- A chest x-ray, an electrocardiogram (a test to monitor the heart's electrical activity), and blood tests may be performed in order to rule out more serious underlying disorders, including heart and lung diseases.

HOW TO TREAT IT

- Rest and avoid exercises or movements that aggravate the inflammation and cause pain; symptoms generally disappear on their own over time.
- Take aspirin or acetaminophen to relieve pain.
- Applying heat (for example, with a heating pad) may provide relief.
- Corticosteroid injections may be used to reduce pain and swelling in more severe cases.

WHEN TO CALL A DOCTOR

- The pain of costochondritis is not serious. However, any intense chest pain warrants immediate emergency medical evaluation, since it may be a sign of a more serious problem, such as a heart attack.

Crohn's Disease

WHAT IS IT?

Crohn's disease, also known as regional ileitis, is a chronic inflammation of the intestinal wall, most commonly in the final portion of the small intestine. The colon or rectum and, less often, the upper digestive tract may also be affected. The inflammation involves deep layers of the intestinal wall, where ulcers and abscesses may form. The ulcers may erode the wall completely, creating abnormal passages (fistulas) to other parts of the intestine, to other organs such as the bladder, or to the skin. Deep cracks (fissures) may also develop in and around the anus. Inflammation may thicken the intestinal wall until the passageway becomes severely obstructed. Symptoms of Crohn's disease appear during flare-ups, which alternate with periods of remission. Some people suffer only one or two attacks before entering into permanent remission; others experience recurrent attacks over a lifetime. Crohn's disease is relatively rare, but the incidence among the general population has been increasing in recent decades.

SYMPTOMS

- Spasms of abdominal pain or cramps, located near the navel or in the lower right abdomen.
- Persistent diarrhea.
- Rectal bleeding or blood in the stool.
- Anal fissures.
- Nausea.
- Fever.
- Fatigue.
- Loss of appetite and weight.
- Systemic complications such as joint pain from arthritis, inflammation of the eyes, and skin lesions from eczema.

WHAT CAUSES IT?

- The cause of Crohn's disease is unknown.
- Hereditary factors seem to play some role in the development of this disorder.
- Various theories suggest these possible causes: viral or bacterial infections, autoimmune disorders, food allergies, or lymphatic obstruction.

PREVENTION

- At present there is no known way to prevent Crohn's disease.

DIAGNOSIS

- Patient history and physical exam are necessary.
- Blood tests may be taken.
- Upper gastrointestinal (GI) series of x-rays are taken to view the small intestine.
- A barium enema may be performed. The barium creates a sharper x-ray image of the colon.
- Sigmoidoscopy (to inspect the lower large intestine) or colonoscopy (to view the entire large intestine) may be performed.
- A biopsy of the colon lining is generally taken during the sigmoidoscopy or colonoscopy to distinguish Crohn's disease from ulcerative colitis.

HOW TO TREAT IT

- For mild attacks, over-the-counter antidiarrheal medications and pain relievers may be taken.
- Anti-inflammatory medications, such as sulfasalazine or corticosteroids, may be recommended.
- Antibiotics may be prescribed to suppress secondary infections.
- Enemas containing corticosteroids or aspirin-like drugs may be used to treat internal inflammation.
- Immunosuppressive drugs may be prescribed on a long-term basis to quell autoimmune activity.
- Dietary changes, vitamin or mineral supplements, or vitamin B_{12} injections, to replace nutrients lost from poor bowel absorption, may be advised.
- In some cases of extremely severe attacks, periods of intravenous feeding may be necessary to allow the bowel to rest.
- Surgery may be required to repair blockages, fistulas, or abscesses in the rectum or intestine.
- In advanced, long-standing cases of Crohn's disease, the damaged portion of the bowel may be removed.

WHEN TO CALL A DOCTOR

- Call a doctor if you experience symptoms of Crohn's disease (especially lower-right abdominal pain, which may signal appendicitis).
- Call a doctor if you experience black or bloody stools, a swollen abdomen, or a fever over 101°F.

Croup

WHAT IS IT?

Croup is a condition marked by obstruction of breathing due to inflammation and narrowing of the air passages. It develops from a respiratory infection, like a cold or flu, and typically lasts up to six days. Symptoms—including the characteristic wheezing and tight, raspy cough—may fluctuate between mild and severe but are usually worse at night. Croup generally affects children up to the age of five. It is more common in boys than girls and is more likely to occur in the winter. Older children and adults are not at risk for croup since their airways are wider and thus resistant to collapse.

WHAT CAUSES IT?

• Viral infections—including flu, measles, and colds—are the most common cause of croup.
• Bacterial infections sometimes lead to croup.

SYMPTOMS
• Loud, barking cough.
• Breathing difficulty, which manifests itself as a wheezing or grunting noise (stridor) during inhalation.
• Hoarseness.
• Chest discomfort.
• Emergency symptoms indicate life-threatening obstruction of the airways and include the following: great difficulty in swallowing; drooling; inability to bend the neck forward; a bluish tinge to the lips; increased breathing difficulty; worsened coughing; extremely rapid heartbeat; high-pitched wheezing noises upon inhaling; loss of consciousness.

PREVENTION

• Wash hands frequently with warm water and soap to prevent spreading the infection to other children.

DIAGNOSIS

• Physical examination and patient history are required.

• A throat culture may be done.
• A neck x-ray or laryngoscopy (using a lighted scope to view the inside of the throat) may be performed to locate specific sites of airway obstruction.

HOW TO TREAT IT

• Have the child inhale moist air from a bowl of steaming water, cool-mist vaporizer, or hot shower, to help relieve congestion during an attack. Having the child breathe cool night air may also help open the airways.
• Sitting up straight makes breathing easier. Infants may be placed in a child seat.
• Acetaminophen may be administered to reduce fever. (Do not give aspirin to children.)
• Be calm and reassure the child, since anxiety and crying aggravate symptoms.
• Antibiotics may be prescribed to treat a bacterial infection and should be taken for the full term prescribed.
• A new therapy involving the inhalation of the steroid budesonide has been shown to relieve symptoms of mild to moderate croup within hours. However, at press time, the drug is still awaiting FDA approval in the United States.
• Hospitalization may be necessary for severe attacks. The child may be placed in a humidified oxygen tent.
• In very serious cases, the doctor may insert a breathing tube down the child's throat through the mouth or through a small incision in the neck (tracheostomy). The tube can usually be removed within 24 hours.

WHEN TO CALL A DOCTOR

• Call a doctor if your child develops noisy, rapid breathing.
• **EMERGENCY** Call an ambulance immediately if your child experiences serious breathing difficulty or develops other emergency symptoms of severe lung obstruction.
• Be alert for signs of ear infections and pneumonia, potential complications of croup that may arise a few days after an attack subsides.

Cushing's Syndrome

WHAT IS IT?

Cushing's syndrome—an uncommon disorder named for the early-twentieth-century American surgeon Harvey Cushing—is caused by elevated blood levels of cortisol (an essential corticosteroid hormone). Cortisol is produced by the cortex of the adrenal glands, grape-size organs located above each kidney that form part of the body's endocrine system. Cortisol secretion is stimulated by the release of adrenocorticotropic hormone, or ACTH, from the pituitary gland (see Hyperpituitarism for more information). Cushing's syndrome is due to overproduction of cortisol by the adrenals or administration of excessive amounts of cortisone in the treatment of a number of diseases. (The disorder is known as Cushing's disease when symptoms are due to increased production of ACTH by a tumor in the pituitary gland. Common complications are hypertension, diabetes, osteoporosis, and peptic ulcer.) Both Cushing's syndrome and Cushing's disease respond well to treatment.

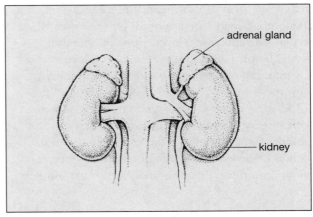

The adrenal glands, located on the top of each kidney, secrete several hormones, including the steroid cortisol, made in the adrenal cortex.

SYMPTOMS

- A round or "moon-shaped" face.
- Fat accumulation on the torso and between the shoulder blades.
- Thin legs and arms.
- Fatigue and muscle weakness.
- Skin changes, including easy bruising; acne; purple stretch marks on the abdomen, thighs, and breasts; thin skin; a reddish appearance of the face.
- Insomnia.
- Changes in mental state, such as mood swings, depression, paranoia, or euphoria.
- In men: growth of breasts (gynomastia), impotence.
- In women: growth of hair (hirsutism), enlargement of the clitoris, and the cessation of menstruation (amenorrhea).
- Back or hip pain from bone fractures due to osteoporosis.

WHAT CAUSES IT?

- Large or long-term doses of oral corticosteroid medications—prescribed to treat disorders such as rheumatoid arthritis, inflammatory bowel disease, or asthma—are now the most common cause of Cushing's syndrome.
- An adrenal tumor or overgrowth (hyperplasia) of adrenal cortex cells may cause Cushing's syndrome.
- A pituitary tumor that secretes excess ACTH overstimulates cortisol production by the adrenal and causes Cushing's disease. Occasionally, tumors elsewhere in the body, such as in the lungs, may produce excess ACTH (ectopic ACTH-producing tumor).

PREVENTION

- If you are taking corticosteroids on a long-term basis, ask your doctor about the lowest possible doses of these medications.

DIAGNOSIS

- Blood and urine tests to measure levels of adrenal hormones.
- CT (computed tomography) scans or MRI (magnetic resonance imaging) of the abdomen or skull (to image the pituitary gland).

HOW TO TREAT IT

- If Cushing's syndrome is caused by long-term treatment with corticosteroid medications, your doctor may gradually reduce the dosage and switch you

Cushing's Syndrome *continued*

to another form of treatment, if possible. Never stop taking prescribed corticosteroids on your own, since serious side effects may occur; slow withdrawal should be planned and supervised by a doctor.

• A pituitary or adrenal tumor can be surgically removed.

• Radiation therapy, either alone or in conjunction with surgery, may be used to treat tumors.

• Medications that inhibit the secretion of cortisol, such as ketoconazole, aminoglutethimide, metyrapone, or mitotane, may be prescribed when surgery is impossible or unsuccessful, or when the tumor is malignant.

• Hormone replacement therapy (temporary or life-long) may be necessary to supplement or replace adrenal and thyroid hormone following surgery or radiation treatment to the pituitary.

WHEN TO CALL A DOCTOR

• Call a doctor if you develop excess fat on your face and torso, accompanied by any of the other symptoms of Cushing's syndrome.

Dermatomyositis

WHAT IS IT?

Dermatomyositis is a rare connective tissue disease caused by inflammation of the muscles and skin. It is an autoimmune disorder, in which the immune system (the body's natural line of defense against disease) inappropriately begins to attack healthy tissues. As dermatomyositis progresses, muscle tissue is wasted and gradually replaced by useless scar tissue. Most commonly affected are the large skeletal muscles

SYMPTOMS
- Red, itchy rash on the face, especially across the cheeks and the bridge of the nose. A rash may form on the knees, knuckles, elbows, or other joints or bony prominences.
- Purple discoloration and swelling of the eyelids, especially apparent upon awakening.
- Skin that feels thicker than normal (over affected areas).
- Weakness, stiffness, and pain in the muscles, especially the muscles of the shoulder and hip. It may even be difficult to perform such simple actions as brushing your hair.
- Cold hands and feet.
- Difficulty speaking or swallowing.
- Bouts of nausea.
- Weight loss.
- Fever.

(those in the arms, shoulders, pelvis, and thighs), as well as heart muscle and the involuntary muscles that control swallowing and breathing. Some people develop polymyositis alone, which results in these muscle problems exclusively; in others, the skin (derma) is involved too, hence the name dermatomyositis. Onset of symptoms may be either sudden or gradual. Dermatomyositis is potentially life-threatening when

vital organs are affected, but the survival rate has improved in recent years (currently about 75 percent of patients survive beyond five years of diagnosis), and the majority of patients improve with treatment. Two-thirds of those afflicted with dermatomyositis are women.

WHAT CAUSES IT?
- The cause of dermatomyositis is unknown.
- Various factors that have been associated with the disorder include allergies, hereditary factors, a history of lung, colon, or breast cancer, and the use of certain medications, such as sulfa drugs, penicillin, antithyroid drugs, gold salts, and thiazide diuretics.

PREVENTION
- Dermatomyositis cannot be prevented at present.

DIAGNOSIS
- Physical examination and patient history are necessary.
- Blood tests are taken.
- Electromyography (which measures electrical activity in the muscles) may be performed.
- A biopsy (tissue sample) of muscle tissue may be taken for laboratory analysis.

HOW TO TREAT IT
- Corticosteroid drugs, such as prednisone, are usually prescribed (often in high doses) to reduce inflammation.
- Immunosuppressant drugs may be used if corticosteroids are not effective in relieving inflammation.
- Physical therapy may be advised to minimize muscle shrinkage.

WHEN TO CALL A DOCTOR
- Call a doctor if you develop symptoms of dermatomyositis.

Diabetes Insipidus

WHAT IS IT?

Diabetes insipidus, not to be confused with the more common diabetes mellitus, is a relatively rare disorder resulting from a failure to produce sufficient amounts of antidiuretic hormone (ADH), also known as vasopressin. ADH, secreted by the posterior pituitary gland, helps the kidneys to reabsorb water and maintain proper fluid balance. If the pituitary fails to produce enough ADH, water is not conserved but simply passed through the kidneys and excreted, typically in very large quantities. More rarely, the kidneys fail to respond properly to ADH; this is known as nephrogenic diabetes insipidus. Dehydration is the primary health risk associated with either form of the disorder. Diabetes insipidus affects both sexes equally, usually between the ages of 10 and 20. With proper treatment, overall prognosis is good (except in cases caused by cancer).

SYMPTOMS

- Frequent and copious urination. Output may be as high as 25 to 35 quarts within 24 hours and may be as frequent as every 30 minutes, even at night.
- Extreme thirst.
- Dry skin.
- Constipation.
- Emergency symptoms of dehydration, including dizziness, weakness, and unconsciousness.

WHAT CAUSES IT?

- In approximately half of all cases, the cause of diabetes insipidus is unknown.
- Hereditary factors appear to play a role in some cases.
- Damage to the pituitary gland from a head injury, a pituitary tumor, radiation therapy, or surgery may lead to diabetes insipidus.

PREVENTION

- There is no known way to prevent diabetes insipidus.

DIAGNOSIS

- Physical exam and patient history are necessary. Diagnosis of diabetes insipidus is suspected when a patient reports unusually large and frequent urine output.
- A urinalysis is done to discover dilute urine (low specific gravity).
- A water deprivation test may be conducted. The patient consumes no fluids for eight hours while urine output and specific gravity are monitored. Patients with diabetes insipidus continue to produce large amounts of urine despite dehydration. Injection of ADH reduces urine volume and produces a concentrated urine in those with pituitary diabetes insipidus (but not nephrogenic diabetes insipidus).
- Blood tests may be taken to assess water and salt balance.

HOW TO TREAT IT

- Vasopressin (synthetic ADH) may be administered (either in a nasal spray or by injection) to replace or supplement the body's ADH production. Such hormone therapy is usually necessary for a lifetime, although if diabetes insipidus is caused by a head injury or surgery, it may be possible to discontinue treatment after a year or so.
- Chlorpropamide (an oral antidiabetic agent) alone may be an effective treatment in mild cases.
- Thiazide diuretics may help the kidneys conserve water.
- To treat nephrogenic diabetes insipidus, your doctor may advise a low-salt diet to reduce thirst and slow the excretion of water. (Nephrogenic diabetes insipidus does not respond to ADH treatment.)
- Drink plenty of fluids to prevent dehydration.
- Consume plenty of high-fiber foods and fruit juices to prevent or treat constipation.

WHEN TO CALL A DOCTOR

- See a doctor immediately if you develop symptoms of diabetes insipidus.
- **EMERGENCY** Call an ambulance if you observe someone lose consciousness.

Diabetes Mellitus

WHAT IS IT?

Diabetes mellitus is a metabolic disorder with abnormally high blood glucose levels (hyperglycemia) as its most prominent feature. During intestinal digestion, carbohydrates and proteins are broken down into simple sugars and amino acids, respectively. The liver converts all of the sugars and some of the amino acids into glucose, a simple sugar that is used for energy by every cell in the body. Glucose passes from the bloodstream into the cells with the help of insulin, a hormone produced by the pancreas (a pear-shaped organ located just below the stomach). By attaching to receptor sites on the surface membrane of a cell, insulin promotes the movement of glucose-transport proteins from the interior of the cell to its surface, where they bind with glucose and carry it into the cell. In diabetes mellitus, several problems may interfere with this process: pancreatic insulin production may be partially or completely impaired, or the cells may become unable to use normal amounts of insulin efficiently.

SYMPTOMS

- Excessive and frequent urination (as often as every hour or so). Nighttime awakening to urinate is common.
- Increased thirst.
- Increased appetite.
- Unintentional weight loss.
- Blurred vision.
- Fatigue and weakness.
- Recurring or persistent infections of the bladder, skin, or gums.
- Numbness and tingling in feet and hands.
- Symptoms of hypoglycemia (see Hypoglycemia for more information).
- Emergency symptoms of hyperosmolar nonketotic states: extreme thirst, lethargy, weakness, mental confusion, coma.
- Emergency symptoms of diabetic ketoacidosis: nausea and vomiting, labored breathing, mental confusion, coma.

These underlying problems in fact distinguish the two main types of the diabetes. In Type I, or insulin-dependent diabetes mellitus (IDDM), also known as juvenile diabetes, the pancreas produces little or no insulin. IDDM develops suddenly and most commonly affects those under 30; the average age of onset is between 12 and 14. However, IDDM accounts for only 7 to 10 percent of cases of diabetes mellitus. In the much more common Type II, or non-insulin-dependent diabetes mellitus (NIDDM), also known as adult-onset diabetes, insulin production by the pancreas is normal or only slightly reduced, but cells are unable to respond efficiently to insulin—a condition referred to as insulin resistance. The onset of NIDDM is usually gradual and affects those over 40, particularly those who are overweight. Infrequently, an adult may develop IDDM.

In both IDDM and NIDDM, the hyperglycemia leads to excretion of glucose in the urine and an accompanying increase in urine production. If inadequate amounts of insulin are administered to patients with IDDM, unrestrained release of fatty acids from adipose (fat) tissue leads to the overproduction of ketone bodies in the liver. Accumulation of ketone bodies can cause a life-threatening condition known as diabetic ketoacidosis (DKA). DKA may occasionally affect those with NIDDM in periods when the body is highly stressed, for example, during a severe infection. Those with NIDDM are susceptible to another life-threatening condition known as a nonketotic hyperosmolar state, characterized by extremely high blood sugar levels. This condition usually occurs in elderly persons with some other serious underlying illness. An episode of either DKA or a nonketotic hyperosmolar state may be the first indication that someone has diabetes.

People with diabetes may also suffer from low blood sugar (hypoglycemia) if too much insulin or oral hypoglycemic agent is given for treatment (see Hypoglycemia for more information).

After 10 to 20 years of diabetes, patients are likely to develop complications, such as vision disorders, kidney damage, and peripheral nerve degeneration (neuropathy). Loss of sensation in the feet may allow injuries to go unchecked and become infected. In addition, people with diabetes are at increased risk for

Diabetes Mellitus *continued*

developing narrowing of the coronary arteries (see Coronary Artery Disease for more information) as well as those supplying the legs. The combination of foot infections and decreased blood supply can lead to gangrene (tissue death), which may require amputation. Diabetes mellitus (and its complications) is the fourth leading cause of death in the United States.

Treatment of IDDM requires between one to four daily injections of insulin. (Insulin cannot be taken orally, since digestive juices would destroy it.) In addition, diet and exercise must be carefully planned to ensure that blood glucose levels are neither too high nor too low. Symptoms of NIDDM may be controlled with a combination of diet, exercise, and weight loss, although medication (including insulin) is often necessary. Treatment is largely a process of self-management. Although there is no cure, almost all people with diabetes are able to control their symptoms and lead full, productive lives.

WHAT CAUSES IT?

• IDDM is an autoimmune disorder, resulting from a mistaken attack by the immune system on otherwise healthy insulin-producing cells in the pancreas.
• Genetic factors are important in NIDDM.
• Obesity predisposes individuals to the development of NIDDM.
• Certain drugs, such as corticosteroids or thiazide diuretics, may increase the risk of NIDDM.
• Other disorders, such as hemochromatosis, chronic pancreatitis, Cushing's syndrome, or hyperpituitarism, may lead to diabetes. Surgical removal of the pancreas may also lead to diabetes.
• Pregnant women may develop diabetes mellitus (gestational diabetes). Gestational diabetes may disappear after childbirth; however, there is an increased risk that affected women will develop NIDDM within 10 years.
• Contrary to popular belief, eating lots of foods rich in sugar does not promote diabetes.

PREVENTION

• To prevent the development of NIDDM, lose weight if you are more than 20 percent overweight, and maintain weight within healthy limits. Exercise regularly.
• There is no known way to prevent IDDM.

• Diabetics should get regular eye examinations to aid in early detection and treatment of diabetes-related vision disorders (diabetic retinopathy).

DIAGNOSIS

• Patient history and physical examination.
• Diagnosis is made when blood tests show abnormally high glucose levels.
• When test results are ambiguous, a glucose tolerance test may be done. A drink containing 75 grams of glucose is swallowed and blood sugar levels are measured every 30 minutes over a two-hour period.
• Urine samples may be analyzed for protein content.
• Blood glycohemoglobin is measured, which indicates average blood glucose levels over the preceding month.

HOW TO TREAT IT

• Daily injections of insulin are necessary to treat IDDM. One to four injections are required every day to control blood glucose levels. Both long-acting and rapid-acting insulin preparations are available; a combination of the two kinds is often prescribed.
• For IDDM, a strict diet and schedule of meals are necessary to control blood glucose levels. Your doctor may recommend a diet low in fat, salt, and cholesterol, and may advise you to see a nutritionist for dietary planning.
• Since both exercise and insulin lower glucose levels, exercise and insulin injections must be timed so that they do not combine to cause a dangerous drop in blood sugar (hypoglycemia).
• Strict adherence to the timetable of injections, meals, and exercise is necessary for proper management of IDDM.
• For NIDDM: A diet low in fat and other calories is necessary to control weight. Exercise is also an important part of proper weight control.
• Oral hypoglycemic drugs, such as tolbutamide, chlorpropamide, glyburide, or glipizide, may be prescribed to treat NIDDM if exercise and diet do not lower glucose levels sufficiently.
• Insulin injections may be necessary in more severe cases of NIDDM, or if a patient with NIDDM contracts an additional illness.
• For both IDDM and NIDDM: Blood tests to mea-

Diabetes Mellitus *continued*

sure glucose levels should be performed as often as your doctor recommends, usually one to four times a day. Your doctor will recommend a blood monitoring device to use at home.

• Careful attention must be paid to the risk factors for atherosclerosis because of its increased occurrence with diabetes. Those suffering from diabetes should not smoke, should reduce dietary saturated fat, cholesterol, and salt, and should take any medications prescribed for high blood pressure.

• Those with diabetes should drink generous amounts of water when stricken with another illness such as the flu. This replaces lost fluid and prevents diabetic coma. When ill, diabetics with IDDM should test their urine for ketones every four to six hours.

• Those with diabetes should practice good foot care and check their feet every day. Nerve damage from diabetes mellitus reduces sensation in the feet, and small foot problems may turn into major infections.

• Laser photocoagulation to prevent the rupture of tiny blood vessels in the eye may be used to treat vision problems due to diabetes mellitus (diabetic retinopathy).

• Dialysis, an artificial blood–filtering process, may be necessary to treat kidney failure. In advanced cases a kidney transplant may be advised (see Renal Failure, Chronic, for more information).

• Amitriptyline or desipramine, medications usually used to treat depression, may be prescribed to relieve the numbness and pain in the limbs (see Peripheral Neuropathy for more information).

• Excellent control of blood glucose levels delays or prevents late complications affecting the eyes, kidneys, and nerves.

• Kidney damage can be slowed by controlling blood pressure and using ACE inhibitors.

• Call the American Diabetes Association for information about support groups in your area.

WHEN TO CALL A DOCTOR

• Call a doctor if you notice a sudden or gradual increase in hunger, thirst, and urine output.

• Call a doctor if you have been diagnosed with diabetes mellitus and an additional illness such as a cold or the flu causes blood sugar levels to go out of control. Do not take over-the-counter medications without first consulting your doctor.

• **EMERGENCY** Call an ambulance if a person with diabetes loses consciousness. Inform the doctor or the rescue worker that the person has diabetes mellitus.

• **EMERGENCY** (NIDDM) Call an ambulance immediately if you develop symptoms of a hyperosmolar nonketotic state, including extreme thirst, lethargy, weakness, and mental confusion.

• **EMERGENCY** (IDDM) Call an ambulance immediately if you develop symptoms of DKA, including dry mouth, dry and flushed skin, sweet or fruity-smelling breath, labored breathing, vomiting, and abdominal pain, with or without excessive urination and extreme thirst.

• **EMERGENCY** (IDDM) Call your doctor right away if urine tests detect the presence of ketones and the steps your doctor has instructed you to take fail to control the problem.

Diarrhea, Acute

WHAT IS IT?

Acute diarrhea, the passage of frequent, loose, or watery stools, is not a disease itself but rather a symptom of an underlying disorder. As food passes through the digestive system, water is normally reabsorbed through the wall of the large intestine. Diarrhea—and, at times, dehydration—results when fluid is not reabsorbed but remains in and is expelled with the fecal matter. Often, diarrhea subsides without treatment within two or three days. However, in infants, the dehydration resulting from acute diarrhea is serious and may be fatal if not treated quickly. The elderly are also more vulnerable.

> ### SYMPTOMS
> - Loose, watery stools.
> - Increased frequency of bowel movements.
> - Abdominal cramping and pain.
> - Emergency symptoms of dehydration in infants: drowsiness; unresponsiveness; slackness of the skin; glazed eyes; a dry, sticky mouth and tongue; persistent crying.

WHAT CAUSES IT?

- Food poisoning from a virus or bacteria.
- Non-food-related viral infections.
- A reaction to certain foods (such as citrus fruits or beans) in some people.
- Large amounts of artificial sweeteners, such as sorbitol, xylitol, and mannitol, which are found in diet foods, chewing gum, vitamins, and other products.
- Alcoholic beverages.
- Some drugs including antihypertensives, drugs to combat heart disease, over-the-counter antacids containing magnesium, and certain antibiotics.
- Emotional stress and anxiety may lead to diarrhea.
- Diseases such as typhoid fever, amebic dysentery, and bacillary dysentery (shigellosis) that produce acute, life-threatening diarrhea.

PREVENTION

- Do not eat food that you suspect has spoiled.
- Avoid foods to which you are sensitive.
- When traveling abroad, drink only bottled or boiled water or other bottled beverages, and only eat cooked foods and peeled fruit. Local water or raw foods may contain bacteria that can cause acute diarrhea.
- Learn ways of coping with emotional stress, and try to avoid stressful situations.

DIAGNOSIS

- Diarrhea may be self-diagnosed by the observation of characteristic symptoms.
- Laboratory stool analysis may be warranted in cases of persistent diarrhea.

HOW TO TREAT IT

- Prevent dehydration by drinking a solution of one teaspoon of salt and four teaspoons of sugar in one quart of water. Measure accurately, since too much salt may worsen dehydration. Drink one pint of this solution per hour while diarrhea lasts. Preventing dehydration is especially important for the elderly.
- Do not take over-the-counter antidiarrheal medications for the first few hours, since the diarrhea may be ridding your body of infectious agents or irritants. If work or other obligations necessitate the use of an antidiarrheal medication, use one containing loperamide (such as Imodium A-D) or bismuth subsalicylate (such as Pepto-Bismol).
- Limit (or avoid) milk products, alcohol, and foods rich in fiber during recovery.
- For infants: While diarrhea persists, do not feed them milk. Instead, feed them an electrolyte solution available from a pharmacist. If diarrhea clears up within two days, reintroduce milk gradually over a 24-hour period. Feed the infant a solution of one part milk and three parts water at first, gradually increasing the amount of milk over the next three feedings. Use a solution of half-milk/half-water for the second feeding; three-quarters milk for the third feeding; undiluted milk for the fourth.

WHEN TO CALL A DOCTOR

- Call a doctor if diarrhea persists for more than 48 hours or is accompanied by lightheadedness, severe cramping, fever over 101°F, or blood in the stool.
- Call a doctor if diarrhea recurs frequently.
- **EMERGENCY** Call a doctor immediately if an infant or an elderly person shows symptoms of dehydration.

Diphtheria

WHAT IS IT?

Diphtheria is a life-threatening disorder caused by a highly contagious bacterial infection. It is especially dangerous when it affects the throat, where it can produce a thick grey membrane that may grow large enough to obstruct breathing. The most serious complications are caused by a toxin produced by the diphtheria bacterium that can damage the heart, nervous system, and, less often, the kidneys (see Myocarditis, Peripheral Neuropathies, and Renal Failure). Diphtheria most often strikes before the age of 15 and is fatal in nearly 10 percent of cases; recovery tends to be slow in those who do survive. Thanks to widespread immunization efforts, however, the disease is now extremely rare in developed parts of the world. In modernized countries the most common infection with the diphtheria bacterium involves the skin and is rarely associated with systemic manifestations.

SYMPTOMS

- Sore throat.
- A thick, grey membrane covering the back of the throat and tonsils, leading to a foul odor.
- Nasal discharge.
- Low-grade fever.
- Headache.
- Rapid pulse, shortness of breath, and other symptoms of heart failure.
- Breathing difficulty in severe cases.
- Swallowing difficulty.
- Paralysis due to involvement of nerves in the face or extremities.

WHAT CAUSES IT?

- Diphtheria is caused by the bacillus *Corynebacterium diphtheriae*, which is usually transmitted via airborne droplets of moisture exhaled by another infected person during sneezing or coughing.
- The diphtheria bacterium may produce a skin infection at the site of a cut or wound.

PREVENTION

- Be certain that you have been inoculated with the DPT (diphtheria, pertussis, and tetanus) vaccine, especially if you are planning to travel to poor, underdeveloped countries. This inoculation is routinely a part of early childhood vaccinations; check your medical records to be sure. If you travel often to countries where you might be at risk of contracting diphtheria, a booster shot every 10 years may be advised.

DIAGNOSIS

- Patient history and physical examination.
- Throat culture.

HOW TO TREAT IT

- If a diagnosis of diphtheria is suspected upon physical examination, diphtheria antitoxin is administered (either intravenously or by intramuscular injection) before laboratory results of the culture confirm the diagnosis. The antitoxin helps to prevent damage caused by the bacterial toxin to vital organs.
- Antibiotics are given to treat the infection.
- Hospitalization is usually required, as intravenous fluids, supplementary oxygen, bed rest, and careful monitoring of heart function are often warranted. If the membrane in the back of the throat obstructs breathing, a tube may be passed through the mouth or nose; in very serious cases a tracheostomy (insertion of a breathing tube through a surgical opening in the throat) may be needed.
- Treatment for congestive heart failure may be necessary.
- All persons who have been in contact with someone infected with diphtheria should be cultured for the bacterium and treated with antibiotics if the culture is positive. Such patients should be given diphtheria toxoid if more than five years have passed since their last immunization.

WHEN TO CALL A DOCTOR

- **EMERGENCY** Symptoms of diphtheria, especially breathing difficulty, require immediate medical attention.
- Make an appointment with a doctor if you believe you have been exposed to the diphtheria bacterium.

Dislocations and Subluxations

WHAT IS IT?

A dislocation is a complete loss of contact between the bone surfaces in a joint that normally meet; a subluxation is a partial loss of contact. Within a normal joint, ligaments hold the bones together so that their surfaces are in close contact, and the entire joint is encased in a membrane (joint capsule). When the bones become dislocated or subluxated (usually because of a violent physical trauma), damage to the ligaments and joint capsule occurs, resulting in severe pain and loss of mobility. Commonly affected joints include those of the shoulders, wrists, fingers, knees, hips, ankles, and feet. Dislocations and subluxations usually respond well to treatment, and normal joint movement is usually restored within two months of the injury. However, in more severe cases a dislocation may involve nerve damage and result in some degree of paralysis.

SYMPTOMS

- Deformity of the affected joint. The joint may be bent at an awkward angle or look misshapen.
- Difficulty moving the affected joint.
- Pain (often severe) or tenderness in the joint.
- Swelling and stiffness within 30 minutes of a physical trauma.

WHAT CAUSES IT?

- Injury is the most common cause of dislocated joints.
- Certain joints, such as the hip, are congenitally prone to dislocations in some people.
- Some joint-tissue diseases, like rheumatoid arthritis, may render affected joints more vulnerable to dislocations.
- Previous injuries of a joint may so weaken surrounding tissues that subsequent dislocation may occur with no apparent cause (so-called spontaneous dislocation).

PREVENTION

- Use protective measures to prevent accidents. Wear seat belts and drive defensively, and wear protective gear when playing sports or working.
- Do not try to lift things that are too heavy.
- Perform warm-up exercises before undertaking any strenuous physical activity.

DIAGNOSIS

- Physical exam and patient history establish a diagnosis.
- X-rays rule out or confirm the condition.

HOW TO TREAT IT

- Get immediate professional medical care; prompt treatment can prevent additional tissue, nerve, and blood vessel damage. Do not try to reposition the joint yourself. On the contrary, the joint should be immobilized with a splint or sling if possible.
- Apply ice to the affected area to reduce swelling while awaiting professional care.
- Do not eat or drink, since a full stomach interferes with the anesthesia that may be necessary during the repositioning of the joint.
- A doctor or other medical personnel will reposition the joint. Local or general anesthesia may be used to reduce pain during the procedure.
- Have your doctor teach you to reposition the joint yourself if spontaneous dislocations tend to occur.
- Surgery may be required to reposition the joint in more severe dislocations. Wire may be used to keep the bones in place.
- A splint, cast, or traction may be required to · immobilize the joint after repositioning, to allow damaged ligaments to heal.
- A program of physical therapy may be prescribed to build strength and mobility after the affected joint has healed.

WHEN TO CALL A DOCTOR

- Call a doctor immediately if you think you have dislocated a joint, since it becomes increasingly difficult to reposition the joint properly as the surrounding tissues swell.
- **EMERGENCY** Call an ambulance or get to a doctor immediately if you experience paralysis, lack of a pulse, or extreme pain near a dislocated joint. This may indicate that the blood supply to the area has been blocked by the injury.

Disseminated Intravascular Coagulation

WHAT IS IT?

Disseminated intravascular coagulation (DIC), also known as defibrination syndrome, is a rare disorder marked by excessive blood coagulation, which paradoxically results in uncontrolled bleeding. Normally, clotting factors cause blood platelets to coagulate into a solid plug at the site of an injury, preventing blood loss from an open vein or artery. In DIC, however, clotting occurs in small blood vessels throughout the body, even where no injury is present. This decreases the available quantity of clotting factors and platelets, thereby increasing the risk of severe bleeding. Furthermore, the body steps up its anticoagulation system to dissolve the numerous clots, which only compounds the likelihood of uncontrolled bleeding. In addition, blockage of blood vessels by clots may damage the kidneys and extremities, and sometimes even the brain, lungs, pituitary and adrenal glands, and the gastrointestinal lining. DIC occurs as a complication of a variety of severe disorders and injuries. Effective treatment requires proper diagnosis and treatment of the underlying disorder.

WHAT CAUSES IT?

• Blood infection (bacterial sepsis) may cause widespread coagulation and subsequent bleeding.

• Leukemia or other systemic cancers may cause disruption of the clotting mechanisms in the blood.
• Extensive, serious burns destroy body tissues and may disturb the normal balance of clotting factors.
• Heatstroke or shock (for example, due to massive blood loss) may lead to DIC.
• Other serious disorders, such as cirrhosis of the liver or cardiac arrest, may cause DIC.
• Complications during pregnancy and childbirth may disrupt the blood's clotting mechanisms.
• Some kinds of surgery, such as cardiopulmonary bypass surgery, may induce DIC.
• A poisonous snakebite may cause excessive coagulation and bleeding.
• Transfusion of an incompatible blood type may induce DIC.

PREVENTION

• Disorders that may lead to DIC require prompt treatment.

DIAGNOSIS

• Blood tests are performed.
• A thorough physical examination and other tests and procedures are required to identify an underlying cause of DIC.

HOW TO TREAT IT

• Hospitalization is necessary to properly treat and monitor DIC.
• Treatment of the underlying disorder is of prime importance.
• Anticoagulants may be used to prevent excessive clotting.
• A transfusion of whole blood, plasma, platelets, or packed red blood cells may be necessary.

WHEN TO CALL A DOCTOR

• **EMERGENCY** Call an ambulance if you develop symptoms of DIC.

SYMPTOMS

• Abnormal bleeding from anywhere in the body, possibly at several sites at once.
• Tiny, red, pinpointlike dots (petechiae).
• Vomiting of blood.
• Bloody or black stools.
• Blood in the urine.
• Vaginal bleeding.
• Unexplained bruises.
• Severe abdominal or back pain.
• Convulsions or loss of consciousness in advanced cases (rare).

Diverticular Disorders

WHAT IS IT?

Diverticulosis is a condition marked by the formation of diverticula—small pouchlike herniations along the wall of the gastrointestinal tract. Most commonly, diverticula appear in the colon, but they may also develop as far up as the throat (pharynx). As many as half of all Americans over the age of 50 have diverticulosis, although few ever have any noticeable symptoms. Diverticulosis only requires treatment if it causes discomfort or complications. In some cases the diverticula become inflamed or infected—a painful condition known as diverticulitis. In severe cases, an inflamed diverticulum may perforate or burst, resulting in abscesses or peritonitis (inflammation of the lining of the abdominal cavity, which may be fatal unless treated immediately). Diverticular diseases are not related to colon cancer.

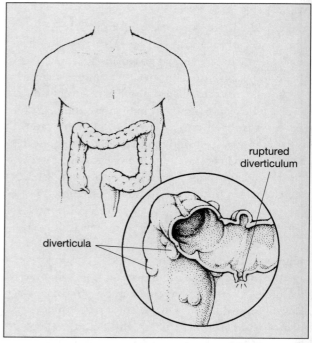

In diverticulosis, small pouches (diverticula) form in weakened spots on the colon wall. If they become inflamed (diverticulitis), they may rupture or bleed.

SYMPTOMS

- Diverticulosis usually causes no symptoms. However, some patients do develop mild complaints, including bloating, gas, nausea, constipation alternating with diarrhea, and tenderness or pain, most often in the lower left abdomen.
- Symptoms are pronounced when a diverticulum becomes inflamed (diverticulitis). Severe abdominal cramping, usually on the lower left side, is the most prominent symptom. Pain may be immediately severe or start off gradually and increase in severity over several days. Other symptoms may include tenderness over the abdomen, fever, nausea, blood in the stool, and impaired bowel function.

WHAT CAUSES IT?

- The cause of diverticulosis is unknown, but there are several risk factors.
- A low-fiber diet—common in industrialized Western countries—is correlated with diverticular disease. Indeed, the disorder is almost unheard of in rural Asian and African societies, where a high-fiber diet is the norm.
- Hereditary factors may play a role in the development of diverticulosis.
- Increased pressure on the colon resulting from straining during bowel movements or from constipation or laxatives may lead to the formation of diverticula.

PREVENTION

- Eat a high-fiber, low-fat diet. Foods high in fiber include fruits, vegetables, and whole-grain breads and cereals.
- Drink plenty of fluids (at least eight full glasses of water per day) to help soften stools.
- Exercise regularly to help maintain intestinal regularity.

DIAGNOSIS

- A barium-swallow x-ray or barium enema may be performed. The barium creates a sharp x-ray image of the digestive tract.
- Colonoscopy (use of a thin, lighted scope to view the colon) may be performed.

Diverticular Disorders *continued*

HOW TO TREAT IT

• Follow prevention tips for diet and exercise. Diet is especially important.

• Your doctor may recommend a laxative containing the fiber psyllium or a stool softener. However, do not take laxatives without consulting your doctor and never use enemas—these may only further aggravate the colon.

• For diverticulitis, your doctor may prescribe antibiotics and bed rest.

• Injections of painkillers may be warranted in severe cases of diverticulitis.

• Antispasmodic drugs may be prescribed to relax the muscles around the digestive tract.

• You may need to have your stomach kept empty (with a tube passed through the mouth into the stomach) and to be fed intravenously to allow inflamed diverticula to heal. You should be able to eat and drink normally when symptoms have subsided (generally in a few days).

• Surgery may be necessary to drain an abscess.

• In severe or recurrent cases, surgery may be necessary to remove the affected part of the colon. In a few cases, a temporary colostomy may be required.

WHEN TO CALL A DOCTOR

• Call a doctor immediately if you experience severe abdominal pain, with or without fever or abdominal bloating.

• Call a doctor if you notice a change in your bowel habits that lasts longer than two weeks, especially if you also experience rectal bleeding.

• Call a doctor if minor symptoms of diverticulosis (nausea, bloating, constipation, and so forth) develop and persist.

Dry Mouth Xerostomia

WHAT IS IT?

Dry mouth, also known as xerostomia, is abnormal dryness of the mucus membranes in the mouth, due to a reduction of the flow or change in the composition of saliva. It can occur as a symptom of many possible underlying disorders or as a side effect of certain medications. Dry mouth is not a serious medical problem in itself, but it may contribute to poor nutrition, psychological discomfort, mouth infections, and tooth decay if left untreated. Medical care is aimed at relieving symptoms and treating the underlying disorder.

WHAT CAUSES IT?

• An impaired or infected salivary gland may lead to dry mouth.
• Dry mouth may occur as a side effect of many medications, including antihypertensive drugs, antidepressants, painkillers, tranquilizers, diuretics, and antihistamines.

SYMPTOMS

• Dry or burning sensation in the mouth.
• Difficulty in chewing, swallowing, tasting, and speaking.
• In advanced cases, cracked lips, changes in the tongue's surface, widespread tooth decay, and mouth ulcers.

• Radiation therapy for tumors in or near the mouth is a possible cause.
• A bone marrow transplant may produce dry mouth.
• Sjögren's syndrome, an autoimmune disorder (wherein the body's own natural defenses against disease inappropriately begin to attack healthy tissue), may lead to dry mouth as well as dry eyes.
• Injury to the head or neck may damage nerve endings and thus interfere with the function of the salivary glands.
• Dry mouth may be associated with neurological changes that occur with brain-centered disorders like a stroke or Alzheimer's disease.
• Nutritional deficiencies may be a cause.
• Fear, stress, anxiety, and depression may lead to dry mouth.
• Some people report the sensation of chronic dry mouth, even though their salivary glands are normal.

PREVENTION

• Eat a healthy, balanced diet.
• Try to limit your exposure to stressful situations.

DIAGNOSIS

• Chronic dry mouth can be self-diagnosed by observation of symptoms. However, your doctor or dentist should be notified. Various tests may be warranted to determine the underlying cause.

HOW TO TREAT IT

• Sip water frequently, especially when speaking or eating. Avoid beverages that contain caffeine or sugar, which may aggravate dryness and tooth decay.
• Chew sugarless gum or suck on sugarless hard candies to stimulate saliva production, or try sucking on a peach pit or a small piece of lemon.
• Avoid tobacco, alcohol, and foods that are salty, spicy, or highly acidic.
• At night, use a humidifier, and keep a glass of water by your bed in case you awaken with dry mouth.
• Use lip balm to prevent the lips from cracking.
• Your dentist may prescribe an artificial saliva solution to moisten the mucus membranes in the mouth.

WHEN TO CALL A DOCTOR

• Make an appointment with your doctor or dentist if you develop dry mouth.

Dupuytren's Contracture

WHAT IS IT?

Dupuytren's contracture, named after the nineteenth-century French surgeon who first described it, is a painless and usually progressive disorder characterized by the hardening of a band of tissue just beneath the skin on the palm of the hand (palmar fascia). For unknown reasons, the tissue hardens and shrinks into a fibrous, scarlike mass. It initially appears as a puckering on the palm of the hand, just below the fingers. As the condition progresses, the contracted tissue pulls one or more of the fingers inward, so that it becomes increasingly difficult, if not impossible, to straighten out the affected digits. Ordinarily, the third and fourth fingers are affected, but the middle and even the index finger are sometimes involved. (Although Dupuytren's contracture typically affects the hands—usually both of them—the feet and toes also are sometimes affected.) In most cases, the condition is nothing to worry about; it is rarely painful, and it causes few limitations. But, should it begin to interfere with normal activities, simple minor surgery can correct the problem.

WHAT CAUSES IT?

• The cause of Dupuytren's contracture is unknown.
• Age, gender, and hereditary factors play a role in the development of Dupuytren's contracture. Older men—particularly those of northern European descent—are most likely to be affected. In fact, one in five Caucasian men over the age of 65 has some signs of the condition.
• Diseases such as epilepsy, alcoholism, and cirrhosis of the liver show some correlation with Dupuytren's contracture.
• Occupations that require handheld tools (especially tools that vibrate, such as jackhammers, electric drills, and chainsaws) may carry an increased risk of developing the condition.

PREVENTION

• There is no known way to prevent Dupuytren's contracture.

DIAGNOSIS

• Physical examination and patient history are usually all that's required to make a diagnosis.

HOW TO TREAT IT

• In more severe cases, surgery may be performed to remove the nodule or band of constricting tissue. A splint is used to hold the digit in position after surgery. Surgery is not necessary unless mobility in the affected area is significantly impaired. Try this test: lay your hand flat, palm and fingers down, on a table. If you cannot lay the hand or fingers flat, consult your doctor.
• In very advanced cases, a skin graft may be necessary to repair and replace damaged tissue.
• Physical therapy may restore mobility and strength in the affected area. However, the ability to perform precision work, such as playing a musical instrument, may not be fully regained. Some numbness may result after surgery if Dupuytren's contracture involved any nearby nerves.

WHEN TO CALL A DOCTOR

• Make an appointment with a doctor if the inability to straighten fingers or toes interferes with normal activities.

SYMPTOMS

• A thickened lump of tissue in the palm of the hand or the sole of the foot.
• Puckering of the skin above the lump.
• Weakness in the grasp.
• Inability to fully straighten one or more fingers or toes, most commonly the third and fourth digits.

Dysentery, Bacillary Shigellosis

WHAT IS IT?

Bacillary dysentery, also known as shigellosis, is a dangerous and extremely contagious bacterial infection of the lining of the colon. Symptoms develop after an incubation period of one to four days, and with proper treatment, they generally subside within 10 days. (Severe cases may last as long as six weeks, but most cases are mild). Shigellosis is most prevalent in children between the ages of one to four years old. Common in overpopulated areas with poor sanitation, shigellosis often occurs in epidemics, so that isolation or quarantine of affected people is required to curb the spread of the disease. Shigellosis is now rare in the United States; most U.S. citizens who do contract it do so while traveling abroad.

SYMPTOMS
- Watery diarrhea that may contain pus, mucus, and blood.
- Straining during bowel movements.
- Abdominal pain.
- Nausea and vomiting.
- Fever.
- Muscle aches all over the body.
- Rapid dehydration and weight loss. (The very young and the elderly are especially susceptible to dehydration.).

WHAT CAUSES IT?
- The shigella bacillus, a bacterium that invades the lining of the colon, is the cause of bacillary dysentery.
- The shigella bacillus is typically spread via contact with the fecal matter of an infected person.
- Failure to wash the hands thoroughly after a bowel movement may help to transmit shigellosis.
- Flies may spread the bacteria from feces as well. (This is more common in areas with poor sanitation.)
- Contaminated food or water may spread the infection.

PREVENTION
- To prevent the spread of infection, wash your hands frequently with warm water and soap, espe-cially after a bowel movement or before handling food. (Since dysentery has an incubation period of up to four days, you may be carrying the disease without realizing it.)
- When traveling abroad or in areas with poor sanitation, drink only bottled or boiled water or other bottled beverages, and eat only cooked foods and peeled fruit.
- Avoid contact with infected persons if possible.

DIAGNOSIS
- Physical examination and patient history are required.
- Stool samples are taken for examination under a microscope and for a laboratory culture to confirm the presence of the shigella bacillus.
- Blood tests are taken to look for electrolyte (essential mineral salt) abnormalities.

HOW TO TREAT IT
- A solution of electrolytes (such as sodium and potassium) and fluids are administered to treat dehydration. In severe cases, fluids must be replaced intravenously.
- While waiting to see the doctor, prevent dehydration by drinking sports drinks, like Gatorade, or a solution of one teaspoon salt and four teaspoons sugar in one quart of water. It is important to measure accurately, because too much salt may worsen dehydration. Drink one pint per hour while diarrhea persists.
- Do not take over-the-counter antidiarrheal medications unless otherwise instructed by your doctor. Diarrhea helps rid the body of infectious organisms.
- Your doctor may prescribe antibiotics to treat the infection. Antibiotics must be taken for the full term of the prescription.
- Isolation from others is required to prevent spread of the disease.

WHEN TO CALL A DOCTOR
- Call a doctor as soon as you notice symptoms of shigellosis. This disease is dangerous and extremely contagious, so it should be treated as soon as possible.

Dyspareunia Painful Intercourse

WHAT IS IT?

Dyspareunia is pain that occurs only (or primarily) during sexual intercourse. It is not a disease but rather a symptom of an underlying physical or psychological disorder. The pain, which can be mild or severe, may occur in the genitals, the pelvic region, or the lower back. The condition is much more common among women. Treatment for dyspareunia is aimed at identifying and properly treating the underlying disorder.

WHAT CAUSES IT?

• For women, causes include vaginismus, a psychological condition characterized by spasms of the vaginal muscles and insufficient vaginal lubrication; scars from an episiotomy (an incision made to facilitate childbirth); thinning and dryness of the vaginal wall due to estrogen deficiencies accompanying menopause or breast-feeding; and inadequate foreplay.
• Disorders that may cause pain upon deep vaginal penetration include pelvic inflammatory disease; ovarian cysts; endometriosis; varicose veins in the pelvis; and ectopic pregnancy.

SYMPTOMS
• Any type of pain that occurs during intercourse—from burning sensations in the genitals caused by infection to lower back pain due to arthritis—qualifies as dyspareunia. The pain may be mild or severe, and it may last throughout sexual activity or occur only under certain circumstances.

• Other causes include infections, such as sexually transmitted diseases, which may irritate the vaginal walls or the skin of the penis; bladder or other urinary tract disorders such as cystitis or urethritis; cancer in the sex organs or the pelvic region; arthritis, especially in the lower back; and allergies to spermicides or to the latex in condoms and diaphragms.

• For men, the condition can result from such disorders as irritation of the skin of the penis due to an allergic rash; physical abnormalities of the penis, like a tight foreskin or a bowed erection (chordee); and infections of the prostate gland or testes.

PREVENTION

• Practice safe sex techniques to reduce the possibility of infection. Use condoms during intercourse.
• Experiment with different coital positions to determine which ones minimize discomfort.

DIAGNOSIS

• Detailed sexual history and physical examination.
• Various laboratory tests may be performed to determine the underlying cause.
• The diagnosis of vaginismus is made only after exclusion of other potential causes.

HOW TO TREAT IT

• Medications are prescribed to treat infections.
• If you suspect an allergy to latex, consult your doctor for alternative methods of birth control and disease prevention.
• If your spermicide is causing discomfort, try a different brand or consider using an alternative method of birth control.
• A water-based lubricant may help ease discomfort and friction. However, avoid oil-based lubricants, such as petroleum jelly, since they dissolve the latex in condoms and may actually promote infection.
• Insertion of a graduated set of dilators into the vagina may be used to treat vaginismus.
• Pain during intercourse due to an episiotomy generally subsides over time.
• Psychological counseling may be advised if no underlying physical anomalies can be identified.

WHEN TO CALL A DOCTOR

• Make an appointment with a doctor if you or your partner is experiencing pain during intercourse.
• Call a doctor if pain worsens or if symptoms do not abate with treatment.

Eardrum, Perforated

WHAT IS IT?

A perforated eardrum is a rip or hole in the tympanic membrane, which lies between the outer ear canal and the middle ear. This translucent membrane receives sound vibrations and transmits them to the tiny bones (ossicles) in the middle ear, the initial step in the process of converting sound waves to nerve impulses. Consequently, when the eardrum is perforated or ruptured, hearing is temporarily compromised. Additionally, a ruptured eardrum provides greater opportunity for bacteria to enter and infect the middle ear. With prompt medical treatment, small perforations generally heal on their own within a month or two. Larger punctures and those that do not heal within three months may require microsurgery to repair or rebuild the eardrum. Once an eardrum is healed, there is usually little or no residual hearing loss.

SYMPTOMS
- Earache or sudden pain in the ear.
- Partial hearing loss.
- Slight bleeding or discharge from the ear. Pain may ease as built-up fluid is released.
- Ringing or buzzing in the ear (tinnitus).

WHAT CAUSES IT?

- A severe middle ear infection (otitis media) may erode the eardrum or cause it to burst.
- Inserting an object (a cotton swab, paper clip, etc.) into the ear may perforate the eardrum.
- A sudden increase or decrease in the air pressure in the outer ear canal relative to that of the middle ear may cause the eardrum to rupture (barotrauma). Changes in pressure strong enough to rupture the eardrum may be caused by a blow to the ear, a nearby explosion, or, sometimes, scuba diving or flying.

PREVENTION

- Do not insert objects, even cotton swabs, into the ear canal, and you should not attempt to clean the ear with alcohol or over-the-counter solutions. If impacted earwax interferes with hearing or causes discomfort, allow your doctor to remove it safely.
- Do not swim in polluted waters, which can cause ear infections.
- Get prompt treatment for ear infections.
- Avoid scuba diving (and flying if possible) when you have an allergy, cold, or throat infection.

DIAGNOSIS

- The doctor will examine the eardrum through an otoscope, a small, lighted viewing instrument.

HOW TO TREAT IT

- If you suspect a ruptured eardrum, see a doctor. In the meantime, cover the affected ear with a clean, dry pad to discourage infection. Take an over-the-counter pain reliever if necessary. Acetaminophen should be given to children instead of aspirin.
- Your doctor may prescribe antibiotics to treat or prevent infection in the middle ear.
- A warm heating pad or towel may be placed over the ear to relieve pain.
- Keep the eardrum dry as it heals. Protect the ear in the shower and when washing your hair; avoid swimming. An ear patch may be recommended for daytime use.
- If the eardrum fails to heal on its own, it may be surgically repaired with a tissue graft (myringoplasty).

WHEN TO CALL A DOCTOR

- Call a doctor if you experience symptoms of a ruptured eardrum.
- Call a doctor if normal hearing is not restored within a month following a ruptured eardrum.

Ear Infection, Middle Otitis Media

WHAT IS IT?

Otitis media is an infection of the middle ear, the cavity between the eardrum and the delicate structures of the inner ear. Typically, it occurs when viruses causing an upper respiratory tract infection (such as a cold) or bacteria migrate along the eustachian tube, the passageway between the nasal passages and the middle ear. The tube may become blocked, thereby preventing the mucus, pus, and other fluids produced during an infection from draining out of the middle ear. This causes pain as these fluids exert pressure on the eardrum, possibly rupturing it. Otitis media is very common in children (because the eustachian tube is smaller), and it tends to recur, especially in winter. With prompt treatment, the chances of full recovery are excellent. A rare, persistent form of the disorder, chronic otitis media, produces milder symptoms; however, if left untreated, it may eventually cause severe structural damage in the ear and skull, resulting in irreversible hearing loss.

SYMPTOMS

- Sensation of fullness in the ear, eventually leading to severe pain.
- Some temporary hearing loss in the affected ear.
- Fever.
- Dizziness.
- Nausea and vomiting.
- Clicking or popping sounds in the ear when moving the jaw.
- Pain when pulling on the earlobe.
- Persistent pus seepage and mild hearing loss, but without earache (the primary symptoms of chronic otitis media).

WHAT CAUSES IT?

- A viral or bacterial infection of the upper respiratory tract is the most common underlying cause of otitis media.

- Nasal allergies or childhood adenoids may cause blockage of the eustachian tube.
- A ruptured eardrum facilitates the entrance of infectious agents into the middle ear.
- Certain groups of people (such as the Navahos) have a hereditary predisposition to ear infections.
- Recurrent bacterial ear infections may result in chronic otitis media.

PREVENTION

- Wash bed linens, towels, and heating pads regularly to prevent reinfection from pus residues. Discard cotton balls and swabs after use.
- Wash hands frequently with soap and warm water to prevent the spread of infection.

DIAGNOSIS

- The doctor will examine the ear canal with an otoscope, a small, lighted viewing instrument.
- A culture of the fluid discharge may be taken.

HOW TO TREAT IT

- Antibiotics may be prescribed to treat a bacterial infection. They should be taken for the full term prescribed.
- Take aspirin or acetaminophen to ease pain and fever. Children should be given acetaminophen only.
- Your doctor may recommend decongestants or antihistamines to treat symptoms.
- A small incision (myringotomy) may be made in the eardrum to allow pus to drain. This incision heals by itself in two to three weeks.
- Surgical removal of enlarged adenoids may be required.
- Rarely, the mastoid process, a bone just behind the ear, becomes infected and must be surgically removed (mastoidectomy).

WHEN TO CALL A DOCTOR

- Call a doctor if you or your child develops an earache that persists despite treatment, especially if symptoms worsen or are accompanied by swelling around the ear, facial twitches, or severe ear pain that suddenly ceases (indicating eardrum rupture).

Ear Infection, Outer Otitis Externa

WHAT IS IT?

Otitis externa, also known as swimmer's ear, is inflammation (often due to infection) of the skin of the outer ear, which includes not only the visible external part of the ear but also the portion of the ear canal that leads up to the eardrum. In some cases, the inflammation may be localized, producing a boil. Although it can be painful and unpleasant, otitis externa is generally not serious and responds well to treatment. However, diabetics, the elderly, and those with weakened immune systems are susceptible to malignant otitis externa, a rare (and noncancerous, despite its name) form of this disorder. Malignant otitis externa may spread to surrounding bones and soft tissues and can be fatal if left untreated.

SYMPTOMS
- Itching in the ear canal in the early stages.
- Ear pain that may worsen when pulling the earlobe.
- Discharge of fluid or pus from the ear canal.
- Redness and swelling of the skin of the ear canal (and occasionally of the external ear).
- A small, painful lump or boil in the ear canal.
- Eczema (patches of broken, flaky, itchy, red, oozing skin) surrounding the opening of the ear.
- Temporary hearing loss due to pus accumulation in the ear canal.
- Fever.

WHAT CAUSES IT?
- Moisture in the ear fosters fungal and certain kinds of bacterial infections. Swimming, especially in polluted water, thus increases the risk of otitis externa, as may showering, washing your hair, or getting caught in the rain.
- Skin disorders, such as eczema or seborrheic dermatitis, may cause inflammation.
- Objects inserted into the ear, like cotton swabs, may irritate the skin or cause small cuts that are vulnerable to infection.
- Hair dyes, shampoos, hairsprays, or chlorinated water may irritate skin in the ear canal.

- Inadequate production of earwax renders the ear more vulnerable to infection.

PREVENTION
- Do not insert objects, even cotton swabs, into the ear canal.
- Do not clean the ear with alcohol or over-the-counter solutions. If earwax interferes with hearing or causes discomfort, your doctor can remove the wax safely.
- Avoid swimming in waters that may be polluted.

DIAGNOSIS
- The doctor will examine the ear canal through an otoscope, a small, lighted viewing instrument.
- A culture of fluid discharge may be taken.

HOW TO TREAT IT
- Over-the-counter pain relievers may be taken. Acetaminophen should be given instead of aspirin to children.
- Your doctor may use a small suction device to remove excess fluid and pus from the ear canal.
- Topical antibiotics or antifungal ear drops may be prescribed to treat infection, in addition to corticosteroid drops to reduce inflammation. A cotton wick may be inserted into the ear to allow medication to travel deeply into the ear canal.
- Oral antibiotics may be given for severe infection.
- Surgical removal of dead tissue may be required to treat malignant otitis externa.
- Codeine or narcotics may be prescribed to relieve severe pain.
- After symptoms disappear, avoid getting water into the ear canal for up to three weeks. During this period, protect your ears when showering or washing your hair; avoid swimming.
- In the event of recurrence, keep a supply of the prescription ear drops on hand to ease symptoms.

WHEN TO CALL A DOCTOR
- Call a doctor if otitis externa symptoms persist for longer than a week despite treatment.
- Those who are diabetic should be sure to notify a doctor when they develop an ear infection.

Eczema Dermatitis

WHAT IS IT?

Eczema or dermatitis is a common inflammatory skin condition. Red raised lesions, oozing, and crusting may be seen in the acute phase; the chronic stage, often brought on by rubbing or scratching, is characterized by scaly, red, thickened patches of skin. The various types of eczema are grouped by cause or appearance, but all types are very itchy and red, and may worsen and spread if scratched. Occasionally, a secondary bacterial infection develops at the irritated site. Eczema is generally not a serious health risk, and in many cases, symptoms may be eased with over-the-counter creams and ointments.

SYMPTOMS

- Itchy patches of dry, swollen, scaly, rough, cracked, or reddened skin.
- Oozing and crusting in the affected areas.
- Coin- or disk-shaped scaly patches of skin (nummular eczema).
- Swollen legs (stasis dermatitis).
- Thick, dry patches of skin in chronic cases.

WHAT CAUSES IT?

- Eczema may be associated with a personal or family history of allergies to foods, pollen, animal dander, and so forth (atopic eczema).
- Eczema may be caused by contact with a variety of substances, including plants such as poison ivy; metals, especially nickel (used in rings and watchbands); rubber or latex; dyes; cosmetics; fragrances; leathers; topical medications; and dishwashing liquid, cleaning agents, and solvents (contact dermatitis).
- Some drugs, such as penicillin, may cause eczema when taken internally by people allergic to them.
- Poor circulation in the legs may lead to eczema (stasis dermatitis).
- The cause of eczema is unknown in some cases.

PREVENTION

- Avoid direct contact with poison ivy, sumac, or oak.
- Avoid direct contact with substances to which you know you are hypersensitive.
- Use a cool-mist humidifier to moisten dry indoor air.

- Apply unscented moisturizer to dry skin as needed.
- Take fewer and shorter baths or showers, and use cool or lukewarm (but not hot) water. Avoid soaps with perfumes or deodorants. Apply moisturizer liberally while the skin is still wet. Gently pat the skin dry; do not rub.
- Wear cotton gloves under rubber gloves to prevent irritation when washing dishes or handling substances containing chemical irritants.
- Do not dress an infant in so many layers that he or she becomes overheated (heat may worsen eczema).

DIAGNOSIS

- Diagnosis may be made upon visual inspection and usually does not require a doctor.
- Blood tests or a skin biopsy may be taken.

HOW TO TREAT IT

- Do not scratch the affected area. Scratching makes eczema worse and can spread the irritation. Covering the affected area with a sterile bandage may help prevent scratching.
- If you come in contact with poison ivy, sumac, or oak, immediately wash the affected area with soap and water to remove the irritating plant chemicals.
- Over-the-counter corticosteroid creams (hydrocortisone) may be used to soothe skin. Oral antihistamines may also help to relieve itching.
- Your doctor may prescribe stronger corticosteroid ointments, or ointments containing coal tar, to soothe inflammation.
- Oral corticosteroid medications may be prescribed for extensive or severe cases that do not respond to topical treatments.
- Special support stockings may be prescribed to improve circulation in the legs to treat stasis dermatitis.
- Wearing cotton clothes next to the skin can be beneficial. Cotton is less irritating than wool, silk, or synthetics.
- Antibiotics may be prescribed to treat a secondary bacterial infection.

WHEN TO CALL A DOCTOR

- Call a doctor if eczema does not respond to self-treatment, is widespread, or is recurrent.

Empyema

WHAT IS IT?

Empyema is an accumulation of pus (which forms as a result of infection) in any body cavity, although the term is generally used to refer to the buildup of pus between the lungs and the membranes (pleura) that surround them. Normally, a small amount of fluid is present inside this space, serving as a lubricant. But if this fluid becomes infected, pus may build up to quantities of a pint or more, exerting pressure on the lungs, which can cause pain and shortness of breath. This disorder has become uncommon since the development of antibiotics. (Empyema may also occur in other organs, resulting in different symptoms. For example, when it affects the gallbladder, abdominal pain and jaundice may occur.)

WHAT CAUSES IT?

• Pleural empyema (within the chest cavity) occurs as a complication of chest surgery, a serious chest injury, or an infection in the lungs (such as pneumonia or tuberculosis) or the pleura.
• Infection elsewhere in the body may spread to the chest cavity and cause pleural empyema.

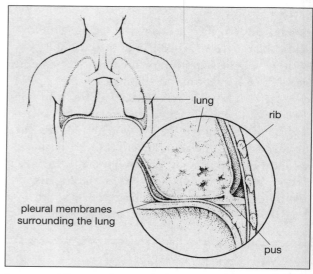

In empyema, the space between the lung and the pleural membranes becomes infected, resulting in a buildup of pus.

SYMPTOMS
• Chest pain, especially when breathing deeply.
• Shortness of breath.
• Dry cough.
• Fever and chills.
• Profuse sweating, including night sweats.
• Exhaustion.
• Weight loss.

PREVENTION
• Prompt treatment for infections, especially of the lungs, helps prevent empyema.

DIAGNOSIS
• A chest x-ray is taken.
• Diagnosis is confirmed by microscopic examination of pus and by culturing it (allowing the infectious agent to grow in the laboratory so that it may be identified). Fluid (or pus) is obtained by thoracentesis, a procedure that involves withdrawing fluid into a syringe after inserting a needle through the chest wall into the pleural cavity.

HOW TO TREAT IT
• Pain relievers, such as aspirin or acetaminophen, are recommended.
• Antibiotics are administered (often intravenously in a hospital) to combat bacterial infection.
• Pus is removed by repeated thoracenteses (see diagnostic information above for definition).
• Surgery may be necessary in severe cases or when the fluid is too thick to be removed by thoracentesis. A drainage tube may be implanted into the chest wall through a small incision (thoracostomy). In some cases a large incision that opens the chest cavity (thoracotomy) may be required.

WHEN TO CALL A DOCTOR
• Call a doctor if you experience the symptoms of empyema or any persistent symptoms of infection.

Encephalitis

WHAT IS IT?

Encephalitis, a rare disorder, is inflammation of the brain, almost always due to a viral infection. In most cases a virus attacks the brain directly after it is spread by a bite from an infected mosquito or, less often, a tick. Encephalitis may occur as an isolated case or in epidemics; most cases occur during the summer and early fall, although infection is possible year-round in warmer regions. Depending on the specific virus involved, the onset of symptoms may be sudden or may take over a week to develop. In some cases a flu-like illness with symptoms of fever, head and muscle aches, and fatigue may be present for several days before more severe symptoms of vomiting, stiff neck, extreme drowsiness, or seizures develop; in other cases severe symptoms may appear immediately. In addition, symptoms may vary among different age groups. In infants, a swelling in the soft spot of the skull (fontanel) and a stiff neck may be pronounced; children may complain of a headache and exhibit a sensitivity to light; in adults, neurological disturbances—both physical and mental—may be prominent. Although most cases of encephalitis are mild and may be mistaken for a cold or flu, in some cases (especially among the very young and very old) encephalitis is life-threatening. The outlook is good for those who survive the first two weeks of the infection; however, neurological symptoms may take many months to subside fully. Severe attacks bear the risk of permanent brain damage or epilepsy. Chemotherapy is available only for infections with the herpes simplex virus. In other cases treatment is aimed at relieving the severity and duration of symptoms.

WHAT CAUSES IT?

• Viral infection causes encephalitis. Most commonly, mosquitoes or ticks acquire an arbovirus from infected domestic animals (especially horses) or wild or domestic birds and may then transfer the virus to humans.
• Occasionally, infections with herpes simplex virus may spread to the brain.
• Human immune deficiency (HIV), measles, chicken pox and infectious mononucleosis may cause an autoimmune encephalitis.
• Rarely, an adverse reaction to a vaccine may lead to encephalitis.

PREVENTION

• Prevent insect bites by using insect repellent containing DEET (N,N-diethyltoluamide) during outdoor summer activities. Apply repellent to clothing; use sparingly on skin.
• Cover exposed skin when in grassy, wooded, or swampy areas where mosquitoes and ticks may be present. Tuck long pants into socks, wear shoes instead of sandals, and wear long-sleeved shirts. Light-colored clothing makes ticks more visible.
• During a more widespread encephalitis outbreak, limit outdoor exposure at times of greatest mosquito activity: early morning, late afternoon, and early evening.
• Use fine-tipped, curved tweezers to remove a tick attached to your skin (see Lyme Disease for more information about tick removal). Do not use petroleum jelly, kerosene, or a lit cigarette to remove a tick; contrary to popular belief, these methods are ineffective and may increase the likelihood of infection.
• If possible, avoid areas where there is an outbreak of encephalitis.

SYMPTOMS

• Headache.
• Fever.
• Nausea and vomiting.
• Fatigue and loss of appetite.
• Double vision, or pupils of different size.
• Speech impairment, loss of hearing.
• Stiff neck and back, due to an associated infection of the meninges—the three layers of tissue covering the brain (see Meningitis for more information).
• Extreme sensitivity to light,
• Mental confusion, irritability, memory loss, personality changes, and hallucinations.
• Seizures.
• Paralysis of one side of the body.
• Drowsiness, gradual loss of consciousness, and coma. Coma may persist for days or weeks.

Encephalitis *continued*

DIAGNOSIS
- Lumbar puncture (spinal tap).
- Blood tests.
- Electroencephalogram (EEG).
- Skull x-rays, CT (computed tomography) scans, or MRI (magnetic resonance imaging).
- In severe cases a brain biopsy may be required to determine the underlying cause and thus guide further treatment. Under general anesthetic, a tiny hole is drilled in the skull, and a needle is used to extract a sample of the affected brain tissue.

HOW TO TREAT IT
- The antiviral drug acyclovir may be administered intravenously to treat encephalitis due to the herpes simplex I or II viruses.
- Oral corticosteroid drugs, such as dexamethasone, may be administered to reduce inflammation of the brain.
- Anticonvulsant drugs, such as phenytoin, may be given to prevent seizures.
- Sedatives may be given to calm the patient.
- Pain relievers, like aspirin, acetaminophen, ibuprofen, or sodium naproxen, may be administered to reduce pain and fever. Aspirin should not be given to children with viral infections, owing to the risk of side effects (see Reye's Syndrome for more information).
- Fluids and electrolytes (such as sodium and potassium) may be administered intravenously to prevent dehydration during treatment, and liquid nutrients may be given through a tube placed in the stomach via the nose.
- A mechanical respirator may be required to aid breathing.
- Antibiotics may be administered to treat an associated bacterial infection.
- Speech, physical, and occupational therapy may be necessary during recovery in cases where a patient has suffered lasting brain damage.

WHEN TO CALL A DOCTOR
- Call a doctor immediately if you or your child develops nausea, severe headache, and a stiff neck, with or without a preceding flu-like illness.
- **EMERGENCY** Call an ambulance immediately if someone loses consciousness.

Endometrial Hyperplasia

WHAT IS IT?

Endometrial hyperplasia is the abnormal thickening of the lining of the uterus due to an increase in the number of endometrial glands. This disorder most often affects young women who are just beginning to menstruate and older women approaching menopause. In most cases endometrial hyperplasia is not a serious health risk. In some women, microscopic examination of endometrial tissue may reveal abnormalities in cellular nuclei, a precancerous disorder sometimes referred to as adenomatous hyperplasia, which may lead to endometrial (uterine) cancer. However, most cases of endometrial hyperplasia are benign and respond well to treatment with hormones or minor surgery. Symptoms of abnormal vaginal bleeding may cease with menopause.

SYMPTOMS

- Vaginal bleeding between menstrual periods or after menopause.
- Heavy menstrual bleeding.
- Periods that last longer than usual.

WHAT CAUSES IT?

- An overproduction of estrogen causes endometrial hyperplasia in young women.
- Unopposed estrogen replacement therapy (taking estrogen without progesterone) in postmenopausal women is associated with a higher incidence of endometrial hyperplasia.
- Young women who have just begun to menstruate, and women who have (or who have had) irregular menstrual cycles, are at greater risk for endometrial hyperplasia when taking estrogen after menopause.

PREVENTION

- While endometrial hyperplasia cannot be prevented, women should have regular pelvic examinations once they reach age 18 or become sexually active, to aid in early detection and treatment of any abnormalities.
- Postmenopausal estrogen replacement should be accompanied by a progestational agent or frequent endometrial biopsies.

DIAGNOSIS

- A Pap smear may be performed (a small sample of cells is scraped from the cervix and examined under the microscope), although a normal Pap smear does not rule out the presence of endometrial cancer.
- A biopsy of endometrial tissue may be taken during a pelvic examination.
- A dilatation and curettage (D&C) may be performed. In this procedure the cervix is widened, and tissue samples are obtained from the uterine lining.
- Blood levels of estrogen are measured.

HOW TO TREAT IT

- In most cases removal of excessive uterine tissue during the diagnostic D&C is all that is needed.
- Postmenopausal women on unopposed estrogen therapy who have recurrent endometrial hyperplasia should discuss with a gynecologist the options of either stopping the therapy or supplementing it with a progestational agent.
- In premenopausal women who have recurrent endometrial hyperplasia, birth control pills may be prescribed for a few months to thin the endometrial lining.
- A hysterectomy, the surgical removal of the uterus (and perhaps other reproductive organs), may be advised for postmenopausal women (or premenopausal women who no longer wish to have children) to reduce the risk of cancer when adenomatous hyperplasia does not respond to progestational agents.

WHEN TO CALL A DOCTOR

- Call a doctor if you develop heavy vaginal bleeding or if you experience vaginal bleeding between periods or after menopause.

Endometrial Polyps

WHAT IS IT?

Endometrial polyps are small, spherical or cylindrical growths on the endometrium, the lining of the uterus. The exact cause of endometrial polyps is not known, but they tend to accompany other conditions involving overgrowth of uterine cells, such as endometrial hyperplasia or uterine fibroids (see Endometrial Hyperplasia or Fibroids, Uterine, for more information). Polyps may appear singly or in clusters and are most common between the ages of 30 and 60, particularly among women over 50. They are usually not a health risk. (The polyps become

---

SYMPTOMS

- No symptoms in many cases.
- Light bleeding or spotting between periods, especially after sexual intercourse.
- Heavy bleeding during menstrual periods.
- Periods that last longer than usual.
- Pelvic cramps.
- Foul-smelling vaginal discharge (if infection occurs).

---

cancerous only in rare cases.) They generally cause no symptoms and, indeed, often go undetected. However, in some instances endometrial polyps may cause heavy menstrual bleeding or bleeding between periods. Occasionally polyps may protrude into the vagina through the cervix, where they may bleed. Cylindrical polyps attached to the uterine wall by a stalk may become twisted, which cuts off their blood supply and leads to infection. In rare cases polyps

may grow large enough to fill or even stretch the uterus and so interfere with conception by blocking the passage of sperm. Endometrial polyps may be easily removed with minor surgery.

WHAT CAUSES IT?

- The cause of endometrial polyps is unknown.

PREVENTION

- While endometrial polyps cannot be prevented, women should have regular pelvic examinations once they reach age 18 or become sexually active, to aid in early detection and treatment of any abnormalities.

DIAGNOSIS

- A pelvic examination may reveal the presence of endometrial polyps that protrude through the cervix.
- A D&C (dilatation and curettage) may be performed. In this procedure the cervix is widened so that the uterine lining can be scraped to obtain a tissue sample.

HOW TO TREAT IT

- Endometrial polyps may be scraped and removed from the uterine lining during the D&C procedure used for diagnosis. The D&C is generally performed at a hospital on an outpatient basis and requires local anesthesia.

WHEN TO CALL A DOCTOR

- Call a doctor if you develop bleeding between periods, or if your periods are heavier or lengthier than normal.

Endometriosis

WHAT IS IT?

Endometriosis is a benign disorder characterized by the presence of endometrial tissue (the tissue that lines the uterus) outside the uterine cavity where it becomes attached to reproductive or abdominal organs. The patches of endometrial tissue swell with blood during menstruation as if they were still in the uterus. Because this blood is trapped within the tissue and cannot be shed through the vagina, blood blisters form, and they may develop further into cysts, scar tissue, or adhesions (fibrous bands that link together other tissues that are normally separated). Cysts may range from the size of a pinhead to a grapefruit; cysts, scars, and adhesions may all lead to infertility. Endometriosis is a common disorder, most prevalent between the ages of 25 and 40. Symptoms vary and are not strictly correlated with the severity of the disease; they may worsen with time, but tend to diminish during pregnancy and cease with menopause. Many women have no symptoms at all. Treatment depends on the severity of symptoms, the age of the woman, and whether she wishes to have children.

WHAT CAUSES IT?

• The cause of endometriosis is unknown. Hereditary factors may be involved.

SYMPTOMS

• Pain in the vagina, lower abdomen, and lower back. Pain often begins just prior to monthly periods, continues during menses, and worsens just after the cessation of blood flow.
• Abnormal or heavy menstrual bleeding.
• Vaginal pain during sexual intercourse (dyspareunia).
• Diarrhea, constipation, or pain during bowel movements.
• Bleeding from the rectum or blood in the urine during menses.
• Nausea and vomiting just prior to monthly periods.
• Infertility. (Endometriosis is one of the most common causes.)

• Hormonal changes or recent pelvic surgery may promote endometriosis.

PREVENTION

• While endometriosis cannot be prevented, women should have regular pelvic examinations once they reach age 18 or become sexually active, to aid in early detection and treatment of any reproductive system abnormalities.

DIAGNOSIS

• A pelvic examination may reveal endometriosis. The doctor presses upon the uterus and ovaries to feel for any abnormalities.
• A definitive diagnosis requires direct visualization of the extrauterine endometrial tissue, usually by laparoscopy, the insertion of a thin, lighted viewing instrument (laparoscope) into the abdomen through a small incision.

HOW TO TREAT IT

• Young women with endometriosis who want children may be advised to have them sooner rather than later.
• Over-the-counter pain relievers may be taken for mild menstrual pain.
• Danazol, progestins, or Gn–RH (gonadotropin-releasing hormone) agonists may be administered to halt menstruation for three to six months in an effort to shrink endometrial tissue.
• Surgical removal of the tissue may be required to relieve severe symptoms or to allow impregnation. Tissue may be destroyed by heat (electrocautery) or removed with lasers during laparoscopy (usually done on an outpatient basis under local anesthesia).
• A hysterectomy, the surgical removal of the uterus (and sometimes other reproductive organs), may be advised in severe cases. Hormone replacement is required if both ovaries are removed.

WHEN TO CALL A DOCTOR

• Call a doctor if you experience severe pain and heavy bleeding during menstruation, with or without additional symptoms of endometriosis.

Epididymitis

WHAT IS IT?

Epididymitis is an infection of the epididymis, a tightly coiled, tubular structure located at the back of each testicle. Newly manufactured sperm cells mature as they slowly pass through the epididymis. The epididymic infection, which almost always affects only one epididymis, is common, easily treated, and not associated with permanent damage; however, epididymitis that affects both sides may lead to sterility if left untreated. Epididymitis does not occur prior to puberty.

WHAT CAUSES IT?

• A bacterial infection is the most common cause of epididymitis. The infection may be sexually transmitted or may spread from a bacterial infection in the bladder, urethra, or prostate.
• Straining upon urination may force urine into the reproductive tract and cause chemical irritation of the epididymis.
• Genital injury is sometimes a cause.
• Urinary tract instrumentation or prostate surgery can lead to epididymitis.

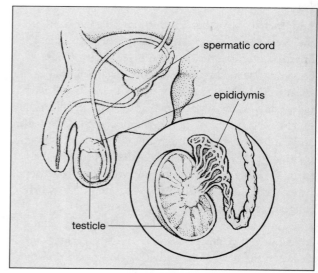

Sperm cells newly produced by the testicles mature during their journey through the long, coiled tubules of the epididymis.

SYMPTOMS

• Rapid onset of pain, heat, and swelling at the back of one testicle (and sometimes both), followed by swelling and hardening of the scrotum.
• Fever.
• Burning on urination.

PREVENTION

• Use a condom to help prevent sexually transmitted disease.
• Obtain prompt treatment for urinary tract infections (see Bladder Infection for more information).

DIAGNOSIS

• Physical examination. A digital rectal examination may be performed by inserting a gloved, lubricated finger into the rectum to feel for abnormalities.

• Samples of urine and prostate gland secretions may be taken.

HOW TO TREAT IT

• Antibiotics are prescribed to treat a bacterial infection. Sexual partners may need to be treated as well.
• Over-the-counter analgesics may be used to ease pain and inflammation.
• Bed rest may be advised until symptoms subside. When resting, it is advised to support the scrotum on a rolled bath towel.
• An ice pack may be used to relieve swelling. (Heat should not be used, because it may damage sperm-producing cells.)
• Sexual activity should be avoided for as long as symptoms persist.
• An athletic supporter may ease discomfort during recuperation.
• Surgical removal of the epididymis may be necessary for very severe or recurrent cases that do not respond to antibiotic therapy.

WHEN TO CALL A DOCTOR

• Call a doctor for any severe or persistent testicular pain or swelling.

Epiglottitis

WHAT IS IT?

Epiglottitis, a medical emergency, is a rare infection of the epiglottis—the small flap of cartilage in the throat that closes upon swallowing to prevent food and liquids from entering the windpipe. When infected, the epiglottis becomes inflamed and swollen, causing rapidly progressive breathing difficulty, especially in children. In an attempt to ease breathing, a person with epiglottitis commonly assumes a characteristic posture of leaning forward in a sitting position with the neck extended. Swelling of the epiglottis may lead to complete blockage of the airway within 12 hours of onset, so immediate treatment is necessary. Hospitalization is necessary so that breathing may be aided by tubes or emergency surgery in the event of complete obstruction of the airway. However, once treatment is initiated, symptoms generally subside within 36 to 48 hours, leaving no permanent damage. Epiglottitis most commonly affects children between the ages of two and eight, but it can occur in adolescents and adults.

WHAT CAUSES IT?

• Bacterial infection causes epiglottitis. The most common cause in children is *H. influenzae* which is highly infectious and may dictate antibiotic treatment of other family members.
• Adults who have a weakened immune system due to leukemia, Hodgkin's disease, AIDS, or chemotherapy treatment for cancer are at higher risk for epiglottitis.

PREVENTION

• As much as possible, try to limit exposure to people with contagious respiratory illnesses.

DIAGNOSIS

• Examination of the throat using a tongue depressor or laryngoscope (a special lighted scope). (There is a danger that this may cause an inflamed epiglottis to completely block the airway, so such an examination should not be attempted at home.)
• Neck x-ray.
• Blood and throat cultures.

HOW TO TREAT IT

• Hospitalization is necessary to treat epiglottitis, since symptoms may quickly become life-threatening.
• Oxygen may be administered to aid breathing.
• Obstruction of the airway may make it necessary to pass a tube down the throat, through the nose or mouth, to permit breathing.
• A temporary surgical opening in the throat, known as a tracheotomy, may be performed in some cases. In this procedure a small tube is surgically inserted into the throat, allowing the patient to breathe. The tube is removed after symptoms and epiglottal inflammation subside.
• Antibiotics are administered intravenously to treat the underlying bacterial infection.
• Fluids may be administered intravenously to prevent dehydration.
• Corticosteroid medications may be given to reduce inflammation of the epiglottis.

WHEN TO CALL A DOCTOR

• **EMERGENCY** Call an ambulance or get to a hospital immediately if you or your child begins to experience swallowing or breathing difficulty, or if your child turns blue or loses consciousness.

SYMPTOMS

• Sore throat.
• Fever.
• Increasing difficulty or pain upon swallowing.
• Drooling.
• Increasingly muffled speech; hoarseness.
• Irritability and restlessness.
• Emergency symptoms: breathing difficulty, a bluish tinge to the skin (cyanosis), loss of consciousness.

Erectile Dysfunction Impotence

WHAT IS IT?

Erectile dysfunction, commonly known as impotence, is the inability to achieve or maintain an erection adequate for sexual intercourse. It may occur at any age but becomes increasingly frequent as men grow older. The mechanisms for erection are fairly complex: A sensory stimulus triggers the brain to send nerve impulses down through the spinal cord. These signals trigger the release of a chemical messenger that causes the vessels supplying blood to the penis to dilate. The rod-shaped spongy tissues (corpora cavernosa) in the penis then fill with blood and expand, pressing against the veins that normally allow blood to drain from the penis, thus producing an erection. Interference with any part of this process—whether psychological or physiological—may cause erectile dysfunction. Although an occasional inability to maintain an erection is common and not a sign of a chronic problem, a doctor should be consulted if impotence persists. Treatment depends upon the underlying cause.

SYMPTOMS
- Inability to achieve or maintain an erection sufficient for sexual intercourse.

WHAT CAUSES IT?

- Emotional and psychological difficulties such as guilt or anxiety (especially performance anxiety, in which fear of not having an erection becomes so distracting that it becomes a self-fulfilling prophecy).
- Conditions that affect the brain and decrease the libido (sex drive), including depression or schizophrenia; use of drugs that act on the central nervous system (sedatives, antidepressants, some antihypertensives, antipsychotics, and alcohol); and chronic illnesses such as heart, lung, kidney, or liver disease, and certain types of cancer.
- Hormonal disturbances that decrease the libido, including diminished testosterone levels, elevated prolactin (due to a pituitary tumor), and hyper- or hypothyroidism.
- Brain disorders (that do not affect libido but that have neurological consequences that affect sexual functioning), including brain tumor and stroke.
- Spinal cord disorders, such as multiple sclerosis or spinal cord trauma.
- Damage to the peripheral nerves due to diabetes mellitus or pelvic surgery for disorders such as prostate enlargement or prostate cancer.
- Other drugs that can sometimes cause sexual dysfunction, including anticholinergics, antihistamines, beta-blockers (and other kinds of antihypertensives), and long-term use of nicotine.
- Peripheral vascular disease (impaired blood flow to the extremities and the penis).
- Fatigue.
- Advancing age.

PREVENTION

- Consume no more than two alcoholic beverages per day.
- Talk to a therapist about improving communication with your sexual partner.

DIAGNOSIS

- Patient history and physical examination are required.
- Blood may be taken to measure testosterone, prolactin, and thyroid hormones.
- Psychological causes may be identified by ruling out a physiological cause. A band of stamps or perforated tape is placed around the penis before sleep. An erection during the night will break the perforations, demonstrating that there is no organic cause for the erectile dysfunction.
- Angiography (x-rays taken after a contrast material is injected into an artery) may be performed to measure blood circulation in the penis.
- The drug papaverine may be injected into the penis to test for vascular problems.

HOW TO TREAT IT

- Psychological counseling may be recommended.
- Avoid nicotine, alcohol, and other drugs.
- Your doctor may change your prescriptions if a medication has caused impotence.
- Testosterone injections are given if blood testosterone levels are low.

Erectile Dysfunction Impotence *continued*

• Hyperthyroidism or hypothyroidism is treated if necessary.

• Bromocriptine therapy is given to correct elevated prolactin levels.

• A special vacuum device may be used to produce an erection. Air is pumped out of a plastic tube placed securely over the penis, and the resulting vacuum stimulates blood flow into the corpora cavernosa within a few minutes. The device is removed and a rubber band is placed at the base of the penis to maintain the erection.

• Surgical implants for the penis are available. In one procedure an inflatable device with a small fluid reservoir is inserted. In another, flexible rods are implanted that can be either bent upward to produce an erection or tucked close to the body.

• Your doctor may advise vascular surgery to improve blood flow to the penis.

• Self-administered injections of papaverine, a vasodilator drug, dilate the blood vessels in the penis to produce an erection. Your doctor will instruct you on the correct injection technique.

WHEN TO CALL A DOCTOR

• Call a doctor if you experience a persistent inability to achieve or maintain an erection.

Esophageal Cancer

WHAT IS IT?
Esophageal cancer is the growth of malignant cells in the esophagus, the passageway from the throat to the stomach. An esophageal cancer blocks the passage of food to the stomach, erodes the esophageal lining, and contributes to the development of fistulas (abnormal channels between normally separate organs) between the esophagus and the trachea (the major airway to the lungs). Although uncommon, esophageal tumors worsen rapidly: by the time symptoms develop, the outlook is poor. In North America this cancer is more common among blacks than whites and affects men more frequently than women. It occurs most often in those over 50. Although a cure may be attempted when the cancer is detected at an early stage, treatment is generally aimed at relieving symptoms and making the patient as comfortable as possible.

WHAT CAUSES IT?
• The cause of esophageal cancer is unknown.
• Smoking and excess consumption of alcohol are believed to be the greatest risk factors.
• Swallowing lye or other corrosive chemicals may lead to esophageal cancer.
• The habit of drinking extremely hot beverages may, over time, damage the esophagus and predispose to cancer.
• Persistent gastric reflux is associated with a higher risk of esophageal cancer (see Gastroesophageal Reflux for more information).

PREVENTION
• Do not smoke.
• Do not drink more than two alcoholic drinks per day.

DIAGNOSIS
• X-ray after swallowing barium to create a clear image of the esophagus.
• Endoscopy (a small, lighted viewing tube inserted into the esophagus through the mouth under local anesthesia).
• A biopsy is performed during the endoscopy to remove a sample of esophageal tissue for examination under a microscope.

HOW TO TREAT IT
• Surgery may be performed in an attempt to remove the tumor.
• If the tumor cannot be completely removed, laser surgery may be used to reduce its size and open a passageway into the stomach.
• Radiation therapy may be used after or in conjunction with surgery to decrease tumor size and prevent its spread.
• Chemotherapy may be used to destroy remaining cancer cells instead of, or in addition to, surgery and radiation therapy.
• An esophageal dilator may be used to widen the stricture. Dilation is usually repeated periodically to maintain the opening.
• Patients unsuitable for surgery may have a plastic tube inserted through the esophagus (intubation) to bypass the site of the tumor.
• An artificial opening in the stomach (gastrostoma) or small intestine (ileostoma) may be created surgically, so that food may bypass the entire esophagus.
• Painkillers and tranquilizers are prescribed to relieve pain and anxiety.

WHEN TO CALL A DOCTOR
• Call a doctor if you experience difficulty in swallowing.

SYMPTOMS
• Progressive swallowing difficulty, first with solid foods, then liquids; painful swallowing.
• Chest pain.
• Weight loss.
• Regurgitation of bloody mucus.
• Regurgitation or vomiting of swallowed food.
• Repeated respiratory infections. Material may spill into the airway and lungs from frequent regurgitation or from an esophago-tracheal fistula.

Esophageal Rupture

WHAT IS IT?

An esophageal rupture, a medical emergency, is a tear in the esophagus, the passageway from the throat to the stomach. The esophagus may be ruptured by forceful vomiting, by damage from swallowing corrosive chemicals, by injury, or by other disorders of the esophagus, such as esophageal cancer (see Esophageal Cancer for more information). Chest pain from a large tear in the esophagus may mimic symptoms of a heart attack (see Myocardial Infarction for more information), although pain from a small tear or perforation may be mild. Leakage of esophageal contents, such as food or vomit, into the neighboring chest cavity can cause a serious bacterial infection or abscess. Treatment usually involves surgery to repair the tear and remove esophageal contents from the chest cavity, combined with antibiotics to prevent or treat a bacterial infection. If the esophagus has been severely damaged, surgical removal of the affected portion of the esophagus may be necessary.

SYMPTOMS

- Mild or severe chest pain that may worsen upon breathing or swallowing.
- Nausea and vomiting; blood in the vomit.
- Fever.
- Rapid, shallow breathing.
- Excessive sweating.

WHAT CAUSES IT?

- Forceful vomiting.
- Swallowing a foreign object.
- Swallowing lye or other corrosive chemicals (see Esophageal Stricture for more information).
- Infection, ulcer, or cancer in the esophagus.
- Accidental injury from insertion of tubes or instruments into the esophagus during medical procedures. (Approximately half of esophageal ruptures are caused this way and usually result in less serious consequences.)
- Trauma, such as an automobile accident.

PREVENTION

- Keep small objects that may be swallowed away from young children.
- Obtain prompt treatment for disorders that cause severe nausea and vomiting.

DIAGNOSIS

- Chest x-ray. You may be required to swallow barium, a contrast material, prior to the x-ray, so that the site of rupture in the esophagus can be clearly identified.

HOW TO TREAT IT

- Surgical repair of the rupture is necessary for all but extremely small tears.
- Suction may be used to empty the esophagus, stomach, and chest cavity of vomit, food, or other matter. Stomach contents and secretions are removed by a nasogastric tube threaded through the nose and esophagus past the site of the rupture into the stomach.
- Intravenous fluids and nutrients may be administered to avoid irritation of the esophagus until the tear has healed.
- Intravenous antibiotics may be administered to treat or prevent an associated bacterial infection. For very small tears that may heal by themselves, antibiotics may be the only treatment necessary.
- In cases of severe esophageal damage, the affected portion of the esophagus may be removed surgically.

WHEN TO CALL A DOCTOR

- **EMERGENCY**. Call an ambulance for any severe chest pain. Heart attack and other serious disorders will need to be ruled out.
- **EMERGENCY** See a doctor immediately if vomiting of blood occurs, with or without other symptoms of esophageal rupture.

Esophageal Stricture

WHAT IS IT?

An esophageal stricture is a narrowing of the esopha-gus, the passageway from the throat to the stomach. Stomach acid, esophageal cancer, accidentally swal-lowed harsh chemicals, and other irritants may injure the esophageal lining, causing inflammation and the formation of scar tissue. This may gradually lead to obstruction of the esophagus, preventing food and fluids from reaching the stomach.

WHAT CAUSES IT?

• Persistent reflux of gastric acid, sometimes associ-ated with hiatal hernia (see Gastroesophageal Reflux and Hiatal Hernia for more).
• Systemic sclerosis (scleroderma), which is often associated with severe reflux and esophageal stricture (see Scleroderma).
• Swallowing lye or other corrosive chemicals.
• Esophageal surgery or protracted use of a nasogas-tric tube (used in hospitals for feeding).
• Esophageal cancer may narrow the esophagus and produce the same symptoms.

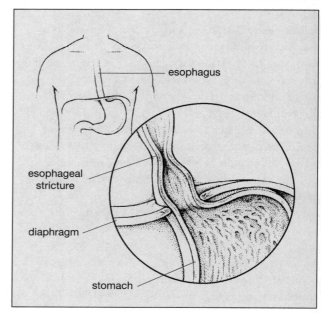

Injury to the lining of the esophagus, the narrowest portion of the digestive tract, may result in esophageal stricture.

SYMPTOMS

• Progressive swallowing difficulty, first with solid foods, then liquids; chest pain after meals; increased salivation.
• Regurgitation of foods and liquids. These may be aspirated into the lungs, causing cough, wheezing, and shortness of breath.
• Weight loss.

PREVENTION

• Store all corrosive chemicals where they will be inaccessible to children.
• Aggressive treatment of chronic gastroesophageal reflux is necessary.

DIAGNOSIS

• Endoscopy (insertion of an illuminated scope into the esophagus through the mouth under local anes-thesia) may be performed.
• Chest x-ray. You may be required to swallow

barium, which helps to create a sharp image of the esophagus on an x-ray.

HOW TO TREAT IT

• Avoid alcohol and spicy foods that may irritate the esophagus.
• Your doctor may advise a diet of liquids or soft foods until food can be swallowed without difficulty.
• Mechanical dilation of the esophagus (esophageal bougienage) may be performed to widen the stricture. Repeated dilations may be necessary if stricture recurs.
• In severe cases the affected portion of the esopha-gus may be removed and replaced with a segment of the large intestine.
• In a few cases patients unsuitable for surgery may have a feeding tube inserted through the stricture. Alternatively, such patients may have a small tube placed into the stomach (gastrostomy), so that food may bypass the esophagus completely.

WHEN TO CALL A DOCTOR

• **EMERGENCY** Call an ambulance if someone has swallowed a corrosive material.
• Call a doctor if you experience progressive diffi-culty in swallowing.

Essential Tremor

WHAT IS IT?

Essential tremor, also known as intention or familial tremor, is a rhythmic shaking movement caused by involuntary muscle contractions. This tremor, termed essential because it is not related to an underlying disorder, most frequently affects the hands and neck; it generally spares the muscles of the torso and lower limbs. Characteristically, essential tremor becomes more pronounced during activities such as writing or using a knife and fork, as distinguished from tremors in Parkinson's disease, which diminish with movement (see Parkinson's Disease for more information). Essential tremor usually develops in middle age or later. Symptoms appear gradually. The most common of the so-called shaking disorders, essential tremor is not a serious health risk. It responds well to treatment and in fact seems to be an indicator of an unusually long life.

WHAT CAUSES IT?

• The cause of essential tremor is unknown.
• Genetic factors play a role in about half of all cases (familial tremor).

SYMPTOMS

• Rhythmic shaking of the hands and fingers and, less frequently, the head, tongue, larynx, eyelids, or other parts of the body. The speed of the shaking movements may be extremely rapid, moderate, or slow.
• Worsening of the tremor under the following conditions: with emotional or physical stress; when voluntarily moving the hands, head, and other muscles; when voluntarily trying to hold the head or hands still.
• Cessation of the tremor when the body is at rest.
• Shaky handwriting.
• Quavering voice.

PREVENTION

• There is no known way to prevent essential tremor.

DIAGNOSIS

• Patient history and physical examination.

HOW TO TREAT IT

• Beta-blocking drugs (commonly used to treat hypertension) such as propranolol are generally the most effective medications for treating essential tremor.
• Other drugs, including anticonvulsants (such as primidone) and tranquilizers (such as clonazepam, lorazepam, or alprazolam), may be used to treat muscle tremors that do not respond to beta-blockers.
• Patients may be advised to drink one glass of wine or one ounce of 80-proof liquor per day, since alcohol has been shown to ease tremors in some cases. However, sometimes a rebound effect occurs, causing the tremor to worsen after the effect of the alcohol has worn off. In addition, some doctors fear the potential risk of alcohol abuse.
• Avoid the consumption of caffeine and other stimulants, which may exacerbate the tremor.
• Regular exercise with one- or two-pound weights may help to reduce shaking in the hands and arms.
• In severe, disabling cases that do not respond satisfactorily to medications, controlled injections of botulinum toxin (which causes the muscle paralysis associated with botulism) into muscles of the forearm or neck may stop tremors.
• Surgical destruction of specific cells within the thalamus, a region of the brain, may provide relief from symptoms in severe cases that do not respond to other forms of treatment, but this is done only as a last resort.

WHEN TO CALL A DOCTOR

• Make an appointment with a doctor if involuntary trembling or shaking of the hands, head, or other muscles interferes with normal activities.

Eye Cancers

WHAT IS IT?

Eye cancer is the growth of malignant cells in the tissues of the eye. In adults, most eye cancers are secondary tumors that spread to the eye from other parts of the body (often the breast, although cancers of the lungs, kidneys, and prostate gland are sometimes involved) via the bloodstream or the lymphatic system. Two primary tumors arise within the eyes: retinoblastomas in children and melanomas in adults. Among children, retinoblastoma is the most common eye cancer; it affects children under age five. Malignant melanoma of the eye is found most frequently in the elderly. Most eye cancers affect only one eye, but retinoblastoma involves both eyes in about one-third of cases. Symptoms may not be evident in the early stages of any form of eye cancer; however, growing tumors may increasingly cause pain and impair vision. Cancer of the eye may spread to the optic nerve, the brain, and the rest of the body (malignant melanoma is particularly quick to spread), so early diagnosis and treatment are important. Treatment for eye cancer is aimed at destroying cancerous cells, relieving symptoms, and preserving sight as much as possible; treatment for secondary eye tumors also involves treating the primary cancer elsewhere in the body.

SYMPTOMS

- Gradual distortion and loss of vision in the affected eye.
- Pain and redness in the affected eye.
- Different color irises in each eye.
- Visible whiteness in the pupil (with retinoblastoma).
- Crossed eyes (with retinoblastoma) where one eye has become blind.
- Bleeding in the eye (with retinoblastoma).
- Black or brown spot on the iris or the white of the eye (with melanoma).
- Bulging eyes (with a secondary tumor located behind the eyeball).

WHAT CAUSES IT?

- The most common cause of eye cancer in adults is the spread of a tumor from some other site in the body.
- Genetic factors play a role in retinoblastoma.

PREVENTION

- If retinoblastoma runs in your family, genetic counseling is advised before having children.
- Newborns and children in families with a history of retinoblastoma should have regular eye examinations.

DIAGNOSIS

- An ophthalmologist will conduct a complete eye examination, possibly using general anesthesia on children.
- Fluorescein angiography (injection of a special dye into a vein to highlight the blood vessels of the eye for a series of photographs) may be done to locate the tumor.
- Skull x-rays, an ultrasound examination, and CT (computed tomography) scans of the head and eye may be performed.

HOW TO TREAT IT

- Laser surgery or cryosurgery (freezing the targeted tissue with liquid nitrogen) may be used to destroy the tumor.
- Radiation therapy may be used to kill cancerous cells, in conjunction with or in lieu of surgery.
- Chemotherapy may be used to halt or limit the spread of the cancer.
- Surgical removal of the eye may be necessary to prevent the cancer from spreading, or when an eye is completely blinded and painful.

WHEN TO CALL A DOCTOR

- Make an appointment with an ophthalmologist if you or your child develops eye pain, redness, or bleeding, loss of vision, or discolored spots on the eye.

Fibrocystic Breast Disease

WHAT IS IT?

Fibrocystic breast disease is characterized by the presence of noncancerous lumps, or cysts, in the breast. The cysts may vary in size, number, and composition; some may be filled with fluid, and others may be solid. Over 60 percent of women develop cysts in the breast, mainly between the ages of 25 and 50. Many doctors believe that the condition represents only a variety of common, natural states or changes in the breast and should not be termed a disease at all. Symptoms of pain and tenderness tend to be more pronounced just prior to menstrual periods. Cysts are not cancerous; however, a biopsy is the only way to make a certain diagnosis of any lump in the breast. Symptoms may disappear after menopause.

WHAT CAUSES IT?

• The cause of fibrocystic breast disease is unknown.
• Estrogen and other ovarian hormones may influence the development of cysts.

PREVENTION

• There is no way to prevent fibrocystic disease. For the purpose of early detection, women should perform monthly breast exams, have a yearly breast exam performed by a doctor or other trained specialist, and begin having mammograms after age 50 (see Breast Cancer for more information).

DIAGNOSIS

• Breast examination or mammography may reveal the presence of a lump in the breast.

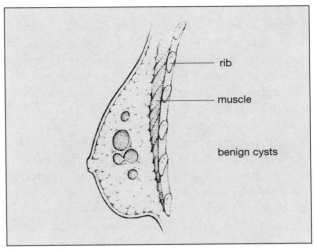

The lumps that characterize fibrocystic breast disease may change in size or feel in response to hormonal changes during the menstrual cycle.

• A biopsy of the lump, using a needle aspiration to extract fluid, or minor surgery to remove solid tissue is the only certain way to determine whether a breast lump or cyst is benign or malignant.

HOW TO TREAT IT

• Needle aspiration or biopsy may drain or remove the lump completely.
• Your doctor may prescribe hormonal treatment to relieve symptoms.
• A full-support bra may help relieve minor breast discomfort.
• Take over-the-counter pain relievers to reduce pain.

WHEN TO CALL A DOCTOR

• Make an appointment with a doctor if you notice the development of a new lump anywhere in the breast or under the arm, especially when no other lumps are present. Most lumps are not cancerous, but a biopsy is necessary for a definite diagnosis.
• Make an appointment with a doctor if you notice that a breast lump has become harder or more painful, changed in size, or if you experience discharge from the nipple.

SYMPTOMS

• One or more lumps or swellings, often painless, anywhere in the breast.
• Discomfort or pain around the lump or in the breast, especially during the week before a menstrual period.
• Changes in the size or symmetry of the breasts.

Fibroids, Uterine

WHAT IS IT?

Uterine fibroids are benign (noncancerous) growths of the muscular wall of the uterus. The growths, which may appear singly or in groups, range from the size of a pea to the size of a grapefruit, and may either be confined to the uterine wall or grow outward on thin stalks. Fibroids often cause no symptoms, unless they grow so large as to press painfully on other organs or even distort the shape of the abdomen. Also, a fibroid with a stalk may become twisted, which cuts off its blood supply and results in sharp, severe pain, requiring emergency surgery. Fibroids are quite common; they generally affect women between ages 30 and 45, and may shrink or disappear with the onset of menopause. The growths rarely become cancerous, although large fibroids may narrow the uterine cavity and lead to miscarriage or infertility.

WHAT CAUSES IT?

• The cause of uterine fibroids is unknown.
• Birth control pills or pregnancy may promote fibroid growth.

Small fibroids in the wall of the uterus may be unnoticeable; larger ones may cause pain, along with menstrual, urinary, or fertility problems.

> ### SYMPTOMS
> • Heavier bleeding during menstrual periods.
> • Abdominal discomfort, fullness, or pain; lower back pain.
> • Frequent urination; constipation.
> • Emergency symptom: sharp, sudden pain in the lower abdomen (when a fibroid with stalk becomes twisted).

PREVENTION

• Women should have regular pelvic exams once they reach age 18 or become sexually active, to aid in early detection and treatment of any abnormalities.
• Women diagnosed with symptomless fibroids should have pelvic examinations once a year so that fibroid growth may be monitored.

DIAGNOSIS

• A pelvic examination, during which a doctor presses upon the uterus and ovaries to feel for any abnormali-ties, may reveal the presence of uterine fibroids.
• A dilatation and curettage, or D&C, widens the cervix and allows a small tissue sample to be scraped from the uterine lining for analysis.
• A pelvic ultrasound scan can confirm the diagnosis.

HOW TO TREAT IT

• Symptomless fibroids rarely require treatment.
• Iron supplements may be advised for heavy bleeding during menstrual periods.
• Surgical removal of the fibroids that leaves the uterus intact (myomectomy) is an option. It may take some investigation to find a doctor to perform a myomectomy.
• Emergency surgery is necessary to remove a twisted fibroid.
• A hysterectomy, the surgical removal of the uterus (and perhaps other reproductive organs), may be recommended for severe or recurrent cases.

WHEN TO CALL A DOCTOR

• Call a gynecologist if you develop symptoms of uterine fibroids.
• **EMERGENCY** Get immediate medical attention for sharp, sudden pain in the lower abdomen.

Fibromyalgia

WHAT IS IT?

Fibromyalgia (previously called fibrositis) is an elusive, poorly understood disorder characterized by generalized fatigue and pain in various muscles, tendons, and ligaments. Pain and fatigue may be persistent or may recur in episodes lasting three to four days at a time. Diagnostic tests show no abnormalities or muscle damage. Fibromyalgia is more common in women between the ages of 20 and 50, although it may strike anyone at any age. This disorder does not lead to joint or muscle damage. Treatment is aimed at the management and relief of symptoms.

WHAT CAUSES IT?

• The cause of fibromyalgia is unknown.
• Sleep disturbances or interruptions, especially of deep sleep (known as stage IV sleep), may provoke a flare-up of fibromyalgia.
• Slack, underused muscles may contribute to fibromyalgia.
• Emotional stress and worry may increase the risk of fibromyalgia.
• Other disorders, such as arthritis or chronic fatigue syndrome, may be associated with fibromyalgia.

PREVENTION

• There is no known way to prevent fibromyalgia.
• Eating a healthy, well-balanced diet and getting regular exercise may help decrease the risk.

SYMPTOMS

• Widespread muscle aches, pains, and stiffness. Physical activity may relieve stiffness but worsen pain. Stiffness is worse upon awakening in the morning and improves in some patients during the course of the day.
• Chronic fatigue, possibly accompanied by insomnia.
• Disturbed sleep patterns and tiredness upon awakening.

DIAGNOSIS

• Patient history and physical examination.
• Although there are no specific tests for fibromyalgia, the diagnosis is strengthened when the physician applies pressure to 18 characteristically painful sites and the patient reports tenderness in at least 11 of them.
• Further tests to rule out rheumatoid arthritis and other diseases may be done. Indeed, a diagnosis of fibromyalgia is dependent upon the exclusion of other disorders.

HOW TO TREAT IT

• Over-the-counter pain relievers may be taken as necessary.
• A regular program of physical exercise may relieve pain and stiffness. Exercise may aggravate pain at first; therefore, in consultation with your doctor, start with low-impact activities such as walking, swimming, and bicycling, sustaining the activity for 20 to 30 minutes at a time. You may slowly work up to more vigorous exercises like jogging, racquetball, or aerobics.
• Antidepressant drugs such as amitriptyline, doxepin, or cyclobenzaprine may be prescribed to promote restful sleep. Antidepressants increase stage IV (deep) sleep, whereas regular sleeping pills interrupt this stage and make fibromyalgia worse.
• A hot bath, heating pad, or massage may provide temporary relief from muscle pain.
• Practice good posture during the day. A firm mattress may help prevent muscle pain at night.
• Psychological counseling may be beneficial and help to ease emotional stress that may trigger painful flare-ups. Relaxation techniques, such as meditation or biofeedback, may help reduce muscle tension and stress.
• Corticosteroids may be injected locally into the affected sites to reduce pain.

WHEN TO CALL A DOCTOR

• Make an appointment with a doctor if you experience symptoms of fibromyalgia for more than three consecutive days, or if symptoms recur.

Fibrous Dysplasia

WHAT IS IT?

Fibrous dysplasia is the replacement of localized areas of bone with abnormal tissue. In fibrous dysplasia, new abnormal tissue fills patches of the bone marrow cavity and replaces the overlying bone. As a result, the bone becomes larger and weaker than normal because the abnormal tissue is laid down in chaotic patterns. This disorder may affect only a single bone (monostotic fibrous dysplasia), and in many cases no symptoms are evident. At the other extreme, polyostotic fibrous dysplasia may attack more than half the bones in the skeleton. Monostotic fibrous dysplasia is generally diagnosed between the ages of 20 and 30, whereas the more severe form of polyostotic fibrous dysplasia may be diagnosed in childhood. Fibrous dysplasia is associated with an increased frequency of other disorders such as hyperpituitarism, hyperthyroidism, or Cushing's syndrome (see Hyperpituitarism, Hyperthyroidism, or Cushing's Syndrome for more informa-

tion). In addition, for unknown reasons fibrous dysplasia may trigger the premature development of secondary sex characteristics in very young girls (precocious puberty). There is no cure for fibrous dysplasia; treatment is aimed at relieving symptoms, reinforcing and strengthening bones, and controlling excess bone growth.

WHAT CAUSES IT?

• The cause of fibrous dysplasia is unknown.

PREVENTION

• There is no known way to prevent fibrous dysplasia.

DIAGNOSIS

• X-rays of the bones.
• A bone biopsy (removal and analysis of tissue samples) may be performed in some cases.

HOW TO TREAT IT

• Over-the-counter pain relievers may be used as necessary.
• Calcitonin, a hormone that regulates bone metabolism, may be prescribed for serious, widespread cases. Such therapy may slow the progression of the disease, although preexisting damage is irreversible.
• Surgical removal of excess and abnormal bone tissue may be required (osteotomy).
• Healthy bone from elsewhere in the skeleton may need to be transplanted, or grafted, onto the affected area to replace dysplastic bone cells.
• Weakened bones may be reinforced by casts or splints.

WHEN TO CALL A DOCTOR

• Call a doctor if you or your child develops bone pain, with or without other symptoms of fibrous dysplasia.

SYMPTOMS

• Bone pain, especially in the ribs, facial bones, and lower leg.
• Walking difficulty.
• Irregular skin discoloration. Irregularly shaped patches of increased pigmentation may be located over affected areas of bone, but may appear anywhere on the skin; in polyostotic fibrous dysplasia, darkened areas of skin may be widespread but limited to only one side of the body.
• Bone fractures or deformities of the bone.
• Enlarged breasts, pubic hair growth, and vaginal bleeding in very young girls.

Food Poisoning

WHAT IS IT?

Food poisoning refers to illness brought on by ingesting foods contaminated with living microorganisms, toxins produced by microorganisms, poisonous chemicals, or poisonous fish, shellfish, or plants (such as mushrooms). The digestive tract is most commonly affected. However, botulism, a life-threatening form of food poisoning, primarily affects the central nervous system and may cause respiratory failure (see Botulism for more information). Food poisoning may result from improper storage and handling of food, such as inadequate refrigeration or touching food with soiled hands or machinery. Symptoms generally develop within one to 48 hours after eating. Some types of food poisoning (notably cholera and shigellosis) may take from three to five days to produce symptoms. Food poisoning is suspected when sudden, acute gastrointestinal symptoms arise. It is difficult to prove that food poisoning is the cause of illness unless several people develop symptoms after sharing a meal or after eating in the same restaurant. Illness often subsides spontaneously after one to five days; however, severe or persistent symptoms require treatment and sometimes hospitalization.

SYMPTOMS
- Diarrhea.
- Abdominal pain and cramps.
- Nausea and vomiting.
- Fever.
- Headaches.
- Bloody stool.

WHAT CAUSES IT?
- Preformed bacterial toxins produced by overgrowth of certain bacteria before food is eaten.
- Contamination with live microorganisms that proliferate in the intestine and may invade tissues or produce toxins.
- Poisonous metals.
- Poisons in fish, shellfish and plants (mushrooms).

PREVENTION
- Wash your hands thoroughly with warm water and soap before preparing food.
- Make sure food is handled, cleaned, cooked, and refrigerated properly.
- Don't buy or use food in rusty, bulging, or leaky cans.
- Don't taste food to check for contamination.
- Don't eat mushrooms you have picked.
- Don't drink raw milk.
- Throw away any questionable leftovers.

DIAGNOSIS
- Vomit, feces, and blood may be cultured.
- If available, samples of suspected foods are examined for contaminants.

HOW TO TREAT IT
- Drink plenty of fluids to prevent dehydration from diarrhea, and take antidiarrheal medications.
- An oral solution containing electrolytes and sugar may be needed to replace minerals lost with severe diarrhea.
- Intravenous fluids may be needed to treat severe dehydration.
- Medication to prevent vomiting may be prescribed in severe cases, although vomiting often helps to rid the body of toxins.
- Antibiotics may be prescribed in some cases, depending upon the specific infectious agent involved.

WHEN TO CALL A DOCTOR
- **EMERGENCY** The elderly, young children, and anyone with a weakened immune system (such as those diagnosed with AIDS or undergoing treatment for cancer) should be taken to a doctor immediately if they develop even mild symptoms of food poisoning, since these people are at greater risk of life-threatening complications.
- Call a doctor if you develop any of the following: sudden, severe diarrhea; a fever over 102°F; bloody diarrhea; severe abdominal pain.
- Call a doctor if food poisoning symptoms do not subside within a week.

Frostbite

WHAT IS IT?

Frostbite is the freezing of skin and damage to underlying blood vessels upon exposure to extreme cold. Blood flow halts in frostbitten skin, and the area must be thawed and rewarmed swiftly to prevent tissue death (gangrene) and infection. The ears, nose, hands, and feet are especially susceptible. Frostbite is sometimes accompanied by a life-threatening drop in internal body temperature, known as hypothermia, which must be treated first (see Hypothermia for more information).

WHAT CAUSES IT?

• Exposure to extremely cold temperatures (32°F or below) for prolonged periods of time causes frostbite. The risk becomes greater as the temperature drops and the wind increases.

• The risk of frostbite increases with impaired circulation. Those with peripheral vascular disease or diabetes mellitus, and those taking beta-blocker drugs, are more vulnerable.

SYMPTOMS

• Initially, a prickling sensation and numbness in the affected area.
• White or bluish gray skin that feels cold, hard, and numb.
• Red, swollen, painful, and blistered skin as skin thaws.

PREVENTION

• Wear several layers of warm, protective clothing when you go out in cold weather. Make sure children are dressed warmly.

• Go inside, if possible, when you feel too cold. Remember that fatigue, lack of oxygen in high elevations, and consumption of alcohol may cause you to disregard discomfort and cold.

• Avoid smoking or drinking before venturing out into extreme cold. Tobacco decreases circulation by constricting blood vessels, and alcohol interferes with the body's ability to regulate temperature.

DIAGNOSIS

• Diagnosis may be made by observation of symptoms and does not require a doctor.
• Your doctor may take an x-ray of the affected area(s).

HOW TO TREAT IT

• Go inside as soon as possible.
• Remove clothing from frostbitten skin and cover the affected area with warm blankets. Do not rub or massage the affected area. If hands are frozen, tuck them under your armpits next to the skin. If the face is frozen, cover it with dry, gloved hands. If feet or toes are frozen, warm them with warm hands or blankets.
• Contrary to popular belief, snow or ice does not help to thaw frostbitten skin.
• Elevate the frozen part to prevent swelling from fluid accumulation (edema).
• Warm, not hot, water (100°F to 108°F) may be used to immerse frozen hands or feet, or the entire body. If the face is frozen, warm, moist towels may be applied to it.
• Drink warm liquids, such as coffee, tea, or cocoa. Do not drink alcoholic beverages, since they actually promote heat loss.
• If possible, do not walk on thawed feet, since skin that has been frostbitten is very delicate.
• Take over-the-counter pain relievers during the thawing process.
• Your doctor may prescribe painkillers to relieve severe pain, and antibiotics to prevent damaged tissue from becoming infected.
• Occasionally, surgery may be necessary to remove damaged tissue. In the uncommon, severe cases where gangrene has set in, affected areas may require amputation.

WHEN TO CALL A DOCTOR

• **EMERGENCY** Call an ambulance or rescue squad if severe frostbite develops. Administer first-aid measures as described above until emergency help arrives.

Gallbladder Disorders

WHAT IS IT?

The gallbladder, a small, pear-shaped organ located just below the liver, concentrates and stores bile, a substance produced by the liver to aid in the digestion of fats. Bile is stored in the gallbladder and secreted during digestion into the duodenum, the portion of the small intestine joined to the stomach. Gallstone formation—known as cholelithiasis—is the most common gallbladder disorder. It usually occurs when excessive amounts of cholesterol in the bile clump together into solid masses. People with hemolytic anemia (marked by rapid destruction of red blood cells) may develop gallstones composed of bilirubin, a bile pigment. The quantity and size of gallstones may vary from one large stone to thousands of tiny ones. More common in women than in men, most gallstones are referred to as "silent gallstones," as they cause no symptoms and so require no treatment. Sometimes, however, gallstones produce acute symptoms by blocking the bile duct or by causing inflammation of the gallbladder, known as cholecystitis. A blocked bile duct is also prone to bacterial infection. In some cases an infected gallbladder may become filled with pus, a condition known as empyema that requires immediate surgery

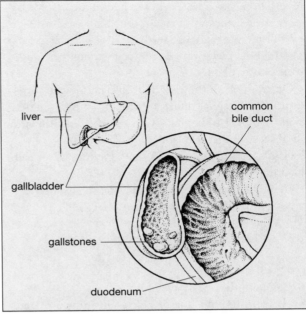

Gallstones may remain in the gallbladder or pass without incident through the bile duct into the duodenum. Symptoms generally do not arise unless stones become trapped in the bile duct or unless the gallbladder becomes inflamed.

(see Empyema for more information). Rarely, the gallbladder may be the site of tumor formation. For reasons that are unclear, gallstones increase the risk of gallbladder cancer; while few people with gallstones develop cancer, the majority of those with gallbladder cancer also have gallstones. Cancer of the gallbladder, which normally strikes at age 70 or older, is inoperable upon diagnosis in 75 percent of cases, and the outlook is generally poor. Treatment for most gallbladder disorders involves surgical removal of the gallbladder (cholecystectomy); gallstones may be dissolved with chemical agents or sound waves, but tend to recur if the gallbladder is not removed. Absence of the gallbladder does not inhibit digestion; bile simply passes directly from the liver into the small intestine.

WHAT CAUSES IT?

- The exact cause of gallstones is unknown, but cholesterol stones are usually associated with an abnormal composition of the bile.
- Age, obesity, a high-calorie diet, very rapid weight

SYMPTOMS

- Moderate to severe pain in the upper-right abdomen, often spreading into the chest, right shoulder, and back. Pain due to gallstones may occur in separate episodes lasting from 30 minutes to four hours. Inflammation of the gallbladder causes pain that gradually increases in severity and may worsen upon deep breathing. Cancer of the gallbladder produces steady pain.
- Possible nausea and vomiting accompanying the attacks of pain.
- Fever and chills (inflammation of the gallbladder).
- Abdominal fullness or bloating.
- Severe belching, heartburn, and gas.
- Weight loss (cancer of the gallbladder).
- Jaundice.

Gallbladder Disorders *continued*

loss, Crohn's disease, cirrhosis, hemolytic disorders, or intestinal surgery increase the risk of gallstones.
• Multiple pregnancies, birth control pills, or estrogen therapy may provoke the development of gallstones in women.
• Obstruction of the bile duct (usually by gallstones), injury, or bacterial infection (usually in conjunction with bile duct obstruction) may lead to inflammation or abscess of the gallbladder.
• Gallstones are associated with a higher risk of gallbladder cancer.
• Hereditary factors may play a role; for example, among certain Native American tribes such as the Pima Indians of Arizona, nearly 70 percent of the women have gallstones by age 30.

PREVENTION
• Maintain ideal body weight.
• Check with your doctor before pursuing any diet for rapid weight loss.

DIAGNOSIS
• Physical examination. The doctor may press on the upper abdomen to feel for an enlarged or tender gallbladder.
• Abdominal x-rays.
• Cholecystography (administration of a contrast material that highlights the gallbladder on an abdominal x-ray).
• Ultrasound scans.
• ERCP (endoscopic retrograde cholangiopancreatogram) is done, in which a thin, lighted, viewing tube (endoscope) is passed down the throat into the small intestine. Contrast material is injected into the bile duct, and x-rays are taken.

HOW TO TREAT IT
• Cholecystectomy, or surgical removal of the gallbladder, is the treatment of choice for most gallbladder disorders and virtually prevents further attacks of gallstones by eliminating their source. Conventional abdominal surgery may be used, although increasingly, a newer procedure called laparoscopic cholecystectomy is preferred. With this method a scope is inserted through small abdominal incisions and then used to excise the gallbladder. The technique dramatically reduces postoperative pain and recovery time.
• Prior to surgery, meperidine or pentazocine is given to relieve pain; intravenous feeding and fluids are initiated, and antibiotics may be administered to prevent or treat an associated bacterial infection.
• In patients who have acute gallbladder inflammation but are too weak for cholecystectomy, a surgical opening in the gallbladder (cholecystostomy) may be created and a tube inserted to drain the gallbladder's contents. Complete removal of the gallbladder may be performed after the patient's condition has improved sufficiently.
• Oral ursodeoxycholic acid or chenodeoxycholic acid—bile acids that dissolve cholesterol gallstones over a period of months or years—may be prescribed. However, such therapy is effective only for small stones composed entirely of cholesterol. It is expensive, it is successful less than 50 percent of the time, and even when it does work, there is a 30 to 50 percent chance that stones will recur in the future.
• A long, thin needle may be used to infuse the solvent methyl tert-butyl ether (MTBE) directly into the gallbladder via a catheter. This method dissolves cholesterol gallstones within one or two days. Again, recurrence is a possibility.
• Sound wave therapy (extracorporeal shock-wave lithotripsy) has been used with limited success to shatter some types of gallstones and avoid surgery.
• Radiation or chemotherapy may be used to treat cancer of the gallbladder.

WHEN TO CALL A DOCTOR
• Call a doctor if you develop severe abdominal pain.
• **EMERGENCY** Call an ambulance if you experience upper-right abdominal pain and nausea accompanied by shortness of breath and sweating, since such symptoms may also signal a heart attack.

Ganglion

WHAT IS IT?

A ganglion is a round swelling or cyst that develops just under the skin near a joint or tendon. The back of the wrist is by far the most common site; however, ganglia may appear elsewhere, including the fingers, ankles, and feet. They vary from the size of a pea to—albeit rarely—the size of a golf ball and are usually painless or only somewhat bothersome. (Paradoxically, smaller ganglia frequently cause more discomfort than larger ones, possibly because they are in the process of expanding.) The thick, clear, jellylike fluid inside of a ganglion is believed to be composed of the same elements as the fluid that lubricates the joints. A buildup of this fluid within a tendon sheath or joint capsule causes these membranes to balloon outward. (Why this buildup occurs is unknown.) Because ganglia pose no health risk and are typically painless, they rarely require treatment and may, in fact, disappear spontaneously without any medical intervention. However, many patients request treatment for cosmetic reasons.

WHAT CAUSES IT?

• The cause of ganglia is unknown.

SYMPTOMS

• An unusual lump under the skin (usually on the wrist), which may feel soft and rubbery, or hard and solid.
• Pain or tenderness in the lump (although this is rare).

PREVENTION

• There is no known way to prevent ganglia.

DIAGNOSIS

• Diagnosis is typically made upon visual inspection of clinical manifestations.
• In rare cases, x-rays or ultrasound may be used to confirm the diagnosis, and other tests may be performed to rule out a more serious disorder, such as a malignant growth, that might cause such a lump.

HOW TO TREAT IT

• Treatment is generally not necessary for a small, painless ganglion unless the patient desires it for cosmetic reasons.
• Your doctor may use a large needle to puncture and drain the ganglion—a procedure known as needle aspiration. An anti-inflammatory corticosteroid medication may then be injected into the affected area. Needle aspiration may eventually need to be repeated, as ganglia treated in this manner have a tendency to recur.
• Surgery may be used to remove a ganglion that recurs or causes discomfort. After such surgery, recurrence is extremely unlikely.

WHEN TO CALL A DOCTOR

• Make an appointment with a doctor if you notice the development of a lump anywhere on your body. A ganglion is nothing to worry about; however, more serious disorders should be ruled out.
• Consult your doctor if a ganglion begins to cause discomfort, interferes with normal activities, or is cosmetically unacceptable to you.

Gastroesophageal Reflux Heartburn

WHAT IS IT?

Gastroesophageal reflux (commonly known as heart-burn, although it has nothing to do with the heart) is the regurgitation of the contents of the stomach and duodenum (the first portion of the small intestine) into the esophagus, the muscular tube through which food travels from the mouth to the stomach. Since the esophagus lacks the protective lining of the stomach, it is easily irritated by digestive juices. The esophagus and the stomach meet at the lower esophageal sphincter (LES), a circular band of muscle that is usually clenched but which opens to permit food to enter the stomach. Reflux occurs when, for a variety of possible reasons, the LES allows some acidic stomach contents to pass upward into the esophagus. Severe, long-standing reflux can cause esophageal scarring (stricture) that causes considerable swallowing difficulty.

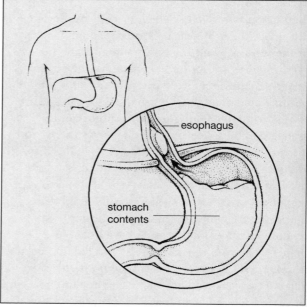

The stomach contains powerful acids and enzymes that are needed to break down proteins. Sometimes, especially following a large meal, stomach contents may be regurgitated into the esophagus (reflux). Since the esophagus is not protectively lined like the stomach, the acid causes a stinging sensation, commonly known as heartburn.

SYMPTOMS

- Burning sensation in the upper chest. In rare cases, pain may radiate to the neck and arms, mimicking a heart attack.
- Difficulty swallowing—especially solid foods.
- Slight regurgitation of food, especially when lying down or bending forward.
- Pain upon swallowing.
- Hoarseness or wheezing from regurgitation into the throat and lungs.
- Rarely, severe chest pain from an esophageal ulcer.

WHAT CAUSES IT?

- Weakness or erratic opening of the LES.
- Hormonal changes and increased abdominal pressure during pregnancy.
- Smoking.
- Overeating and obesity. (Hiatal hernia—protrusion of a portion of the stomach through the diaphragm into the chest cavity—was once thought to be a common cause of reflux, but now is believed to cause symptoms only infrequently.)
- Fatty, spicy, acidic, or caffeinated foods and drinks.
- Excessive consumption of alcohol.
- Certain anti-inflammatory drugs, such as aspirin, cortisone, or arthritis medications.

PREVENTION

- Avoid overeating or eating within two or three hours of going to bed, and avoid napping after a meal. Also, don't exercise immediately after eating.
- Avoid tight pants, girdles, and belts.
- Lose weight if you are overweight.
- Avoid excessive consumption of alcoholic beverages.
- Don't smoke.

DIAGNOSIS

- Patient history usually indicates the diagnosis.
- X-rays are taken after the patient swallows barium, which clearly outlines the esophagus and stomach.
- Endoscopy (the insertion of a lighted scope into the esophagus through the mouth) may be performed.
- Esophageal acidity may be measured.
- When it is difficult to distinguish heartburn from chest pain due to heart disease, acid may be infused

Gastroesophageal Reflux Heartburn *continued*

into the esophagus (Bernstein test) in an effort to duplicate the pain, thereby revealing its cause.

HOW TO TREAT IT
• Follow preventive measures.
• Elevate the head of the bed by six inches to reduce reflux at night.
• Take an over-the-counter antacid (that does not contain calcium) one hour before and three hours after meals and at bedtime to relieve pain and discomfort. Long-term use of antacids may lead to metabolic problems, so check with a doctor if you need more than occasional relief.
• Your doctor may prescribe medication to suppress the secretion of stomach acids, to tighten the LES, or to speed the passage of food from the stomach to the small intestine. Medications include Bethanechol, Metoclopramide, H2-antagonists (cimetidine, ranitidine, famotidine), and Omeprazole. These drugs are usually very effective and are the treatment of choice when simple self-care methods fail.
• In severe cases, surgery may be necessary to repair a large hiatal hernia or to tighten the LES.

WHEN TO CALL A DOCTOR
• Call a doctor if symptoms of heartburn persist despite self-treatment.
• **EMERGENCY** Call an ambulance if you experience severe chest pain, as this may signal a heart attack.

Genital Herpes

WHAT IS IT?

Genital herpes is a viral infection characterized by outbreaks of painful sores on the genitals. Most often it spreads through sexual contact. It can also spread by contact with contaminated hands (though this is rare). Once infected, a person carries the virus permanently in a latent form in the nerve cells; there is no cure. Symptoms are not always present. The initial attack and recurrences generally last from one to three weeks, after which the infection may go into remission for months or years at a time. Subsequent attacks tend to be less severe, and in about one-third of cases, permanent remission follows the initial outbreak. Genital herpes is highly contagious, and one partner may transmit it to another even when no visible sores or lesions are present. It is more easily transferred from men to women than vice versa; it may also be transferred to babies of infected mothers during childbirth, possibly causing blindness, retardation, or even death. Genital herpes is also a risk factor for HIV infection.

SYMPTOMS

- Pain or itching in the genital area.
- Watery blisters in the genital area that break to form painful, shallow ulcers. The ulcers scab over and disappear spontaneously within three weeks. Occasionally, blisters and ulcers around the mouth may accompany genital sores.
- Painful urination in women.
- Fever, fatigue, loss of appetite, and enlarged lymph nodes in the groin (typically occurring only with the initial attack).
- Possibly, headache (in those who develop viral meningitis).

WHAT CAUSES IT?

- Herpes simplex virus Type II is the most common cause of genital herpes.
- Herpes simplex virus Type I, the virus that commonly causes cold sores around the mouth, may also cause genital herpes.
- Recurrence in both sexes may be triggered by sexual intercourse, exposure to ultraviolet light, fatigue, injury, heat, cold, and stress. In women, recurrence may also be triggered by menstrual periods.
- People with weakened immune systems, such as those undergoing cancer treatment or those with AIDS, are at greater risk of severe cases of genital herpes.

PREVENTION

- Avoid sexual contact if symptoms are present in either partner.
- Latex condoms during sexual intercourse reduce the risk of transmission, but they are not foolproof, since they rarely cover all infected areas.
- To prevent ultraviolet light from triggering a recurrence of genital herpes, use sunscreen (SPF 15 or higher) before going outdoors.

DIAGNOSIS

- Patient history and physical examination.
- Culture of fluid from blisters or sores.
- Microscopic examination of scrapings from a lesion.

HOW TO TREAT IT

- Treatment is aimed at relieving symptoms. The antiviral drug acyclovir may be prescribed in topical or oral form to lessen the duration and severity of outbreaks. Acyclovir is less effective for recurrences.
- Take aspirin, acetaminophen, or ibuprofen to relieve pain.
- Since open sores increase the risk of bacterial infection, your doctor may prescribe antibiotics.
- Frequent warm baths may lessen discomfort during an outbreak.
- Women may urinate through a small tube, such as a toilet-paper roll, to prevent urine from irritating open sores on the vagina.
- A cesarean section may be necessary for pregnant women who have genital herpes, in order to avoid transferring the infection to the infant during childbirth. The mother and infant may both be treated with acyclovir.

WHEN TO CALL A DOCTOR

- Call a doctor if you develop symptoms of genital herpes.

Genital Warts

WHAT IS IT?

Genital warts, also known as condylomata acuminata, are small growths in the genital area, commonly appearing around the vaginal opening or inside the vagina on the cervix, around the anus, on the penis, and on the perineum (the area between the genitals and anus). They are highly contagious, and are most commonly spread through sexual or other intimate body contact. It may take from eight to 18 months after infection for a wart to appear. In addition, the virus may remain in skin tissues even after warts are removed, making recurrence common. Conditions producing excess vaginal moisture and discharge, such as yeast infections or pregnancy, may encourage wart growth in women. Genital warts are linked to an increased risk of cervical and penile cancer. It is thus important for women who have had genital warts to have a Pap smear annually, so that if cancer develops, it may be detected early. Other sexually transmitted diseases, such as syphilis or gonorrhea, may be transmitted at the same time as the virus that causes genital warts.

SYMPTOMS
- Small, red, round or flat, itchy bumps on or around the vagina, anus, penis, or perineum.
- Several warts may grow together into a cauliflower-like configuration.

WHAT CAUSES IT?
- The human papilloma virus (HPV) causes genital warts. Most of the more than 60 strains of the virus produce only harmless warts, but some have been associated with greater risk of cervical or penile cancer.
- Genital warts may be spread by sexual intercourse.
- It is possible for warts on the fingers (also caused by a strain of HPV) to be transferred to the genital area, although this is uncommon.

- Genital warts in children may be evidence of sexual abuse.

PREVENTION
- Use a latex condom during sexual intercourse to help prevent spreading or contracting the disease.

DIAGNOSIS
- Patient history and physical examination. Women's pelvic examinations should include a Pap smear (a test in which a small sample of cells is scraped from the cervix); in addition, the doctor may examine the vagina with a colposcope (a magnifying instrument for viewing the inside of the vagina and the cervix).
- Blood samples may be taken to rule out other sexually transmitted diseases.
- A culture of vaginal or penile discharge may be taken to rule out gonorrhea.
- A biopsy (removal and analysis of tissue samples) may be performed to rule out cancer.

HOW TO TREAT IT
- A doctor may apply podophyllin or trichloroacetic acid, chemical solutions that gradually destroy warts.
- Genital warts may be removed by applying liquid nitrogen, which freezes and thus destroys warts (cryosurgery). Warts may also be burned away with an electric probe (electrocauterization) or destroyed with laser surgery.
- The sexual partner(s) of the infected person should be examined as well.
- Do not attempt to remove genital warts using over-the-counter wart preparations. Such chemical solutions are too harsh for sensitive genital skin and may cause disfigurement.

WHEN TO CALL A DOCTOR
- Make an appointment with a doctor if you or your sexual partner displays symptoms of genital warts.

Gingivitis

WHAT IS IT?

Gingivitis is an inflammation of the gums (gingiva), usually caused by the buildup of plaque at the base of the teeth. Bacteria within this sticky, colorless substance produce toxins that can inflame the gums, causing them to bleed and recede. Without proper dental care, gingivitis may lead to more serious periodontitis (involving destruction of the bone that anchors the teeth in place) and eventual tooth loss.

WHAT CAUSES IT?

• Poor or improper oral hygiene is the most common cause.
• Poor nutrition, certain chronic diseases (such as diabetes), hormonal changes (such as those that occur with pregnancy or menopause), and some medications (including anticonvulsants) may promote gingivitis.

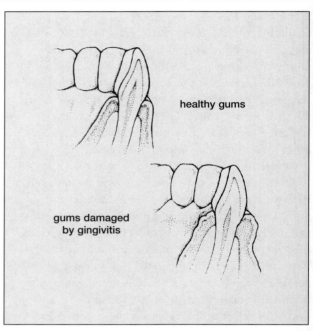

In gingivitis, plaque builds up on the teeth and irritates the gums. Eventually, plaque wedges into pockets between the teeth and gums, damaging the gums and causing them to recede.

SYMPTOMS
• Red, shiny, swollen, tender gums that bleed easily, for example, upon brushing the teeth.
• Bad breath.

PREVENTION

• Brush your teeth at least twice a day using a soft nylon-bristle toothbrush. Scrub with a gentle circular motion, then whisk the brush up (on lower teeth) and down (on upper teeth), away from the gums. Brushing teeth too vigorously will only erode the gums. Be sure to clean the inside surfaces of the teeth (nearest to your tongue), since plaque deposits tend to be heavy there.
• Brush your tongue; it collects the same bacteria that stick to your teeth.
• Floss after brushing. With a gentle sawing motion, ease the floss between the teeth, forming a crescent against one side of a tooth. Use your thumbs and index fingers to stabilize the floss. Gingerly scrape up and down, from just under the gum line to the top of the teeth.
• Consider using irrigation devices such as Waterpik or plaque removal devices such as Interplak—but check with your dentist first.
• See a dentist at least once a year. Professional cleaning is required to remove deposits of hardened plaque (tartar).
• Limit your consumption of sugary drinks and sweet, starchy, or sticky foods, which stimulate the production of acid and lead to tooth and gum decay. Fruits and vegetables with high fiber content help to clean teeth and prevent gingivitis.

DIAGNOSIS

• An oral examination by a dentist is required to determine the extent of gum disease.

HOW TO TREAT IT

• Follow preventive tips for proper dental care.
• Your dentist will scrape plaque and tartar off teeth and may prescribe an antibacterial mouthwash.
• Vitamin supplements may be recommended to treat a nutritional deficiency.

WHEN TO CALL A DOCTOR

• Make an appointment with a dentist if you develop symptoms of gingivitis.

Glaucoma

WHAT IS IT?

Glaucoma is a sight-threatening disorder marked by an increase in intraocular pressure (IOP), that is, the pressure within the eyeball. It occurs as a result of an excess buildup of aqueous humor—the clear fluid inside the eyeball that provides nutrients to and carries waste products away from the lens and cornea of the eye, the only parts of the body with no blood supply. Each day, the eye produces about one teaspoon of aqueous humor. Normally, this fluid escapes from the eye, through a spongy mesh of connective tissue called the trabecular network, at the same rate at which it is produced. In glaucoma, production of aqueous humor exceeds the rate of its escape. There are two forms of glaucoma: open angle and closed angle. Open-angle glaucoma, which accounts for 90 percent of all cases, is a slow, progressive disease that produces no symptoms in its early stages. By contrast, closed-angle glaucoma is relatively uncommon and is characterized by rapid and extreme elevations of IOP, causing acute symptoms such as severe eye pain and rapid loss of vision. Both types of glaucoma may lead to blindness by damaging the optic nerve; however, early detection and treatment can usually control IOP and prevent severe vision loss. Glaucoma is most prevalent among those over 40.

WHAT CAUSES IT?

• It is theorized that open-angle glaucoma occurs when, for reasons not completely understood, the trabecular network becomes partially blocked. IOP builds up as more aqueous humor is formed, but pressure doesn't rise high enough to cause any

Aqueous humor passes through the anterior chamber between the lens and the cornea. It is then drained through the spongelike trabecular meshwork, and funnelled into the body's circulatory system through a passageway known as the canal of Schlemm. If the trabecular meshwork becomes clogged, drainage of the aqueous humor is impaired and pressure within the eye (intraocular pressure) increases.

noticeable symptoms initially. When IOP remains elevated or continues to rise, however, fibers in the optic nerve are compressed and destroyed, leading to a gradual loss of vision over a period of years.
• Closed-angle glaucoma is caused by a sudden blockage near the iris that prevents aqueous humor from reaching the trabecular network. This results in the rapid onset of extremely high IOP that may cause severe, permanent vision loss within a day or two.
• A family history of visual-field loss due to glaucoma increases the risk of optic nerve damage. Evidence also suggests that cardiovascular disease, diabetes, and myopia (nearsightedness) increase the risk of nerve damage from glaucoma.

PREVENTION

• While there is no way to prevent glaucoma, early detection and treatment may prevent damage to the optic nerve. See an ophthalmologist for a complete

SYMPTOMS

• Open-angle glaucoma: gradual loss of peripheral vision, marked by blind spots.
• Closed-angle glaucoma: acute attacks involving severe eye pain, nausea and vomiting, blurred vision, and the appearance of rainbow-colored halos around lights.

Glaucoma *continued*

eye exam every two years after age 50. (Those of African descent should start having such exams at age 40.)

DIAGNOSIS

• Tonometry (use of an instrument to apply slight pressure upon the eyeball to measure IOP).
• Ophthalmoscopy (in which the pupils are dilated with eye drops so that the optic nerve may be magnified and examined with an ophthalmoscope, a lighted viewing instrument).
• Perimetry (a visual-field test that determines the extent of peripheral vision).

HOW TO TREAT IT

• Open-angle glaucoma can often be treated with lifelong medical therapy alone. Eye drops—which have fewer overall side effects than oral medications—are the first line of treatment. Three types of eye drops are used: miotics, adrenergic agonists, and beta-blockers. Miotics (drugs that constrict the pupil) and adrenergic agonists increase the outflow of aqueous humor. Beta-blockers diminish the production of aqueous humor. Eye drops must be applied two to four times a day, regularly and on schedule, to maximize IOP control.
• Carbonic anhydrase inhibitor pills are generally used when optic nerve damage continues or seems highly likely despite maximal topical treatment. These oral medications initially lower IOP by 20 to 30 percent on average, but significant systemic side effects (such as numbness or tingling in the extremities, malaise, and loss of appetite) and occasional serious complications (such as kidney stones and blood abnormalities) can limit their use.
• Periodic ophthalmologic examinations are essential throughout medical therapy. These may initially be required daily or weekly for those with severe nerve damage or extreme elevations of IOP, or only every three to six months for patients with stable IOP and minimal optic nerve damage.
• About 10 percent of those with open-angle glaucoma require surgery, when drug therapy fails or when the patient has a medical condition (such as hypertension or severe heart or lung disease) that precludes maximal drug therapy. The two most common surgical procedures—laser trabecular surgery and filtration surgery—reduce ocular pressure by opening a passage for aqueous humor. While results are generally very favorable, complications such as cataracts may occur, and repeat procedures may be required.
• Unless high IOP is relieved promptly during an acute attack of closed-angle glaucoma, blindness can occur within a day or two. Removal of a part of the iris (iridectomy) creates a drainage path for the aqueous humor. Iridectomy in the other eye is generally recommended owing to the high likelihood that it will be involved in a future acute attack.

WHEN TO CALL A DOCTOR

• Contact an ophthalmologist right away if your develop any symptoms of glaucoma.
• See an ophthalmologist for a complete eye exam every two years after age 50. (Those of African descent should start having such exams at age 40.)

Glomerulonephritis, Acute

WHAT IS IT?

Acute glomerulonephritis is a term used to describe a number of underlying disorders that cause a sudden inflammation of the glomeruli, the tiny structures in the kidneys that filter waste products from the blood. Inflammation of the glomeruli impedes the filtering process, trapping waste products in the blood and allowing red blood cells and proteins to escape into the urine. Kidney malfunction may also lead to high blood pressure and fluid retention. Acute glomerulonephritis is most common among children, often occurring after a streptococcal infection of the throat or sometimes the skin. Although a few severe cases (about 5 percent) lead to kidney failure, most subside spontaneously within two weeks to several months.

WHAT CAUSES IT?

• Acute glomerulonephritis may occur as a complication of a bacterial infection. A throat or skin infection can trigger the production of substances called immune complexes, which circulate through the bloodstream. These may become trapped in the tiny glomeruli, causing inflammation and interfering with normal kidney function, usually within six to 14 days of the initial infection.
• Viral or parasitic infections, such as mononucleosis, measles, hepatitis B, and malaria, may be a cause.
• Autoimmune disorders, like systemic lupus erythematosus or other causes of vasculitis (inflammation of small blood vessels) may produce glomerulonephritis and persistent kidney damage.

Blood enters the kidney through the renal artery; wastes are filtered out in the tiny glomeruli and excreted as urine through the ureter. Damaged glomeruli allow proteins and red blood cells to escape too.

PREVENTION

• There is no way to prevent acute glomerulonephritis.

DIAGNOSIS

• Patient history and physical examination.
• Blood and urine tests.
• A kidney biopsy (using a tissue sample taken with a needle) may be done if symptoms persist or if an underlying systemic disorder is suspected.

HOW TO TREAT IT

• High blood pressure is treated with antihypertensives.
• Diuretics and a low-salt diet may be used to reduce excess water retention and increase urine output.
• If the disorder is the result of an underlying bacterial infection, antibiotics may be prescribed.
• Short-term kidney dialysis is sometimes needed.

WHEN TO CALL A DOCTOR

• Call a doctor if you or your child develop symptoms of acute glomerulonephritis.

SYMPTOMS

• Abrupt onset of blood in the urine (urine color may range from light brown to bright red).
• Passing only small amounts of urine.
• Swelling of the ankles or the tissues around the eyes, due to fluid accumulation (edema).
• Shortness of breath, due to fluid accumulation in the lungs.
• In severe cases, symptoms of kidney failure, including fatigue, nausea and vomiting, loss of appetite, overall itching, headaches, flank pain, fever, and impaired vision.

Glomerulonephritis, Chronic

WHAT IS IT?

Chronic glomerulonephritis, an uncommon kidney disorder, is marked by slow, cumulative damage to the tiny blood filters in the kidneys. These filters, known as glomeruli, remove waste products from the blood. In chronic glomerulonephritis, inflammation of the glomeruli impedes the filtering process, trapping waste products in the blood while allowing red blood cells and proteins to escape into the urine, eventually producing the characteristic symptoms of blood in the urine and swelling around the eyes and in the ankles. The disorder commonly causes high blood pressure as well. Long-term inflammation produces scarring (sclerosis) of the kidneys, which may lead to kidney failure in severe cases. Damage may progress without symptoms for months or years; by the time symptoms finally appear, the course of the disorder may be irreversible.

SYMPTOMS

- Blood in the urine (urine color may range from light brown to bright red).
- Passing only small amounts of urine.
- Swelling of the ankles, the tissues around the eyes, or other parts of the body, due to fluid accumulation (edema).
- Shortness of breath, due to fluid accumulation in the lungs.
- In severe cases, symptoms of kidney failure, including fatigue; nausea and vomiting; loss of appetite; overall itching; headaches; flank pain; fever; and impaired vision.

WHAT CAUSES IT?

- The specific cause of most cases of chronic glomerulonephritis is unknown.
- Viral infections, like malaria, chicken pox, mononucleosis, and acquired immune deficiency syndrome (AIDS), may lead to chronic glomerulonephritis.
- Autoimmune disorders, such as systemic lupus erythematosus, or other causes of vasculitis (inflammation of small blood vessels) may cause chronic glomerulonephritis.
- Acute glomerulonephritis may, after a symptomless period of many years, reappear as chronic glomerulonephritis.

PREVENTION

- There is no known way to prevent chronic glomerulonephritis.

DIAGNOSIS

- Blood and urine tests.
- An intravenous pyelogram may be performed, in which a material that creates a sharp x-ray image of the kidney is injected.
- A kidney biopsy may be performed. Under local anesthesia, the doctor inserts a needle into the kidney through the back to extract a small sample of tissue.

HOW TO TREAT IT

- Antihypertensive drugs may be prescribed to reduce high blood pressure.
- Diuretics may be prescribed to reduce excess fluid retention and increase urine production.
- Your doctor may advise you to eat a low-protein, low-salt diet and to take iron or vitamin supplements.
- Antibiotics may be prescribed to treat associated bacterial infections.
- In severe cases where kidney failure occurs, dialysis may be necessary. Dialysis performs the functions of the kidney by removing waste products and excess fluid from the blood when the kidney cannot (see Renal Failure, Chronic for more information).
- A kidney transplant is an alternative to dialysis in cases of kidney failure.

WHEN TO CALL A DOCTOR

- Call a doctor if you develop symptoms of chronic glomerulonephritis.

Goiter

WHAT IS IT?

A goiter is an enlargement or swelling of the thyroid, a gland in the throat that secretes a hormone which regulates body growth and metabolism. Goiters vary in size from a small lump to a huge swelling in the neck and, though sometimes unsightly, are generally painless. Rarely, a goiter may press against the trachea or esophagus, causing difficulty in breathing or swallowing. The disorder affects women four times more often than men.

WHAT CAUSES IT?

• Goiters can be caused by insufficient amounts of iodine in the diet. This is now rare in the United States since the advent of iodized salt.
• A goiter is a common manifestation of Hashimoto's thyroiditis and Graves' disease, two serious thyroid disorders.
• Goiters may appear in women because of hormonal changes that occur with pregnancy, adolescence, menopause, or the use of birth control pills.
• Certain drugs designed to slow thyroid hormone production may cause goiters.
• A benign or malignant tumor of the thyroid gland may result in a goiter.

SYMPTOMS

• A swelling in the neck, ranging from a barely noticeable lump to a large growth.
• Difficulty in breathing or swallowing (although these symptoms are rare).

PREVENTION

• There is no known way to prevent goiter except in cases caused by a dietary insufficiency of iodine.

DIAGNOSIS

• Patient history and physical exam are necessary.
• Blood tests, taken to evaluate the functional status of the thyroid gland, may also help to determine the underlying cause of the goiter.

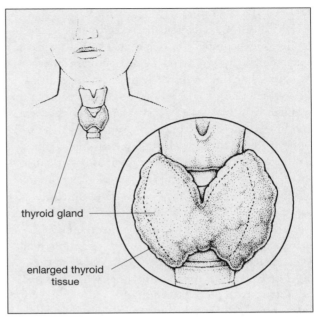

thyroid gland

enlarged thyroid tissue

Hyperthyroidism and other disorders affecting the butterfly-shaped thyroid in the neck can cause the gland to enlarge, resulting in a goiter.

• Thyroid scan with radioactive iodine or an ultrasound exam may be done to obtain an image of the thyroid gland.
• Fine needle biopsy may be performed to rule out malignancy.

HOW TO TREAT IT

• Your doctor may alter your prescription if the goiter is due to a medication.
• Surgical removal of all or part of the thyroid may be necessary if the goiter is large, causes difficulty in breathing or swallowing, or is due to a malignant tumor.
• A diet that includes iodized salt and fish is advised in the unlikely event of iodine deficiency.
• Thyroid-hormone-replacement therapy may ease the demand on the gland to produce thyroid hormone, which may cause it to decrease in size.

WHEN TO CALL A DOCTOR

• Call a doctor for any swelling in the neck.

Gonorrhea

WHAT IS IT?

Gonorrhea is a contagious bacterial infection, most commonly acquired through sexual contact with an infected partner. In men, the disease often infects the urethra (the conduit in the penis that carries urine and sperm) and may spread to other structures in the genitals or urinary tract. In women, gonorrhea usually infects the cervix but may eventually spread to other parts of the reproductive system (uterus and fallopian tubes), a condition known as pelvic inflammatory disease, which can lead to infertility. Less commonly, infections may occur in the throat, rectum, or eyes. Symptoms usually develop within two to 10 days after exposure, although many people, particularly women, experience no symptoms at all. This disease generally strikes people between the ages of 18 and 30, particularly those who have had multiple sexual partners. Left untreated, the infection may spread via the bloodstream to the joints and tendons as well as to valves in the heart. With proper treatment, however, prognosis is excellent, although reinfection is common.

WHAT CAUSES IT?

• Gonorrhea is most often contracted via sexual contact, including anal, oral, and vaginal intercourse.

SYMPTOMS

• Pain during urination.
• Yellowish, puslike discharge from the penis or vagina.
• Rarely, pain during sexual intercourse.
• Redness or swelling at the infection site.
• Abnormal vaginal bleeding or lower abdominal pain in women (although these are rare).
• Sore throat (due to orally contracted infection); unusual rectal discharge or constant urge to move the bowels (in the case of anal infection).

• An infected pregnant mother may transmit the disease to her baby during childbirth. This may cause blindness in the infant.
• Touching the eyes with contaminated hands can result in a gonococcal eye infection.

PREVENTION

• Abstinence or maintaining a monogamous sexual relationship are the only sure ways to prevent sexually transmitted gonorrhea.
• Men are advised to use a latex condom during sex.
• Wash the genitals with soap and water before and after sexual contact.

DIAGNOSIS

• Diagnosis is confirmed by taking a culture of the discharge or infected tissue.

HOW TO TREAT IT

• A doctor will prescribe antibiotics such as ampicillin. Tetracycline is often prescribed as well to treat other sexually transmitted infections that commonly coexist with gonorrhea. Take antibiotics for the full term prescribed.
• Abstain from sexual activity until you are assured by your doctor that the infection is completely cured.
• A week after the initial diagnosis, a follow-up visit to the doctor is recommended.
• Nonprescription pain relievers may be used to ease discomfort.
• Gonorrhea in the eye is treated with intravenous antibiotics as well as irrigation of the eye with an antibiotic solution.

WHEN TO CALL A DOCTOR

• See a doctor if you develop any of the symptoms of gonorrhea.
• If you discover that a sexual partner has gonorrhea, consult a doctor.

Gout

WHAT IS IT?

Gout is a systemic disorder (that is, one affecting an entire organ system), marked by elevated blood levels of uric acid, one of the body's waste products. This buildup in the blood can be caused by overproduction of uric acid, impaired excretion of it in the urine, or sometimes a combination of both. As it accumulates in the bloodstream, uric acid may form crystals in the joints. Thus, gout is often first recognized by inflammation of a single joint. The immune system typically reacts to these crystals as if they were foreign invaders and releases substances that produce inflammation. The affected joint becomes swollen, red, warm, and severely painful. Often, the first episode of gout affects the base of the big toe. Although symptoms gradually subside within a week, subsequent attacks are likely. These generally strike with no warning, occur with increased frequency, and affect a greater number of joints, such as the knees, elbows, hands, feet, or wrists. Elevated uric acid levels in the blood, if untreated, may result in kidney stones or deposition of uric acid in the kidneys, possibly causing kidney failure. About 90 percent of those affected with gout are men over 40. In women, the disorder usually strikes after menopause.

SYMPTOMS
- Sudden and severe pain in a joint, often the big toe.
- Swelling and redness around the affected joint.
- Fever (in some cases).
- Kidney stone symptoms.

WHAT CAUSES IT?
- Genetic factors are often involved; one in four gout sufferers has a family history of the disorder.
- A kidney malfunction may result in a buildup of uric acid and thus an attack of gout.
- Certain antibiotics and diuretics may raise uric acid levels and promote gout.
- Obesity and high blood pressure are risk factors.
- Contrary to popular belief, foods high in purines (like liver, anchovies, kidneys, sweetbreads, and nuts) do not provoke attacks of gout.
- Chemotherapy may raise uric acid levels as it rapidly destroys cells.

PREVENTION
- There is no known way to prevent gout, but after the first attack, the risk of a recurrence can be minimized.
- Daily doses of colchicine can reduce the frequency of attacks.
- Control your weight, but do not fast, since this may raise uric acid levels.
- Avoid excessive alcohol consumption.
- Several medications, including allopurinol (which blocks uric acid formation) and the uricosuric drugs, probenecid and sulfinpyrazone (which increase uric acid excretion in the urine), reduce uric acid levels.

DIAGNOSIS
- To confirm the diagnosis, fluid from the affected joint will be removed and analyzed for the presence of uric acid crystals.
- Blood samples will be taken and measured for uric acid levels.
- X-rays are taken to look for permanent joint damage in people with chronic gout.

HOW TO TREAT IT
- A doctor may prescribe colchicine to relieve pain and decrease swelling. During an acute episode of gout, this is taken hourly until symptoms subside or until side effects (nausea, vomiting, cramps, and diarrhea) begin.
- Because of colchicine's side effects, NSAIDs (nonsteroidal anti-inflammatory drugs) have recently become the treatment of choice for gout.
- Your doctor may prescribe more powerful analgesics, including codeine or meperidine, for rapid relief of severe pain.
- Corticosteroids may be administered in pill form or by direct injections into the joint.
- Bed rest may be necessary. The weight of blankets and sheets may cause pain, so try making a tent of the bedding to keep it from touching the affected area.

WHEN TO CALL YOUR DOCTOR
- Call a doctor if you experience any of the symptoms of gout.

Hammer Toe and Mallet Toe

WHAT IS IT?

A hammer toe is a deformity of the middle joint of a toe, producing a clenched, clawlike appearance in the affected digit. The tendons in the toe become abnormally contracted, causing the toe to bend downward, which, in turn, forces the joint to protrude upward. A mallet toe is a deformity in which the end joint of a toe becomes bent downward, so that the toe curls underneath itself. In either case, the affected joints are stiff and the toe cannot be straightened out. Constant rubbing against shoes may furthermore cause a painful corn (a round patch of rough, thickened, calloused skin) to develop over the joint or at the tip of the affected toe. Hammer and mallet toes may occur in any toe, although the second toe is the most common site. These deformities are often painful and limit the toe's range of motion—sometimes requiring surgery.

SYMPTOMS

- A toe (usually the second digit, next to the big toe) that is clenched into a painful, clawlike position (hammertoe). As the toe points downward, the middle joint may protrude upward.
- A toe with an end joint that curls under itself (mallet toe).
- A painful corn on top of the bent joint or at the tip of the affected toe, because of persistent rubbing against shoes.
- Pain in the toes that interferes with walking, jogging, dancing, and other normal activities, possibly leading to gait changes.

WHAT CAUSES IT?

- Wearing shoes that are too short or that have pointed toes may produce hammer toe.
- Long-term diabetes mellitus commonly produces nerve damage involving the feet and so may lead to hammer toe.
- The cause of mallet toe is unknown.

PREVENTION

- Wear wide, comfortable shoes that have plenty of room for the toes.

DIAGNOSIS

- Examination of the affected toe is required.
- X-rays may be taken.

HOW TO TREAT IT

- Wear wide shoes with resilient soles. Avoid wearing shoes with pointed toes.
- Commercially available felt pads or cushions may ease pressure from the shoe on the toe. Toe caps (small, padded sleeves that fit around the tip of the toe) may relieve the pain of hammer toe.
- Arch supports or an orthotic shoe insert prescribed by your doctor or podiatrist may help to redistribute weight on the foot. These devices do not cure the problem but may ease the symptoms of either hammer toe or mallet toe.
- Surgery to realign the affected joint may be recommended if pain persists despite treatment.

WHEN TO CALL A DOCTOR

- Make an appointment with your regular doctor or a podiatrist if you experience continuing pain on account of a hammer toe or mallet toe or if the affected toe interferes with walking or other activities.

Headache, Cluster

WHAT IS IT?

Cluster headaches are characterized by sudden, intensely painful headaches occurring on one side of the head, centering around one eye. They tend to occur repeatedly, night after night, in periods or "clusters" of several weeks or months at a time. Pain usually appears one to three hours after falling asleep, during rapid eye movement (REM) sleep, and lasts for about an hour or more. Clusters may be separated by symptom-free months or years. Rarely, cluster headaches may be chronic, lasting for several years. This disorder is four times more common in men than women and most commonly strikes between the ages of 20 and 40. Although cluster headaches may produce severe pain, they do not cause permanent harm (such as brain damage) and do not lead to other disorders.

WHAT CAUSES IT?

• The cause of cluster headaches is unknown.
• Substances that may trigger headaches include alcohol, nicotine, and nitroglycerin (used in the treatment of angina).
• Certain foods have been implicated, specifically, those containing tyramine. Such foods include pepperoni, red wine, chicken livers, active yeast preparations, and camembert, cheddar, and other aged cheeses.
• Heavy smokers and drinkers are at greater risk for cluster headaches.
• Stress, overwork, or emotional duress may promote cluster headaches.

SYMPTOMS

• Steady, intense pain around one eye, lasting from 30 minutes to two hours. Pain may spread to affect one entire side of the head.
• Nasal blockage on the affected side, later followed by profuse watery nasal discharge.
• Bloodshot, watery eye. Pupil may be constricted and eyelid may droop.
• Swollen cheek.
• Flushed face.

PREVENTION

• Avoid substances that appear to trigger headaches. Keep a detailed headache diary to help identify possible culprits. Record daily food and drink, activities, and the duration and severity of headaches.
• Avoid cigarettes and excessive alcohol consumption.

DIAGNOSIS

• Patient history and physical examination.
• Tests may be performed to rule out sinusitis, glaucoma, cerebral aneurysm, or other disorders that may produce symptoms similar to those of cluster headaches.

HOW TO TREAT IT

• Do not lie down during an episode—this often worsens the pain.
• Standard over-the-counter pain relievers often work too slowly to relieve the pain of a cluster headache.
• Your doctor may prescribe inhalation of 100 percent oxygen for five to 15 minutes at the beginning of an episode to relieve pain.
• Your doctor may prescribe ergotamine tartrate, which may relieve pain at the first sign of a headache. A more effective approach is to prevent headaches by taking one of a number of different medications (steroids, anti-inflammatories, antidepressants, and antihypertensive drugs) throughout the duration of a cluster.
• Surgery to sever certain nerves near the site of the headaches may be recommended in severe cases that do not respond to other therapy. Surgery provides relief about two-thirds of the time but may have serious side effects, including muscle weakness and loss of sensation in some areas of the face.

WHEN TO CALL A DOCTOR

• Call a doctor immediately if you have never had a cluster headache, and you develop a sudden, intense headache centered on one eye. Other, more severe disorders may produce similar symptoms.
• Make an appointment with a doctor if your headaches are not responding to treatment.

Headache, Migraine

WHAT IS IT?

A migraine is a throbbing, intensely painful headache, usually beginning on one side of the head and sometimes preceded by distinct early warning symptoms. Incapacitating pain may last for up to two days, and the frequency of episodes may vary from several times per week to once every few years. Migraines afflict about 10 percent of the population, usually first appearing during childhood or adolescence, and are more common among women than men. There is no cure, but symptoms can be prevented or controlled with proper treatment.

WHAT CAUSES IT?

• The precise cause of migraines is unknown, although it appears that abnormal constriction, followed by dilation, of arteries supplying the brain may be involved.
• Hereditary factors may play a role.
• Factors that may trigger migraines include foods containing the chemical tyramine (for example, nuts, chicken livers, red wine, and aged cheeses); stress and overwork; menstrual periods; birth control pills; bright lights; and changes in the weather.

network of arteries
in the brain

Migraines may begin as a spasm in the arteries of the brain, reducing its blood supply. The arteries then dilate to meet the brain's energy needs—but this also triggers the release of pain-causing chemicals.

> ### SYMPTOMS
> • Severe, throbbing pain, usually beginning on one side of the head, lasting up to two days.
> • Nausea and vomiting; possible diarrhea.
> • Sensitivity or aversion to light.
> • Early warning symptoms of classic migraine: temporary blind spots or blindness and other visual disturbances (such as seeing patterns of flashing lights); dizziness; numbness on one side of the face; weakness of an arm or leg; fatigue and listlessness.

PREVENTION

• Keep a daily record of food and drink to help identify possible triggers, and then avoid suspected items.
• Eat in moderation and at the same time every day.
• Allow time for relaxation and recreation.
• Avoid oversleeping, since it may lead to a migraine.

DIAGNOSIS

• Patient history and physical examination.

HOW TO TREAT IT

• Take over-the-counter analgesics for mild attacks.
• Lie down in a dark, quiet room while symptoms last. An ice pack on the forehead may be soothing.
• Your doctor may prescribe a combination of medications to prevent or relieve symptoms. Ergotamine tartrate and a new drug, Sumatriptan (currently available only in injectable form in the United States), may relieve symptoms of a severe migraine if taken at the onset of the headache. Drugs that may be taken to prevent an attack include propanolol, diazepam, amitriptyline, and methysergide maleate.
• Biofeedback—a technique in which the patient learns voluntary control over certain physiological responses—may be used to treat migraines.
• Relaxation training may be advised.

WHEN TO CALL A DOCTOR

• Call a doctor if headaches are severe, frequent, or persist for more than 24 hours, if there is a change in the pattern of your headaches, or if you experience speech difficulty.

Headache, Tension

WHAT IS IT?

Tension headaches, the most common type of headache in adults, are named so because it was once theorized that tensing and stretching of the scalp and neck muscles caused the pain. However, it is now known that muscle tension does not cause such headaches (although it may exacerbate them). The true cause remains unknown. In approximately half of cases, tension headaches are accompanied by some contraction and dilation of blood vessels in the brain, a condition usually referred to as a vascular headache. Additionally, a patient may suffer simultaneously from both tension headaches and migraines (a severe form of vascular headache; see Headache, Migraine, for more information). Pain and pressure from tension headaches may last continuously for days or weeks at a time (unlike other types of headaches, which are generally of much shorter duration). Tension headaches most commonly affect people of middle age and older. Treatment is aimed at relieving symptoms.

SYMPTOMS

- Steady pain or pressure in the scalp, temples, or back of the head. Unlike migraines, which typically affect only one side of the head, the pain of a tension headache involves both sides. (Also unlike migraines, tension headaches rarely cause nausea and vomiting.) Pain may be dull, intense, sharp, or diffuse, and persist for days or even months at a time.
- Pain or pressure that may feel like a constricting band encircling the head.
- Slight dizziness.
- Ringing in the ears (tinnitus).

WHAT CAUSES IT?

- The cause of tension headaches is unknown. However, certain conditions may promote the onset of a tension headache, including poor posture due to stress and fatigue; depression or anxiety; too little or too much sleep; a noisy or poorly ventilated environment; physically exhausting work; eyestrain; and the onset of menstrual periods.
- Contrary to popular belief, mental concentration in itself does not cause headaches; eyestrain or poor posture from hunching over a desk are likely culprits in such cases.

PREVENTION

- Get plenty of rest.
- Allow time in your schedule for regular exercise and relaxation.

DIAGNOSIS

- Patient history and physical examination. Diagnosis does not require a doctor.
- In severe or persistent cases, a doctor may perform some or all of the following tests: urinalysis, vision tests, sinus or skull x-ray, or a CT (computed tomography) scan of the brain.

HOW TO TREAT IT

- Over-the-counter pain relievers may be taken as needed. Aspirin may be the best of these for headaches.
- Massaging the muscles of the scalp and neck may help reduce pain.
- A hot bath may help relax muscles and ease the headache.
- A brief nap or even a rest in a dark, quiet room may be helpful.
- Antidepressants or tranquilizers may be prescribed in some cases to relieve severe or persistent pain.
- Biofeedback—a technique that fosters voluntary control over certain of the body's activities such as skin temperature—may be used to treat tension headaches.
- Relaxation training may be advised.

WHEN TO CALL A DOCTOR

- Call a doctor if headache is severe, persists more than 24 hours, or is accompanied by other symptoms, such as fever, drowsiness, nausea and vomiting, or blurred vision.

Heatstroke

WHAT IS IT?

Heatstroke is a medical emergency that occurs when overexposure to intense heat (but not necessarily direct sunlight) overwhelms the body's internal heat-regulating mechanisms. Consequently, the protective sweating reflex ceases to function, even though evaporation of sweat on the skin's surface is one of the primary means for the dissipation of excess heat. Body temperature subsequently soars to dangerous heights (104°F or above—in some cases as high as 107°F). Unless emergency medical assistance is obtained promptly, shock, coma, brain damage, kidney failure, or even death may result. Infants and the elderly are at the greatest risk of severe consequences.

SYMPTOMS

- Body temperature of over 104°F.
- Headaches, dizziness.
- Hot, dry, red skin. Skin appears gray in later stages.
- Conspicuous absence of sweating, despite high body temperature. (Profuse sweating may occur initially but then cease as the body's temperature-regulating mechanisms break down.)
- Rapid heartbeat.
- Rapid and shallow breathing.
- Dilated pupils.
- Muscle cramps.
- Confusion, delirium, or stupor, progressing to seizures or loss of consciousness.

WHAT CAUSES IT?

- Prolonged exposure to hot climates and high humidity.
- Dehydration or insufficient fluid intake.
- Electrolyte disturbances (imbalances in mineral salts, such as potassium, calcium, and magnesium).
- Impaired sweat gland function (which may be congenital).
- Strenuous work or exercise in hot climates.
- Alcohol consumption and overeating increase risk.
- Risk of heatstroke is greater among older people (as internal temperature-regulating mechanisms become less responsive with age) and overweight people (as extra layers of body fat tend to retain heat).
- Certain medications, including diuretics and antihistamines, may increase risk of heatstroke.
- Preexisting heart disease and diabetes are risk factors.
- A recent dehydrating illness (that is, one that involved excessive vomiting or diarrhea) increases susceptibility.

PREVENTION

- In hot, humid weather, increase fluid intake, wear light clothing, take frequent cool baths, try to remain in a cool (preferably air-conditioned) environment, and avoid alcohol and strenuous activity. These recommendations are especially important for the elderly, the chronically ill, or the very young.
- The body gradually adjusts to hotter climates over a period of one to three weeks. When the weather changes or you travel to warmer environs, spend increasingly longer amounts of time in the heat, followed by periods of rest in cool conditions to promote full acclimatization.

DIAGNOSIS

- Diagnosis is generally evident from the symptoms and history.
- Urine and blood tests may be performed to determine a heatstroke victim's degree of dehydration.

TREATMENT

- Heatstroke is an emergency: summon professional medical assistance at once.
- While waiting for emergency help to arrive, move the patient into a shady area or, ideally, an air-conditioned room. Elevate his or her feet. Loosen or remove clothing. Cover the body with a wet sheet or continually apply a wet cloth or sponge. Fan the person and offer cool liquids.
- Professional treatment involves controlled, gradual cooling of the patient, fluid and electrolyte replacement (via oral or intravenous delivery), and tranquilizers to control seizures.

WHEN TO CALL YOUR DOCTOR

- **EMERGENCY** Call an ambulance if signs of heatstroke develop.

Hemochromatosis

WHAT IS IT?

Hemochromatosis (one of the most common genetic disorders) is characterized by the increased absorption of iron by the intestine, resulting in an excessive accumulation of iron in the liver, pancreas, heart, testes, and other organs. Quantities of iron stored in the body increase very gradually over many years. Symptoms thus often do not appear until late middle age, but by the time they do, the disease may be very advanced. Excess iron in the pancreas may lead to diabetes mellitus, while excess iron in the liver may lead to cirrhosis of the liver, liver cancer, and liver failure. Untreated hemochromatosis may also lead to congestive heart failure. Early detection and treatment are essential for staving off symptoms and complications. The gene for the disease is recessive, meaning that both parents must carry it for a child to have a chance of developing it. Men from high-risk families are 10 times more likely to develop the disease than women; men have a greater iron intake to begin with (because they tend to consume more food), and for much of their lives, women lose iron every month during menstruation. Boys from high-risk families should be tested at the onset of puberty, and girls before age 20.

WHAT CAUSES IT?

- A genetic disorder results in excess iron storage.
- Years of increased absorption of iron from the diet, iron supplements, or, rarely, the exclusive use of iron cookware may lead to hemochromatosis in those who are genetically predisposed.
- Excessive alcohol intake contributes to liver damage and increases iron absorption.
- Patients with defective red blood cell formation (for example, because of thalassemia) may accumulate excessive iron from repeated blood transfusions (secondary hemochromatosis).

PREVENTION

- If you are at risk for hemochromatosis, limit your intake of foods high in iron, such as liver, red meats, and iron-enriched breads and cereals.
- Do not take iron supplements unless otherwise advised by your doctor.

DIAGNOSIS

- Tests measuring the blood levels of iron and ferritin (an iron-containing protein) often establish diagnosis.
- CT (computer tomography) scans or MRI (magnetic resonance imaging) may reveal organ abnormalities, which help determine the severity of the disorder.
- A liver biopsy (removal of a small sample of liver tissue with a needle) is the most definitive test.

HOW TO TREAT IT

- Periodic withdrawal of blood (venesection) is necessary to rid the body of excess iron. This may be needed weekly for several years in severe cases; when iron stores have been reduced to normal, venesection is required only three or four times per year.
- Testosterone therapy may be administered to men to correct loss of sexual desire and changes in secondary sexual traits.
- A diet low in iron-rich foods may be advised, although a completely iron-free diet is not necessary.
- Administration of the medication deferoxamine is required to remove iron in patients with secondary hemochromatosis.

WHEN TO CALL A DOCTOR

- Call a doctor if you develop symptoms of hemochromatosis.
- Be sure to schedule diagnostic screening for hemochromatosis if you have a family history of it.

SYMPTOMS

- Changes in skin coloration (possibly a bronze tinge or a slate-gray appearance) due to both increased melanin and iron deposits in the skin.
- Chronic abdominal pain.
- Joint pain.
- Drowsiness, weakness, and lethargy.
- Impaired mental faculties.
- In men, a decrease in the size of the testes, loss of sexual desire, and impotence.
- Irregular heartbeat and other symptoms of congestive heart failure.
- Excessive thirst and urination and other symptoms of diabetes.

Hemophilia

WHAT IS IT?

Hemophilia is the most common inherited blood coagulation disorder, affecting nearly one out of every 10,000 males. (Females may inherit the gene and be carriers for the disease, but are otherwise unaffected.) Outcome varies; the lower the amount of coagulation factors, the more severe the disease. Mild hemophilia may go undiagnosed until adulthood when prolonged bleeding occurs following surgery or an injury; moderate cases may cause a few bouts of uncontrolled bleeding during the patient's lifetime; severe cases are marked by frequent episodes of bleeding. The development of hematomas—accumulations of blood inside an organ, muscle, soft tissue, or body cavity—can cause potentially serious secondary symptoms. For example, a hematoma in the neck or throat may cause breathing obstruction. Bleeding into the brain may cause severe headaches, personality changes, paralysis, coma, or even death. About half of all hemophiliacs experience bleeding into the joints (hemarthrosis), resulting in arthritis-like symptoms. Also, because hemophiliacs often require numerous transfusions of blood products, they are at increased risk for blood-borne infections such as hepatitis or AIDS, although such risks have diminished thanks to improvements in the methods of preparation of blood products and recent efforts to screen donated blood. With current medical treatment and vigilant self-care, even patients with severe hemophilia may live relatively normal lives.

SYMPTOMS

- Frequent and extensive bruises.
- Prolonged bleeding that may not occur until several days after an injury or a procedure such as tooth extraction.
- Spontaneous bleeding for no apparent reason.
- Painful uncontrolled bleeding into joints or muscles, causing swelling, tenderness, and possibly deformity. Joint pain may precede clear-cut evidence of bleeding.
- Blood in the urine or stool.
- Headache, paralysis, or coma from bleeding into the brain.

WHAT CAUSES IT?

- Hemophilia A, which accounts for 80 percent of cases, results from genetic deficiency of Factor VIII, also known as antihemophilic factor. Hemophilia B results from a deficiency in Factor IX. Both factors are necessary for normal blood coagulation. Because the genes for the factors are carried on the X chromosomes, hemophilia only affects males; women may be carriers and pass the disorder to their offspring.

PREVENTION

- There is no way to prevent hemophilia, although those with a family history of it may benefit from genetic counseling when considering having a child.

DIAGNOSIS

- Patient history (including family history) and physical examination are necessary.
- Blood tests are taken to measure clotting time and blood levels of Factors VIII and IX.

HOW TO TREAT IT

- Avoid activities that carry a high risk of injury.
- Do not use medications such as aspirin that promote bleeding.
- A bleeding episode can be stopped by intravenous infusion of the missing clotting factor. Factor VIII can often be administered by the patient himself; early treatment is best. Two main types of Factor VIII preparations are available: a frozen concentrate that must be thawed before infusion and a powder that is refrigerated and reconstituted just prior to use.
- Regular preventive doses of clotting factors may be taken in severe cases, but such treatment is very expensive. Patients on a home care regimen require clinical evaluation every six months to a year.
- Episodes of uncontrollable bleeding require hospitalization and prolonged infusions of clotting factor.
- Physical therapy may be advised to rehabilitate damaged joints. Activities such as swimming are encouraged; contact sports should be avoided.
- In 10 to 20 percent of patients, development of an inhibitor to Factor VIII renders treatment ineffective.

WHEN TO CALL A DOCTOR

- See a doctor for any bout of uncontrolled bleeding.

Hemorrhoids

WHAT IS IT?

Hemorrhoids (also called piles) are distended varicose veins in the anus. All veins are lined with valves that permit blood to flow in only one direction (back to the heart). Excess pressure on these valves can cause them to weaken and fail, allowing blood to flow in the wrong direction or to stagnate. The vein may engorge with blood, which, in the anus, results in a hemorrhoid. While hemorrhoids are often painless, the swollen wall of the vein is fragile and thus prone to rupture and bleeding. Stagnant blood promotes formation of blood clots in the vein, which are typically painful and, in severe cases, may require surgery. Hemorrhoids usually affect people between the ages of 20 and 50 and are especially common in those who are pregnant or obese, owing to increased pressure within the veins of the lower abdomen.

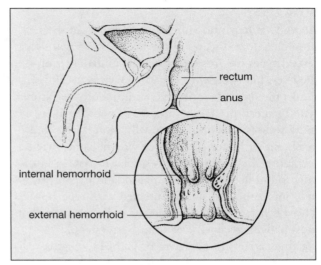

External hemorrhoids affect veins in or near the anal opening; internal hemorrhoids are located further up, in the rectum.

WHAT CAUSES IT?

• Straining during bowel movements is a primary cause. (A diet low in fiber can result in constipation, which in turn encourages the tendency to strain during bowel movements.)
• Pregnancy, childbirth, and obesity increase the risk of hemorrhoids.
• Prolonged standing or sitting may be causes.
• Loss of muscle tone due to old age, an episiotomy, or rectal surgery can promote hemorrhoids.

SYMPTOMS

• Bright red blood on the toilet paper, the stool, or in the toilet bowl following a bowel movement.
• Pain, especially during bowel movements.
• Anal itching.
• Mucus discharge from the anus.

PREVENTION

• A high-fiber diet including fresh fruit, vegetables, and whole-grain breads and cereals is recommended.
• Drink plenty of water.
• Don't strain during bowel movements or stay on the toilet longer than necessary.

DIAGNOSIS

• Patient history and examination of the anus and rectum are necessary. A doctor may detect internal hemorrhoids with a proctoscope or anoscope.
• Barium enema x-rays may be ordered.

HOW TO TREAT IT

• Wash the anal area gently but thoroughly after each bowel movement, using a soft tissue and warm water.
• For external hemorrhoids, apply an ice compress.
• Frequent warm baths or sitz baths can relieve mild symptoms of pain and itching.
• Anesthetic suppositories and topical corticosteroids (such as hydrocortisone) may ease pain and swelling.
• An injection of a solution that turns the hemorrhoid to scar tissue may be used (sclerotherapy).
• Some hemorrhoids may be tied off using a rubber band (rubber band ligation).
• In severe cases, surgical removal (hemorrhoidectomy) may be necessary.

WHEN TO CALL A DOCTOR

• If hemorrhoids do not improve with home treatment, see a doctor.
• Rectal bleeding always warrants a doctor's attention; more serious disorders such as colon cancer must be ruled out.

Hepatitis, Acute Viral

WHAT IS IT?

Acute viral hepatitis is the most common of the serious contagious diseases of the liver. It is caused by several types of viruses that produce inflammation of the liver. Infection with hepatitis A virus usually results in complete recovery and immunity to future type A infection. The symptoms of hepatitis B, a more serious infection, are usually more severe and persistent (although all types of viral hepatitis may be asymptomatic). Hepatitis E is similar to type A but is only found near the Indian Ocean, and hepatitis D only infects people already infected with type B. There is no specific treatment for these disorders, but most patients recover over time. Some people become carriers of Hepatitis B, C, or D—that is, they remain infectious long after all symptoms have cleared. In some cases, both type B and type C (formerly known as non-A, non-B hepatitis) may lead to chronic (persistent) hepatitis, cirrhosis, and liver cancer.

SYMPTOMS
- General discomfort.
- Fever.
- Fatigue.
- Loss of appetite.
- Nausea and vomiting.
- Aching muscles or joints.
- Abdominal discomfort or pain.
- Jaundice.
- Dark urine and pale stools.

WHAT CAUSES IT?
- Viruses cause acute hepatitis.
- Hepatitis A and E are spread by contact with the fecal matter of an infected person, via contaminated fingers, food, or water.
- Raw shellfish from polluted waters may cause hepatitis A.
- Hepatitis B, C, and D may be spread by exposure to contaminated blood (both fresh and dried) on infected needles, during a blood transfusion, or during sexual intercourse.

- Hepatitis B may be transmitted to an infant at childbirth by an infected mother.

PREVENTION
- Hepatitis types A and B vaccines are advised prior to traveling to areas where hepatitis infection rates are high. Type B vaccines are also recommended for people in high-risk categories, such as health-care workers, people with multiple sexual partners, renal dialysis patients, and children born to infected mothers.
- Wash your hands with warm water and soap after a bowel movement or before handling food, especially if you have hepatitis A or E or if you are caring for someone with the infection. (Since hepatitis is contagious for weeks before symptoms develop, people may carry and spread the disease without realizing it.)
- When traveling abroad or in areas with poor sanitation, drink only bottled water or other bottled beverages and eat only cooked foods and peeled fruit.
- Use condoms during sexual intercourse to help prevent the spread of hepatitis B. Avoid intimate contact with infected persons if possible.
- Sterile or disposable needles should be used in acupuncture, ear piercing, or tattooing. Ask about sterilization procedures in advance.

DIAGNOSIS
- Blood tests for the virus or antibodies to the virus are taken.

HOW TO TREAT IT
- Avoid alcoholic beverages during recovery.
- Rest as needed.
- Increase caloric intake. Several small meals daily rather than a few large ones may help combat nausea and loss of appetite.
- In severe cases, temporary intravenous feeding may be necessary.

WHEN TO CALL A DOCTOR
- Call a doctor if you develop symptoms of acute viral hepatitis.
- Call a doctor if you have been exposed to someone known to have acute viral hepatitis.

Hepatitis, Chronic

WHAT IS IT?

Chronic hepatitis is characterized by ongoing inflammation of the liver and destruction (necrosis) of liver cells that persists for more than six to 12 months. There are two main forms: persistent and active (in rare cases the former may develop into the latter). Symptoms may be mild or vague with either form of the disease. Chronic persistent hepatitis progresses slowly and often subsides spontaneously, although it may take many months, or even years, to do so. Chronic active hepatitis is a more dangerous condition because the destruction of liver cells results in the development of scar tissue in the liver (cirrhosis) and may ultimately lead to liver failure. However, with adequate treatment most patients with chronic active hepatitis recover within one to three years.

WHAT CAUSES IT?

• An acute infection of hepatitis B or C may develop into chronic hepatitis.
• Years of excessive alcohol consumption may lead to chronic hepatitis.
• Autoimmune disorders (in which the immune system attacks body tissues) and, rarely, metabolic disorders (such as Wilson's disease, in which excess amounts of copper are stored in the liver) may be a cause.
• In rare instances some medications, such as dantrolene, nitrofurantoin, and the sulfonamides, may lead to chronic hepatitis, as may long-term use of aspirin or acetaminophen.
• In some cases the cause is unknown.

PREVENTION

• Consume no more than two alcoholic drinks per day. If you suspect that you may have a drinking problem, seek help at once.
• A hepatitis B vaccination is recommended for those at high risk, such as health care workers, and before traveling to areas where hepatitis is common.

DIAGNOSIS

• Patient history and physical examination.
• Blood tests. (Recently, a specific blood test for hepatitis C was put into use.)
• Liver biopsy (removal of a small sample of tissue with a needle). It is almost always necessary for a diagnosis.

HOW TO TREAT IT

• Do not consume alcoholic beverages.
• Corticosteroids, with or without an immunosuppressant drug such as azathioprine, may be prescribed to treat cases of chronic active hepatitis not caused by the hepatitis B virus.
• Alpha-interferon may be prescribed to treat chronic active hepatitis caused by the hepatitis B or C viruses.
• Continued observation may be the only treatment advised for chronic persistent hepatitis.
• Your doctor may change your prescription(s) to relieve symptoms caused by medications.
• Lifelong treatment of any underlying metabolic disorder (such as Wilson's disease) is necessary.
• Liver transplantation may be recommended when the liver has been severely damaged.

WHEN TO CALL A DOCTOR

• Call a doctor if you develop symptoms of chronic hepatitis.
• Call a doctor if you have had jaundice or an acute hepatitis infection and symptoms persist despite treatment.

SYMPTOMS

• General discomfort.
• Fatigue.
• Loss of appetite.
• Nausea and vomiting.
• Jaundice.
• Small, red, spidery veins on the surface of the skin (spider telangiectasias).
• Pain or tenderness in the upper right abdomen.
• Abdominal swelling (when cirrhosis develops as a result of chronic active hepatitis).
• Fever (chronic active hepatitis).
• In women (especially when autoimmune chronic hepatitis is involved): cessation of menstruation (amenorrhea), acne, the appearance of male-pattern facial hair, and joint pain.

Herpes Zoster Shingles

WHAT IS IT?

Herpes zoster, also known as shingles, is a disorder caused by varicella zoster, the same virus that causes chicken pox. After an attack of chicken pox, usually a childhood disease, the virus does not die but rather lies dormant in the nerve cells that extend from the spinal cord or the brain. Years later, the virus may be reactivated and migrate along the path of the nerve to the surface of the skin, where it causes a rash of painful blisters. While it is generally not a dangerous condition, shingles can be extremely painful and often causes lingering nerve pain (postherpetic neuralgia) for months or even years after the rash is gone. This disorder only affects those who have previously had chicken pox and usually strikes after the age of 50. Usually only one attack occurs, lasting for two or three weeks. Outlook is good unless the virus spreads to the brain.

WHAT CAUSES IT?

• How or why shingles occurs is uncertain. It is believed that the virus reactivates when the immune system—owing to age, illness, stress, or the use of immunosuppressant drugs—becomes too weak to keep the virus in a state of dormancy. Indeed, it's been demonstrated that immunosuppressed patients (those with disorders such as Hodgkin's disease or treated with immunosuppressive drugs) are at increased risk for herpes zoster.

The lines demarcate the regions of skin supplied by individual nerves stemming from the spinal cord. When shingles strikes, the rash is usually confined to one of these narrow bands.

PREVENTION

• There is no known way to prevent herpes zoster.

DIAGNOSIS

• Appearance of typical skin lesions and a prior history of chicken pox or shingles indicate herpes zoster.
• A culture of the skin lesions may be taken to confirm the diagnosis.

HOW TO TREAT IT

• Apply cool, wet compresses or ice packs.
• Use over-the-counter pain relievers.
• Calamine lotion and oatmeal or cornstarch baths can help relieve itching.
• During the early stages, acyclovir, an antiviral drug, may stem the progression of the rash and speed healing.
• Corticosteroids or tranquilizers may be used for more serious cases of postherpetic neuralgia.
• In severe cases, neural blocking agents may be used to prevent pain signals from reaching the brain.

WHEN TO CALL A DOCTOR

• Call a doctor if you develop symptoms of herpes zoster.
• See a doctor or ophthalmologist immediately if herpes zoster is accompanied by eye pain.

SYMPTOMS

• In early stages, a sensation of tingling followed by pain (often accompanied by fever and headache), preceding the development of the rash by several days.
• Severe pain and itching in a bandlike rash of small, red, fluid-filled blisters on one side of the torso, arms, legs, or face lasting from about one to four weeks. About 10 days after their appearance, blisters dry up into scabs.
• Pain that persists for months or years after skin lesions have healed (postherpetic neuralgia).

Hiatal Hernia

WHAT IS IT?

A hiatal hernia occurs when a portion of the stomach slides upward into the chest cavity through the esophageal hiatus (opening) of the diaphragm, the sheet of muscle separating the chest cavity from the abdominal cavity. The condition is quite common, particularly among those over 50, and is rarely serious. Indeed, less than 20 percent ever experience any symptoms. However, weakness of the muscular ring (lower esophageal sphincter) that maintains a one-way flow from esophagus to stomach may accompany a hiatal hernia. In some cases, this may permit stomach acid to back up into the esophagus, which does not have a protective lining like the stomach, resulting in the sensation of heartburn. In severe cases (which are rare), a substantial portion of the stomach may slip into the chest cavity, leading to internal bleeding and iron deficiency anemia. Very rarely, blood flow to the herniated portion of the stomach may be cut off (strangulation), requiring immediate surgery.

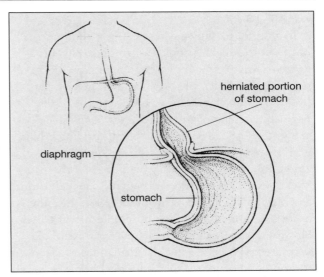

A hiatal hernia results when a portion of the stomach slides upward from the abdominal cavity, through the hiatus (the opening in the diaphragm muscle), and into the chest cavity.

SYMPTOMS

- Heartburn one to four hours after eating.
- Belching.
- Regurgitation.
- Swallowing difficulty, bleeding, severe pain, and shock in very rare, severe cases.

WHAT CAUSES IT?

- Most often, muscle weakness due to normal aging.
- Congenital abnormalities in the diaphragm.
- Increased pressure in the abdominal cavity due to pregnancy, obesity, ascites (fluid in the abdominal cavity), coughing, sneezing, vomiting, straining during bowel movements, or physical exertion such as lifting.

DIAGNOSIS

- Endoscopy (use of a thin, flexible tube to view the esophagus and stomach).
- Chest x-rays.
- Barium-swallow x-ray (using barium to render a sharp x-ray image of the digestive tract).

PREVENTION

- There is no known way to prevent hiatal hernia.

HOW TO TREAT IT

- Eat small meals, avoid high-fat foods and alcohol, and avoid lying down two or three hours after eating—practices intended to prevent heartburn.
- Take antacids when heartburn strikes. However, if prolonged use of antacids becomes necessary, see your doctor. Long-term antacid use can cause diarrhea and metabolic problems.
- Avoid cigarettes completely.
- Raise the head of your bed at least six inches by placing books or bricks under the back legs; this will prevent stomach acid from reaching the esophagus while you recline.
- Avoid constrictive clothing like tight belts, pants, girdles, or pantyhose.
- Avoid straining during bowel movements.
- Rarely, when symptoms are chronic and severe, a doctor may recommend surgery to tighten the lower esophageal sphincter. This procedure has a high rate of success.

WHEN TO SEE A DOCTOR

- See a doctor if you experience persistent heartburn.

Hydrocele

WHAT IS IT?

A hydrocele is a fluid-filled swelling around one or both testicles. Each testicle is surrounded by a two-layered sheath or sac (not to be confused with the scrotum, the pouch of skin in which the testicles hang). The small amount of lubricating fluid that is normally present between the layers of the sheath allows the testicles to move freely. If too much fluid is produced, or too little is absorbed, an excess amount may accumulate between the two sheath layers, forming a hydrocele. (A hydrocele is thus not an enlargement of the testicle itself.) This disorder is more common among men of middle age or older. However, some young boys may have a hydrocele associated with an inguinal hernia, a localized protrusion of a portion of the abdominal lining, located in the channel where the testicles descended from the abdomen. In these cases, the channel did not close properly after descent of the testicles, and excess fluid may leak into the hydrocele sac from the abdominal lining. Hydroceles are not a health risk, rarely cause pain, and, in adult men, require treatment only when the swelling causes discomfort.

SYMPTOMS
• A soft, painless swelling in the scrotum.

WHAT CAUSES IT?

• In most cases the cause of a hydrocele is unknown, but overproduction or decreased absorption of the normal cushioning fluid appears to be involved.
• Injury to the testicles may lead to a hydrocele.
• An inguinal hernia may produce a hydrocele in young boys.

PREVENTION

• There is no known way to prevent hydrocele.
• Regular self-examination of the testes aids in early diagnosis and treatment of any abnormalities (see Testicular Cancer for more information).

DIAGNOSIS

• The doctor will gently palpate the testicles to determine the size and consistency of any lumps.
• The doctor may shine a bright light on the scrotum to determine the nature of the swelling. Since hydroceles are composed of watery fluid, they are relatively transparent and allow the light to shine through. (A tumor or other mass would appear opaque.)
• An ultrasound examination may confirm the diagnosis.

HOW TO TREAT IT

• In young boys, surgery (through a small incision in the abdomen) to close the inguinal hernia eliminates the cause of the hydrocele.
• Excess fluid may be removed with a needle and syringe (needle aspiration) under local anesthesia; however, with this method the hydrocele tends to recur. Needle aspiration also carries the risk of infection.
• In adult men, surgery (through a small incision in the scrotum) may be used to tighten or remove the testicle sheaths and permanently eliminate a hydrocele.

WHEN TO CALL A DOCTOR

• Call a doctor if you notice an unusual growth or swelling in the testicles. While a hydrocele is not a health risk, an examination by a doctor is warranted to rule out more serious disorders.

Hydrocephalus

WHAT IS IT?

Hydrocephalus is an uncommon disorder involving the overaccumulation of cerebrospinal fluid (CSF) in the fluid-filled spaces, or ventricles, within the brain. CSF is secreted into the ventricles, circulates around the brain tissue, and is then absorbed by tiny finger-like projections from the membranes surrounding the brain. If the flow of CSF is blocked, or if a defect interferes with fluid reabsorption, pressure increases upon the brain. Newborns and the elderly are most susceptible to this disorder. In infants, increased CSF pressure forces the soft bones of the head apart, producing an abnormally large head. The onset of hydrocephalus may be sudden or gradual; in either case, it can cause permanent brain damage in all age groups, so prompt treatment is essential.

WHAT CAUSES IT?

• In infants, causes include congenital malformations, injury during birth, bacterial meningitis, and viral infections.
• In both children and adults, causes include brain hemorrhage and brain tumor.
• In adults, causes include head injury and meningitis (an inflammation of the membranes surrounding the brain due to infection).
• In adults, the cause is sometimes unknown.

PREVENTION

• There is no known way to prevent hydrocephalus.

SYMPTOMS
• Abnormal enlargement of the head (in infants).
• Projectile vomiting (in infants).
• Convulsions or seizures (in infants).
• Severe headache.
• Loss of appetite.
• Mental confusion and deterioration, including irritability, loss of memory, anxiety, paranoia, apathy, impaired judgment, or speech disturbances.
• Unsteadiness when walking.
• Urinary incontinence.

ventricles

normal flow of CSF

Cerebrospinal fluid (CSF) is produced in the ventricles deep within the brain and then flows into the spaces around the brain and spinal cord. Hydrocephalus is marked by blockage of the normal flow of CSF and consequential enlargement of the ventricles.

DIAGNOSIS

• The circumference of a newborn's head is measured at birth. Enlargement suggests hydrocephalus.
• X-rays, CT (computed tomography) scans, and MRI (magnetic resonance imaging) of the skull.
• Lumbar puncture (spinal tap).

HOW TO TREAT IT

• Surgical insertion of a drainage tube, or shunt, is necessary to circumvent blockage or to drain excess CSF in both children and adults. The shunt allows excess CSF to flow into a vein in the neck, and thus into the bloodstream, or the abdominal cavity, where it is reabsorbed. The shunt is usually permanent. If placed in an infant, the shunt must be periodically replaced as the child grows.

WHEN TO CALL A DOCTOR

• Symptoms of hydrocephalus warrant immediate medical attention to prevent or minimize potential brain damage.
• **EMERGENCY** Call a doctor immediately if a child with a shunt for hydrocephalus exhibits vomiting, irritability, or convulsions. These may be signs of shunt malfunction.

Hypercholesterolemia High Cholesterol

WHAT IS IT?

Hypercholesterolemia is a disorder characterized by high levels of blood cholesterol, mainly carried on low-density lipoprotein (LDL). Lipoproteins are particles formed in the liver to transport cholesterol and other fats through the bloodstream. Because fats do not dissolve in water, they cannot travel through the body unaided. Cholesterol is manufactured primarily in the liver and then carried to the cells throughout the body by LDL. Cholesterol is returned to the liver from other body cells by another lipoprotein, high-density lipoprotein, or HDL. From there, cholesterol is secreted into the bile, either unchanged or after being converted to bile acids. Cholesterol is essential for the formation of cell membranes and the manufacture of some hormones, but it is not required in the diet, because the liver generally produces all the cholesterol the body needs. If cholesterol levels in the blood are elevated, particularly when HDL levels are low, LDL can deposit it in the arterial walls. These deposits represent the first stage of atherosclerosis, or so-called hardening of the arteries. There are no symptoms of hypercholesterolemia, so preventive measures and regular measurement of cholesterol levels are important for those in high-risk categories. Left untreated, hypercholesterolemia can eventually lead to coronary artery disease and the possibility of a heart attack.

WHAT CAUSES IT?

• Hereditary factors (familial hypercholesterolemia) appear to be the primary cause.

SYMPTOMS

• There are no symptoms, except in very advanced cases that have gone untreated for a long time. When cholesterol levels are very high, cholesterol may be deposited as yellow nodules (xanthomas) in tendons or just below the skin at the elbows, knees, or under the eyes.

• A diet high in saturated fat and cholesterol increases blood cholesterol levels.
• Other disorders, such as diabetes mellitus, Cushing's syndrome, and hypothyroidism, may promote hypercholesterolemia.

PREVENTION

• Eat a diet low in saturated fats and cholesterol. A diet rich in water-soluble fiber tends to lower blood cholesterol.
• Exercise regularly, and try to lose weight if you are more than 20 percent overweight.
• Drink alcoholic beverages in moderation—no more than two per day. A number of studies indicate that such moderate alcohol consumption helps to raise levels of beneficial HDL; however, consumption in excess of this amount has harmful effects.

DIAGNOSIS

• Patient history and physical examination.
• Blood cholesterol tests.

HOW TO TREAT IT

• Follow preventive tips. Lifestyle changes alone are frequently all that is necessary.
• Medications specifically designed to reduce blood cholesterol levels, like cholestyramine, colestipol, statins (lovastatin, pravastatin, simvastatin, and fluvastatin), or large doses of niacin, may be prescribed when dietary modifications prove inadequate.
• In rare cases when cholesterol levels are extremely high, blood plasma removal may be recommended.

WHEN TO CALL A DOCTOR

• Make an appointment with your doctor to get your cholesterol levels checked if you are in a high-risk category for coronary artery disease.
• Make an appointment with your doctor for a blood cholesterol test if any member of your immediate family is diagnosed with familial hypercholesterolemia.

Hyperparathyroidism

WHAT IS IT?

Hyperparathyroidism is marked by overactivity of one or more of the parathyroid glands, the four pea-size glands embedded in the corners of the thyroid gland at the base of the neck. These glands produce parathyroid hormone (PTH), a chemical that, along with vitamin D and calcitonin (a hormone manufactured in the thyroid gland), regulates blood calcium levels. Excess PTH due to hyperparathyroidism results in unusually high levels of blood calcium (hypercalcemia), most of which is released from calcium stores in the bones. Eventually, the loss of calcium may lead to weakened bones (see Osteomalacia). Excess calcium in the blood may also lead to calcinosis—the deposition of calcium salts in various body tissues, including the kidneys, skin, tendons, and cartilage—resulting in kidney disorders, arthritis,

SYMPTOMS

- Generalized discomfort.
- Muscle aches or weakness.
- Arthritic joint pain.
- Heartbeat irregularities.
- Constipation, nausea, vomiting, loss of appetite.
- Fatigue, lethargy, confusion, depression, psychosis, or other mental changes, possibly resulting in coma (due to hypercalcemia).
- Increased thirst and urine output (due to kidney involvement).
- Frequent or unexplained bone fractures.
- Chronic low back pain or upper abdominal pain (due to peptic ulcer or pancreatitis).

or other problems. The kidneys excrete in the urine large amounts of calcium, which can, over time, cause kidney stones or renal damage. Two other problems associated with hyperparathyroidism are peptic ulcers and pancreatitis. In many cases, hyperparathyroidism causes few if any symptoms and is only discovered during a routine blood test. However, a sudden attack of severe hypercalcemia can be a life-threatening emergency. This relatively rare disorder is most common among women over 40.

WHAT CAUSES IT?

- Most often, a benign tumor (adenoma) on one or more of the parathyroid glands is the cause.
- In about 20 percent of patients, the disorder is due to generalized enlargement (hyperplasia) of all four parathyroid glands.
- Other disorders, including chronic renal failure and vitamin D deficiency (rickets), can cause secondary hyperparathyroidism by lowering blood calcium levels. The parathyroids then secrete excessive amounts of PTH to return blood calcium levels to normal.
- Long-term use of certain drugs like laxatives and phenytoin (an anticonvulsant used to treat seizures) may lead to the disorder.

PREVENTION

- There is no way to prevent hyperparathyroidism.

DIAGNOSIS

- Patient history and physical exam are necessary.
- High blood levels of calcium and low levels of phosphorous indicate hyperparathyroidism.
- Calcium levels in the urine are measured.
- Measuring blood levels of PTH confirms diagnosis.
- X-rays may be taken to assess loss of bone mass.

HOW TO TREAT IT

- In cases producing no obvious symptoms, careful, regular monitoring may be all that is required.
- High fluid intake and low calcium intake are recommended in patients with high levels of calcium in their blood or urine.
- In symptomatic cases, surgical removal of abnormal parathyroid tissue usually cures the disorder. If an abnormal growth cannot be located and subsequently removed, all but half of one of the four parathyroid glands may be removed. (Following surgery, the remaining parathyroid tissue may produce insufficient amounts of PTH, requiring treatment for hypoparathyroidism.) Surgery is indicated if blood calcium levels are too high or if there is evidence of bone or kidney damage.

WHEN TO CALL A DOCTOR

- See a doctor for regular checkups or if you experience symptoms of hyperparathyroidism.

Hyperpituitarism

WHAT IS IT?

One form of hyperpituitarism—marked by an overproduction of growth hormone by the pituitary gland—is a rare, chronic disorder known as acromegaly in adults and gigantism in children. The pituitary, a peanut-size organ located at the base of the brain, is the most important gland in the body's endocrine, or hormonal, system. It produces a number of essential hormones; one of these, human growth hormone (HGH or somatotropin), is responsible for regulating growth during childhood. Normally, as people reach adulthood, less HGH is produced. Overproduction of HGH in children results in exaggerated height. (The most dramatic case of gigantism on record is a child who grew to a height of nearly nine feet.) When onset of the disorder occurs during adulthood (acromegaly), bones can no longer increase in length but progressively thicken instead. This results in gradual enlargement of the hands, feet, jaw, forehead, nose, and ears and produces the coarse facial features characteristic of the disorder. The internal organs also become abnormally enlarged. Thus, acromegaly often reduces life expectancy and, if left untreated, may lead to blind-ness, arthritis, infertility, diabetes, high blood pressure, heart valve failure, and coronary artery disease.

WHAT CAUSES IT?

• A benign pituitary tumor (adenoma) is the most common cause of HGH overproduction.
• Rarely, a tumor in the hypothalamus (the region of the brain directly behind the pituitary gland) may overstimulate production of HGH.

PREVENTION

• There is no way to prevent hyperpituitarism.

DIAGNOSIS

• Patient history and physical examination, including visual-field tests.
• Blood tests revealing elevated levels of HGH that are not fully reduced by administration of glucose.
• Measurement of elevated levels of somatomedin-C (IGF-1) in the blood.
• CT (computed tomography) scans and MRI (magnetic resonance imaging) to detect a pituitary tumor.
• X-rays to detect increased bone mass.

HOW TO TREAT IT

• Surgical removal of the underlying tumor is the treatment of choice. It is not uncommon for HGH levels to return to normal within hours of surgery and for soft tissue (but not bony) enlargement to subside rapidly.
• Radiation, alone or after surgery, may be performed to shrink the tumor (or prevent its recurrence).
• In some cases, lifetime hormone replacement therapy with thyroid or adrenal-steroid hormones may be necessary if surgery or radiation damages the remaining pituitary gland.
• Medications such as bromocriptine or octreotide may be prescribed to decrease tumor size and regulate HGH secretion. However, doses must be administered daily in large amounts, and effectiveness is limited, so medication is usually only supplemental to radiation or surgery.

WHEN TO CALL A DOCTOR

• See a doctor if you or your child develop symptoms of hyperpituitarism.

SYMPTOMS

• In children: excessive height due to abrupt, accelerated growth (not to be confused with normal adolescent growth spurts).
• In adults: enlarged hands, feet, forehead, and jaw bones; broadened head and neck; coarsened facial features; widely spaced teeth; impotence in men; cessation of menstrual periods (amenorrhea) and excess facial hair (hirsutism) in women.
• In both children and adults: fatigue and muscle weakness; profuse sweating; weight gain; oily skin; sinus congestion; increased tongue size; hollow-sounding voice; oversleeping; joint pain; tingling sensations in the hands; sudden mood changes.
• Headaches and impaired vision may occur as tumor growth exerts pressure within the skull.

Hypertension High Blood Pressure

WHAT IS IT?

Hypertension is characterized by a persistent increase in the force that the blood exerts upon the walls of the arteries. It's normal for this force to increase with stress or physical exertion, but with hypertension, the patient's blood pressure is high even at rest. Blood pressure is measured with two numbers: systolic and diastolic. It is measured in millimeters of mercury (abbreviated mm Hg) using a device called a sphygmomanometer. The first (systolic) number represents the force of blood against the walls of the arteries when the heart contracts to pump blood to the rest of the body. The second (diastolic) number represents the pressure within the arteries as the heart relaxes and refills with blood (which explains why the diastolic number is always lower than the systolic measurement). Hypertension is defined as a blood pressure reading greater than 140/90. Some 60 million Americans have hypertension, but only about half of them know it, primarily because it so rarely causes any noticeable symptoms and is usually detected only incidentally during a routine physical examination. But left untreated,

During the systolic phase of the heartbeat, the heart contracts powerfully to pump blood out to the rest of the body; during the diastolic phase, it relaxes as its lower chambers fill with blood to be expelled during the next contraction. Blood pressure readings are commonly given as a pair of numbers (for example, 120/80). The first number refers to the force the blood exerts against the walls of the arteries during the systolic phase; the second number corresponds to the force maintained during the diastolic phase.

SYMPTOMS

- Symptoms are rare with uncomplicated hypertension. However, the following may occur when blood pressure is dangerously high:
- Headaches.
- Dizziness or ringing in the ears.
- Palpitations.
- Nosebleeds.
- Numbness or tingling in the hands or feet.
- Drowsiness or confusion.

hypertension promotes arteriosclerosis (narrowing of the arteries) and increases the risk of heart attack, stroke, kidney damage, and destruction of tiny blood vessels in the eye, which can result in visual loss. For these reasons, hypertension is often called "the silent killer." Fortunately, if detected early and treated properly, the prognosis is good.

WHAT CAUSES IT?

- In more than 90 percent of cases, no single identifiable cause can be pinpointed, but risk factors include a family history of hypertension, sex (women are at one-half to two-thirds the risk of men), race (incidence is up to twice as great among blacks as whites), emotional stress, sedentary lifestyle, and aging. Obesity, excessive alcohol consumption, cigarette smoking, and a high-sodium diet also increase the risk of hypertension.
- When an underlying cause can be identified, this is known as secondary hypertension. Such causes include kidney disorders, adrenal tumors, and pregnancy.

PREVENTION

- Keep weight within a healthy, normal range.
- Avoid cigarettes and restrict alcohol intake to no more than two drinks per day.

Hypertension High Blood Pressure *continued*

• Aim to get at least 20 minutes of vigorous aerobic exercise (like jogging, biking, dancing, or swimming) per day, three or four days per week.
• Limit sodium intake to less than 2,500 milligrams per day.

DIAGNOSIS

• Diagnosis requires accurate measurements of elevated blood pressure on at least three different occasions over a period of a week or more. Some people exhibit "white coat hypertension," wherein blood pressure is consistently high in a clinical setting but is normal when accurately measured at home. Other people sporadically alternate between normal and high readings (known as labile hypertension). Such patients may be asked to wear a portable monitor that automatically records their blood periodically over the course of a day or so.
• Blood tests to look for kidney damage and EKG to check for heart damage (both possible complications of hypertension) will be performed.

TREATMENT

• The first line of treatment for essential hypertension involves adopting the healthy lifestyle measures outlined above in Prevention. Mild hypertension may respond positively to these measures and thus require no further medical therapy. For example, some studies indicate that as many as 30 percent of those with high blood pressure (specifically, the type known as sodium-sensitive hypertension) can control it by lowering their salt intake.

• If lifestyle changes prove inadequate, your doctor will prescribe one or more of the many available drugs. Diuretics (or "water pills") increase elimination of salt and water and thus reduce overall body-fluid volume. Beta-blockers interfere with nerve receptors in the heart, causing it to beat less forcefully. Calcium channel blockers reduce the ability of arterial walls to constrict. ACE inhibitors prevent the formation of a hormone that constricts blood vessels. Alpha-blockers and central alpha agonists interfere with nerve impulses that cause arteries to constrict. Vasodilators relax and so dilate the arterial walls. Some diuretics deplete the body's levels of potassium, thus requiring potassium supplementation.
• For secondary hypertension, the underlying disease must be identified and treated.

WHEN TO CALL A DOCTOR

• All adults should have their blood pressure checked at least once a year. This is especially applicable if you are male, over age 40, overweight (particularly if you have been overweight since youth), sedentary, or if you have a family history of hypertension or heart disease.
• Notify your doctor if you experience any unpleasant side effects from antihypertensive drugs. Adjustments in your prescription may eliminate the problem; never elect to stop taking your medication without consulting your doctor.
• Get prompt medical attention if you experience symptoms such as ringing in the ears, dizziness, or recurrent headaches or nosebleeds—these may be signs of dangerously high blood pressure.

Hyperthyroidism

WHAT IS IT?

Hyperthyroidism is a disorder caused by excessive production of thyroid hormone by the thyroid, a gland in the neck that regulates body growth and metabolism. Normally, the pituitary gland, located deep in the brain, produces a hormone (thyroid-stimulating hormone or TSH) that regulates the thyroid gland's output of thyroid hormone. Most often, hyperthyroidism is due to autonomous (unregulated by TSH) overproduction of thyroid hormone by an enlarged gland (Graves' disease). This is believed to be an autoimmune disorder. Less commonly, the disorder may be caused by the growth of a single thyroid nodule that produces abnormally high amounts of thyroid hormone. Excess thyroid hormone speeds up all metabolic activity in the body (including the rate at which calories are burned) and may result in a myriad of symptoms; some can be mistaken as the result of stress or anxiety. While hyperthyroidism is eminently treatable, severe cases can be fatal if not adequately controlled. The disorder most commonly affects those between 30 and 40 years of age and is five times more frequent in women than men.

WHAT CAUSES IT?

• Graves' disease is considered an autoimmune disorder, wherein antibodies that attack thyroid tissue stimulate a constant production of thyroid hormone.
• Hyperthyroidism and other thyroid disorders run in families, although the exact genetic mechanisms are unknown.
• An excessive amount of iodine in the diet and, possibly, emotional stress may trigger the disorder in those predisposed to it.

PREVENTION

• There is no known way to prevent hyperthyroidism.

DIAGNOSIS

• Patient history and physical exam often point to the correct diagnosis. Indicators of hyperthyroidism include elevated heart rate, nervousness, tremor, sweating, appearance of goiter, and bulging eyes.
• Blood tests show high levels of thyroid hormones and low levels of TSH.
• A thyroid scan is taken following the administration of radioactive iodine to detect an isolated nodule overproducing thyroid hormone.

HOW TO TREAT IT

• Orally administered radioactive iodine is now the preferred method of treatment. As the thyroid absorbs the iodine, radiation destroys parts of the gland, so that it produces less thyroid hormone.
• Propylthiouracil or methimazole, two drugs that inhibit production of thyroid hormone, may be prescribed. Symptoms usually subside within several weeks; however, drug therapy must usually be continued for at least a year.
• Surgery to remove a large portion of the thyroid may be recommended for patients with extreme thyroid enlargement.
• Hyperthyroid patients will require frequent medical supervision throughout their lives. One risk of radioactive iodine treatment or surgery is that the thyroid will end up producing too little thyroid hormone (hypothyroidism), which then requires lifelong supplemental therapy with thyroid hormone.

WHEN TO CALL A DOCTOR

• Contact your doctor if you experience the symptoms of hyperthyroidism.

SYMPTOMS

• Weight loss despite an increase in appetite and food consumption.
• Anxiety, restlessness, and insomnia.
• Rapid heartbeat or palpitations.
• Tremors in the fingers or tongue.
• Increased sweating and intolerance to heat; insensitivity to cold.
• Bulging, watery eyes that feel gritty; an increased sensitivity to light.
• Swelling in the neck (goiter).
• Fatigue and muscle weakness.
• Increased frequency of bowel movements or diarrhea.
• Unusually light or absent menstrual periods.

Hyphema

WHAT IS IT?

Hyphema is a visible accumulation of blood in front of the iris (the colored portion) of the eye, usually resulting from an injury. While the outermost layers or whites of the eyeball contain capillaries (small blood vessels), the internal chambers of the eye normally contain no blood vessels. Instead, the eye has its own special circulatory system, consisting primarily of a transparent liquid known as aqueous humor. However, if a capillary in the white of the eye bursts for any reason, blood may seep into the aqueous humor and cause visual problems. Aqueous humor flows constantly across the iris and is reabsorbed by a network of small veins that empty into the bloodstream. The blood from hyphema is usually carried away from the eye by the flow of the aqueous humor within a matter of days, and vision returns to normal. However, a blood clot may block the small veins responsible for reabsorbing the aqueous humor, causing it to build up in the eyeball. This may result in damage to the optic nerve or glaucoma, a sight-threatening increase in pressure within the intraocular space (see Glaucoma for more information). The risk of glaucoma is greater in cases when, after the blood has disappeared, there is subsequent rebleeding and recurrence of hyphema.

WHAT CAUSES IT?

• An injury to the eye, with a blunt instrument or by a puncture, is the most common cause of hyphema.
• Severe inflammation of the iris may lead to hyphema.

SYMPTOMS

• A visible pool of blood in front of the iris (the colored portion) of the eye.
• Vision problems.
• Eye pain (due to injury or cancer).

• A blood vessel abnormality may cause blood to leak into the front portion of the eye.
• Retinoblastoma, a form of eye cancer, may cause hyphema (see Eye Cancers for more information).

PREVENTION

• Take care to avoid accidents involving the eyes.

DIAGNOSIS

• Patient history and eye examination.
• A thorough eye examination is performed by an ophthalmologist if injury has occurred or if inflammation, blood vessel abnormality, or cancer is a suspected cause.

HOW TO TREAT IT

• Bed rest and hospitalization may be required to allow damaged blood vessels in the eye to heal and to check for further bleeding and glaucoma. Administration of eyedrops that prevent movement of damaged blood vessels in the eye make the eye extremely sensitive to light. Therefore, a patch is placed over the eye during recuperation.
• To prevent glaucoma, your ophthalmologist may prescribe eyedrops, such as timolol and acetazolamide, which reduce pressure inside the eyeball, or hyperosmotic agents (which draw fluid away from the inside of the eye), such as mannitol, glycerol, or sorbitol.
• Surgery may be required to evacuate blood from the eye in severe cases. The ophthalmologist will create a small temporary opening, or drain, in the eye, so that the bloody aqueous fluid may be drawn out; this drain may be surgically reopened if hyphema recurs.

WHEN TO CALL A DOCTOR

• Call an ophthalmologist immediately if you develop hyphema or if hyphema recurs after treatment.

Hypoglycemia

WHAT IS IT?

Hypoglycemia is an abnormally low blood sugar level, arising from an imbalance in the rate at which glucose (a simple sugar) is released from the liver and used by other body tissues. Glucose is absolutely essential as an energy source for the cells of the central nervous system. Insulin regulates glucose levels in the blood and stimulates glucose entry into the cells. Too little glucose in the blood starves the cells of energy, which triggers the release of adrenaline. This produces the symptoms of a hypoglycemic episode, characterized by a sudden attack of anxiety, shakiness, dizziness, and excess perspiration. Such episodes are generally not dangerous, since the symptoms incite people to ingest a sugar-containing food

---

SYMPTOMS

- Adrenaline-triggered symptoms: anxiety, hunger, a tingling sensation in the hands, palpitations, profuse perspiration, shakiness, or weakness.
- Symptoms of nighttime hypoglycemia: nightmares, restlessness, and profuse perspiration.
- Slower-onset symptoms, due to inadequate supply of glucose to the brain: agitation, amnesia, confusion, dizziness, disorientation, feeling cold, headache, impaired vision, lack of coordination, numbness, or personality changes.
- Emergency symptoms: seizures, transient paralysis of one side of the body, or loss of consciousness.

---

or drink, and the adrenaline (and other hormones) released tend to help restore blood sugar levels to normal. However, prolonged, severe hypoglycemia may be very dangerous, as it gradually and insidiously starves the brain of glucose, which may lead to disorientation and confusion, eventually progressing to seizures, partial paralysis, or loss of consciousness. If left untreated, hypoglycemia may ultimately result in permanent brain damage and, in rare cases, even death. There are two types of hypoglycemic episodes:

those that occur two to five hours after eating, known as postprandial hypoglycemia, and those that occur after an extended period without food (usually overnight), known as fasting hypoglycemia. Postprandial hypoglycemia may be unpleasant but is usually not serious, since it may be corrected easily by eating or drinking and by the action of hormones. Fasting hypoglycemia—which most commonly occurs among diabetics when too much insulin is administered—is potentially very dangerous, because of the risk of brain damage. In many cases, however, hypoglycemia may be managed by carefully following specific diet and lifestyle guidelines (see Diabetes Mellitus for more information).

WHAT CAUSES IT?

- In most cases of postprandial hypoglycemia, the cause is unknown. It may occur, however, as one of the early manifestations of diabetes mellitus, or following stomach surgery.
- The most common cause of fasting hypoglycemia is the administration of too much insulin to a diabetic patient. Risk is increased among these patients by overexercising or missing meals.
- Other causes of fasting hypoglycemia include excessive alcohol ingestion, insulin-producing tumors of the pancreas (insulinoma), tumors in other organs, adrenal or pituitary insufficiency, rampant leukemia, congestive heart failure, chronic kidney failure, severe liver failure, and some childhood metabolic disorders, such as fructose intolerance and galactosemia.
- Occasionally, hypoglycemia may be triggered by excessive amounts of certain medications, including aspirin (especially among children), as well as propranolol and other beta-blockers, and oral hypoglycemic agents.

PREVENTION

- Diabetics should carefully abide by their regimen of diet, medication, exercise, and blood glucose monitoring, and should always carry some fast-acting carbohydrate (glucose tablets, hard candies, gumdrops, or fruit juice) to consume at the first sign of symptoms. Also, insulin-treated diabetics should never travel for more than two hours in a car, plane,

Hypoglycemia *continued*

or train without having some sort of slow-acting carbohydrate food (such as peanut butter crackers) available for a snack.

• Those who experience postprandial hypoglycemic episodes should eat five or six small meals per day that are low in simple carbohydrates and high in protein, fat, and fiber.

DIAGNOSIS

• Diagnosis in those who do not have diabetes requires demonstration of low blood glucose levels accompanied by the usual symptoms. Depending on the type of hypoglycemia, blood glucose is measured either during a glucose tolerance test or after an overnight fast. Further tests and a detailed patient history are then necessary to determine the underlying cause of hypoglycemia.

• Diabetics can verify and document episodes of hypoglycemia with home blood glucose monitoring.

HOW TO TREAT IT

• If you sense a hypoglycemic episode coming on, stop all activity. If you are driving a car, for example, pull over.

• Consume one portion of any fast-acting carbohydrate: four ounces of fruit juice or sugared drink; some candy, such as six or seven jelly beans, or three large marshmallows; or one-half tube Glutose (80-g container). If you do not feel better quickly, consume

one more portion. However, do not eat chocolate, since the fat in it slows absorption of sugar into the bloodstream.

• Instruct your family and friends to give you a small drink of fruit juice or to smear syrup inside your mouth if you become disoriented or uncooperative (symptoms of worsening hypoglycemia).

• Instruct your family and friends how to administer an injection of glucagon, a hormone that helps raise your blood sugar level, in the event you lose consciousness from hypoglycemia. After the injection they should call an ambulance and, in the meantime, not attempt to give food or fluids, and most certainly not administer insulin.

• Your doctor may adjust or change your medication if you are receiving too much insulin or if you are taking one of the other drugs that sometimes triggers hypoglycemia in those who are susceptible.

• Surgery is required to treat a pancreatic tumor (insulinoma) and sometimes involves removing most of the pancreas. In cases where surgery is not an option, chemotherapy may be used to destroy cancerous cells.

WHEN TO CALL A DOCTOR

• **EMERGENCY** Call an ambulance immediately if someone loses consciousness.

• Call a doctor if you develop symptoms of hypoglycemia.

Hypoparathyroidism

WHAT IS IT?

Hypoparathyroidism is a common disorder that occurs when the parathyroid glands (the four pea-size glands embedded in the corners of the thyroid gland at the base of the neck) fail to produce sufficient quantities of parathyroid hormone (PTH), which helps regulate the blood level of calcium by its actions on the bones and the kidneys. Lack of PTH results in reduced levels of calcium in the blood, which can produce a variety of neurological and muscle abnormalities, from paresthesia (numbness or a burning or prickling sensation) to tetany (hyperexcitability of the nerves, characterized by painful spasms, twitching, and cramps in the face, hands, arms, throat, and sometimes the feet). Such symptoms usually subside with treatment, although the disorder tends to develop gradually, so that by the time it is treated, it may have already caused certain irreversible complications such as cataracts or basal ganglion calcifications. When hypoparathyroidism occurs during childhood and is not treated properly, it may result in poor tooth development and, sometimes, mental retardation. Otherwise, when diagnosis is established early in the course of the disorder, prognosis is good.

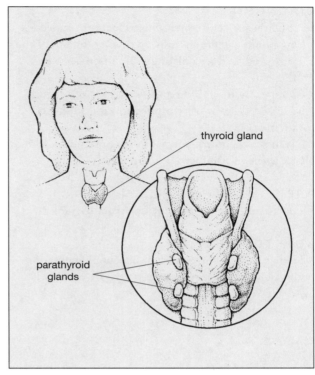

The four, small, round parathyroid glands are located within the lobes of the thyroid gland, which sits atop the trachea (windpipe).

SYMPTOMS

- Tingling and numbness or burning and prickling sensations in the face, hands, fingertips, or elsewhere.
- Painful, uncontrollable muscle spasms or cramps in the face, hands, and feet (tetany).
- Breathing or swallowing difficulty.
- Dry, lusterless skin and hair; split or cracked nails.
- Abnormal tooth development in children.
- Cataracts.
- Psychosis (in very severe cases).
- Seizures (in rare cases).
- Mental retardation when the disorder is left untreated in children.

WHAT CAUSES IT?

- The most common causes of hypoparathyroidism in adults are the accidental removal of parathyroid tissue during thyroid or other neck surgery and the removal or destruction of substantial portions of the parathyroid glands during the treatment of hyperparathyroidism.
- In children, hypoparathyroidism most often results from destruction of thyroid gland as a result of an autoimmune disorder.
- Hypoparathyroidism may occur when the parathyroid tissue is destroyed by amyloidosis (the build-up of a starchy protein in tissues and organs), hemochromatosis (excess iron storage), or malignant (cancerous) tumors.
- Rarely, an infant may be born without parathyroid glands or with a congenital malfunction of the glands.

Hypoparathyroidism *continued*

DIAGNOSIS
• Patient history and physical examination are needed.
• Low blood calcium is suspected when tetany of the hand is produced by inflating a blood pressure cuff on the arm.
• Abnormally low blood concentrations of calcium (and elevated levels of phosphorus) indicate hypoparathyroidism.
• Diagnosis is confirmed by the measurement of low blood levels of parathyroid hormone.

PREVENTION
• There is no way to prevent hypoparathyroidism.

HOW TO TREAT IT
• Therapy usually involves lifelong supplementation with calcium and very large amounts of vitamin D (which, along with PTH, is essential in maintaining proper blood levels of calcium).
• Severe muscle spasms (tetany) or convulsions may require hospitalization. Intravenous infusions of calcium provide temporary but immediate relief. Sedatives and anticonvulsants may also be administered.
• Regular periodic monitoring of blood calcium levels is essential.

WHEN TO CALL A DOCTOR
• Consult a doctor if you experience painful muscle spasms or cramps, or recurrent tingling, numbness, or burning sensations, especially if such symptoms occur in conjunction with other symptoms of hypoparathyroidism.
• **EMERGENCY** Get immediate medical attention if breathing difficulty or seizures occur.

Hypopituitarism

WHAT IS IT?

Hypopituitarism is a rare disorder involving under-production of hormones by the pituitary gland. The pituitary, deep in the brain, is the most important gland in the body's endocrine, or hormonal, system. One of the six hormones produced by the anterior portion of the pituitary is human growth hormone (HGH). In children, HGH deficiency may lead to impaired growth, or dwarfism. Early diagnosis and administration of HGH can correct this hormonal deficiency and result in near-normal height. Deficiencies in other pituitary hormones produce a wide variety of symptoms; in panhypopituitarism, the most dramatic form of this disorder, deficiencies occur in all pituitary hormones. Since pituitary hormones stimulate hormone production in other glands, hypopituitarism may have a snowball effect, resulting in deficiencies of adrenal, thyroid, and sex hormones (see Hypoglycemia, Diabetes Insipidus, Addison's Disease, and Hypothyroidism for more information).

SYMPTOMS

- Growth retardation in children and adolescents.
- Partial or total impairment of sexual maturation.
- Weakness.
- Nausea and vomiting.
- Hoarseness.
- Intolerance to cold.
- Slow heartbeat.
- Slowed or impaired thinking.
- Extreme thirst combined with excessive urination (due to diabetes insipidus, a disorder of the posterior pituitary), dehydration, constipation.
- Fine wrinkles next to the eyes and mouth, dry skin, depigmentation of the skin, loss of axillary and pubic hair.
- In women: cessation of menstruation (amenorrhea), breast atrophy, vaginal dryness, absence of milk production in new mothers (Sheehan's syndrome).
- In men: loss of libido and potency, reduced muscular strength, shrinking and softening of the testes, decreased secondary hair growth.

WHAT CAUSES IT?

- A tumor, in or near the pituitary gland, is the most common cause of hypopituitarism.
- Pituitary surgery or radiation is a potential cause.
- Hypopituitarism may develop in the postpartum period (Sheehan's syndrome) because of necrosis (tissue death) in the pituitary as it outgrows its blood supply during pregnancy.
- Inflammatory processes such as those that occur with tuberculosis are a possible cause.
- Infiltration of the pituitary by a starchy protein (amyloidosis) or iron (hemachromatosis) may result in hypopituitarism.

PREVENTION

- There is no way to prevent hypopituitarism.

DIAGNOSIS

- Patient history and physical examination.
- Blood tests to measure levels of pituitary, thyroid, and adrenal hormones.
- X-rays, CT (computed tomography) scans, or MRI (magnetic resonance imaging) to detect a tumor.

HOW TO TREAT IT

- Lifelong hormonal replacement therapy is necessary. The specific hormones needed will depend on the nature of the patient's deficiency. To treat adult panhypopituitarism, it is necessary to replace thyroid and adrenal hormones and, in men, testosterone.
- HGH replacement therapy is necessary for children and adolescents to obtain near-normal growth.
- In some cases, doses of corticosteroids (such as hydrocortisone or prednisone) must be increased during periods of stress, illness, infection or surgery.
- It may be necessary to reduce insulin dosage in diabetics who develop hypopituitarism.
- If a tumor causes hypopituitarism, surgery or radiation therapy may be warranted.

WHEN TO CALL A DOCTOR

- Call a doctor if you or your child develop any of the symptoms of hypopituitarism.
- **EMERGENCY** Nausea, vomiting, extreme weakness, dehydration, and fever suggest adrenal insufficiency that may require emergency medical care.

Hypothermia

WHAT IS IT?

Hypothermia is a drop in internal body temperature to a below-normal level. When the body's core temperature drops too low, the heart rate and metabolism slow dramatically, oxygen consumption decreases, loss of consciousness may ensue, and eventually, cardiac arrest may occur. Body temperature below 94°F indicates moderate to severe hypothermia; temperatures between 94°F and 97°F indicate mild hypothermia. The lower the temperature, the more severe the symptoms. (Incidentally, many household thermometers do not register temperatures below 94°F and thus are not reliable indicators of severe hypothermia.) Hypothermia may develop even at moderate external temperatures of 30°F to 50°F, especially in windy or wet weather. (Water conducts heat away from the body about 25 times faster than air.) The elderly are particularly vulnerable, since the ability to regulate body temperature diminishes with age. Hypothermia is the most common killer of outdoor recreationists and constitutes a medical emergency.

SYMPTOMS

- Shivering.
- Numbness.
- Pallor, or a bluish or grayish tinge to the skin (cyanosis).
- Slurred speech.
- Confusion.
- Stumbling.
- Emergency symptoms: drowsiness, dramatically decreased pulse and breathing rate, dilated pupils, loss of consciousness.

WHAT CAUSES IT?

- Exposure to cold air or water, especially in wind and rain. Hypothermia may occur indoors as well, especially among infants or the elderly.
- Risk factors include alcohol use; diabetes mellitus; disorders of the pituitary, thyroid, or adrenal glands; fatigue; and use of beta-blocking drugs (often prescribed to treat hypertension).

PREVENTION

- Wear several layers of warm, woolen clothing in cold or wet weather. Don't stay out too long in the cold if you can help it. Be aware that fatigue, lack of oxygen in high elevations, and alcohol may lead you to disregard discomfort due to cold.
- Avoid nicotine and alcohol before venturing out in cold weather; both interfere with the body's ability to regulate temperature.
- Check often on elderly relatives or friends during cold weather.

DIAGNOSIS

- Diagnosis may be made by observation of symptoms and does not require a doctor.
- A doctor may use a special low-reading thermometer to measure body temperature.

HOW TO TREAT IT

- Call an ambulance or emergency rescue team immediately.
- Someone suffering from hypothermia outdoors should go, or be brought, inside as soon as possible. Wet clothing should be removed and replaced with dry clothing, blankets, or a warm sleeping bag. Make sure the top of the head is covered.
- Skin-to-skin contact is effective for rewarming. Concentrate on rewarming the torso, since rewarming the limbs may in fact draw blood away from the vital organs.
- The patient should lie still until help arrives. Activity forces cold blood from the extremities into the body's core, reducing internal temperature even further. Be very cautious moving an unconscious victim, since heart arrhythmias may result if cold blood from the extremities returns to the heart.
- Warm drinks may be given. Do not offer alcoholic beverages, as they promote heat loss.
- A doctor may administer intravenous fluids. In severe cases, the patient's own blood will be extracted, warmed, and returned to the body.

WHEN TO CALL A DOCTOR

- **EMERGENCY** Call an ambulance or rescue squad if hypothermia develops. Administer first-aid measures as described above until emergency help arrives.

Hypothyroidism

WHAT IS IT?

Hypothyroidism occurs when the thyroid, a gland in the neck that controls body growth and metabolism, produces insufficient amounts of thyroid hormone, thereby slowing all metabolic processes in the body. Symptoms depend on the degree of thyroid deficiency and may develop slowly over many years. (When full-blown symptoms do occur, the condition is known as myxedema.) Although hypothyroidism can occur at any age and in both sexes, it is most common in women over the age of 50. The disorder can be completely controlled with proper treatment. In rare cases, however, severe untreated hypothyroidism may result in myxedema coma, a life-threatening condition that may be precipitated by illness, sedatives, cold weather, surgery, or injury. Untreated hypothyroidism occurring during infancy results in mental retardation and dwarfism (cretinism).

WHAT CAUSES IT?

• Hypothyroidism is frequently due to an autoimmune disorder (such as Hashimoto's disease), wherein the body's natural defenses against infection mistakenly attack the healthy tissue (in this case, the thyroid).
• Hypothyroidism may occur when the pituitary gland, located at the base of the brain, fails to

The thyroid (from the Greek word for "shield," referring to the gland's shape) sits atop the trachea (windpipe) at the base of the neck.

produce sufficient quantities of thyroid-stimulating hormone (TSH), a regulator of the thyroid gland.
• The disorder may occur following surgical removal of the thyroid gland to treat hyperthyroidism or thyroid cancer.
• Medical treatments for hyperthyroidism may also result in hypothyroidism. Radioactive iodine treatment results in permanent hypothyroidism about half the time; hypothyroidism due to antithyroid drugs persists only for as long as the drugs are taken.
• Certain drugs such as lithium can interfere with thyroid function.
• In rare cases, an insufficient dietary intake of iodine may cause hypothyroidism.
• Infants may be born with thyroid defects or with no thyroid at all (very rare).
• Risk of hypothyroidism is greater among those who are over 50 years old, obese, or female.

DIAGNOSIS

• Patient history and physical examination are necessary. Slowed heart and pulse rates, low blood pressure,

SYMPTOMS

• Fatigue, lethargy, and slowed movement.
• Intolerance to cold.
• Unexplained weight gain.
• Constipation.
• Dry, thickened, flaky skin.
• Muscle cramps and weakness.
• Deepened voice.
• Lack of interest in sex.
• Possibly, goiter (swelling in the neck).
• Abnormally heavy, prolonged menstrual periods.
• Puffiness around the eyes.
• Dry, lifeless hair or hair loss.
• Impaired mental faculties.

Hypothyroidism *continued*

and low body temperature suggest hypothyroidism.
• Blood tests are taken to determine levels of thyroid hormone and TSH. (TSH is the most sensitive test for hypothyroidism.)

PREVENTION
• There is no known way to prevent hypothyroidism, although diagnostic screening allows for early detection and treatment in those at risk for congenital hypothyroidism.

HOW TO TREAT IT
• Lifelong hormone replacement therapy with thyroid hormone (thyroxine) is necessary. The lowest effective dose is determined and then maintained. (In the elderly and those with coronary artery disease, hormone replacement is started with a small dose and gradually increased. It is controversial whether or not to initiate such therapy at all in those with slightly elevated TSH but no symptoms.)
• If a large goiter causes breathing or swallowing difficulty, surgical removal may be required.
• Hospitalization is necessary for treatment of myxedema coma (a life-threatening form of hypothyroidism). Intravenous thyroid hormone replacement, as well as steroid therapy, will usually be administered. In addition, oxygen, artificial respiration, fluid replacement, and other intensive care measures may be warranted.

WHEN TO CALL A DOCTOR
• If you experience the symptoms of hypothyroidism, consult a doctor as soon as possible.

IgA Deficiency

WHAT IS IT?

IgA deficiency is a defect in the immune system characterized by an inadequate amount of the antibody known as immunoglobulin A (IgA). Antibodies are large proteins produced by the body to fight infections caused by invaders, such as bacteria, viruses, fungi, parasites, and other foreign agents. The immune system responds to the protein component (antigens) of these invaders by producing large quantities of specific antibodies, including IgA. These antibodies bind to the antigens on the surface of an invader (bacteria, for example) and prevent them from multiplying, thus halting the spread of disease in the body. IgA is found in the saliva, mucus membranes, and intestinal secretions, where

SYMPTOMS
• Frequent or chronic infections of the sinuses, lungs, ears, upper respiratory tract, or gastrointestinal tract.

it may serve as the first line of defense against various sinus, respiratory, and gastrointestinal infections. Consequently, a deficiency of IgA heightens one's vulnerability to such infections. People with IgA deficiency are also more susceptible to certain other disorders, including autoimmune diseases such as rheumatoid arthritis, systemic lupus erythematosus, and chronic hepatitis; respiratory allergies and asthma; irritable bowel disease; and some types of cancer, such as squamous cell carcinoma of the lungs and thymoma (cancer of the thymus gland). However, many people with IgA deficiency are relatively healthy and do not suffer from these infections and disorders as much as might be expected. There is currently no cure, so treatment is aimed at easing symptoms and controlling associated diseases. IgA deficiency is the most common immunodeficiency disorder among Caucasians, affecting roughly one in every 600 people.

WHAT CAUSES IT?
• IgA deficiency is most often a hereditary disorder.
• Some drugs, including certain anticonvulsants, may result in a temporary IgA deficiency.

PREVENTION
• There is no known way to prevent IgA deficiency.

DIAGNOSIS
• The diagnosis is made by detecting low levels of IgA in the blood and the saliva.

HOW TO TREAT IT
• Antibiotics are prescribed to treat bacterial infections. These should be taken for the full term prescribed.
• Nonprescription pain relievers may be taken to treat minor pain and fever. Acetaminophen (not aspirin) should be given to children.
• Measures must be taken to control underlying disorders that may be associated with IgA deficiency. These include malignant tumors, asthma, and autoimmune disorders (such as rheumatoid arthritis and systemic lupus erythematosus).

WHEN TO CALL A DOCTOR
• Make an appointment with a doctor if you or your child develop frequent or persistent infections.

Impacted Teeth

WHAT IS IT?

An impacted tooth is one that cannot emerge normally from the gums and becomes displaced. Most often, the third molars (wisdom teeth) that emerge in the late teens or early twenties become impacted because the jaw is too small to properly accommodate any more teeth. A tooth may also be positioned at an angle before it emerges and thus travel sideways instead of straight. Finally, another tooth may stand as an obstacle and cause a new tooth to emerge crookedly or prevent it from emerging altogether. Although wisdom teeth are most frequently affected, any tooth may be impacted. Often, impacted teeth cause no symptoms and require no treatment. However, in some cases impaction may cause pain or put pressure on other teeth, resulting in misalignment of the bite; in other cases an improperly placed or partially emerged tooth may easily trap food debris and encourage infection and inflammation of the gums. When impaction produces such symptoms, extraction of the tooth is generally advised.

WHAT CAUSES IT?

• Overcrowding of the teeth within the jaw may cause impacted teeth.
• Faulty alignment of teeth may result in misplacement and impaction.

PREVENTION

• Proper dental care during childhood and adolescence, including orthodontic braces if necessary, may prevent impaction.

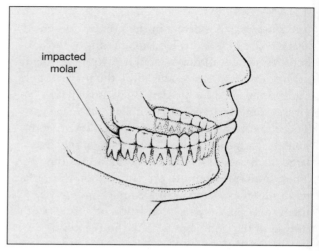

Impacted third molars (wisdom teeth) are very common. Perhaps one explanation is that modern *Homo sapiens* has a smaller jaw than his hominidal ancestors but similar-size teeth.

• See a dentist at least once a year for an examination and professional cleaning.

DIAGNOSIS

• Dental examination.
• Dental x-rays.

HOW TO TREAT IT

• Until you can see a dentist, take over-the-counter pain relievers for minor tooth pain and discomfort. Rinsing with mouthwash or a solution of warm salt water may be soothing as well.
• Antibiotics are prescribed when bacterial infection occurs at the site of the impacted tooth.
• Surgical extraction is the definitive treatment for an impacted tooth that causes problems. Depending upon the position of the tooth, extraction may be performed in the dentist's office under local anesthesia; more complicated extractions are performed by an oral surgeon and may require general anesthesia.

WHEN TO CALL A DOCTOR

• Make an appointment with a dentist if you develop tooth or gum pain.

SYMPTOMS

• Tooth or gum pain.
• Recurring infections at the site of the impacted tooth.
• Foul taste in the mouth and bad breath due to trapped food debris or gum infection.
• Headaches.

Infectious Arthritis

WHAT IS IT?

Infectious arthritis is joint inflammation due to infection by one of any number of various micro-organisms. The infectious organism may enter the joint directly from a wound, or it may spread from a nearby infection (such as a boil), but most often it travels to the joint via the bloodstream from an infection elsewhere in the body. The knee and other weight-bearing joints are the ones most commonly affected. Infectious arthritis is not a permanent condition and does not lead to other forms of joint inflammation, such as osteoarthritis or rheumatoid arthritis. However, if left untreated, it may cause lasting stiffness and limitation of movement in the affected joint.

SYMPTOMS

- A painful, red, warm, swollen, and stiff joint. (Viral arthritis commonly affects more than one joint.)
- Fever (possibly as high as 104°F) and chills.
- Fatigue.
- Skin rash (with Lyme arthritis, as well as gonorrheal, syphilitic, and some varieties of viral arthritis).

WHAT CAUSES IT?

- A bacterial infection in another part of the body may invade a joint (usually only one) and result in infectious arthritis, typically accompanied by severe illness, pain, and fever. Staphylococcus, the strain of bacteria that causes skin infections (boils), is the most common underlying cause, but various other strains may produce infectious arthritis too, including those that cause strep throat, gonorrhea, and tuberculosis. Most cases of bacterial arthritis tend to be acute but relatively short-lived, except for those associated with tuberculosis, which tend to be more mild and progress gradually over a period of months. Gonococcal arthritis is the most common variety among sexually active young men and women, and unlike the other types of bacterial arthritis, it may affect several joints at once, especially those in the hands and wrists.

- Viral infection, including the viruses that cause hepatitis B, rubella, mumps, infectious mononucleosis, and herpes, may cause infectious arthritis. In some cases, the rubella vaccine may be a cause as well. Viral arthritis often affects multiple joints but generally leaves no permanent damage.
- Fungal infection may cause infectious arthritis; it typically progresses more slowly and is more mild than bacterial arthritis.
- Lyme disease, transmitted by a tick bite, may cause recurrent bouts of infectious arthritis (Lyme arthritis) despite initial treatment.
- Syphilis may cause infectious arthritis, although this is now quite rare.
- Factors that heighten risk for infectious arthritis include rheumatoid arthritis or gout; immunosuppressive therapy; systemic illness; corticosteroid injections; recent arthroscopy, prosthetic joint replacement, or injections into a joint; intravenous drug use; and joint injury.

PREVENTION

- Obtain prompt treatment for infections elsewhere in the body.

DIAGNOSIS

- Fluid culture from the swollen joint. Fluid may be withdrawn with a needle and syringe (arthrocentesis). Surgery (arthrotomy) may be required to obtain fluid from some joints, like the hip.
- Blood culture.
- X-rays, CT (computed tomography) scans, or MRI (magnetic resonance imaging).

HOW TO TREAT IT

- Antibiotics are prescribed to treat bacterial infections and Lyme arthritis. These drugs should be taken for the full term prescribed—which may be as long as six weeks or more in severe cases—even if symptoms subside before that time. Failure to do so can permit the strongest, most virulent strains of the underlying organism to survive and multiply, which may result in an even more severe rebound infection that is harder to treat. For acute bacterial infections, antibiotics are often initially delivered in very high doses by injection.

Infectious Arthritis *continued*

• Aspirin or other nonsteroidal anti-inflammatory drugs (NSAIDs) may be administered to reduce pain and inflammation in viral infections.

• More potent painkillers, such as narcotics, may be prescribed in severe cases.

• Amphotericin B, an antifungal antibiotic, may be used for fungal infections.

• Your doctor will drain fluid from the affected joint daily, sometimes as often as several times per day, during the first week of treatment.

• Surgery (arthrotomy) may be required for fluid drainage of some joints, such as the hip or shoulder.

• Infection in a prosthetic joint usually requires removal of the prosthesis. A new one can be implanted after intensive treatment cures the infection.

• Immobilization of the joint is necessary during the healing process. This may require bed rest in addition to a cast or splint.

• Physical therapy may be necessary after the infection has subsided, to regain mobility and strength in the affected joint.

WHEN TO CALL A DOCTOR

• Call a doctor immediately if you develop symptoms of infectious arthritis. Prompt treatment may help prevent permanent damage to the joint.

• Call a doctor immediately if you have rheumatoid arthritis or gout and you develop arthritic symptoms that do not respond to the medication prescribed for flare-ups.

Influenza

WHAT IS IT?

Influenza, commonly know as the flu, is a highly contagious viral infection of the respiratory tract. Often occurring as an epidemic, flu results from three kinds of *Myxovirus influenzae*: types A, B and C. Type A viruses tend to be the most virulent, and constantly mutate into new strains, making immunization against them difficult. Thus, type A influenza is most often responsible for large epidemics. The type B virus, generally a less severe variety, mutates occasionally, causing smaller, more localized outbreaks. Type C, which causes only mild illness resembling a common cold, is a very stable virus. During an initial bout with a type C infection, the body produces antibodies that confer 491immunity against future infections. Symptoms of all types of influenza usually appear following an incubation period of one to four days after initial exposure, and run their course over a period of seven to 10 days. Occasionally, however, the virus may lead to further, potentially serious complications such as bacterial bronchitis, pneumonia, or sinusitis; the elderly, the very young, and those who suffer from major chronic illnesses are particularly vulnerable to such risks.

SYMPTOMS
- Sudden onset of chills and fever (usually between 101°F and 104°F).
- Muscle aches.
- Dry cough.
- Sore throat and hoarseness.
- Headache.
- Loss of appetite.
- Nasal congestion or runny nasal discharge.
- Chest pain.

WHAT CAUSES IT?
- Influenza is usually contracted by inhaling contaminated droplets expelled into the air during coughing or sneezing by an infected person. Most often, outbreaks occur in winter, when people tend to remain inside and are in close proximity to one another.

DIAGNOSIS
- Diagnosis is usually self-evident from symptoms; a visit to a doctor is rarely necessary.

PREVENTION
- A yearly flu vaccination is recommended for those at high risk of developing complications. Conditions that confer high risk include chronic heart or kidney disease; chronic lung disease (including asthma, emphysema, chronic bronchitis, tuberculosis, or cystic fibrosis); diabetes mellitus or other chronic metabolic disorders; severe anemia; and depressed immunity due to diseases (such as AIDS) or medical treatments (such as chemotherapy for cancer). Also, those over age 65 or who live in a nursing facility are at heightened risk. The vaccine should be administered well before the beginning of flu season (as early as October 15 but no later than Thanksgiving) to provide maximum protection.
- Avoid close contact with those infected with influenza.

HOW TO TREAT IT
- Get plenty of bed rest, preferably in a warm, well-ventilated room.
- Take over-the-counter pain relievers to ease aches and reduce fever. (Give acetaminophen, not aspirin, to children.)
- Drink plenty of fluids to keep mucus secretions thin and easy to expel.
- Drink warm liquids or gargle with salt water to alleviate a sore throat.
- A cool-mist humidifier may help to thin mucus secretions.
- For the elderly or those with a serious chronic illness, the antiviral drug amantadine may help reduce the severity of symptoms from type A infections if administered within 24 hours of onset.

WHEN TO CALL A DOCTOR
- See a doctor if flu symptoms do not improve after a week to 10 days.
- Those with any of the conditions that carry a high risk of complications (see Prevention above) should consult a doctor immediately if flu exacerbates an underlying illness.

Inguinal Hernia

WHAT IS IT?

A hernia (sometimes referred to as a rupture) is a protrusion of soft tissue, such as a portion of the intestine, through a weak spot in a muscle, usually in the abdominal wall. The most common type—the inguinal hernia—occurs where the abdomen meets the thigh in the groin region. Men are more susceptible to this type of hernia because of a residual weakness along the path (inguinal canal) where the testicles descended into the scrotum prior to birth. But any weakness in the abdominal wall—whether due to injury, strain, aging, or a congenital defect—can promote the formation of one of the two types of inguinal hernia. In a direct inguinal hernia (the more common of the two), the abdominal organs push through a weak spot in the abdominal wall to create a visible bulge in the groin area. In an indirect inguinal hernia, which only occurs in men, the tissue protrudes farther down through the inguinal canal, entering the scrotum. In either case, if the hernia can be pushed back into the abdominal cavity, it is said to be "reducible," which, while not an immediate health threat, eventually requires surgical repair. If it cannot be pushed back, the hernia is "nonreducible" (or incarcerated), a condition that may lead to dangerous complications including the obstruction of the flow of the intestinal contents or obstruction of intestinal blood supply (strangulation), leading to tissue death. Intestinal obstruction produces nausea, vomiting, loss of appetite, and abdominal pain and usually requires prompt surgery. A strangulated hernia is extremely painful and requires immediate emergency surgery.

In a direct inguinal hernia, a portion of the intestine pushes through a weak spot in the abdominal wall and may result in a visible bulge in the groin.

SYMPTOMS

- A lump in the groin area that may be evident only when standing or straining and that disappears when reclining.
- Pain at the site of the lump, especially when lifting a heavy object.
- Swelling of the scrotum.
- Excruciating abdominal pain (if strangulation occurs).
- Nausea, vomiting, loss of appetite, and pain (if intestinal obstruction occurs).

WHAT CAUSES IT?

- Congenital or age-related weakness in the abdominal wall.
- In males, improper closure of the abdominal cavity during gestation.
- Increase in pressure within the abdominal cavity owing to heavy lifting, straining, obesity, or pregnancy.

PREVENTION

- When lifting heavy objects, bend your knees, keeping the object close to your chest. Lift using your leg muscles and keep your back straight. Don't strain or hold your breath while lifting.

DIAGNOSIS

- Patient history and physical examination are usually all that are required. Observation of a protrusion in the groin when the patient strains or coughs during examination indicates diagnosis of an inguinal hernia.

Inguinal Hernia *continued*

HOW TO TREAT IT

• In simple cases, the preferred treatment is herniorrhaphy, in which soft tissue is pushed back into the abdominal cavity and the weak spot is sewn closed. This is now one of the safest and most common of all major operations. Formerly, it required hospitalization, several days of bed rest, and weeks of restricted activity. Thanks to improved techniques, the procedure is now usually done on an outpatient basis under local anesthesia, and the patient can usually return to a normal schedule within a week.

• Larger hernias may warrant hernioplasty, in which a piece of nylon mesh is sutured in place to reinforce the abdominal wall. New muscle eventually grows over the mesh.

• Strangulated hernias require surgical removal of the affected portion of intestine.

• An externally worn truss, once a common remedy, is generally no longer recommended, as it does nothing to address the risk of intestinal strangulation or other associated problems. However, a truss may be useful for those who are too frail to withstand an operation.

WHEN TO CALL A DOCTOR

• See a doctor if you develop the symptoms of inguinal hernia.

• **EMERGENCY** Severe lower abdominal pain warrants immediate medical care; it may be a sign of intestinal obstruction or strangulation.

Insomnia

WHAT IS IT?

Insomnia—difficulty in falling or staying asleep, or waking up too early—is the most common sleep disorder. It may affect people of any age, but its prevalence increases with advancing years. Note that sleep requirements vary greatly: some people need nine hours of sleep per night; some do fine with five. Many who complain of insomnia sleep more than they think they do. Although persistent insomnia may be frustrating and even debilitating, self-treatment is often successful.

SYMPTOMS

- Difficulty falling asleep.
- Waking often during the night or waking significantly earlier than desired.
- Daytime fatigue, drowsiness, inability to concentrate, or irritability.

WHAT CAUSES IT?

- Psychological distress—due to emotional upset, a different or noisy sleeping environment, or worrying about the next day—is the most common cause of insomnia. Chronic anxiety, depression, and mania may cause more persistent sleep disturbances.
- Caffeine and other stimulants are common causes. Even a cup or two of coffee or tea during the day may lead to insomnia in susceptible people.
- Alcoholic beverages disrupt the sleep cycle and cause frequent awakenings. Chronic alcoholism may cause sleeping problems that persist for years, even after drinking is discontinued.
- Paradoxically, sleeping pills may cause insomnia. They tend to lose their effectiveness after a few weeks, and withdrawal may cause rebound insomnia.
- Other disorders—including certain heart or lung conditions, an overactive thyroid gland, gastrointestinal disorders, arthritis, and many more—may cause insomnia. Prostate disorders, kidney disease, and diabetes may cause frequent awakenings throughout the night, owing to the need to urinate.
- Other causes include a sedentary lifestyle, exercising vigorously too late in the day, recent surgery, and pregnancy (especially the last month).

PREVENTION

- Avoid or minimize caffeinated beverages.
- Within three hours of going to bed, do not drink alcoholic beverages, smoke, or eat a large meal (although a small bedtime snack may be advised).
- Avoid taking amphetamines or other stimulants (unless directed otherwise by your doctor).
- Moderate exercise during the day should help you feel tired at night.
- If possible, go to bed and get up at set times each day, and resist the temptation to take unscheduled naps.
- Prior to bedtime, restrict reading or television watching to light, calming, or even slightly dull topics, and try to avoid worrying. (It may help to set aside a regular time during the day to think about problems and possible solutions.) Take a warm bath or drink a glass of warm milk to relax.
- Use your bed only for sleeping and intimacy; that is, don't watch television, talk on the phone, or do paperwork in bed.

DIAGNOSIS

- Your doctor may ask you to keep a log of sleeping patterns.
- In cases with no obvious cause, the doctor may advise an overnight stay at a sleep-study laboratory to monitor brain-wave patterns, breathing, muscle activity, and other body functions.

HOW TO TREAT IT

- Follow preventive tips.
- If you are unable to fall asleep or if you wake up and cannot get back to sleep, get out of bed and stay up until you feel tired and drowsy.
- Psychological counseling may help relieve the anxiety or depression that prevent sleep.
- Your doctor may prescribe a benzodiazepine tranquilizer (such as Valium or Xanax) to be taken on a short-term basis. Use such medications only under a doctor's supervision.

WHEN TO CALL A DOCTOR

- Make an appointment with a doctor if insomnia interferes with normal activities and persists despite self-treatment.

Intervertebral Disk, Herniated

WHAT IS IT?

A herniated disk, also known as a prolapsed or slipped disk, is a protrusion of the central portion of one of the flat, circular pads found in the joints between the bones of the spine (vertebrae). Each disk has a soft and gelatinous inner portion, surrounded by a tough outer ring. Weakness or trauma may allow the inner portion to push through the outer ring—in some cases compressing one of the spinal nerves, which causes pain and numbness in the neck or along an arm or leg. The intervertebral disks in the neck and especially the lumbar spine are the most likely to rupture. A prolapsed disk can cause symptoms by pressing either on a nerve leaving the spinal cord or on the spinal cord itself.

WHAT CAUSES IT?

• Neck or back injury is the most common cause.
• Weak muscles, obesity, or a sedentary lifestyle may put uneven stress on the spine and cause a herniated disk.
• Herniated disks are more prevalent among men under age 45, after which the growth of extra fibrous tissue around the disks affords greater spinal stability.
• Risk increases again among the elderly, owing to disk degeneration.

PREVENTION

• Bend and lift from the knees, not the waist. Do not strain to lift things that are too heavy.
• Follow a program of moderate, regular exercise to strengthen back and abdominal muscles. Warm up thoroughly before engaging in strenuous activity.
• Lose weight if you are more than 20 percent overweight.

SYMPTOMS

• Back or neck pain that worsens with movement, bending forward, coughing, sneezing, or straining.
• Pain, tingling, or numbness in the buttocks or a leg (sciatica) or an arm, usually on one side.

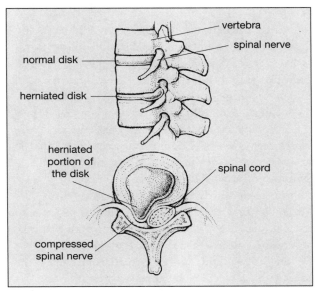

If one of the disks between a pair of vertebrae becomes herniated, it may press on a spinal nerve or the spinal cord, causing symptoms.

DIAGNOSIS

• Patient history and physical examination.
• CT (computed tomography) scans or MRI (magnetic resonance imaging).

HOW TO TREAT IT

• Several days to several weeks of total bed rest often affords complete relief of symptoms.
• Use an ice or heat pack to relieve pain.
• Analgesics, muscle relaxants, and anti–inflammatory medications may be prescribed.
• Removal of the disk through a needle may be performed in some cases.
• Surgery to remove the herniated disk (laminectomy) and, more rarely, to fuse the adjoining vertebrae may be performed in severe cases.
• During recovery, a supportive collar and an extra-firm mattress may be advised. A back brace may be used to provide support during activity.

WHEN TO CALL A DOCTOR

• See a doctor if you develop herniated disk symptoms.
• **EMERGENCY** Call an ambulance immediately if a person suffers a serious back or neck injury. Make sure the patient remains still until help arrives, since any movement may damage the spinal cord.

Intestinal Obstruction

WHAT IS IT?

Intestinal obstruction is a partial or total blockage of the small or large intestine, which impedes the normal passage of digested matter through the intestinal tract, preventing the excretion of feces and, in cases of total blockage, even gas. Symptoms depend on the location of the obstruction and whether it is partial or complete. Blockage in the small intestine causes paroxysms of abdominal pain and vomiting that may lead to dehydration and possibly shock. Symptoms (intractable constipation and pain) develop more slowly in large-bowel obstruction. A partial blockage that allows only liquid to pass can result in diarrhea instead. The most obvious feature of intestinal obstruction is progressive abdominal swelling as gas, fluid, and fecal matter build up. If the obstruction restricts blood supply to the intestine, there is an increased risk of tissue death or intestinal perforation, both life-threatening conditions. Complete blockage of the small intestine, if left untreated, can cause death within hours.

SYMPTOMS
- Intermittent bouts of painful cramping.
- Vomiting.
- Progressively painful abdominal swelling.
- Progressive constipation, leading to an inability to pass feces or, sometimes, even gas.
- Uncontrollable hiccuping.
- Diarrhea (occurs with partial obstruction).
- Low-grade fever (less than 100°F).
- Weakness or dizziness.
- Breath odor.

WHAT CAUSES IT?

- Adhesions (internal scar tissue) from prior abdominal surgery. (These are the most common cause of bowel obstruction.)
- A strangulated hernia (a portion of small intestine protruding through a weak spot in the abdominal wall, so that its blood supply is cut off).
- Colon cancer.
- Diverticulitis (inflammation of small balloonlike pouches along the wall of the colon).

- Volvulus (a twist or knot in the bowel).
- Intussusception (collapse of one segment of intestine into an adjacent segment, much like a telescope).
- Impacted food or feces.
- Gallstones.
- Rarely, a swallowed foreign object that becomes lodged in the digestive tract.
- In paralytic (or adynamic) ileus, the intestine ceases to contract and move its contents along. It almost invariably follows abdominal surgery and lasts a few days before (unlike other causes) it resolves on its own.

DIAGNOSIS

- Patient history and physical examination.
- X-rays to locate the site of obstruction.
- Colonoscopy (use of a flexible, lighted viewing tube to inspect the large intestine).
- Barium enema. (Barium provides a clear image of the colon on an x-ray.)

PREVENTION

- Follow a high-fiber diet.

HOW TO TREAT IT

- Intestinal obstruction is a medical emergency requiring immediate professional treatment. Do not attempt to treat it yourself using enemas or laxatives.
- Initially, doctors will decompress the distended abdomen by removing fluid and gas through a long flexible tube passed through the nose or mouth into the stomach.
- In most cases, surgery is necessary to clear a mechanical intestinal obstruction. Six to eight hours of preoperative preparation are often necessary to restore fluid and electrolyte (essential mineral) balances, in order to prevent dehydration and shock.
- Bowel resection may be necessary. After removal of the affected portion of the intestine, the severed ends may be rejoined, although ileostomy or colostomy (surgeries in which an abdominal opening is made so that intestinal waste products may empty into an external bag) may be necessary.

WHEN TO CALL A DOCTOR

- **EMERGENCY** If you experience the symptoms of intestinal obstruction, get immediate medical attention.

Irritable Bladder

WHAT IS IT?

Irritable bladder is a catchall term for any persistent condition that provokes the muscles in the bladder to contract involuntarily, resulting in a sudden, urgent, uncontrollable need to urinate (urge incontinence). Numerous stimuli can intermittently irritate the bladder and override conscious attempts to inhibit the voiding reflex, sometimes resulting in large-volume accidents that may occur either during the day or while sleeping. The mechanisms that trigger irritable bladder are sometimes difficult to determine; identifying an underlying cause often leads to effective treatment. Irritable bladder is fairly common, especially among women.

> ## SYMPTOMS
> - Sudden urgent need to urinate.
> - Accidental voiding of urine, sometimes in large volumes.
> - Frequent urination, both during the day and at night.

WHAT CAUSES IT?

- In many cases the cause is unknown.
- Urinary tract infections.
- Bladder stones.
- Pregnancy.
- Damage to the nerves that control bladder function, causing excessive contraction of the bladder.
- Obstruction of the outflow of urine, for example, because of a tumor, urethral stricture, or an enlarged prostate.
- A reaction to the use of a urinary catheter, as is sometimes needed in the hospital.

PREVENTION

- Because it is difficult to identify the underlying cause of irritable bladder, the disorder is difficult to prevent.

DIAGNOSIS

- Patient history and physical examination.
- An "incontinence chart" or voiding record of the time, amount, and circumstances of urination.
- Catheterization of the bladder to measure the amount of urine remaining after urination.
- Observation of the effects of filling the bladder through a catheter.
- Microscopic examination and culture of urine, to determine if a urinary tract infection underlies the problem.
- Cytoscopy (use of a lighted scope to view the bladder).
- A voiding cystogram (an x-ray taken while the patient urinates).

HOW TO TREAT IT

- When irritable bladder is due to bacterial infection, antibiotics are given.
- In some cases bladder control can be regained or improved with a technique known as bladder training. The technique begins by scheduling a bathroom visit every two hours, whether the patient needs to use the bathroom or not. The interval is gradually increased by a half hour at a time, toward a goal of four-hour intervals. In many cases the body adapts to this schedule, eliminating incontinence.
- Antispasmodic, antihypertensive, and other drugs may be prescribed to relax bladder muscles and so prevent uncontrolled contractions of the bladder.
- Although adult diapers and pads are widely advocated by advertisers, they may actually promote complications, so they are not recommended for anything but very short-term use unless otherwise advised by a doctor.

WHEN TO CALL A DOCTOR

- Consult a doctor for any repeated episodes of urinary incontinence.

Irritable Bowel Syndrome

WHAT IS IT?

Irritable bowel syndrome (IBS) is a common gastrointestinal disorder (often referred to as spastic colon) characterized by intermittent periods of constipation and diarrhea. After partly digested food leaves the stomach, it is moved along through the small and then the large intestine by regular contractions (peristalsis) of the muscles in the intestinal wall. In IBS, these muscles go into spasm and move residues either too quickly (causing diarrhea) or too slowly (causing constipation). IBS should not be confused with the more serious irritable bowel diseases (see Colitis, Ulcerative, and Crohn's Disease). There is no cure for IBS; however, it is often possible to relieve symptoms with a combination of diet and stress management. IBS is more common in women than men.

SYMPTOMS

- Constipation or diarrhea, or alternating bouts of both.
- Diarrhea.
- Excess gas.
- A feeling that the bowels do not empty completely.
- Abdominal cramps, pain, or bloating.
- Nausea.

WHAT CAUSES IT?

- The cause of IBS is unknown.
- Emotional stress may be a contributing factor.
- Certain foods may trigger flare-ups. Common irritants include high-fat foods like bacon, poultry skin, vegetable oils, and margarine; dairy products such as milk, ice cream, cheese, and butter; and gas-producing foods like beans and broccoli.

PREVENTION

- There is no known way to prevent irritable bowel syndrome; however, those who are diagnosed with IBS can learn to minimize symptomatic episodes through dietary modifications and stress management techniques (such as meditation or biofeedback).

DIAGNOSIS

- Patient history and physical examination. Diagnosis is made by ruling out other disorders, such as cancer and regional enteritis.
- A barium enema may be necessary. Barium creates a clear image of the colon on an x-ray.
- A small, lighted viewing tube may be used to inspect part or all of the large intestine (sigmoidoscopy or colonoscopy).

HOW TO TREAT IT

- Eat a low-fat diet.
- Experiment with fiber intake in the diet. Some people find that symptoms are relieved by a diet rich in high-fiber foods (raw fruits and vegetables, bran, whole-grain breads, and dried legumes). Others find that a high-fiber diet increases symptoms.
- Smaller, more frequent meals may be easier to digest.
- Psychological counseling may aid in stress management.
- Regular, moderate exercise may reduce stress and relieve symptoms.
- Your doctor may prescribe laxatives, antidiarrheal medications, antispasmodics, bulk-forming agents (psyllium), or tranquilizers.
- Don't smoke.

WHEN TO CALL A DOCTOR

- Make an appointment with a doctor if symptoms of IBS interfere with normal activities.

Jaw Dislocation or Fracture

WHAT IS IT?

Dislocation of the jaw occurs when the lower jaw-bone (mandible) becomes displaced from one or both of the joints connecting it to the base of the skull (temporomandibular joints). Because these joints tend to be unstable, they are the ones most commonly dislocated, and recurrences are likely following an initial incident. A jaw fracture is a break in the mandible, usually due to a forceful blow. A severe jaw fracture warrants immediate emergency medical care.

WHAT CAUSES IT?

• Automobile crashes, industrial accidents, and falls are the most common causes of jaw injury. Sports injuries and physical assault are also common causes.
• Some people have especially weak temporomandibular joints, so that opening the mouth very widely—for example during yawning or eating a large sandwich—may cause the jaw to dislocate.

PREVENTION

• Wear seat belts in the car and drive defensively. Wear a helmet if you ride a motorcycle or bicycle.
• Wear protective head gear when playing sports.

DIAGNOSIS

• Patient history and physical examination.
• X-rays of the jawbone (mandible) and temporo-mandibular joints.
• CT (computed tomography) scans of the facial and skull bones.

HOW TO TREAT IT

• A simple dislocated jaw often may be snapped back into place. However, recurrent dislocations

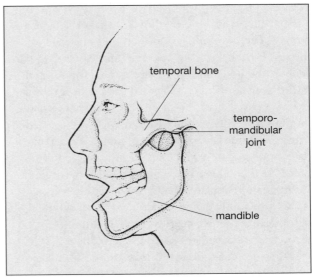

The mandible (jawbone) can become dislocated from the temporo-mandibular joint fairly easily; extreme force may fracture the mandible.

warrant examination and evaluation by a doctor.
• Get to an emergency room immediately for more serious jaw injuries (fractures or very painful dislocations).
• Do not try to talk with an injured jaw; write notes instead.
• The doctor or oral surgeon may insert a tube through the mouth and into the throat to ease breathing.
• The doctor will reset the jaw manually (for a minor dislocation) or surgically (for a severe dislocation or fracture). After it is reset, a fractured jaw is immobilized by wiring the upper and lower teeth together while the bones heal.
• A liquid diet is necessary during recovery (a fracture may take up to six weeks to mend). Do not resume eating solid foods without your doctor's permission.
• Analgesics and muscle relaxants may be prescribed.
• During recovery from a dislocation, avoid opening your mouth too widely. For example, put your fist under your jaw when yawning.

WHEN TO CALL A DOCTOR

• **EMERGENCY** See a doctor or call an ambulance immediately if you sustain a serious jaw injury.

SYMPTOMS

• Inability to close the mouth normally.
• Painful, swollen, or numb jaw.
• Misalignment of teeth.
• Speaking difficulty.
• Drooling.
• Emergency symptoms: breathing difficulty, heavy bleeding.

Kidney Cancer

WHAT IS IT?

Kidney cancer is the growth of malignant cells in a kidney. The two kidneys, located on either side of the lower back, regulate the fluid and electrolyte balance in the body and filter wastes out of the blood into the urine. Urine collects in the portion of the kidney known as the renal pelvis; from there it passes through a narrow conduit (the ureter) to the bladder. There are three distinct types of kidney cancer: Renal cell carcinoma (RCC) and transitional cell cancer (TCC) affect adults almost exclusively, while Wilms' tumor usually affects children under five. RCC (previously called hypernephroma), which arises in tiny tubules deep within the kidney, accounts for 85 percent of all kidney cancers. TCC arises in the renal pelvis and may also be found in the ureter and bladder. The affected kidney is removed unless the cancer has spread to distant sites. Only one kidney is necessary, as the remaining one compensates for the kidney that is removed. With early diagnosis and treatment, the outlook for kidney cancer is optimistic, especially for Wilms' tumor.

SYMPTOMS

- Blood in the urine. Urine may appear dark, smoky, or cloudy.
- Abdominal pain.
- Pain or discomfort in the lower back.
- Abdominal mass (especially in Wilms' tumor).
- General feeling of poor health.
- Fever (with RCC).
- Fatigue.
- Nausea and vomiting.
- Loss of appetite and weight loss.
- A variety of systemic symptoms due to hormones produced by RCC.

WHAT CAUSES IT?

- The cause of kidney cancer is unknown.
- Hereditary factors may play a role in RCC.
- Smokers have a greater risk of kidney cancer.
- Those on dialysis for kidney failure have a greater risk of RCC.
- High blood pressure may be a risk factor for RCC.
- Overuse of analgesics, like aspirin and phenacetin, is associated with greater risk of TCC.
- Toxic industrial chemicals may promote TCC.

PREVENTION

- Don't smoke.
- Avoid high doses or long-term use of analgesics unless recommended by a doctor.

DIAGNOSIS

- Patient history and physical examination. The doctor will press upon the flanks and abdomen to detect any abnormal solid masses.
- Urine is examined for blood.
- An x-ray of the kidney may be taken after injection with a contrasting dye (intravenous pyelogram).
- Ultrasound, CT (computed tomography) scans, and MRI (magnetic resonance imaging) may be done to determine the nature of a kidney abnormality and to see if cancer has spread.
- If tests do not reveal whether a kidney growth is solid or cystic, a needle may be inserted through the back (under local anesthesia) to check for fluid.
- Cystoscopy (the use of a thin, lighted tube that allows a surgeon to see the bladder directly) may help to diagnose TCC.
- Chest x-rays and bone scans may be used to determine if cancer has spread.

HOW TO TREAT IT

- Surgical removal of the affected kidney (nephrectomy) is almost always recommended, unless RCC has spread to distant sites. For TCC, the ureter and part of the bladder may also be removed.
- Radiation and chemotherapy may be used to destroy cancer cells prior to, in conjunction with, or (if cancer has spread to distant sites) in lieu of surgery.
- Experiments with various forms of immunotherapy (interferon, interleukin-2, activated lymphocytes) have shown some promise for RCC that has spread.
- Wilms' tumor responds well to a combination of nephrectomy, radiation, and chemotherapy.

WHEN TO CALL A DOCTOR

- Call a doctor if you notice blood in the urine or if you develop other symptoms of kidney cancer.

Kidney Cysts

WHAT IS IT?

Cysts (spherical, thin-walled fluid-filled sacs) may develop within the tissues of the kidneys singly or in groups. Single kidney cysts are not a health risk and are common after age 50. While cancer or infection may develop within a cyst, such complications are very rare. However, polycystic kidney disease, a common inherited disorder, may lead to the formation of hundreds of cysts, abnormally enlarged kidneys, and eventual kidney failure. (The disease may also cause cysts to develop in many other organs, especially the liver.) Some children are born with the full-fledged disorder (usually resulting in stillbirth or death during infancy), and others develop it early in life. More often, however, symptoms of polycystic kidney disease begin by ages 30 to 40. Major complications include respiratory distress, liver disease, kidney failure, hypertension, and congestive heart failure. There is yet no cure for polycystic kidney disease; goals of treatment are to preserve kidney function as much as possible, to prevent complications, and to alleviate symptoms. Renal failure is rare before age 40, and normal kidney function is maintained in about half of patients at the age of 70.

WHAT CAUSES IT?

• The cause of single kidney cysts is unknown.
• In adults, polycystic kidney disease is inherited and, in fact, is the most common hereditary disease in the U.S.

SYMPTOMS

• Pain or tenderness in the lower back or abdomen.
• Blood in the urine.
• Frequent need to urinate at night (nocturia).
• In infants, visibly enlarged, protruding kidneys.
• Burning on urination and abdominal pain due to associated urinary tract infections (see Bladder Infection for more information).
• Frequent urination, fatigue, swollen ankles, shortness of breath, and itching skin due to end-stage renal disease (see Renal Failure, Chronic for more information).

PREVENTION

• There is no known way to prevent either kidney cysts or polycystic kidney disease.
• If you have a family history of polycystic kidney disease, get regular checkups to aid in early diagnosis.

DIAGNOSIS

• Patient history and physical examination. The doctor will press on the flanks and abdomen to detect any solid, abnormal masses.
• Diagnosis of polycystic kidney disease in infants is confirmed by the presence of large bulges below the ribs on either side of the body.
• Blood and urine tests.
• Ultrasound or CT (computed tomography) scans of the kidneys.
• A test, known as gene linkage analysis, can detect the genetic abnormality responsible for polycystic kidney disease, but the test is expensive and rarely necessary.

HOW TO TREAT IT

• Asymptomatic cases do not require treatment.
• Needle aspiration, in which the doctor inserts a needle into the kidney to drain an enlarged or painful cyst, may be done.
• Antibiotics may be prescribed to treat associated urinary tract infections. Antibiotics should be taken for the full term prescribed.
• Antihypertensive drugs may be prescribed to treat associated high blood pressure.
• Dialysis is necessary should kidney failure occur. This procedure filters the blood artificially, removing waste products and excess fluid when the kidney can no longer perform these functions (see Renal Failure, Chronic for more information).
• A kidney transplant is an alternative to dialysis in cases of kidney failure.

WHEN TO CALL A DOCTOR

• Call a doctor if you develop symptoms of kidney cysts or polycystic kidney disease.
• Make an appointment with a doctor if you have a family history of polycystic kidney disease. Genetic counseling may be advised for those considering having children.

Kidney Infection Pyelonephritis

WHAT IS IT?

Pyelonephritis is an infection of the kidneys, most often caused by bacteria. The kidneys filter waste products from the blood and produce urine, which passes to the bladder via the ureters (see illustration). The bladder stores urine, which leaves the body via the urethra. Normally, urine is sterile; it contains no bacteria or other microorganisms. However, bacteria may enter the urethra and travel back up the urine stream to the kidneys, causing an infection. (In most cases, these are bacteria that normally inhabit the anal area with no ill effect.) Bacteria may also travel to the kidneys from infections elsewhere in the body via the bloodstream. Typically, acute pyelonephritis resolves without treatment and also responds well to antibiotics. On the other hand, recurrent or persistent kidney infection, known as chronic pyelonephritis—while rare—may lead to scarring of the kidneys and, in severe cases, kidney failure. Kidney infections are more common in women, because the urethra is considerably shorter and so provides less of a barrier to bacteria.

WHAT CAUSES IT?

• Most often, pyelonephritis is caused by a bacterial infection; fungal infections may also be a cause.
• A greater risk of kidney infection is associated with kidney stones, bladder tumors, enlargement of the

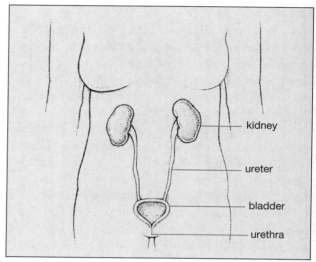

Most urinary tract infections remain confined to the urethra or bladder, but sometimes an infection ascends the ureters to involve the kidneys.

prostate, obstructive lesions of the urinary tract, venereal disease, diabetes mellitus, or the use of a urinary catheter.
• In women, the risk of kidney infection increases with pregnancy and sexual activity.

PREVENTION

• Women should practice careful hygiene. After using the toilet, wipe from front to back to avoid spreading fecal bacteria to the urethra.

DIAGNOSIS

• Patient history and physical examination.
• Urine sample for culture and microscopic analysis.

HOW TO TREAT IT

• Antibiotics are often prescribed to fight the infection and should be taken for the full term indicated.
• Take over-the-counter pain relievers to reduce fever and discomfort, and get sufficient bed rest.
• Drink eight or more glasses of water per day.
• Surgical correction may be needed if a urinary tract obstruction causes recurrent pyelonephritis.

WHEN TO CALL A DOCTOR

• Call a doctor immediately if you develop symptoms of a kidney infection.

SYMPTOMS

• Fever and chills.
• Sudden, intense, persistent pain in the lower back. Pain may be worse on one side and may intensify with movement.
• Joint and muscle pain.
• Nausea and vomiting.
• Burning on urination; frequent and urgent urination; cloudy or discolored urine, possibly with a strange odor (due to an associated bladder infection).
• Fatigue.
• Chronic pyelonephritis generally causes no symptoms until enough renal damage occurs to induce kidney failure.

Labyrinthitis

WHAT IS IT?

Labyrinthitis is an inflammation of the semicircular canals—the three small, curved tubes in the inner ear that help maintain balance. Each canal is filled with a fluid called endolymph and contains tiny calcium stones known as otoliths. The walls of these canals are lined with patches of hairlike fibers. Movement of the head causes the otoliths to move and press upon the fibers. When bent, these fibers send signals to the brain so it can calculate the head's position. Inflammation of the semicircular canals interferes with this process, sending conflicting signals to the brain, which causes severe dizziness and nausea. Although the symptoms may be frightening, labyrinthitis is not serious, and full spontaneous recovery is common.

WHAT CAUSES IT?

- Bacterial or viral infections.
- Allergies.
- Alcohol abuse.
- Certain medications, such as aminoglycosides.
- Head injury.
- Labyrinthitis may occur as a complication of cholesteatoma, a cystlike tumor in the middle or inner ear (see Cholesteatoma for more information).

SYMPTOMS

- Acute onset of vertigo (severe dizziness or a spinning sensation, and loss of balance).
- Nausea and vomiting.
- Ringing in the ears (tinnitus).
- Hearing loss in the affected ear (when labyrinthitis is a complication of a bacterial infection of the inner ear).

PREVENTION

- Obtain prompt treatment for ear infections, bacterial infections elsewhere in the body, and allergies (especially allergies of the upper respiratory tract).
- Drink alcoholic beverages in moderation.

DIAGNOSIS

- Patient history and physical examination are necessary.
- A culture of any discharge from the ear will be taken.

The vestibular labyrinth, deep in the inner ear, is comprised of several structures necessary for balance, including the semicircular canals.

HOW TO TREAT IT

- No specific cure exists for labyrinthitis. Treatment is aimed at easing symptoms as recovery occurs spontaneously, usually after a period of several weeks.
- When labyrinthitis is caused by a bacterial infection, antibiotics will be prescribed, often in large doses.
- Fluid replacement is needed to prevent dehydration if severe vomiting has occurred. This may be done orally or, in severe cases, intravenously.
- Medications such as meclizine (an antihistamine with an antinausea effect), prochlorperazine (an antinausea drug), scopolamine (a motion-sickness drug), and diazepam (a tranquilizer) may be prescribed.
- Rarely, surgery may be required to drain pus from the middle ear or to remove a cholesteatoma (see Ear Infection, Middle and Cholesteatoma for more information).
- During recovery, try to avoid positions that trigger or exacerbate dizziness. Rest in bed in a dark, quiet room with your head immobilized between pillows.
- Until vertigo subsides, do not drive, climb ladders, operate heavy machinery, or perform other activities in which loss of balance may be especially dangerous.

WHEN TO CALL A DOCTOR

- See your doctor if you experience persistent dizziness or other symptoms of labyrinthitis.

Lactose Intolerance

WHAT IS IT?

Lactose intolerance is an impaired ability to digest lactose, a type of sugar found in milk and dairy products. During digestion, lactose is broken down into two simple sugars by lactase, an enzyme found in the small intestine. However, if an insufficient amount of this enzyme is produced, lactose cannot be properly digested, resulting in abdominal discomfort within 30 minutes to two hours after consuming milk or milk-based foods. The degree of lactose intolerance varies from person to person. In most cases, the ability to digest lactose is present at birth but is lost, either suddenly or gradually, between the ages of three and 20. The condition is very common; indeed, it is estimated that over 70 percent of the world's adult population cannot digest lactose, with the exception of people of northern European descent, of whom less than 20 percent are lactose intolerant. Most African-Americans, Asians, and Native Americans produce little or no lactase. Lactose intolerance is not a health risk, and symptoms may be controlled by following simple dietary measures.

SYMPTOMS
- Abdominal pain, cramps, and bloating.
- Excessive gas.
- Diarrhea.
- Audible bowel noises.
- Weight loss or slow growth in infants and young children.

WHAT CAUSES IT?

- Hereditary factors play a role in lactose intolerance.
- Some chronic gastrointestinal disorders, such as irritable bowel disease, regional enteritis, and ulcerative colitis, may cause lactose intolerance.
- In infants, an intestinal infection such as gastroenteritis may cause temporary lactose intolerance.

PREVENTION

- There is no known way to prevent lactose intolerance (although treatment can prevent symptoms).

DIAGNOSIS

- Lactose intolerance is suspected when stomach upset occurs shortly after consuming milk or other dairy products.
- Ability to absorb lactose can be determined by administering lactose orally and measuring the resulting rise in blood glucose (lactose tolerance test), or by measuring the amount of hydrogen subsequently exhaled in the breath (hydrogen breath test).

HOW TO TREAT IT

- Eliminate or reduce the amount of dairy products in your diet, including milk, cream, cheese, butter, and ice cream. Experiment: you may be able to tolerate moderate amounts of milk if consumed with a meal; also, the fat in whole milk may make it easier to digest than skim milk. Lactose-reduced milk with 70 percent less lactose is available.
- Add lactase drops to milk or swallow lactase tablets or caplets just prior to meals. The lactase in these over-the-counter supplements will break down most lactose in dairy products.
- Try yogurt with live cultures. Yogurt contains less lactose than milk, and the bacteria predigest much of what remains. Look for live or active cultures listed on the label (especially bulgaricus cultures).
- Hard, aged cheeses, like cheddar and parmesan, are very low in lactose.
- Substitute soy milk (a liquid made from soybeans) for cow's milk. Soy milk may be fed to babies, poured on cereal, and used in baking.
- Be aware that lactose is commonly found in many foods, including baked goods such as breads, cookies, and cakes; pancake mixes; some powdered drinks such as cocoa and flavored coffees; processed meats such as frankfurters; and some canned and powdered soups.
- Many medications contain lactose as an additive—check with your pharmacist.
- Make sure to get enough calcium in your diet. Broccoli, calcium-fortified orange juice, amaranth (a grain), and legumes are good choices. Your doctor may advise calcium supplements as well.

WHEN TO CALL A DOCTOR

- See your doctor if self-treatment for lactose intolerance does not relieve abdominal discomfort.

Laryngeal Cancer

WHAT IS IT?

Laryngeal cancer is the growth of malignant cells in the larynx (also known as the voice box), an organ composed of the vocal cords and a structure known as the epiglottis, a flap of tissue that prevents food from entering the airway while swallowing. The larynx is located between the pharynx, or throat, and the trachea (the windpipe). Laryngeal cancer can almost always be cured if detected early enough. Thus, it is essential to be alert to persistent hoarseness—the disease's cardinal and often only symptom. Treatment is most successful when the tumor is restricted to the vocal cords. The outlook is less optimistic for cancers that have spread from the larynx to nearby lymph nodes or to other parts of the body via the bloodstream. Some 11,000 cases of laryngeal cancer are diagnosed each year, mostly in those over 50, and 3,700 people die from it annually. Men are affected far more often than women—accounting for about 9,300 annual cases.

WHAT CAUSES IT?

• Like other cancers of the oral and respiratory system, the risk of laryngeal cancer is higher among those who smoke or otherwise use tobacco.
• Heavy use of alcohol is also associated with laryngeal cancer. The combination of drinking and smoking significantly increases risk.

PREVENTION

• Avoid tobacco use and excessive alcohol consumption.

SYMPTOMS

• Hoarseness or other changes in voice quality that persist more than a week or recur.
• Symptoms of cancers arising in parts of the throat other than the vocal cords: swallowing difficulty and pain; a lump or swelling in the neck.
• In late stages: pain, a cough, and breathing difficulty.
• Unintentional weight loss.

DIAGNOSIS

• Patient history (including alcohol and tobacco habits) and physical examination are needed.
• You may be sent to an ear, nose, and throat (ENT) specialist, who will do an indirect laryngoscopy (examination of the throat using a bright light and a pair of mirrors).
• A direct laryngoscopy (use of a flexible lighted scope to inspect the larynx) may be done if the visual exam is suspicious. This is usually performed under sedation or general anesthesia.
• A biopsy (microscopic examination of a tissue sample) may be taken to confirm the diagnosis when cancer is suspected.
• CT (computed tomography) or MRI (magnetic resonance imaging) scans may be done to determine the extent of a tumor.

HOW TO TREAT IT

• Early tumors confined to the vocal cords can be treated successfully with radiation, which can destroy the tumor while leaving the voice intact.
• Laser surgery can also treat some early tumors without affecting the ability to speak.
• More advanced cancers often require a laryngectomy—removal of the larynx. Most often, this will cure the cancer but will result in the loss of normal speaking ability. In such cases a speech therapist can teach the patient alternate means of speaking, such as using the esophagus (the tube through which food passes) as a substitute for the vocal cords, sometimes with the assistance of a surgically placed valve. Speech may also be synthesized with vibrating electromechanical aids placed against the throat.
• Surgery is often followed by radiation.
• Chemotherapy may be tried in advanced cases to prevent or arrest the spread of cancer and to ease symptoms.
• Administration of isotretinoin may reduce the likelihood of recurrence.
• Cure of laryngeal cancer is unlikely if the patient continues to smoke.

WHEN TO CALL A DOCTOR

• Call a doctor if hoarseness persists for more than a week or recurs frequently.

Laryngitis

WHAT IS IT?

Laryngitis is inflammation of the larynx or voice box, the structure in the throat containing the vocal cords. It occurs in two forms: acute, which lasts only a few days; and chronic, which persists over a period of weeks or months. The most common symptom of either form is hoarseness that may, within several days, progress to partial or total loss of the voice. Fever, sore throat, and swallowing difficulty may occur as well. Children face the added risk of encountering breathing difficulty, because the opening of a child's larynx is narrow to begin with, and inflammation restricts the air passages even further (see Croup). Laryngitis may result from prolonged straining of the voice. It may also occur as an isolated local infection of the larynx or as part of another, more serious underlying disorder, such as pneumonia or tuberculosis. In most cases, however, it is a minor ailment and clears up on its own within a few days or weeks.

SYMPTOMS
- Hoarseness.
- Sore throat.
- Weak or absent voice.
- Sensation of a lump in the throat or constant need to clear the throat.
- Dry cough.
- Possibly, fever.

WHAT CAUSES IT?
- Acute laryngitis is most often due to a viral infection, including the common cold and influenza. Bacterial infections (such as tonsillitis, bronchitis, and pneumonia) less commonly cause laryngitis.
- Acute laryngitis may result from excessive strain on the vocal cords, as occurs with activities such as yelling, cheering, singing, or public speaking.
- Postnasal drip, allergies, or inhalation of smoke, fumes, or caustic chemicals can irritate the larynx and cause inflammation.
- Chronic laryngitis may be caused by excessive alcohol consumption, smoking, or constant exposure to dust or chemical irritants like paint remover.
- Chronic upper respiratory tract disorders such as sinusitis, bronchitis, nasal polyps, and allergies can cause chronic laryngitis.
- Repeated episodes of acute laryngitis may eventually lead to chronic laryngitis.
- Gastroesophageal reflux (heartburn) may ulcerate the larynx.

DIAGNOSIS
- Physical examination and patient history.
- Laryngoscopy (viewing the larynx with a flexible, lighted scope).
- Throat culture (if bacterial infection is suspected).

PREVENTION
- Receive prompt treatment for upper respiratory infections.
- Avoid straining your voice.

HOW TO TREAT IT
- If laryngitis is caused by a bacterial infection, antibiotics will be prescribed.
- Avoid speaking during recovery; write notes instead. Be aware that whispering puts greater strain on the vocal cords than normal speaking.
- Inhale steam from a bowl of hot water or a warm shower.
- Drink warm, soothing liquids (but do not drink alcoholic beverages).
- Try a cool-mist humidifier; increased moisture in the air may ease a sore throat. Avoid air-conditioning.
- Nonprescription pain relievers and throat lozenges can ease discomfort.
- Smokers should avoid cigarettes until symptoms have subsided. Giving up smoking entirely is advised for everyone, but for those with chronic laryngitis it is essential.
- The underlying cause of chronic laryngitis must be diagnosed and treated.

WHEN TO CALL A DOCTOR
- If you have the symptoms of laryngitis for more than two weeks despite self-care measures, see a doctor.
- Chronic hoarseness warrants a doctor's attention; it may be an early symptom of laryngeal cancer.
- Call a doctor if symptoms appear in a child who is three months old or younger.

Legionnaire's Disease

WHAT IS IT?

Legionnaire's disease is a form of bacterial pneumonia that may occur in sporadic isolated cases or, more commonly, as a localized epidemic, affecting groups of people aboard a cruise ship or staying in a hotel. Symptoms develop within two days to a week after infection. Progressively severe pneumonia frequently occurs soon thereafter and lasts an additional week. This is followed by either a gradual recovery or by progressively worsening congestion in the lungs that

---

SYMPTOMS

- Headache.
- High fever and shaking chills.
- Muscle aches and stiffness.
- Dry cough in early stages; cough with bloody sputum later.
- Shortness of breath.
- Chest pain.
- Diarrhea.
- Nausea and vomiting.
- Mental confusion, disorientation, and delirium.

---

causes serious breathing difficulty. (In a milder form of the disease known as Pontiac syndrome, symptoms subside in a few days, although fatigue may persist for several weeks.) The prognosis for Legionnaire's disease largely depends on the age and the general health of the patient. Younger people usually recover fully, while the elderly or those in poor health are at risk for potentially fatal respiratory failure. Legionnaire's disease most often affects those who are middle-aged or older and is most prevalent in late summer or early fall.

WHAT CAUSES IT?

- Legionnaire's disease is caused by the *Legionella pneumophila* bacterium, which breeds readily in warm, moist places. Most outbreaks of the disease occur when these bacteria contaminate the air-conditioning systems of large public buildings and are transmitted via airborne vapor droplets. (The infection does not spread from person to person.)
- Smoking and excessive alcohol consumption increase the risk of infection among those exposed to the bacterium.
- Chronic, debilitating illness, such as kidney failure, emphysema, or diabetes mellitus, increases the risk.

DIAGNOSIS

- Patient history and physical examination are necessary.
- A culture of respiratory mucus may be taken.
- Blood cultures may be taken.
- A chest x-ray will be done.
- A lung biopsy may be performed (rarely).

PREVENTION

- Cooling and heating systems should be cleaned and inspected regularly and all filters changed as necessary.

HOW TO TREAT IT

- Hospitalization is usually required.
- Erythromycin (the most effective antibiotic against the *Legionella pneumophila* bacterium) is often given intravenously. This usually alleviates symptoms quickly.
- Intravenous replenishment of fluids and electrolytes (essential mineral salts) may be required.
- Aspirin or aspirin-like drugs are used to reduce fever and ease discomfort.
- Supplementary oxygen may be administered, or in severe cases, a mechanical respirator may be required.

WHEN TO CALL A DOCTOR

- If you develop the symptoms of Legionnaire's disease, call your doctor immediately.
- If, during or after treatment, you experience severe chest pain, bluish nails, lips, or skin, or bloody sputum, see a doctor.

Leukemias

WHAT IS IT?

Leukemia is a disease of the blood-producing structures—the bone marrow and the lymphatic system (the spleen, liver, and lymph nodes)—in which a large number of abnormal white blood cells are produced. Malignant cells are released into the blood, where they circulate throughout the body and may infiltrate other body tissues. Blood contains three broad types of cells. Red blood cells carry oxygen; platelets are crucial for clotting; white blood cells fight infections and are part of the body's immune system. White blood cells are further subdivided into two major types. Myelocytes destroy bacteria and other foreign invaders by engulfing them; lymphocytes produce antibodies that bind to infectious agents to prevent them from multiplying. Immature white blood cells, known as blasts, are produced by the bone marrow and lymphatic system but are not released into the bloodstream until they mature. Normally, the body produces only enough white cells to replace the ones that have died. However, in leukemia, too many blasts and mature white cells are produced. Excessive numbers of white cells in the bone marrow interfere with the production of other types of blood cells. The resulting lack of red cells starves body tissues of oxygen; deficiency of platelets greatly increases the risk of hemorrhage; lack of certain white cells can compromise the immune system. Leukemic cells may spread from the blood to other structures in the body, including the liver, the skin, and the central nervous system.

The different types of leukemia are classified as acute and chronic, according to how quickly the disease tends to progress, and by the type of white cell affected. The acute leukemias are rapidly progressing diseases, usually requiring immediate treatment. The chronic leukemias have two phases, gradual and acute. During the gradual phase, which may last for years, symptoms often do not occur, and treatment may be unnecessary; however, the symptoms and rapid progress of the acute phase of chronic leukemia resemble those of the acute leukemias.

Acute and chronic leukemias are further distinguished by the type of white blood cell affected: acute and chronic myelogenous leukemia (AML and CML) affect myelocytes; acute and chronic lymphocytic leukemia (ALL and CLL) and hairy cell leukemia affect lymphocytes; acute monocytic leukemia affects monocytes. Hairy cell leukemia is a rare chronic leukemia marked by the production of abnormal lymphocytes with irregular hairlike protrusions. Overall, leukemias account for about 5 percent of cancers in the United States. Half of the cases of leukemia are the acute leukemias; ALL is the most common cancer in children, while over 80 percent of cases of AML occur in adults. Of the chronic leukemias, CLL is the most common overall, comprising over one-third of cases in the United States, and CML accounts for one-fifth of cases. Despite leukemia's reputation as a childhood disease, it mainly affects people over 60, especially men. Treatment can bring about remission, although relapse is common,

---

SYMPTOMS

- No symptoms associated with the early stages of the chronic leukemias.
- General feeling of poor health (ALL, AML, CLL, CML, hairy cell leukemia).
- Fever and night sweats due to associated bacterial, viral, or fungal infections. Infections may be frequent because of the weakened immune system and the absence of enough myelocytes for proper defense (ALL, AML, CLL, CML, hairy cell leukemia).
- Severe fatigue, pallor, and breathing difficulty, due to anemia (ALL, AML, CLL, CML).
- Headaches and seizures due to associated meningitis (ALL, AML).
- Increased bruising and bleeding (ALL, AML, CML).
- Bone pain, especially in the legs (ALL, CML, hairy cell leukemia).
- Abdominal pain, nausea, and abdominal distention (ALL, CML, hairy cell leukemia).
- Loss of appetite and weight loss (AML, CLL, CML).
- Swollen glands due to enlarged lymph nodes and spleen (AML, CLL).
- Palpitations (CLL).
- Joint pain due to gout (CML).

Leukemias *continued*

so ongoing treatment is often necessary. In children, the treatment of acute lymphocytic leukemia is a modern success story: 50 to 70 percent achieve long-term remission and are considered cured.

WHAT CAUSES IT?
• The cause of leukemia is unknown.
• Hereditary factors play a role. A genetic abnormality known as the Philadelphia chromosome causes CML; approximately 10 percent of people with ALL have also been shown to have the Philadelphia chromosome.
• Some industrial chemicals, such as benzene, a petroleum derivative, may be associated with leukemia.
• Prolonged exposure to x-rays or radiation (as used in cancer treatment) may lead to leukemia.
• Some medications used in chemotherapy, such as the alkylating agents Mustargen, Leukeran, Cytoxan, and busulfan, may carry a higher risk of leukemia.
• The human T-cell leukemia virus is involved in a rare type of leukemia known as adult T-cell leukemia.

PREVENTION
• Limit exposure to toxic chemicals, as well as to x-rays and other forms of radiation, to reduce the risk of ALL, AML, and CML.

DIAGNOSIS
• Examination of the number of red cells, platelets, and different types of white cells in the blood.
• Bone marrow aspiration or biopsy. A sample of bone marrow is usually taken from the hip bone.
• Cytological (cell) studies are performed to determine the presence of the Philadelphia chromosome.

HOW TO TREAT IT
• Chemotherapy is used to treat the acute leukemias and the acute phases of the chronic leukemias. High doses are used to induce remission, and lower maintenance doses may be continued for months or years to prevent relapses. Bone marrow from the patient may be extracted during a remission and preserved in a frozen state. Removal protects the bone marrow from damage during treatment of a relapse with high doses of chemotherapeutic drugs, after which the preserved marrow cells are given back to the patient.

• Radiation therapy may be used to destroy leukemia cells in the cerebrospinal fluid, central nervous system, spleen, and lymph nodes (ALL, CLL, CML).
• Corticosteroids, usually prednisone, may be prescribed prior to or in addition to chemotherapy (ALL, CLL, the acute phase of CML).
• Bone marrow transplantation may be used to treat and possibly cure leukemia (ALL, AML, CML) if a compatible donor can be found. Bone marrow is more difficult to match than blood; the best results occur with a sibling donor. If that is not possible, a search to find a compatible donor may be done through the National Bone Marrow Registry. Before transplant, the patient is given intensive chemotherapy or total body radiation to destroy leukemia cells. Bone marrow may also be extracted from the patient, subjected to chemotherapy or radiation, and then returned.
• Interferon has been highly successful in the treatment of hairy cell leukemia, with more than 90 percent of patients expected to survive more than five years. Interferon may also be used in the treatment of chronic myelogenous leukemia.
• Surgery to remove an enlarged spleen, one of the sites of white-blood-cell production, may be necessary in hairy cell leukemia and CLL.
• For all forms of leukemia, transfusions of blood, red cells, or platelets may be used during treatment to maintain adequate levels of blood components.
• Analgesics may be prescribed for all forms of leukemia.
• Antibiotics or antifungal medications may be needed to treat associated infections in all forms of leukemia. Common infections are dangerous for the leukemia patient, since both the cancer and its treatment suppress the body's immune system.

WHEN TO CALL A DOCTOR
• Call a doctor if you notice an increased tendency to bruise or bleed, or if you develop severe fatigue, breathing difficulty, bone pain, appetite or weight loss, abdominal pain, swollen glands, palpitations, or fever.
• Call a doctor if your child develops bone pain, an increased tendency to bruise or bleed, fever, or severe fatigue.

Lice

WHAT IS IT?

Lice are small, yellowish gray, wingless insects that live on the body and feed on human blood. There are three species: head lice, pubic lice (crabs), and body lice. Head lice live on and suck blood from the scalp, leaving red spots that may itch severely. Constant scratching may lead to a secondary skin infection. The females lay small, pale, football-shaped eggs (nits) on the hair shafts close to the scalp. These eggs hatch within seven days and then usually live for several weeks. Head lice are spread through direct contact with an infested person. Body lice live in

---

SYMPTOMS

- Intense itching, usually in hair-covered areas.
- Redness and flaking of the skin.
- Tiny red bite marks.
- Visible lice on clothing.
- Visible nits (eggs) on hair shafts.

---

and lay their eggs on clothing and go to the body only when they need to feed. They may transmit typhus or relapsing fever (both infectious diseases characterized by a rash and fever), although this is quite rare. Body lice usually affect people who do not change their clothes often enough. Pubic lice live in pubic hair and are usually transmitted during sexual contact. Less commonly, they may infest beards, armpit hair, and hair around the anus. In general, those at greatest risk for lice infestation are school children and those living in nursing homes or in other crowded or unsanitary conditions. Although lice are terribly annoying and spread quite easily, they are fairly easy to treat and rarely pose a serious health risk.

WHAT CAUSES IT?

- Living in an overcrowded or unhygienic environment increases the risk of lice infestation.
- Lice may be contracted from an infested toilet seat.
- Schoolchildren are often affected because of their close daily contact with schoolmates and the use of communal closets.

- Head lice can be transmitted through use of an infested hairbrush, comb, hat, or set of headphones.
- Pubic lice are most often transmitted through sexual contact with an infected partner but may also be transmitted through contact with infested bedding.

DIAGNOSIS

- Diagnosis is usually based on self-examination. Lice and their eggs, while minuscule, are visible on hair shafts, skin, and clothes.

PREVENTION

- Check your children periodically for lice and nits, especially during peak season (August through November).
- Do not wear the same clothes for more than a day or two. Launder clothes often.
- Bathe or shower frequently.
- Do not share combs, hairbrushes, hats, or other headwear with others.

HOW TO TREAT IT

- Several over-the-counter lotions are available to treat lice. These products should be applied to all infected areas of the body, left on for 12 hours, and washed off. Then, using a fine-tooth comb, remove any dead lice or nits from the hair shafts. One or two more applications of the lotion may be necessary.
- Several shampoos are available for the treatment of head lice. Repeated use of these over several days is usually required.
- Combs and hairbrushes should be washed in very hot soapy water to kill any attached eggs.
- Infested clothing should be washed in very hot water and dried on a high heat cycle for at least 20 minutes.
- Items like towels, bedding, rugs, upholstery, mattresses, and children's stuffed toys should be thoroughly cleaned (or burned if necessary) to avoid reinfestation.

WHEN TO CALL A DOCTOR

- Call a doctor if symptoms persist despite self-treatment.

Liver Tumors

WHAT IS IT?

A liver tumor is an abnormal growth of cells—at times benign but far more often malignant—in the liver. Benign growths may cause symptoms and require treatment in rare cases, but generally they are not a health risk. Malignant tumors are classified as either primary or secondary. Primary tumors, which are relatively uncommon in North America, originate in the liver, either from the liver cells themselves (hepatoma or hepatocellular carcinoma) or from cells of the bile ducts (cholangiocarcinoma). Much more common are secondary, or metastatic, tumors that have spread to the liver from cancers elsewhere in the body. Next to the lymph nodes, the liver is the most common site for the spread of cancer. The outlook for both primary and secondary liver cancers is poor; they are usually fatal within six months to one year of diagnosis. Treatment is aimed at relieving symptoms. Benign tumors are more common among women; malignant ones more common among men.

SYMPTOMS
- Usually no symptoms in early stages.
- Pain or discomfort in the upper-right portion of the abdomen.
- Abdominal swelling.
- General feeling of poor health.
- Loss of appetite and weight.
- Nausea and vomiting.
- Fever.
- Profuse sweating.
- Jaundice.
- Severe fatigue, pale complexion, and breathing difficulty due to associated anemia.

WHAT CAUSES IT?
- The cause of primary liver tumors is unknown.
- The risk of primary liver cancer is increased in patients with cirrhosis, whether due to hepatitis B or C infection, hemochromatosis, or alcoholism.
- Exposure to toxic chemicals, such as polyvinyl chloride vapors or arsenic, may lead to liver cancer.
- Aflatoxins (molds that grow on incorrectly stored peanuts and grains) may contribute to liver cancer.
- Metastatic tumors may spread to the liver from virtually anywhere else, but most commonly from cancers of the colon, stomach, pancreas, lung, and breast.
- The use of oral contraceptives is associated with some benign liver tumors, although this is rare.

PREVENTION
- Consume no more than two alcoholic drinks per day. If you suspect that you may have a drinking problem, seek help immediately. You will need to avoid alcohol completely if you have cirrhosis, and a doctor or support group may help you with this.
- Try to limit exposure to toxic chemicals, like insecticides, herbicides, cleaning solvents, paint thinner, and engine exhaust.
- Get regular checkups if you have a history of hepatitis B or C infections, hemochromatosis, or cirrhosis.

DIAGNOSIS
- Patient history and physical examination. The doctor will press upon the liver to detect any swelling or solid masses.
- Blood tests.
- Ultrasound, CT (computed tomography) scans, or MRI (magnetic resonance imaging) of the liver may be performed.
- A liver biopsy may be performed. Under local anesthesia, a needle is inserted under the ribs and into the liver to extract a small tissue sample for analysis.
- Exploratory surgery may be necessary in some cases.

HOW TO TREAT IT
- Benign tumors that cause symptoms may be removed surgically.
- Chemotherapy may be used to destroy cancerous cells.
- Surgical removal of a single small malignant tumor may be performed. However, surgery is not advised for large malignant tumors or widespread cancer.
- Radiation therapy is used in some cases.
- Liver transplantation is a rare option.

WHEN TO CALL A DOCTOR
- Any symptoms of a liver tumor warrant a doctor's attention.

Lung Abscess

WHAT IS IT?

A lung abscess is a pus-filled cavity within the lungs. Now uncommon, lung abscesses usually result from a severe infection such as pneumonia or tuberculosis or from the inhalation (aspiration) of infectious material from the mouth. An abscess may also develop if a bronchial passage becomes blocked by vomit, food, or some other foreign matter that has trapped lung secretions, allowing them to accumulate and become infected. Generally, coughing expels material that may potentially block the lungs, preventing the formation of abscesses. However, loss of consciousness, for example, owing to a head injury, anesthesia for surgery, or the abuse of drugs or alcohol, may allow infectious material to be aspirated into the lungs and remain there. A tumor may also block bronchial passages and lead to an abscess. An embolus (blot clot) in the blood vessels of the lungs can lead to death of lung tissue and cause an abscess to form. Symptoms may develop over a period of days or weeks. The incidence of lung abscesses has decreased substantially since the advent of antibiotics. Lung abscesses are not contagious and generally respond well to a prolonged course of antibiotics.

SYMPTOMS
- Fever and chills.
- Profuse sweating.
- General feeling of poor health.
- Loss of appetite and weight loss.
- Chest pain.
- Deep cough that may produce foul-tasting or bloody sputum.
- Clubbing of the fingers.
- Fatigue.

WHAT CAUSES IT?
- Lung abscess may occur as a complication of a bacterial infection, such as pneumonia or tuberculosis (although this has become less common).
- Fungal infection of the lungs may lead to a lung abscess.
- Inhalation of foreign matter into the lungs may lead to an abscess, especially in the presence of a tooth abscess or an infection of the gums (see Periodontitis).
- A lung tumor may block bronchial passages (see Lung Cancer for more information).
- Immunocompromised patients, such as those with AIDS or those undergoing treatment for cancer, are prone to lung abscesses.

PREVENTION
- Obtain prompt treatment for upper respiratory infections.

DIAGNOSIS
- Patient history and physical examination.
- Blood and sputum cultures.
- Chest x-rays. If a lung abscess is found, x-rays will be taken periodically throughout treatment to monitor progress.
- CT (computed tomography) scans.
- At times, bronchoscopy (passage of a thin, hollow, flexible tube through the mouth into the windpipe to allow the main bronchial passages to be viewed).

HOW TO TREAT IT
- Antibiotics are prescribed to treat a lung abscess involving a bacterial infection (including tuberculosis or bacterial pneumonia). These should be taken for the full term prescribed (often six weeks or more), even if fever and cough subside within a shorter period.
- Antifungal drugs may be prescribed to treat an underlying fungal infection.
- Your doctor may show you how to drain mucus from your lungs by assuming various positions that lower your head below your torso (a technique known as postural drainage).
- Bronchoscopy may be used to aid drainage in some cases, depending upon the location and size of the abscess. Pus may be drawn out through the scope.
- Surgery may be performed to drain the abscess or, more often, to remove the infected lobe of the lung if the abscess does not respond to antibiotics.

WHEN TO CALL A DOCTOR
- Call a doctor for shortness of breath, wheezing, high fever with chills, or fainting spells, or if a respiratory infection worsens despite treatment.

Lung Cancer

WHAT IS IT?

Lung cancer, the growth of malignant cells in the lungs, is the leading cause of death from cancer in the United States for both men and women. The types of primary lung cancer (cancer that originates in the lungs) may be grouped into two broad categories: small-cell carcinoma and several forms of lung cancer collectively termed non-small-cell carcinoma. Small-cell carcinoma spreads very quickly and is more difficult to treat (although the outlook is poor in all types of lung cancer), and the majority of patients die within a year of diagnosis. Primary lung cancer may spread to essentially any organ—for example, the brain or the bones—where it may produce more disabling symptoms and be more deadly than the primary tumor itself. Most cases occur between the ages of 45 and 75, after years of exposure to cigarette smoke or other pollutants. Primary lung cancer is, in many instances, preventable; over 90 percent of cases are caused by smoking. Nonsmokers have only a small risk, and those who quit smoking—even after smoking for years—greatly reduce their risk. The lungs are also a frequent site of metastatic, or secondary, cancer that has spread from elsewhere in the body. Such tumors are almost always incurable.

WHAT CAUSES IT?

• Cigarette smoking is by far the most common cause of primary lung cancer.
• Air pollution, including so-called passive or second-hand smoke, traffic fumes, and smokestack emissions, may contribute to lung cancer.
• Exposure to toxic substances, such as radon and other radioactive gases, asbestos, and arsenic, may cause lung cancer.
• Chronic bronchitis is associated with an increased risk of lung cancer (see Chronic Obstructive Pulmonary Disease for more information).

PREVENTION

• Don't smoke; try to limit your exposure to second-hand smoke and air pollution.
• Homes may be tested for radon using a kit available in most hardware stores.

DIAGNOSIS

• Patient history and physical examination.
• Sputum sample.
• Chest x-rays, CT (computed tomography), and MRI (magnetic resonance imaging) scans.
• Bronchoscopy (passage of a thin, hollow, flexible tube through the mouth into the windpipe to allow the main bronchial passages to be viewed).
• A biopsy of cancerous tissue is essential to guide treatment decisions.

HOW TO TREAT IT

• Surgical removal is the preferred treatment for non-small-cell carcinomas that have not yet spread. Part or all of the affected lung may be removed, depending on tumor size and location.
• Chemotherapy is used to treat small-cell carcinomas (which are inoperable). High doses of several chemotherapeutic agents are used in an attempt to destroy the tumor.
• Radiation therapy may be used to treat non-small-cell carcinoma in addition to surgery, or for patients ineligible for surgery. In some cases radiation may be used in addition to chemotherapy to treat small-cell carcinoma.

WHEN TO CALL A DOCTOR

• Call a doctor if you develop symptoms of lung cancer.
• Get regular lung examinations if you are 45 or over and smoke heavily.

SYMPTOMS

• Deep cough, sometimes with bloody sputum.
• Wheezing and shortness of breath.
• Chest pain.
• Pain in the shoulder and arm.
• Fever.
• Fatigue.
• Loss of appetite leading to weight loss.
• Clubbed fingers.
• Hoarseness.
• Swollen neck and face; swallowing difficulty.
• Enlarged lymph nodes in the neck.

Lyme Disease

WHAT IS IT?

Lyme disease is an infection caused by a bacterial spirochete (corkscrew-shaped organism) spread by a bite from an infected tick. It is named after the community of Old Lyme, Connecticut, where the disease was first identified. Lyme disease may affect several organ systems, and symptoms vary widely, some arising months or even years after a bite. Left untreated, the infection may affect the brain, heart, and joints, resulting in a type of chronic arthritis (see Infectious Arthritis for more information). The specific kinds of ticks that carry the infection are prevalent in New England, along both U.S. coasts, and in the upper Midwest. They are tiny: adults are the size of a pinhead; nymphs smaller still. Between 20 and 60 percent of ticks carry the bacteria, but there is little risk of infection if the tick is removed within 48 hours. Lyme disease is preventable; it responds well to treatment, especially if given in the early stages of infection, and it subsides spontaneously in some cases.

WHAT CAUSES IT?

• A bacterial infection causes Lyme disease. Ticks acquire the disease from infected mice and deer and may then transfer the bacteria to humans.

SYMPTOMS

• Within two to 30 days after a bite: a small, red, flat or slightly raised lesion at the site of the tick bite, surrounded by a round, bull's-eye-like, red rash with a pale center. The rash may increase in size for several weeks before fading, and similar lesions may appear at other sites. The affected area does not itch but may feel warm to the touch.

• Within 30 days: flu-like symptoms of fever and chills, extreme fatigue, headaches, muscle and joint aches.

• Within several weeks or months: heart palpitations, shortness of breath, temporary facial paralysis, joint pain and swelling.

• Within two years: chronic joint pain, especially in the knees (Lyme arthritis), in about 60 percent of infected people who are not treated.

PREVENTION

• Cover exposed skin when in grassy or wooded areas where ticks may be present. Tuck long pants into socks, wear shoes instead of sandals, and wear long-sleeved shirts. Light-colored clothing makes ticks easier to see.

• Use insect repellent containing DEET (N,N-diethyltoluamide) during outdoor summer activities. Apply repellent to clothing; use sparingly on skin.

• Check skin, clothing, and pets for ticks after an outing. Pets should wear tick-repellent collars.

• Use fine-tipped, curved tweezers to remove a tick attached to your skin. Grasp the tick as close to the skin as possible and pull steadily and firmly to remove it. Avoid squeezing the bloated abdomen, as this may inject bacteria into your skin or bloodstream. Do not touch the tick with your hands, since bacteria from a crushed tick may penetrate even unbroken skin. Preserve the tick by dropping it in rubbing alcohol. Immediately wash your hands and apply antiseptic to the bite.

• Do not use petroleum jelly, kerosene, or a lighted match or cigarette to remove the tick. Contrary to popular belief, these methods are ineffective and may increase the likelihood of infection.

DIAGNOSIS

• Patient history and physical examination.

• Blood tests. Standardized tests to detect Lyme disease do not yet exist, so results may be inconclusive.

• A preserved tick may be examined to determine if it is the type that carries the infectious bacteria.

HOW TO TREAT IT

• Antibiotics are prescribed for as long as 20 days to treat the early stages of Lyme disease, when cures are much more likely.

• Antibiotics may need to be taken for a month or longer to treat chronic arthritis.

• Take over-the-counter pain relievers to reduce fever and inflammation.

• Corticosteroids may be prescribed to treat severe joint pain and inflammation.

WHEN TO CALL A DOCTOR

• Call a doctor if you have symptoms of Lyme disease.

Lymphoma, Hodgkin's Hodgkin's Disease

WHAT IS IT?

Hodgkin's lymphoma is an uncommon form of cancer involving lymphatic tissue in the lymph nodes and spleen. Lymph nodes produce lymphocytes, a type of white blood cell that is crucial in regulating and carrying out most of the activities of the immune system. In Hodgkin's disease, cells in the lymphatic tissues grow in a rapid and uncontrolled manner—the defining characteristic of cancer. If not treated in time, the cancer may spread to other organs, such as the lungs, liver, and bone marrow. In addition, the proliferation of abnormal lymphocytes reduces the number of healthy lymphocytes. The resulting impairment of the immune system leaves the body susceptible to serious infection. However, with prompt detection and treatment, prognosis is good—more than 75 percent of adults diagnosed with Hodgkin's are curable. The mortality rate is dropping more rapidly for this disease than for any other type of cancer in the United States, largely because of advances in therapy. Hodgkin's disease, more common among men, most often affects those between the ages of 15 and 35, and those older than 55.

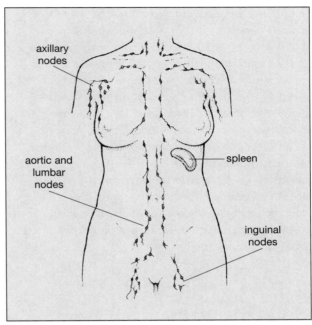

The lymphatic system (which includes the spleen) is comprised of a vast network of glands or nodes essential to the immune system.

SYMPTOMS

- Painless, gradual swelling of lymph nodes, especially in the neck, underarms, or groin. (In a few cases, lymph nodes enlarge rapidly and painfully or may fluctuate in size.)
- Fever, chills, or night sweats.
- Persistent fatigue.
- Weight loss and loss of appetite.
- Itching that worsens as the disease progresses.

WHAT CAUSES IT?

- The cause of Hodgkin's disease is unknown, although hereditary factors may play a role. The incidence appears to be higher among those with immune system disorders or receiving immuno-suppressant drugs (used after organ transplants, for example).

PREVENTION

- There is no way to prevent Hodgkin's lymphoma.

DIAGNOSIS

- Patient history and physical examination.
- Lymph node biopsy, in which a portion of an enlarged lymph node is removed and examined under the microscope. Presence of a specific type of cell (Reed-Sternberg cell) characteristic of Hodgkin's disease provides a definitive diagnosis.
- Other tests, including blood tests; liver, spleen, and bone marrow biopsies; chest x-rays and abdominal CT (computed tomography) scans; and bone or lung scans may be done to determine the extent of lymph node and other organ involvement.

HOW TO TREAT IT

- Successful treatment is based heavily upon a process known as staging, which depends upon the presence or absence of general symptoms, use of a battery of tests to determine how far the cancer has spread, and the microscopic appearance of the lymphatic tissue.
- Radiation therapy alone is used for Stage I as well as for Stage II cancers. Stage I is the earliest and least serious stage, involving only one lymph node region

Lymphoma, Hodgkin's Hodgkin's Disease *continued*

or one organ outside the lymph nodes. Stage II involves two or more lymph node regions or one extralymphatic organ and its nearby nodes, grouped on the same side of the diaphragm muscle, which separates the abdominal and chest cavities.

• Radiation is used in combination with chemotherapy for Stage III Hodgkin's, in which cancer affects lymph nodes above and below the diaphragm.

• Combinations of chemotherapeutic agents alone are used for patients with Stage IV disease (in which cancer has spread widely to other organs), as well as those who relapse after radiation alone. Such therapy, while generally producing the worst side effects of all treatment options, often leads to prolonged or even complete remissions.

• Autologous bone marrow transplantation, in which healthy bone marrow is removed prior to treatment and replaced afterward, may be recommended to preserve bone marrow cells while the rest of the body is subjected to intensive chemotherapy or radiation.

WHEN TO CALL A DOCTOR

• While most incidences of enlarged glands are not a sign of cancer, see a doctor if the swelling persists longer than two weeks, especially if accompanied by fever or night sweats.

• EMERGENCY See a doctor immediately for the sudden onset of a high fever, loss of bladder or bowel control, or numbness in the arms or legs—all potential signs of Hodgkin's disease complications.

Lymphoma, Non-Hodgkin's

WHAT IS IT?

Lymphoma is a relatively rare form of cancer involving lymphatic tissue in the lymph nodes and spleen. Lymph nodes produce lymphocytes, a type of white blood cell that is crucial in regulating and carrying out most of the activities of the immune system. In lymphoma, cells in the lymphatic system begin to grow in a rapid and uncontrolled manner—the defining characteristic of cancer. Hodgkin's disease, the most common form of lymphoma (see Lymphoma, Hodgkin's), has several features that distinguish it from the other types, which are grouped together and collectively known as non-Hodgkin's lymphoma (nHL). The more than 10 kinds of nHL are categorized according to cell type and how fast they grow: low grade (slow growing), intermediate grade, and high grade (rapidly growing). If not treated in time, even low-grade nHL may eventually spread to other organs, such as the lungs, liver, and central nervous system. In addition, the proliferation of abnormal lymphocytes reduces the number of healthy lymphocytes. The resulting impairment of the immune system leaves the body susceptible to serious infection. Prognosis depends upon the grade and the extent of the disease but is generally not as favorable as that for Hodgkin's disease, since nHL is more likely to spread to other organs and has usually done so by the time it is diagnosed.

WHAT CAUSES IT?

• The cause of nHL is unknown, although there is evidence that a viral component may be involved.

• Incidence appears to be higher in those with immune system disorders or those receiving immunosuppressant drugs (used after organ transplants, for example).

PREVENTION

• Non-Hodgkin's lymphoma is not preventable.

DIAGNOSIS

• Patient history and physical examination.
• Lymph node or bone marrow biopsies, in which tissue is removed for microscopic examination.
• Other tests, including blood tests, liver and spleen scans, chest x-rays, or abdominal CT (computed tomography) scans may be done to determine the extent of lymph node and other organ involvement.

HOW TO TREAT IT

• Treatment choices are based upon a process known as staging, which depends upon the presence or absence of general symptoms, use of a battery of tests to determine how far the cancer has spread, and the microscopic appearance of the lymphatic tissue.
• Radiation therapy alone is used for lymphomas (especially low-grade varieties) confined to a single lymph node region or well-defined organ site.
• Since nHL has usually spread by the time it is diagnosed, chemotherapy with a combination of several anticancer agents (like cyclophosphamide, doxorubicin, and vincristine) and corticosteroids may be used, with or without radiation.
• In more severe cases autologous bone marrow donation (in which healthy bone marrow is removed prior to treatment and replaced afterward) may be recommended to preserve marrow while the rest of the body is subjected to intensive chemotherapy or radiation.

WHEN TO CALL A DOCTOR

• While most incidences of enlarged glands are not a sign of cancer, see a doctor if the swelling persists longer than two weeks, especially if accompanied by fever or night sweats.
• **EMERGENCY** See a doctor immediately for the sudden onset of a high fever, intractable constipation, urinary incontinence, or numbness in the arms or legs—all potential signs of lymphoma complications.

SYMPTOMS

• Painless, gradual swelling of the lymph nodes, especially in the neck, underarms, or groin.
• Enlarged tonsils and adenoids.
• Fever, chills, or night sweats.
• Breathing difficulty and coughing in children.
• Persistent fatigue.
• Weight loss and loss of appetite.
• Itching, which worsens as disease progresses.
• Rarely: nausea, vomiting, or abdominal pain.

Macular Degeneration, Age-Related

WHAT IS IT?

The macula is the central and most sensitive portion of the retina, the layer of tissue in the eye that contains the light-receptive nerve cells essential for sight. For unknown reasons, at about age 50 or 60 the macula begins to break down to some extent, resulting in the condition known as age-related macular degeneration (AMD). As the macula deteriorates, central vision and the ability to distinguish fine detail become increasingly impaired, even though peripheral vision remains unaffected. If macular function is lost completely, activities such as reading become impossible. There are two forms of AMD: "dry" (also known as nonexudative or atrophic) and "wet" (exudative). About 90 percent of those with AMD have the nonexudative form, which—while irreversible and essentially untreatable—tends to progress slowly and may stabilize for periods of time, so that most patients experience no serious vision loss. However, in exudative AMD—the more serious form of the disorder—fine blood vessels at the back of the eye proliferate and begin to leak or exude fluid. This may scar the macula, resulting in permanent loss of central vision in a matter of days or weeks. Wet AMD may develop suddenly at any time in patients with dry AMD. In either form, macular degeneration is usually painless and most often affects one eye at a time, but it may eventually occur in both. AMD is the leading cause of severe and irreversible vision loss in the U.S.

WHAT CAUSES IT?

• The cause is unknown, although aging is clearly a risk factor; some evidence of AMD can be detected in approximately one-quarter of all people over the age of 65 and in one-third of those over 80.
• Other risk factors include hyperopia (farsightedness), cigarette smoking, light-colored eyes, and a family history of AMD.

PREVENTION

• There is no known way to prevent macular degeneration.

DIAGNOSIS

• Eye examination by an ophthalmologist is necessary.
• When exudative AMD is suspected, diagnosis is confirmed with fluorescein angiography, which involves injection of a special dye into the bloodstream and allows clear photographic images of the blood vessels in the eye to be taken.

HOW TO TREAT IT

• There are no ways to arrest or reverse the course of dry AMD; however, patients are continually monitored for the onset of wet AMD. In the meantime, the following low-vision optical aids may be useful: high-power reading glasses; a small telescope that can be mounted on one lens of your eyeglasses; a pocket telescope for reading street signs; and a closed-circuit television hookup that can magnify a written page as much as 60 times and display the image on a television screen.
• If detected early enough, exudative AMD can be treated with laser surgery. The intense beam of light destroys the new leaking blood vessels and so retards the progress of the disorder. Such surgery should be performed only by an ophthalmologist with special training and experience.
• Careful follow-up is essential for all AMD patients.

WHEN TO CALL A DOCTOR

• See an ophthalmologist if you develop the symptoms of macular degeneration.
• Those diagnosed with macular degeneration are given a simple home test, known as an Amsler grid, with which they can monitor their own visual changes. Any worsening of symptoms warrants an immediate visit to an ophthalmologist.

SYMPTOMS

• Increasingly blurred central vision.
• Haziness, grayness, or blank spots in the central field of vision.
• Visual distortion. Straight lines appear bent; objects may appear smaller than they actually are.
• Dulled color perception.
• Difficulty reading or doing close work.

Malabsorption

WHAT IS IT?

Malabsorption syndrome is a term for any condition in which one or more essential nutrients or minerals are not properly absorbed by the intestines. Lipids (fats) are the most commonly malabsorbed nutrients, but proteins and amino acids, carbohydrates, electrolytes (such as sodium and potassium), vitamins, and minerals (such as iron and calcium) may be poorly absorbed as well. A multitude of different disorders can result in malabsorption; outlook depends upon the success in treating the underlying cause. Symptoms may range from bouts of gas, diarrhea, and stomach cramps that occur only when certain foods are consumed (see Lactose Intolerance) to emaciation and other signs of severe malnutrition.

WHAT CAUSES IT?

• Any defect in the functioning of the digestive system (for example, an inadequate production of bile salts by the liver, or digestive enzymes by the pancreas or cells in the lining of the intestine) can prevent the proper breakdown of foods necessary for the absorption of nutrients.
• Inflammation or other abnormalities (see Crohn's Disease and Amyloidosis) in the mucus membrane that lines the intestine may prevent nutrients from passing through the intestinal wall.

The small intestine is lined with tiny projections, called villi, that afford optimal surface area for the absorption of fluids and nutrients.

• Surgery to remove diseased segments of the intestine may result in short bowel syndrome, characterized by an inadequate amount of absorptive surface within the organ.
• Infections including acute infectious enteritis and tapeworm or other parasites may inhibit proper digestion. Some infections may result in an overgrowth of intestinal bacteria, which may also lead to malabsorption. Those with AIDS are particularly prone to malabsorption, since the disease damages immune defenses against secondary infections that may cause digestive problems.
• Any obstruction of the lymphatic system, as may occur with lymphomas and tuberculosis, may also interfere with nutrient absorption.
• Certain cardiovascular problems may result in malabsorption (see Congestive Heart Failure and Pericarditis).
• Malabsorption may be induced by certain medications, such as cholestyramine (a cholesterol-lowering drug), neomycin (an antibiotic), colchicine (an anti-gout drug), and certain laxatives.
• Other diseases, including diabetes mellitus, hyper- and hypothyroidism, and carcinoid syndrome, may cause malabsorption for reasons that are unclear.

SYMPTOMS
• Diarrhea.
• Stools that float and are bulky, greasy, and unusually malodorous.
• Excessive gas.
• Abdominal discomfort or cramps, especially after eating.
• Fatigue.
• Weight loss or emaciation.
• Night blindness (from vitamin A malabsorption).
• Easy bruising (from vitamin K malabsorption).
• Bone pain and painful muscle contractions (calcium malabsorption).
• Pallor and other symptoms of anemia.

Malabsorption *continued*

PREVENTION

• Malabsorption is preventable only when the underlying cause (such as an infection) is preventable.

DIAGNOSIS

• Patient history and physical examination.
• Blood tests for anemia and other nutritional deficiencies.
• Stool samples.
• Culture of the microorganisms inhabiting the intestine.
• Breath tests to detect lactose intolerance or bacterial overgrowth in the small intestine.
• Biopsy of intestinal tissue (may be taken during endoscopy; i.e., visual inspection of the bowel with a flexible, lighted scope).
• Barium swallow or enema (use of barium to create a clear x-ray image of the intestine).

HOW TO TREAT IT

• The underlying disorder causing malabsorption must be diagnosed and treated. For instance, antibiotics are given to cure an infection.
• In some cases the only treatment necessary is to avoid certain foods that trigger or exacerbate symptoms. For example, those with lactose intolerance should avoid milk products; those with nontropical sprue may be cured by avoiding all foods containing gluten (a protein found in wheat, rye, oats, and barley).
• Nutritional supplements may be prescribed, including calcium, magnesium, iron, and vitamins A, B, D, and K.
• Pancreatic enzymes may be prescribed to correct insufficient production of them.
• Corticosteroids may improve absorption in some cases.
• In many cases a high carbohydrate, low-fat diet is recommended.

WHEN TO CALL A DOCTOR

• Call a doctor if diarrhea or other symptoms of digestive problems persist for more than three days.

Malaria

WHAT IS IT?

Malaria is an acute infectious disease, usually transmitted by the bite of a mosquito. Single-celled parasites (plasmodia) carried by the mosquito enter the bloodstream and travel to the liver. There, they mature and proliferate for several days or weeks and cause no symptoms. Eventually, however, the plasmodia reenter the bloodstream and infect the red blood cells. After multiplying for two to three days, the parasites cause massive destruction of the red cells. This initiates the classic cycle of malaria symptoms that last 12 to 24 hours. It begins as a period of uncontrollable shivering and chills, followed by a fever as high as 105°F. Finally, a period of profuse sweating occurs, which helps the body temperature return to normal. The patient is left exhausted but otherwise temporarily free of symptoms. However,

---

SYMPTOMS
- Headache.
- Sudden chills and uncontrollable shivering.
- High fever.
- Nausea and vomiting.
- Rapid, shallow breathing.
- Profuse perspiration accompanied by a drop in body temperature.
- Muscle aches and pain.

---

plasmodia released from dying red cells and those continuing to multiply in the liver infect other red cells and cause repeated attacks, usually every two to three days. If untreated, attacks can continue for years and may be fatal, although the body gradually builds up defenses against the disease. While malaria is rarely life-threatening, one form of the disease, caused by the parasite *Plasmodium falciparum,* releases all of the parasites into the bloodstream at once and produces a single severe attack that is sometimes fatal. Falciparum malaria may be complicated by kidney failure or disseminated intravascular coagulation (DIC).

WHAT CAUSES IT?

- Malaria is caused by single-celled parasites (plasmodia), usually transmitted to their human hosts via the bite of an infected female anopheles mosquito. This disease is most common in rural, tropical areas.
- Malaria may be spread during a blood transfusion or by sharing needles for intravenous drug use.
- Infected mothers can transmit malaria to their unborn children.

DIAGNOSIS

- Patient history and physical exam are necessary.
- Blood smears are examined for parasites.

PREVENTION

- Before departing for a tropical or subtropical area, see your doctor or, preferably, go to a travel clinic where you can obtain information on the types of malaria presently found in the area of your destination. Recommendations may include taking the antimalarial drug chloroquine before leaving and for at least four weeks after returning. In certain areas, such as Southeast Asia, Colombia, and Kenya, plasmodia are resistant to chloroquine. For trips to such places, the drug Fansidar (a combination of sulfadoxine and pyrimethamine) may be taken along and administered if malaria symptoms arise at any point. This drug does not usually cure malaria but forestalls symptoms until proper treatment can be sought.
- When in mosquito-infested areas, put mosquito netting over beds, use insect repellents, and install window screens. Stay indoors between dusk and dawn, the hours when mosquitoes feed.

HOW TO TREAT IT

- Hospitalization is usually required. The drug chloroquine is administered to kill parasites in the blood. To kill chloroquine-resistant plasmodia, a combination of quinine and Fansidar may be given.
- For malaria other than that due to *Plasmodium falciparum* (which causes only one attack), an additional drug, primaquine, must be taken for two weeks. This kills parasites in the liver, thereby preventing recurrent attacks.

WHEN TO CALL A DOCTOR

- Contact your doctor before traveling to areas where malaria is prevalent.
- See a doctor if malaria symptoms develop or recur.

Mastoiditis

WHAT IS IT?

Mastoiditis is a bacterial infection and inflammation of the hollow "air cells" within the honeycomb-like mastoid process—the bone located just behind the ear, near the jaw bone. In most cases, mastoiditis results when an ear infection spreads to the mucus membrane surrounding the mastoid process and eventually to the walls of the bone itself. If the infection persists, it may begin to destroy the delicate structures of the mastoid. This can result in hearing loss and, without treatment, continued destruction of bone in the skull. Mastoiditis most often affects children; indeed, before the advent of antibiotics, it was a common cause of childhood mortality. Currently, the prospects of full recovery are very good. However, if not treated promptly, mastoiditis may lead to further complications, including meningitis, facial paralysis, labyrinthitis, and brain abscess, in addition to hearing loss and bone destruction.

SYMPTOMS
- Earache, often severe.
- Redness, swelling, and tenderness in the region behind the ear.
- Fever, sometimes spiking to very high temperatures.
- Headaches.
- Discharge from the ear.
- Hearing loss.

WHAT CAUSES IT?
- Most commonly, mastoiditis occurs when a bacterial infection of the middle ear (otitis media) spreads to the mastoid process.

- Chronic systemic diseases (those that affect entire organ systems) may increase the likelihood of various other infections, including mastoiditis.
- Suppression of the body's immune system (as occurs with the use of certain medications or with diseases such as AIDS) is conducive to secondary infections such as mastoiditis.

PREVENTION
- Get prompt treatment for ear, sinus, and other infections.

DIAGNOSIS
- Patient history and physical examination.
- Head x-rays or CT (computed tomography) scans.
- A culture of the fluid discharge from the ear will be taken.

HOW TO TREAT IT
- Intensive antibiotic treatment is required, generally delivered by injection. Additionally, oral antibiotics may be prescribed for weeks afterward. Mastoiditis is, however, often resistant to antibiotic therapy, since it is difficult for medications to reach sufficiently deep into the bone tissue of the mastoid process.
- Surgical drainage of the middle ear (myringotomy) may be needed to treat an underlying ear infection.
- If antibiotics fail to cure the infection, mastoidectomy (surgical removal of all or part of the mastoid process) may be recommended. Following such surgery, antibiotic therapy is likely to be continued for several weeks to prevent further infection.

WHEN TO CALL A DOCTOR
- Call your doctor if an ear infection persists despite treatment or if new symptoms arise.

Measles Rubeola

WHAT IS IT?

Measles (also known as rubeola) is a highly contagious viral infection that primarily affects the respiratory tract. Symptoms appear in a predictable sequence: After an incubation period of one to two weeks (at which time the disease is most communicable), fever, runny nose, and a dry cough develop. By the third day, fever subsides somewhat and tiny gray bumps (Koplik's spots) appear inside the mouth. On subsequent days, fever rises again and the spotted skin rash characteristic of measles appears. Typically, within a week of onset, all symptoms (including the rash) begin to fade and the disease is no longer contagious. Measles is one of the most serious preventable childhood illnesses. Fortunately, large-scale immunization efforts in the United States and Canada have, over the past 25 years, reduced the incidence of measles by 99 percent—although it is still a major cause of childhood mortality in underdeveloped countries. Although the outlook is very optimistic, on rare occasions spread of the virus or a secondary bacterial infection can lead to serious complications, including middle ear infections (otitis media), pneumonia, and encephalitis (inflammation of the brain).

SYMPTOMS

- Cough.
- Fever.
- Watery nasal discharge.
- Red, watering eyes.
- Sore throat.
- Aversion to light.
- Loss of appetite.
- Muscle aches.
- General feeling of poor health.
- Small grayish bumps (Koplik's spots), surrounded by a red halo, on the lining of the mouth (appearing three or four days after the onset of initial symptoms).
- Red, slightly itchy bumps that gradually spread all over the body, usually within five days of the onset of symptoms.

WHAT CAUSES IT?

- Measles is caused by the paramyxovirus, which is most commonly spread by airborne respiratory droplets from an infected person.

PREVENTION

- Children should be inoculated with the MMR (measles, mumps, rubella) vaccine at the age of 15 months. A booster shot is generally recommended between four and six years of age. (Teenagers and young adults who have not had this second shot are at risk of contracting measles.)
- Gamma globulin (a substance derived from human blood containing antibodies to most types of infection) may be given to those who have been exposed to measles but have not been properly immunized.

DIAGNOSIS

- Physical examination and patient history are necessary.
- In rare cases when diagnosis is uncertain, blood, mucus, or urine samples may be taken to identify the measles virus.

HOW TO TREAT IT

- Treatment is aimed at making the patient as comfortable as possible, since there is no specific remedy for measles. In most cases, the disease remits on its own after about 10 days. In the meantime, bed rest, nonprescription pain relievers, and humidified air are advised.
- In some cases, doctors may administer an injection of gamma globulin antibodies, which battle the virus and thus may ease the severity of the infection.
- Antibiotics may be required if a secondary bacterial infection (such as bacterial pneumonia) occurs.

WHEN TO CALL A DOCTOR

- Call a doctor if symptoms do not begin to ease after one week, or if earache, heavy cough, or severe lethargy develop. These are signs of impending complications.
- **EMERGENCY** Get medical help immediately if generalized bleeding from skin lesions (hemorrhagic measles) or convulsions occur. (Both symptoms are extremely rare.)

Megacolon, Toxic

WHAT IS IT?

Toxic megacolon is a serious condition characterized by swelling and dilation of the large intestine due to inflammation of the intestinal wall and accumulation of excessive amounts of gas. It primarily occurs in association with a severe attack of inflammatory bowel disease—either ulcerative colitis or Crohn's disease (see Colitis, Ulcerative, and Crohn's Disease for more information). Bacterial infections of the colon and certain drugs can also cause toxic megacolon. The disorder produces extreme illness and is life-threatening; treatment requires hospitalization, and surgery may be required to remove the affected portion of the intestine. For adults, the prognosis for toxic megacolon varies; there is a danger of widespread blood poisoning (see Septic Shock), extensive hemorrhaging from the colon, perforation of the colon (see Peritonitis) and blockage of the arteries that supply blood to the lungs (see Pulmonary Embolism for more information).

SYMPTOMS
- Acute illness most often preceded by increased intensity of ulcerative colitis or Crohn's disease symptoms, which include abdominal pain, diarrhea, possibly leading to dehydration, and blood in the stool.
- Abdominal distension and tenderness.
- High fever.
- Rapid heart rate.
- Pallor.
- Mental changes.
- Shock.

WHAT CAUSES IT?

- Ulcerative colitis or Crohn's disease in the colon are the most common causes of toxic megacolon. In such patients, discontinuing or decreasing prescribed dosages of anti-inflammatory medications, such as sulfasalazine or one of the 5-aminosalicylic acid (5-ASA) drugs, may trigger an episode of toxic megacolon.
- Some medications—including narcotics (such as morphine and codeine), anticholinergic agents (such as scopolamine and atropine), and some antidepressants—may lead to toxic megacolon.

PREVENTION

- Do not discontinue medications for ulcerative colitis or Crohn's disease unless otherwise advised by your doctor.

DIAGNOSIS

- Patient history, especially of prior diagnosis of inflammatory bowel disease.
- Blood tests for anemia and for high white-cell count.
- Abdominal x-rays.
- Stool cultures to detect an underlying infection.
- Colonoscopy (insertion of a thin, lighted viewing tube into the rectum) may be performed to inspect the bowel.
- A biopsy of the colon lining may be taken during colonoscopy.

HOW TO TREAT IT

- Prompt hospitalization is required. Doctors will attempt to relieve the distended bowel and prevent intestinal perforation (which results in peritonitis) by passing a small tube through the nose or mouth into the colon to remove gas and fluids.
- Intravenous solutions and nutrients are given. (Nothing can be given by mouth.)
- Blood transfusions are given if necessary.
- Antibiotics may be prescribed to prevent or treat associated bacterial infection or blood poisoning due to septic shock.
- Surgery may be required if the medical treatment of toxic megacolon fails to relieve the distention and symptoms of toxicity. The affected portion of the large intestine is removed, and the remaining sections are sewn together (a procedure known as bowel resection). In some cases it may be necessary to create a temporary or permanent colostomy, in which the end of the remaining upper portion of the colon is brought through an opening created in the abdominal wall. Wastes pass through this opening into a bag, instead of being eliminated rectally.

WHEN TO CALL A DOCTOR

- **EMERGENCY** See a doctor immediately for severe abdominal pain and distention accompanied by fever.

Melanoma

WHAT IS IT?

Melanoma is the least common form of skin cancer but by far the most deadly—and recently, the incidence of melanoma has been increasing. In women, for example, only the incidence of lung cancer is rising more quickly. Melanoma develops in the melanocytes, cells located in the epidermis and eyes that produce the dark pigment melanin, which serves to protect the skin from ultraviolet radiation. People with darker skin produce more melanin and generally are at less risk for melanoma (and other types of skin cancer) than those with pale skin. However, although there is a relationship between sunburn (especially repeated sunburns in childhood) and skin cancers, this relationship is less clear for melanoma, and the exact cause of skin cancer remains unknown. Melanomas may develop anywhere on the body, although the most common sites are areas frequently exposed to the sun, such as the face, neck, and arms. (Melanoma in the eye is uncommon and is mostly confined to the elderly; see Eye Cancers for more information.) Left untreated, melanoma may quickly spread to other parts of the body—making it the most dangerous type of skin cancer. Fortunately, with early detection and treatment, melanoma is almost always curable.

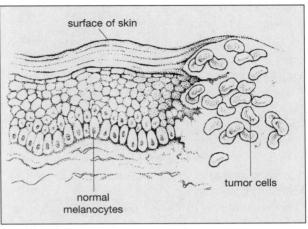

Overexposure to ultraviolet rays may damage the pigment-producing melanocytes in the skin, resulting in cancerous cells.

WHAT CAUSES IT?

- The cause of melanoma is unknown.
- Exposure to ultraviolet (UV) radiation from the sun or from artificial sources (such as sunlamps) may promote melanoma. Skin damage and melanoma risk increase with cumulative UV exposure.
- Hereditary factors may play a role in some forms of melanoma.
- Those with pale skin, blue or green eyes, and red or blond hair are most at risk for skin cancer.
- The presence of many moles on the skin is a risk factor.
- The risk of melanoma increases steadily with age.
- The erosion of the atmosphere's protective ozone layer is allowing more ultraviolet radiation to reach the earth's surface, increasing the risk of skin cancer.

PREVENTION

- Perform regular skin self-examinations: once a year for those with a low risk of skin cancer; more often for those in high-risk categories. Stand in front of a mirror and slowly inspect the entire surface of the skin, checking for changes in existing moles and for the appearance of any new skin abnormalities. Do not neglect hard-to-see areas; a second mirror may help. Regular self-examination aids in early diagnosis and treatment.
- Avoid exposure to direct sunlight between 10AM and 2PM, whenever possible.

SYMPTOMS

- Change in the appearance of a mole. These changes, known as the ABCDs of melanoma, may include any of the following: asymmetry, irregular borders, variations in color, and a diameter larger than a pencil eraser.
- An irregularly shaped, flat, or raised patch anywhere on the skin. The patch or bump may be black, brown, blue, red, white, or multicolored; it may feel tender, itchy, or hard and may ooze or bleed.
- A black or brown spot on the iris or the white of the eye; change of color of an iris; gradual loss of vision; pain and redness in the affected eye.

Melanoma *continued*

• Block the sun's rays by wearing protective clothing, like hats and long-sleeved shirts.

• A half hour before going outside, apply a sunscreen lotion containing PABA (para-aminobenzoic acid) with a sun protection factor (SPF) of 15 or higher. Reapply often, especially after swimming or perspiring heavily.

• Avoid sunlamps and tanning booths.

• Make sure children follow steps for proper sun protection, since sun exposure and sunburn during childhood and adolescence increase the likelihood of skin damage later in life.

• People who have had one episode of melanoma are at greater risk of developing others in the future. For this reason, preventive measures are especially important after initial diagnosis.

DIAGNOSIS

• A biopsy is done to remove part or all of a suspicious skin growth, and the tissue is sent to a laboratory for analysis.

• A complete eye examination is conducted by an ophthalmologist, possibly with the patient under general anesthesia, if melanoma in the eye is suspected.

HOW TO TREAT IT

• Surgery to remove cancerous skin cells and some of the surrounding skin is required. In some cases, neighboring lymph nodes may be removed to prevent the cancer from spreading.

• A skin flap may be used as a patch after the removal of large melanomas.

• Chemotherapy and radiation therapy may be used in advanced cases of melanoma to forestall cancer growth and thus ease symptoms (although these treatments rarely result in a cure).

• Laser surgery, cryosurgery (in which liquid nitrogen is used to freeze the targeted tissue), or radiation therapy may be used to destroy cancerous cells in the eye.

WHEN TO CALL A DOCTOR

• Make an appointment with a dermatologist if you notice a change in the appearance of your skin. Most skin growths are harmless, but a biopsy is necessary to determine the presence or absence of cancer.

• Make regular follow-up appointments with a dermatologist after an episode of melanoma, because of the increased likelihood of subsequent episodes.

• Make regular appointments with a dermatologist for skin cancer screenings if you are in a high-risk category for melanoma or other skin cancers.

• Make an appointment with an ophthalmologist if you develop symptoms of melanoma in the eye.

Ménière's Disease

WHAT IS IT?

Ménière's disease is characterized by a buildup of excess fluid in the labyrinth, the part of the inner ear that controls balance. The excess fluid leads to increased pressure that distorts (and occasionally ruptures) labyrinth membranes, causing episodes of severe vertigo (the sensation of spinning), ringing in the ears, and fluctuating hearing loss. The disorder usually affects one ear, but in about a third of cases it subsequently affects the other. Symptoms arise in periodic acute attacks, which may last from several minutes to several days. These attacks may occur as often as every few weeks or as infrequently as every few years. In most cases, the disorder is mild and will disappear spontaneously; in other cases, attacks may become increasingly frequent and severe. Over time, hearing loss and ringing in the ears may persist between attacks. In the most severe cases, deafness in one or both ears may occur. Ménière's disease usually strikes between the ages of 30 and 60 and affects men slightly more than women.

SYMPTOMS

- A sudden attack of vertigo, often severe enough to disrupt the sense of balance and cause a fall (usually to the side of the affected ear). Frequently triggers nausea and vomiting as well.
- Hearing impairment or loss.
- Ringing or buzzing in the ears (tinnitus).
- Pressure, fullness, or a feeling of blockage in the affected ear.
- Sweating.
- Giddiness.

WHAT CAUSES IT?

- It appears that Ménière's disease may result from the overproduction or decreased absorption of endolymph, a fluid produced naturally in the ear. Why this occurs, however, remains unclear.
- In some women with the disease, premenstrual retention of fluid may precipitate an attack.

PREVENTION

- There are no known ways to prevent Ménière's disease.

DIAGNOSIS

- Patient history and physical examination.
- Audiometry (measurement of hearing ability).
- X-rays to rule out other disorders that may cause similar symptoms.
- A caloric stimulation test, in which water of different temperatures is instilled into the ear canals, causing the eyes to reflexively flicker in a predictable way (nystagmus), which indicates whether or not there is nerve damage in the ear.

HOW TO TREAT IT

- Lie still during an acute attack. Avoid reading and bright lights, as these may exacerbate dizziness and nausea.
- Drugs such as atropine may be prescribed to control nausea and vomiting and to reduce vertigo.
- Antihistamines such as diphenhydramine may help to ease symptoms during a severe attack, or they may be taken preventively to ward off attacks.
- Mild sedatives may be prescribed for those who suffer anxiety during a severe attack.
- Diuretics and a low-sodium diet may be recommended to reduce the overall amount of fluid in the body, and thus reduce the accumulation of endolymph fluid in the ear.
- If the disorder persists and causes very severe or frequent attacks, several surgical options are available, including drilling a hole in the bones of the middle ear to drain excess fluid; severing the nerve involved; or removal of the affected portion of the labyrinth. Such methods are effective but may result in irreversible hearing loss.

WHEN TO CALL A DOCTOR

- Call your doctor or an ear, nose, and throat specialist (otolaryngologist) if you experience persistent dizziness, ringing in the ears, fluctuating hearing loss, or other symptoms of Ménière's disease.

Meningitis

WHAT IS IT?

Meningitis is inflammation of the meninges, the three thin layers of tissue that cover the brain. It is almost always due to an infection—usually one that has spread to the meninges from elsewhere in the body. (In rare cases meningitis may also be caused by tumors or exposure to chemical irritants.) Three major types of infections cause meningitis—bacterial, viral, and fungal—and the nature and severity of symptoms vary depending on the specific microorganism involved. For example, viral meningitis— the most common type—typically causes mild symptoms such as headache and malaise and usually gets better on its own in a week or two. On the other hand, bacterial meningitis (usually affecting infants and young children) is a serious medical emergency that may cause brain damage or even be fatal if left untreated. Other types of meningitis (such as those caused by a fungus or tuberculosis) tend to progress slowly but may also lead to brain damage and death if not treated. Immediate treatment should thus be sought even for mild symptoms of meningitis. Prompt diagnosis and treatment allows most people to recover fully, with no permanent neurological damage.

WHAT CAUSES IT?

• Bacterial, viral, or fungal infection causes meningitis. Meningococcal meningitis (a bacterial variety that is the most dangerous) may occur in epidemic outbreaks.

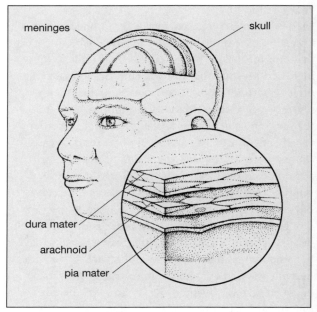

Between the brain and skull are three protective membranes: the meninges. Swelling due to inflammation of the meninges (meningitis) may exert potentially harmful pressure on the brain.

• A higher risk of meningitis is associated with head injury, brain surgery, cancer in or around the brain, acute otitis media (middle ear infection), pneumonia, syphilis, tuberculosis, exposure to chemical irritants, and alcoholism.
• Anyone whose immune system is weakened—for example, by AIDS or cancer chemotherapy—is at greater risk of meningitis.

PREVENTION

• Obtain prompt treatment for bacterial infections elsewhere in the body, especially ear and upper respiratory infections.
• Vaccines can protect against outbreaks of meningococcal meningitis in groups such as military recruits.
• Antibiotics may be administered to prevent infection in those who are in close contact with others infected with meningococcal meningitis.

DIAGNOSIS

• Lumbar puncture (spinal tap) to examine under the microscope spinal fluid for cells and organisms and to culture for bacterial or fungal growth.
• Blood cultures.

SYMPTOMS

• Fever (may be very high in cases of bacterial meningitis).
• Headache, possibly severe.
• Stiff neck.
• Nausea and vomiting.
• Aversion to light.
• Poor feeding in infants.
• With bacterial meningitis: mental confusion, drowsiness, seizures, and loss of consciousness.
• With meningococcal meningitis: red, blotchy skin rash.

Meningitis *continued*

• CT (computed tomography) scans or MRI (magnetic resonance imaging) may be performed during treatment.

HOW TO TREAT IT

• Hospitalization is required for bacterial meningitis. Antibiotics are given in large doses, often intravenously. Corticosteroids may be given to reduce inflammation; tranquilizers may be prescribed to prevent seizures.

• A respirator may be necessary if the patient loses consciousness.

• Antibiotics are ineffective against viral meningitis, which is usually mild anyway and is overcome by the body's own defenses within a week or two. Treatment is thus is aimed at relieving symptoms: bed rest, plenty of fluids, and over-the-counter pain relievers are recommended.

• Antifungal medication is prescribed to treat a fungal infection.

• Antitubercular medications are given for tubercular meningitis.

WHEN TO CALL A DOCTOR

• **EMERGENCY** Call a doctor immediately if you or your child develops symptoms of meningitis.

Mesenteric Ischemia

WHAT IS IT?

Mesenteric ischemia is an uncommon condition characterized by obstruction of one of the arteries to the intestines. Blockage occurs when a blood clot forms at a site already narrowed by atherosclerosis (mesenteric thrombosis), when plaques gradually build up in the arterial walls, or when an embolus (a blood clot from a distant site) lodges in an artery. Less often, mesenteric ischemia results from blockage of a vein leading away from the intestine. Total obstruction of a mesenteric artery due to severe atherosclerosis may be preceded by a period of "abdominal angina"—abdominal pain that begins 20 to 30 minutes after eating and lasts for several hours. Obstruction due to an embolus occurs without warning. Complete blockage of a mesenteric artery causes death of the affected portion of the intestine. Treatment involves removing any permanently damaged portion of the intestine and, if possible, removal of the embolus or bypassing the portion of the artery obstructed by the clot; prognosis is generally grim.

WHAT CAUSES IT?

• Mesenteric thrombosis occurs in people with far-advanced atherosclerosis (see Coronary Artery Disease).
• An embolus in the mesenteric arteries is most common in patients with atrial fibrillation (see Cardiac Arrhythmias), artificial heart valves, and valvular heart disease (see Valvular Heart Disease).
• Oral contraceptives may increase the danger of occlusion of mesenteric veins.

PREVENTION

• As much as possible, observe heart-healthy behaviors, such as maintaining a healthy diet, engaging in regular aerobic exercise, and avoiding cigarettes.

DIAGNOSIS

• Patient history and physical examination.
• Abdominal x-ray.
• For "abdominal angina," a barium-swallow test (use of barium to help create a clear image of the intestines on an x-ray) or a CT (computed tomography) scan may be followed by angiography (x-ray of the blood vessels after injection of a contrast agent).
• If complete blockage of a mesenteric artery is suspected, immediate angiography is done to locate the blockage, followed by emergency surgery if diagnosis is confirmed. When the diagnosis is strongly suspected, surgery may be initiated without angiography.

HOW TO TREAT IT

• When blockage of the mesenteric blood supply is only partial, surgical options include arterial bypass graft (rerouting blood flow around the damaged portion of the artery) and percutaneous transluminal angioplasty (inflation of a tiny balloon, routed via a catheter, at the narrowed point inside the artery, to compress the plaque and widen the passageway).
• Complete occlusion requires immediate surgery. The damaged portion of the intestine is removed and the remaining ends sewn together (bowel resection).
• A second operation is often needed 24 to 36 hours later to remove dead bowel that was not apparent at the time of the first procedure.
• Heparin, an anticoagulant, may be administered after surgery to reduce the risk of subsequent clots.

WHEN TO CALL A DOCTOR

• **EMERGENCY** Call an ambulance immediately if you experience severe, unremitting abdominal pain or cramping, especially if accompanied by other symptoms of mesenteric ischemia.

SYMPTOMS

• Abdominal angina: intermittent dull or cramping pain beginning 20 to 30 minutes after a meal and lasting for several hours.
• Severe, cramping abdominal pain, usually beginning around the navel. Pain later becomes steady throughout the abdomen.
• Weight loss.
• Abdominal swelling.
• Nausea and vomiting.
• Fever.
• Diarrhea or constipation.
• Rectal bleeding or bloody stools.
• Rapid heartbeat.

Mitral Valve Prolapse

WHAT IS IT?

In mitral valve prolapse (MVP)—also known as floppy valve syndrome—the valve between the heart's left atrium (upper chamber) and left ventricle (lower chamber) does not close normally and pro-lapses (balloons outward) into the atrium. Disquiet-ing as a heart valve abnormality may sound, MVP is typically harmless and causes no symptoms. How-ever, in less than 4 percent of cases, blood may flow backward (regurgitate) through the valve from the ventricle to the atrium—perhaps enough to interfere with blood supply to the body. This may produce mild to serious symptoms and require treatment. Often discovered in early adulthood, MVP affects nearly 5 percent of the population.

WHAT CAUSES IT?

- The cause of MVP is most likely genetic.
- Women are twice as likely to develop MVP as men, especially women who are thin or who have scoliosis (curvature of the spine) or other types of skeletal abnormalities of the chest.

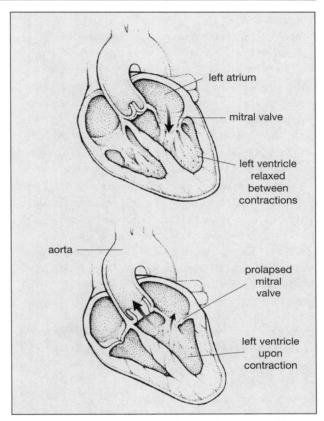

When the heart contracts, a prolapsed mitral valve may allow blood to reflux back into the left atrium, rather than enter the aorta exclusively.

SYMPTOMS

- In the majority of cases, MVP causes no symptoms. In more serious cases, however, the following may occur:
- Heart palpitations (in 10 to 15 percent of cases).
- Shortness of breath, especially when lying flat.
- Recurrent lightheadedness, especially when arising from a chair or bed; possible fainting.
- General fatigue or weakness.

PREVENTION

- There is no known way to prevent MVP.

DIAGNOSIS

- MVP is typically discovered during a routine checkup, as the condition produces characteristic sounds that can be heard through a stethoscope.
- Echocardiography (the use of ultrasound to map the structure and motion of the heart) confirms diagnosis.

HOW TO TREAT IT

- Treatment is rarely needed. However, those with MVP should have regular checkups. Periodic echocar-diograms may be needed to evaluate a patient's status.
- Those with MVP are at increased risk for endo-carditis (infection of a heart valve), and so may be given preventive antibiotics prior to any dental or surgical procedure.
- Beta-blocking drugs (often used for high blood pressure) may be prescribed for patients with fre-quent or bothersome palpitations. However, these drugs may exacerbate fatigue.
- For the most severe and debilitating cases of MVP, surgery to reconstruct or replace the prolapsed valve may be recommended.

WHEN TO CALL A DOCTOR

- See a doctor for frequent dizziness or palpitations.

Mononucleosis, Infectious

WHAT IS IT?

Infectious mononucleosis is an acute infection stemming from the Epstein-Barr virus or, more rarely, the cytomegalovirus, both members of the herpes family. It most often affects children, adolescents, and young adults and is particularly common among college students in the early fall and again in the spring. Once the virus enters the body, it multiplies in lymphocytes, a type of white blood cell. The characteristic sore throat, fever, and debilitating fatigue usually emerge after an incubation period of about 10 days in children and from 30 to 50 days in adults. Acute symptoms usually disappear after about six to 10 days, although some residual weakness and fatigue may linger for two to three months. Mononucleosis is usually not serious; major complications—which may include infection of the brain or heart or rupture of the spleen—are very rare.

SYMPTOMS
- Headaches.
- Weakness and fatigue.
- Sore throat and enlarged tonsils.
- Swollen lymph glands in the neck, armpits, and groin.
- Fever (with fluctuating temperatures that peak during the evening at about 101°F to 102°F).
- Loss of appetite.
- Stiff or sore muscles.
- Temporary jaundice, due to mild, reversible liver damage.

WHAT CAUSES IT?

- Mononucleosis is frequently transmitted via saliva, hence the nickname "the kissing disease." It may also be spread via mouth-to-hand-to-mouth contact or by sharing towels or utensils.
- The infection may be transmitted during a blood transfusion.

PREVENTION

- Avoid mouth-to-mouth or hand-to-mouth contact as well as sharing towels or utensils with persons known to be infected with mononucleosis.

DIAGNOSIS

- Diagnosis is suspected in those who exhibit the classic triad of symptoms—sore throat, swollen lymph glands, and fever—upon physical examination.
- A high white-blood-cell count and the presence of "atypical" lymphocytes in the blood are characteristic findings.
- A positive heterophile antibody test (a blood test that reveals the presence of specific antibodies against the virus) confirms the diagnosis.
- Liver function tests may be done.

HOW TO TREAT IT

- There is no specific treatment for infectious mononucleosis; however, the vast majority of people recover on their own within four to six weeks. Bed rest is essential when symptoms are most acute. A normal schedule of activity can be gradually resumed as symptoms subside.
- Take over-the-counter analgesics to reduce fever and to relieve headaches, body aches, and sore throat. (Children should be given acetaminophen instead of aspirin.)
- Drink water and fruit juice to help relieve fever and prevent dehydration.
- Gargle with one-half teaspoon of salt in a glass of warm water several times a day to relieve sore throat.
- In rare cases, corticosteroids may be prescribed to reduce tonsil inflammation, should it become severe enough to obstruct breathing.
- Approximately 20 percent of those with infectious mononucleosis will also be simultaneously infected with strep throat, which requires antibiotic therapy for at least 10 days.
- In rare cases, mononucleosis causes a rupture of the spleen, which requires immediate emergency surgery.

WHEN TO CALL A DOCTOR

- If you experience any of the symptoms of infectious mononucleosis, call a doctor.
- **EMERGENCY** If you have been diagnosed with infectious mononucleosis and you feel sudden sharp pains in the upper left side of your abdomen, get professional medical care immediately. This may be an indication of a ruptured spleen.

Multiple Myeloma

WHAT IS IT?

Multiple myeloma is a form of cancer resulting from the overproduction of a single clone of plasma cells, a type of white blood cell produced in the bone marrow. Plasma cells proliferate in the marrow, infiltrate adjacent bone tissue, and may spread throughout the skeleton, resulting in bone pain and fractures of fragile, brittle bones. (Some patients develop a single plasma cell tumor, known as a plasmacytoma, in a bone or elsewhere.) Proliferation of plasma cells interferes with the formation of red cells (causing anemia), platelets (increasing the risk of hemorrhage), and white cells (increasing susceptibility to infection). Symptoms may arise from kidney failure, hypercalcemia (high levels of blood calcium, due to bone breakdown), and compression of the spinal cord due to collapse of the vertebrae. Myeloma also involves the production of large amounts of a type of immunoglobulin (antibody) termed myeloma protein. Multiple myeloma most often affects those over 50 and is usually fatal within two years of diagnosis. While there is no cure, treatment can prolong life and improve the quality of life of the patient.

WHAT CAUSES IT?

- The cause of multiple myeloma is unknown, although genetic factors may play a role.
- Risk increases with age and exposure to radiation.

PREVENTION

- Try to minimize exposure to radiation.

DIAGNOSIS

- Patient history and physical examination.
- Blood tests for myeloma protein, calcium levels, and numbers of red cells, platelets, and white cells.
- Urine examination for myeloma protein.
- Bone marrow biopsy, usually taken from the hip.
- X-rays of the chest, spine, or other sites of pain.

HOW TO TREAT IT

- Stay as active as possible to maintain bone strength, since inactivity hastens bone loss. Since bones may be brittle, your doctor or physical therapist should supervise any program of activity.
- Combination chemotherapy, often including corticosteroids (usually prednisone), is used to destroy cancerous cells.
- Radiation therapy is effective for plasmacytomas.
- Radiation is also used to relieve bone pain and spinal cord compression.
- Surgery may be necessary to repair bone fractures.
- Plasmapheresis, a procedure that filters excess waste products out of the blood artificially, may be performed in the event of kidney failure.
- Analgesics are administered to reduce pain.
- Antibiotics may be prescribed to treat associated bacterial infections.

WHEN TO CALL A DOCTOR

- Call a doctor for bone pain or for the emergency symptoms of hypercalcemia or kidney failure.

SYMPTOMS

- Bone pain, especially along the spine, that worsens with movement.
- Unexplained bone fractures. The collapse of affected vertebrae may cause loss of height and compression of the spinal cord, which may result in the inability to urinate and pain or paralysis of the legs.
- Fatigue, pallor, and shortness of breath, due to associated anemia.
- Frequent bacterial infections, due to a weakened immune system.
- Increased bruising and bleeding (for example, from the nose or gums).
- Headache and visual disturbances.
- Symptoms of hypercalcemia (high blood levels of calcium), which include generalized discomfort; muscle aches or weakness; arthritic joint pain; heartbeat irregularities; constipation, nausea, vomiting, and loss of appetite; and fatigue, lethargy, confusion, depression, psychosis, or other mental changes, possibly resulting in coma.
- Symptoms of kidney failure (see Renal Failure, Acute).

Multiple Sclerosis

WHAT IS IT?

Multiple sclerosis (MS) is a disorder characterized by destruction of the protective outer casings of the nerves within the central nervous system (the brain, optic nerve, and spinal cord). The nerve casings, known as myelin sheaths, are composed mostly of fats; they insulate the nerves and increase the speed of electrical transmissions. In MS, patchy areas of the sheaths are destroyed (demyelinated) and replaced by scar tissue (called plaques)—a process known as sclerosis—at multiple sites throughout the central nervous system (hence the name of the disorder). Sclerosis impairs electrical conduction, thus

---

SYMPTOMS

- Severe fatigue.
- Muscle weakness and spasticity in the arms and legs.
- Muscle spasms.
- Eye pain and visual disturbances, including blurry vision, loss of vision in one eye, or a sudden inability to distinguish colors (optic neuritis).
- Double vision.
- Tingling or pins-and-needles sensations.
- Disturbances in the gait; loss of coordination.
- Vertigo with nausea and vomiting.
- Slurred speech.
- Loss of bladder control and constipation.
- Emotional depression and mood swings.
- Mental confusion or loss of memory.
- Paralysis of one side of the face.
- Partial or complete paralysis of the body.

---

reducing or eliminating transmission of nerve impulses within the affected areas. Symptoms wax and wane unpredictably and vary widely from patient to patient. For example, sclerosis of the optic nerves may cause vision disturbances, and sclerosis of the nerves that control the muscles may lead to spasticity, weakness, muscle spasms, or paralysis. Different symptoms may occur in combination and may vary greatly over time. The cause is unknown; however, current research suggests that MS might be an autoimmune disorder, in which the immune system attacks some of the body's own cells, mistaking them for foreign invaders. MS occurs in two major forms. In relapsing/remitting MS, which afflicts about 70 percent of MS patients, a series of flare-ups or attacks are separated by periods of normal or near-normal health. Such remissions may be short or may last for months or years. In a few cases, remission is permanent, but many patients gradually accumulate permanent neurological deficits. The other type of MS, chronic/progressive, gradually worsens without remission; a rare version is fatal within several months of onset. MS is rare in children and in people over 60; the first episode usually occurs between the ages of 20 and 50. Women are affected more often than men. Average survival after diagnosis is more than 35 years, but destruction of the myelin sheaths eventually results in a combination of nerve, muscle, and, occasionally, brain damage. However, many people retain much of their neuromuscular function for years and are able to pursue a wide range of normal activities with the help of supportive therapy. Currently, treatment is aimed at reducing the severity of attacks, relieving the problems caused by neurological deficits, and providing psychological support.

WHAT CAUSES IT?

- The cause of multiple sclerosis is unknown.
- Hereditary factors may play a role.
- Environmental factors may be associated with multiple sclerosis; the majority of cases occurs in temperate climates.
- Some theories suggest that multiple sclerosis may be caused by a virus or other infectious agent.
- There is some evidence of an autoimmune component.

PREVENTION

- There is no known way to prevent multiple sclerosis.

DIAGNOSIS

- No definitive diagnostic test exists for MS, and several attacks may occur before diagnosis is certain. The following procedures may be performed:

Multiple Sclerosis *continued*

- Patient history and careful neurological and eye examination.
- Lumbar puncture (spinal tap).
- MRI (magnetic resonance imaging) to detect plaques of scar tissue even in the absence of associated symptoms.
- Tests to detect abnormalities of vision and other sensory modalities.
- Nerve conduction studies.

HOW TO TREAT IT

- Oral corticosteroids, such as prednisone, may be prescribed to shorten the duration and reduce the severity of attacks.
- Your doctor may prescribe Betaseron interferon (beta-Ib) injections, a form of biological therapy, to treat MS. This medication is synthetically engineered to be identical to a naturally occurring protein and reduces the frequency and severity of attacks by altering the body's immune responses.
- Your doctor may prescribe antispasmodics or tranquilizers, including diazepam, to relax spastic muscles and provide pain relief; amantadine to treat fatigue; and antidepressants to treat associated depression.
- A variety of medications may be administered to treat incontinence, frequency, hesitancy, and other bladder-control problems.
- Try not to become overheated. Avoid sunbathing, heavy exertion, and hot baths, and obtain prompt treatment for fevers, since raised body temperature may trigger or worsen symptoms. Taking a cool shower, swimming, or sitting in an air-conditioned room may relieve the severity of symptoms during an attack.
- Pursue a program of moderate exercise to help keep muscles as flexible and strong as possible.
- A combination of physical and occupational therapy may help patients adjust to muscular and sensory changes.
- Psychological counseling may help patients and their families cope with depression and the lifestyle changes imposed by MS.
- Be wary of unproven remedies, such as bee venom.
- Obtain more information by contacting your local chapter of the National Multiple Sclerosis Society.

WHEN TO CALL A DOCTOR

- Call a doctor if you develop any of the symptoms of MS, especially if you have suffered several episodes or attacks.

Mumps

WHAT IS IT?

Mumps is an acute illness characterized by swelling of the parotid glands, just below and in front of the ear, and at times, the salivary glands under the jaw. It occurs most often in children ages two through 12, although unvaccinated adults are susceptible too. The patient is contagious for about one week before and two weeks after the onset of symptoms, which occurs about two to three weeks after exposure to the mumps virus. Preliminary symptoms (headache, sore muscles, appetite loss, and low-grade fever) usually persist for 24 hours, followed by an earache that is aggravated by chewing, soreness and swelling of the parotid glands on either or both sides, and moderate fever. About 20 percent of men and adolescent boys experience pain and swelling in one or both testes (orchitis), which in rare cases may cause sterility. Although uncomfortable, mumps is usually harmless, and symptoms normally subside within 10 days. Occasional complications include meningitis (inflammation of membranes around the brain) and pancreatitis (inflammation of the pancreas), but these usually resolve with no permanent adverse effects.

The incidence of mumps in the United States has drastically diminished over the past few decades owing to increased childhood immunization efforts. In almost all cases, those who do get the mumps have lifelong immunity to reinfection.

WHAT CAUSES IT?

• The disorder is transmitted by direct contact with infectious saliva or by inhalation of airborne moisture droplets containing the paramyxovirus.

PREVENTION

• The MMR (measles, mumps, rubella) vaccine should be given to children after the age of 15 months.
• Immunization within 24 hours of exposure to the mumps.

DIAGNOSIS

• Patient history and physical exam are necessary. Diagnosis is generally based on the presence of the characteristic symptoms (particularly, swelling of the salivary glands).
• Diagnosis may be confirmed by a saliva or urine culture or with a blood test for antibodies against the mumps virus.

HOW TO TREAT IT

• Use acetaminophen or ibuprofen to reduce fever and relieve discomfort. (Aspirin should not be given to children under 12.)
• Bed rest is advised for the duration of the fever.
• Ice packs or heating pads may ease the pain of swollen glands.
• Adequate fluid intake is essential to prevent dehydration due to fever. Extreme swallowing difficulty may warrant intravenous fluid replacement.
• For males with orchitis, doctors may prescribe stronger painkillers as well as corticosteroids to reduce inflammation.

WHEN TO CALL A DOCTOR

• Get professional medical care promptly if mumps symptoms occur in conjunction with severe headache, unusual drowsiness, persistent vomiting or abdominal pain, or convulsions.

SYMPTOMS

• Soreness and swelling of the parotid glands on one or both sides. Discomfort may range from vague tenderness to obvious pain when opening the mouth or swallowing.
• Fever, usually lasting about two or three days.
• Sore muscles.
• Loss of appetite.
• Headache.
• Earache that is aggravated by chewing.
• In men and adolescent boys, swelling in one or both testes (often subsides within four days).
• Headache, aversion to light, lethargy, and a stiff neck (which may indicate meningitis).
• Upper abdominal pain, nausea, and vomiting (which may indicate pancreatitis).
• Lower abdominal discomfort in women (may indicate swelling of the ovaries, which is rare).
• Many children with mumps have no symptoms.

Muscular Dystrophy

WHAT IS IT?

Muscular dystrophy (MD) is a term used to describe a number of inherited disorders characterized by progressive weakness and wasting of the muscles. The most common and severe type is Duchenne's MD, in which a genetic defect leads to the formation of an abnormal type of muscle protein called dystrophin. Others include Becker's MD, limb-girdle MD, facioscapulohumeral MD, and myotonic dystrophy. The types of MD are classified according to the location of muscles involved, the age that symptoms appear, the rate that symptoms progress, and the manner in which the defective gene is passed on. (For example, the genes for Duchenne's and Becker's MD are X-linked recessives; that is, they generally affect boys only but are carried and passed on by women.) Symptoms and prognosis vary, depending on the type of MD. The disease may affect some or all muscles, may develop during childhood or adulthood, may progress very gradually or rapidly, and may or may not become severely disabling. Boys with Duchenne's MD are usually in a wheelchair by the age of 12 and rarely live past age 20; on the other hand, people with facioscapulohumeral MD often have a normal life span and usually remain able to walk, since the leg muscles are only mildly affected. Also, in some types of MD, the rate of progression and the extent of disability varies substantially from patient to patient. Most forms of MD affect the heart muscle and thus result in cardiomyopathy.

WHAT CAUSES IT?

• All forms of MD result from some type of genetic defect. In the majority of cases, the defect is inherited and affects various relatives throughout a family, but it in a few cases, the disorder may result from a new genetic mutation.

PREVENTION

• If you have a family history of MD, you may choose to see a genetic counselor before planning to have a child. Genetic tests can determine whether or not you are a carrier of the MD gene or if an unborn child has MD.

DIAGNOSIS

• Patient history and physical exam are necessary.
• A muscle biopsy (removal of a small tissue sample for microscopic examination) will be performed to confirm the diagnosis.
• Electrical activity in the muscles may be measured and analyzed (electromyography).

HOW TO TREAT IT

• There is no specific treatment to cure or halt the progression of MD.
• Physical therapy, exercise, orthopedic appliances (such as braces or wheelchairs), or corrective orthopedic surgery may help to preserve muscle function and prevent joint contractures as much as possible and improve quality of life.

WHEN TO CALL A DOCTOR

• If you or your child appears to be exhibiting the symptoms of muscular dystrophy, call a doctor.
• Consult a doctor if there is a history of muscular dystrophy in your or your spouse's family and you are considering having a child.

SYMPTOMS

• Progressive muscle wasting, weakness, and loss of function. (The muscle groups affected depends on the type of MD.)
• In Duchenne's MD, delayed development of basic muscle skills and coordination in children. Common signs include poor balance with frequent falls, walking difficulty with waddling gait and calf pain, and limited range of movement. Muscular and skeletal deformities, including backward curvature of the spine with protruding abdomen, are likely. Respiratory failure may occur.
• Obesity.
• Joint contractures.
• Cataracts, frontal baldness, drooping eyelids, gonadal atrophy, and mental impairment (with myotonic dystrophy).
• Intellectual impairment (occurs in various types of MD).

Myasthenia Gravis

WHAT IS IT?

Myasthenia gravis is a chronic autoimmune disorder characterized by weakness and rapid fatigue of the muscles. Antibodies, which normally fight infection, attack and inactivate muscle cell receptors that, in response to nerve impulses, permit the muscles to contract. Muscles with a reduced number of functioning receptors become weak, and voluntary control is dulled. In almost all cases muscles in the face are involved first, causing drooping eyelids and changes in speech and facial appearance. In about 85 percent of patients, muscles in the arms and legs are

---

SYMPTOMS
- Drooping eyelids.
- Double vision.
- Facial weakness characterized by a "snarling" expression when attempting to smile.
- Difficulty chewing.
- Slurred and nasal-sounding speech.
- Muscle weakness in the arms and legs, making it difficult to walk, stand up, or grasp objects.
- Severe breathing and swallowing difficulty (myasthenic crisis).

---

affected later. Muscles tend to tire after brief periods of use but recover with rest. The degree of weakness tends to fluctuate throughout the day; cycles of partial remissions alternating with debilitating relapses are common throughout the course of the disease. While there is no cure, highly effective treatments allow most patients to return to full, productive lives. The disorder may, however, become life-threatening and require emergency care in the case of a myasthenic crisis, when severe muscle weakness interferes with breathing or swallowing. Myasthenia gravis most often affects women between the ages of 20 and 30 and, less commonly, men between 50 and 70.

WHAT CAUSES IT?

- Myasthenia gravis occurs when, for reasons that remain unclear, antibodies produced by the body's immune system begin to inactivate receptors for acetylcholine that allow muscle fibers to respond to nerve impulses. The thymus (a gland in the chest and

a component of the immune system) appears to play a role in the disease; overgrowth of the gland (hyperplasia) appears in 65 percent of cases, while tumors of the thymus (thymomas) appear in 10 percent.

PREVENTION

- There is no way to prevent myasthenia gravis.

DIAGNOSIS

- Patient history and physical exam. Injection of a drug that temporarily improves muscle function in myasthenia gravis patients is given. Immediate gains in muscle strength indicate a positive diagnosis.
- Electromyography (measurement of the electrical activity of the muscles).
- CT or MRI scan of the upper chest to look for thymus enlargement or a tumor.
- Blood tests for acetylcholine-receptor antibodies.

HOW TO TREAT IT

- Acetylcholine released from nerves is rapidly inactivated by the enzyme cholinesterase. Agents that block this enzyme (anticholinesterase drugs) allow high levels of acetylcholine to accumulate at muscle receptor sites, thus enhancing their responsiveness to nerve impulses. These drugs alleviate symptoms but become less effective as the disease progresses.
- Removal of the thymus (thymectomy) results in improvement in 85 percent of patients, including complete remission in 35 percent.
- Long-term use of corticosteroids or other immunosuppressive drugs may reduce the body's autoimmune activity and improve symptoms of weakness.
- Plasmapheresis (a procedure involving partial removal of blood plasma while blood cells are returned to circulation) may be used to remove the antibodies that inactivate muscle receptors. It is used prior to surgery or to provide short-term relief in severe cases.
- Hospitalization and intensive care are needed during myasthenic crises.

WHEN TO CALL A DOCTOR

- Call a doctor if you develop the symptoms of myasthenia gravis.
- **EMERGENCY** Swallowing or breathing difficulty require immediate medical attention.

Myelofibrosis

WHAT IS IT?

Myelofibrosis is a disorder characterized by a progressive replacement of normal bone marrow cells with useless fibrous tissue. This impairs the marrow's ability to manufacture healthy blood cells (including red cells, white cells, and platelets). In some types of myelofibrosis, abnormal neoplastic cells that normally reside in the bone marrow migrate to and lodge in other organs, such as the spleen, liver, and lymph nodes, where they cause these organs to enlarge. Myelofibrosis tends to develop gradually in people over the age of 50 for no apparent cause; this is known as primary myelofibrosis. Symptoms normally do not appear until several years after the onset of the disease. The most common initial symptoms—fatigue, weakness, and appetite loss—are due to the anemia that results from insufficient red-blood-cell production. But eventually, severe complications—such as congestive heart failure, infection, and kidney failure—occur. Indeed, average survival time is estimated at four to five years after diagnosis of myelofibrosis; one quarter of patients live up to 15 years. Treatment is aimed at relieving symptoms. Secondary myelofibrosis is the term used when the disorder results from some other disease that damages the bone marrow. It may also occur if bone marrow is exposed to certain industrial toxins or to radiation.

SYMPTOMS

- Weakness and fatigue; heart palpitations; shortness of breath; pallor; loss of weight and appetite (due to anemia).
- Easy bleeding and bruising; clusters of pinpoint-size hemorrhages (petechiae) on the skin (due to platelet insufficiency).
- Fever and night sweats (due to insufficient white cells).
- Bone pain (in some cases).
- Attacks of gouty arthritis.
- Jaundice (due to liver damage).
- Abdominal pain, fullness, or breathing difficulty (due to enlargement of the spleen and liver).

WHAT CAUSES IT?

- The cause of primary myelofibrosis is unknown.
- Secondary myelofibrosis arises as a result of some other disease that affects the bone marrow (such as metastatic cancer, Hodgkin's disease, polycythemia vera, tuberculosis, Gaucher's disease, or Paget's disease), or from exposure to certain toxins (such as benzene) or to radiation, including x-rays.

PREVENTION

- There is no known way to prevent myelofibrosis, except in cases caused by exposure to radiation or industrial chemicals.

DIAGNOSIS

- Patient history and physical examination are necessary. An enlarged spleen and, in later stages of the disease, an enlarged liver are characteristic of myelofibrosis.
- Blood tests show abnormal numbers and appearance of blood cells.
- A bone marrow biopsy is necessary for a definite diagnosis, as myelofibrosis is often difficult to distinguish from certain other blood disorders.

HOW TO TREAT IT

- There is currently no effective treatment to cure or slow the progression of myelofibrosis.
- Blood transfusions may be administered, as needed, to treat anemia.
- Androgens (male hormones) may be administered to stimulate red-blood-cell production. Such treatment is temporarily effective in nearly half of all cases.
- The antigout drug allopurinol is prescribed for patients exhibiting gouty arthritis.
- Surgical removal of the spleen (splenectomy) may be indicated in cases where spleen enlargement causes severe problems for the patient.
- Treatment of the underlying disease is essential for secondary myelofibrosis.

WHEN TO CALL A DOCTOR

- If you experience the symptoms of myelofibrosis, call a doctor.

Myocardial Infarction Heart Attack

WHAT IS IT?

A myocardial infarction, commonly known as a heart attack, is a medical emergency that occurs when a portion of the heart is deprived of oxygen because of blockage of one of the coronary arteries, which supply the heart muscle (myocardium) with blood. Lack of oxygen causes characteristic chest pain and death of myocardial tissue. Heart attacks are more likely to occur when arteries have already been substantially narrowed by years of coronary artery disease (see Coronary Artery Disease for more information). Plaque—composed of cholesterol-rich fatty deposits, collagen and other proteins, and excess smooth muscle cells—builds up in the arterial walls, a process known as atherosclerosis. Arterial walls thicken and narrow, inhibiting the flow of blood into the heart. When arterial walls have been roughened by plaque deposits, it becomes much easier for blood clots to form along the surface of the plaque. If the clots grow, or if they detach from their place of origin and are carried along the artery, they may block a coronary artery completely, causing a heart attack. Arteries may also narrow suddenly as a result of an arterial spasm. A third of all heart attacks occur with no prior warning signs. In the remainder, attacks of chest pain (angina) brought about by stress or exer-

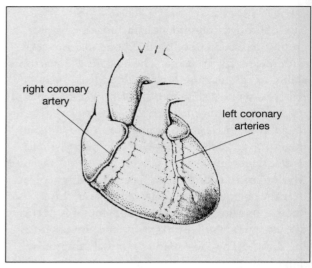

right coronary artery

left coronary arteries

If a blood clot forms in a coronary artery narrowed by atherosclerotic plaque, the blockage may starve heart muscle of oxygen-rich blood, causing the chest pain and tissue death associated with a heart attack.

tion occur periodically for months or years prior to a heart attack. In some cases a mild heart attack produces no symptoms—a so-called silent heart attack.

Prompt emergency medical attention is crucial: if treatment is received within a few hours of the onset of a heart attack, chances for survival are good. Improved treatment methods—including the administration of thrombolytic (clot dissolving) drugs and angioplasty (inflation of a tiny balloon at the site of the blockage to widen the artery and permit the flow of blood through the artery)—have led to a steady decrease in mortality from heart attacks. However, the best treatment remains prevention. The process of atherosclerosis may be halted or even reversed with fairly simple measures, and the risk of myocardial infarction can thus be reduced.

WHAT CAUSES IT?

• Blood clots that block a coronary artery are the most common cause of heart attacks. Clots develop on plaque in a coronary artery. Pieces of the clot may also be carried along the coronary artery and cause an obstruction.

• Severely narrowed arteries due to atherosclerosis underlie the development of a heart attack.

• Cigarette smoking, high blood pressure, high blood

SYMPTOMS

• Chest pain or pressure, tightness, squeezing, burning, aching, or heaviness in the chest, lasting longer than 10 minutes. The pain or discomfort is usually located in the center of the chest just under the breastbone and may radiate down the arm (especially the left), up into the neck, or along the jaw line.
• Shortness of breath.
• Profuse sweating.
• Dizziness.
• Muscle weakness.
• Nausea and vomiting.
• A choking sensation.
• Anxiety, or a feeling of impending doom.
• No symptoms occur with a silent heart attack.

Myocardial Infarction Heart Attack *continued*

cholesterol levels, a diet rich in saturated fat (especially animal fat), obesity, lack of exercise, and diabetes mellitus all promote atherosclerosis and thus increase the risk of heart attacks.
• A family history of early or premature heart attacks (before the age of 55 in men and 65 in women) increases the risk of heart attack.
• Men have a significantly higher risk of heart attack than premenopausal women. The risk for post-menopausal women approaches that of men, however, as estrogen production decreases with menopause.
• Risk increases with age; heart attacks are most common after age 65.
• A spasm of the muscles of the arterial walls may cause a heart attack by narrowing an artery. Spasms may be triggered by smoking, extreme emotional stress, or exposure to very cold air or water.
• Abuse of cocaine or amphetamines may cause a sudden heart attack even in those with no signs of heart disease.
• Heavy exertion, such as shoveling snow, or carrying heavy objects up stairs, and severe emotional stress may trigger a heart attack in those who have led a sedentary lifestyle.
• Having had one heart attack increases the risk of future heart attacks.

PREVENTION

• Don't smoke. Your doctor may recommend methods for quitting, including nicotine patches.
• Eat a diet low in fat, cholesterol, and salt.
• Pursue a program of moderate, regular exercise. People over age 50 who have led a sedentary lifestyle should check with a doctor before beginning an exercise program.
• Lose weight if you are more than 20 percent overweight.
• Your doctor may advise you to take a low dose of aspirin regularly. Aspirin reduces the tendency for the blood to clot, thereby decreasing the risk of heart attack. However, such a regimen should only be initiated under a doctor's expressed recommendation.
• Women at or approaching menopause should discuss the cardioprotective benefits of estrogen replacement therapy with their doctors.

DIAGNOSIS

• Patient history and physical examination. Diagnosis will often be made immediately upon examination by a doctor or emergency response technician.
• An electrocardiogram (ECG or EKG) will be performed to measure changes in the electrical activity of the heart resulting from abnormalities in the flow of blood.
• Blood tests measure the release of enzymes from damaged heart muscle into the bloodstream.
• A coronary angiography is performed to locate the arterial blockage prior to angioplasty or bypass surgery. In this procedure a tiny catheter is inserted into an artery in a leg or arm and threaded up the artery to the heart. A contrast material is then injected from the end of the catheter into the coronary arteries, and a high-speed series of x-rays is taken.

HOW TO TREAT IT

• It is advised to chew on aspirin at the onset of the symptoms of a heart attack. It may help break up the clot.
• Emergency treatment and immediate hospitalization is necessary in the event of a heart attack.
• A stopped heartbeat must be restarted immediately by cardiopulmonary resuscitation (CPR) or by a device known as an electrical defibrillator.
• Thrombolytic, or clot-dissolving, drugs such as tissue plasminogen activator (tPA), streptokinase, or urokinase may be injected immediately to dissolve arterial blockage. This technique is most effective within three hours of the onset of a heart attack.
• Painkillers such as morphine or meperidine are administered to relieve pain.
• Nitroglycerin may be given to reduce the heart's oxygen demands and lower blood pressure.
• Antiarrhythmic drugs such as lidocaine or procainamide may be administered to maintain a regular heartbeat.
• Oxygen may be administered through nasal tubes.
• Antihypertensive drugs such as beta-blockers, ACE inhibitors, or calcium channel blockers may be administered to lower blood pressure and reduce the heart's oxygen demand. The effect of these drugs may be enhanced by diuretics.

Myocardial Infarction Heart Attack *continued*

• Anticoagulants such as heparin, aspirin, or warfarin may be administered to reduce the risk of blood clots.

• Digitalis glycosides may be prescribed in some cases to strengthen heart muscle contraction. (In the United States, digoxin is the most commonly prescribed type of digitalis.)

• Dopamine or dobutamine may be administered to increase blood flow to the heart and strengthen the heartbeat.

• Blocked arteries may be opened or widened by percutaneous transluminal coronary angioplasty (PTCA). A small balloon is inserted into an artery, guided with a catheter to the narrowed point in the coronary artery, and then inflated. This compresses the plaque, widens the passageway, and improves blood flow.

• Coronary bypass surgery may be performed to restore adequate blood flow to the heart muscle. A mammary artery or a vein from the leg is grafted onto the narrowed coronary artery to circumvent the blocked portion.

• Electronic implants, such as a pacemaker or a defibrillator, may be surgically attached to the heart to maintain strong, regular contractions of the heart muscle.

• A heart transplant may be advised in severe cases when heart muscle has been badly damaged. The survival rate for heart transplant is 80 percent after one year and over 60 percent after four years.

• During recovery, follow prevention tips to reduce the risk of another heart attack.

• Contact your local chapter of the American Heart Association for information about support groups.

WHEN TO CALL A DOCTOR

• **EMERGENCY** Call an ambulance if you experience crushing chest pain, with or without nausea, vomiting, profuse sweating, breathlessness, weakness, or intense feelings of dread.

• **EMERGENCY** Call an ambulance if chest pain from previously diagnosed angina does not subside after 10 to 15 minutes.

• **EMERGENCY** Call an ambulance the first time you experience intense chest pain.

Myocarditis

WHAT IS IT?

Myocarditis is an inflammation of the heart muscle (myocardium), usually due to a viral infection. In many cases myocarditis produces no noticeable symptoms, although severe cases may cause serious disturbances of the heartbeat (cardiac arrhythmia), weakness of the heart muscle (cardiomyopathy), heart failure, or sudden cardiac arrest. While in most instances the inflammation subsides on its own without treatment and without causing permanent damage, more severe cases or those that become chronic may require hospitalization and medical treatment. Myocarditis can affect people of all ages. Because it is often asymptomatic, it is sometimes diagnosed only after a young adult with heart damage due to chronic myocarditis dies unexpectedly during strenuous exercise. Patients with viral myocarditis often exhibit inflammation of the pericardium (pericarditis) as well.

SYMPTOMS
- In many cases there are no symptoms.
- Fatigue.
- Shortness of breath.
- Heart palpitations or rapid heartbeat.
- Fever.
- Chest pain.

WHAT CAUSES IT?

- Viral infection, including Coxsackie virus, measles, rubella, influenza, and polio-, adeno-, and echo-viruses, is the most common cause of myocarditis in the United States.
- Bacterial infection is a rare cause.
- Radiation therapy for cancer (especially lung or breast carcinoma and Hodgkin's disease).
- Excessive alcohol consumption.
- Certain chemicals and drugs (such as immuno-suppressants).
- Parasitic infections such as trichinosis and toxoplasmosis (both rare in the United States).

- Chagas' disease, due to the parasite *Trypanosoma cruzi* (a common cause of heart disease in Central and South America).
- Toxins released in the course of diphtheria infections.
- Rheumatic fever.
- Lyme disease.

PREVENTION

- Vaccinations for diphtheria, tetanus, measles, German measles, and polio should be kept current.
- Get prompt treatment for infections, especially those of the upper respiratory system.

DIAGNOSIS

- Patient history and physical examination.
- Blood tests.
- ECG (electrocardiogram), which measures the electrical activity of the heart.
- Endomyocardial biopsy (removal of a small sample of heart muscle with a needle for analysis) provides a definitive diagnosis.

HOW TO TREAT IT

- Most cases subside in a few weeks without medical treatment. Studies have indicated that exercise may be risky for those with myocarditis, so all strenuous activity should be avoided. Bed rest is generally recommended in severe cases during convalescence to minimize the work load on the heart. A low-salt diet and abstinence from alcohol may also be advised.
- Antibiotics are prescribed for bacterial infection.
- In some cases corticosteroid drugs may be prescribed to reduce inflammation of the myocardium and to speed recovery.
- Appropriate medications may be needed to treat congestive heart failure or arrhythmias.

WHEN TO CALL A DOCTOR

- Call a doctor if you develop the symptoms of myocarditis, especially if you have a recent history of infection.

Nasal Polyps

WHAT IS IT?

Nasal polyps are benign growths or swellings in the lining of the nasal cavity. (They should not be confused with potentially cancerous polyps that may develop, for example, in the colon.) Nasal polyps are caused by an overproduction of fluid in the cells of the mucus membrane, usually due to persistent irritation from an underlying chronic allergy or recurrent nasal or sinus infections. They may occur singly, but more often polyps appear in clusters in both sides of the nose. They are generally not a serious health threat but may grow large enough or numerous enough to obstruct the airways and cause breathing difficulty. Also, they may block drainage of the sinuses and foster recurrent sinus infections. Nasal polyps usually respond well to treatment, although they tend to recur. Incidence is higher among adults than children.

SYMPTOMS
- Feeling of blockage in the nose or sinuses.
- Loss of the sense of smell.
- Dull pain or pressure in the face.
- Recurrent headaches.
- Nasal discharge.
- Breathing difficulty.

WHAT CAUSES IT?

- Nasal polyps usually result from persistent irritation caused by a chronic allergy (allergic rhinitis), which triggers swelling and fluid retention in the mucus membrane of the nasal cavity.
- Recurrent or persistent nasal and sinus infections increase the risk of developing nasal polyps.

PREVENTION

- There is no known way to prevent nasal polyps.

DIAGNOSIS

- Patient history and physical examination are necessary. The doctor is likely to use a nasal speculum, a device that distends the nostrils and permits easy viewing of the interior of the nasal cavity.
- X-rays may be taken of the sinuses and nasal passages.

HOW TO TREAT IT

- The first line of treatment is the same as for allergies: antihistamines, nasal decongestants, inhaled corticosteroid spray, or allergy shots. Many people respond well to one or several of these therapies; however, relief may only be temporary.
- Antibiotics may be prescribed if an infection is present.
- A topical astringent may be applied to shrink a swollen polyp.
- The most reliable and long-lasting treatment of polyps is surgical removal (polypectomy). This minor procedure, usually requiring only local anesthesia, is traditionally performed with a wire snare. However, many surgeons now prefer to use an endoscope (a slender optical viewing tube that can be inserted into the nose), which permits a more precise and complete excision of the polyp, thereby reducing the likelihood that it will recur at the same site.
- Frequent recurrence of polyps may require more invasive surgery to open the sinus cavities and remove diseased tissue.
- Over-the-counter pain relievers may be used. A special note: People who are prone to nasal polyps should use acetaminophen rather than aspirin, since (for reasons that remain unclear) these same people also tend to be allergic to aspirin.

WHEN TO CALL A DOCTOR

- If you experience the symptoms of nasal polyps, make an appointment to see a doctor. You will most likely be referred to an ear, nose, and throat specialist (otolaryngologist) for further examination and treatment.
- If you experience persistent or excessive bleeding, high fever, or unrelenting pain after surgical removal of nasal polyps, contact a doctor immediately.

Nephrotic Syndrome

WHAT IS IT?

Nephrotic syndrome is a condition marked by the loss of large amounts of protein through the urine. A number of different diseases can result in the syndrome; however, in many cases it is caused by kidney damage of unknown origin, especially in children, in whom it is most common. Nephrotic syndrome arises from damage to the glomeruli, the tiny structures in the kidneys that filter blood. Small chemical substances, including waste products, pass through the glomerular membrane, but proteins are too large to cross an intact membrane. However, if the glomeruli are damaged, proteins may escape into the urine. Loss of large amounts of protein through the urine lowers albumin levels in the blood, which prevents fluid in the body tissues from returning to the bloodstream, producing the swelling (edema) characteristic of this syndrome. Major complications include protein malnutrition, occlusion of major veins by blood clots, and renal failure. Children with nephrotic syndrome are more vulnerable to systemic infections. The outcome depends on the underlying cause of the syndrome.

WHAT CAUSES IT?

• Acute glomerulonephritis, especially following a streptococcal infection, as well as other types of glomerular disease, are the most common causes of nephrotic syndrome (see Glomerulonephritis, Acute, for more information).
• Other disorders can cause the syndrome, including diabetes mellitus, systemic lupus erythematosus, amyloidosis, hypertension, hepatitis B, and cancer.
• Some toxins and medications, such as heroin, gold, mercury, lead, mesantoin, and perchlorate, may damage the kidneys.
• Allergic reactions to bee stings and poison ivy may result in nephrotic syndrome.
• The cause of some cases is unknown.

PREVENTION

• Treatment of potential underlying causes may prevent the onset of nephrotic syndrome.

DIAGNOSIS

• Blood tests show a reduction in albumin and an increase in triglycerides and cholesterol.
• Urine protein loss is measured. Urine is also examined for red and white blood cells.
• A kidney biopsy may be performed. Under local anesthesia a needle is inserted into the kidney through the back to extract a small tissue sample.

HOW TO TREAT IT

• A low-salt diet may help reduce fluid retention.
• Adequate dietary protein is needed to replace that which is lost in the urine.
• Diuretics are used to reduce excess fluid retention and increase urine output.
• Long-term anticoagulant treatment may be needed in those with the tendency to form blood clots.
• Antihypertensive drugs may be prescribed to reduce associated high blood pressure.
• Antibiotics may be prescribed to treat associated bacterial infections.
• Corticosteroids may reduce protein loss in the urine.
• Intravenous albumin may be given to increase plasma protein levels when extremely low blood albumin levels cause severe symptoms. However, the albumin is rapidly excreted in the urine.
• Chemotherapeutic drugs used to treat cancer are also effective in preventing relapses of nephrotic syndrome and may be used in addition to steroids.

WHEN TO CALL A DOCTOR

• Call a doctor for symptoms of nephrotic syndrome.
• **EMERGENCY** Call your doctor immediately if symptoms of kidney failure develop, including fatigue, nausea and vomiting, loss of appetite, itching, headaches, or impaired vision.

SYMPTOMS

• Swelling of the abdomen, the tissues around the eyes, and the ankles, due to fluid retention.
• Weight increase owing to fluid retention.
• Shortness of breath due to fluid retention in the lungs.
• Decreased amount of urine.
• Diarrhea.
• Loss of appetite.
• Fatigue.

Neuralgia

WHAT IS IT?

Neuralgia refers to a range of disorders marked by spasms of pain along the path of a nerve. Some forms are named for the nerves they affect. For example, trigeminal neuralgia, also known as tic douloureux, affects the trigeminal (fifth cranial) nerve that supplies sensation to the face, causing brief but intense spasms of pain on one side of the lips, gums, cheek, chin, or, rarely, around the eyes. Other forms of neuralgia are associated with specific diseases. Postherpetic neuralgia, for example, can arise after a case of shingles and causes a dull, burning pain that may persist for months or even years. Facial neuralgia may also be a feature of multiple sclerosis or migraines. Neuralgia tends to affect people over 50. Trigeminal neuralgia is fairly common, particularly in older women; postherpetic neuralgia is also common, while the other forms of neuralgia are rare. Although painful, neuralgia is not life-threatening.

WHAT CAUSES IT?

- In most cases the cause is unknown.
- Some cases may be due to compression of the nerve by blood vessels or a tumor.
- Herpes zoster infection (shingles) precedes postherpetic neuralgia.
- Multiple sclerosis is a cause of neuralgia in those younger than 50.

PREVENTION

- There are no known ways to prevent neuralgia.

The trigeminal nerve has three distinct branches. Neuralgia in any one of them produces pain within the regions indicated.

DIAGNOSIS

- Neuralgia is identified by its characteristic symptoms.
- X-rays or computed tomography (CT) may be done to rule out other conditions, such as tumors.

HOW TO TREAT IT

- Over-the-counter pain relievers may be of some use.
- The topical cream Zostrix (capsaicin), along with physical therapy, may ease postherpetic neuralgia.
- The drug carbamazepine helps in about 75 percent of cases of trigeminal neuralgia, but a third of patients cannot tolerate the drug.
- More invasive procedures may be warranted if drug treatment fails. The most commonly used approach delivers high-frequency sound waves or electrical currents to the nerve to reduce its sensitivity. This often helps but causes lingering numbness and, if the region around the eye is involved, may result in corneal damage. Also, neuralgia may eventually recur.
- Another approach involves exploratory surgery to look for and loosen any blood vessels that may be compressing the nerve. This approach provides long-term relief in most cases but can require up to a week of hospitalization and, like all major surgeries, carries significant risks.

WHEN TO CALL A DOCTOR

- Call a doctor if you experience persistent pain that does not respond to over-the-counter treatment.

SYMPTOMS

- Brief, staccato bursts of excruciating pain, typically lasting from a few seconds to a minute or two.
- Recurrent pain in the same location, often in bouts lasting weeks at a time. Between bouts, there may be weeks or months with no pain.
- Pain triggered by touching specific areas of the skin or by talking, chewing, shaving, brushing the teeth, or swallowing. Bursts of dull dental or sinus pain may be an early sign of trigeminal neuralgia.

Neurogenic Bladder

WHAT IS IT?

Neurogenic bladder is impaired bladder function resulting from damage to the nerves that govern the urinary tract. Various nerves converge in the area of the bladder and serve to control the muscles of the urinary tract, which include the sphincter muscles that normally form a tight ring around the urethra to hold urine back until it is voluntarily released. A variety of factors can damage these nerves and cause urinary incontinence. In some cases spontaneous nerve impulses to the bladder trigger spastic, unexpected bladder contractions, resulting in accidental voiding of sometimes large amounts of urine. In other types of neurogenic bladder conditions, the bladder may become flaccid and distended and cease to contract fully, resulting in only partial emptying and continual dribbling of small amounts of urine. Rashes may erupt in areas of skin irritated by urine. Stagnant urine in the bladder also increases the risks of bladder stone formation and urinary tract infections. Such infections, when severe, can lead to life-threatening kidney failure. In some patients there is partial loss of anal sphincter control as well. Neurogenic bladder can occur at any age, but it is especially common among the elderly.

SYMPTOMS

- Urinary incontinence, characterized by either the involuntary release of large volumes of urine or continuous dribbling of small amounts. Bed-wetting may occur.
- Frequent urination.
- Persistent urge to urinate despite recent voiding; constant feeling that the bladder is not completely empty.
- Pain or burning on urination.

WHAT CAUSES IT?

- Spinal cord injuries resulting in paralysis.
- Other disorders that may produce neurogenic bladder as they progress. Such disorders include syphilis, diabetes mellitus, brain or spinal cord tumors, stroke, ruptured or herniated intervertebral disk, and degenerative neurological diseases such as multiple sclerosis and amyotrophic lateral sclerosis (Lou Gehrig's disease).
- A congenital spinal cord abnormality (that is, one that is present at birth), such as spina bifida.
- Long-term effects of alcoholism.

PREVENTION

- There are no known ways to prevent neurogenic bladder.

DIAGNOSIS

- A thorough patient history is essential. It is useful to keep a 24-hour record of urination patterns, including the approximate volume of urine voided, how urgently you feel the need to urinate, and any factors that may aggravate incontinence. It is also important to report any medications you are taking.
- Physical examination will likely include a rectal, genital, and abdominal exam to check for enlargement of the bladder or other abnormalities.
- A complete neurological exam is essential.
- X-rays or an ultrasound scan may be taken during urination (voiding cystography).
- Tests to measure urine output are conducted. To determine whether urine is retained after voiding, the doctor may insert a catheter into the bladder. To determine whether leakage occurs, a full-bladder stress test may be necessary: the bladder is filled to capacity via a catheter, and the patient is then asked to bend over, cough, or walk.
- Urine and blood samples may be taken to look for abnormalities, including infections and underlying disorders that might be causing or aggravating the condition.
- Spinal x-rays.

HOW TO TREAT IT

- A urinary catheter (drainage tube) can be used continuously by patients who have sudden, unexpected bladder contractions. Women usually fare better with such therapy; men are more prone to developing urinary tract infections and complications, including abscess formation.
- Patients suffering from bladder paralysis can be taught to insert a catheter several times a day to drain the bladder completely and so prevent urine retention

Neurogenic Bladder *continued*

that may lead to bladder stones and infections.

• Various medications may help to improve bladder muscle control and to prevent involuntary muscle contractions. Muscle relaxants, antispasmodics, and anticholinergic drugs (which block the neurotransmitter acetylcholine), such as propantheline, oxybutynin, and imipramine, are helpful in some cases.

• Bethanechol is the most commonly prescribed drug to help stimulate bladder contractions in patients who retain urine.

• A device that stimulates bladder contraction with electrical impulses may be used, although such therapy is considered experimental.

• Surgery may be performed to widen the sphincter to decrease resistance in the bladder outlet and thus maximize bladder emptying. In other cases the sphincter or lower pelvic muscles may be surgically tightened to improve bladder control.

• In very severe cases surgery may be done to reroute the flow of urine so that it empties into the intestine or into an externally worn receptacle.

WHEN TO CALL A DOCTOR

• Call a doctor if you experience recurrent urinary incontinence. Don't allow embarrassment to prevent you from seeking professional help.

Obesity

WHAT IS IT?

Obesity is conventionally defined as an excess of stored fat resulting in a body weight that is 20 percent or greater than what is accepted as ideal for a person's height and body type. It is not in itself a disease, but obesity does represent a serious health risk. Mortality rates and the incidence of high blood pressure, heart disease, and diabetes mellitus are substantially higher in obese adults, especially in those whose excessive fat is stored in the abdomen rather than in the hips. Certain types of cancer are also more common among those who are overweight. Excess weight places greater stress on the back, hips, and knees, which may aggravate arthritis. In addition, obesity is often accompanied by poor self-image, psychological distress, and diminished quality of life. Health care professionals have come to realize, however, that losing weight and keeping it off is extraordinarily difficult. Nonetheless, a sensible balanced diet and a regular regimen of moderate exercise confer valuable health benefits and so are advised for everyone, regardless of weight.

SYMPTOMS
• Body weight of 20 percent or greater than the recommended ideal.

WHAT CAUSES IT?

• Obesity results from an imbalance between caloric intake and energy expenditure. At times, obesity may result from habitually excessive food intake or from extremely limited physical activity. There is evidence, however, that some people gain weight because they have a lower basal metabolic rate; that is, they burn fewer calories to maintain everyday body functions, such as breathing, heart contractions, and digestion.
• Hereditary, environmental, and psychological factors all play a role in obesity.

PREVENTION

• Establish healthy eating habits; maintain a nutritious, low-fat, high-carbohydrate diet.
• Exercise regularly and stay as active as possible.

DIAGNOSIS

• Height and weight is compared to standard tables.
• Blood tests for complications of diabetes are taken.
• Circumference of waist and hips are measured; a waist-to-hips ratio of greater than one indicates more dangerous abdominal obesity.

HOW TO TREAT IT

• In many cases doctors and nutritionists advise a diet of no less than 1,200 calories per day, made up of nutritious, low-fat, low-calorie foods such as fruits, vegetables, whole grains, lean meat or fish, and low-fat dairy products. It is particularly important to avoid fat as much as possible.
• Avoid crash diets, fasting, or appetite suppressants, which may reduce weight over the short term but rarely produce sustained weight loss, since they do not alter usual eating habits and may induce metabolic changes that actually promote weight gain.
• Try to engage in regular, vigorous aerobic exercise, like running, biking, or swimming, for at least 30 minutes a day, four times a week. If this is not possible, even walking or gardening is helpful.
• For the grossly obese, doctors may advise a very low-calorie liquid diet program (800–900 calories per day), but such a program should be conducted only under careful medical supervision.
• Because health hazards appear to result from frequent fluctuations in weight (yo-yo dieting), weight loss efforts should only be undertaken after a firm resolve is made to maintain any weight loss achieved.
• In rare cases when obesity is life-threatening, doctors may resort to extraordinary measures, including wiring the jaw shut for several weeks, surgery to staple the stomach and reduce its size, or cutting or suctioning away fat (liposuction). However, the long-term success of these methods is questionable, and severe complications are possible.
• Therapy or counseling may help to confront underlying psychological and emotional reasons for overeating. Support groups are often helpful.

WHEN TO CALL A DOCTOR

• If you are obese and unable to change your eating and exercise habits to lose weight, see a doctor or nutritionist.

Optic Neuritis

WHAT IS IT?

Optic neuritis, an inflammation or demyelination (progressive loss of the protective sheaths around a nerve) of the optic nerve in one or both eyes, may interfere with the transmission of nerve impulses from the optic nerve to the brain, causing sudden blurring or other visual impairment. Usually, central vision and color perception are affected the most. Although rare, some cases progress from blurring to total temporary blindness in the affected eye(s) within a matter of days. Underlying conditions that can damage the optic nerve include multiple sclerosis and various infections, such as syphilis. In the majority of cases, symptoms disappear spontaneously and normal or nearly normal vision is restored within a few months; however, attacks may recur and can eventually lead to permanent visual loss, depending on the underlying cause.

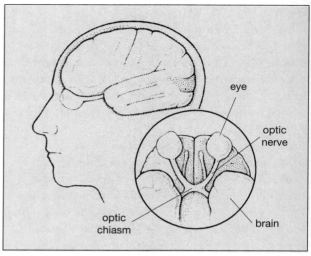

At the optic chiasm, some of the fibers of either of the two optic nerves cross over to the optic tract on the opposite side. Optic neuritis is characterized by inflammation of any part of this nerve structure.

SYMPTOMS
- Impaired central vision or color perception in one or both eyes.
- Partial or total vision loss within a period of several hours to several days. If both eyes are involved, the second eye may be affected several days or weeks later.
- Pain when moving or touching the affected eye or eyes, especially in the first several days after the onset of symptoms.

WHAT CAUSES IT?
- An episode of optic neuritis may be one of the earliest indications of multiple sclerosis (MS), a disease in which the protective sheaths (myelin) surrounding the nerves are gradually destroyed. Indeed, by some estimates, 35 percent of men and 75 percent of women who develop optic neuritis will develop MS within the ensuing 15 years; conversely, 40 percent of MS patients experience at least one episode of optic neuritis.
- Optic neuritis may also be caused by inflammation due to infection of the tissues surrounding the optic nerve.

PREVENTION
- There are no known ways to prevent optic neuritis.

DIAGNOSIS
- A thorough eye examination is required. Inspection with an ophthalmoscope (a lighted instrument that permits viewing of the internal structures of the eye) often reveals only normal conditions during the early stages, but later examinations may uncover characteristic signs of optic neuritis.
- Visual field and color perception tests may be performed.
- Tests may be required to rule out serious underlying diseases associated with optic nerve damage. If multiple sclerosis or temporal arteritis is suspected, the doctor will recommend further testing.

HOW TO TREAT IT
- In most cases, partial or full recovery of vision will occur within several months without treatment .
- Corticosteroids may be prescribed to speed natural recovery, but they cannot prevent or lessen the severity of subsequent attacks.

WHEN TO CALL A DOCTOR
- If you experience any vision loss or impairment, contact an ophthalmologist immediately.

Oral Cancers

WHAT IS IT?
Oral cancer is the growth of malignant cells in any part of the oral cavity, which includes the lips, gums, tongue, cheeks, floor or roof of the mouth, and tonsils. The most common site is the lip, followed by the tongue, and then other locations. The primary risk factor for all types of oral cancer is the use of tobacco in any form. Symptoms vary depending on the location of the cancer but usually include ulcerations that are initially painless. In more advanced stages, the cancer spreads, most often to the lymph nodes in the neck or under the jaw. Treatment depends on the location and stage of the malignancy and the age and overall health of the patient, but it usually involves surgery, radiation, or both. Prognosis is good if the cancer is detected and treated in its early stages, before it has spread. In most cases, lip cancer is very treatable because it is easier to detect, while prognosis for tongue cancer is not as good, particularly if the lesion is near the rear of the mouth and hard to see. Oral cancers account for about 5 percent of all cancers. Risk increases with age; the majority of cases occur in people over 45, with men at twice the risk as women.

SYMPTOMS
- A skin lesion or ulcerations in some area of the mouth that persist or worsen over time. In early stages, such lesions are often painless.
- Difficulty speaking, eating, and swallowing, in more advanced cases.
- Bad breath.
- Abnormal sense of taste.
- An enlarging growth on the lip that crusts over and bleeds when the crust is removed.
- A sore throat or burning sensation in the mouth during advanced stages, especially when eating or drinking.
- White patches (leukoplakia) or velvety red patches (erythroplakia). (These must be watched carefully, as they may be precancerous.)

WHAT CAUSES IT?
- The cause of oral cancer is unknown, but the following risk factors have been identified:
- The use of tobacco in any form (smoking, chewing, or dipping).
- Long-term heavy alcohol use.
- Nutritional deficiencies (including lack of vitamin A, certain B vitamins, and iron).
- Years of exposure to sunlight (a risk factor for lip cancer).
- Infections with herpes simplex or human papillomavirus.

PREVENTION
- Avoid all tobacco products.
- Avoid excessive alcohol use.
- Regular dental checkups and periodic self-examination of the mouth may help detect cancer in its early stages.

DIAGNOSIS
- Patient history and examination of the mouth and neck are necessary.
- A small sample of affected tissue is removed (biopsy) for microscopic examination of the cells to determine if cancer is present.
- X-rays of the head or chest may be performed to detect if the cancer has spread.

HOW TO TREAT IT
- Surgery to remove the tumor, the surrounding tissue, and possibly the lymph nodes in the neck is generally recommended.
- Radiation therapy is often advised when there is suspicion that cancer may have spread. It may be administered externally (for example, with x-rays) or internally (by implanting pellets into the tumor).
- Speech therapy and other kinds of occupational therapy may be part of rehabilitation.
- A wide variety of plastic-surgery techniques are available to correct disfigurement.

WHEN TO CALL A DOCTOR
- Contact your doctor or dentist if you develop any mouth lesion that fails to heal within two weeks to a month.

Orchitis

WHAT IS IT?

Orchitis is the inflammation of one or both of the testicles because of infection. Indeed, orchitis is the most common complication of mumps in adult males, occurring in up to one-fourth of men who contract mumps after puberty. Orchitis is character-ized by swelling and severe pain in the testes, which usually begins to subside after three to seven days. Most of the time the affected testicles return to nor-mal size and function, but complications may include testicular atrophy and, rarely, infertility. Two-thirds of cases affect only one testicle; involvement of both carries a higher risk of infertility. Orchitis is most common among males 15 to 25 years old.

SYMPTOMS
- Severe pain in the scrotum or in the affected testicle.
- Swelling and a feeling of heaviness, usually on one side of the scrotum.
- Fever.

WHAT CAUSES IT?

- Orchitis is most often caused by a viral infection, especially the virus responsible for mumps.
- Bacterial infections of the epididymis (the long, tightly coiled, sperm conduit that rests on the back of each testicle) or the prostate may spread to the testes.
- Testicular inflammation may be a manifestation of sexually transmitted diseases such as syphilis and chlamydia.

PREVENTION

- Be sure you have been immunized with the MMR (measles, mumps, rubella) vaccine.
- Practice safe sex behaviors, such as monogamy and condom use.

DIAGNOSIS

- Patient history and physical examination are necessary.
- Urinalysis and urine culture are performed to screen for an underlying bacterial infection.

HOW TO TREAT IT

- Antibiotics are prescribed for bacterial infections. Sexual partners may also need to be treated.
- If orchitis is due to a virus, treatment is aimed exclusively at relieving symptoms (as antibiotics are effective against bacterial but not viral infections). Analgesic drugs, bed rest with support of the scro-tum, and the application of ice packs may help to ease the pain of orchitis.

WHEN TO CALL A DOCTOR

- Call your doctor if you develop any persistent pain or swelling in the scrotum. It is likely that you will be referred to a urologist. A careful urological evalu-ation is necessary to rule out other disorders such as epididymitis and testicular torsion, which produce similar symptoms to orchitis.

Osteoarthritis

WHAT IS IT?

Osteoarthritis —also known as degenerative joint disease—is the gradual age-related deterioration of cartilage within the joints, causing pain and sometimes deformity. (Joint inflammation is uncommon.) It is the most common form of arthritis: nearly all people have developed some degree of osteoarthritis in one or more joints by the age of 60. It can occur in any joint, but most commonly osteoarthritis affects the fingers, neck, spine, hips, knees, and feet. As the elastic cartilage that serves as a cushion between bones breaks down, bone ends may rub together, causing them to develop uneven outgrowths called osteophytes, or spurs, that may grind against each other as the joint moves. Damage usually develops gradually over a period of years. In some people, symptoms remain mild or even fade; in others, symptoms grow progressively worse until they are severely disabling. Affected joints may begin to lose their shape and alignment, and weakness and wasting of the muscles surrounding the joints may occur if pain and stiffness prevent normal motion. Osteoarthritis has no impact on longevity (unlike some other forms of arthritis), but it can diminish the overall quality of life of its sufferers. There is no cure, but a number of treatments can ease pain and minimize disability.

WHAT CAUSES IT?

• Osteoarthritis occurs as a normal part of aging, owing to years of cumulative wear and tear on the joints. Obesity increases the risk of developing osteoarthritis in weight-bearing joints (the back, hips, and knees).
• Trauma or overuse of a joint can hasten the development of osteoarthritis. This is common among athletes and those whose occupations require constant repetitive motions, such as pianists, typists, machinists, and dancers.

PREVENTION

• Maintain a healthy weight.
• As much as possible avoid repetitive activities that may lead to joint overuse.

DIAGNOSIS

• Patient history and physical examination.
• X-rays.
• In rare cases when diagnosis is in question, fluid may be drawn from the affected joint through a needle for laboratory analysis.

HOW TO TREAT IT

• Pain relievers, including acetaminophen, and non-steroidal anti-inflammatory drugs (NSAIDs), such as ibuprofen, naproxen, and salsalate, are the first line of treatment.
• Cold packs, warm compresses, heat lamps, and warm baths or showers may bring relief.
• Splints, braces, neck collars, crutches, or canes may provide support and limit stress on the affected joint.
• A regular exercise program under the guidance of a doctor or physical therapist is recommended. The right program can help maintain flexibility, strengthen muscles (and thus lessen stress on joints), and improve overall fitness.
• Corticosteroid injections may be advised for relief of severe pain.
• A variety of surgical procedures may be warranted in severe cases, including arthroscopy (insertion into the affected joint of a thin, flexible viewing scope that can be used to smooth or repair cartilage) and arthroplasty (total joint replacement).

WHEN TO CALL A DOCTOR

• If symptoms of osteoarthritis begin to interfere with the enjoyment of normal activities, call a doctor.

SYMPTOMS

• Joint pain that is aggravated by movement and relieved by rest.
• Stiffness, especially in the morning or after exercise, and loss of flexibility in the affected joints.
• Knobby overgrowths on the joints closest to the fingertips (Heberden's nodes) or on the middle joints of the fingers.
• Audible crackling noises upon joint movement.
• Changes in gait.
• Redness, warmth, and swelling of a joint (rare).

Osteomalacia and Rickets

WHAT IS IT?

Osteomalacia is a disorder marked by inadequate or defective mineralization of the skeleton, resulting in soft or fragile bones. It typically occurs either when there are insufficient amounts of vitamin D in the diet or, more commonly, when the body is unable to properly absorb and metabolize vitamin D, which is essential for the absorption of the calcium needed to maintain strong, healthy bones. When the disease occurs in children, it is known as rickets and tends to produce obvious skeletal deformities such as bowed legs. The disease has more subtle manifestations in adults and may be difficult to diagnose or to differentiate from osteoporosis, although in some cases repeated pressure on soft bones can lead to fractures or mild deformities. In adults, when osteomalacia is due to a vitamin D deficiency, treatment usually cures the problem within six months. In children, the disease may be arrested with treatment, although skeletal deformities may be permanent. While common in underdeveloped countries, rickets is now rare in Western nations.

SYMPTOMS

- Bone pain in the arms, legs, spine, and especially the hips.
- Muscle weakness, waddling gait.
- Unexplained bone fractures or deformities.
- Painful spasms or cramps in the face, hands, and feet due to low levels of calcium in the blood (rare).
- In rickets: bowed limbs (especially the legs), pot belly, waddling gait, disturbed growth.

WHAT CAUSES IT?

- A chief cause of osteomalacia is intestinal malabsorption of vitamin D, which may result from a number of causes (see Malabsorption).
- Low levels of vitamin D lead to secretion of excessive amounts of parathyroid hormone, which in turn mobilizes calcium from the bones and increases the loss of phosphorus in the urine.
- Inadequate exposure to sunlight reduces the amount of vitamin D produced naturally by the skin.

- Dietary deficiency of vitamin D is rarely a cause.
- Chronic renal failure and complications of hemodialysis are potential causes.
- Chronic acidosis (an abnormal state of reduced alkalinity in the blood or body tissues, usually due to renal failure) may lead to osteomalacia.
- Osteomalacia may occur as a side effect of some anticonvulsant drugs used to treat epilepsy. They interfere with normal activation of vitamin D.
- Several rare hereditary disorders can cause hypophosphatemia (low phosphorus levels in the blood), resulting in osteomalacia.
- Hypophosphatemia may result from chronic use of nonabsorbable antacids.

PREVENTION

- Dietary intake of vitamin D–fortified foods (such as milk products) and adequate exposure to sunlight may help prevent vitamin D deficiency.

DIAGNOSIS

- Patient history and physical examination.
- X-rays to evaluate bone mass and fractures.
- Blood tests to measure calcium, phosphorus, and vitamin D levels.
- Bone biopsy in some cases.

HOW TO TREAT IT

- Oral supplements of vitamin D are given, sometimes in conjunction with calcium.
- For osteomalacia due to intestinal malabsorption, large doses of oral vitamin D or injections of vitamin D may be needed. Such patients may also benefit from treatments with artificial ultraviolet light and calcium supplements.
- Osteomalacia due to chronic renal failure requires correction of the acidosis.
- Disorders leading to low blood phosphorus are treated with large oral phosphate supplements plus vitamin D metabolites.
- Skeletal deformities may be corrected surgically.

WHEN TO CALL A DOCTOR

- Consult a doctor if you or your child experiences bone pain, unexplained fractures, or apparent limb deformities.

Osteomyelitis

WHAT IS IT?

Osteomyelitis is infection of the bone. The infection can originate in another part of the body (in the throat or skin, for example) and spread to the bones via the bloodstream, or develop after a bone fracture has broken the skin and becomes infected directly. The infected bone becomes inflamed, resulting in severe bone pain, fever, and the formation of pus. Single episodes of the disorder, known as acute osteomyelitis, are most common in the arm and leg bones of rapidly growing children. Chronic osteomyelitis, a rare and stubborn form of the condition, causes persistent bone pain for years. This form of

SYMPTOMS
- Pain, often excruciating, in the affected bone.
- Heat, swelling, tenderness, redness, and restricted movement in the affected area.
- High fever.
- Fatigue and malaise.
- Tachycardia (rapid heart beat).

the disease may also lead to complications, including skin abscess, bone deformity, cessation of bone growth in children, and amyloidosis (the deposition of a starchy protein into tissues and vital organs). Chronic osteomyelitis is more prevalent among adults and most often affects the pelvis or vertebrae. With prompt attention, acute osteomyelitis can usually be treated successfully with antibiotics; chronic osteomyelitis, however, is more difficult to treat and normally requires surgery to remove the affected bone. With the advent of antibiotics and higher standards of nutrition in developed countries, osteomyelitis of either form had become increasingly rare.

WHAT CAUSES IT?
- Acute osteomyelitis occurs when infectious organisms—usually bacteria—invade bone tissue. (More rarely, a fungal infection is the cause.) A bone is more susceptible to infection after a blunt physical trauma or fracture.

- Possible causes of chronic osteomyelitis include an acute case that is ignored or fails to respond to treatment; a compound bone fracture; and tuberculosis that spreads to the bone from elsewhere in the body.

PREVENTION
- Get prompt and thorough medical treatment for any bacterial infection before it can spread to the bones or other organs.

DIAGNOSIS
- Blood cultures may identify the organism responsible for infection.
- Bone scans can provide early detection of osteomyelitis; bone x-rays may also detect osteomyelitis, but usually only two to three weeks after infection.
- Biopsy of a small sample of tissue or pus can be taken to identify the infectious organism if blood cultures fail.

HOW TO TREAT IT
- Acute osteomyelitis can usually be cured with an extended course of antibiotics, given orally or intravenously over a period of weeks or months.
- Bed rest and immobilization of the affected area may be advised.
- If antibiotics fail to cure the infection, surgery to drain pus and remove infected or dead tissue may be warranted.
- The only effective treatment for chronic osteomyelitis is surgical removal of the affected bone tissue. Bone grafting may be necessary in such cases.

WHEN TO CALL A DOCTOR
- If you experience the symptoms of osteomyelitis, see a doctor right away.
- If you develop any sign of complication during treatment for osteomyelitis (formation of or increased drainage from an abscess, fever, unbearable pain), see a doctor immediately.
- If you previously had osteomyelitis and experience any of the symptoms of recurrence, see a doctor as soon as possible.

Osteoporosis

WHAT IS IT?

Osteoporosis is characterized by a loss of bone mass due to depletion of minerals essential to bone formation (phosphorus and especially calcium). Affected bones become porous and brittle and susceptible to fractures. The wrists, hips, and vertebrae in the spine are the most common sites of fractures due to osteoporosis. The disorder is very common among people over the age of 70 and affects women four times more often than men, owing to hormonal changes that occur with menopause.

WHAT CAUSES IT?

• Some degree of loss of bone mass is a normal part of aging, but a number of factors hasten osteoporosis, including reduced estrogen levels after menopause; dietary calcium deficiency; physical inactivity; smoking; excessive alcohol use; and being underweight.
• Hereditary factors may be involved. For example, Caucasian women have a higher incidence of osteoporosis than others.
• Osteoporosis may occur as a consequence of an underlying condition, such as hyperthyroidism, premature menopause (before age 45), chronic lung diseases, and Cushing's disease (excessive production of corticosteroids by the adrenal glands). It may also arise from long-term use of corticosteroid drugs or heparin (an anticoagulant).

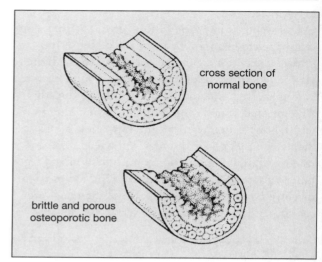

cross section of normal bone

brittle and porous osteoporotic bone

Rich stores of calcium make normal bones remarkably strong. Osteoporosis weakens bone by robbing it of its mineral content.

diet alone, which is the case for most people.
• Regular weight-bearing exercise is important.

DIAGNOSIS

• Patient history and physical examination.
• Bone density scan.
• X-rays or other imaging tests, such as CT (computed tomography) scans. Routine x-rays, however, do not detect osteoporosis until 25 percent or more bone mass has been lost.
• Blood or urine tests or a bone biopsy to detect or rule out secondary disorders as the cause of bone loss.

HOW TO TREAT IT

• Take over-the-counter analgesics for minor pain.
• Prompt estrogen replacement therapy can slow the progress of osteoporosis in postmenopausal women.
• High doses of calcitonin (a hormone that regulates the body's calcium usage) can slow bone loss and may in fact add bone mass. Another drug, etidronate, has been shown to produce similar results.
• Calcium supplementation may be advised.
• Exercise and physical therapy may preserve function.

WHEN TO CALL A DOCTOR

• Call a doctor for any symptoms of osteoporosis.
• If you have osteoporosis and pain develops after any strain or injury, see a doctor immediately.

> **SYMPTOMS**
> • Lower back pain.
> • Gradual loss of height and stooping posture.
> • Wrist, hip, or vertebral fractures.

PREVENTION

• Estrogen replacement is highly effective in preventing osteoporosis in postmenopausal women. Estrogen must be started soon after menopause because bone loss accelerates rapidly at that time.
• A diet rich in calcium and vitamin D protects against osteoporosis. Calcium supplementation is recommended for postmenopausal women and others at risk for osteoporosis if a daily intake of 1,500 milligrams of calcium cannot be achieved through

Otosclerosis

WHAT IS IT?

Otosclerosis is a disorder caused by abnormal growth of spongy bone tissue at the junction of the inner ear and middle ear, resulting in gradual hearing loss. The overgrowth of bone impedes and, in the majority of cases, eventually immobilizes the stapes, one of the three tiny bones in the middle ear that mechanically conduct sound waves into the inner ear. This results in what is known as conductive hearing loss. In some cases, however, excess bone growth may eventually spread to the inner ear, causing damage to the nerves involved in hearing (sensorineural hearing loss), which is far more difficult to treat than conductive hearing loss. Otosclerosis may occur in one ear alone, but most often it affects both, either simultaneously or in succession. In general, hearing loss progresses gradually over a period of 10 to 15 years, usually leading to total deafness. Partial or total hearing can be restored, however, with a surgical procedure called a stapedectomy. Otosclerosis is fairly common, affecting one out of every 200 people, usually between the ages of 15 and 30, and is especially prevalent among Caucasians. Incidence is twice as high in women as in men.

WHAT CAUSES IT?

• Otosclerosis appears to be an inherited disorder; many of those who develop it report a family history of hearing loss.

SYMPTOMS

• Gradual and progressive hearing loss.
• Ringing or noises in the ears (tinnitus).
• Dizziness.
• A tendency to speak softly.
• Improved ability to perceive spoken words in environments with background noise. (The opposite is true with many other types of hearing loss, including that which commonly occurs with age.)

• Pregnancy may trigger the onset of symptoms or accelerate the rate of hearing loss in those with active otosclerosis.

PREVENTION

• There is no know way to prevent otosclerosis.

DIAGNOSIS

• Diagnosis is suspected in patients who have a blood relative with known otosclerosis or early hearing loss.
• Hearing tests will be performed to determine the type and degree of hearing loss. If the doctor suspects otosclerosis, especially if a patient has a family history of the disorder, more specialized hearing tests will be conducted.

HOW TO TREAT IT

• Stapedectomy (surgical removal of the stapes and replacement with an artificial prosthesis) is the only method to cure or at least arrest the progress of otosclerosis. The procedure is often highly successful, significantly improving hearing in the majority of cases. Since there is a small risk that the surgery will result in total deafness in the operated ear, stapedectomy is normally performed on only one ear at a time.
• Hearing aids can be very effective for people with otosclerosis when stapedectomy is not possible. Also, a hearing aid may be required to augment hearing after stapedectomy.

WHEN TO CALL A DOCTOR

• Contact an otolaryngologist (ear, nose, and throat specialist) or ask your regular family practitioner to recommend one if you experience any degree of hearing loss.
• If you have had stapedectomy surgery for otosclerosis and you experience any sign of postoperative infection (pain, dizziness, fever), call a doctor immediately.

Ovarian Cancer

WHAT IS IT?

Ovarian cancer occurs when cancer cells form malignant tumors in one or often both ovaries. With about 20,000 new cases diagnosed each year, ovarian cancer is the seventh most common type of cancer in women. Although the overall incidence is relatively low, the death rate from ovarian cancer is very high. It is the most deadly of all gynecologic cancers and the fourth most common cause of cancer-related death in women. The reason for the low survival rate is that ovarian cancer usually produces no noticeable symptoms in its early stages, and there is

---

SYMPTOMS

- In early stages there are usually no symptoms.
- Vague abdominal discomfort, indigestion, or other mild gastrointestinal problems.
- Abdominal swelling or bloating.
- Pelvic fullness or pressure.
- Urinary frequency.
- Unexplained vaginal bleeding or abnormal menstrual cycles.
- Weight loss.

---

currently no simple test to screen for it. Consequently, the disease is usually not diagnosed until symptoms appear and the cancer has spread. Occasionally, the disease is first suspected during a routine pelvic examination. Prognosis varies depending on the type and the stage of the disease, but the overall five-year survival rate is between 30 and 40 percent. It is therefore important to keep up with regular pelvic examinations, since diagnosis and treatment of ovarian cancer in the earliest stages yields nearly a 75 percent five-year survival rate. Owing to recent advances in treatment, the survival rate has improved even among women with late-stage disease, and some types of ovarian cancers can now be cured.

WHAT CAUSES IT?

- The cause of ovarian cancer is unknown. It is most common among postmenopausal women. Women who have not had children are at increased risk; those who have used oral contraceptives are at decreased risk.

PREVENTION

- There are no known ways to prevent ovarian cancer. Scheduling regular pelvic examinations, however, may help to detect ovarian cancer at an earlier, more treatable stage.

DIAGNOSIS

- Patient history and physical exam are necessary.
- Abdominal ultrasound or CT (computed tomography) scans are used to locate tumors.

HOW TO TREAT IT

- When cancer is strongly suspected, surgery (known as exploratory laparotomy) is performed to confirm the diagnosis and determine the extent of the disease (staging) in order to plan the future course of treatment. Tumors found during this procedure are removed, if possible, and examined under a microscope.
- Most often, both ovaries are removed. In addition, the fallopian tubes, uterus, or nearby lymph glands may be removed as well if they appear to be affected.
- Surgery is usually followed by chemotherapy or radiation to shrink or destroy any remaining cancer sites.
- Follow-up "second-look" surgery may be scheduled at some point during the course of therapy to evaluate the efficacy of treatment and to remove any new malignancies (although the value of second-look surgery is controversial).

WHEN TO CALL A DOCTOR

- If you experience any of the symptoms of ovarian cancer, see a doctor immediately.

Ovarian Cysts, Benign

WHAT IS IT?

An ovarian cyst is an abnormal, fluid-filled sac that forms in the ovary. Ovarian cysts are common and, in the vast majority of cases, they are benign (non-cancerous). They vary in size and may occur at different sites in the ovary; the most common type develops when an egg-producing follicle does not rupture and release the egg but instead swells with fluid and forms a follicular cyst. Benign ovarian cysts often cause no symptoms and are discovered incidentally during a routine pelvic examination. In some cases, however, they may alter hormone production in the ovaries or grow large enough to produce noticeable symptoms. Cysts often disappear on their own without treatment, but in some cases they may require surgical removal. In rare cases, a cyst that twists or ruptures may cause serious complications warranting emergency surgery.

WHAT CAUSES IT?

• The cause of ovarian cysts is unknown.

PREVENTION

• There are no known ways to prevent ovarian cysts.

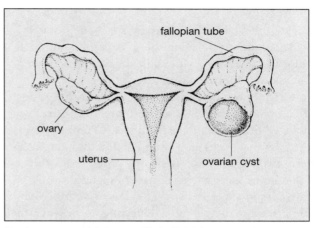

Ovarian cysts are globular sacs filled with fluid or semisolid material. They are typically detected during a routine pelvic examination.

DIAGNOSIS

• Gynecological examination is necessary. If a lump or mass in the ovary is detected, further tests are necessary to rule out the possibility of ovarian cancer.
• Abdominal or pelvic ultrasonography may be performed.
• A minor procedure called laparoscopy (insertion of a scope through a small incision in the abdomen to view the ovaries) may be used to confirm the diagnosis and determine the size and position of the cyst.

HOW TO TREAT IT

• Ovarian cysts often disappear without treatment.
• Surgery to remove the cyst may be needed if cancer is suspected, if the cyst does not go away, or if it causes symptoms. In many cases it can be taken out without damaging the ovary, but sometimes the ovary may have to be removed.
• In some cases ovarian cyst may be drained during laparoscopy (see Diagnosis).

WHEN TO CALL A DOCTOR

• If you experience any of the symptoms of ovarian cysts, call a gynecologist.
• **EMERGENCY** If you have been diagnosed with an ovarian cyst and you experience sudden, sharp abdominal pain, fever, or vomiting, see a doctor immediately.

SYMPTOMS

• In many cases ovarian cysts cause no symptoms.
• Mild abdominal ache.
• Abdominal swelling or a feeling of fullness or pressure.
• Pain during sexual intercourse.
• Menstrual irregularities including absence of menstrual bleeding (amenorrhea), heavy bleeding (menorrhagia), and painful periods (dysmenorrhea).
• Unusual hair growth on the face and body, caused by an increased production of masculinizing hormones.
• Sudden, sharp abdominal pain, fever, and nausea if a cyst becomes twisted or ruptures.
• Painful, frequent urination—or urinary retention—if a cyst presses against the bladder (rare).

Paget's Disease

WHAT IS IT?

Paget's disease is a slowly progressive bone disorder, most commonly affecting the spine, hip, skull, thigh, shin, and upper arm, although almost any bone may be involved. Bone is continuously broken down and restored. In the initial stages of Paget's disease, too much bone is broken down and, to compensate, new bone is formed at an increased rate. Often, however, the new bone cells are laid down in a disordered pattern, making the bone weak and prone to fractures. In addition, overgrowth of new bone results in deformities in affected areas. The disease is most common in those older than 40, affecting up to 3 percent of the population in some parts of the world. Most cases are mild and tend to progress slowly. Advanced cases, however, may cause pain, deformity, incapacitation, hearing loss, or heart failure. Malignant bone cancer (sarcoma), the most serious complication, occurs in less than 1 percent of cases.

SYMPTOMS

- Most cases go unnoticed and are discovered incidentally when x-rays or blood tests are taken for another reason. In more severe cases symptoms may occur and are highly variable.
- Bone pain (usually persistent and sometimes severe).
- Neck or back pain (especially the lower back), which may radiate to the buttocks or legs.
- Pain or stiffness in the joints (especially the hips, knees, or shoulders), resembling osteoarthritis.
- Warmth in the skin overlying affected bones.
- Unexplained bone fractures.
- Bone swelling or deformities, including bowed legs, skull enlargement around the eyes and forehead, barrel-shaped chest, or bent spine causing reduced height.
- Hearing loss.
- Headache, dizziness, ringing in the ears.

WHAT CAUSES IT?

- The cause of Paget's disease is unknown, although viral infection strongly appears to play a role. Indeed, the disease has been reported to occur within families but is not transmitted from one generation to another—a finding consistent with an infectious disorder.

PREVENTION

- There are no specific preventive measures.
- For those with Paget's disease, regular checkups are advised to screen for early bone cancer or to detect hearing loss.

DIAGNOSIS

- X-rays or bone scans are taken.
- Blood or urine tests may point to the diagnosis.
- A bone biopsy may be required.

HOW TO TREAT IT

- Most patients never develop symptoms and so do not require treatment.
- Over-the-counter (OTC) analgesics (aspirin, ibuprofen, acetaminophen) may be used to reduce pain and inflammation.
- Prescription anti-inflammatory drugs may be needed when OTC products prove to be inadequate.
- Drugs (such as calcitonin and etidronate) that correct the abnormally rapid bone metabolism may be prescribed in serious cases. Although they may cause side effects, these medications may completely halt the progress of the disease in some patients, but the damage that has already occurred is usually irreversible.
- Orthopedic surgery may be indicated. For example, if bone deformities lead to difficulty in walking, hip replacement or reshaping the leg bones may be performed to improve gait.

WHEN TO CALL A DOCTOR

- See your doctor if symptoms of Paget's disease develop.

Pancreatic Cancer

WHAT IS IT?

Pancreatic cancer, currently the fifth leading cause of death from cancer, is the growth of malignant cells in the pancreas, a pear-shaped organ located just below and behind the stomach. The pancreas secretes digestive enzymes into the small intestine via the common bile duct, and islet cells of the pancreas secrete hormones (insulin and glucagon) into the blood. Pancreatic cancer impairs the digestive process and may block the bile duct as it grows. Most cases occur after age 50; men are affected slightly more often than women. A cure is sometimes possible with early diagnosis and surgical removal. However, pancreatic cancer is extremely difficult to diagnose and has usually spread by the time symptoms appear, so cures are uncommon. Islet cell tumors (insulinomas) are much less common. They release excessive amounts of insulin, causing low blood glucose (hypoglycemia). Only about 10 percent of insulinomas are malignant, and the symptoms of hypoglycemia can be eliminated by surgical removal of the tumor.

WHAT CAUSES IT?

• The cause of pancreatic cancer is unknown.
• Pancreatic cancer is two to three times more common in heavy smokers than nonsmokers.
• Exposure to solvents, petroleum, and coal-tar compounds may lead to pancreatic cancer.
• Hereditary pancreatitis may be associated with a greater risk of pancreatic cancer.
• There is no evidence that drinking large amounts of coffee or alcohol causes pancreatic cancer.

PREVENTION

• Minimize exposure to toxic chemicals at home and in the workplace, and avoid cigarettes.

DIAGNOSIS

• Chest and abdominal x-rays are performed initially.
• Ultrasound scans or CT (computed tomography) scans detect about 80 percent of cases. Further tests are performed if diagnosis is questionable.
• ERCP (endoscopic retrograde cholangiopancreatogram) is done, in which a thin, lighted, viewing tube (endoscope) is passed down the throat into the small intestine. Contrast material is injected into the bile duct, and x-rays are taken. The endoscope may also be used to take a biopsy.
• Diagnosis is confirmed by biopsy of pancreatic tissue. A tissue sample may be extracted with a needle; in some cases exploratory abdominal surgery is needed.

HOW TO TREAT IT

• Surgical removal of the tumor is possible with a relatively small tumor that has not yet spread, which may prolong survival time. Surgery may involve removal of the entire pancreas as well as a portion of the small intestine.
• Surgery to bypass a bile duct blocked by the tumor may be performed to relieve symptoms.
• Chemotherapy in combination with radiation therapy may destroy cancerous cells and ease symptoms.
• Analgesics or narcotics are administered to reduce pain. Antihistamines or amphetamines may be used to enhance analgesic effects. In cases of severe pain, the relevant nerves may be cut or destroyed by an alcohol injection at the time of surgery.
• Tablets containing pancreatic enzymes may be prescribed if food is poorly absorbed because of a blockage of pancreatic secretions.

WHEN TO CALL A DOCTOR

• Call a doctor for symptoms of pancreatic cancer.

SYMPTOMS

• Pain in the upper-central or right abdomen. The pain may spread to the back and may be relieved by sitting up and leaning forward.
• Jaundice.
• Itching skin.
• Nausea and vomiting.
• Diarrhea or constipation, dark-colored urine, or pale stools.
• A feeling of fullness.
• Loss of appetite and weight loss.
• Fatigue, depression, and mood swings.
• Shakiness, irritability, profuse perspiration, chills, dizziness, or muscle spasms in patients with an islet cell tumor, due to associated hypoglycemia (see Hypoglycemia for more).

Pancreatitis

WHAT IS IT?

Pancreatitis is inflammation of the pancreas, an organ that produces digestive enzymes and hormones (insulin and glucagon). Acute attacks of pancreatitis usually subside within several days to a week but carry the risk of life-threatening complications, including shock and infection in a collection of fluid near the pancreas (pseudocyst). Chronic pancreatitis involving permanent damage to the pancreas may follow recurrent attacks of acute pancreatitis or be due to persistent smoldering inflammation. Possible long-term complications include inadequate absorption of nutrients and diabetes mellitus.

SYMPTOMS

- Acute pancreatitis: moderate to severe abdominal pain that may spread to the chest, back, and sides (and is often worse when lying down); nausea and vomiting; abdominal bloating; mild fever; clammy skin.
- Chronic pancreatitis: constant or episodic abdominal pain; weight loss; bulky, floating stools.

WHAT CAUSES IT?

- Gallbladder disease is often a cause of acute attacks.
- Alcoholism is commonly associated with both acute and chronic pancreatitis.
- Less common causes of acute attacks: injury to the pancreas; use of certain drugs (including immunosuppressants, corticosteroids, and sulfa drugs); peptic ulcer; high triglycerides; viral infection such as mumps.
- Other causes of chronic pancreatitis: recurrent acute pancreatitis; cystic fibrosis (in children); malnutrition.
- In rare cases pancreatitis is hereditary.
- In many cases the cause cannot be determined.

PREVENTION

- Avoid excessive alcohol use.

DIAGNOSIS

- Medical history and physical examination.
- Blood tests.
- X-rays, ultrasound, or CT (computed tomography).

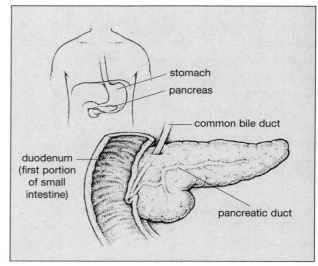

The pancreas, located just below and behind the stomach, manufactures crucial hormones and digestive enzymes.

- ERCP (endoscopic retrograde cholangiopancreatogram) is done, in which a thin, lighted, viewing tube (endoscope) is passed down the throat into the small intestine. Contrast material is injected into the bile duct, and x-rays are taken.
- Stool tests, pancreatic function tests, and other tests may be needed to confirm chronic cases.

HOW TO TREAT IT

- Acute attacks require hospitalization. The stomach is emptied of its contents, and intravenous fluids and painkillers are given. Patients are not allowed to eat for several days to a week; antibiotics may be given to treat an associated infection.
- Surgery to remove gallstones may be necessary.
- Narcotic painkillers may be needed for severe pain.
- Alcohol and large, fatty meals should be avoided by those with the chronic form of the illness.
- Pancreatic enzyme pills are usually prescribed for patients with chronic pancreatitis, to aid in digestion.
- Insulin may be needed if diabetes develops.
- Chronic pancreatitis occasionally requires partial or total removal of the pancreas (pancreatectomy) or surgery to deaden the nerves that transmit the pain.

WHEN TO CALL A DOCTOR

- See a doctor right away for symptoms of pancreatitis.

Parkinson's Disease

WHAT IS IT?

Parkinson's disease, named after the English doctor who first described it in 1817, is caused by the progressive death of neurons within the basal ganglia, a region of the brain responsible for the coordination of muscular activity. Nerve cells (neurons) communicate with one another by releasing highly specialized chemicals called neurotransmitters. Basal ganglia produce the neurotransmitter dopamine, which helps control communication between the nerves and muscles and is essential for fast, smooth, and efficient movement. In Parkinson's disease, dopamine-producing neurons gradually deteriorate and reduce the amount of dopamine production. This results in the progressive shaking, stiffness, and uncoordinated movements characteristic of the disorder. Parkinson's disease, the most common degenerative disease of the nervous system, is most frequent between the ages of 60 and 70. Men are affected more often than women. Symptoms usually begin gradually and may not be noticeable at first, or may be mistakenly attributed to aging. Although there is no definitive diagnostic test for Parkinson's disease, worsening of symptoms over time eventually allows a diagnosis to be made with certainty. The cause of Parkinson's disease remains unknown, and there is as yet no cure. However, medications can alleviate many symptoms and greatly improve the quality of life for patients.

SYMPTOMS

- Rhythmic shaking of the hands (pill-roll tremor) and head, especially at rest or in moments of anxiety.
- Cessation or lessening of the tremor with movement and sleep.
- Stiff, jerky, or slowed movements.
- Difficulty in changing position; for example, from sitting to standing or from standing to walking.
- A temporary inability to move (in some cases).
- Hesitant gait with small, shuffling steps.
- Loss of balance.
- Stooped posture.
- Rigid facial expression.
- Difficulty in swallowing.
- Drooling.
- Oily skin and scalp (seborrhea).
- Shaky, cramped handwriting.
- Quavering, expressionless voice, and mumbling.
- Bowel or bladder dysfunction, including incontinence and constipation.
- Emotional depression and anxiety.
- Gradual confusion, loss of memory, and other mental disorders (in some severe cases).

WHAT CAUSES IT?

- The cause of Parkinson's disease is unknown in most cases.
- Brain injury, tumors, post-influenza encephalitis, and possibly carbon monoxide poisoning may lead to Parkinson's disease in some cases.
- The use of phenothiazine tranquilizers may cause Parkinson's disease.
- Some theories suggest that hereditary factors may play a role.
- Environmental factors, including early or prolonged exposure to the chemicals in herbicides and pesticides, may be associated with an increased risk of the disease.

PREVENTION

- There are no known measures for preventing Parkinson's disease.

DIAGNOSIS

- Patient history and physical examination.
- CT (computed tomography) scans, PET (positive emission tomography) scans, or MRI (magnetic resonance imaging).

HOW TO TREAT IT

- Treatment may not be necessary in the early stages.
- The medication levodopa (L-dopa) is the treatment of choice to relieve symptoms of Parkinson's disease. Within the brain, L-dopa is converted to the missing neurotransmitter, dopamine. L-dopa is usually combined with a decarboxylase inhibitor (carbidopa or

Parkinson's Disease *continued*

benserazide) to enhance efficiency and limit side effects of L–dopa by preventing the conversion of L–dopa to dopamine from occurring outside of the brain. (Side effects include nausea and vomiting, and dizziness when sitting or standing up from a reclining position.) Since the effectiveness of L–dopa decreases with time—becoming essentially ineffective after five or six years—doctors often withhold the drug until symptoms interfere greatly with normal activities.

• Deprenyl, also known as selegiline, may be prescribed immediately upon diagnosis. This drug slows the progression of symptoms by blocking an enzyme in the brain that breaks down dopamine, thus postponing the time when L–dopa becomes necessary.

• Anticholinergic drugs (which block certain nerve impulses), such as trihexyphenidyl, benztropine mesylate, and antihistamines (such as diphenhydramine) may be prescribed to reduce tremor and stiffness.

• Amantadine, which increases the release of dopamine in the brain, may be prescribed to reduce tremor, stiffness, and difficulty in movement.

• Brain surgery (cryothalamotomy) to destroy part of the thalamus may be occasionally recommended, since it has been shown to reduce tremor. However, since the surgery does not relieve muscle rigidity or loss of voluntary movement and may result in further brain damage, it is used only in very severe cases.

• Implantation of fetal tissue into the basal ganglia has shown promise in a few patients.

• Patients should stay active and exercise regularly to keep muscles as flexible as possible.

• Physical and speech therapy may help patients adapt to the limitations imposed by the disease.

• Psychological counseling may be advised for patients to combat depression and provide emotional support. Family members of Parkinson's patients may also benefit from counseling.

• To allow L–dopa to work better, your doctor may advise dietary changes, such as consuming the majority of the daily protein allotment in the evening meal and maintaining a seven–to–one ratio of carbohydrates to protein.

• Call your local branch of the National Parkinson Foundation or the United Parkinson Foundation for more information, results of current research, and support groups in your area.

WHEN TO CALL A DOCTOR

• Call a doctor if you develop symptoms of Parkinson's disease.

• Call a doctor if new, unexpected symptoms develop during treatment, since the medications prescribed may have significant side effects.

Pelvic Inflammatory Disease

WHAT IS IT?

Pelvic inflammatory disease (PID), a condition marked by acute, persistent, or recurrent infection of the internal female reproductive organs (including the cervix, uterus, and fallopian tubes), is one of the most frequent causes of pelvic pain in women. In most cases proper treatment leads to full recovery within a week, although recurrence is common. If untreated, however, PID may lead to serious complications, including life-threatening abdominal abscess, infection of the abdominal cavity (peritonitis), and septicemia (blood poisoning). In addition, PID may scar the fallopian tube, significantly increasing the risks of infertility and ectopic pregnancy (which occurs when a fertilized egg becomes trapped in the fallopian tube before it can settle in the uterus).

SYMPTOMS

- Dull, aching pain and tenderness in the lower abdomen or back.
- Pain during intercourse.
- Low-grade fever, possibly with chills.
- Irregular, absent, or unusually heavy menstrual periods.
- Bad-smelling, copious vaginal discharge.
- Frequent, painful urination.
- Loss of appetite.
- Nausea and vomiting.

WHAT CAUSES IT?

- Infection usually begins in the cervix, extends into the uterus and fallopian tubes, and then involves the pelvic cavity.
- Various infectious agents, especially those that cause chlamydia and gonorrhea, can be transmitted by a sexual partner to cause PID.
- Less often, PID may be caused by using an intrauterine contraceptive device (IUD), or it may occur in the aftermath of a miscarriage, full-term pregnancy, or a gynecological procedure such as endometrial biopsy or dilatation and curettage (D&C).
- Risk factors include sexual activity at a young age, multiple sexual partners, and never having borne children. Use of oral contraceptives appears to reduce risk.

- Occasionally, infection may spread from other organs, as a complication of appendicitis for example.

PREVENTION

- Monogamy, abstinence, or the use of condoms protects against sexually transmitted infections.
- To help prevent infection after minor gynecologic procedures such as dilatation and curettage, avoid douching or intercourse for at least seven days. Report any fever, increased vaginal discharge, or pain after such procedures.

DIAGNOSIS

- A gynecologic pelvic exam is needed. PID is difficult to diagnose, since it is hard to distinguish from other types of pelvic diseases (such as endometriosis).
- Cultures of swab samples of vaginal discharge may identify underlying infectious agents.
- Laparoscopy (inspection of the pelvic organs with a small, slender scope passed through either the vagina or a small abdominal incision) may be carried out to identify the infectious agents or to detect an abscess.

HOW TO TREAT IT

- If PID appears likely, antibiotics are often prescribed immediately, since delaying treatment is risky. Therapy can be adjusted after lab results are known.
- Bed rest and pain relievers are recommended.
- Hospitalization may be advised for more serious cases, if the diagnosis is uncertain, the patient is pregnant or an adolescent, or if the infection fails to respond to outpatient treatment. Treatment may include intravenous antibiotics and surgical drainage of the abscess. A ruptured abscess is life-threatening and may require a complete hysterectomy.
- Surgery may also be considered for complicated or persistent cases that do not respond to antibiotics.
- Male sexual partners—even asymptomatic ones—should be treated for gonorrhea and chlamydia, since a successfully treated woman may become reinfected by an infected partner.

WHEN TO CALL A DOCTOR

- If PID symptoms appear, especially a high fever and severe pain in the lower abdomen, see your physician or gynecologist immediately.

Pemphigus

WHAT IS IT?

Pemphigus is an uncommon chronic disorder characterized by extensive blistering of the skin and mouth. It is believed to be an autoimmune disease—an unexplained attack and destruction of healthy cells by the body's immune system. In pemphigus, antibodies directed against the surface of a particular type of skin cell interfere with adhesion between cells, which leads to a loosening and separation of one of the layers of the skin. Easy blistering is the result. Blisters usually first appear in the mouth; months later, lesions may appear on almost any area of the skin, as well as on the lining of the esophagus, vagina, or cervix. Pemphigus most often affects people between the ages of 40 and 60, particularly those of Mediterranean descent. Potentially debilitating flare-ups tend to alternate with periods of remission that may occur even with treatment. Although the blisters often heal without scarring, skin color in involved areas may permanently darken and, more seriously, the blisters tend to break easily to form open sores that are prone to infection. Without treatment pemphigus can be fatal within months or years because of severe complications, including widespread infection of ruptured blisters and dehydration. Although there is no cure, treatment can control the disease, and long-term remission is possible.

SYMPTOMS

- Blisters in the mouth or on the lips (often an early sign).
- Recurrent, fragile blisters affecting many areas of the skin.

WHAT CAUSES IT?

- It is unknown what causes the autoimmune response that results in pemphigus. Genetic factors appear to be involved.
- Certain drugs, including penicillamine (used to treat rheumatoid arthritis) and captopril (used to treat high blood pressure), may trigger a limited form of the condition; however, symptoms subside when the patient stops taking the drug.

PREVENTION

- No specific measures can be taken to prevent pemphigus.

DIAGNOSIS

- Patient history and physical examination, especially of the skin and mucus membranes, is necessary.
- A small sample of skin (biopsy) will be removed and examined under a microscope.
- Uninvolved areas of the skin may slough off easily when rubbed with a finger or cotton swab.
- Cultures for bacterial growth are taken from areas of infection.

HOW TO TREAT IT

- Long-term oral corticosteroid therapy is prescribed—often in high doses—to keep the blistering under control. Drugs that suppress the immune system (methotrexate, azathioprine) may also be prescribed. Drugs that contain gold salts, often used to treat rheumatoid arthritis, may help to control pemphigus. (Why such compounds are effective is unknown.) Drug treatment often helps to prevent blister formation and can lead to long-term remission, but serious side effects including cataracts and diabetes mellitus may occur
- Antibiotic lotions may be used to prevent infection of mild to moderate blistering.
- Anesthetic lozenges can help to alleviate the pain from mouth sores. Corticosteroid drugs may be injected for more serious cases of mouth lesions.
- Severe flare-ups are treated similarly to severe burns, including hospitalization in an intensive care or burn unit. Intravenous fluids and antibiotics are given to prevent dehydration and infection. If severe blistering in the mouth prevents normal eating or drinking, intravenous feeding may be necessary.

WHEN TO CALL A DOCTOR

- Call a doctor if blisters arise in the mouth and persist or begin to spread across the skin.
- If you have already been diagnosed with pemphigus, call a doctor if you feel generally unwell, have fever, chills, or muscle or joint aches, or if the skin exudes a strange odor in spite of bathing.

Penile Cancer

WHAT IS IT?

Penile cancer is the growth of malignant cells in the skin or underlying tissues of the penis. The cancer cells tend to arise on the glans (head) of the penis or, in uncircumcised men, on the foreskin, although they may arise anywhere on the penis. If left untreated, the cancer typically spreads, first to the deeper layers of penile tissue, then to nearby lymph nodes in the groin or to blood vessels, and finally to distant sites throughout the body. Most penile cancers are slow-growing, although some are highly aggressive, spreading to the lymph nodes over the course of months. Any suspicious growth on the penis therefore requires prompt medical attention. Cancer of the penis is rare in the United States, particularly among circumcised men. As with any malignancy, penile cancer may be life-threatening. However, if detected and treated early (before it spreads to lymph nodes), cure is likely.

SYMPTOMS

- A wartlike lump, pimple, sore, or ulcer on the penis, usually near the glans (head).
- Bleeding or unusual discharge from the penis.
- Painful urination (as cancer progresses).
- Enlarged lymph nodes in the groin (indicating spread of cancer).

WHAT CAUSES IT?

- The cause is unknown, but the risk is higher in uncircumcised men, particularly in those who do not wash the area around the foreskin thoroughly.
- Risk appears to be greater among cigarette smokers and in those with a history of leukoplakia of the penis (a precancerous condition marked by white, scaly patches of skin), balanitis (an inflammation of the head of the penis), or an epithelial horn (an abnormal skin growth) on the penis.
- Sexually transmitted diseases (especially genital warts) are associated with increased risk.

PREVENTION

- Perform monthly self-examinations to detect penile cancer at an early, more treatable stage.

DIAGNOSIS

- If a growth looks suspicious, a small sample of affected skin (biopsy) is removed for examination.
- If the tissue is found to be cancerous, additional tests are performed to see whether the cancer has spread to other parts of the body (a process known as staging).

HOW TO TREAT IT

- Treatment generally depends on how far the cancer has spread, as well as the age and overall health of the patient.
- Surgery is the most common form of treatment. Cancer confined to the foreskin in uncircumcised men can be cured by circumcision alone.
- Radiation therapy may be effective for slow-growing tumors detected at an early stage.
- Surgery is especially warranted for rapidly growing tumors and those that have spread into deeper tissues of the penis. If the cancer does not appear to have spread very far, the surgeon may remove the tumor and a small area of surrounding normal tissue (in case any cancer cells have invaded there), sparing as much of the penis as possible. In more advanced cases removal of most or all of the penis and, often, affected lymph nodes in the groin may be required. Subsequent plastic surgery may be performed in such cases to help restore the appearance and function of the penis.
- If cancer has spread to distant sites, radiation or chemotherapy may be used to reduce discomfort.
- Psychological counseling and support groups may be helpful.

WHEN TO CALL A DOCTOR

- Call a doctor if any suspicious sore or growth appears on the penis or if any symptoms of penile cancer arise.

Peptic Ulcer

WHAT IS IT?

Peptic ulcers are craterlike erosions in the lining of the stomach, the duodenum (the part of the small intestine just past the stomach), and rarely, the esophagus. Duodenal ulcers are about three times more common than stomach (gastric) ulcers. Normally, glands in the stomach secrete acid and the enzyme pepsin (hence the name peptic ulcer) that help to break down foods in the digestive process. The stomach and duodenum meanwhile secrete mucus to protect against harm from pepsin and gastric acid. In peptic ulcer disease the digestive tract's defensive mechanisms break down, often as a result of infection with the bacterium *Helicobacter pylori*. Consequently, even small amounts of stomach acid can cause corrosion. Each year, about 1 percent of Americans develop peptic ulcers, and overall, up to 10 percent of the population will have an ulcer at some point during their lives. All ages may be affected (including children), although ulcers most often affect those over 30. Ulcers commonly recur: even after an ulcer has healed, new ones often arise throughout the patient's lifetime, either in the original location or elsewhere. Therefore, current ulcer drugs, which mostly act to reduce levels of stomach acids, must often be taken on a long-term basis. The development of newer,

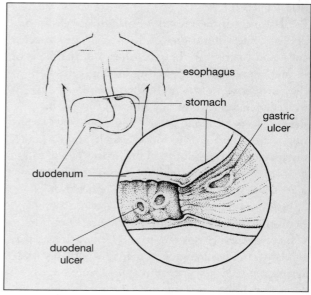

Peptic ulcers may arise anywhere in the lining of the stomach or the duodenum (or, more rarely, the esophagus).

short-term drug regimens directed against *H. pylori* may significantly lower the high rate of ulcer recurrence. Although peptic ulcers are rarely a major health threat, they sometimes lead to serious complications, such as bleeding, obstruction of the digestive tract due to scarring, or the creation of a hole or tear (perforation) in the digestive tract, which can lead to severe, life-threatening infection of the abdominal cavity (peritonitis). In addition, in a small percentage of cases a persistent stomach ulcer may be cancerous. (The same is not true for duodenal ulcers.) For most ulcers, treatment is highly effective in controlling symptoms and preventing serious complications.

WHAT CAUSES IT?

• At least 80 percent of ulcers are believed to be caused by infection of the digestive tract with *H. pylori* bacteria. It's not known how the infection spreads, although it may be transmitted orally. *H. pylori* infects about 60 percent of Americans by age 60, but most of those infected do not develop ulcers. Rather, the bacteria merely increase the chances of developing an ulcer by weakening the stomach's protective mechanisms and making the lining of the digestive tract susceptible to corrosion by

---

SYMPTOMS

• No symptoms in some patients.
• Gnawing pain in the upper stomach area several hours after a meal (duodenal ulcer) or dull, aching pain, often right after a meal (gastric ulcer). Pain may radiate to the back or behind the breastbone, resembling heartburn.
• Feeling hungry an hour or two after meals.
• Indigestion, nausea, vomiting, and weight loss.
• Emergency symptoms: black, tarry, or bloody stools; vomiting of blood or material resembling coffee grounds (signs of potentially serious bleeding). Searing abdominal pain could indicate that an ulcer has eroded completely through the digestive tract (perforation). Such complications require immediate emergency medical attention.

Peptic Ulcer *continued*

stomach acids. Once an ulcer has developed, various secondary factors can aggravate it, including alcohol, caffeine, dietary factors, smoking, and stress.

• In the past, excessive production of stomach acid was thought to be the primary cause of ulcers. It is now recognized that many people with ulcers actually have normal or even slightly less-than-normal amounts of stomach acid. However, because mechanisms that protect the digestive tract lining are weakened (in most cases by *H. pylori),* even small amounts of stomach acid can cause (or delay the healing of) ulcers. The exception is ulcers caused by certain kinds of pancreatic or duodenal tumors that secrete the hormone gastrin, which causes massive amounts of acid secretion (Zollinger-Ellison syndrome).

• Long-term use of aspirin and other nonsteroidal anti-inflammatory drugs, like ibuprofen or naproxen, can lead to ulcers by irritating the lining of the digestive tract.

• Hereditary factors also appear to play a role. The chances of developing an ulcer are greater if a close family member has had the disease.

PREVENTION

• Avoid long-term use of aspirin or nonsteroidal anti-inflammatory drugs if possible. Anyone who must take these drugs on a long-term basis, such as those with arthritis, may benefit from the prescription drug misoprostol.

• To help prevent ulcer recurrence, carefully follow instructions for any ulcer drugs prescribed. Try to minimize stress, do not smoke, and avoid foods or drinks that have caused flare-ups in the past.

DIAGNOSIS

• Patient history and physical exam are necessary.

• An upper GI series (which involves swallowing a solution containing barium to create a clear x-ray image of the digestive tract) may show active ulcers or scarring caused by past ulcers.

• Endoscopy (in which a flexible scope is guided down the throat and into the stomach and duodenum) allows ulcers to be viewed directly. A small sample of the ulcer (biopsy) may be taken at the same time to test for cancer.

• Biopsies can also detect the presence of *H. pylori,*

but this method is invasive and expensive. Quick office tests for the detection of this bacterium are currently under development.

HOW TO TREAT IT

• For those with mild disease (one or two periods of symptoms per year), prescription drugs that reduce secretion of stomach acid (cimetidine, ranitidine, famotidine, nizatidine, or omeprazole) or that coat the lining of the stomach (sucralfate) usually relieve pain within a week, although ulcers take about eight weeks to heal. Antacids may also help, although they may interfere with the actions of the prescription drugs if both are taken in close succession.

• Antibiotics directed against *H. pylori* bacteria are generally reserved for those with more serious disease who do not respond to other ulcer medications, as the long-term effectiveness and side effects of this approach are still being evaluated. A combination of two antibiotics (usually metronidazole and tetracycline) are usually taken for at least two weeks, along with a bismuth-containing antacid (such as Pepto-Bismol). Prescription antacids may also be given to help speed the healing of ulcers. Combination antibiotic regimens prevent ulcer recurrences in about 90 percent of cases.

• Surgery may be needed for bleeding, obstruction or perforation of the digestive tract, or intractable pain.

• Sensible eating, including a diet rich in fiber, is recommended. Many dietary measures advocated in the past—such as eating bland foods, eating many small meals a day rather than three larger meals, or drinking milk—do not appear to help. Indeed, milk may actually increase stomach acid production, although one or two glasses a day is usually not harmful. Coffee, tea, caffeinated sodas, and fruit juices high in acid should be avoided if they seem to cause irritation. Avoid excessive alcohol consumption.

• Do not smoke.

WHEN TO CALL A DOCTOR

• Call a doctor for symptoms of peptic ulcer disease.

• **EMERGENCY** For those with ulcers, any signs of bleeding or perforation, including vomiting blood, black tarry stools, or severe abdominal pain, require immediate emergency medical attention.

Pericarditis

WHAT IS IT?

Pericarditis is inflammation of the pericardium, the membrane that surrounds and protects the heart. It occurs in two forms: acute (sudden and short-lived) and chronic (persistent over long periods). The most common type of acute pericarditis, caused by a viral infection, generally resolves spontaneously with no permanent damage, even without treatment. Acute pericarditis due to bacterial infection, however, may cause fluid to accumulate in the space between the pericardium and the heart (pericardial effusion) and interfere with the heart's ability to function properly. This may result in severe symptoms and may even be fatal unless fluid is promptly removed from the pericardial sac. In chronic pericarditis, ongoing inflammation scars and thickens the pericardium (constrictive pericarditis) so that it constricts the heart and hinders the heart's ability to fill with blood returning from the great veins. Constrictive pericarditis nearly always leads to progressive heart failure; surgical intervention is often beneficial.

SYMPTOMS

- Acute pericarditis: severe, sudden chest pain that may spread to the neck, back, shoulders, or arms, and is often worse when breathing deeply or changing position and relieved by sitting up or leaning forward; fever.
- Pericardial effusion: breathing difficulty or ill-defined pain or fullness in the chest.
- Chronic pericarditis: swelling in the legs and abdomen due to fluid retention; breathing difficulty; fatigue.

WHAT CAUSES IT?

- Acute pericarditis may result from a number of underlying disorders, including viral, bacterial, or fungal infection; heart attack; rheumatic fever; lupus erythematosus; rheumatoid arthritis; severe hypothyroidism; metastatic cancer; and kidney failure.
- Acute pericarditis may occur following a chest injury or open heart surgery.
- Chronic pericarditis may develop from recurrent acute cases.
- Chronic cases may result from a chronic infection such as tuberculosis.
- In some cases the cause is unknown.

PREVENTION

- There are no specific measures to prevent pericarditis.

DIAGNOSIS

- Medical history and physical examination, including listening for abnormal heart sounds with a stethoscope.
- Blood and urine tests.
- Chest x-rays.
- Electrocardiogram (ECG), which measures electrical activity in the heart.
- Echocardiography (ultrasound imaging of the heart).
- Culture of pericardial fluid taken through a needle to identify infectious organisms.

HOW TO TREAT IT

- The underlying cause is treated if possible. For example, antibiotics are given for bacterial infections.
- Analgesics (including aspirin and ibuprofen) are used to reduce pain and inflammation.
- Diuretics may be used to reduce fluid retention.
- Bed rest and restricted activity are essential.
- Surgical drainage of fluid with a needle (pericardiocentesis) may be required for severe pericardial effusion.
- Partial or total surgical removal of the pericardium (pericardectomy), the treatment of choice for chronic pericarditis, often yields excellent results.

WHEN TO CALL A DOCTOR

- If you experience any symptom of pericarditis, get to a doctor immediately.

Periodontitis

WHAT IS IT?

Periodontitis is inflammation of the periodontia—the tissues that surround and support the teeth, including the gums and the bony tooth sockets in the upper and lower jaw. The disease begins as gingivitis (inflammation of the gums, usually due to inadequate dental hygiene) which progresses without treatment. Gingivitis occurs when dental plaque (a sticky substance made of mucus, food particles, and bacteria) and calculus (the hardened deposit composed of mineralized plaque and saliva) irritate and inflame gum tissue, causing it to gradually erode. Over time, the gums recede and small pockets form between the gums and teeth. As these pockets deepen, they trap increasing amounts of plaque and calculus. Bacteria in the plaques produce enzymes that erode the bones and ligaments which support the teeth, causing the teeth to loosen from their sockets. Pus tends to form as the periodontia fall prey to infection. In some cases an acute infection may cause an abscess to form. Eventually, bone erosion is so extensive that the affected teeth fall out. Indeed, periodontitis—not tooth decay—is the major cause of adult tooth loss in the United States.

WHAT CAUSES IT?

• Periodontitis results when gingivitis is left untreated or is treated too late, and so progresses beyond the gums to affect the deeper tissues of the periodontia.

SYMPTOMS

- Red, shiny, swollen, tender gums that bleed easily.
- Bad breath and an unpleasant taste in the mouth.
- Toothache, exacerbated by hot, cold, or sweet foods or liquids.
- One or more loose or missing teeth.
- Pus appearing at the gumline.
- Intense toothache and fever (if abscess occurs).

PREVENTION

• Practice careful oral hygiene (see Gingivitis for more information) and see a dentist at least once a year for a routine cleaning and checkup.

DIAGNOSIS

• A complete dental examination is necessary. The dentist will measure the depth of gum pockets to assess the extent of the disease.
• Dental x-rays are taken to determine how much underlying bone has been lost.

HOW TO TREAT IT

• If the disease is discovered early enough, it may be possible to reverse its progress simply by having a dentist remove plaque and calculus from the root surfaces of the teeth. Afterward, a strict self-care program of brushing and flossing is required.
• A minor surgical procedure known as gingivectomy may be performed to cut away affected gum tissue. The gum line is then covered with a special paste (periodontal pack) that remains in place for one to two weeks, while the gums grow back in their proper place.
• A similar procedure, gingivoplasty, may be performed to reshape the gums in a manner that discourages them from forming pockets.
• More advanced cases may require flap surgery. In this procedure a flap of gum tissue is cut and peeled back so that the teeth and underlying bones may be cleaned and recontoured. The flap of gum is then sutured back into place.
• Occasionally, surgical grafting with bone or a bone substitute may be needed to restore damaged underlying bone.
• Loose teeth may be anchored to other teeth by splinting them together; in some cases affected teeth must be extracted to prevent further spread of the disease. Dentures or permanent dental implants may then be used to replace missing teeth.

WHEN TO CALL A DOCTOR

• Make an appointment with a dentist right away if you experience bleeding gums or loose teeth.

Peripheral Neuropathies

WHAT IS IT?

Peripheral neuropathies are a group of disorders characterized by the degeneration of the nerves involved in the communication between the central nervous system (the brain and spinal cord) and the rest of the body. Peripheral nerves transmit sensory signals back to the central nervous system, and signals from the brain to the muscles. Neuropathies are caused by a wide variety of underlying disorders, and nerve function may be lost in a number of ways: the nerve fibers themselves (axons) may degenerate; the myelin sheaths that cover and protect the nerves may erode; and in some cases there

---

SYMPTOMS

- A tingling sensation followed by numbness and pain, commonly beginning in the hands or feet and spreading toward the center of the body. The facial muscles are also frequently affected. The pain may be severe with diabetes mellitus or alcoholism.
- Muscle weakness.
- Loss of bladder or bowel control.
- Unsteady gait.
- Emergency symptoms: difficulty in breathing, paralysis.

---

is a loss of blood supply to a nerve. The mononeuropathies are conditions that affect a single nerve (see Bell's Palsy and Carpal Tunnel Syndrome for more information); polyneuropathies affect multiple nerves that may be distributed throughout the body. Symptoms vary according to which nerves are affected. Most often, symptoms develop gradually over months or years; however, in Guillain-Barré syndrome, an uncommon form of polyneuropathy, severe symptoms appear within days. (Recovery from Guillain-Barré may also be relatively rapid in many cases.) Peripheral neuropathies are most common in men between the ages of 30 and 50. Symptoms may arise from degeneration of the sensory neurons, the motor neurons, or both. Fortunately, because these disorders often leave the cell bodies of the nerves intact, the nerves can regenerate; thus,

chances for recovery may be good. However, prognosis and specific treatment depend on the underlying disorder.

WHAT CAUSES IT?

- Many disorders, including alcoholism, diabetes mellitus, rheumatoid arthritis, systemic lupus erythematosus, amyloidosis, and uremia, may cause peripheral neuropathy.
- Malnutrition, especially a vitamin deficiency, may lead to peripheral neuropathy.
- A viral infection, rabies and flu vaccines, or surgery may sometimes be associated with Guillain-Barré syndrome.
- A number of medications, especially isoniazid, pyridoxine, and vincristine, can cause peripheral neuropathy.
- Exposure to toxic chemicals, including lead, mercury, arsenic, and the chemicals in pesticides and herbicides, may lead to peripheral neuropathy.
- Nerve damage may be caused by injuries or by repeated jarring, such as that brought on by operating a jackhammer.
- Exposure to cold temperatures may produce nerve damage (see Hypothermia for more information).
- Some cancers, including multiple myeloma, lung cancer, and leukemia, may cause peripheral neuropathy.
- Some types of peripheral neuropathy are hereditary.
- The cause is unknown in some cases.

PREVENTION

- Consume no more than two alcoholic drinks per day. If you suspect that you may have a drinking problem, seek help from a doctor or support group immediately.
- Eat a healthy, balanced diet.
- Try to reduce or eliminate exposure to toxic chemicals at home and in the workplace.

DIAGNOSIS

- Patient history and physical examination.
- Electromyography may be performed. In this procedure, needle electrodes are inserted into various muscles to measure electrical activity associated with nerve function.

Peripheral Neuropathies *continued*

- A variety of tests may be given to evaluate reflexes and nerve performance.
- Lumbar puncture (spinal tap).
- Blood tests.
- X-rays.
- Biopsies of nerve or muscle tissue.

HOW TO TREAT IT

- Strict control of diabetes through medication, diet, and exercise may allow diabetic neuropathy to subside either partially or completely, depending upon the extent of the nerve damage.
- Diabetics should practice good foot care and check their feet every day. Peripheral neuropathy reduces sensation in affected areas, so minor foot problems may go unnoticed and develop into major infections.
- Alcohol-induced neuropathy requires complete abstinence from alcohol.
- Multivitamin supplements may be recommended.
- Exposure to toxic chemicals should be reduced or eliminated as much as possible.
- Plasmapheresis (a procedure that involves partial removal of blood plasma while the blood cells are returned to circulation) may be performed to speed recovery from Guillain-Barré syndrome by filtering out irritating or dangerous antibodies from the bloodstream.
- Hospitalization is recommended for treatment of Guillain-Barré syndrome, since it may worsen unpredictably and be life-threatening before recovery begins. Breathing and swallowing difficulties are treated with supplemental oxygen and intravenous feeding.
- Over-the-counter pain relievers may be taken to reduce pain.
- Physical therapy is advised to help regain muscle function. Canes, walkers, or wheelchairs may be temporarily useful, and rails near stairs and in the bathroom are recommended to prevent falls.

WHEN TO CALL A DOCTOR

- **EMERGENCY** Call an ambulance if you or someone in your presence experiences breathing difficulty, widespread muscle tingling or numbness, or paralysis.
- Call a doctor if you develop symptoms of peripheral neuropathy.
- Call a doctor if, after being diagnosed with peripheral neuropathy, you develop sores or open wounds on the hands and feet.

Peripheral Vascular Disease

WHAT IS IT?

Peripheral vascular disease results from a narrowing of the arteries in the legs and sometimes the arms, generally due to atherosclerosis, the buildup of plaque in the arterial walls. Plaque—composed of cholesterol-rich fatty deposits, collagen, other proteins, and excess smooth muscle cells—gradually accumulates in the arteries. Thickening of the arterial walls narrows the vascular channels and impedes blood flow. During walking or other activity the narrowed arteries are unable to supply enough blood and oxygen to the muscles, causing pain (intermittent claudication), most commonly in the calves. Peripheral vascular disease is more common in men over age 50, although one form can affect some male smokers as early as age 20. Diabetes greatly increases the risk of peripheral vascular disease, especially in women. The disease may worsen if left untreated, in some cases even leading to tissue death (gangrene). Peripheral vascular disease shares the same risk factors as the more dangerous coronary artery disease, and the diseases often occur together.

WHAT CAUSES IT?

• Atherosclerosis is the most common cause of peripheral vascular disease.
• Smoking is the greatest risk factor.
• Obesity, a sedentary lifestyle, high cholesterol levels, and high blood pressure contribute to atherosclerosis.

SYMPTOMS

• Muscle pain in the calves or thighs of one or both legs that occurs when walking, especially fast or uphill. Pain subsides with rest. It may also occur in the fingers, arms, buttocks, lower back, or the arch of the foot.
• Impotence (erectile dysfunction).
• Symptoms of severe disease: muscle pain at rest that worsens at night; discolored or blue toes; cold or numb feet; numbness in the affected area when at rest; open sores on the feet or legs; heightened sensitivity to cold, or weak or absent pulse in the affected limb; scaly or hairless skin over the affected area.

• People with diabetes mellitus are at increased risk.
• Medications that reduce blood pressure, such as beta-blockers, may starve some muscles of blood.

PREVENTION

• Don't smoke.
• Exercise regularly.
• Eat a diet low in saturated fat, cholesterol, and salt.
• Lose weight if necessary.

DIAGNOSIS

• Patient history and physical examination.
• X-rays of the arteries are taken after the injection of a contrast material (angiography).
• Ultrasound or MRI (magnetic resonance imaging).

HOW TO TREAT IT

• Follow prevention tips.
• Each day, take a walk and continue until leg pain develops. Rest for a short time to let the pain subside, then continue walking. Gradually, the distance that can be traveled painlessly will increase.
• Pentoxifylline (Trental), a blood-viscosity reducing agent, may be prescribed to improve blood flow.
• Practice good foot care and check your feet every day. Poor circulation due to peripheral vascular disease slows the healing of sores. Spotting problems early may help to prevent minor foot problems from becoming major infections.
• Diabetics must maintain scrupulous control over their blood sugar levels.
• Daily doses of aspirin may be prescribed to prevent blood clots that can lead to heart attack or stroke.
• Cholesterol-lowering drugs may be prescribed for those with unhealthy blood cholesterol levels that cannot be controlled by lifestyle changes alone.
• In severe cases angioplasty to dilate the narrowed portion of the artery, or bypass surgery to reroute blood around the narrowed artery, may be necessary.
• In extreme cases when gangrene is spreading uncontrollably, amputation of the affected limb may be required.

WHEN TO CALL A DOCTOR

• Make an appointment with a doctor if you repeatedly develop muscle pain when walking or at rest.

Peritonitis

WHAT IS IT?

Peritonitis is a serious disorder caused by an inflammation of the peritoneum, most often due to a bacterial infection. The peritoneum is a two-layered membrane that lines the abdominal cavity and encloses the stomach, intestines, and other abdominal organs. This membrane supports the abdominal organs and protects them from infection; however, occasionally the peritoneum itself may become infected by bacteria or other microorganisms. Infection usually spreads from organs within the abdomen. The inflammation may affect the entire peritoneum or be confined to a walled-off, pus-filled cavity (abscess). A rupture anywhere along the gastrointestinal tract is the most common pathway for entry of an infectious agent into the peritoneum. Peritonitis is a medical emergency: the muscles within the walls of the intestine become paralyzed and the forward movement of intestinal contents stops (ileus). However, since the advent of antibiotics, most people recover fully from peritonitis with proper treatment.

SYMPTOMS

- Acute onset of severe, steady pain throughout the abdomen or localized in one area of the abdomen. Pain may persist for several hours and is worsened by movement or pressure on the abdomen.
- Boardlike rigidity of the abdomen, due to contraction of the muscles of the abdominal wall.
- Swollen or bloated abdomen.
- Chills and fever, with profuse perspiration.
- Nausea and vomiting.
- Weakness.
- Pale, cold skin.
- Shock.

WHAT CAUSES IT?

- Many different types of bacteria can cause peritonitis, particularly those found within the intestine.
- Tuberculosis and fungal and parasitical infection may cause a less acute form of peritonitis.
- Perforation of the gastrointestinal tract, due to a stab or bullet wound, peptic ulcer, colon cancer, appendicitis, or diverticulitis, may allow bacteria-laden gastric material to enter the abdominal cavity and cause peritonitis.
- Abdominal surgery occasionally results in peritonitis.
- Infection of the fallopian tubes, which are adjacent to the peritoneum, may cause peritonitis.
- Cirrhosis of the liver may promote the development of bacterial peritonitis.
- Systemic lupus erythematosus may cause a noninfectious inflammation of the peritoneum.

PREVENTION

- Obtain prompt treatment for any infections or abdominal injuries or diseases.
- Antibiotics prescribed for any disorder should be taken for the full term as directed.

DIAGNOSIS

- Patient history and physical examination.
- Blood tests will show elevated white count.
- Abdominal x-rays, ultrasound exams, and CT (computed tomography) scans.
- Exploratory abdominal surgery (laparotomy) may be necessary.

HOW TO TREAT IT

- Large doses of antibiotics are administered intravenously to treat bacterial peritonitis.
- Surgery is often necessary when peritonitis is due to a disorder that has caused perforation along the intestinal tract, for example, a peptic ulcer or a burst appendix.
- Intravenous fluids and feeding may be necessary to prevent dehydration and to allow the intestines to rest.
- Analgesics may be administered to reduce pain.
- Antifungal medication is prescribed to treat fungal peritonitis.
- A tube passed through the nose into the intestine is attached to a suction device to remove contents from a temporarily paralyzed intestine.

WHEN TO CALL A DOCTOR

- **EMERGENCY** See a doctor or call an ambulance immediately if you experience severe abdominal pain that persists longer than 10 or 20 minutes, accompanied by any other symptoms of peritonitis.

Peritonsillar Abscess Quinsy

WHAT IS IT?
Peritonsillar abscess (also known as quinsy) is a pus-producing infection occurring in the cavity at the back of the throat, near the tonsils. Quinsy is usually a complication of tonsillitis, a bacterial infection of the tonsils. The infection may spread to the soft palate (the back of the roof of the mouth) or may travel down the throat into the chest. If left untreated, the infection may attack the membranes that surround the heart and lungs, known as the pericardium and the pleura, respectively. Infections of these membranes may eventually produce serious,

---

SYMPTOMS
- A sore throat that suddenly intensifies in severity, often spreading to the soft palate.
- Pain or difficulty in swallowing. Ear pain may occur during swallowing.
- Drooling.
- Swollen neck.
- Fever.
- Headache.
- Enlarged lymph nodes (swollen glands) in the neck.

---

even life-threatening, complications, including fluid accumulation around the heart or lungs, chest pain, and breathing difficulty (see Pericarditis for more information). Also, in rare cases, swelling around the roof of the mouth may become severe enough to interfere with breathing. Although peritonsillar abscess occurs more often in young adults, it is uncommon even among that age group. This disorder may

respond well to antibiotics, but surgical drainage is often needed. An abscess may recur if the tonsils are not removed.

WHAT CAUSES IT?
- Bacterial infection of the tonsils is the underlying cause of peritonsillar abscess.

PREVENTION
- Obtain prompt treatment for sore throats and other upper respiratory infections.

DIAGNOSIS
- Examination of the throat and palate.

HOW TO TREAT IT
- Antibiotics administered to treat peritonsillar abscess should be taken for the full term prescribed.
- Surgery may be necessary to drain a large, pus-filled abscess.
- Pain relievers may be taken as necessary to reduce fever and pain.
- Patients should gargle with warm salt water to soothe a sore throat during recovery and consume plenty of additional nonalcoholic liquids.
- Surgery to remove the tonsils (tonsillectomy) may be advised to prevent recurrence of peritonsillar abscess, but the operation is usually delayed until the infected abscess has subsided. Tonsillectomy may be reserved for those with recurrent peritonsillar abscess.

WHEN TO CALL A DOCTOR
- Call a doctor if you develop symptoms of a peritonsillar abscess.

Pharyngitis

WHAT IS IT?

Pharyngitis—often simply referred to as a sore throat—is inflammation of the pharynx, the portion of the throat that lies just beyond the back of the roof of the mouth and stretches to the Adam's apple (larynx). It usually occurs when viruses (or sometimes, bacteria) from a cold, flu, or sinus infection involve the throat. Pharyngitis is very common but rarely serious. Most cases clear up on their own after three to 10 days and require no therapy other than pain relievers to ease discomfort. Rarely, though, tissues in the throat may swell considerably and obstruct breathing—a life-threatening condition. In addition, strep throat (caused by streptococcus bacteria) requires antibiotics to prevent complications, including rheumatic fever, a condition that can permanently damage the heart valves. Diphtheria is a rare but serious bacterial variety of pharyngitis.

SYMPTOMS
- Sore or red, raw throat.
- Difficulty speaking or swallowing.
- Tender, swollen lymph nodes (glands) in the neck.
- Fever.
- Headache.
- Earache.

WHAT CAUSES IT?

- Most cases are caused by viral infection.
- About 5 percent of cases are caused by bacterial infections (including strep) or other microorganisms.
- Some cases are caused by contact with toxic fumes or chemicals, long-term exposure to cigarette smoke or polluted, dry, or dusty air, or excessive alcohol consumption.
- Persistent infections elsewhere in the head, such as the sinuses or mouth, can cause lingering, or chronic, pharyngitis.

PREVENTION

- Avoid cigarette smoke, excessive alcohol, or other substances that can irritate the throat.
- A humidifier or air purifier may help if dust or dryness causes irritation.

DIAGNOSIS

- A doctor will examine the throat and may take a throat swab culture to test for strep or other bacteria.

HOW TO TREAT IT

- Symptoms such as sore throat or fever can be treated with nonprescription pain relievers such as aspirin. Gargling with a half teaspoon of salt dissolved in a glass of warm water or using antiseptic lozenges or sprays may also provide temporary relief.
- Antibiotics are prescribed for pharyngitis caused by bacteria. These drugs are effective in killing bacteria and certain other microorganisms, but not viruses. If the diagnosis is strep throat, it is very important to continue the antibiotics for at least 10 to 14 days, even if sore throat and other symptoms subside, to assure that all of the bacteria are eliminated. Strep infection can lead to rheumatic fever (which may permanently damage the heart valves).
- Pharyngitis caused by viruses clears up on its own; antibiotics are not effective against viral infections, so treatment is aimed at easing symptoms.
- Do not smoke; curb alcohol intake. Smoke and alcohol irritate the throat.
- Persistent pharyngitis caused by exposure to toxic fumes, air pollution, or industrial chemicals is treated by reducing or eliminating exposure to the noxious agent.

WHEN TO CALL A DOCTOR

- Call a doctor if a sore throat is unusually severe, is accompanied by high fever, or doesn't seem to be getting better after a few days.
- **EMERGENCY** If sore throat escalates to the point of causing breathing difficulty or inability to swallow liquids, get to an emergency room at once.

Pheochromocytoma

WHAT IS IT?

Pheochromocytoma is a rare type of tumor that usually develops in the inner portion (medulla) of the adrenals, the small glands located atop each kidney. The tumor causes excess release of epinephrine (adrenaline) and norepinephrine (noradrenaline), two hormones that help to regulate heart rate and blood pressure. The primary effect of the tumor is to cause intermittent or sustained periods of high blood pressure. Sporadic surges in blood pressure are marked by a rapid or pounding heartbeat, palpitations, headache, sweating, and extreme anxiety. Symptomatic attacks are sometimes brought on by emotional upset, a change in posture, or certain medications and tend to increase in frequency, duration, and severity if the tumor is left untreated. Treatment should be initiated as early as possible to prevent the long-term consequences of high blood pressure, which include heart disease, stroke, and kidney damage. (In patients with sustained high blood pressure, the hypertension may persist even after removal of the tumor.) Pheochromocytomas can develop at any age but are most common in young to middle-aged adults. Most cases are benign (noncancerous) and arise in only one adrenal gland without spreading. Sometimes tumors arise on both adrenals (especially in people with familial pheochromocytoma) or at other sites in the abdomen or chest. About 10 percent of pheochromocytomas are malignant (cancerous) and may spread to distant sites. Tumors that have spread are difficult to treat and prove fatal within five years in more than half of such cases. Benign tumors, on the other hand, are usually completely curable with surgery.

WHAT CAUSES IT?

• The cause of pheochromocytomas is unknown.
• Some people with a rare inherited syndrome called multiple endocrine neoplasia develop pheochromocytomas in association with medullary thyroid tumors and overproduction of parathyroid hormone (hyperparathyroidism).

PREVENTION

• There is no way to prevent pheochromocytoma.

DIAGNOSIS

• Blood and urine samples are taken to check for high levels of epinephrine, norepinephrine, and their breakdown products. Blood tests may show a high blood glucose level.
• Computed tomography (CT) scans or magnetic resonance imaging (MRI) of the abdomen usually identifies an adrenal tumor.
• An angiogram (injection of a contrasting material into the blood vessels to make them clearly visible on a series of x-rays) is occasionally performed.

HOW TO TREAT IT

• Surgical removal of the tumor (adrenalectomy) is possible in most cases and usually leads to cure and full recovery. The earlier the tumor is treated the better. Surrounding healthy tissue may be removed as well if there is concern that the cancer may have spread locally. Drugs are given to control blood pressure for several weeks prior to the operation.
• If a malignant tumor has spread to other sites, radiation or chemotherapy may be tried, although results are generally disappointing.
• In a small percentage of cases, recurrence of tumors after surgery requires additional surgery.
• Drugs to lower blood pressure are used when hypertension persists after removal of a benign pheochromocytoma or in cases of malignant tumors.

WHEN TO CALL A DOCTOR

• See a doctor for symptoms of pheochromocytoma.

SYMPTOMS

• Headache, often severe.
• Palpitations, or rapid or pounding heartbeat.
• Excessive sweating.
• Lightheadedness, especially when arising from a sitting position.
• Chest pain.
• Abdominal pain.
• Constipation.
• Weight loss.
• Nervousness, irritability, or anxiety.
• Mental confusion or psychosis.

Pinworms

WHAT IS IT?

Pinworms are slender, white, threadlike worms, about a third of an inch long, that can infest the intestinal tract. Infestation with these parasites begins when pinworm eggs are swallowed and lodge in the intestine, where they hatch and mature. Two to six weeks later, the adult worm exits the anus to lay new eggs, often during the night when the host is sleeping. Pinworms are more of a nuisance than a serious health problem. The main complaint is intense anal itching, due to the irritation caused by worms migrating across the skin. In general, the body's immune system eliminates pinworms living in the intestine within several months. However, eggs are usually dispersed in bedding material or clothing and may spread via the fingers or even through the air, making reingestion of eggs and a new cycle of infestation common—not just among those who were originally affected but among other members of the household as well. Pinworms are very common, affecting up to 10 percent of the population, especially children. With medical care and scrupulous hygiene, however, reinfestation can be avoided.

SYMPTOMS
- Anal itching or pain.
- Irritability or fidgetiness.
- Restless sleep.
- Vaginal itching, pain, or discharge. This occurs infrequently when adult worms migrate across the skin to the vagina.

WHAT CAUSES IT?

- Swallowing pinworm eggs initiates a cycle of infection. Most often, eggs are spread when a child scratches the anus, allowing the eggs to be transported on the fingers or beneath the fingernails, where they can then contaminate food, dishes, toys, or play areas.

PREVENTION

- It is difficult to prevent an initial outbreak of pinworms. However, the following measures can be used to prevent reinfestation once the first outbreak has occurred:
- Wash the hands thoroughly before eating and after handling potentially infected objects, such as children's toys.
- Wash the hands after handling pets, as they may become infected during an outbreak as well.
- Keep fingernails short so they are less likely to pick up eggs.
- Shower frequently.
- Wash sheets, bedding, pajamas, underwear, towels, dishes, toilet seats—or any items likely to be infected—in very hot or even boiling water. Ironing sheets and clothes will also help to kill pinworm eggs.

DIAGNOSIS

- Adult worms are sometimes seen around the anal area at night or in bowel movements. A doctor can supply a piece of cellulose tape to be applied to the anal area during the night or in the early morning. The tape is then examined under a microscope for worms or eggs to confirm the diagnosis.

HOW TO TREAT IT

- Everyone in the household is treated with anti-worm drugs, since other family members are at high risk of being infected. Usually, a dose of mebendazole or pyrantel pamoate is given, followed by a second dose two weeks later. These medicines are very effective in killing worms.
- Creams or ointments that relieve anal itching and may contain substances that kill the worms can be prescribed.
- Careful hygiene is essential to prevent reinfection. The measures recommended under Prevention (see above) should be followed during the treatment period and for several weeks afterward.
- A veterinarian can help rid a pet of pinworms.

WHEN TO CALL A DOCTOR

- Call a doctor if symptoms of pinworm infestation occur.

Plantar Fasciitis

WHAT IS IT?

Plantar fasciitis is inflammation, usually due to injury, of the plantar fascia, the ligament between the front of the heel bone and the base of the toes that helps to support the arch. Excess stress absorbed by the foot may irritate or tear the plantar fascia, making this a common disorder among athletes, especially runners. Although plantar fasciitis may take up to a year to heal fully, it is not a serious health risk, and proper rest and stretching techniques may promote faster healing.

WHAT CAUSES IT?

• A tendency for the foot to roll inward (pronation) upon walking.
• Stress on the heel due to repeated hard pounding or quick turns, often from long-distance running, jogging, or basketball.
• Wearing shoes that lack proper heel support or that have thin or stiff soles.
• Age-related loss of resiliency in the ligaments.
• Some forms of arthritis, such as ankylosing spondylitis or Reiter's syndrome.

SYMPTOMS

• Sharp or burning pain directly under the heel. Pain worsens upon running or walking.

PREVENTION

• Wear running shoes with proper cushioning.
• Avoid exercising on nonresilient surfaces such as concrete.

DIAGNOSIS

• Patient history and physical examination.

HOW TO TREAT IT

• Rest the foot as much as possible, especially during the first week. Avoid running or jogging; instead, substitute exercises that do not put undue stress on the injured ligament, like bicycling or swimming.

• Apply ice to the tender area daily to reduce inflammation. Try rolling the arch of the foot over an empty tennis-ball can that has been filled with water and frozen; this both cools and stretches the affected area.
• Take over-the-counter pain relievers to reduce pain and inflammation.
• Insert an over-the-counter heel-support cushion into your shoe. Cut a hole in the pad to relieve pressure on the tender area if necessary. Try to avoid walking barefoot, since it may put added stress on the plantar ligament.
• Stretch the ligament with the following exercises. Each position should be held for 30 seconds, and each exercise repeated six times; the entire series should be performed three times daily if possible:
• Sit on a table with your knees bent. Loop a towel under the ball of the injured foot and pull, flexing the front of your foot upward. Keep your knee bent and try to press your foot against the towel.
• Perform the exercise as above with the leg extended straight out in front of you. Keep the leg straight during the stretch.
• Sit on a chair and cross the ankle of the injured foot over the opposite knee. Slowly push your toes backward with your hand until you feel the stretch in the bottom of the foot.
• Stand facing a wall, about one foot away, with the injured foot about six inches farther back. Put your hands on the wall and gently lean forward, stretching the lower calf.
• Stand facing a wall, about two feet away, with the injured foot about six inches farther back. Keep both feet slightly turned out. Put your hands on the wall and gently lean forward, bending the front knee and keeping the back heel on the floor.
• Rarely, surgery to repair the ligament may be recommended.

WHEN TO CALL A DOCTOR

• Make an appointment with a doctor if pain does not subside within four to six weeks.
• Call a doctor if pain is severe.

Plantar Warts

WHAT IS IT?

Plantar warts are noncancerous skin growths that develop on the soles of the foot. Like all warts, they are caused by a virus (human papillomavirus). Various features set plantar warts apart from so-called common warts (which typically form raised dome-shaped skin lesions on the fingers and other areas) and genital warts. First, plantar warts arise exclusively on the bottoms of the feet. Pressure from body weight tends to make plantar warts grow inward, just beneath the skin's surface, and a rough, thickened layer of skin (callus) typically grows over the wart. A plantar wart may feel like a pebble in the shoe; however, in some cases it causes intense pain, particularly if it lies on the heel or ball of the foot. Second, plantar warts do not tend to spread to other sites on the body and are not contagious to other people. They usually appear singly, although a variant, the mosaic wart, consists of multiple small lesions. Finally, unlike genital warts, which have been linked to serious health problems such as genital cancer, plantar warts pose no such risks. Several treatment sessions may be necessary to cure plantar warts, but a doctor can usually eliminate even the most stubborn cases.

SYMPTOMS

- A bumpy, white, tender skin growth on the bottom of the foot, usually surrounded by a callus.
- Pain or discomfort when putting weight on the affected foot.

WHAT CAUSES IT?

- Plantar warts, like other warts, are caused by the human papillomavirus, which may enter the skin through a cut or crack. There it incubates for several months before developing into a wart. For unknown reasons the incidence is highest among adolescents.

PREVENTION

- There are no known ways to prevent plantar warts.

DIAGNOSIS

- A doctor can identify a plantar wart by its characteristic appearance. Cutting off the surface layer reveals a soft, cauliflower-like central portion that is speckled with small, clotted blood vessels resembling splinters.

HOW TO TREAT IT

- Painless plantar warts may need no treatment, as they tend to disappear on their own, usually within a year or two. However, if the wart is painful and interferes with walking, treatment is warranted.
- Home treatment can be attempted, although plantar warts (unlike common warts) tend to be rather difficult to treat and often require professional care. One approach involves nightly applications of salicylic-acid plasters, which are available in drug stores.
- See a physician or podiatrist for warts that fail to respond to self-treatment. (You should not attempt to cut off warts or the calluses that may cover them.) Usually, the doctor will first cut away any thickened skin over the wart. It can then be treated with any of several techniques.
- Frozen liquid nitrogen may be applied to the wart (cryosurgery), which may cause it to blister and fall off within a couple of days. Alternatively, the wart may be burned off using acidic chemicals or a beam of electric current or laser light. These approaches generally cause minimal discomfort, although large or deep warts may require local anesthesia. Several treatment sessions may be necessary, since the thickness of the plantar surface makes it more resistant to treatment, and because warts tend to grow back.
- In especially stubborn cases, complete surgical removal of the wart may be necessary.

WHEN TO CALL A DOCTOR

- See your doctor or a podiatrist if a plantar wart is painful and interferes with walking.

Platelet Function Disorders

WHAT IS IT?

Various disorders can affect platelets, the components of the blood that help blood to clot. Normally, platelets are formed continuously in the bone marrow. From there, they are released into the blood, where they circulate and help with wound healing. For example, after a simple cut, platelets flowing by the damaged area collect, form a small clot that stanches blood flow, and release various substances that help the wound to heal. Most platelet disorders are due to an insufficient number of platelets, a condition known as thrombocytopenia. This condition results either from inadequate production of platelets in the bone marrow or from their excessive destruction in the bloodstream. Less often, the number of circulating platelets is normal, but they are defective and function improperly. In either case deficient platelet function can lead to excessive bleeding. The most common result is for blood to leak slowly from minute tears in the smallest blood vessels (capillaries), causing bright or dark red pinpoint-size hemorrhages, called petechiae, to appear on the skin. Petechiae often occur on the lower legs (where gravity exerts increased pressure on blood vessel walls), on the inside of the cheeks (owing to pressure from chewing), or along areas constricted by tight clothing (such as brassiere straps). Petechiae are harmless, but they may be a harbinger of more serious internal bleeding, particularly bleeding from the gastrointestinal tract or from blood vessels in the brain (a potentially life-threatening complication known as intracranial hemorrhage). There are a wide variety of causes of platelet disorders, and they can occur at any age. Some are hereditary disorders that may become obvious as early as infancy; for example, there may be excessive bleeding following circumcision. In older people, platelet disorders may become manifest after a dental extraction or surgical procedure. Outcome varies widely, depending on the cause and severity of the disorder. Some forms are mild and lifelong, with only minor bruising or limited periods of excessive bleeding; others arise suddenly and may be fatal. In general, older patients seem to be at higher risk of serious complications like intracranial hemorrhage.

WHAT CAUSES IT?

• In many cases, platelet disorders are believed to be due to an autoimmune disorder (an attack, for unknown reasons, by the body's immune system against its own healthy cells). In this case, platelets are destroyed prematurely as they circulate in the blood. A common unexplained autoimmune disorder is called idiopathic thrombocytopenic purpura (IPP), and platelets are rapidly destroyed in systemic lupus erythematosus, also an autoimmune disorder.
• Certain types of leukemia or bone marrow invasion by cancer can give rise to decreased platelet function.
• A number of infections, including rubella, mononucleosis, bacterial blood infections, malaria, hepatitis, and human immunodeficiency virus (HIV), can cause platelet disorders.
• A wide variety of drugs are capable of causing platelet disorders in a small percentage of people. Some of these drugs are very commonly used, including aspirin, ibuprofen, and antibiotics such as penicillin. Others include quinidine and quinine (used to treat malaria) and illicit intravenous drugs.
• In aplastic anemia, a rare but very serious condition, production of platelets (and other blood cells) in the bone marrow is severely suppressed. It can be

SYMPTOMS

• Minor bleeding just under the surface of the skin or in the mouth. Usually appears as multiple tiny, pinpoint-size specks (petechiae) on the lower legs or inner cheeks.
• Bleeding of the gums or blood blisters in the mouth.
• Nosebleeds.
• Easy bruising.
• Prolonged menstrual periods.
• Prolonged bleeding after a minor cut or after dental or surgical procedures.
• Emergency symptoms: sudden onset of severe headache, nausea, vomiting, vision loss, or confusion—signs of brain hemorrhage; black or tarry stools may indicate bleeding from the gastrointestinal tract.

Platelet Function Disorders *continued*

induced by radiation or chemotherapy drugs (for cancer), gold compounds (used to treat arthritis), the antibiotic chloramphenicol, or exposure to organic solvent fumes, including benzene and glue. It also sometimes occurs in those with acute hepatitis, but in many cases the cause cannot be determined.

• Chronic alcoholism or deficiencies of certain B vitamins can cause platelet disorders.

• Massive blood transfusions can cause a temporary platelet deficiency, exacerbated at times by an immune reaction to the donor's blood that leads to platelet destruction.

• Various genetic defects can cause inherited platelet disorders.

• Disseminated intravascular coagulation (DIC) involves impaired platelet function.

• Chemotherapy and radiation treatments for cancer or leukemia may destroy platelets.

PREVENTION

• There are no known ways to prevent platelet function disorders.

DIAGNOSIS

• Patient history should include all drugs being taken and family history of bleeding disorders.

• Blood samples will be taken for a platelet count and to test platelet function.

• Bleeding time (how long it takes for a small puncture wound to stop bleeding) is measured.

• A bone marrow biopsy (removal of tissue through a needle inserted into the hip or thigh) may be necessary to determine whether adequate numbers of platelets are being manufactured.

HOW TO TREAT IT

• All patients should avoid aspirin and other drugs that can affect platelets until the condition clears.

Those whose only symptoms are petechiae may need no additional treatment.

• For those with more serious bleeding disorders, transfusions of platelets are given until the underlying defect is corrected and the body produces enough healthy platelets on its own. Those with chronic or inherited forms of the disease may require transfusions whenever bleeding problems arise or before surgical or dental procedures are performed.

• If a drug is found to be the cause, discontinuation of the drug usually resolves the problem quickly.

• Corticosteroid drugs may be prescribed to suppress the destruction of platelets by the immune system. The disorder often improves within several weeks and may disappear completely. Other immunosuppressive drugs may be tried as well.

• Those who continue to have platelet defects despite corticosteroids or other forms of therapy may benefit from surgical removal of the spleen (splenectomy). The spleen acts to remove worn out blood cells, including platelets, but in those with platelet disorders, it can become enlarged and overactive and thus stall recovery. Splenectomy—used especially in those with IPP—brings about long-term remissions in many patients without causing other long-term side effects.

WHEN TO CALL A DOCTOR

• See a doctor if you have symptoms of a bleeding disorder.

• If you have already been diagnosed with a platelet disorder, call a doctor if you notice increased bruising or new areas of petechiae or if you begin bleeding from the nose or gums.

• **EMERGENCY** Get to an emergency room immediately if symptoms of internal bleeding from the gastrointestinal tract (black, tarry stools) or brain (severe headache, nausea, vision loss) occur.

Pleurisy and Pleural Effusion

WHAT IS IT?

Pleurisy is inflammation of the pleura—the delicate, two-layered membrane that encases the lungs and lines the inside of the chest cavity. The space between the pleura is normally bathed in a lubricating fluid that ensures smooth expansion and contraction of the membranes during breathing. With pleurisy, an area of the pleura becomes inflamed and roughened, causing the two layers of the membrane to rub together painfully. Pleurisy can affect people of any age. Most cases are due to infections and, with treatment, clear up in a few days or weeks. However, some cases are caused by more serious underlying disorders, such as systemic lupus erythematosus or a pulmonary embolism. If inflammation is severe, fluid may accumulate in the pleural space—a condition known as pleural effusion. The excess fluid often provides lubrication that eases pain, but the extra pressure may compress the underlying lung and make breathing difficult. Pleurisy and pleural effusion are not diseases themselves so much as manifestations of an underlying disorder, and outcome depends on the seriousness of the underlying cause.

SYMPTOMS

- Pleurisy symptoms: chest pain that is usually sharp and fleeting, but may be mild and continuous. Pain is made worse by deep breathing, coughing, sneezing, or moving the affected area and may radiate to the shoulder, lower chest, or abdomen, but it usually affects only one side of the body.
- Fever and chills.
- Headache.
- Weakness.
- Rapid, shallow breathing.
- Dry cough.
- Generally no symptoms for pleural effusion. However, if it is very large, especially if it affects both sides of the chest, pleural effusion may cause shortness of breath.

WHAT CAUSES IT?

- Pleurisy is often caused by lung or chest infections, including tuberculosis, pneumonia, and viral infections. Pleurodynia, a viral infection that most often affects children, may cause outbreaks of pleurisy among family members.
- Pulmonary embolism (a blood clot in an artery of the lung) is a life-threatening cause of pleurisy.
- Other causes include autoimmune disorders (like lupus or rheumatoid arthritis), chest injury, and sickle cell disease.
- Pleural effusion may result from pleurisy, a tumor in the pleura (mesothelioma), cancer that has spread from the lung or elsewhere, heart failure, liver disease, kidney disease, or pancreatitis.

PREVENTION

- There is no known way to prevent pleurisy.

DIAGNOSIS

- Patient history and physical examination.
- Chest x-rays.
- Ultrasound or CT (computed tomography) scans of the chest.
- Aspiration (withdrawal of fluid from the pleural space with a needle) and biopsy may be done at the same time.

HOW TO TREAT IT

- Underlying disorders are treated. For example, antibiotics are given for bacterial pneumonias.
- Over-the-counter pain relievers are recommended. Wrapping the chest loosely in elastic bandages may also help to ease pain.
- If pleural effusion makes breathing difficult, fluid may be withdrawn with a needle (thoracentesis).
- For very severe cases of recurrent pleural effusion—such as those that may occur with inoperable cancer—doxycycline (an antibiotic) or an anticancer drug is injected into the pleural space. The drugs cause scarring and fusion of the two pleural layers, thus preventing future recurrences.

WHEN TO CALL A DOCTOR

- Call a doctor if symptoms of pleurisy develop, particularly if they are accompanied by fever.

Pneumonia

WHAT IS IT?

Pneumonia, a general term encompassing many different diseases, is inflammation of the lungs. Although usually caused by an infectious microorganism, such inflammation may also be caused by the inhalation of irritating gases or particles. The lungs have a complex system of defense: frequent branching and narrowing of the bronchial passages make it difficult for invaders to penetrate the lungs deeply; millions of tiny hairs, or cilia, in the bronchial lining constantly sweep particles out of the airways; the cough reflex forces irritating substances out of the lungs at high speed; and white blood cells, known as phagocytes, engulf and destroy infectious agents. Despite these defenses, pneumonia is still common. Inflammation may be limited to a single area (lobar pneumonia) or may occur in patches throughout the lungs (bronchopneumonia). An accumulation of fluid in the air sacs (alveoli) of the lungs impairs transfer of oxygen to the bloodstream. The body's cells may thus become starved of oxygen, and in severe cases complete respiratory failure may result. Until the development of antibiotics, pneumonia was the number one cause of death in this country, and recently, strains of the most common cause of bacterial pneumonia (*Streptococcus pneumoniae*) have emerged that are penicillin resistant. Pneumonia, especially deadly among the elderly or those already weakened by underlying illness, remains among the 10 leading causes of death today. Nevertheless, despite the serious health risks posed by the disease, the outlook for complete recovery is good, especially with early diagnosis and treatment. For the elderly and members of other high-risk groups, a vaccine is available that provides long-term protection against 23 different strains of *Streptococcus pneumoniae* (which account for 90 percent of cases of pneumococcal pneumonia).

WHAT CAUSES IT?

- Viral or bacterial infections are the most common causes of pneumonia.
- Other microorganisms may sometimes cause pneumonia; for example, fungal and parasitic pneumonia commonly affects those with AIDS.
- Although bacteria are usually inhaled, they may spread to the lungs from elsewhere in the body via the bloodstream.
- Inhalation of chemical irritants, like poisonous gases, may lead to pneumonia.
- Vomit inhaled into the lungs, which may occur when a person loses consciousness, may cause what is known as aspiration pneumonia.
- Infancy or very old age, smoking, recent surgery, hospitalization, the use of chemotherapy and other immunosuppressive drugs, and the prolonged use of antibiotics are risk factors of pneumonia.
- Other conditions, including asthma, chronic bronchitis, poorly controlled diabetes mellitus, AIDS, alcoholism, Hodgkin's disease, leukemia, multiple myeloma, and chronic kidney disease, increase the risk both of contracting pneumonia and of encountering more severe complications.

PREVENTION

- Don't smoke.
- People at high risk for pneumonia should be

SYMPTOMS

- Fever (over 100°F, possibly as high as 105°F) and chills.
- Cough, possibly with bloody sputum. (A cough may persist for six to eight weeks after the infection, especially a viral infection, subsides.)
- Chest pain upon inhalation.
- Shortness of breath.
- Headache, sore throat, and muscle pain.
- Nasal discharge.
- General feeling of poor health.
- Weakness and fatigue.
- Profuse perspiration.
- Loss of appetite.
- In severe cases: breathing difficulty, blue tinge to the skin, mental confusion.
- General note: Symptoms vary greatly depending on the type of pneumonia involved, and the elderly and very sick people tend to have less-pronounced symptoms and less fever, even though pneumonia is more dangerous among such patients.

Pneumonia *continued*

immunized against pneumococcal pneumonia. These people include those over 65; those with heart, lung, or kidney disease, diabetes mellitus, or weakened immune systems; and alcoholics. The vaccine is required only once; it provides long-term protection and is between 60 to 80 percent effective.
• An annual flu vaccination may also be recommended, since pneumonia is a common complication of severe influenza among those in high-risk groups.

DIAGNOSIS
• Patient history and physical examination.
• Blood and sputum cultures.
• Chest x-rays.
• A biopsy of lung tissue may be performed in severe cases.

HOW TO TREAT IT
• Antibiotics or other antimicrobial drugs are prescribed to treat a bacterial infection and should be taken for the full term prescribed. Stopping the medication too soon may produce a relapse of pneumonia more severe than the initial attack.
• Antifungal drugs, such as amphotericin B, are prescribed to treat a fungal infection.
• Antiviral drugs such as ribavirin, acyclovir, and ganciclovir sodium are effective against some types of viral infection.
• Your doctor may recommend analgesics to reduce fever and pain. Check with your doctor before taking over-the-counter pain relievers, because they are not recommended for some types of bacterial pneumonia.

• Take an over-the-counter cough suppressant containing dextromethorphan if you have a persistent dry cough. However, if you are coughing up sputum, suppressing the cough may encourage mucus accumulation in the lungs, potentially leading to serious complications.
• Your doctor will instruct you how to drain mucus from your lungs by assuming various positions that lower your head below your torso (a technique known as postural drainage).
• Inhale steam, use a humidifier, or take hot showers, and drink at least eight glasses of water a day to loosen lung secretions and make them easier to expel.
• Rest in bed until fever subsides.
• Hospitalization may be recommended, especially during the early stages, since pneumonia may unexpectedly become severe within hours.
• Oxygen may be administered through a mask to aid breathing. In severe cases an artificial respirator may be required.
• Excess fluid in the space surrounding the lungs may be removed by aspiration with a syringe and needle inserted through the chest wall (thoracentesis).

WHEN TO CALL A DOCTOR
• Call a doctor if you develop symptoms of pneumonia, especially a fever above 100°F, shortness of breath even when lying down, or bloody sputum from coughing.
• **EMERGENCY** Call an ambulance if you experience difficulty in breathing or if a blue tinge to the skin appears.

Pneumothorax

WHAT IS IT?

Pneumothorax is an accumulation of air in the pleural space (that is, between the pleura, the two layers of membrane that cover each lung and the inner chest wall), resulting in partial or total collapse of the affected lung. The different types of pneumothorax (spontaneous, secondary, traumatic, and tension) are distinguished by their cause. Treatment and outcome depend upon severity.

WHAT CAUSES IT?

• Spontaneous pneumothorax occurs when an air-filled blister known as a bleb ruptures within the upper part of the lung. Blebs are believed to be congenital or hereditary in origin; smoking may be a contributing factor. Scuba diving or high altitudes may precipitate the rupture of a bleb. This type of pneumothorax is most common among tall, thin, and otherwise healthy men between the ages of 20 and 40, and recurs in about one-third of patients.
• Secondary pneumothorax (usually far more serious than spontaneous pneumothorax) occurs as a complication of some underlying lung disorder, including chronic obstructive pulmonary disease, cystic fibrosis, tuberculosis, and certain types of pneumonia.
• Traumatic pneumothorax results from a direct puncture or laceration of the pleura, which may occur with a stab wound or rib fracture, or as a complication of a medical procedure.
• A tension pneumothorax develops when air entering the pleural space during inhalation becomes trapped and cannot escape during exhalation.

PREVENTION

• Don't smoke.
• Seek prompt treatment for any existing lung disorders, such as tuberculosis or asthma.

SYMPTOMS

• Shortness of breath (of varying degrees) and tightness in the chest.
• Chest pain, usually sudden and sharp.
• Bluish skin, bulging neck veins, and weak rapid pulse (in severe cases).

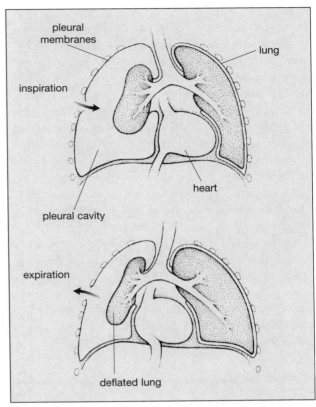

In traumatic pneumothorax, air enters the pleural cavity upon inspiration and exits on expiration, while the lung remains deflated. Tension pneumothorax results when air cannot escape during expiration.

DIAGNOSIS

• Patient history, examination, and chest x-rays.

HOW TO TREAT IT

• A small pneumothorax may heal on its own; a few days of monitoring in a hospital may be advised.
• More serious cases may require removal of air by suction through a needle or catheter. Using this procedure, the lung usually reexpands over several days.
• Recurrent spontaneous pneumothorax may warrant installation of irritants into pleural space to cause the layers to fuse together.
• Surgery may be considered to repair a lung lesion causing secondary pneumothorax.

WHEN TO CALL A DOCTOR

• If you experience the symptoms of a pneumothorax, see a doctor immediately.

Poliomyelitis

WHAT IS IT?

Poliomyelitis, also known as infantile paralysis or polio, is a highly contagious viral infection. In its most severe form, polio may cause rapid and irreversible paralysis and until recently was one of the most feared infectious diseases, often occurring in epidemics. Postpolio syndrome or postpoliomyelitic progressive muscular atrophy may occur 30 years or more after the initial infection, gradually producing additional muscle weakness, atrophy, and pain. Polio is preventable by immunization and has virtually disappeared in this country; however, the danger from this disease still exists. The dramatic decline in cases of polio has created a false sense of security; fewer children in the United States have been receiving the vaccine, so the number of people vulnerable to the infection is rising. Polio is still common in much of the world, and there is no cure; therefore, until the poliovirus is destroyed, immunization remains essential for protection.

SYMPTOMS

- Fever.
- Headache and sore throat.
- Stiff neck and back.
- Nausea and vomiting.
- Difficulty in swallowing.
- Muscle pain, weakness, or spasms.
- Constipation and urine retention.
- Swollen or bloated abdomen.
- Irritability.
- Emergency symptoms: muscle paralysis; breathing difficulty.

WHAT CAUSES IT?

- Poliomyelitis is caused by a viral infection by one of the three forms of poliovirus.
- The virus may be spread through contact with contaminated food and water, or by infected saliva expelled during coughing or sneezing.

PREVENTION

- A series of vaccines is recommended to begin at two months of age, repeated at four and 18 months of age, and followed by a booster shot when the child enters school (between the ages of four and six).
- In adults, immunization against polio is only recommended before traveling to an area where polio is common.

DIAGNOSIS

- Patient history and physical examination.
- Blood tests.
- Lumbar puncture (spinal tap).

HOW TO TREAT IT

- Bed rest is advised until severe symptoms subside.
- Pain relievers may be administered to reduce fever, pain, and muscle spasms.
- Your doctor may prescribe bethanechol to treat urinary retention and antibiotics to fight an associated bacterial infection of the urinary tract.
- A urinary catheter, a thin tube attached to a storage bag used to collect urine, may be necessary if bladder control has been lost because of paralysis.
- Artificial respiration may be required if breathing is impaired; in some cases a surgical opening (tracheotomy) in the throat may be necessary.
- Physical therapy is necessary in cases of temporary or permanent paralysis. Mechanical aids such as braces, crutches, a wheelchair, and special shoes may aid in mobility.
- Occupational and psychological therapy may help patients adapt to the limitations imposed by the disease.

WHEN TO CALL A DOCTOR

- Call a doctor immediately if you or your child develop symptoms of polio, or if you may have been exposed to the virus and you are not immunized.
- **EMERGENCY** Call an ambulance if someone experiences breathing difficulty or develops paralysis in any of the limbs.
- Make an appointment with your doctor to receive the polio vaccine if you have not been immunized and plan to travel where polio is common.

Polycystic Ovaries

WHAT IS IT?

Polycystic ovarian disease, also known as the Stein-Leventhal syndrome, is characterized by the formation of cysts (spherical, thin-walled nodules filled with a thin fluid) within both ovaries. Each ovary contains an abundance of structures known as ovarian follicles. Roughly once a month, hormones stimulate a single follicle to grow and rise to the ovarian surface, where it bursts and releases an egg. At the same time, hormones cause the uterine wall to thicken to provide support if the egg becomes fertilized. The egg passes out of the ovary, through the fallopian tube, and into the uterus. If fertilization does not occur, the thickened uterine lining sloughs off and the egg, excess lining, and blood are all released through the vagina during menstruation. However, in polycystic ovarian disease the follicles

---

SYMPTOMS
- Absent or irregular menstrual periods.
- Infertility.
- Abnormal growth of facial hair (hirsutism).
- Obesity.
- Acne.

---

grow but do not burst; instead of releasing an egg, the follicle forms a cyst just under the ovary's surface. Normal menstrual periods are present early in puberty but taper off or cease as the ovaries begin to produce cysts instead of eggs; eventually, both ovaries become filled with tiny cysts. Lack of ovulation results in the cessation of menstrual periods, infertility, and overproduction of the male sex hormone testosterone by the ovaries. The reason for cyst development is not fully understood, but it is believed to involve an imbalance in the production of two pituitary hormones, luteinizing hormone (LH) and follicle-stimulating hormone (FSH). Other common features of this disorder are obesity, acne, and the abnormal growth of male-pattern facial hair. Polycystic ovarian disease affects women between the ages of 15 and 30. If left untreated, the relative excess of estrogen compared to progesterone may increase the risk of uterine cancer later in life. However, the disease often responds well to treatment, which may restore fertility and eliminate symptoms. Specific treatment depends on the individual needs of the patient, especially whether or not she wishes to have children in the future.

WHAT CAUSES IT?
- The cause of polycystic ovarian disease is unknown.

PREVENTION
- There is no known way to prevent polycystic ovarian disease.

DIAGNOSIS
- Patient history and pelvic examination. The gynecologist may gently press on the abdomen to detect enlarged ovaries.
- Blood tests to measure levels of LH, FSH, testosterone, and other hormones that affect the ovaries.
- Ultrasound scans.
- Laparoscopic abdominal surgery (use of a lighted scope that is inserted into the abdomen through small incisions) may confirm the diagnosis.

HOW TO TREAT IT
- For those who wish to become pregnant, clomiphene citrate, a fertility drug, or hormones such as human menopausal gonadotropin and human chorionic gonadotropin may be prescribed to induce ovulation. Rarely, laparoscopic surgery to reduce the size of the ovary (wedge resection) may be performed to create more favorable conditions for ovulation.
- For those who do not wish to become pregnant, oral contraceptives or progestins such as medroxyprogesterone acetate may be prescribed to suppress ovulation and reduce the risk of uterine cancer later in life.

WHEN TO CALL A DOCTOR
- Call your gynecologist if you develop symptoms of polycystic ovarian disease.

Polycythemia Vera

WHAT IS IT?

Polycythemia vera is an uncommon blood disorder characterized by a pathological overproduction of red blood cells in the bone marrow; often, white blood cells and platelets are overproduced as well. Each type of blood cell performs an essential function: red cells carry oxygen, platelets are crucial for clotting, and white cells can engulf infectious agents and thus serve as part of the body's immune system. Red blood cells and platelets, and most types of white blood cells, are produced by the bone marrow and released into the bloodstream as they mature. Normally, the marrow produces only enough new cells to replace the ones that have died. However, in polycythemia vera new blood cells are produced in excess. The overabundance of red blood cells and platelets increases the viscosity or thickness of blood,

---

SYMPTOMS

- Frequent headaches and a feeling of pressure in the head.
- Dizziness and ringing in the ears (tinnitus).
- Fatigue.
- Blurred or double vision.
- Flushed or itching skin. Itching may worsen after a hot bath.
- Night sweats.
- Frequent nosebleeds and bruises.
- Shortness of breath.
- Weight loss.

---

resulting in a greater frequency of blood clots in both the arteries and veins. This produces a substantially greater risk of stroke or heart attack. There is also a higher risk of excess bleeding, due to defective platelets or possibly to blood vessels that have enlarged to accommodate the extra cells. Late in the disease, the spleen may enlarge markedly and trap enough platelets and white cells to reduce their levels in the blood. Polycythemia vera is associated with a greater risk of acute leukemia (see Leukemias for more information). Symptoms develop gradually. This disorder affects people over 40 and is slightly more common in men than in women. If left untreated, polycythemia vera may be fatal within two years; stroke and heart attack are the most common causes of death. However, with treatment and control of the disease, the majority of patients survive more than 10 years after initial diagnosis.

WHAT CAUSES IT?

- The cause of polycythemia vera is unknown.
- A hereditary component may be involved; for example, people of Jewish descent appear to be at greater risk of polycythemia vera.

PREVENTION

- Polycythemia vera cannot be prevented.

DIAGNOSIS

- Patient history and physical examination.
- Blood and urine tests.
- Bone marrow aspiration or biopsy. A sample of bone marrow is withdrawn from the hip bone with a long needle and syringe.
- When diagnosis is questionable, an intravenous pyelogram (injecting into a vein a chemical substance that outlines the kidneys clearly on an x-ray) or a CT (computed tomography) scan may be done.

HOW TO TREAT IT

- Phlebotomy, or blood removal, is performed to eliminate excess red blood cells and to decrease blood viscosity. At first it may be necessary to withdraw a pint of blood every few days; with time, phlebotomy may only be necessary once or twice per year.
- Chemotherapy or radioactive phosphorus may be given (either in addition to phlebotomy or instead of it) to suppress production of excess blood cells in the bone marrow. (Both of these types of therapy may increase the danger of leukemia.)
- Medications to relieve itching (such as cyproheptadine or cimetidine) may be prescribed.
- Rarely, surgery to remove an enlarged spleen may be necessary if it fails to shrink with treatment.

WHEN TO CALL A DOCTOR

- Make an appointment with a doctor if you develop symptoms of polycythemia vera.

Presbycusis

WHAT IS IT?

Presbycusis—the gradual loss of hearing that accompanies aging—is a type of sensorineural or perceptive hearing loss that is brought on by degeneration of nerve cells of the inner ear. (This may be contrasted with typically more treatable conductive hearing losses, which occur when earwax, fluid, a tumor, or a tear in the eardrum physically interferes with the transmission of sound through the structures of the ear.) Like many types of sensorineural hearing loss, presbycusis is most noticeably characterized by difficulty understanding speech, especially in the presence of background noise (common in restaurants, for example). Presbycusis is not necessarily an inevitable part of aging; many people in their 80s hear perfectly well. Individual risk factors determine the degree of hearing loss a person will experience with age. A decline in auditory neurons may begin as early as 30 or 40 years old, although presbycusis rarely becomes noticeable before the age of 55. By age 65, one in every three people has some degree of hearing loss.

SYMPTOMS
- Progressive hearing loss.
- Inability to discern high-frequency sounds.
- Difficulty understanding speech, especially in noisy or crowded environments.

WHAT CAUSES IT?
- Presbycusis is caused by age-related degeneration of sensory cells of the inner ear.
- Cumulative lifetime exposure to excessive noise can hasten presbycusis.
- Atherosclerosis (the buildup of cholesterol-based plaques in the arteries) may deprive structures in the ear of sufficient blood supply.

- Certain drugs, such as aminoglycoside, may be toxic to tissues in the inner ear.
- A hereditary predisposition appears to be involved.

PREVENTION
- Avoid loud sounds and noisy places as much as possible throughout your lifetime. Use earplugs whenever such conditions cannot be avoided.

DIAGNOSIS
- Patient history and hearing tests (audiometry) are necessary. Examination is usually conducted by an audiologist (hearing specialist).
- Other procedures, including blood tests, x-rays, CT (computed tomography) scans, and an electroencephalogram or EEG (measurement of the electrical activity in the brain) may be ordered to rule out other possible causes of hearing problems.

HOW TO TREAT IT
- Generally, the only remedy available for presbycusis is a hearing aid. Resist the temptation to go directly to a hearing-aid supplier or to order from companies that advertise on television or in print. They typically charge too much and cannot provide the quality of medical attention you need. Go instead to a certified audiologist, preferably one recommended by your primary-care physician. Advances in technology have made hearing aids more effective and better suited to individual needs than ever.
- An audiologist may provide counseling and non-medical rehabilitation techniques, such as lip-reading.

WHEN TO CALL A DOCTOR
- Consult your doctor if you experience any degree of hearing difficulty. You will likely be referred to an audiologist or an otolaryngologist (ear, nose, and throat specialist) for testing and diagnosis.

Presbyopia

WHAT IS IT?

Presbyopia is an inability to focus on close objects, which occurs as the lens of the eye progressively loses its flexibility—a normal consequence of aging. The lens—the focusing mechanism in the eye located just behind the pupil—expands and contracts to provide clarity over a range of distances. At rest, the lens is fully expanded and focused for distance vision. A tiny muscle in the eye causes the lens to contract and thicken for accurate near vision. As the lens hardens and becomes less flexible with age, it becomes increasingly difficult to focus at close range. Sometime after age 40, most people notice that close objects seem more blurry, and that newspapers and books must be held at arm's length to be read. Prescription reading glasses compensate for this loss of focusing power. Those who already require glasses to correct other vision problems, such as nearsightedness or astigmatism, may need bi- or trifocal lenses when presbyopia develops. Presbyopia is not a serious health risk and does not lead to blindness.

As the lens loses its flexibility with age, it becomes difficult for the ciliary muscles to compress it to the thickness required for near vision.

SYMPTOMS
- Blurred vision at close range.
- Eyestrain.
- Headaches.

WHAT CAUSES IT?
- Aging causes the lens in the eye to harden and become less flexible.

PREVENTION
- Presbyopia cannot be prevented.
- Contrary to popular belief, vision cannot be improved by refusing to wear prescription lenses if you need them or by performing so-called vision-strengthening exercises.

DIAGNOSIS
- An ophthalmologist will perform a complete eye examination.

HOW TO TREAT IT
- Eyeglasses are prescribed to allow nearby objects to be seen clearly. Some people may need bifocals, trifocals, or more than one pair of glasses if additional vision problems exist; others may only need reading glasses.
- The prescription for eyeglasses may need to be updated approximately every two years as lens flexibility is progressively lost. After age 65, the eye's lens becomes completely inflexible, so the prescription for corrective lenses usually stabilizes.
- Use goggles or a sports strap to secure glasses during sports or other strenuous physical activities.

WHEN TO CALL A DOCTOR
- Make an appointment with an ophthalmologist or optometrist if it becomes difficult to see nearby objects clearly.

Proctitis

WHAT IS IT?

Proctitis is an inflammation of the rectum. Located at the lower portion of the digestive tract, the rectum connects the large intestine, or colon, to the anus, where fecal matter exits the body. After leaving the stomach, food residues are slowly pushed through the small and large intestine by slow, rhythmic muscular contractions, known as peristalsis. Nutrients are absorbed into the body through the lining of the small intestine, while peristalsis forces waste products, or stool, into the rectum, where they are eliminated via the anus. Inflammation may occur owing to a variety of causes; symptoms vary according to the cause and the severity of the inflammation. Proctitis usually responds well to treatment, except in cases caused by genital herpes, since there is no cure for herpes yet. However, in such cases treatment may relieve symptoms, and episodes tend to become milder over time (see Genital Herpes for more information).

SYMPTOMS

- Painful, frequent bowel movements.
- Straining at stool (tenesmus).
- Rectal pain, itching, and cramps.
- Bloody, pus- or mucus-filled discharge.
- Constipation or diarrhea.
- Fever.
- Blisters or open sores in or around the anus and rectum (due to bacterial or viral infection).
- Pain in the lower back, difficulty in urination, and impotence (due to genital herpes).

WHAT CAUSES IT?

- Inflammatory bowel disease, which may affect much of the lower digestive tract, may cause proctitis (see Colitis, Ulcerative, and Crohn's Disease for more information).
- A bacterial or viral infection, including dysentery, gonorrhea, syphilis, chlamydia, and genital herpes, may cause proctitis (see specific disorders for more information).
- Anal intercourse may lead to proctitis, either by injuring the anus or rectum or by spreading sexually transmitted infections.
- Rare causes of proctitis include tuberculosis, amoebiasis, and tissue damage due to radiation.
- The cause of proctitis is sometimes unknown.

PREVENTION

- Use latex condoms during sexual intercourse to reduce the risk of sexually transmitted disease.

DIAGNOSIS

- A blood test for syphilis is taken if sexually transmitted proctitis is suspected.
- Discharge of mucus or pus is cultured for bacteria and examined under the microscope.
- Your doctor may perform a proctoscopy by passing an illuminated scope though the anus to allow a visual examination of the rectum.
- A biopsy of the colon lining may be taken during proctoscopy.

HOW TO TREAT IT

- Antibiotics are prescribed to treat a bacterial infection and should be taken for the full term indicated.
- Corticosteroid suppositories or mesalamine (suppositories or oral tablets) may be prescribed to treat proctitis due to inflammatory bowel disease.
- Treatment for herpes is aimed at relieving symptoms. The antiviral drug acyclovir may be prescribed in topical form to lessen severity and pain, and in oral form to lessen the length and frequency of outbreaks.
- Over-the-counter pain relievers may be taken to reduce pain and inflammation.
- Frequent warm baths may ease rectal discomfort.

WHEN TO CALL A DOCTOR

- Call a doctor if you develop discomfort or pain in the rectum or if bowel movements become difficult, painful, or bloody.

Prostate Cancer

WHAT IS IT?

Prostate cancer is the growth of malignant cells in the prostate, a walnut-size gland located just below the bladder in men, which produces about 30 percent of the fluid portion of semen. Prostate cancer is widespread, and its incidence has been rising; it is the most common cancer in men and is second only to lung cancer as a cause of mortality. Indeed, autopsy studies have shown that 60 to 70 percent of all men who reach the age of 80 have at least some microscopic evidence of prostate cancer. Often there are no symptoms until the cancer has spread beyond the prostate, highlighting the importance of regular checkups. Because prostate cancer tends to grow very slowly and take years to spread, immediate and aggressive treatment may not be advised in older men. For such patients a diagnosis of prostate cancer may warrant a strategy of

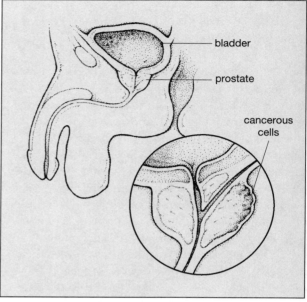

The prostate gland, located just beneath the bladder, commonly enlarges in men over 50; rarely, the growth is cancerous.

SYMPTOMS

- Frequent or urgent need to urinate; delayed or interrupted urinary stream; dribbling.
- Pain upon urination.
- Blood in the urine.
- Painful ejaculation.
- Pain in the pelvis or lower back.

"watchful waiting." This involves regular examinations and blood tests, but treatment is undertaken only if evidence indicates tumor growth. The specific treatment plan depends upon a number of factors: the patient's age, the characteristics of the cancerous cells, the size of the tumor, whether cancer appears to have spread to other sites, and the risk of complications. Prostate cancer may be cured by removing the prostate gland before the cancer has spread. However, much controversy prevails about when to advise surgery because it is not possible to predict which cancers will spread and which will not. There is no cure once the cancer has spread beyond the prostate. In some cases though, prostate cancer never spreads, and in general, the outlook is good when the cancer is detected early.

WHAT CAUSES IT?

- The cause of prostate cancer is unknown.
- Male hormones (androgens), especially testosterone, stimulate the growth of prostate cancer.
- Hereditary factors may play a role.
- Prolonged exposure to chemicals used in the rubber industry, or to cadmium, may increase the risk of prostate cancer.
- A diet high in animal fat may be associated with a greater risk of prostate cancer.
- The incidence of prostate cancer is higher among black men.

PREVENTION

- Men over 40 should have regular digital rectal examinations (a rectal examination of the prostate with a gloved finger) and measurements of PSA (see Diagnosis) to aid in early detection and treatment.
- A diet low in animal fat may decrease the risk and severity of prostate cancer.

DIAGNOSIS

- Patient history and physical examination, including a digital rectal examination.

Prostate Cancer *continued*

• Blood tests. The prostate specific antigen (PSA) blood test is a useful tool for early detection. PSA, an enzyme secreted by the cells lining the prostate, functions to liquefy semen after ejaculation. Normally, little PSA enters the blood, but prostate cancer tends to boost levels of PSA in the bloodstream. However, since nonmalignant abnormalities such as benign x hyperplasia and prostatitis may also cause increased blood levels of PSA, other tests are often necessary to determine the diagnosis. (See Prostatic Hyperplasia, Benign, or Prostatitis for more information.)

• Urine tests.

• Transrectal ultrasonography (ultrasound scans with a rectal probe).

• Multiple biopsies of the prostate are necessary to confirm the diagnosis. Small tissue samples are obtained with a needle inserted into the prostate through the rectum.

HOW TO TREAT IT

• Since prostate cancer tends to grow very slowly, a common management strategy is watchful waiting, which involves regular physical examinations and measurements of PSA to monitor the progress of the tumor, with more aggressive treatment advised when warranted. Watchful waiting is often recommended for men in their seventies and eighties.

• Total surgical removal of the prostate gland (radical prostatectomy) is the most common treatment; it may include removal of nearby lymph nodes in some cases. New, nerve-sparing surgical techniques have greatly reduced the risk of impotence and incontinence. Surgery is generally recommended for men in their fifties and sixties.

• Radiation therapy to destroy cancerous cells may be recommended for somewhat older men or those who are unable to withstand surgery. (Chemotherapy, which is useful in the treatment of some types of cancer, has not been effective in the treatment of prostate cancer.)

• In advanced cases when the cancer has spread, surgical removal of the testicles (orchiectomy) or hormone therapy (which involves either the administration of female hormones or hormones that block the release or function of male hormones) may slow the growth of prostate cancer and thus minimize or arrest the further spread of the cancer.

WHEN TO CALL A DOCTOR

• Call a doctor if you experience difficult, painful, or unusually frequent urination.

Prostatic Hyperplasia, Benign

WHAT IS IT?

Benign prostatic hyperplasia (BPH) is a nodular, irregular enlargement of the prostate, a walnut-size gland located just below the bladder in men, which produces about 30 percent of the fluid portion of semen. Since the prostate surrounds the urethra, the passageway through which urine empties from the bladder, enlargement of the prostate may eventually constrict the urethra and thus interfere with urination. An enlarged prostate may also cause the muscular bladder wall to enlarge, as stronger contractions are necessary to push urine through a narrowed urethra. Increased size of the wall of the bladder reduces its capacity for urine and results in the need for frequent urination. BPH is common, and its incidence increases with age; some degree of BPH is present in 75 percent of men over 50. There is no evidence that BPH leads to prostate cancer; however, symptoms of both disorders are similar, and it is possible to have BPH and prostate cancer at the same time. BPH responds well to treatment.

WHAT CAUSES IT?

• The cause of BPH is unknown.
• Male sex hormones play a role in the development of BPH.

SYMPTOMS

• Frequent or urgent need to urinate; delayed, weak, or interrupted urinary stream; dribbling.
• Pain upon urination.
• Urge to urinate several times a night (nocturia).
• Blood in the urine.

PREVENTION

• There is as yet no way to prevent BPH.

DIAGNOSIS

• Patient history and physical examination, which includes a digital rectal examination. In this procedure, the doctor inserts a gloved finger into the rectum and presses on the prostate gland to check for enlargement.
• Tests to measure the rate of urine flow.

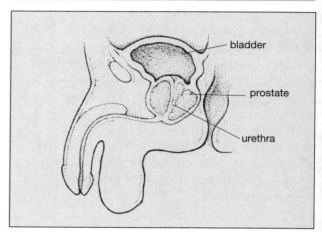

An enlarged prostate (common among men over 50) may constrict the urethra, impeding the passage of urine from the bladder.

• Urine tests and cultures.
• Measurement of pressure within the bladder.

HOW TO TREAT IT

• Treatment may be unnecessary for mild symptoms.
• Avoid excess alcohol or fluid intake, especially at night.
• Your doctor may prescribe medication such as finasteride (Proscar) to shrink the prostate or terazosin (Hytrin) to alleviate urinary difficulties.
• Removal of excess tissue from an enlarged prostate via transurethral resection of the prostate (TURP) is the most common surgical treatment. A thin, lighted viewing tube is passed through the penis into the urethra. A minuscule cutting tool at the end of the tube is used to excise prostate tissue that is pressing upon the urethra.
• Surgical removal via an abdominal incision may be necessary when the prostate is unusually large.
• Balloon dilation, in which a small balloon is inserted into the urethra via a catheter and inflated, may be performed to widen a narrowed urethra. However, this procedure may not prevent recurrence of BPH and is gradually losing favor among experts.
• Antibiotics may be prescribed for associated bacterial infections.

WHEN TO CALL A DOCTOR

• Call a doctor if you develop symptoms of BPH.

Prostatitis

WHAT IS IT?

Prostatitis is an acute or chronic inflammation of the prostate, a walnut-size gland located just below the bladder in men, which produces about 30 percent of the fluid portion of semen. Inflammation may be caused by an infection. Acute prostatitis is characterized by the sudden onset of symptoms; chronic prostatitis causes persistent, long-term symptoms that are similar but less severe. A bacterial infection is usually the cause of acute prostatitis and is responsible for about 5 percent of cases of chronic prostatitis, the majority of which are due to unknown causes. Chronic prostatitis may affect as many as 35 percent of men over 50. An inflamed prostate may press upon the urethra and completely block the flow of urine. Additionally, if left untreated, acute prostatitis may lead to a prostate abscess, an infected, pus-filled cavity. Treatment for the acute and chronic forms of prostatitis may differ considerably.

SYMPTOMS

- Fever and chills (with acute prostatitis).
- Urinary difficulty, frequency, or urgency.
- Pain upon urination.
- Blood in the urine.
- Feeling of fullness in the bladder.
- Painful ejaculation, blood in the semen, or impotence (with chronic prostatitis).
- Pain in the pelvis or lower back.

WHAT CAUSES IT?

- The cause of prostatitis is unknown in most cases.
- Bacterial infection may cause acute and chronic prostatitis; infection usually ascends through the urethra to the prostate, and it may be transmitted sexually.
- The use of a urinary catheter increases the risk of prostatitis.
- Acute prostatitis may lead to chronic prostatitis in some cases.
- Risk of acute prostatitis is higher among men between the ages of 20 to 40 who have multiple sex partners and who practice high-risk behaviors, such as anal intercourse or failure to use condoms.

PREVENTION

- Use condoms to prevent the spread of sexually transmitted disease.
- Get prompt treatment for any urinary tract infections.

DIAGNOSIS

- Patient history and physical examination, which includes a digital rectal examination. In this procedure, the doctor inserts a gloved finger into the rectum to press on the prostate gland.
- Microscopic examination and culture of secretions expressed from the prostate during digital rectal exam.
- Culture and microscopic analysis of urine.
- Ultrasound scans, which may be helpful in detecting an abscess.

HOW TO TREAT IT

- Hospitalization is often necessary to treat acute prostatitis. Intravenous antibiotics are given for bacterial infections, and a urinary catheter may be required to permit urination.
- Oral antibiotics are prescribed to treat acute and chronic prostatitis and should be taken for the full term prescribed (from four to 12 weeks).
- Caffeinated and alcoholic beverages should be avoided until symptoms subside, since the diuretic effect of these drinks increases urinary frequency.
- Warm baths may provide some relief from symptoms of chronic prostatitis.
- Over-the-counter pain analgesics may be taken as necessary to reduce pain and fever.
- If the prostate has become abscessed, surgical drainage is needed.
- Stress reduction techniques may be advised to help patients manage nonbacterial chronic prostatitis.

WHEN TO CALL A DOCTOR

- Call a doctor if you become unable to urinate or if you develop difficult or painful urination.

Psoriasis

WHAT IS IT?

Psoriasis is a common, persistent skin disorder, characterized by patches of raised, red bumps covered with white, flaking scales. The rash generally develops on the scalp, knees, or elbows, although it may affect any area of the skin. The production of skin cells at affected sites is accelerated, either chronically or intermittently. Normally, new skin cells are constantly produced in the deepest layer of skin. From there, they rise to the top layer—the epidermis— where dead surface cells are shed, a process that normally takes about 28 days. However, in areas affected by psoriasis, new cells only take three to four days to reach the skin's surface, and the accumulation of excess cells causes the characteristic scaly rash. Lesions may continue to enlarge slowly, or flare-ups of psoriasis may be separated by periods of remission. First attacks usually begin between the ages of 10 and 30 years. In rare cases the rash may cover the entire surface of the skin—this is a medical emergency requiring immediate treatment. Although most cases of psoriasis can be controlled with treatment and do not represent a serious health risk, psoriasis cannot be cured and may be painful and unpleasant to live with.

SYMPTOMS
- Patches of red, raised bumps with silvery, flaking scales, commonly located on the scalp, knees, elbows, or buttocks. The patches may be itchy or painful.
- Itching skin.
- Loosened, pitted, discolored nails.
- Joint pain and stiffness.
- Emergency symptoms: patches covering the entire skin; fever; fatigue.

WHAT CAUSES IT?
- The cause of psoriasis is unknown.
- Hereditary factors may play a role.
- Flare-ups may be triggered by alcohol, stress, cold temperatures, or skin injury.

PREVENTION
- There is no known way to prevent psoriasis.
- Avoiding alcoholic beverages and limiting exposure to stress, cold temperatures, and skin injuries (such as cuts or scrapes) may prevent flare-ups of psoriasis.

DIAGNOSIS
- Diagnosis is generally made by viewing the skin.
- A skin biopsy confirms the diagnosis.

HOW TO TREAT IT
- Use moisturizing skin creams to prevent dryness.
- Creams or ointments containing cortisone may be applied to relieve symptoms.
- Preparations and shampoos containing coal tar may soothe irritated skin.
- Controlled exposure to ultraviolet light, in combination with psoralens, drugs that increase skin sensitivity to those wavelengths, may be used to subdue the rash.
- Bathing with mineral salts or oatmeal soothes the skin and encourages healing.
- In severe cases an anticancer drug such as methotrexate may be used to slow the production of skin cells.
- A vitamin A derivative, topical tretinoin (Retin-A), may be used for some forms of psoriasis when other treatments fail.
- Check with your doctor regarding any prescriptions you may take for other conditions. Some medications that may worsen symptoms of psoriasis include propanolol and other antihypertensives; lithium (an antidepressant); quinidine (an antiarrhythmic); indomethacin (an anti-inflammatory); and antimalarial drugs.
- Contact the National Psoriasis Foundation for information about support groups in your area.

WHEN TO CALL A DOCTOR
- Make an appointment with a doctor if symptoms do not respond to self-treatment.
- **EMERGENCY** Call a doctor immediately if you develop widespread psoriasis, with or without fever, joint pain, and fatigue.

Pulmonary Edema

WHAT IS IT?

Pulmonary edema, a medical emergency, is an accumulation of fluid in the lungs. Most often a consequence of congestive heart failure, pulmonary edema typically occurs when the heart is unable to pump blood out through the arteries as quickly as it is returned to the heart through the veins. Failure of the left side of the heart (left ventricle) causes blood to accumulate in the veins of the lungs (pulmonary veins), producing a dangerous rise in blood pressure within these veins. Sustained high pressure in the pulmonary veins eventually forces some fluid from the blood into the surrounding microscopic air sacs, or alveoli, that

---

> **SYMPTOMS**
> - Severe breathing difficulty, including wheezing; rapid, shallow breathing; and a feeling of suffocation.
> - Cough, dry at first, but later producing pink, frothy sputum.
> - Fatigue.
> - Profuse perspiration.
> - Blue tinge to the nails, lips, or skin.
> - Palpitations.
> - Anxiety and restlessness.
> - Loss of consciousness.

---

transfer oxygen to the bloodstream. As the alveoli fill with fluid, they can no longer provide adequate amounts of oxygen to the body. Symptoms, especially severe breathing difficulty, develop over the course of a few hours and are life-threatening. Although the outlook for pulmonary edema is favorable if treated in time, the overall outcome for the patient depends upon the nature of the underlying disorder. Adults at high risk for heart failure are most commonly affected.

A less common form of the disease, high-altitude pulmonary edema (which may occur while mountain-climbing, for instance) is also life-threatening if not treated quickly. Strenuous activity upon arrival at high altitudes may cause a dangerous rise in the pressure in the pulmonary veins, forcing fluid out of the veins into the alveoli. After becoming acclimated to the altitude, strenuous activity does not pose such a risk. High-altitude pulmonary edema most often affects young adults under age 25 who are unacclimatized to the altitude but otherwise in good health. Symptoms appear within 24 to 72 hours and necessitate immediate descent to a lower altitude for treatment. (Air travelers are generally not at risk for this disorder because commercial airplane cabins are pressurized.)

WHAT CAUSES IT?
- Congestive heart failure due to hypertension, aortic or mitral valve disease, cardiomyopathy are common causes of pulmonary edema (see discussions of these disorders for more information).
- A heart attack may cause pulmonary edema.
- A variety of other conditions, such as lung infections, extensive burns, liver or kidney disease, Hodgkin's disease, pneumothorax, or nutritional deficiencies, may lead to pulmonary edema in some cases.
- Overdoses of heroin, morphine, and other narcotics may lead to pulmonary edema.
- Rapid ascent to high altitudes followed immediately by heavy exertion may cause high-altitude pulmonary edema.

PREVENTION
- To prevent heart disease, don't smoke; eat a healthy, balanced diet; exercise regularly; and lose weight if you are more than 20 percent overweight.
- Allow a few days to adjust to a higher altitude before engaging in strenuous physical activity. If you have an existing heart condition, your doctor may alter your medication prior to a high-altitude trip.

DIAGNOSIS
- Patient history and examination of the chest is necessary.
- Blood samples are taken to measure oxygen and carbon dioxide content.
- A chest x-ray may be taken.
- Radionuclide scanning, in which a small amount of radioactive gas is inhaled prior to x-rays, may highlight blocked portions of the lungs.

Pulmonary Edema *continued*

• An electrocardiogram (ECG or EKG) may be performed to identify a a heart rhythm disturbance or evidence of a heart attack.

HOW TO TREAT IT

• Call an ambulance or go to the nearest emergency room immediately. While waiting for an ambulance, sit upright. If possible, sit facing backward on an armless chair, with your raised arms resting on the chair back, to ease breathing.
• Pure oxygen is administered through a face mask or nasal tube or by an assisted positive pressure ventilator, which mechanically aids breathing.
• Morphine is given to relieve anxiety and to decrease the force of blood flow through the lungs.
• Diuretics, such as furosemide, bumetanide, or ethacrynic acid, are administered to promote excretion of excess fluids.

• Sodium nitroprusside or digoxin may be prescribed to dilate the arteries and strengthen the contractions of the heart muscle.
• Inhaled bronchodilating drugs, such as aminophylline, may be administered to relax constricted bronchial passages.
• It is imperative to return to a lower altitude immediately to obtain emergency medical care for high-altitude pulmonary edema. If possible, ask a ranger to call a helicopter if someone becomes too disabled to walk.

WHEN TO CALL A DOCTOR

• **EMERGENCY** Call an ambulance immediately if you develop symptoms of pulmonary edema.
• **EMERGENCY** Descend immediately to a lower altitude and call for emergency medical treatment if you develop high-altitude pulmonary edema.

Pulmonary Embolism

WHAT IS IT?

A pulmonary embolism is a blood clot that travels through the veins to block a pulmonary artery, one of the vessels that carries blood to the lungs to be oxygenated. In most cases the blood clot (thrombus) originates in a leg vein, owing to a condition known as deep-vein thrombosis; the next most common site is the right chamber of the heart. Part or all of a loosened thrombus may pass through the right side of the heart and be carried into the pulmonary arteries. (Clumps of cancerous cells, fat, or bubbles of air in the bloodstream may also form emboli, although this is rare.) An embolus lodges in the main pulmonary artery or one of the smaller ones, cutting off the blood flow through the affected portion of the lungs. Symptoms occur suddenly; severity depends on the size and number of emboli. Although some small emboli dissolve on their own, the disorder may quickly turn fatal if a large enough portion of the lungs is affected by either one large embolus or many smaller ones. Approximately one case in 10 results in sudden death. The first hour of a pulmonary embolism is crucial, so emergency treatment should be sought immediately; patients who survive long enough to be diagnosed usually recover. In the United States, over a half million cases of pulmonary embolism occur per year. Outlook is most favorable among younger patients. Pulmonary embolism affects significantly more women than men (in an approximately two-to-one ratio).

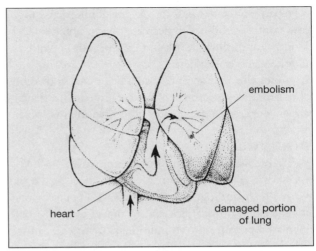

As the heart pumps blood into the lungs to be oxygenated, a blood clot carried in the bloodstream may lodge in a pulmonary artery.

WHAT CAUSES IT?

• A blood clot dislodged from a leg vein is the most common cause of pulmonary embolism.
• Rarely, an air bubble or a clump of cancerous cells, fat, bacteria, or other material may lodge in a pulmonary artery.
• Risk factors include pregnancy; recent surgery; previous heart attack or stroke; prolonged bed rest (for example, while recovering from an illness); obesity; smoking; bone fractures, especially of the hip or leg bones; cancer, especially of the lungs, breast, or liver; and family history of venous thrombosis or pulmonary embolism.
• Those with heart disease, emphysema, or chronic bronchitis are at greater risk of severe consequences from pulmonary embolism (see Coronary Artery Disease or Chronic Obstructive Pulmonary Disease for more information).

PREVENTION

• Prescription elastic support hose may be worn to prevent deep-vein thrombosis in the legs among those at risk. Try not to cross the legs when sitting, as this promotes thrombus development.
• Regular doses of aspirin may be prescribed to prevent the development of blood clots for those at high risk.

SYMPTOMS

• Sudden onset of chest pain, which is usually sharp and made worse by taking a deep breath.
• Sudden shortness of breath.
• Cough, possibly with bloody sputum.
• Profuse perspiration.
• Anxiety.
• Palpitations or rapid heartbeat.
• Lightheadedness.
• Emergency symptom: loss of consciousness.

Pulmonary Embolism *continued*

• Heparin, an anticoagulant, may be administered in low, continuous doses to decrease the possibility of blood clots in those at risk (for example, those with chronic venous insufficiency, congestive heart failure, or those who have recently had a heart attack) or those about to undergo surgery. After surgery, such patients are encouraged to get up and walk as soon as possible.

DIAGNOSIS

• Patient history and physical examination.
• Chest x-ray.
• An electrocardiogram (ECG or EKG) is performed to rule out a heart attack and to detect evidence of increased pressure in the pulmonary arteries or of other serious cardiovascular conditions.
• Radionuclide scanning, which involves inhaling a small amount of radioactive gas and injection of radioactive particles into the bloodstream, may highlight blocked portions of the lungs on an x-ray scan.
• Pulmonary arteriography (injection of a contrast material into the pulmonary arteries prior to taking a series of x-rays) is the only certain way to identify pulmonary embolism and thus establish a definitive diagnosis.

HOW TO TREAT IT

• Anticoagulant drugs, like heparin and warfarin, are administered to prevent further blood clots.
• Thrombolytic (clot dissolving) medications such as tPA (tissue plasminogen activator), streptokinase, or urokinase may be injected into the bloodstream to clear the blockage.
• Analgesics are given to relieve pain.
• Oxygen may be administered via respirator.
• Emergency treatment is necessary for a suspected pulmonary embolism. Immediate surgical removal may be necessary when a large embolus is blocking a major pulmonary artery.

WHEN TO CALL A DOCTOR

• **EMERGENCY** Call an ambulance immediately if you or someone in your presence develops sudden, severe chest pain and shortness of breath, along with feelings of great apprehension or dread. In addition to pulmonary embolism, such symptoms may also be indications of a heart attack or other serious cardiovascular crisis.
• **EMERGENCY** Call an ambulance immediately any time someone unexpectedly loses consciousness.

Rabies Hydrophobia

WHAT IS IT?

Rabies is a severe viral infection of the brain that primarily affects animals, both wild and domestic. Raccoons, skunks, bats, foxes, and other mammals may be rabid; domestic dogs and cats can also become infected. Rabies may be transferred to humans through the saliva of an infected animal, usually by a bite, although the virus can also enter the bloodstream via a lick over broken skin. The rabies virus travels to the brain and attacks the central nervous system. Rabies is fatal in humans unless measures are taken right away to prevent the disease from developing, so if you are bitten by an animal, see a doctor immediately. Do not wait to see if rabies develops—once symptoms appear, the course of the disease is irreversible despite treatment, and death occurs within a few days. Symptoms most often emerge in four to eight weeks, but anywhere from 10 days to several years may lapse between the bite and the appearance of symptoms. Treatment consists of a series of vaccines and is effective only if administered in time.

SYMPTOMS

- Initial symptoms: fever, muscle aches, headaches, general sense of illness, loss of appetite, tingling and muscle twitches at the site of the bite.
- Violent muscle spasms provoked by swallowing liquids (hence the name hydrophobia).
- Agitation and violent behavior. Periods of rage alternate with periods of calmness, but lucid periods quickly become shorter and less frequent as the disease progresses.
- Mental confusion.
- Convulsions, paralysis, and coma.
- Drooling due to excessive salivation and difficulty swallowing.

WHAT CAUSES IT?

- Viral infection causes rabies.

PREVENTION

- Immunize pets against rabies. Less than 10 cases of rabies have been reported in the United States since 1980, thanks to extensive animal-vaccination programs.
- Those in high-risk occupations, like veterinarians and other animal handlers, hunters, and cave-explorers, should receive an annual rabies vaccine.
- Stray animals in areas where rabies is common are often killed by local authorities to prevent the spread of the disease.
- A quarantine is imposed on imported animals in countries where rabies is not present, such as England, Japan, and Australia.

DIAGNOSIS

- Patient history and physical examination.
- Every effort should be made to capture the animal inflicting the bite so that its brain can be tested for the presence of the virus. Healthy-appearing domestic animals are kept under observation for 10 days to watch for the development of any behavioral abnormalities.

HOW TO TREAT IT

- Call a doctor immediately if you are bitten by an animal.
- Wash the wound gently but thoroughly with soap and water and then apply antiseptic.
- Postexposure immunization (within two days of a bite) usually prevents the disease from developing. Two types of immunization are necessary: a passive immunization provides antibodies for immediate protection against the rabies virus; the active vaccine provokes the production of antiviral antibodies for long-term protection against the virus. Half the passive vaccine is injected around the wound, the other half injected into a muscle; the active vaccine is administered in a series of five injections over several weeks. People who have already received the vaccine (those in high-risk occupations) need only receive the active vaccine for treatment.
- Antibiotics and a tetanus booster shot may be given to prevent associated bacterial infections.
- Hospitalization is necessary if symptoms appear; however, the outlook is unfavorable at this point.

WHEN TO CALL A DOCTOR

- **EMERGENCY** See a doctor immediately if you have been bitten by an animal; do not wait for symptoms of rabies to appear.

Refractive Disorders

WHAT IS IT?

Refractive disorders—which include myopia (near-sightedness), hyperopia (farsightedness), and astigmatism—are common, correctable vision problems. Light enters the eye through the cornea, the thin, transparent membrane covering the eye, and then the pupil, the dark area in the center of the iris. The lens, located behind the pupil, focuses the light rays onto the retina, the layer of light-sensitive cells that line the back of the eye. Refractive disorders arise when irregularities in the shape or strength of these structures distort the focus and impair vision. In myopia, objects at a distance appear out of focus; in hyperopia, nearby objects are unclear. In astigmatism, the cornea is not evenly curved, producing blurriness or uneven degrees of distortion in portions of the visual field. Astigmatism may be combined with either myopia or hyperopia in the same eye. In addition, the lens becomes progressively less flexible after age 40, impairing close vision (see Presbyopia for more information). Refractive disorders may be corrected with glasses or contact lenses.

In nearsightedness (myopia), light is focused at a point just short of the retina; in farsightedness (hyperopia), just beyond the retina.

SYMPTOMS
- Blurred vision at a distance (myopia).
- Blurred vision of nearby objects, possibly causing eyestrain and headaches (hyperopia).
- Uneven degrees of blurriness in portions of the visual field (astigmatism).

WHAT CAUSES IT?
- Hereditary factors play a role.

PREVENTION
- Contrary to popular belief, vision cannot be improved by refusing to wear glasses if you need them or by performing so-called eye exercises.

DIAGNOSIS
- An ophthalmologist will perform an eye examination.

HOW TO TREAT IT
- Glasses or contact lenses are prescribed to correct vision. The prescription is updated as vision changes.
- During sports or other strenuous physical activities, use goggles to protect your eyes or a sports strap to secure glasses.
- A form of surgery, known as radial keratotomy (RK), may correct mild to moderate myopia. Several tiny incisions are made (with a laser or by conventional means) to flatten the cornea and correct the focus, eliminating the need for glasses. However, the long-term effects of the surgery are not fully known.

WHEN TO CALL A DOCTOR
- Make an appointment with an ophthalmologist or optometrist if you or your child is having vision problems.

Renal Artery Stenosis

WHAT IS IT?

Renal artery stenosis is a blockage of one of the arteries that supplies blood to the kidneys. Once the renal artery or one of its branches becomes blocked, the blood supply to the kidney is partially or completely cut off; the affected kidney tissue may be damaged irreversibly. The unaffected kidney compensates for the decrease in function of the other one. Sudden total occlusion of a renal artery may cause acute onset of vague pain in the flanks, nausea, and vomiting. These symptoms generally disappear in three to four days. More often, however, renal artery stenosis has no symptoms. The most common indication of it is high blood pressure that responds poorly to regular treatment measures. Although chronic kidney failure may be a possibility if both kidneys are affected (or if someone has only one kidney), in many cases blockage may be reduced or eliminated with treatment, and kidney function may improve.

SYMPTOMS
- Usually no symptoms. Renal artery stenosis is typically detected only when a physical examination reveals high blood pressure (also symptomless), and further tests are performed to determine the underlying cause.
- Dull flank pain, nausea, and vomiting may occur for a few days if sudden total occlusion of a renal artery occurs.

WHAT CAUSES IT?

- The buildup of plaque in the arteries (atherosclerosis) may cause renal artery stenosis.
- In those of middle age or older, blockage of a renal artery is usually due to a blood clot that has broken free from the heart and been carried by the bloodstream to lodge in an artery in a kidney.
- A renal artery may become obstructed by a fragment of plaque material that breaks off of an artery wall and travels to the kidney.
- An inherited disorder called fibromuscular dysplasia causes abnormal thickening of the arterial walls and may thus block the renal artery. This disorder primarily affects women between the ages of 20 and 40.

PREVENTION

- Other than maintaining a healthy weight, diet, and lifestyle to avoid the buildup of plaque in the arteries, there are no specific measures to prevent renal artery stenosis.

DIAGNOSIS

- Patient history and physical examination.
- Urine and blood samples.
- Renal vein occlusion is suspected when blood pressure is unusually high, particularly hard to control, or rises suddenly in a person with previously normal blood pressure. Under such circumstances the tests described below may be done.
- An x-ray of the kidney may be taken after injection with a material that creates a clear x-ray image of the kidneys (intravenous pyelogram).
- A similar procedure, renal arteriography, allows the exact location of the blockage to be determined.
- Ultrasound, CT (computed tomography) scans, or MRI (magnetic resonance imaging) may be done.

HOW TO TREAT IT

- Fibrinolytic (clot dissolving) therapy may be administered to break up the artery-blocking clot.
- Percutaneous transluminal angioplasty may be performed. In this procedure, a tiny balloon on the tip of a catheter is threaded through the artery. At the narrowed or blocked point, the balloon is inflated to widen the passageway.
- Antihypertensive drugs may be needed to lower associated high blood pressure.
- Surgery may be performed to remove a blockage that is extensive or calcified (hardened). In cases of extensive damage to the arterial walls, tissue from an artery elsewhere in the body may be grafted onto the renal artery.
- Long-term administration of anticoagulant drugs may be prescribed to prevent future blood clots.

WHEN TO CALL A DOCTOR

- Call a doctor immediately if you notice a decrease in urine output (an indication of kidney failure) or develop lower back pain accompanied by nausea and vomiting and possibly fever (indications of death of kidney tissue due to sudden blockage of a renal artery).

Renal Calculi Kidney Stones

WHAT IS IT?
Renal calculi, also known as kidney stones, form when substances (such as calcium oxalate) in the urine concentrate and coalesce into hard, solid lumps in the kidney. During the production of urine, the two kidneys regulate the fluid and electrolyte balance in the body and filter wastes out of the blood. Urine collects in the portion of the kidney known as the renal pelvis; the urine then passes from the kidney to the bladder via a narrow tube called the ureter. Calcium oxalate and calcium phosphate stones account for about 80 percent of renal calculi. The next most common stone is composed of uric acid. Kidney stones may form in the renal pelvis if the urine becomes too concentrated, if excessive amounts of calcium are absorbed from the intestine or released from bone, or if a bacterial infection alters the pH (acidity) of the urine. The stones may then pass through the ureter into the bladder before they are eliminated from the body with the urine. Some stones are so small that they cause no symptoms and pass painlessly on their own; large stones may never leave the kidney and can be detected only if an abdominal x-ray is taken for other reasons. Sometimes, however, a stone enters the ureter and produces intermittent severe pain (known as renal colic) that continues until the stone has reached the blad-

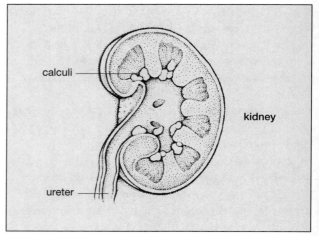

Renal calculi can cause substantial pain if they become lodged in the ureter. Most kidney stones pass spontaneously.

der; this process may take a few hours or up to several days. The pain of a single attack is usually felt on only one side of the body; however, stones tend to recur and may develop in the other kidney, causing pain on that side. Symptoms subside once the stone is passed. Recurrence is common, and treatment is aimed at relieving symptoms, dissolving or removing existing stones, and preventing recurrence. Kidney stones are common, especially among young and middle-aged adults, and men are affected much more frequently than women.

WHAT CAUSES IT?
• The most common cause of kidney stones is unexplained excessive absorption of calcium from the intestine, resulting in increased calcium in the urine (hypercalciuria).
• High blood calcium levels (for example, from hyperparathyroidism or vitamin D intoxication) lead to hypercalciuria and kidney stones.
• Recurrent urinary tract infections may create a chemical environment conducive to the development of kidney stones.
• Irritable bowel disease, Crohn's disease, or a diet high in oxalic acid (found in rhubarb, spinach, leafy vegetables, and coffee) increases the excretion of oxalate in the urine.
• High blood uric acid levels, sometimes associated

SYMPTOMS
• Intermittent pain, sometimes excruciating, beginning in the lower back below the ribs and traveling downward through the lower abdomen to the groin. Men may experience pain in the testes and penis as the stone passes.
• Interruption of the urine stream, inability to urinate except in certain positions, frequent urge to urinate but with only small amounts of urine passed.
• Bloody, cloudy, or darkened urine.
• Nausea and vomiting.
• Burning upon urination; fever (due to an associated bacterial infection—see Kidney Infection for more information).

Renal Calculi Kidney Stones *continued*

with symptoms of gout, may lead to the formation of uric acid stones.

• Mild, persistent dehydration concentrates the urine and may lead to stone formation.

• Hereditary factors may be associated with stone formation.

• In some cases the cause of kidney stones is unknown.

PREVENTION

• Drink at least eight glasses of water a day, and eat a healthy, well-balanced diet.

• Dietary changes may be advised to prevent recurrence. Specific changes, such as avoiding calcium or foods containing oxalic acid (found in rhubarb, spinach, leafy vegetables, and coffee), will depend on the type of kidney stone involved.

• Medications, such as thiazide diuretics, phosphate-based compounds, allopurinol, sodium or potassium citrate, or large doses of calcium or magnesium, may be administered to help prevent recurrence of stones. The type of medication varies according to the exact composition of the stone. An effort is made to increase the acidity of the urine in people with calcium stones and to decrease urine acidity in those with uric acid stones.

DIAGNOSIS

• Patient history and physical examination.

• Blood sample to measure calcium and uric acid levels.

• Urine culture and examination for cells and crystals.

• In cases when stones recur, your doctor may ask you to collect urine over a 24-hour period in order to measure the amount of calcium and uric acid excreted.

• Abdominal x-rays, following injection of an iodine-based dye into the kidneys (pyelography).

• Laboratory analysis of the chemical content of any stone that is passed and captured.

HOW TO TREAT IT

• To encourage a small stone to pass, drink at least three liters of water daily to flush the stone into the bladder. Urinate through a piece of gauze to trap the stone when it does pass, so it can be analyzed.

• Over-the-counter pain relievers are recommended.

• Antibiotics may be prescribed to treat an associated bacterial infection.

• In more severe cases hospitalization may be advised, and narcotic painkillers are prescribed to relieve pain.

• Antispasmodic drugs may be prescribed to help the ureter muscles relax and ease passing of the stone.

• Larger stones can be pulverized with a treatment called extracorporeal shock-wave lithotripsy, which aims concentrated bursts of sound waves at the stones. The tiny fragments then pass into the bladder and are excreted.

• Abdominal surgery may be performed to remove the stone.

• Surgery to remove an overactive parathyroid gland may be performed in cases where stones have resulted from hyperparathyroidism.

• Surgery to remove the kidney may be required in advanced cases that do not respond to other forms of treatment. Only one kidney is necessary for normal body function; if a diseased kidney is removed, the remaining one compensates for the loss.

WHEN TO CALL A DOCTOR

• Call a doctor if you develop symptoms of kidney stones.

Renal Failure, Acute

WHAT IS IT?

Acute renal failure—or kidney failure—occurs when both kidneys suddenly stop functioning. The kidneys regulate the chemical and fluid balance in the body and filter waste products out of the blood and into the urine. Acute renal failure may occur via a number of different mechanisms, including kidney disorders, partial or complete blockage of the passage of urine, and a decrease in the blood volume, following severe blood loss for example. Symptoms may develop over several days: the amount of urine passed may be greatly reduced, and fluid that should be excreted accumulates in bodily tissues, producing weight gain and swelling, especially in the ankles. Acute renal failure is a life-threatening condition, as excessive amounts of water, minerals like potassium, and waste products, all normally eliminated in the urine by the kidneys, accumulate in the body. Acute renal failure usually responds well to treatment; kidney function may be fully regained within several months after normal blood volume is restored or an obstruction to urine flow is released. However, acute renal failure due to a kidney disorder may occasionally progress to chronic renal failure, and the long-term outlook ultimately depends upon the response of the underlying disorder to treatment.

SYMPTOMS

- Passing only small amounts of urine.
- Weight gain and swelling of the ankles and face, due to fluid accumulation (edema).
- Loss of appetite.
- Nausea and vomiting.
- Widespread itching.
- Fatigue.
- Late stage symptoms if renal failure is not treated successfully: shortness of breath, due to fluid retention in the lungs; unexplained bruising or bleeding; drowsiness; mental confusion; muscle spasms or seizures; loss of consciousness.

WHAT CAUSES IT?

- Depletion of blood volume from severe injury with associated blood loss or dehydration is a common cause of acute renal failure. Reduced blood flow to the kidney due to diminished blood volume may damage the kidneys.
- Some kidney disorders, such as acute glomerulo-nephritis, may cause acute renal failure (see Glomerulonephritis, Acute, for more information).
- Tumors, kidney stones, or an enlarged prostate gland may obstruct both ureters or the urethra, impeding the flow of urine and damaging the kidneys.
- Other disorders may cause the kidneys to fail, including polycystic kidney disease, systemic lupus erythematosus, diabetes mellitus, congestive heart failure, heart attack, liver disease, acute pancreatitis, and multiple myeloma (see specific disorders for more information).
- Poisoning with heavy metals such as cadmium, lead, mercury, or gold may lead to kidney damage.
- Chemotherapeutic agents and certain antibiotics such as streptomycin may lead to kidney failure, especially in those with underlying kidney disease.
- Long-term high doses of acetaminophen or non-steroidal anti-inflammatory drugs, such as ibuprofen and naproxen sodium, may cause kidney damage.
- The radiographic contrast materials used to highlight blood vessels or organs in some x-ray procedures may induce kidney failure in those at higher risk.
- The release of the protein myoglobin from the muscles, because of muscle injury, heat stroke, drug or alcohol overdose, or severe infection may lead to acute kidney failure.
- Those who have had one kidney removed are more vulnerable to severe complications of kidney damage.
- Rarely, women may develop acute renal failure as a complication of childbirth.

PREVENTION

- Treatment of potential underlying causes may prevent acute renal failure.

DIAGNOSIS

- Patient history and physical examination.
- Ultrasound scans.

Renal Failure, Acute *continued*

• Blood and urine tests.
• An x-ray of the kidney may be taken after injection with a contrasting dye (intravenous pyelogram) to locate an obstruction to urine flow.
• A kidney biopsy may be done. After local anesthesia is administered, the doctor inserts a needle into the kidney through the back to extract a small sample of tissue.

HOW TO TREAT IT

• The underlying cause of kidney failure must be treated. Emergency medical treatment may be necessary in the event of severe injury and may include surgery to repair damaged tissues, intravenous fluids to reverse dehydration, and blood transfusion to replace the blood lost.
• Surgery may be necessary to remove an obstruction of the urinary tract.
• Diuretics may be prescribed to reduce fluid retention and increase urine output.
• There are a number of post-emergency measures that are important to a full recovery. A low-salt, low-protein, high-carbohydrate diet, vitamin supplementation, and restriction of fluid intake may all be recommended.
• Antibiotics may be prescribed to treat associated bacterial infections and should be taken for the full term indicated.
• Antihypertensive drugs may be prescribed to treat associated high blood pressure.
• Glucose, sodium bicarbonate, and other substances may be given intravenously until kidney function is regained, in order to maintain proper levels of these substances in the bloodstream.
• Temporary dialysis, an artificial blood-filtering process, may be necessary until kidney function is regained. There are several types of dialysis. In hemodialysis, blood is pumped from the body into an artificial kidney machine, or dialyzer, where it is filtered before being returned to the body. Hemodialysis must be performed for about nine hours weekly (usually in three sessions). Peritoneal dialysis is another option. In this procedure, a catheter is inserted into the abdomen, and a special fluid, known as dialysate, is circulated through the peritoneum, the membrane lining the abdominal cavity, to draw impurities out of the bloodstream. Peritoneal dialysis must be performed for a total of 30 to 40 hours per week; however, indwelling catheters make it possible for the patient to move about during dialysis. In milder cases dialysis may be used early in treatment to prevent further complications; in more severe cases dialysis may be required for a longer period of time.
• Contact your local chapter of the National Kidney Foundation for more information.

WHEN TO CALL A DOCTOR

• **EMERGENCY** Call a doctor immediately if you develop symptoms of acute renal failure, including decreased urine output, nausea, shortness of breath, and swollen ankles.

Renal Failure, Chronic

WHAT IS IT?

Chronic renal, or kidney, failure occurs when both kidneys gradually cease to function. Within the kidneys are numerous tiny structures (glomeruli) that filter waste products from the blood and retain larger substances, such as proteins. Waste products and excess water then accumulate in the bladder until excreted as urine. In chronic kidney failure, the kidneys suffer progressive damage over a number of years. As kidney tissue is destroyed by injury or inflammation, the remaining healthy tissue compensates for the loss of function. The extra work overloads the previously undamaged portions of the kidneys, causing more damage, until eventually the entire kidney may cease to function (a condition known as end-stage renal failure). The kidneys are resilient organs; over 90 percent of the kidneys may be damaged before symptoms appear (although symptoms may develop earlier if the weakened kidney is subjected to a sudden stress, such as an infection, dehydration, or use of a kidney-damaging drug). As excessive amounts of water, minerals like potassium, and waste products accumulate in the body, chronic renal failure becomes a life-threatening condition. However, if the underlying disease is treated and further damage can be controlled, the onset of end-stage renal failure may be delayed for up to 10 to 20 years. End-stage renal failure may be treated with dialysis or kidney transplantation; either can prolong life and allow participation in many normal activities.

WHAT CAUSES IT?

• Diabetes mellitus and hypertension are the most common causes of chronic renal failure.
• Primary kidney disorders, such as acute and chronic glomerulonephritis, polycystic kidney disease, and kidney infection, may lead to chronic renal failure (see specific disorders for more information).
• High blood pressure can both cause and be caused by progressive damage to the kidneys.
• Tumors, kidney stones, or an enlarged prostate gland may obstruct the urinary tract, impair the flow of urine, and thus damage the kidneys.
• Long-term use of large doses of nonsteroidal anti-inflammatory drugs such as ibuprofen or naproxen sodium may lead to chronic renal failure.
• Poisoning with heavy metals like cadmium, lead, mercury, or gold may lead to kidney failure.
• Certain antibiotics (like streptomycin), antifungal drugs, and immunosuppressants may damage the kidney and lead to kidney failure.
• The contrast substances used in some x-ray procedures may induce kidney failure in those with weakened kidneys.
• Kidneys damaged by any disorder are more prone to chronic infection.
• Hypercalcemia (excess blood levels of calcium, which occurs with hyperthyroidism for example) and elevated levels of uric acid may lead to chronic renal failure.
• Those who have had one kidney removed are more vulnerable to severe complications from kidney damage.

PREVENTION

• Treatment of potential underlying causes (especially drug therapy for hypertension and scrupulous control of diabetes) may prevent or delay development of chronic renal failure.

SYMPTOMS

• Frequent urination; passing only small amounts of urine.
• General feeling of poor health.
• Symptoms of end-stage renal failure due to the accumulation of waste products in the blood (uremia): swelling of the ankles or the tissues around the eyes, due to fluid retention (edema); shortness of breath, due to fluid accumulation in the lungs; nausea and vomiting; loss of appetite and weight loss; frequent hiccups; bad breath; furred tongue; pain in the chest and bones; overall itching; yellowish or brownish tinge to pale skin; tiny white crystals upon the skin (uremic frost); unexplained bruising or bleeding, including bleeding gums; cessation of menstrual periods in women (amenorrhea); fatigue and drowsiness; mental confusion; muscle spasms or seizures; loss of consciousness.

Renal Failure, Chronic *continued*

DIAGNOSIS

• Patient history and physical examination.
• Blood and urine tests.
• An x-ray of the kidney may be taken after injection with a contrasting dye (intravenous pyelogram).
• Ultrasound or CT (computed tomography) scans, or MRI (magnetic resonance imaging) of the abdominal area.
• A kidney biopsy may be done. After local anesthesia is administered to the patient, the doctor inserts a needle into the kidney through the back to extract a small sample of tissue.

HOW TO TREAT IT

• A low-salt, low-protein, high-carbohydrate diet, restricted fluid intake, and vitamin supplements may be recommended.
• Surgery may be necessary to remove an obstruction in the urinary tract.
• Antibiotics may be prescribed to treat associated bacterial infections.
• Antihypertensive drugs are prescribed to control associated high blood pressure.
• Medications may be needed to treat congestive heart failure.
• Anemia can be treated with erythropoietin, which stimulates blood cell formation.
• Sodium bicarbonate or calcium carbonate is administered to treat the excessive accumulation of body acids (renal acidosis).
• Phosphate-binding agents, calcium supplements, and vitamin D are given to prevent secondary hyperparathyroidism, which may produce further kidney damage.
• Dialysis, an artificial blood-filtering process, is nec-essary once a significant portion of kidney function has been lost. There are several types of dialysis. In hemodialysis, blood is pumped from the body into an artificial kidney machine, or dialyzer, where it is filtered before being returned to the body. Hemodialysis must be performed for about nine hours weekly (usually in three sessions). Peritoneal dialysis is another option. In this procedure a catheter is inserted into the abdomen, and a fluid known as dialysate is circulated through the peritoneum, the membrane lining the abdominal cavity, to draw impurities out of the bloodstream. Peritoneal dialysis must be performed two to three times per week for a total of 30 to 40 hours. An alternative form of this therapy uses a self-contained system that allows the patient to instill and empty his or her own dialysate every few hours, thus eliminating the need for a hospital stay.
• A kidney transplant offers an alternative to dialysis in cases of end-stage renal failure. Successful transplantation may cure kidney failure, but potential donors must be matched carefully for compatibility; family members of the patient are most likely to be compatible. Recipients of a kidney transplant must remain on immunosuppressive drugs to prevent rejection of the transplant.
• Contact your local chapter of the National Kidney Foundation for information about support groups.

WHEN TO CALL A DOCTOR

• **EMERGENCY** Call a doctor if you experience frequent urination, nausea and vomiting, swelling around the ankles, shortness of breath, a yellowish tinge to the skin, or any other symptoms of chronic renal failure.

Renal Vein Thrombosis

WHAT IS IT?

Renal vein thrombosis (RVT), an uncommon disorder, is a blood clot in one of the veins that carries blood from the kidneys back to the heart. In infants, the condition may occur suddenly and result in kidney failure and severe acute illness. In adults, the condition may be mild. In many cases part of the blood clot may separate from the renal vein and lodge in a pulmonary artery, where the clot, known as an embolism, may produce symptoms of chest pain and shortness of breath (see Pulmonary Embolism for more information). In many cases RVT subsides spontaneously over time.

WHAT CAUSES IT?

• Injury to the abdomen or lower back may result in RVT.
• Diarrhea with severe associated dehydration is the most common cause in children.
• In adults, RVT is almost always a result of some underlying illness.
• Malignant kidney tumors that extend into the renal vein can lead to RVT.
• Some types of nephrotic syndrome are frequently associated with RVT (see Nephrotic Syndrome for more information).
• Pregnancy or the use of oral contraceptives increases the risk.

PREVENTION

• There is no known way to prevent renal vein thrombosis.

SYMPTOMS

• Pain, usually mild, in the lower back and side.
• In infants: fever and chills; blood in the urine.
• Chest pain; shortness of breath; cough, possibly with bloody sputum; profuse perspiration; anxiety; palpitations, due to associated pulmonary emboli.

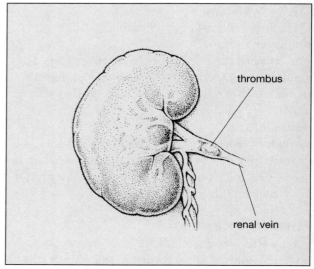

Blood is filtered in the kidneys, then returns to the heart via the renal veins. A thrombus (blood clot) lodged in a renal vein impedes this flow.

DIAGNOSIS

• Patient history and physical examination.
• Urine sample.
• Renal venography (injection of a contrast material into the renal vein prior to x-rays), ultrasound scans, CT (computed tomography) scans, or MRI (magnetic resonance imaging) may be performed to locate a blood clot.

HOW TO TREAT IT

• Streptokinase, an enzyme, may be administered to dissolve blood clots.
• Anticoagulant medications may be prescribed on a long-term basis to reduce the risk of a pulmonary embolus.
• In infants with life-threatening cases, surgical removal of the affected kidney may be required.

WHEN TO CALL A DOCTOR

• Call a doctor if you develop nagging, persistent pain in the lower back or side, or if you experience shortness of breath and chest pain.

Restless Legs Syndrome

WHAT IS IT?

Restless legs syndrome has been characterized as "an unusual, almost indescribable sensation" in the muscles that leaves its sufferers with an irresistible urge to move their legs for relief. Symptoms may last for an hour or more. It commonly occurs at night or during rest, usually within five to 30 minutes after lying down, but prior to the onset of sleep. (It may also occur during the day in some cases.) Generally, the feeling is not painful—just odd and unpleasant—often described as a crawling sensation in the muscles of the calves (although it can occur in the thighs and feet or, more rarely, in the arms). Sufferers find that the only way to ease the sensation is to kick their legs or get up and walk around—thus, it is a common underlying cause of insomnia. It occurs most often in older individuals, especially women. Restless legs syndrome, although unpleasant and annoying, does not constitute a major health risk, nor is it an early warning sign of a more serious neuromuscular disorder such as Parkinson's disease.

SYMPTOMS
- Unpleasant crawling sensations inside the calves, experienced while lying down but still awake. These sensations may also be felt in the thighs, feet, or arms.
- Irresistible urge to move the legs (or other affected muscles).
- Involuntary jerking movements of the legs during sleep.
- Daytime fatigue due to difficulty sleeping.

WHAT CAUSES IT?
- The exact cause of restless legs syndrome is unknown, but some studies suggest the symptoms are related to low levels of the neurotransmitter dopamine in the brain.
- Pregnancy is associated with a higher incidence of restless legs syndrome.
- Iron-deficiency anemia, rheumatoid arthritis, diabetes mellitus, lung disease, or kidney disease may predispose to restless legs syndrome.
- Hereditary factors may play a role.
- Emotional stress or the regular use of caffeine or tobacco may provoke or worsen symptoms.
- Certain medications, such as antihistamines, may cause restless legs as a side effect.

PREVENTION
- Avoid nicotine and large amounts of caffeine.

DIAGNOSIS
- Diagnosis is based upon the characteristic symptoms.
- Physical examination may be performed to rule out other disorders; no known pathological changes are associated with restless legs syndrome.

HOW TO TREAT IT
- Follow prevention tips.
- Walk around for 10 to 15 minutes prior to going to bed, to stretch the leg muscles and promote restful sleep. Flexing or massaging the leg muscles before going to bed may help relieve symptoms.
- Keep feet and calves warm with heavy socks, a heating pad, or a hot water bottle; a warm bath may help relax muscles. (Diabetics should wrap a hot water bottle in a heavy towel first to prevent accidental burns due to diabetic neuropathy.)
- For some people, cold compresses, leaving the legs uncovered, or soaking the feet in cool water may relieve symptoms.
- Make sure your iron intake is adequate. Some sufferers may need iron supplement pills to maintain sufficient levels.
- Stress management techniques or psychological counseling may help relieve anxiety and emotional strain.
- In more severe cases that cause repeated sleep disturbances, low doses of the antiparkinsonian drug L-dopa or tranquilizers such as clonazepam may be prescribed to relieve symptoms.
- Your doctor may alter prescriptions for any medications suspected of causing restless legs syndrome.

WHEN TO CALL A DOCTOR
- Make an appointment with a doctor if restless legs symptoms interfere with sleep.

Retinal Detachment

WHAT IS IT?

Retinal detachment is a vision-threatening condition that results when the retina, the layer of light-sensitive cells lining the back surface of the eye, becomes separated from the back wall of the eye, which contains blood vessels that nourish the retina. The retina is also attached in places to the vitreous body, a transparent, jellylike substance that fills the eye. In some cases detachment follows a small tear or hole in the retina; more often, however, age-related shrinkage or degeneration of the vitreous body causes part of the retina to lift away. The vitreous humor then seeps between the retina and the back wall of the eye, causing a progressively larger area of detachment over a period of hours or days. The retina must be reconnected as soon as possible to prevent permanent vision loss in the affected eye.

WHAT CAUSES IT?

• Eye injury may tear the retina.
• The risk of spontaneous retinal detachment increases with age.
• Hereditary factors may play a role.
• A disease called cytomegalovirus retinitis, common among AIDS patients, may cause retinal detachment.
• Those with severe myopia (nearsightedness), tumors or inflammation in or around the eye, diabetes mellitus, or a family history of retinal detachment are at greater risk.
• Cataract surgery may increase the risk of the disorder.

SYMPTOMS

• Sudden appearance of floating spots or flashes of light in the visual field.
• Blurred or wavy vision.
• Vision loss. It may seem as if a cobweb or curtain obscures part of the field of vision.

PREVENTION

• Use protective gear, such as goggles or helmets, during vigorous activities like motorcycling or in-line skating.
• Regular eye examinations may aid in early detection.

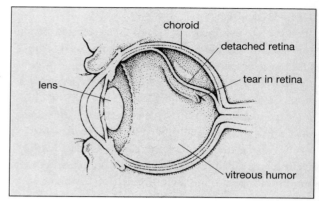

If the retina becomes detached from the choroid (the thin, blood-vessel-rich membrane surrounding the eye), vitreous humor may seep in and behind the retina and cause further detachment.

DIAGNOSIS

• Eye examination by an ophthalmologist.
• Ultrasound scans.
• Fluorescein angiography (injection of a special dye into the bloodstream that allows clear photographic images to be taken of the blood vessels in the eye).

HOW TO TREAT IT

• In most cases the retina is reattached by laser surgery or cryosurgery (use of liquid nitrogen to freeze the targeted tissue). These procedures produce scarring around the edges of the retina, sealing it into place.
• In cases of more severe detachment, more complex surgical procedures may be necessary.
• Medicated eyedrops and ointments are prescribed to aid healing.
• The FDA recently approved an injectable silicone-based oil that can be injected into the eye to hold the retina in place for indefinite periods; this treatment is reserved for complicated cases that cannot be corrected by standard surgery.
• Over-the-counter pain relievers are advised.
• Dark glasses may be recommended to protect the eye after surgery, and prescription lenses may be needed to help correct permanent visual deficits.

WHEN TO CALL A DOCTOR

• **EMERGENCY** See an ophthalmologist immediately if you develop sudden symptoms of flashing lights, black spots in the field of vision, or visual loss.

Retinal Vessel Occlusion

WHAT IS IT?

Retinal vessel occlusion is a blockage in one of the tiny veins or arteries that supply the retina, the layer of light-sensitive cells lining the back surface of the eye. Occlusion of the retinal artery is a sight-threatening emergency. If blood flow is not re-established within a few hours, death of the light-sensitive cells produces permanent loss of vision in the affected eye. Blockage may be due to a blood clot or, more often, an embolus from a blood clot or a fragment of atherosclerotic plaque that has broken away from the site of its origin and has been carried by the bloodstream to lodge in an artery. An embolus lodged in the main retinal artery or one of its branches will cut off the blood supply to the affected eye. By contrast, retinal vein occlusion is not a medical emergency, and there is no effective treatment. However, because blood cannot escape from the blocked vein, it may seep into the vitreous humor, the transparent, jellylike substance that fills the eye, clouding the vision in the affected eye. The vision may clear spontaneously or remain permanently clouded. Symptoms of retinal vessel occlusion occur suddenly with abrupt, painless vision loss. Treatment is sometimes initiated even before diagnosis is complete, since quick action may save the retina in some cases. Unfortunately, partial loss of vision is rarely prevented even with prompt treatment. Retinal vessel occlusion is more common among the elderly.

WHAT CAUSES IT?

• A blood clot, an embolus composed of a blood clot or atherosclerotic plaque, or cancerous cells may block a retinal blood vessel.

SYMPTOMS

• Sudden loss of vision in one eye. Vision loss may be complete or partial.
• Sudden blurred vision in one eye.

• The early stages of chronic glaucoma may predispose to retinal vein occlusion (see Glaucoma for more information).
• Other conditions, such as high blood pressure, diabetes mellitus, and polycythemia vera, may be associated with retinal vessel occlusion.

PREVENTION

• While there is no definitive way to prevent retinal vessel blockage, regular eye examinations may aid in early detection of potential disorders.

DIAGNOSIS

• An eye examination by an ophthalmologist is necessary.
• A complete patient history and physical examination may be required to diagnose the underlying cause.

HOW TO TREAT IT

• Breathing into a paper bag to increase the amount of carbon dioxide in the blood may permit the arteries to dilate or widen, releasing the blockage.
• A doctor may apply firm, intermittent pressure to the eye with the heel of the hand (pressing on the eye for a few seconds, suddenly releasing the pressure, then repeating the procedure), to try and dislodge the blockage.
• Anticoagulant drugs, such as aspirin, heparin, or warfarin, may be administered to prevent further clot formation.
• Ophthalmologists may use special procedures to clear the blockage.
• Antihypertensive drugs may be prescribed to treat associated high blood pressure.

WHEN TO CALL A DOCTOR

• **EMERGENCY** Call an ambulance or see an ophthalmologist immediately if you experience sudden vision loss.

Reye's Syndrome

WHAT IS IT?

Reye's syndrome is a rare, life-threatening disorder that almost exclusively affects children under age 16 (although, rarely, cases have been reported in adults). Now widely recognized since it was first identified as a distinct disease in 1963, Reye's syndrome is characterized by swelling and inflammation of the brain and liver. The cause is unknown; however, aspirin may act as a trigger of the disease in children, especially when taken for viral infections such as influenza, chicken pox, or the common cold. Symptoms of Reye's syndrome generally appear during the recovery phase of the viral infection, and the disease

---

SYMPTOMS

- Severe nausea and vomiting.
- Drowsiness; lethargy.
- Palpitations.
- Mental confusion, hyperactivity, disorientation, or memory loss.
- Severe symptoms: seizures, loss of consciousness, cessation of breathing.

---

progresses rapidly, often resulting in a coma. The outcome is dependent upon the severity of the symptoms, especially the length of the coma. Reye's syndrome has been fatal in up to 50 percent of cases, but this percentage has been decreasing in recent years with advances in treatment. Those who survive generally recover fully, with the exception of those few who suffer permanent brain damage. Early detection and treatment may limit damage from the disease and increase the likelihood of survival; however, prevention remains the most important component in combating Reye's syndrome.

WHAT CAUSES IT?

- The cause of Reye's syndrome is unknown.
- Aspirin may trigger Reye's syndrome in children, especially when given for viral infections.

- The primary damage is to the liver; brain injury results from the metabolic disturbances created by the acute liver abnormalities.

PREVENTION

- Do not give aspirin to those under 16 years of age. Acetaminophen or ibuprofen should be used instead to relieve pain and fever.

DIAGNOSIS

- Patient history and physical examination.
- Blood tests.
- Lumbar puncture (spinal tap).
- Liver biopsy may be done, but it is generally not needed. After local anesthesia is administered to the patient, the doctor inserts a needle under the ribs into the liver to extract a small sample of tissue for microscopic examination.

HOW TO TREAT IT

- Hospitalization in an intensive care unit is usually necessary.
- Intravenous fluids are given to restore blood electrolytes to normal and maintain blood glucose levels.
- Dexamethasone, a corticosteroid medication, may be given to reduce inflammation of brain tissue.
- Mannitol, a diuretic drug, may be administered to reduce pressure on the brain.
- Temporary dialysis may be necessary. Dialysis performs the functions of the kidney by removing waste products and excess fluid from the blood when the kidney cannot (see Renal Failure, Acute, for more information).
- A mechanical respirator may be necessary in the event the child stops breathing.
- In some cases surgery may be performed to reduce swelling and pressure on the brain.

WHEN TO CALL A DOCTOR

- **EMERGENCY** Call an ambulance immediately if a child starts to vomit and becomes excessively drowsy in the aftermath of a viral infection.

Rheumatic Fever

WHAT IS IT?

Rheumatic fever is an inflammatory disease that occasionally occurs as a delayed complication of a streptococcal infection of the upper respiratory tract (usually strep throat). The disease is characterized by inflammation of one or more organ sites throughout the body, including the joints (hence the name "rheumatic," or joint-related, fever), the heart, the skin, and the central nervous system. Symptoms typically appear within one to five weeks after a group A streptococcal infection and include fever, painful and swollen joints, and a skin rash. Untreated attacks usually subside in about three months. With prompt diagnosis and treatment, the disease is usually short-lived, although symptoms may continue for as long as six months with severe heart involvement. The most serious manifestations of rheumatic fever involve the heart muscle and valves. Congestive heart failure can develop and may be fatal. The only long-term complication of rheumatic fever is valvular heart disease, a thickening or distortion in the heart valves that prevents them from closing properly or opening fully. Such damage may not be detected for many years. About 15 percent of patients with rheumatic fever develop Sydenham's chorea (also known as St. Vitus' dance), which is characterized by emotional instability and involuntary jerking movements of the limbs or facial muscles. Rheumatic fever may occur in isolated instances or as part of an epidemic outbreak affecting numerous people, although in the United States, antibiotics and improved public health conditions have kept the incidence in check. Like strep infections in general, rheumatic fever is most common among children between the ages of five and 15.

WHAT CAUSES IT?

• Rheumatic fever is believed to result from an immune response by the body to specific strains of streptococcal bacteria. This immune reaction, and not the infection per se, produces the inflammatory lesions in the various tissues throughout the body.

PREVENTION

• Get prompt treatment for a sore throat that lasts more than 48 hours, especially if accompanied by a fever. Timely administration of antibiotics may prevent the development of rheumatic fever.

DIAGNOSIS

• Patient history and physical examination. A characteristic heart murmur may be detected with a stethoscope if the disease has affected a heart valve.
• Blood tests for the presence of antibodies against streptococcal proteins.
• Throat culture, to detect a streptococcal infection.
• An electrocardiogram (or ECG, a measurement of the heart's electrical activity) may be done to detect carditis or other heart abnormalities.

HOW TO TREAT IT

• Antibiotics, usually penicillin or erythromycin, are given to eliminate streptococcal bacteria even though they are usually absent by the time rheumatic fever occurs.
• Aspirin or another anti-inflammatory drug is usually given to control joint pain and swelling.

SYMPTOMS

• Sore throat precedes the illness by some weeks.
• Swollen, painful joints, especially the knees, ankles, wrists, and elbows. Arthritis symptoms often move sequentially from one joint to another.
• Fever.
• Excessive fatigue.
• Evanescent raised, red patches on the skin, in a curved latticelike pattern.
• Small, painless, pea-size lumps or nodules beneath the skin, commonly appearing on the hands, elbows, knees, scalp, shoulder blades, and spine.
• Acute abdominal pain.
• Involuntary, jerky movements and extreme emotional instability (Sydenham's chorea).

Rheumatic Fever *continued*

• For more severe inflammation, corticosteroids may be needed.

• For mild to moderate rheumatic fever, two to 12 weeks of bed rest are necessary.

• Penicillin, taken daily by mouth or, less often, by monthly injection, is continued for years to prevent reinfection.

• Prophylactic penicillin or amoxicillin may be required prior to dental or surgical procedures throughout the patient's life.

• Sedatives and tranquilizers (such as diazepam or chlorpromazine) may be prescribed to treat Sydenham's chorea, the unusual complication of rheumatic fever that causes jerky, uncontrolled movements and mood swings.

WHEN TO CALL A DOCTOR

• If you have a sore throat that persists for more than 48 hours, especially if it is accompanied by a fever, consult your doctor.

Rheumatoid Arthritis

WHAT IS IT?

Rheumatoid arthritis is a common, persistent systemic disorder that can cause inflammation of joints throughout the body. Joints contain a number of structures that allow for ease of movement. The ends of the bones in a joint are protected from rubbing together by an elastic cushioning material, known as cartilage. The entire joint is surrounded by a capsule, known as the synovial sac. A thin layer of tissue (synovial membrane) lines the sac and secretes synovial fluid, which provides lubrication to ease movement. In the early stage of rheumatoid arthritis, the synovial membrane becomes inflamed and thickened, causing pain and limiting joint movement. As the disease progresses, the cartilage and the ends of the bones themselves erode, resulting in severe joint damage and deformity. Joint pain is often preceded by nonspecific symptoms, such as fever, fatigue, and loss of appetite, and by stiffness, particularly in the morning. The disorder can affect the joints of the hands, feet, wrists, elbows, shoulders, knees, hips, ankles, and neck. Symptoms tend to occur symmetrically; joints on both sides of the body are usually affected at the same time. In some cases other organ systems of the body—including the eyes, heart, and lung—may become inflamed too. Symptoms occur in lengthy episodes that may be separated by remission periods of reduced or total absence of pain and stiffness.

As rheumatoid arthritis attacks and inflames joint tissues, joints may lose their shape and alignment, possibly resulting in severe deformity.

Between 50 and 75 percent of patients experience a remission within one to two years after the first episode. Current research suggests that rheumatoid arthritis is an autoimmune disorder caused by an attack of the immune system on some of the body's own cells. The disease usually develops between the ages of 20 and 50, and its prevalence increases with age; women are affected approximately three times more frequently than men. Treatment is aimed at relieving pain and inflammation, preventing joint deformity, and preserving function.

WHAT CAUSES IT?
- The cause of rheumatoid arthritis is unknown.
- Genetic factors may play a role.
- Some theories suggest that a virus may be associated with the development of rheumatoid arthritis.
- Flare-ups of rheumatoid arthritis may be triggered by emotional stress.

PREVENTION
- There is no known way to prevent rheumatoid arthritis.

DIAGNOSIS
- Patient history and physical examination. There is no specific diagnostic test for rheumatoid arthritis; long-term observation of joint changes may be necessary for definitive diagnosis.

SYMPTOMS
- Early symptoms, preceding obvious joint involvement: fatigue and weakness; low-grade fever; general feeling of poor health; loss of appetite and weight loss.
- Red, swollen, painful joints that may be warm to the touch. With long-term rheumatoid arthritis, joints may become bent and gnarled.
- Stiffness (often the second manifestation), especially after awakening in the morning.
- Red, painless skin lumps, known as rheumatoid nodules, on the elbows, ears, nose, knees, toes, or the back of the scalp.
- Chest pain and breathing difficulty.
- Dry mouth and dry, painful eyes.

Rheumatoid Arthritis *continued*

• Blood tests for a number of autoimmune rheumatoid factors, low white-blood-cell count, or anemia.
• X-rays of the affected joints.
• Synovial fluid analysis. Under local anesthetic, synovial fluid is drawn from the affected joint with a needle.

HOW TO TREAT IT

• To reduce fever and treat pain, your doctor may prescribe large doses of aspirin, or one of the many other nonsteroidal anti-inflammatory drugs (NSAIDs), such as ibuprofen, naproxen sodium, nabumetone, or salsalate.
• Hot or cold compresses may provide some pain relief.
• Get plenty of rest. People with rheumatoid arthritis often need over 10 hours of sleep per night, or eight hours per night and a two-hour nap during the day, and may need more during severe episodes.
• Creams or lotions containing capsaicin may be applied to relieve minor joint pain. Preparations containing camphor, menthol, or turpentine oil may mask pain and provide some relief from minor symptoms.
• Contrary to popular belief, there is no evidence that bee venom relieves or cures rheumatoid arthritis.
• As the disease progresses, drugs usually used to treat malaria, such as hydroxychloroquine sulfate, may also be prescribed to relieve symptoms of rheumatoid arthritis. The drug's effects may not be felt for three to six months.
• A solution containing gold salts may be taken orally or injected intramuscularly to reduce inflammation and pain.
• Methotrexate, an antimetabolite drug, may be prescribed to subdue the immune system. If symptoms persist, immunosuppressants such as azathioprine or cyclophosphamide may be tried.
• Penicillamine, a drug derived from penicillin, may be prescribed to relieve symptoms if other drugs are ineffective.
• Corticosteroids, such as prednisone, offer quick relief from symptoms of rheumatoid arthritis. Because prednisone has serious side effects when used for extended periods, it is often reserved for severe flare-ups of the disease or when other treatments are ineffective.
• Splints may be prescribed to relieve pain by immobilizing the joints during severe episodes.
• Your doctor may prescribe an exercise program or may advise you to see a physical therapist. While exercise that is too vigorous may worsen symptoms, some regular activity is necessary to maintain full motion of the joints and prevent muscle atrophy. You will be taught gentle exercises to increase the range of motion of the joints. Some movements are easier to perform in a pool or hot tub, since water helps support the body.
• Surgery to remove the diseased synovial membrane from affected joints (synovectomy) may be performed in advanced cases.
• Surgery to remove the damaged joint and replace it with a mechanical joint (arthroplasty, or total joint replacement) may be performed in advanced cases. The hip and the knee joints are the ones most often replaced, but joints in the shoulders, elbows, hands, and feet may be replaced as well.

WHEN TO CALL A DOCTOR

• Make an appointment with a doctor if painful joints interfere with normal activities.

Rheumatoid Arthritis, Juvenile

WHAT IS IT?

Juvenile rheumatoid arthritis is an uncommon childhood condition characterized by persistent or recurrent joint inflammation. Joints contain a number of structures and fluids that allow for ease of movement. The ends of the bones in a joint are protected from rubbing together by an elastic cushioning material, known as cartilage. The entire joint is surrounded by a capsule, known as the synovial sac. A thin layer of tissue (synovial membrane) lines the sac and secretes synovial fluid, which provides lubrication to ease

SYMPTOMS

- Red, swollen, painful joints that may be warm to the touch.
- Stiffness, especially after awakening in the morning.
- Fatigue and muscle weakness.
- Fever that may spike as the day progresses. The child's temperature is often normal in the morning but may reach 103°F by the end of each day.
- Red or pink skin rash.
- General feeling of poor health.
- Abdominal pain.
- Loss of appetite and weight loss.
- Chest pain and breathing difficulty (Still's disease).
- Red, painful eyes from inflammation of the iris (Still's disease).
- Anemia (Still's disease).
- Enlarged lymph nodes (Still's disease).

movement. Inflammation may thicken, erode, or otherwise damage these structures, causing pain and limiting movement. Most cases of juvenile rheumatoid arthritis have clinical features significantly different from those of the type of rheumatoid arthritis seen in adults (see Rheumatoid Arthritis for specific information about that disorder). There are three main types of juvenile arthritis: pauciarticular and polyarticular juvenile rheumatoid arthritis, and Still's disease (also known as systemic juvenile arthritis). Pauciarticular juvenile rheumatoid arthritis, which

accounts for approximately 40 percent of cases, causes pain, swelling, and stiffness in four or fewer joints. Polyarticular juvenile rheumatoid arthritis, a more severe form of the disease that accounts for another 40 percent of cases, causes pain, swelling, and stiffness in a number of joints throughout the skeleton. In Still's disease, which accounts for the remaining 20 percent of cases, the child may exhibit symptoms of general illness, including fever, rash, and abdominal pain that last for several weeks and precede symptoms of joint pain and stiffness by several months. Still's disease may cause inflammation of the eyes and lining of the lungs (pleura) or heart (pericardium). Unlike the other forms of juvenile arthritis, Still's disease may also occasionally affect adults. Joint symptoms of juvenile rheumatoid arthritis tend to occur in episodes of several weeks, separated by remission periods when symptoms subside. With frequent or severe episodes, bone growth may be uneven or abnormal; however, permanent joint deformity only occurs in 10 percent of affected children. Current research suggests that juvenile rheumatoid arthritis is an autoimmune disorder, an attack by the immune system on some of the body's own cells. The disease usually appears between the ages of two and four, or nine and 12. In most cases symptoms disappear around the age of puberty, and girls are affected more often than boys. Treatment is aimed at relieving symptoms, preventing deformity, and maintaining optimal joint function throughout the duration of the disease.

WHAT CAUSES IT?

- The cause of juvenile rheumatoid arthritis is unknown.
- Genetic factors may play a role.

PREVENTION

- There is no known way to prevent juvenile rheumatoid arthritis.

DIAGNOSIS

- Patient history and physical examination. There is no specific diagnostic test for juvenile rheumatoid arthritis, and long-term observation may be necessary for definitive diagnosis.

Rheumatoid Arthritis, Juvenile *continued*

• Blood tests.
• X-rays of the affected joints.
• Synovial fluid analysis may be performed. In this procedure a local anesthetic is administered to desensitize the affected joint, and synovial fluid is then withdrawn from the joint capsule with a needle.

HOW TO TREAT IT

• To reduce fever and treat minor pain, your doctor may prescribe large doses of aspirin, or one of the many other nonsteroidal anti-inflammatory drugs (NSAIDs), such as tolmetin or naproxen sodium.
• Hot or cold compresses applied to the joints may offer some pain relief.
• Creams or lotions containing capsaicin may be applied to relieve minor joint pain. Preparations containing camphor, menthol, or turpentine oil may mask pain and provide some relief from minor symptoms.
• In severe cases, stronger medications may be prescribed to relieve pain and inflammation, including the antimalarial drug hydroxychloroquine sulfate, gold salts administered by injection or by mouth, immunosuppressive drugs, such as methotrexate, azathioprine, or cyclophosphamide, and the penicillin-derived drug penicillamine.
• Corticosteroids, such as prednisone, offer quick relief from symptoms of juvenile rheumatoid arthritis but have serious side effects; they are used only in the smallest possible doses and only when other treatments prove ineffective.
• Plenty of rest is required. Children with juvenile rheumatoid arthritis often need to sleep longer than average at night and may need to take naps during the day.
• Your child's doctor may prescribe an exercise program or may advise that your child see a physical therapist. While exercise that is too vigorous may worsen symptoms, some regular activity is necessary to prevent limitation of joint movements and to prevent muscle weakness and atrophy. Gentle exercises are taught to increase the range of motion in affected joints. Some movements are easier to perform in a pool or hot tub, since water helps support the body.
• Splints may be prescribed to relieve pain by immobilizing affected joints during severe episodes.
• Contact your local chapter of the Arthritis Foundation for information about support groups in your area.

WHEN TO CALL A DOCTOR

• Make an appointment with a doctor if your child develops painful or stiff joints.

Ringworm Dermatophytosis

WHAT IS IT?

Ringworm is a skin infection caused not by a worm but by several different species of fungus collectively referred to as tinea. The fungus causes scaly, round, itchy patches to develop on various parts of the body, including the scalp, groin, nails, feet, and the skin under the beard. Most people in the United States have had at least one form of ringworm, which is moderately infectious. Prompt treatment with topical antifungal agents usually clears up most cases within a few weeks.

WHAT CAUSES IT?

• Infection by one or more of the different tinea fungi causes ringworm. Exposure to animals (especially cats and dogs) with a fungal infection is one mode of transmission.

SYMPTOMS

• On the scalp: bald patches and scales.
• On the skin: round, red patches that grow to about one inch across. As the patch radiates outward, the central area heals, leaving a red ring where the infection remains active (hence the name "ringworm").
• Under a beard: an itchy, scaling rash.
• On the feet: dry scaling and fissuring of the skin between the toes and on the arch (Athlete's foot).
• On the nails: red, swollen, and painful fingernails or toenails.
• People with athlete's foot may develop a nonspecific (possibly allergic) dermatitis at other sites on the feet or hands that clears when the fungal infection is fully treated.

PREVENTION

• Do not share towels or shoes.
• Thoroughly dry the feet after taking a bath or shower, and after swimming.
• Avoid lengthy stays in an overheated, humid environment, like the areas around indoor swimming pools. Warmth, moisture, and darkness encourage the growth of fungi.

• Avoid contact with infected pets as much as possible. Seek prompt veterinary treatment for any skin conditions your pet exhibits.

DIAGNOSIS

• Ringworm is suspected by observation of the characteristic red-bordered rash.
• Culture and microscopic examination of skin, pus, or hair shafts may be needed to confirm the diagnosis.

HOW TO TREAT IT

• Ringworm can often be cured with over-the-counter antifungal creams or solutions. Effective medications include those containing clotrimazole, miconazole nitrate, and ketoconazole. Generally, these preparations are applied twice daily; the infection should begin to fade within a week. Continuing treatment for the recommended amount of time will help ensure eradication of the fungus.
• If over-the-counter treatments fail, a more powerful oral agent (griseofulvin) or topical antifungal medication may be prescribed. Topical or low-potency corticosteroids may be prescribed as well to ease itching and speed healing.
• Keep affected areas as clean and dry as possible; talcum or medicated powders may be used.
• If a fungal infection begins to blister or ooze, apply damp compresses to help clear out the affected areas. Do not break blisters, as this encourages further infection.
• If you have ringworm of the groin area (jock itch), wear cotton underwear and change it more than once a day. If the feet are affected (Athlete's foot), change socks frequently to keep feet as dry as possible.
• Sterilize any clothing, towels, or bedding that have touched the lesions.

WHEN TO CALL A DOCTOR

• Call your doctor if your symptoms do not improve or if infection continues to spread after several weeks of over-the-counter treatment.
• Call a doctor if you develop new, unexplained symptoms, which may be side effects from the medications used to treat ringworm.

Rocky Mountain Spotted Fever

WHAT IS IT?

Rocky Mountain spotted fever is an illness caused by a microorganism that infects humans through the bite of a tick. A severe headache, fever, and rash typically appear within one week of infection. The disease gets its name from the Rocky Mountain area where it was first reported, but its occurrence is widespread in the United States; cases are most common in the southern Atlantic states. The wood tick and dog tick are the primary carriers, and either can be found in both city and woodland locales. More than 90 percent of cases occur between April 1 and September 30, the time of year when ticks are most prevalent. Children and adolescents account for nearly half of cases, primarily because of increased tick exposure through outdoor activity. Untreated, especially in older patients, Rocky Mountain spotted fever may result in heart failure, pneumonia, or coma, and is fatal in 20 to 30 percent of cases.

WHAT CAUSES IT?

• A bite from a tick infected with the microorganism *R. rickettsii*.

SYMPTOMS

• Severe headache, chills and a high fever that reaches 103°F to 104°F within the first two days.
• A rash appears between the second and sixth day of illness. It begins at the wrists and ankles and within 24 hours spreads to the rest of the body and face. In about 10 percent of patients, the rash does not occur or is barely noticeable, particularly in males and persons with dark skin.
• Nausea, vomiting, diarrhea, and abdominal pain.
• A dry cough.
• Muscle aches.
• Heightened sensitivity to light.

• The organism invades and multiplies in cells lining the arteries and veins throughout the body, causing vasculitis.

PREVENTION

• Minimize contact with ticks and tick-infested areas.
• Wear protective clothing and use insect repellent on exposed skin and clothes.
• Inspect your body several times a day for ticks when visiting a tick-infested area.
• Check dogs for ticks; ticks may infect the animal and establish a host for further transmission.
• Remove an attached tick with tweezers: grasp it as close to the skin as possible, being careful not to squeeze the body of the tick, which may spew infectious microorganisms into the bloodstream. Pull the tick steadily upward without twisting and do not handle it after removal. Transmission is unlikely unless the tick has been attached for a number of hours.
• Wash the bite area with soap and water or antiseptic to destroy any contaminants.

DIAGNOSIS

• A patient history should include any recent outdoor activities or travel in tick-infested areas.
• Microscopic examination of a biopsy of skin or rash is the only way to make a conclusive diagnosis early in the disease.

HOW TO TREAT IT

• Antibiotic drug therapy (usually tetracycline or chloramphenicol) should be administered as early as possible in the course of illness. If treatment is delayed until the rash is widespread, therapy is less effective.
• If untreated, the illness often abates after two weeks and convalescence is usually rapid.

WHEN TO CALL A DOCTOR

• Call a doctor when there are symptoms of rash, fever, headache and weakness, regardless of whether or not a tick bite is evident. Conclusive diagnosis and appropriate treatment are only available through a physician.

Roseola

WHAT IS IT?

Roseola, also known as exanthem subitum, is a common childhood viral infection. After a symptom-free incubation period of five to 12 days, a sudden, high fever develops. The fever may persist for three to five days. During this time the child may become irritable and, in a few cases, experience febrile (fever-induced) convulsions. On the fourth or fifth day of the illness, the fever subsides abruptly, and a rash appears on the torso. The rash, consisting of small, red, flat areas, each about two millimeters in diameter, may quickly spread outward to the neck and face, as well as to the arms and legs. The rash often subsides after one or two days; in some cases it only persists for a few hours. By the time the rash appears, the child typically feels better and is no longer contagious. Roseola occurs exclusively in children, especially between the ages of six months to two years, and is more prevalent during the spring and fall. The disease is not a serious health risk, and no further complications arise after the infection subsides. Treatment is aimed at relieving symptoms while they last.

WHAT CAUSES IT?

• The human herpes virus 6 causes roseola.
• Exposure to an infected child may spread the virus to other children.

SYMPTOMS

• Sudden onset of fever (possibly as high as 105°F).
• Irritability.
• Skin rash on the torso that usually spreads to the neck, face, arms, or legs.
• Sore throat.
• Swollen glands in the neck.
• Possible convulsions.

PREVENTION

• Follow proper sanitary measures, such as washing hands after using the bathroom and before handling food, to help prevent the spread of infectious disease.
• If possible, avoid exposing your child to another child with roseola.

DIAGNOSIS

• Diagnosis is based primarily on patient history and physical examination, since there is no specific test for roseola.
• Throat or blood cultures may be performed to rule out the possibility of other illnesses.

HOW TO TREAT IT

• Acetaminophen may be given to reduce fever. Do not give aspirin, which increases the risk of Reye's syndrome, a rare but life-threatening inflammation of the brain and liver in children (see Reye's Syndrome for more information).
• Sponge baths with cool water are recommended as a way to reduce fever.
• Sedatives or anticonvulsant medications may be prescribed if seizures occur.
• Follow prevention tips to halt the spread of infection.
• Strenuous physical activity should be avoided during periods of high fever.

WHEN TO CALL A DOCTOR

• Call a doctor if a young child develops a high fever, with or without swollen glands. High fever can indicate a number of potentially serious disorders that may require professional treatment.
• EMERGENCY See your doctor immediately or get to an emergency room if your child experiences convulsions.

Rotator Cuff Injury

WHAT IS IT?

Rotator cuff injury is an inflammation or tear in the ligaments or tendons of the rotator cuff, the group of four muscles and tendons that forms, in part, the roof of the shoulder joint. The muscles of the rotator cuff make it possible to lift and rotate the arm, and when the tendons are repeatedly stressed or torn, shoulder pain occurs and mobility of the arm becomes limited. Injuries vary in severity: in rotator cuff tendinitis, the humerus, or long bone of the upper arm, rubs against a tendon causing microscopic tears and inflammation; in rotator cuff tear, the more serious injury, a rupture of a tendon causes sharp pain and may severely limit arm movement. Rehabilitation for most injuries is usually accomplished within six months, and long-term physical therapy is seldom necessary.

WHAT CAUSES IT?

• Repeated stress to the shoulder from activities such as sports or heavy labor.
• Trauma to the shoulder, such as falling on an outstretched arm or lifting heavy objects.
• Wearing out the shoulder by years of continual use, as in golfer's shoulder, usually occurring between the ages of 60 and 75.

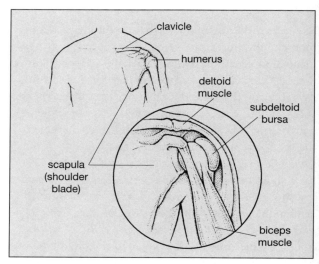

The structures of the rotator cuff lie just beneath the deltoid muscle, providing stability to the humerus where it enters the shoulder socket.

SYMPTOMS

• Tenderness in the shoulder region, often worse at night.
• Pain aggravated by rotating or lifting the arm, especially to an angle of 90 degrees or higher.
• Sudden, sharp pain in the shoulder that radiates down to the elbow.
• Pain and weakness in the shoulder that may last several months or longer with a chronic or untreated injury.

PREVENTION

• Exercise that increases strength and flexibility of the rotator cuff muscles will reduce the likelihood of injury.
• As much as possible, avoid activities that repeatedly stress the shoulder joint.

DIAGNOSIS

• Physical exam may include range of motion tests to determine the extent of injury: a mild tear is most painful when the arm is raised between 60 and 90 degrees; a complete tear renders the arm incapable of being raised above the head.
• Arthrography, an x-ray technique using dye injection, may be used to examine joint tissues in the shoulder.

HOW TO TREAT IT

• Apply hot compresses to the shoulder.
• Take over-the-counter analgesics such as aspirin, acetaminophen, ibuprofen, or naproxen sodium.
• Partial immobilization with a sling may be recommended for a limited time.
• Exercise (after the pain subsides) may be recommended. With supervised physical therapy a mild tear can usually be rehabilitated within six months.
• Corticosteroids may be injected directly into the affected area to reduce pain and swelling.
• Surgery is often required to repair a ruptured tendon, usually on an outpatient basis under local anesthetic.

WHEN TO CALL A DOCTOR

• Call a doctor if routine motions such as lifting your arm to comb your hair become difficult and painful, or if you experience a sharp, wrenching pain or other trauma to the shoulder.

Rubella

WHAT IS IT?

Rubella, also known as German measles, is a contagious viral infection. Neither as severe nor as contagious as measles, another rash-producing viral infection, the most characteristic symptom of rubella is a nonitchy skin rash that lasts for a few days before fading. Symptoms vary widely between children and adults; children may have few if any symptoms except the rash, while adults may develop more pronounced symptoms. In any case, rubella is usually a mild infection that goes away on its own without complications. However, if contracted by a women in the first four months of pregnancy, the virus may cause miscarriage, stillbirth, or serious birth defects in the developing fetus, a condition known as congenital rubella syndrome. All women not immunized as children are therefore advised to receive the rubella vaccine.

WHAT CAUSES IT?

• A viral infection causes rubella.
• The virus may be spread by infected saliva expelled during coughing or sneezing, or by sustained, close contact (for example, within a household or school).

SYMPTOMS

• A mild skin rash that lasts for about three days, spreading from the face to the torso, arms, and legs before fading.
• Mild fever (102°F or lower).
• General feeling of poor health.
• Nasal discharge.
• Sore throat.
• Red, bloodshot eyes.
• Joint aches.
• Enlarged lymph glands.

PREVENTION

• Children should be vaccinated at 15 months of age; a combination vaccine for measles, mumps, and rubella (known as MMR) is usually administered. (During rubella epidemics, which are now rare in the United States, doctors may recommend that the vaccine be given to children as young as 12 months.) Some areas also require a rubella booster shot between the ages of four and six, or 11 and 12.
• All women not immunized as children should receive the rubella vaccine. Effective birth control should be used for three months after the vaccine, to prevent congenital rubella syndrome in a developing fetus. Pregnant women, however, should not receive the rubella vaccine.
• Children or adults with compromised immune systems (for example, those with AIDS or those undergoing treatment with immunosuppressive drugs) should not receive the rubella vaccine.

DIAGNOSIS

• Diagnosis is strongly suggested upon patient history and physical examination, although rubella can be easily mistaken for other viral illnesses. In cases of a rubella epidemic, other tests are generally not necessary.
• Blood tests that reveal antibodies to the virus can confirm diagnosis.

HOW TO TREAT IT

• Acetaminophen, ibuprofen, or naproxen sodium may be given to a child to reduce fever and relieve headache. Do not give aspirin to those younger than age 16, since aspirin increases the risk of Reye's syndrome, a rare but life-threatening inflammation of the brain and liver in children (see Reye's Syndrome for more information). Adults may take the analgesic of their choice.

WHEN TO CALL A DOCTOR

• Call a doctor if you develop a stiff neck, severe headache, visual disturbances, or other symptoms of meningitis during or after a rubella infection (see Meningitis for more information).
• Call a doctor if you are pregnant, or suspect that you might be, and you believe you may have been exposed to rubella.
• See your doctor if you become pregnant and have not been immunized.

Salivary Gland Disorders

WHAT IS IT?

The three sets of salivary glands, located at the sides of the mouth below the ears (parotid glands), below the jaw (submandibular glands), and in the floor of the mouth (sublingual glands), secrete saliva into the mouth through tiny ducts. Saliva aids in swallowing, prevents infection, and helps keep the mouth and teeth clean. The salivary glands can malfunction in a number of ways: too much or too little saliva may be produced; the glands may become infected; the ducts may be blocked by a plug, known as a stone; rarely, tumors (either cancerous or benign) may develop within the glands. Treatments depend upon the underlying problem. If one salivary gland needs to be removed (say, in the case of a malignant tumor), the remaining glands compensate and produce adequate amounts of saliva.

WHAT CAUSES IT?

• Bacteria and viruses may cause salivary gland infections (see Mumps or AIDS for more information).
• Chemicals in saliva may solidify into a salivary duct stone.
• The cause of salivary gland tumors is unknown.
• Swelling of the salivary glands or a decrease in salivation may be caused by other disorders, such as diabetes mellitus, cirrhosis, Sjögren's syndrome,

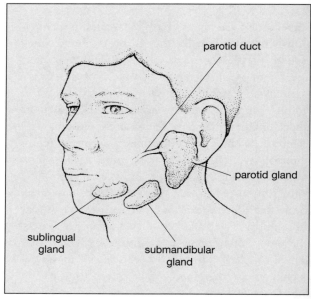

The salivary glands are each comprised of thousands of sacs that produce saliva, which is secreted into the mouth through ducts.

depression, and dehydration; treatments such as radiation therapy to the head and neck; and medications including antihistamines, antidepressants, and some combinations of antihypertensive drugs.
• Excessive salivation may be caused by certain salivary gland infections.

PREVENTION

• There is no known way to prevent salivary gland disorders.

DIAGNOSIS

• Patient history and physical examination, either by a physician or dentist.
• Dental x-rays.
• CT (computed tomography) scans.
• Biopsy of affected salivary glands.

HOW TO TREAT IT

• Antibiotics are prescribed to treat bacterial infections of the salivary glands.
• Antifungal agents may be needed to treat yeast infections of the mouth occurring in those with decreased saliva.

SYMPTOMS

• Decreased or increased salivation.
• Swelling around the mouth or in front of the ears. Painful swelling is associated with salivary gland infections and salivary duct stones; painless swelling that develops gradually may be due to salivary gland tumors or the conditions described above in "What Causes It?"
• Mouth pain, especially at mealtimes.
• Bad taste in the mouth (salivary gland infection).
• Fever (salivary gland infection).
• Increase in dental cavities and difficulty swallowing owing to decreased salivation (see Sjögren's Syndrome).

Salivary Gland Disorders *continued*

• Over-the-counter analgesics can be taken for pain relief. Aspirin should not be dispensed to children under 16 (see Reye's Syndrome for more information).

• Sugarless gum or sour candies can help stimulate salivation. Increased fluid intake is also recommended for dry mouth.

• Saliva substitutes (solutions containing 2 percent methylcellulose) may be prescribed, especially to be used at night. In severe cases the drug pilocarpine may be prescribed to increase saliva production (see Sjögren's Syndrome).

• Rinsing the mouth several times daily with a solution of salt or baking soda in warm water is advised to wash away pus from an infected salivary duct.

• Surgery may be performed to remove a stone blocking the salivary duct, to remove a tumor, or to widen the opening of the duct.

• Surgical removal of the entire salivary gland may be required for malignant tumors and may be advised in cases of recurrent infection.

• Radiation therapy may be needed to destroy cancerous cells. Prognosis for salivary tumors is quite favorable if they are detected early.

WHEN TO CALL A DOCTOR
• Make an appointment with a doctor if you develop pain or swelling in or around the mouth or if you experience an increase or decrease in saliva production.

Sarcoidosis

WHAT IS IT?

Sarcoidosis is a relatively common disease characterized by an accumulation of inflammatory cells that may occur in tissues throughout the body, most often in the lungs, lymph nodes, eyes, and skin. Although the cause is unknown, sarcoidosis is thought to be an autoimmune disorder—an attack of the immune system on certain of the body's own cells. Symptoms depend on which organs are affected; in many cases no symptoms appear at all. Most cases of sarcoidosis subside spontaneously within two or three years; long-term or chronic sarcoidosis accounts for only 10 percent of cases. The most serious manifestations of sarcoidosis result from damage to the lungs. Symptoms may be relieved with corticosteroid drugs; however, since the disease may be mild and most cases subside even without treatment, the decision to prescribe corticosteroids is based upon the likelihood of complications developing in the lungs, eyes, or other organs. Sarcoidosis is more common between the ages of 20 and 40, although it may strike anyone at any age; in the United States, African Americans are affected more frequently than Caucasians.

WHAT CAUSES IT?

• The cause of sarcoidosis is unknown.

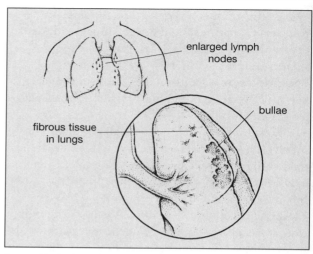

In sarcoidosis, the accumulation of inflammatory cells in various tissues may produce scarlike fibrous tissue or thin-walled blisters (bullae) in the lungs, and enlargement of the lymph nodes.

SYMPTOMS

• Sarcoidosis may cause no symptoms.
• Fatigue, aching muscles, general feeling of poor health.
• Fever.
• Breathing difficulty, dry cough, hoarseness, wheezing.
• Swollen lymph nodes.
• Blurred vision; painful, red, dry eyes; aversion to light (photophobia).
• Painful joints.
• Loss of appetite leading to weight loss.
• Reddish skin bumps on the legs; swollen bluish purple areas on the face.

PREVENTION

• There is no known way to prevent sarcoidosis.

DIAGNOSIS

• Diagnosis is suspected from patient history, physical examination, and chest x-ray.
• Confirmation of the diagnosis requires a biopsy, often of lung tissue obtained by bronchoscopy (the passage of a thin, flexible viewing tube through the mouth and throat into the lungs).
• Skin lesions or other sites may be biopsied.

HOW TO TREAT IT

• Corticosteroid drugs such as prednisone are prescribed to reduce inflammation and relieve symptoms. When the lungs are involved, such therapy may be sustained for a year or more, then withdrawn to see if spontaneous remission has occurred. Relapses may require indefinite steroid therapy.
• Chloroquine (a drug usually used to treat malaria) is often useful in the treatment of skin lesions.

WHEN TO CALL A DOCTOR

• Call a doctor if you develop persistent shortness of breath, fever, unexplained weight loss, or other symptoms of sarcoidosis.

Scabies

WHAT IS IT?

Scabies is a disorder caused by a skin infestation of a burrowing mite. The tiny mite digs under the uppermost layer of the skin and lays several eggs. The skin becomes sensitized to the mite over a period of about two weeks, until finally a skin eruption of small blisters occurs, causing intense itching. Scratching may collect the mites and eggs under the fingernails and help transmit them to other parts of the body. The warm folds of the skin, such as those of the wrists, the underarms, the genitals and the webs between the fingers, are most commonly affected. In infants and small children, the blisters may be more generally distributed, appearing on the face and neck, palms, and soles. With treatment, itching usually subsides quickly, and all traces of the disease generally disappear within one or two weeks.

WHAT CAUSES IT?

• The female mite burrows into the upper layer of skin and lays two or three eggs daily for up to 60 days if undetected or untreated. Within three weeks newly hatched larvae mature and begin a continuing cycle of infection. Itching is due to a reaction to the mite and its products.
• Physical contact with an infested person or with contaminated clothing or bedding may spread scabies. (Casual transmission, as between schoolmates, is uncommon.) Family members and bed mates are at the highest risk. Children under 15 are usually the first members of the family to get scabies.
• Crowded, institutional, or unsanitary living conditions also increase the risk.

PREVENTION

• Practice good personal hygiene; wash clothes and bedding often.
• Avoid physical contact with persons, clothing, or bedding that may be infested with scabies.

DIAGNOSIS

• Diagnosis is suspected upon visual inspection of burrows or lesions.
• Confirmation of the diagnosis requires observation of the mite upon microscopic examination of a skin scraping.

HOW TO TREAT IT

• A topical scabicide such as lindane, crotamiton, or permethrin is prescribed and applied after bathing. Scabicides are not recommended for children under six or pregnant women, where a milder sulfur solution is preferred.
• Oral antihistamines (like diphenhydramine) may help ease itching, as may topical emollients.
• Antibiotics may be required to treat secondary bacterial infections.
• Bed linen and clothes used for two to three days prior to treatment should be thoroughly washed in hot water. The mite cannot live more than three days without a host.
• Family members, even without symptoms, may also be treated.

WHEN TO CALL A DOCTOR

• Call a doctor if you experience intense itching and over-the-counter remedies fail to relieve it.

SYMPTOMS

• Small, red, itchy blisters, which break easily when scratched. Open blisters are prone to secondary infection.
• Severe itching, typically concentrated in the wrists, armpits, genitals, the folds of the breasts, buttocks, or elbows, and between the fingers. Itching is often worse at night or after a hot bath.
• Visible trailing burrows on the skin, especially between the fingers, which characteristically appear as dotted lines or wavy gray ridges resembling pencil marks.
• Small blisters without trailing burrows (indicating canine scabies, also highly contagious, acquired from a dog with mange).
• Severe scaling and crusting of the skin (in a rarer form known as Norwegian or crusted scabies, seen in persons with weakened immune systems and characterized by mild itching but extreme mite infestation).

Scleritis and Episcleritis

WHAT IS IT?

Scleritis and episcleritis are inflammations of the outer protective layers of tissue that form the eyeball's shell. The deepest layer is the sclera, known commonly as the white of the eye. The transparent tissue covering the sclera is the episclera, which in turn is covered by a fine membrane called the conjunctiva. Inflammation of the episclera—or episcleritis—often resembles a localized form of conjunctivitis, but episcleritis is not accompanied by the watery or pus-filled discharge typical of conjunctivitis. Episcleritis is usually a minor disorder that does not permanently damage the eye and generally resolves on its own within a week or two. Its presence occasionally indicates an underlying disease such as rheumatoid arthritis. Scleritis, a less common but more serious disease, most often occurs in association with an underlying systemic or autoimmune disorder, usually in people between the ages of 30 and 60.

WHAT CAUSES IT?

• The cause of episcleritis and scleritis is unknown.
• Both episcleritis and scleritis may be associated with a systemic disorder, that is, one affecting other organ systems in the body. Such disorders include autoimmune rheumatoid diseases (rheumatoid arthritis, scleroderma, lupus), inflammatory bowel disease, and tuberculosis.
• Herpes zoster involving the eye can lead to scleritis.

PREVENTION

• There is no known way to prevent episcleritis or scleritis.

DIAGNOSIS

• Patient history and an eye examination by an ophthalmologist.
• A general physical examination by a medical doctor may be required to identify an associated underlying disease.

HOW TO TREAT IT

• In episcleritis, steroids in drop or ointment form may be prescribed to reduce inflammation.
• The course of scleritis often parallels the activity and treatment of the associated systemic disorder. Corticosteroids, in tablet or eyedrop form, may reduce inflammation in some patients. Cycloplegic drugs may be administered to dilate the pupil, which may prevent scarring and alleviate pain somewhat. Immunosuppressive drugs may be prescribed in more severe cases.
• Surgery may be required for scleritis if the sclera has perforated.

WHEN TO CALL A DOCTOR

• If you suspect you have either episcleritis or scleritis, consult an ophthalmologist immediately.

SYMPTOMS

• A red or violet, slightly raised patch on the white of the eye, usually only a fraction of an inch in diameter.
• Sharp, severe eye pain that intensifies when the eye is moved.
• Dull, aching pain in one or both eyes, often worse at night. In some cases pain is severe.
• Aversion or increased sensitivity to light.
• Blurred vision.

Scleroderma Systemic Sclerosis

WHAT IS IT?

Scleroderma is characterized by the overgrowth of fibrous connective tissue in the skin and some internal organs. The disease, which means hardening (sclero) of the skin (derma), was initially thought to affect only the skin. It was later recognized that vital organs may be affected as well. The disease begins when fibroblasts and other cells that manufacture the protein collagen (a major component of connective tissue) spontaneously overproduce dense, inelastic, scarlike connective tissue. Circulation may be affected as the buildup of dense tissue chokes off the flow of blood through the tiny capillary blood vessels. When internal organs (typically the esophagus, lungs, kidneys, or heart) are involved, fibrous tissue slowly infiltrates organ tissues, interfering with normal organ function. This may lead to life-threatening conditions such as severe lung disease or kidney failure. Scleroderma usually evolves gradually over a number of years; outcome depends on the organ systems involved. Occasionally, the disease goes into remission. Onset is usually between 30 and 50 years of age; women are affected more than men.

SYMPTOMS

- Distinctive change of skin color from white to blue as blood vessels constrict in response to cold, and then to red as circulation returns during rewarming (Raynaud's phenomenon). Such episodes are often painful.
- Numbness, coldness, and blue appearance in the fingers or toes.
- Shiny or waxy appearance of skin.
- Puffiness, thickening, and tightening of the skin, especially on the face, arms, and hands.
- Changes in pigmentation.
- Joint pain and stiffness.
- Heartburn, especially when lying down or bending over.
- Tightness in the throat; swallowing difficulty.
- Shortness of breath after minimal exertion.
- Fatigue and weakness.
- Persistent slight fever.
- High blood pressure; symptoms of renal failure.

WHAT CAUSES IT?

- The cause of scleroderma is unknown, although it appears to be an autoimmune disorder (an attack by the body's defenses on healthy tissue).
- Exposure to silica dust, vinyl chloride, epoxy resins, and hydrocarbons has been implicated.

PREVENTION

- There is no known way to prevent scleroderma or to arrest its progression.

DIAGNOSIS

- Frequently, the diagnosis may be determined upon patient history and physical examination alone.
- Blood tests and skin biopsy may be taken to rule out other connective tissue disorders.

HOW TO TREAT IT

- No definitive medical therapy has been proven effective for scleroderma; treatment is aimed at minimizing symptoms and complications.
- Immunosuppressive drugs such as azathioprine or penicillamine may help inhibit excess collagen production in some patients.
- Skin lotions and bath oils may be used to soften the skin. Regular exercise and massage may help to maintain skin pliability as well.
- Antacids, frequent small meals, and elevation of the head of the bed are recommended for patients with heartburn.
- Drugs may be prescribed to aid circulation and so reduce the incidence of Raynaud's phenomenon.
- Inflammation of the heart or joints may be eased by corticosteroids.
- Hypertension (which occurs when the kidneys are affected) is treated with drug therapy.
- Dialysis may be needed in those with impaired kidney function.
- Patients with heart failure require treatment with digitalis and diuretics.

WHEN TO CALL A DOCTOR

- Call a doctor if patches of skin become tight, shiny, and lose their elasticity or if you experience symptoms of poor circulation, difficulty in swallowing, or shortness of breath.

Scoliosis

WHAT IS IT?

Scoliosis is a sideways, or lateral, curvature of the spine. A curve to one side, most often in the thoracic (chest) portion of the spine, leads to compensatory bends in the lumbar (lower back) and cervical (neck) portions of the backbone. The resulting S-shape of the spine causes the chest cavity to be enlarged on the wide part of the curve and compressed on the narrow side. Lung capacity may be seriously reduced, depending on the severity of the deformity, and heart and respiratory problems may result. The disorder is usually accompanied by a forward or backward curvature, known respectively as kyphosis (humpback) and lordosis (swayback). Scoliosis usually begins in the years of rapid skeletal growth, between the ages of four and nine, or in the early teens. Adolescent girls are four times more likely to be affected. Progression usually slows by early adulthood. Scoliosis may worsen with age as a result of osteoporosis or loss of muscle strength. When detected early, minor deformities may be halted by spine-strengthening exercises and by wearing a brace. More severe cases may require surgery.

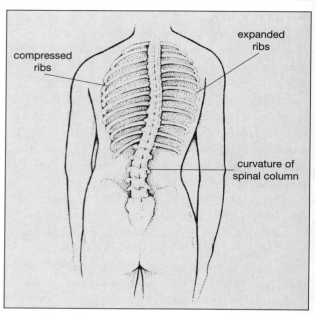

Scoliosis compresses the rib cage on one side and expands it on the other. This may diminish lung capacity on the compressed side.

SYMPTOMS
- A visible S-shaped curve in the spine.
- Pain in the lower back (lumbar region).
- Breathing difficulty after minimal exertion.
- Rapid, shallow breathing, particularly in older patients, when the chest wall becomes less flexible with age.

WHAT CAUSES IT?
- In 80 percent of cases, the cause is unknown.
- In 20 percent of cases, scoliosis can be attributed to abnormalities such as uneven leg lengths; poor posture; weakness of the spinal muscles due to neuromuscular disease, as in poliomyelitis; spinal injury, such as a prolapsed disk; or acquired or inherited defects in the vertebrae.

PREVENTION
- There is no known way to prevent scoliosis, but its progression may be arrested after it is diagnosed.

DIAGNOSIS
- Patient history and physical examination.
- Spinal x-rays.

HOW TO TREAT IT
- When the deformity is slight or associated with muscular weakness, exercises may be recommended.
- Frequent monitoring is necessary during the rapid growth years to detect significant changes.
- Prolapsed disk injury may often be treated with bed rest alone.
- An orthopedic shoe can compensate for uneven leg lengths.
- A hinged plaster jacket or adjustable metal brace, fitted by an orthopedic surgeon, may be used to arrest curvature and immobilize the spine.
- Curvature greater than 45 degrees requires surgery. Bone grafting is done to fuse the vertebrae and so straighten the spine.

WHEN TO CALL A DOCTOR
- Call a doctor if you suspect scoliosis in yourself or your child, since curvature is often worse than it appears, and early treatment can halt its progression.

Seizures

WHAT IS IT?

Seizures are alterations in neurologic function resulting from bursts of abnormal electrical activity in the brain. In normal brain function, electrical charges flow from one neuron to the other along pathways that establish orderly patterns of thought and behavior. Seizures are initiated by the sudden onset of repetitive, synchronized discharges from many neurons that can cause radical changes in consciousness, sensation, and muscle control. The many different types of seizures can be grouped into two broad categories: generalized and partial (or focal). In generalized seizures, abnormal electrical activity may occur anywhere in the brain, while in partial seizures, abnormal activity is isolated to one area of the brain. Perhaps the best-known type of generalized seizure is the grand mal seizure: sudden loss of consciousness followed by violent full-body convulsions lasting several minutes. The patient has no memory of the event and is usually confused and drowsy for some time afterward. The petit mal seizure—another type of generalized seizure—is characterized by a blank look, staring, and loss of awareness, but not muscle convulsions. Like the grand mal, there is typically no memory of the event afterward. An untreated person may experience hundreds of petit mal seizures daily, each one lasting only a few seconds. However, these are only two of many different types of seizures. Partial (or focal) seizures may trigger isolated, localized movements—such as chewing, lip smacking, or swallowing—or merely produce odd sensations, such as transient prickling or numbness. Disorders producing recurrent seizures are known as the epilepsies; seizures may also occur as one-time events, such as those triggered by high fevers in children. Epilepsy occurs in approximately 1 to 2 percent of the population. Generally, seizures last a few seconds to a few minutes at a time. Prolonged grand mal seizures (status epilepticus), or those that recur in rapid succession, require emergency medical treatment.

Although there is generally no cure, epilepsy can usually be controlled with a variety of anticonvulsant medications. Children with petit mal epilepsy often outgrow it as they reach late adolescence and young adulthood. For other types of seizures, anticonvulsant medication can often be discontinued after a patient has been seizure-free for two to five years. Finally, brain surgery is an option if seizures are severe or resistant to medication. After surgery, seizures may subside completely or almost completely, and mental functioning is often improved.

SYMPTOMS

- Warning symptoms (known as an aura) prior to a seizure: sensations of strange odors, sounds, sights, or feelings; feeling of déjà vu; nausea. Each person generally has a consistent aura, although aura sensations vary widely from person to person.
- Petit mal or absence seizure: loss of awareness and lack of responsiveness; staring; twitching of the arm or head.
- Grand mal seizure: loss of consciousness; muscle rigidity followed by twitching or jerking; loss of bladder and bowel control. Most grand mal seizures are not preceded by an aura. After the seizure: no memory of the event; confusion; sleepiness; headache.
- Focal seizure: uncontrollable twitching of one part of the body, such as the hand, which may spread to nearby muscles or the entire body. The patient may remain conscious during a focal seizure.
- Temporal lobe seizure: loss of awareness; sudden, bizarre behavior, such as laughing or becoming angry for no apparent reason; repetitive lip smacking, chewing motions, or picking at clothes. Temporal lobe seizures may be preceded by an aura lasting a few seconds.
- Febrile seizure: rapid rise or fall in temperature; loss of consciousness; muscle convulsions characteristic of a grand mal seizure. Febrile seizures are usually isolated events that do not recur.

WHAT CAUSES IT?

- Sudden, explosive, highly synchronized firing of neurons in the brain—the cause of which is unidentifiable in about half of all cases.

Seizures *continued*

• Brain damage due to prior head trauma, such as an automobile accident, sports injury, or a fall.
• Withdrawal from alcohol, illicit drugs, or anticonvulsant medication.
• Brain tumor or stroke.
• Infection of the brain or its surrounding tissues (see Meningitis and Encephalitis).
• High fevers, which commonly cause seizures in children under five (febrile seizure).
• Congenital brain damage due to illness, injury, or infection during pregnancy that affects the development of the fetal nervous system.
• Chemical imbalances such as low blood sugar, calcium, or sodium levels, or severe vitamin deficiency.
• Conditions that affect the central nervous system, such as cerebral palsy and multiple sclerosis.
• Sleep deprivation or physical stress.

PREVENTION
• There is no known way to prevent epilepsy, but medications can control seizures in most cases.

DIAGNOSIS
• Patient history and physical examination.
• Electroencephalogram (EEG). In this procedure, electrodes are attached to the patient's head to measure electrical activity in the brain. A series of EEGs may be taken over a period of time to obtain a complete picture of brain activity.
• Skull x-ray; CT (computed tomography), PET (positron-emission tomography), or SPECT (single-photon emission computed tomography) scans of the brain; MRI (magnetic resonance imaging).

• Proper diagnosis of the type of seizure is important for selecting the most appropriate drug treatment.

HOW TO TREAT IT
• Do not try to restrain someone having a seizure. If the person falls, try to ease the descent to the ground. Move objects out of the way to prevent accidental injury, then stand aside. Do not try to insert your fingers into the mouth of someone having a seizure; contrary to popular belief, people do not swallow their tongues during seizures, and attempting to force their mouth open may cause injury to them or you. After muscle convulsions have ceased, roll the person to one side to prevent choking on fluids or vomit. When the person regains consciousness, offer reassurance. The person may need to sleep for a while after a seizure.
• Treatment is unnecessary for seizures caused by high fevers in children.
• Anticonvulsant medications, such as carbamazepine, phenytoin, phenobarbital, valproate, ethosuximide, clonazepam, and primidone, may be prescribed.
• Brain surgery may be advised in severe cases to remove tumors, scar tissue, or vascular malformations, or to interrupt paths of abnormal electrical activity.

WHEN TO CALL A DOCTOR
• Call a doctor if you or your child suffers a seizure for the first time.
• **EMERGENCY** Call an ambulance if a seizure lasts for more than five minutes, or if the person has another seizure before regaining consciousness.

Septic Shock

WHAT IS IT?

Septic shock, a life-threatening medical emergency, is the result of an invasion of the bloodstream by infectious agents (septicemia), usually bacteria. In an inflammatory response to the infectious organisms or their toxic products, substances are released that cause blood vessels to dilate, cardiac output to decline, and fluids to leak from small blood vessels into the tissues. Blood pressure then drops precipitously (septic shock), starving the body's cells of oxygen-carrying blood. Deprived of oxygen and injured by tissue factors, cells begin to die. Cell damage can rapidly lead to multiple organ-system failure of the liver, lungs, brain, kidneys, and heart. Failure of any of the vital organs can be fatal. Septic shock occurs most commonly among hospitalized patients, especially those with severe infections or undergoing surgery. Early recognition of the signs leading up to shock and immediate treatment are imperative, since full-blown septic shock is fatal in over two-thirds of cases despite modern therapeutic measures.

WHAT CAUSES IT?

• A bacterial infection is the most common cause of septic shock. Puncture wounds, deep cuts, burns, surgical procedures, or the use of a urinary catheter facilitate the entrance of bacteria into the bloodstream.

SYMPTOMS

• Rapid, shallow breathing (hyperventilation).
• Changes in consciousness or mental state, such as confusion, agitation, disorientation, or coma.
• Sudden high fever and chills.
• Severe fatigue and weakness.
• Cold hands and feet; bluish tinge to the skin.
• Nausea and vomiting.
• Diarrhea.
• Decreased urine output.
• Prostration.
• Rapid heartbeat.

• Rarely, viral or fungal infections cause septic shock.
• Risk factors for developing septic shock and for suffering more severe consequences include other disorders, such as diabetes mellitus, advanced cancer, and cirrhosis of the liver; severe injury or burns; surgery; and a weakened immune system due to AIDS or treatment for cancer, for example. Newborns and the elderly are also at higher risk.

PREVENTION

• Obtain prompt treatment for bacterial infections, wounds, or burns.

DIAGNOSIS

• Diagnosis may be presumed immediately upon physical examination, patient history, and observation of characteristic symptoms; since septic shock is an emergency, treatment is initiated prior to laboratory confirmation of diagnosis.
• Blood cultures provide a definitive diagnosis.

HOW TO TREAT IT

• Hospitalization in an intensive care unit is necessary.
• Intravenous antibiotics are administered to treat the bacterial infection.
• Intravenous fluids and blood transfusions are given to restore adequate fluid volume in the circulatory system and to counteract severe anemia.
• If administration of fluids fails to restore blood pressure to acceptable levels, a vasopressor (blood vessel constricting) drug such as dopamine may be given to increase blood pressure.
• Mechanical respiration through a mask or nasal tubes may be required to supply adequate oxygen.
• Surgery to drain or remove an abscess or to cleanse a wound of foreign material is performed as needed.

WHEN TO CALL A DOCTOR

• **EMERGENCY** Call an ambulance immediately if someone begins to hyperventilate and becomes confused and disoriented, with or without fever, nausea, or a blue tinge to the skin.

Shin Splints

WHAT IS IT?

Shin splints occur when one of the bones in the calf (usually the tibia) or its surrounding muscles or tendons become injured and inflamed. During exercise, the lower leg muscles enlarge and press against the compartment formed by the two bones of the lower leg. Repeated stress and pressure can cause irritation of the muscles, tendons, ligaments, or bones, and result in the pain known as shin splints. In more severe cases the physical stress may cause a hairline fracture in the tibia. When the pain is located on the outer side of the calf, it is known as anterior shin splints, and when it is on the inner side, posterior shin splints. These injuries are common in joggers, dancers, or anyone whose exercise routine or occupation involves pounding the feet on hard surfaces. In most cases three weeks of rest followed by a regimen of proper conditioning will allow the patient to safely return to his or her full complement of normal activities.

SYMPTOMS

- Pain, with either a gradual or abrupt onset, which usually occurs during or just after exercise.
- Persistent aching pain in the front or side of the lower leg.

WHAT CAUSES IT?

- Inadequate warm-up prior to exercise.
- Muscle fatigue or exercising to excess.
- Running on uneven or hard surfaces such as concrete, or excessive running uphill.
- Inadequate training or improper technique.
- Improper or worn-out footwear that no longer absorbs impact sufficiently.

PREVENTION

- Be sure to stretch calf muscles thoroughly in your regular warm-up before exercise.
- Use proper athletic footwear with good support.
- Run on grass or dirt paths instead of concrete.
- Avoid sudden increases in the intensity of your workout.

DIAGNOSIS

- Diagnosis is based primarily on patient history and presentation of symptoms.
- Examination of the foot and lower leg helps to establish any anatomical predisposition, such as slew or flat feet, both of which are frequently associated with posterior shin splints.
- An x-ray or bone scan may be used to diagnose a hairline stress fracture when symptoms are prolonged or recurrent.

HOW TO TREAT IT

- Rest, usually for two or three weeks, is the most common recommendation and may be combined with physical therapy to strengthen any affected muscles.
- A temporary switch to low-impact activities such as bicycling or swimming is advised if high-impact exercise (like aerobic dancing or running) appears to have caused shin splints.
- Wear shoes that are well cushioned and provide good support.
- For pain, take over-the-counter anti-inflammatory drugs such as aspirin or ibuprofen.
- Ice packs may be recommended for swelling and inflammation.
- Heat, in the form of whirlpool or hot soaks, may reduce discomfort.
- Ace bandages may provide comfort and support.
- Stretching exercises and self-massage may ease pain.
- A podiatrist or orthopedist may recommend an orthotic device (a specially fitted insert) to place in your shoes. Orthotics help to correct structural anomalies that promote repeated episodes of shin splints.
- In rare cases a surgical procedure known as fasciotomy (severing of the ligaments involved in repeated muscle and joint strain) may be warranted to treat severe and persistent shin splints.

WHEN TO CALL A DOCTOR

- If shin pain persists for more than three weeks despite self-treatment, consult your doctor. You may be referred to a podiatrist or orthopedist for further evaluation and treatment.

Sinusitis

WHAT IS IT?

Sinusitis is an inflammation of one or more of the four sets of facial sinus cavities, usually due to infection. When irritated, the mucus membrane lining the sinus may swell and block the small drainage channels that permit mucus to flow into the nose. The buildup in pressure often results in headache, nasal congestion, and facial pain. Acute sinusitis is a common disorder that often follows a cold or flu; chronic sinusitis refers to persistent or recurrent episodes that are generally milder than acute cases. Sinusitis often subsides on its own and responds well to home treatment. In rare cases, however, infection may spread to the eyes or the brain, possibly leading to vision loss, meningitis, or brain abscess.

WHAT CAUSES IT?

- A viral or bacterial infection that spreads to the sinuses from the nose.
- Anatomical irregularities, such as a deviated septum or nasal polyps.
- Swimming in contaminated water.
- Infection spread from abscesses in the upper teeth.
- Chronic sinusitis may be caused by irritation from dust, air pollutants, or excessive exposure to tobacco smoke, or result from an untreated acute condition.

PREVENTION

- If you have allergies, control them by limiting exposure to allergens and using antihistamines.

SYMPTOMS

- Headache pain and pressure concentrated over one or both eyes (frontal sinusitis).
- Pain in the cheek bones (maxillary sinusitis).
- Swelling in the upper eyelids (ethmoid sinusitis).
- Tenderness over the affected sinus.
- Pain behind the eyes (sphenoid sinusitis).
- A yellowish green nasal discharge.
- Persistent nasal blockage and forced breathing through the mouth, following a cold or the flu.
- Fever and chills.
- Dental pain, usually in the upper jaw.

- When you have a cold, use a cool-mist humidifier and sleep with your head slightly elevated to promote drainage.
- Chronic sinusitis sufferers should avoid tobacco smoke and alcohol (its diuretic effect thickens mucus) and should drink plenty of liquids to loosen nasal secretions.

DIAGNOSIS

- Patient history and physical examination.
- Removal of fluid from the maxillary sinus with a needle may be necessary to determine the type of bacterial infection.
- X-rays may be used to locate areas of blockage.

HOW TO TREAT IT

- Inhale steam from a basin of hot water.
- Over-the-counter oral or nasal decongestants may reduce swelling. Nasal decongestants should not be used for more than three days in order to avoid even more severe "rebound congestion" that occurs when usage is stopped. People with high blood pressure, heart disease, arrhythmias, or glaucoma should check with their doctors before using decongestants.
- Nonprescription pain relievers, ice packs, or warm compresses may soothe sinus pain. In severe cases codeine may be prescribed.
- Antihistamines are used to treat allergic sinusitis.
- Steroid nasal sprays may be prescribed to reduce pain and inflammation.
- Antibiotics are prescribed for bacterial infections.
- Endoscopy, use of a flexible fiber-optic scope, may be used to survey the sinuses and clear blockage.
- Surgery may be needed to drain or repair sinuses in very rare cases. Early surgical drainage is often recommended for frontal sinusitis.
- Hospitalization and intravenous antibiotics are required for severe bacterial sinusitis.

WHEN TO CALL A DOCTOR

- Call a doctor if symptoms persist longer than two weeks or are accompanied by bloody nasal discharge.
- **EMERGENCY** Get to a doctor right away if you develop redness, pain, or bulging (proptosis) of an eye, paralysis of eye movements, or nausea and vomiting in association with other symptoms of sinusitis.

Sjögren's Syndrome

WHAT IS IT?

Sjögren's syndrome is a type of autoimmune disorder in which, for reasons unknown, the body's defenses against infection mistakenly attack cells in the salivary and lacrimal (tear) glands. The result is extreme dryness in the mucus membranes of the mouth and eyes, which may lead to dental cavities and corneal infections. Other glands may be affected too, such as those that produce vaginal lubrication. Vaginal dryness is thus a symptom in women, who develop Sjögren's syndrome 10 times more often than men (usually in their 30s or 40s). Other tissues may be affected too, especially the kidneys, lungs, and nervous system. Lymph glands often become enlarged, and Sjögren's patients have a higher incidence of lymphoma (see Lymphoma, Non-Hodgkin's, for more). The disorder may occur on its own or in conjunction with other autoimmune disorders (secondary Sjögren's syndrome); as many as 30 percent of those with rheumatoid arthritis also develop Sjögren's syndrome. In uncomplicated cases symptoms can be eased with treatment, and the outlook is generally favorable.

WHAT CAUSES IT?

• The cause of Sjögren's is unknown, although a hereditary predisposition appears to be involved.

SYMPTOMS

• Dry, red, painful eyes.
• Dry, painful mouth; swallowing difficulty; frequent dental cavities.
• Reduced ability to distinguish taste and smells.
• Hoarseness and dry cough that worsens in cold weather.
• Dry skin.
• Swelling of the salivary glands just in front of the ears (parotid glands).
• Vaginal dryness.
• Joint pain.
• Fatigue.
• Raynaud's phenomenon: distinctive change of skin color from white to blue as blood vessels constrict in response to cold, and then to red as circulation returns during rewarming.

• Other autoimmune disorders are associated with a higher risk of Sjögren's syndrome (see Rheumatoid Arthritis, Systemic Lupus Erythematosus, or Scleroderma for more information).

PREVENTION

• There is no way to prevent Sjögren's syndrome.

DIAGNOSIS

• Patient history and physical examination.
• Blood tests for indicators of autoimmune activity.
• Biopsy and microscopic examination of a tissue sample from the salivary glands or lip.

HOW TO TREAT IT

• There is no cure for Sjögren's syndrome; treatment is aimed at relieving symptoms.
• Artificial tear solutions containing methylcellulose or saline eyedrops are used to treat dry eyes.
• Sugarless gum or sour candies can help stimulate salivation.
• Increased fluid intake is important, but alcohol and caffeine should be avoided, since they have a diuretic effect that can exacerbate dryness.
• Saliva-substitute solutions, which also contain methylcellulose, may be recommended. In severe cases the drug pilocarpine may be prescribed to increase saliva production.
• Vigilant dental hygiene is essential for the prevention of cavities.
• Antibiotics may be prescribed to treat associated bacterial infections in the eyes or eyelids.
• Over-the-counter water-based lubricants may be used to counteract vaginal dryness. Your doctor may recommend using a gel containing propionic acid.
• For dry skin, moisturizing creams should be applied right after bathing, while skin is still moist.
• In very severe cases corticosteroids such as prednisone or short-term courses of immunosuppressive drugs may be administered to treat life-threatening vital organ involvement.

WHEN TO CALL A DOCTOR

• Make an appointment with a doctor if you develop persistent dryness in the mucus membranes of the eyes, mouth, nasal passages, or vagina.

Sleep Apnea

WHAT IS IT?

Sleep apnea is a disorder characterized by repeated cessation of breathing for brief periods during sleep. Most common among obese, middle-aged men, apnea can usually be attributed to excessive relaxation during sleep of the muscles at the back of the throat—a consequence of getting older or gaining extra weight. The sagging folds of muscle may block the upper airway (obstructive sleep apnea) a dozen to hundreds of times a night. After 10 to 100 seconds, the demand for oxygen grows critical and the sleeper gasps or snores abruptly in characteristically loud, staccato bursts in the struggle to regain normal breathing. (In a rare form of the disorder known as central sleep apnea, the airways remain open but the chest muscles are not stimulated to function for repeated short periods. A third form, mixed sleep apnea, combines airway obstruction with chest muscle inactivity.) The sleeper rarely awakens fully during these episodes but is aroused briefly and tends to arise tired and unrefreshed the next morning, since apnea prevents the sufferer from reaching deeper stages of sleep. Severe, persistent cases of sleep apnea may promote serious cardiovascular problems, such as high blood pressure, abnormal heart rhythms, and heart failure. Treatment varies according to the cause and severity of symptoms.

SYMPTOMS

- Breathing cessation interrupted by loud, abrupt bursts of snoring or snorting.
- Excessive daytime sleepiness.
- Morning headache.
- Difficulty concentrating; memory loss; personality changes.

WHAT CAUSES IT?

- Excess weight combined with loss of muscle tone at the base of the throat.
- Alcohol and sedatives promote apnea.
- Hormonal changes due to menopause may produce sleep apnea in some women.
- Incidence increases with age.
- The cause of central sleep apnea is unknown.

PREVENTION

- Maintain a healthy weight.
- Avoid sleeping pills and do not consume alcoholic beverages within two or three hours before bedtime.

DIAGNOSIS

- Patient history and physical examination. History may include reports from roommates or bed mates. A tape recording of nighttime snoring may also be useful in making a diagnosis.
- Further evaluation at a sleep center or from an ear, nose, and throat specialist may be recommended to pinpoint the underlying causes of sleep apnea and to devise a suitable treatment strategy.
- Laboratory tests may include chest x-rays, tests of blood-oxygen levels during periods of apnea, and electrocardiogram.

HOW TO TREAT IT

- Weight loss is a key part of management for those who are overweight.
- A tennis ball may be sewn to the back of pajamas to prevent sleeping on one's back, a position that encourages episodes of sleep apnea.
- Medications such as the antidepressant protriptyline, or the hormonal supplement medroxyprogesterone, may relieve symptoms in some cases.
- A device known as continuous positive airway pressure (CPAP) may be prescribed. With CPAP, a mask is worn over the nose and mouth; air is forced through the mask throughout the night to keep the airways open.
- Surgery may be performed to improve breathing in severe cases. Anatomical obstruction in the back of the throat may be corrected, or in life-threatening cases a small opening in the throat (tracheostomy) may be created to bypass the blocked airway.

WHEN TO CALL A DOCTOR

- Make an appointment with a doctor if you develop extremely loud snoring with periods of silence, or if excessive daytime sleepiness interferes with normal activities.

Spinal Cord Trauma

WHAT IS IT?

Injury to the spinal cord is a medical emergency that may result in severe and permanent disability. The spinal cord—which along with the brain comprises the central nervous system—is a bundle of nerve cells that may travel almost the entire length of the spine, connecting the brain to the nerves in the rest of the body. The vertebrae, the small bones that make up the spine, form a bony tunnel that surrounds the cord and protects it from injury; however, if a blow is severe enough, or if the bones are weakened by disease, the spinal cord is vulnerable to damage. Destroyed nerve cells cannot regenerate; injury to the spinal cord may thus result in

---

SYMPTOMS
- Intense localized back or neck pain.
- Swelling at the site of injury.
- Weakness, numbness, tingling, and impaired sensation in the limbs and trunk below the injured area of the spinal cord.
- Paralysis of the legs (paraplegia) or of both the arms and legs (quadriplegia).
- Loss of bowel and bladder control.
- Erectile dysfunction.
- Breathing difficulty.
- Shock.

---

permanent paralysis of the legs (paraplegia) or, in the case of a neck injury, the arms, trunk, and legs (quadriplegia). About half of the cases of spinal cord injury involve the neck. However, partial or complete recovery may be expected in cases when neurons in the spinal cord have been traumatized but not completely destroyed. Outcome thus depends upon both the severity and the specific location of the injury: damage to the spinal cord will affect nerves at the level of the injury and below.

WHAT CAUSES IT?
- Injury, from motor vehicle or sports accidents, falls, or gun shot wounds, is the most common cause of spinal cord trauma.

- Displaced or broken vertebrae can damage the spinal cord directly.
- Swelling of nearby tissues, or a blood clot, may compress the spinal cord.
- Trauma may damage the cord by interrupting its blood supply.
- Those with bones weakened by osteoporosis, rheumatoid arthritis, or bone cancer are at greater risk for spinal cord damage.

PREVENTION
- Drive defensively and wear seat belts. Be sure water is sufficiently deep before diving. Wear protective gear when playing sports.
- Get enough calcium to reduce the risk of osteoporosis. Hormone replacement therapy may be recommended to postmenopausal women to prevent osteoporosis.

DIAGNOSIS
- Patient history and physical examination.
- X-rays of the spine.
- CT (computed tomography) scans or MRI (magnetic resonance imaging).
- X-rays may be taken after injection of a contrast medium (myelography) to outline the spinal cord.

HOW TO TREAT IT
- Call an ambulance immediately. Do not attempt to move someone who may have a spinal cord injury.
- Careful immobilization of the head and back by means of traction, splints, and braces is necessary to prevent further damage.
- Oxygen may be supplied through a small tube inserted into the nose if breathing is impaired owing to paralysis of respiratory muscles.
- Intravenous methylprednisolone, a corticosteroid drug, may be administered within the first eight hours of injury to minimize the extent of nerve damage.
- Surgical decompression of the spinal cord may restore some function if cord damage is incomplete.
- Long-term use of a urinary catheter may be necessary if bladder control is lost.
- Special prescription support hose and anticoagu-

Spinal Cord Trauma *continued*

lant drugs such as heparin help prevent the formation of blood clots in immobilized limbs and the resultant pulmonary emboli.

• Tube feedings may be needed to provide ample nutrition.

• Wheelchairs may be needed for those with permanent paralysis.

• Frequent repositioning helps avoid skin breakdown (bed sores) over pressure points.

• Extensive physical therapy can prevent immobilization of joints and contractures of muscle.

• Occupational and emotional therapy help patients and their families cope with major lifestyle changes.

WHEN TO CALL A DOCTOR

• **EMERGENCY** Call an ambulance immediately if you suspect someone has sustained a back or neck injury. Do not attempt to move the person, and do not allow him or her to sit up, since any movement may cause further damage to the spinal cord.

Spinal Stenosis

WHAT IS IT?

Spinal stenosis is a narrowing of the spinal canal, the cavity within the vertebral column through which the spinal cord passes. Nerves leaving and entering the spinal cord are called nerve roots; they pass through the vertebral column through small canals. Arthritic changes that cause overgrowth of vertebral bones may compress the spinal cord or the nerve roots, impairing sensation and muscle strength in the affected portion of the body. Most common among people in their 50s and 60s, spinal stenosis affects the lumbar (lower back) portion of the spine, causing pain, numbness, and weakness in the lower back and legs. Symptoms may disappear and sensation may be fully regained if pressure on the nerve roots and spinal cord can be relieved with treatment.

WHAT CAUSES IT?

• Disorders that involve arthritic degeneration and abnormal overgrowth of bone tissue, such as osteoarthritis or Paget's Disease, may cause spinal stenosis (see Osteoarthritis or Paget's Disease for more information).

Overgrowth of the vertebrae narrows the spinal canal. This may compress the spinal cord or spinal nerves, causing pain and numbness.

SYMPTOMS

• Back pain that may radiate to the buttocks and legs. Pain worsens with activity.
• Numbness in the buttocks and legs.
• Weakness in the legs.

PREVENTION

• There is no way to prevent spinal stenosis.

DIAGNOSIS

• Patient history and physical examination. Reflexes in the legs are tested to assess nerve involvement.
• X-rays of the spine.
• CT (computed tomography) scans or MRI (magnetic resonance imaging).

HOW TO TREAT IT

• Losing weight and toning the abdominal muscles through exercise may reduce pressure on the spine. Check with your doctor before beginning any weight-loss program or new exercise regimen.
• A lumbosacral support (a type of corset available at certain pharmacies or medical-supply stores) may be recommended to discourage spinal motion that causes pain. Such a support may help ease walking and exercise but should not be worn all day.
• Anti-inflammatory drugs may be used to relieve pain.
• If pain prevents normal activities despite self-care and medication, surgery to relieve pressure on the nerves (known as decompression surgery) may be warranted. The surgeon opens the spinal column where narrowing has occurred and removes the constricting bone or fibrous tissue. The opening through which nerve roots pass may be widened; if an excessive amount of bone is removed, the affected vertebrae may be fused together to increase spinal stability. Physical therapy may aid in rehabilitation following surgery.

WHEN TO CALL A DOCTOR

• Call a doctor if you develop persistent pain, numbness, or weakness in the back, legs, or neck.

Spinal Tumor

WHAT IS IT?

A spinal tumor is an abnormal growth of cells located either within the spinal cord itself or, much more often, in its surrounding membranes and tissues. The spinal cord, which along with the brain comprises the central nervous system, is a bundle of nerve cells encased in a protective membrane that travels almost the entire length of the spine, connecting the brain to the nerves in the rest of the body. Tumors affecting the spinal cord are uncommon; they may be either benign or malignant. However, even benign tumors can compress the spinal cord, leading to irreversible paralysis (see Spinal Cord Trauma for more information), or impinge upon nerves as they leave the spinal cord. Malignant tumors rarely originate in the spinal cord itself; most often, cancer compressing the spinal cord has spread from elsewhere in the body to the bones of the spine (vertebrae) or originated in the vertebrae. Benign tumors usually grow slowly, but malignant tumors may increase in size in a matter of days; symptoms may be limited to back pain or may include numbness, loss of sensation, and weakness, generally beginning in the legs. Both benign and malignant tumors can damage the spinal cord by interrupting its blood supply. After diagnosis of a malignant tumor, rapid treatment is necessary to limit damage and to prevent irreversible paraplegia.

SYMPTOMS

- Constant back pain that may spread in a horizontal band around the chest or abdomen. Pain may be described as a burning sensation and may worsen upon exertion, lying down, and coughing or sneezing.
- Numbness, tingling, and muscle weakness usually beginning in the legs.
- Loss of pain and temperature sensation below the site of the tumor.
- Loss of bladder and bowel control.

WHAT CAUSES IT?

- The cause of spinal tumors is unknown.
- Cancer that originates elsewhere in the body, such as the breast, lungs, or prostate, may spread to the vertebrae.

PREVENTION

- There is no known way to prevent spinal tumors.
- Regular examinations of the prostate in men and the breasts in women aid in early detection and treatment of tumors in those areas (see Breast Cancer and Prostate Cancer for more information).

DIAGNOSIS

- Patient history and physical examination.
- X-rays of the spine.
- MRI (magnetic resonance imaging).
- CT (computed tomography) scans, with injection of a contrast material (myelography), may be performed in some cases.
- Lumbar puncture (spinal tap), to analyze a sample of cerebrospinal fluid.
- Biopsy of the tumor may be required to confirm the diagnosis.

HOW TO TREAT IT

- Surgery may be performed promptly to reduce compression of the spinal cord by removing part or all of the tumor.
- Large doses of corticosteroid drugs, such as dexamethasone, may be administered to reduce swelling.
- Radiation therapy may be required in addition to or instead of surgery to treat malignant tumors.
- Chemotherapy may be advised in some cases to treat malignant tumors.
- Physical, occupational, and emotional therapy may be recommended to patients and their families to help them cope with major lifestyle changes.

WHEN TO CALL A DOCTOR

- Call a doctor if you develop severe, persistent back pain, with or without numbness, tingling, or muscle weakness.

Spondylosis, Cervical

WHAT IS IT?

Cervical spondylosis is a general term for degeneration of the structures in the cervical, or neck, region of the spine. The seven cervical vertebrae constitute the top portion of the spine, the long, flexible column of bones that supports the skeleton and protects the spinal cord. Flat, circular pads of cartilage known as intervertebral disks serve as cushions between the vertebrae and allow for smooth movement. In spondylosis, rupture of a disk, overgrowth of the vertebrae or the ligaments that support the spine, or any combination of these may compress the spinal cord or the spinal nerves leaving or entering the spinal cord, causing pain and other symptoms (see Spinal Stenosis or Intervertebral Disk, Herniated, for more information). Spondylosis is common among those of middle age and older; many cases are mild and respond well to self-treatment.

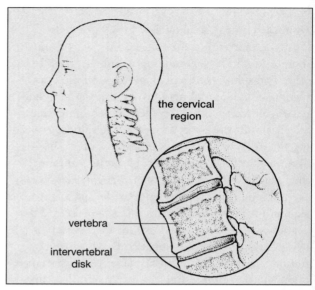

The cervical region of the spine is comprised of the seven uppermost vertebrae in the spinal column and their supporting structures.

SYMPTOMS
- Pain and stiffness in the neck and shoulders. Pain may radiate to the arms and may worsen upon coughing or sneezing.
- Tingling or numbness in the hands and feet.
- Weakness in the arms and legs.
- Gait irregularities or walking difficulty in advanced cases.
- Impaired bladder control in very advanced cases.

WHAT CAUSES IT?
- The cause of spondylosis is unknown.
- Risk increases with age.
- Prior neck injuries may increase the risk of developing spondylosis.

PREVENTION
- There is no way to prevent cervical spondylosis.

DIAGNOSIS
- Patient history and physical examination are needed.
- Spinal x-rays or a CT (computed tomography) scan usually confirms the diagnosis.
- Myelography (injection of a contrast material into the space around the spinal cord to highlight spinal abnormalities on a series of x-rays) is sometimes performed.

HOW TO TREAT IT
- Mild cases of cervical spondylosis may resolve on their own. Rest and immobilization of the neck with a brace may aid in recovery.
- Over-the-counter analgesics may be used for minor pain. For more severe cases prescription painkillers, muscle relaxants, or tranquilizers may be warranted.
- Traction therapy may be required if pain is persistent. This is usually done on an outpatient basis in sessions of 15 to 30 minutes at a time, although one or two weeks of hospitalization is sometimes advised.
- In advanced cases surgery may be performed to relieve pressure on the spinal nerves. This is done by removing bony overgrowth in the vertebrae or by fusing affected vertebrae together to prevent harmful joint movement, or both.
- Regular exercise or physical therapy may be recommended.

WHEN TO CALL A DOCTOR
- Call a doctor if persistent neck pain does not respond to self-treatment.

Sprains and Strains

WHAT IS IT?

Although the terms sprain and strain are used loosely and have no precise clinical definition, a sprain generally refers to an injury to a ligament—one of the tough, fibrous cords within a joint that connects the bones together. Strain refers to muscle injury. Sprains and strains often occur together in or near a joint, since joints absorb the stress of movement and are vulnerable to being twisted or wrenched; the ankle and the knee are the most common sites of such injuries. In mild cases the force of the injury tears a few fibers of the ligament or muscle, causing mild to moderate pain and swelling, which usually subside within a few days. A more violent injury may completely tear a ligament or muscle and involve bone damage (see Dislocations and Subluxations, or Bone Fractures, for more information). With proper care, most sprains and strains heal completely without complication.

SYMPTOMS
- Mild to severe pain in the affected joint that worsens with movement or the application of pressure.
- Swelling, redness, or bruising around the affected joint.
- In severe cases, loss of mobility in the affected joint.

WHAT CAUSES IT?

- Sprains and strains occur as a result of an injury, when the joint is subjected to more physical force than it can withstand. Athletes, dancers, and those who perform manual labor commonly suffer such injuries.
- Previous sprains may so weaken the ligaments that recurrence is possible with only minor pressure.
- The risk of sprains and strains increases with obesity and poor muscular conditioning.

PREVENTION

- Perform warm-up exercises before undertaking any strenuous physical activity.
- Wear a brace or elastic support, or tape or wrap joints, before engaging in vigorous physical activity.
- Engage in regular, moderate exercise to keep muscles and joints strong and flexible.

DIAGNOSIS

- Patient history and physical examination.
- X-rays of the affected joint to rule out a bone fracture or other underlying problem.

HOW TO TREAT IT

- Follow first-aid measures for a sprain or strain, which can be easily remembered with the acronym RICE, short for rest, ice, compression, and elevation.
- *Rest* the injured area. Try not to move or put pressure on the affected joint. A sling or splint may be recommended to immobilize the joint and allow damaged ligaments or muscles to heal.
- *Ice* the affected area to reduce swelling. After 24 hours, either ice or heat may be applied to reduce pain.
- *Compress* the joint by wrapping it in an Ace bandage to help reduce swelling and pain.
- *Elevate* the joint to reduce swelling.
- Take over-the-counter pain relievers to treat minor pain. Your doctor may prescribe stronger analgesics for more severe pain.
- Surgery may be required in severe cases to repair torn ligaments or muscles.
- After the pain has subsided, gently exercise the joint to regain strength and mobility. A physician or physical therapist may help to devise an exercise program to aid in rehabilitation.

WHEN TO CALL A DOCTOR

- Call a doctor if you experience severe pain after straining or spraining a joint, or if joint pain persists for more than two or three days after the initial injury despite self-treatment.

Stomach Cancer

WHAT IS IT?

Stomach cancer results from the growth of abnormal cells in the lining of the stomach. More than 90 percent of gastric cancers are adenocarcinomas, arising from cells lining the stomach wall; lymphomas account for 3 to 7 percent of stomach cancers (see Lymphoma, non-Hodgkin's). Men over 50 are most commonly affected. The incidence of stomach cancer has decreased dramatically in the United States in the last 50 years; the reason for this is unknown, although dietary factors and the refrigeration of foods (which has decreased the need for chemical preservatives) are implicated. Complete surgical removal of the tumor is the only cure; unfortunately, by the time symptoms occur, adenocarcinomas are often too large to be completely excised, and cancer is likely to have spread to other sites. Early detection greatly increases the chances that treatment may be initiated in time. Survival rates for lymphomas of the stomach are improved with a combination of surgery and chemotherapy.

WHAT CAUSES IT?

• The cause of stomach tumors is unknown.
• Environmental factors appear to play a role. Geographic areas where colorectal cancer is common (such as the United States) often have a low incidence of stomach cancer.
• Consumption of foods that contain nitrates or nitrites—chemicals commonly used in processed foods as preservatives—is implicated in stomach cancer risk, although there is no definitive proof of this hypothesis. Salty, pickled, barbecued, or smoked foods are believed to pose the highest risk.
• Surgical removal of a portion of the stomach (gastrectomy), chronic inflammation of the stomach lining (gastritis), and pernicious anemia increase the risk of stomach cancer.
• Hereditary factors may play a role. For reasons that are unknown, there is a higher incidence of stomach cancers among people with type-A blood.

PREVENTION

• Limit your intake of salty, pickled, and smoked foods (such as bacon, smoked or salted fish, and pickled vegetables).
• Regular checkups, especially a test for traces of blood in the stool, may aid in early detection and treatment.

DIAGNOSIS

• Patient history and physical examination.
• Stool samples (guaiac test). Microscopic traces of blood in the stool may indicate digestive tract tumors.
• Tumors can be detected with x-rays done after the patient swallows barium to highlight the stomach.
• Gastroscopy may be performed, in which a thin, flexible, viewing tube (gastroscope) is passed into the stomach via the throat.
• Biopsy of the stomach lining may be taken with the gastroscope to confirm diagnosis.

HOW TO TREAT IT

• Surgery to remove as much of the tumor as possible is the primary treatment. Part or all of the stomach, nearby lymph nodes, the pancreas, and the spleen may also be removed if it is suspected that cancer may have spread to these sites.
• Radiation therapy may be administered instead of or in addition to surgery to relieve pain and bleeding.
• Chemotherapy may be warranted.

WHEN TO CALL A DOCTOR

• Call a doctor if you develop symptoms of persistent stomach pain, abdominal fullness, or nausea.

SYMPTOMS

• No symptoms in most cases of small, surgically curable stomach cancers.
• Stomach discomfort or pain. Pain occurs after meals and is not relieved by soothing foods or antacids.
• Nausea and vomiting.
• Gas, heartburn, regurgitation, and belching.
• Loss of appetite and weight.
• Abdominal fullness or bloating.
• Difficulty in swallowing.
• Weakness and fatigue, due to associated anemia.
• Black, tarry stools.

Strabismus

WHAT IS IT?

Strabismus—a common disorder often referred to as crossed eyes or lazy eye—is a misalignment of the eyes. Normally, the six tiny muscles attached to each eye assure that the eyes work in parallel; coordinated eye movement allows for three-dimensional vision and proper depth perception. Impairment of the eye muscles or the nerves that control them may prevent the eyes from focusing together, resulting in double vision. In young children—in whom strabismus is most prevalent—the brain reacts to the double image by ignoring signals from the deviating or weaker eye. If left untreated, this may result in permanent vision loss in the affected eye; a child will not simply outgrow strabismus. However, if the child is treated before the age of five or six, normal vision may be preserved. When strabismus occurs in adults, it is often a sign of some underlying disorder.

In divergent strabismus (shown here), the deviating eye turns outward; in convergent strabismus, the eye turns toward the bridge of the nose.

SYMPTOMS
- Uncoordinated, divergent eye movements.
- Impaired vision in the affected eye.
- Double vision.
- Faulty depth perception.

WHAT CAUSES IT?
- Impaired development of the ocular muscles may cause strabismus in children.
- Hereditary factors may play a role.
- Increased risk is associated with farsightedness (hyperopia).
- In adults, strabismus may occur as a complication of an underlying disorder, including diabetes mellitus, multiple sclerosis, cancer, and stroke.
- Fatigue, stress, or illness can sometimes cause temporary strabismus.

PREVENTION
- There is no known way to prevent strabismus.

DIAGNOSIS
- Eye examination by an ophthalmologist.
- Patient history and physical examination may be necessary, especially in adults, to diagnose an underlying disorder.

HOW TO TREAT IT
- Initial therapy involves attempts to strengthen the muscles of the weaker eye and so regain coordination of both eyes. An eye patch or eyedrops that temporarily blur the vision may be used in the unaffected eye to encourage increased use of the weakened eye.
- Eyeglasses may be prescribed to correct farsightedness and other vision defects.
- Surgical repositioning of the muscles that control eye movement may be necessary to bring about re-alignment; more than one operation may be required.

WHEN TO CALL A DOCTOR
- Call a doctor or ophthalmologist if your child's eyes seem misaligned (although occasional crossed eyes in infants less than three months old is normal and nothing to worry about).
- Call a doctor or ophthalmologist if you develop double vision.

Streptococcal Infections

WHAT IS IT?

Streptococcal infections are among the most common bacterial infections. There are many different strains of the bacteria; a number of them inhabit the mouth, intestine, and vagina without ill effect. However, these bacteria may cause infections elsewhere in the body, such as the urinary tract (see Bladder Infection for more information), or produce symptoms if the immune system fails to prevent the bacteria from proliferating. The most common site of streptococcal infection is the throat. Strep may also infect the skin, ears, tonsils, urinary tract, heart valves, and other areas of the body. Most cases of strep respond well to antibiotics, although occasionally strep may lead to rheumatic fever or acute glomerulonephritis (see these disorders for more information).

WHAT CAUSES IT?

• Streptococcal bacteria may be spread through the air by the sneeze or cough of an infected person or by physical contact. Strep spreads easily in homes, schools, and other areas where people are in close and continued contact with each other.
• Infants, the elderly, and people with weakened immune systems, such as those infected with the human immunodeficiency virus (HIV) or undergoing chemotherapy for cancer, are at greater risk for the more serious complications of strep infections.

PREVENTION

• Wash hands frequently with soap and warm water, especially after visiting public places.
• Don't share towels or drinking glasses.
• Try to limit exposure to people who are coughing or sneezing.

DIAGNOSIS

• Patient history and physical examination.
• Throat culture (if strep throat is suspected).
• Culture of any lesion or discharge.

HOW TO TREAT IT

• Treatment varies depending on the location and nature of the infection. In general, antibiotics—usually penicillin or erythromycin—are prescribed to treat strep infections and must be taken for the full term prescribed (often 10 days or more). Stopping the medication early can result in an even more virulent recurrence of the infection (rebound infection). In severe cases antibiotics may be administered by injection.
• Over-the-counter pain relievers may be used to reduce pain and fever.
• Abscesses may need to be surgically drained.

WHEN TO CALL A DOCTOR

• Call a doctor if you develop a sudden sore throat and fever.
• Call a doctor if a skin wound becomes infected, or if you or your child develops a red, crusting rash anywhere on the body.

SYMPTOMS

• Symptoms depend on the location and nature of the specific infection, but may include the following:
• Fever.
• Headache.
• Swollen lymph glands.
• General feeling of poor health.
• Fatigue.
• Loss of appetite.
• Sudden, severe sore throat that is aggravated by swallowing.
• Nasal discharge.
• Red skin rash.

Stroke

WHAT IS IT?

A stroke is a medical emergency caused either by obstruction of an artery carrying blood to the brain or rupture of one of the cerebral arteries. Lack of oxygen due to blockage of the blood supply may quickly lead to cell death and permanent brain damage, since brain cells cannot regenerate. Strokes are more likely to occur when arteries have already been substantially narrowed by atherosclerotic plaques. Blood flow through narrow arteries is reduced, and blood clots are more likely to form along the uneven surface of the plaque. A clot formed in a carotid artery in the neck or a cerebral (brain) artery can block the artery at the site. Clots may also form elsewhere, become detached, and ultimately block a cerebral artery, causing a stroke. About 80 percent of strokes are due to blockage in either an artery in the brain or in one of the carotid arteries in the neck. The remaining 20 percent of strokes result from a rupture of an artery in the brain (see Brain Hemorrhage for more information). This type of stroke is generally the most life-threatening, primarily because of the excessive pressure the hemorrhage exerts on brain tissue. Although incidence is highest among those over 65, a stroke may strike anyone at any age. Symptoms vary depending upon the portion of the

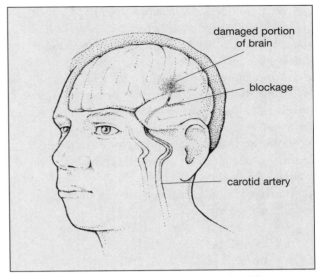

damaged portion of brain

blockage

carotid artery

The carotid arteries are the main blood vessels from the heart to the brain. In the most common type of stroke, blockage in a cerebral or carotid artery cuts off the blood supply to a portion of brain tissue.

brain affected, but they almost always come on very suddenly. There is as yet no cure, and two-thirds of cases result in permanent disability or death; indeed, strokes are the third leading cause of death in the United States. Prevention is key.

WHAT CAUSES IT?

• Blood clots that obstruct an atherosclerotic carotid or cerebral artery are the most common cause of stroke.

• An embolus (a fragment of plaque, tissue, or blood clot) may develop in the heart and travel to the brain to cause a stroke. Emboli are most likely to develop in association with cardiac arrhythmias (especially atrial fibrillation), valvular heart disease, myocardial infarction, or cardiomyopathy (see these disorders for more information).

• An aneurysm (a balloon-like weak spot in an arterial wall) in a cerebral artery may burst or leak, resulting in a stroke.

• Hypertension is the greatest risk factor for stroke.

• Severely narrowed arteries due to atherosclerosis increase the risk of stroke.

• Use of cocaine or amphetamines may boost blood pressure to dangerously high levels and cause a stroke.

• Risk is high among those who have experienced

SYMPTOMS

• Sudden, severe headache. (All stroke symptoms almost always come on suddenly.)
• Weakness or paralysis on all or on one side of the face or body.
• Numbness, and tingling in one or both arms or legs.
• Speech difficulty or loss.
• Difficulty in swallowing.
• Nausea and vomiting.
• Total blindness or partial loss of vision, double vision, dilated pupils, or crossed eyes due to partial inability to move the eye.
• Dizziness, mental confusion, or sudden loss of consciousness.
• Memory loss.

Stroke *continued*

one or more transient ischemic attacks (TIAs)—a temporary blockage in an artery that lasts for less than 24 hours (usually only a few minutes) and causes no brain damage. (See Transient Ischemic Attack for more information.)

• A family history of stroke, early or premature heart attacks, atherosclerosis, or high blood pressure, increases the risk of stroke.

• Smoking, alcohol abuse, high blood cholesterol levels, a diet high in fat (especially animal fat), obesity, lack of exercise, diabetes mellitus, and oral contraceptive use all may increase the risk of stroke.

• Risk increases with age.

PREVENTION

• Don't smoke.

• Eat a diet low in fat, cholesterol, and salt.

• Engage in moderate, regular exercise. Check with a doctor before beginning an exercise program.

• Lose weight if you are more than 20 percent overweight.

• Consume no more than two alcoholic beverages per day.

• Low daily doses of aspirin or the antiplatelet drug ticlopidine may be prescribed to reduce the chances of blood clot formation in those who have had a TIA or are otherwise at high risk for stroke.

• Hypertension must be treated aggressively.

• The anticoagulant warfarin (Coumadin) may be prescribed for those with atrial fibrillation to prevent blood clot formation.

• Patients who show evidence of substantial atherosclerotic narrowing in the carotid arteries (the two main blood vessels in the neck supplying the brain) may be good candidates for carotid endarterectomy, a surgical procedure to clear away plaque deposits in these arteries.

DIAGNOSIS

• Diagnosis is often made immediately upon examination by a doctor or emergency rescue technician.

• Blood tests are taken.

• CT (computed tomography) scans or MRI (magnetic resonance imaging) may be used to locate an abnormal blood vessel or an area of brain damage.

• Ultrasound scans of carotid arteries reveal narrowing due to atherosclerotic plaque.

• Angiography may be performed to locate the arterial blockage. In this procedure, a tiny catheter is inserted into an artery in the groin (femoral artery) and threaded up to the carotid artery in the neck. A contrast material is injected to produce a clear x-ray image of the carotid and cerebral arteries.

• An electrocardiogram (ECG or EKG) is performed to detect a cardiac arrhythmia or heart damage from a myocardial infarction.

HOW TO TREAT IT

• Emergency treatment and immediate hospitalization is necessary in the event of a stroke. Life support measures may be required.

• If the stroke is caused by arterial blockage due to a blood clot, thrombolytic (clot-dissolving) drugs such as streptokinase or anticoagulants (such as heparin or warfarin) may be administered.

• If the stroke is the result of a cerebral hemorrhage, physicians will immediately take measures to reduce blood pressure of hypertensive patients in order to minimize flow of blood from the ruptured artery.

• Long-term therapy following a stroke may include antiplatelet medications such as aspirin or dipyridamole (to prevent future clots), antihypertensives, and diuretics.

• Special railings, braces, canes, wheelchairs, or other devices may be necessary to help increase mobility for those with partial paralysis.

• Physical, speech, occupational, and emotional therapy helps patients and their families cope with major lifestyle changes.

• Those with extensive disabilities may require professional in-home medical care.

WHEN TO CALL A DOCTOR

• **EMERGENCY** Call an ambulance immediately if you or someone in your presence exhibits stroke symptoms.

Styles

WHAT IS IT?

A stye is a common problem caused by a bacterial infection of an eyelash follicle. The infection causes a small, red, painful bump to form at the base of the eyelash. Generally, the stye enlarges over several days as the infected follicle fills with pus; then it usually subsides within three to seven days, or it may rupture. The bump should not be squeezed, since this may spread the infection and cause other styes to develop. Also, the bacteria that produce a stye are contagious, so care should be taken to avoid touching the eyes or sharing towels, washcloths, and cosmetics. Styes are not a serious health risk, and they do not affect vision. Although styes often recur, they usually respond well to self-treatment. In some cases, however, an untreated stye may lead to cellulitis (a more widespread infection of the skin) of the eyelid.

WHAT CAUSES IT?

• Styes generally occur when an eyelash follicle becomes infected with staphylococcal bacteria.

When the follicle of an eyelash becomes infected, it produces a stye—a swollen, pus-filled bump on the eyelid.

DIAGNOSIS

• Diagnosis can usually be made upon visual inspection and does not normally require a doctor.
• If an abscess occurs, a culture of the pus is taken to identify the infectious agent.

HOW TO TREAT IT

• Hold a warm compress (a soft, clean towel or cloth that has been soaked in warm water and wrung dry) against the affected eye for 10 to 15 minutes. Repeat the procedure two to four times per day until the stye drains (usually three to seven days). Use a new compress each time so as not to perpetuate the infection.
• Do not squeeze the stye; let it drain on its own.
• Antibiotic eye drops or ointment may be prescribed. Use as directed and be careful not to allow the tip of the bottle or tube to touch the eyes.
• A doctor may lance and drain a stye if it persists or enlarges despite treatment.

WHEN TO CALL A DOCTOR

• Call a doctor if a stye does not respond to self-treatment within a week or two, or if it enlarges despite treatment.

> **SYMPTOMS**
> • Small, red, painful bump at the base of an eyelash.
> • A gritty sensation or a feeling that there is something in the eye.
> • Copious watering of the affected eye.

PREVENTION

• Avoid touching the eyes.
• Wash hands frequently with soap and warm water.
• Do not share towels or washcloths.
• Change your towel and pillowcase often.
• Do not share eye makeup; replace cosmetics every four to six months.

Syphilis

WHAT IS IT?

Syphilis, a bacterial infection, is a highly contagious sexually transmitted disease. Once infection occurs, the bacteria travel quickly through the bloodstream and lymphatic system of the infected person and give rise to a wide variety of symptoms. If not treated, syphilis progresses through three main stages: primary (three to four weeks after infection), secondary (four to eight weeks later), and tertiary (one to 30 years after infection). The skin lesions of both primary and secondary syphilis heal spontaneously over a period of several weeks to months. The secondary and tertiary stages are separated by a latent period during which the patient displays no symptoms and appears healthy. Latency usually lasts for years—often for the lifetime of the patient. A person infected with syphilis is extremely contagious during the primary and secondary stages, but not during the latent and tertiary phases. Adequate treatment with antibiotics during the primary or secondary stages cures the infection. Untreated syphilis that progresses to the tertiary stage may damage tissue in the heart, brain, spinal cord, eyes, and other organs, and can be fatal. Although tertiary symptoms appear in only about 30 percent of untreated patients, by the time these symptoms have developed, tissue destruction is widespread, and antibiotic treatment is no longer effective. Therefore, early detection and treatment of syphilis are crucial.

WHAT CAUSES IT?

• Infection by the *Treponema pallidum* bacterium causes syphilis.
• Syphilis is spread by sexual intercourse and anal intercourse. Those with multiple sexual partners are at higher risk. Incidence of primary syphilis in the United States had declined steadily until a resurgence occurred in the past 15 years, especially among male homosexuals.
• Infected pregnant women may transfer syphilis to the fetus. Syphilis may also be transferred to the baby during childbirth.

PREVENTION

• Use latex condoms during sexual intercourse to reduce the risk of transmission. A mutually monogamous relationship is safest.

DIAGNOSIS

• Patient history and physical examination.
• Blood tests for antibodies against the bacteria.
• Microscopic examination of fluid from lesions.
• Lumbar puncture (spinal tap).

HOW TO TREAT IT

• Intramuscular injections of penicillin can cure primary or secondary syphilis. Other antibiotics are used in people allergic to penicillin. Sexual partners may be treated as well.
• To prevent the spread of the syphilis, avoid sexual intercourse during treatment and until at least two follow-up examinations show no evidence of infection.

WHEN TO CALL A DOCTOR

• Call a doctor if you or your sexual partner develops a painless sore on the mouth or genital area.
• Call a doctor if you have had sexual contact with someone you suspect may have syphilis.

SYMPTOMS

• Primary syphilis (three to four weeks after infection): a painless ulcer (chancre) on the penis, vagina, cervix, rectal area, or mouth. Enlarged lymph nodes in the region of the chancre.
• Secondary syphilis (four to eight weeks later): low fever; headache; sore throat; general feeling of poor health; hair loss; skin rash, especially on the palms of the hands and the soles of the feet; gray plaques in the mouth; enlarged, painless lymph nodes in the neck, armpit, or groin.
• Tertiary syphilis (five to 30 years after infection): loss of balance; loss of bladder control; sudden severe pains; loss of sensation in the legs, paralysis; impotence; personality changes; dementia or insanity; blindness; symptoms of congestive heart failure due to damage to the aortic valve.

Systemic Lupus Erythematosus

WHAT IS IT?

Systemic lupus erythematosus, also known as lupus or SLE, is a persistent inflammation that may affect many organs throughout the body, including the cardiovascular, renal, neurological, and musculoskeletal systems. The precise cause of SLE is unknown. However, it is known that SLE is an autoimmune disorder: antibodies formed by the immune system attack some of the body's own cells. Inflammation typically occurs in the joints (arthritis), and inflammation of the skin may cause a characteristic butterfly rash on the face, as well as an increased sensitivity to the sun. Symptoms vary widely depending upon which organ systems are involved, and occur in a series of flare-ups or episodes separated by periods of normal or near-normal health. In severe cases SLE may lead to kidney or heart failure and can be fatal. However, SLE is often mild; many people never experience the most severe symptoms of the disease and, with treatment, are able to pursue a wide range of normal activities. Women are affected eight to 10 times more frequently than men. An increased incidence of SLE is found among people of Asian and African descent and members of some Native American tribes. SLE usually develops between the ages of 15 and 35, although it may occur at any age. Currently, treatment is aimed at relieving the severity of episodes and limiting the progression of the disease.

WHAT CAUSES IT?

• SLE is an autoimmune disorder, the exact underlying mechanisms of which remain unclear.
• Hereditary factors and sex hormones may play a role.
• Episodes may be triggered by ultraviolet radiation (as in sun exposure), infection, childbirth, abortion, or stress.
• Many drugs, including hydralazine (an antihypertensive), procainamide (a drug used to treat heart rhythm disturbances), or chlorpromazine (a tranquilizer), and certain foods, such as alfalfa sprouts, may cause a temporary SLE-like illness in some people that disappears when the medication is discontinued.
• Some theories suggest that a virus may be responsible for the development of SLE.

PREVENTION

• There is no known way to prevent SLE.

DIAGNOSIS

• Patient history and physical examination. Long-term observation may be necessary for definitive diagnosis, which requires the presence of at least four of the symptoms of SLE.
• Blood tests for autoimmune antibodies, anemia, and decreased numbers of white blood cells and platelets.
• Urine tests for excessive protein and red blood cells.

SYMPTOMS

• Fever.
• Fatigue.
• General feeling of poor health.
• Loss of appetite and weight loss.
• Abdominal pain, nausea, and vomiting.
• Headache.
• Joint pain and swelling (see Rheumatoid Arthritis).
• Red rash (butterfly rash) over both cheeks and the bridge of the nose, and rashes elsewhere on the body.
• Increased skin sensitivity to sun exposure.
• Small, painless ulcers in the mucus membranes of the nose and mouth.
• Increased susceptibility to infections (due to a weakened immune system).
• Blurred or worsening vision.
• Unusual bruising or bleeding; jaundice; dark urine; palpitations or irregular heartbeat (see Anemia, Hemolytic).
• Enlarged glands (lymph nodes).
• Swelling of the abdomen, the tissues around the eyes, and the ankles; weight gain; shortness of breath; decreased amount of urine (see Nephrotic Syndrome).
• Cough and chest pain (see Pleurisy).
• A tingling sensation or pain in the muscles, stiffness, spasms, seizures, numbness, or temporary paralysis.
• Emotional depression, anxiety, mental confusion, personality changes, or psychosis.

Systemic Lupus Erythematosus *continued*

• A kidney biopsy may be done. The doctor inserts a needle into the kidney through the back (under local anesthesia) to extract a small sample of tissue.
• Lumbar puncture (spinal tap).
• CT (computed tomography) scans or MRI (magnetic resonance imaging).

HOW TO TREAT IT

• Treatment may be unnecessary for mild symptoms.
• Take aspirin or other over-the-counter pain relievers to reduce fever and treat minor pain.
• Apply warm compresses to relieve joint pain.
• Get plenty of rest. People with SLE often need over 10 hours of sleep per night and may need more during episodes of active disease.
• Oral corticosteroids, such as prednisone, may be prescribed to hold the immune system in check and so treat many of the different symptoms of SLE.
• Immunosuppressive drugs, including higher doses of corticosteroids as well as chemotherapeutic medications, may be prescribed to subdue the immune system.
• Hydroxychloroquine, an antimalarial drug, may be prescribed to relieve skin rash and pain from arthritis.
• Anticonvulsants may be prescribed to treat seizures.
• Warfarin sodium, an anticoagulant, may be pre-scribed to prevent blood clots and reduce the possibility of heart attack and stroke.
• Antibiotics are prescribed to treat associated bacterial infections.
• Your doctor may change your prescriptions for certain medications if they are suspected of causing drug-induced SLE.
• Apply a sunscreen lotion containing PABA (para-aminobenzoic acid) with a sun protection factor (SPF) of 15 or higher. Avoid exposure to direct sunlight between 10 AM and 2 PM whenever possible.
• Your doctor may recommend a low-salt diet. Calcium and vitamin D supplements may be advised for some patients.
• Dialysis may be needed to treat kidney failure. This procedure filters the blood artificially, removing waste products and excess fluid when the kidneys cannot (see Renal Failure, Chronic, for more information).
• A kidney transplant is an alternative to dialysis in cases of kidney failure.

WHEN TO CALL A DOCTOR

• Make an appointment with a doctor if you develop symptoms of SLE.
• Make an appointment with a doctor if, after being diagnosed with SLE, symptoms worsen or new symptoms develop.

Tapeworm Infestation

WHAT IS IT?

Three types of tapeworms—flat, segmented worms—can inhabit the digestive tract of humans: *Diphyllobothrium latum* (fish tapeworm), *Taenia saginatum* (beef tapeworm), and *Taenia solium* (pork tapeworm). Once inside the intestine, a tapeworm attaches itself to the intestinal wall with the suction cups and hooks on its head, and absorbs food through the entire surface of its body. Tapeworms vary in length from less than an inch to more than 30 feet, and some may survive for over 25 years in the body. Tapeworm larvae are most often ingested while eating raw or undercooked fish, beef, or pork; poor sanitary practices increase the risk of infestation. In humans, the adult worm remains in the intestine; however, the larvae of some tapeworms such as *Taenia solium* may form cysts in organs throughout the body (known as cysticercosis and echinococcosis). While tapeworm infestation generally causes few if any symptoms, the cysts formed by the larvae may produce serious and widespread symptoms. Tapeworm infestation, although unpleasant, is easily treated.

WHAT CAUSES IT?

• Ingestion of raw or undercooked freshwater fish, beef, or pork that contain tapeworm cysts causes tapeworm infestation.

SYMPTOMS

• Hunger, fatigue, loss of appetite, and unintentional weight loss.
• Abdominal pain or discomfort.
• Diarrhea and excess gas.
• Nausea and vomiting.
• Anal itching or inflammation.
• White, mobile, ribbonlike worm segments in stool, clothing, or bedclothes.
• Fever, headache, muscle pain, seizures, bone fractures, eye pain, vision loss, memory loss, and personality changes (in advanced cases of cysticercosis and echinococcosis).
• Symptoms of pernicious anemia (see this disorder for more) due to the uptake of vitamin B_{12} by the fish tapeworm.

• Fish from lakes polluted with raw sewage are more likely to be infested.
• Poor sanitary conditions may promote infestation by tapeworm eggs and lead to cysticercosis or echinococcosis.

PREVENTION

• Thoroughly cook fish, beef, and pork before eating.
• Avoid dishes made with raw meat or fish, such as steak tartare, sushi, and ceviche.
• Wash hands vigorously with soap and warm water after using the toilet and before handling food.

DIAGNOSIS

• Patient history and physical examination.
• Stool samples or anal scrapings to detect eggs or worm segments.
• Abdominal x-rays. X-rays may be taken of other areas if cysticercosis or echinococcosis is suspected.
• CT (computed tomography) scans or MRI (magnetic resonance imaging) may be done to detect cysts in the brain.

HOW TO TREAT IT

• Worm-killing medications, such as niclosamide or praziquantel, are prescribed. The duration of treatment and strength of dosage depend upon the type of tapeworm.
• Injections of vitamin B_{12} may be administered to treat pernicious anemia associated with fish tapeworm infestation.
• Surgery is performed to excise cysts when possible. Cysts may be killed with an injection of an alcohol or saline solution prior to surgery.
• Mebendazole, flubendazole, or albendazole may be prescribed to destroy cysts in patients for whom surgery is not advised, or who have extensive cysts.
• Corticosteroid drugs may be prescribed to treat inflammation caused by a cyst.
• Anticonvulsant drugs may be prescribed to control seizures.

WHEN TO CALL A DOCTOR

• Call a doctor if you notice worm segments or eggs in your stool or clothing, or if you develop unexplained hunger, fatigue, nausea or abdominal pain.

Temporomandibular Joint Syndrome

WHAT IS IT?
Temporomandibular joint syndrome is characterized by pain and inflammation in the temporomandibular joints (TMJs), where both sides of the lower jaw (mandible) are attached to the skull. Normally, the muscles and ligaments in the TMJ stabilize, cushion, and guide the mandible's movements during eating, speaking, and other activities. TMJ syndrome occurs when these muscles and ligaments do not work together in a coordinated manner. For unknown reasons, 90 percent of TMJ sufferers are women.

SYMPTOMS
- Headaches; earaches; or muscle aches in the neck, shoulders, or upper back.
- Pain and swelling in the jaw or at the TMJ.
- Clicking, popping, or scraping noises upon opening or closing the jaw.
- The jaw may temporarily lock in position.
- Tenderness of the muscles used for chewing.

WHAT CAUSES IT?
- Clenching and grinding the teeth (bruxism) is a common cause of TMJ syndrome. Bruxism often occurs during sleep, although the sleeper may be unaware of it.
- Emotional stress may lead to bruxism.
- Improper alignment of the teeth (malocclusion) is a common cause of TMJ syndrome.
- Bad posture (for example, thrusting the chin forward), a blow to the jaw, whiplash, or eating chewy foods can promote TMJ pain.
- Arthritis is an uncommon cause of TMJ syndrome.

PREVENTION
- Try not to grind the teeth or clench the jaw as a reaction to stress.

- See your dentist regularly.
- Practice correct posture to avoid muscle strain in the head and neck.

DIAGNOSIS
- Patient history and exam by a dentist or doctor.
- X-rays, CT (computed tomography) scans, or MRI (magnetic resonance imaging) of the TMJ may be done (although they usually show no abnormality).

HOW TO TREAT IT
- Follow prevention tips above.
- Take a nonprescription pain reliever.
- A hot or cold pack may provide temporary pain relief.
- Tranquilizers or muscle relaxants may be prescribed, and to reduce severe inflammation, corticosteroids may be injected into the TMJ.
- At times when symptoms are particularly troublesome, eat soft foods and avoid chewing gum.
- Your dentist may grind tooth surfaces to correct malocclusion, prescribe a removable plastic or rubber mold that fits over the teeth at night to prevent bruxism, or prepare a type of splint to be worn in the mouth during the day.
- Biofeedback (a technique for gaining voluntary control over certain of the body's reactions to stress and other stimuli) may be recommended. Relaxation training or physical therapy to lessen muscle tension may also be advised.
- In severe cases surgery may be recommended to repair damaged joint tissue and to correct bone defects. Surgery should only be considered as a last resort, however, because of the risk of severe complications. Always get a second opinion.

WHEN TO CALL A DOCTOR
- Call a doctor if symptoms of TMJ syndrome interfere with normal activities.

Tendinitis

WHAT IS IT?

Tendinitis is inflammation of a tendon, one of the fibrous cords that join a muscle to a bone. Injury or repetitive overuse can cause microscopic tears and painful swelling in a tendon. Sites most commonly affected include the shoulder (golfer's shoulder), the elbow (tennis elbow), the wrist (DeQuervain's wrist), the fingers (trigger finger), and the ankle (Achilles heel). When the muscles in the affected area are used regularly despite pain, the injured tendon may be slow to heal. While many cases of tendinitis last no more than two weeks and are usually alleviated by rest and proper conditioning, repeated use of the injured tendon may lead to chronic tendinitis, characterized by scarring of the involved tissues and limited flexibility. Those over 40 are most prone to the chronic form of tendinitis.

SYMPTOMS
- Pain in the affected area.
- Tenderness, often worse at night, disturbing sleep.
- Limited joint movement.
- Muscle spasms concurrent with pain.
- Sudden pain, often accompanied by a snapping sound, with the rupture of an Achilles tendon.

WHAT CAUSES IT?
- Overuse due to prolonged, repetitive movements as required by tennis, golf, bowling, and certain occupations, like carpentry and painting.
- Sudden physical trauma, such as falling on an arm, twisting an ankle, or lifting heavy objects.
- Inadequate conditioning or insufficient warm-up prior to exercise.
- Degenerative changes owing to aging and years of continual use.
- Calcium deposits in a tendon (calcific tendinitis).

PREVENTION
- Avoid highly repetitious movements, or interrupt them with activities requiring other muscle groups.
- Engage in regular, moderate exercise to maintain strength and flexibility.
- Be sure to stretch and warm up adequately before engaging in exercise or other demanding physical activity.
- Use flexible-soled footwear with good support when exercising, and use elastic ankle supports, especially if you have weak ankles.

DIAGNOSIS
- Patient history including recent physical activity.
- Physical examination may include range-of-motion tests to determine the area and extent of injury.
- Arthrography (injection of a contrast material into a joint to create a clear x-ray image of soft tissues) may be used to identify tendon damage.
- Ultrasound or MRI (magnetic resonance imaging) scans may be used to identify minor tears.

HOW TO TREAT IT
- Rest is essential, although gentle exercise may be advised to prevent stiffness. Slings or splints may be prescribed for a few days to immobilize the injured area.
- Take over-the-counter anti-inflammatory drugs like aspirin.
- Ice packs should be used immediately after an injury to reduce swelling; later, hot compresses may soothe discomfort.
- Corticosteroids may be injected directly into the affected area to relieve pain and inflammation (not recommended for Achilles tendinitis, where injections may weaken or rupture the tendon).
- Surgery to repair the tendon may be required if the tendon is torn.
- Temporarily switch to low-impact exercise, like bicycling or swimming, if you suspect high-impact exercise is responsible.

WHEN TO CALL A DOCTOR
- Call a doctor if muscle or joint pain persists for more than two weeks and interferes with ordinary activities despite treatment with rest and pain relievers.

Testicular Cancer

WHAT IS IT?

Testicular cancer is the growth of malignant cells in the testicles. In almost all cases only one testicle is involved. While relatively rare, testicular cancer is the most common cancer among young men; incidence is highest between the ages of 15 and 34, and quite rare beyond age 40. The disease disproportionately affects white men. Prognosis depends heavily upon whether or not the cancer has spread to other organs, but is often good, and the cure rate is very high when testicular cancer is detected and treated early.

WHAT CAUSES IT?

• The exact cause is unknown, but the incidence of testicular cancer is significantly higher among men in whom one or both testicles failed to descend from the abdominal cavity into the scrotum prior to birth (cryptorchism).
• Other predisposing factors include a history of inguinal hernia in childhood (see Inguinal Hernia) and testicular inflammation that occurs in conjunction with mumps (see Orchitis and Mumps).

SYMPTOMS
• A firm, painless lump or nodule on one of the testicles.
• A feeling of heaviness or hardness in a testicle.
• Rarely, testicular pain.
• Breast growth or nipple tenderness.
• In advanced cases: swollen lymph glands; abdominal or back pain; urinary difficulty; fatigue; weight loss; cough or breathing difficulty (due to spread of cancer to the lungs).

PREVENTION

• There is no way to prevent testicular cancer, but vigilant monthly self-examination can aid in early detection, which promises a very favorable prognosis. The best time to perform self-examination is after a warm shower, when the scrotum is soft and pliable.

DIAGNOSIS

• Patient history and physical examination are needed. A special bright light can be shined through the scrotum to aid in diagnosis; tumors will appear opaque, while other abnormalities (such as a hydrocele or a spermatocele) will appear translucent.
• Blood tests for specific biochemical markers of testicular cancer can be used to track the response to treatment and detect the recurrence of cancer.
• An ultrasound scan can confirm the presence of a solid mass.
• Chest x-rays and CT (computed tomography) scans of the abdomen and pelvis are used to evaluate the stage of any tumors and to determine whether cancer has spread beyond the testicle. Treatment strategy depends heavily upon results of these tests and the type of cell causing the cancer, determined by microscopic examination of testicular tissue.

HOW TO TREAT IT

• Once a tumor is detected by diagnostic procedures, the affected testicle must be removed. A biopsy to confirm diagnosis is not done since it may promote the spread of the cancer.
• The course of further treatment depends on the cell type of the tumor. Seminomas are treated with radiation to pelvic and abdominal lymph nodes. Other types of cancer (nonseminomas) require surgical removal of these lymph nodes.
• Chemotherapy is used if either type of cancer has spread to other sites in the body. These treatments often result in infertility.
• Men who discover they have testicular cancer and wish to have children in the future may consider preserving sperm in a sperm bank prior to treatment. The approximate two-week delay in therapy appears to have little effect on outcome.
• The removed testicle may be replaced with a prosthesis; fertility is maintained if the other testicle is unaffected. If need be, regular hormone injections can be given to preserve normal sexual functioning.

WHEN TO CALL A DOCTOR

• Make an appointment with your doctor right away if you discover a lump on one of your testicles. While any testicular abnormality is cause for concern, an actual lump is frequently a sign of cancer, and the sooner treatment is sought, the greater the likelihood of a complete cure.

Testicular Torsion

WHAT IS IT?

Each testicle is suspended within the scrotum from one of the two spermatic cords. These cords, in addition to providing a conduit for sperm manufactured in the testis, also contain blood vessels that supply the testicle. Testicular torsion involves an abnormal twisting of a testicle and its spermatic cord, so that testicular blood supply is cut off (strangulation). The condition is extremely painful, and if prompt treatment is not obtained, permanent damage may occur within

SYMPTOMS

- Excruciating pain and tenderness in the affected testicle. Pain may radiate into the lower abdomen.
- Swelling, unusual firmness, and redness of the scrotum. Affected testicle may appear to be positioned higher than normal.
- Nausea and vomiting.
- Faintness or fainting.

hours, rendering the affected testicle unable to produce sperm. In 90 percent of cases, torsion involves only one testicle; sperm production still occurs in the unaffected testicle, and fertility persists despite a diminished sperm count. In rare cases the testicle somehow becomes untwisted by itself, resulting in immediate relief; subsequent evaluation by a physician is essential nonetheless, so that recurrence can be prevented and more serious disorders, including testicular cancer, may be ruled out. Testicular torsion is most common between the ages of 12 and 18, although it can happen at any age, including infancy.

WHAT CAUSES IT?

- Testicular torsion usually occurs spontaneously for no apparent reason; indeed, it may even occur during sleep. The patient may be predisposed to the condition because of a congenital abnormality or weakness in the structures within the scrotum.

- Torsion sometimes occurs following very strenuous activity.

PREVENTION

- Testicular torsion is difficult to anticipate and thus difficult to prevent; in any case, use an athletic supporter when engaged in strenuous physical activities.

DIAGNOSIS

- Patient history and physical examination suggest the diagnosis. Since testicular torsion is an emergency, treatment is generally initiated at once, without any special tests.
- An ultrasound scan may be done to rule out other disorders (such as epididymitis or strangulated hernia) that produce similar symptoms.
- Diagnosis is confirmed by visual inspection of the twisted spermatic cord during the minor surgical procedure used to correct testicular torsion.

HOW TO TREAT IT

- Immediate medical treatment is imperative. The doctor will first attempt to properly reposition the testicle by gentle manipulation.
- If manipulation fails, a small incision is made in the scrotum and the testicle is rotated to untwist the spermatic cord.
- In most cases—whether torsion is corrected by manipulation or surgery—the testicle is surgically anchored to the side of the scrotum (orchiopexy) to prevent recurrences. As a precaution, the unaffected testicle may be anchored in place too.
- If treatment is not received soon enough (within a few hours) and the testicle has begun to atrophy and die, it may have to be removed (orchiectomy) and replaced with a prosthesis.

WHEN TO CALL A DOCTOR

- **EMERGENCY** Get immediate medical attention for any severe testicular pain or injury. Even if the pain eases on its own, the likelihood of recurrence or complications warrants examination by a doctor.

Tetanus

WHAT IS IT?

Tetanus is a life-threatening disease caused by a toxin produced by bacteria that typically enter the body as a dormant form (spore) through a deep cut or puncture wound. The spores require an environment with a low oxygen content for about seven to 10 days in order to be activated to the growing form of the bacteria that produces the toxin. The toxin travels along nerves to the spinal cord, where it produces muscle rigidity and spasms. Tetanus is sometimes called lockjaw, because difficulty opening the mouth is often the first symptom, and rigidity may become so severe the jaw is frozen shut. The bacterial spores of *Clostridium tetani* are found worldwide in soil, dust, animal feces, and, occasionally, human feces. Incidence is highest in rural areas with warm climates or in any population that is not immunized or is only partially immunized. Persons over 50 are most commonly affected, usually because they have not gotten booster vaccinations. Severity ranges from mild muscle stiffness to convulsive spasms that can choke or suffocate the victim by blocking the respiratory airway. The illness usually lasts from four to six weeks, but infection rarely occurs when a person is properly immunized. Aggressive treatment has reduced the overall mortality rate to less than 25 percent in the United States, and incidence is now rare in this country.

SYMPTOMS

- Muscle rigidity and pain, typically in the jaw, neck, back, and abdomen.
- Muscle spasms, often first felt in the jaw and neck, that may progress to painful spasms throughout the body.
- Pain and tingling at the wound site.
- Swallowing or breathing difficulty.
- Grimacing due to involuntary constriction of facial muscles.
- Irritability.
- Drooling.
- In severe cases: high fever, profuse sweating, rapid heartbeat, or heart rhythm disturbances.

WHAT CAUSES IT?

- Bacterial infection from *C. tetani*, which usually enters the body through a wound—for example, a puncture from a nail. Less often, tetanus follows a burn, surgery, or injection of illicit drugs into the skin.

PREVENTION

- Immunization should be initiated in early infancy. The DTP vaccine (diphtheria, tetanus, and pertussis) is most often used.
- Get a booster shot every ten years or after sustaining a deep wound.
- Clean wounds with soap and water and apply an antiseptic, such as hydrogen peroxide.

DIAGNOSIS

- Patient history should include any prior tetanus immunization, allergic reactions to immunizations or penicillin, and recent wounds.
- Diagnosis is generally based on characteristic clinical findings.
- Wound cultures may be taken, although not all patients with tetanus produce a positive test result.

HOW TO TREAT IT

- Deep, often surgical, cleansing of the wound is commonly performed to eliminate invading bacteria.
- Antitoxin should be administered immediately to neutralize the bacterial toxin.
- Antibiotics (usually penicillin) are administered intravenously.
- Muscle relaxants may be used to relieve muscle stiffness.
- Neuromuscular blockers (drugs that block nerve-to-muscle signals) may be administered to control violent spasms, especially if they threaten breathing.
- For patients with severe breathing difficulty, tracheostomy (the implantation of a breathing tube through a surgical opening in the throat) may be needed, along with mechanical ventilation.
- Tetanus vaccine may be administered.

WHEN TO CALL A DOCTOR

- **EMERGENCY** Get immediate medical attention whether or not a wound is present if you begin to suffer from unusual muscle spasms and stiffness.

Thrombophlebitis

WHAT IS IT?

Thrombophlebitis is inflammation of a vein (usually in an extremity, especially one of the legs) that occurs in response to a blood clot in the vessel. When it occurs in a vein near the surface of the skin, it is known as superficial thrombophlebitis, a minor disorder commonly identified by a red, tender vein. Deep-vein thrombophlebitis (affecting the larger veins further below the skin's surface) is more serious. It may produce less-pronounced symptoms at first—indeed, half of all cases are asymptomatic—but carries the risks of pulmonary embolism (when the clot detaches from its place of origin and travels to the lung) and chronic venous insufficiency (impaired outflow of blood through the veins), resulting in dermatitis, increased pigmentation, and swelling. Thrombophlebitis is common; incidence is higher among women and older people.

> ### SYMPTOMS
> - Superficial thrombophlebitis: a red, engorged, cordlike vein, associated with localized swelling, pain, or tenderness.
> - Deep-vein thrombophlebitis: generalized swelling, warmth, and redness in the affected limb; distention of superficial veins; bluish skin color in the limb or toes (cyanosis); rarely, fever and chills.

WHAT CAUSES IT?

- Stagnation of blood flow due to immobility. This is common among bedridden patients (such as heart patients and those who have undergone any type of major or orthopedic surgery, especially of the hip or knee), as well as healthy persons who must sit or lie still for an extended period—for example, on a long flight or car ride.
- Blood vessel injury, caused by trauma, intravenous catheters or needles, chemotherapeutic agents, or infectious organisms.
- Conditions that increase the tendency for blood to coagulate, such as a familial deficiency in anticlotting factors or disorders like systemic lupus erythematosus.
- Pregnancy and varicose veins are associated with a higher risk of superficial vein thrombophlebitis.
- Deep-vein thrombophlebitis is associated with a number of different cancers.

PREVENTION

- Stand up and walk around periodically on long trips.
- Following a heart attack or major surgery, low doses of an anticoagulant such as heparin or warfarin may be recommended. Getting up and walking around again as soon as possible is also advised.

DIAGNOSIS

- Superficial thrombophlebitis can usually be diagnosed from patient history and physical examination alone. Deep-vein thrombophlebitis is more elusive and often requires further tests.
- Venography (x-rays following the injection of a contrast material into the affected vein) is a highly accurate means of identifying an obstructing clot.
- Ultrasound may be used to identify altered blood flow caused by an obstructing clot.

HOW TO TREAT IT

- Superficial thrombophlebitis may be treated with warm compresses and anti-inflammatory drugs to relieve discomfort, and elevation of the affected limb to reduce swelling. A few days of rest are advised.
- Hospitalization may be required for deep-vein thrombophlebitis. Bed rest and elevation of the affected limb are essential. An anticoagulant, usually heparin, is administered intravenously for seven to 10 days to inhibit further clotting. Oral anticoagulants such as warfarin are then given for three to 12 months depending on the site of the thrombophlebitis.
- Thrombolytic (clot dissolving) agents such as streptokinase or urokinase may be injected in some cases.
- Special elastic support stockings may be prescribed to aid circulation in the lower limbs.
- Surgery may be advised to tie off the affected vein to prevent the clot from migrating to the lungs (pulmonary embolism).

WHEN TO CALL A DOCTOR

- Call a doctor if you have a painful, swollen vein that does not disappear in a few weeks, or if you have unexplained swelling in an arm or leg.

Thyroid Cancer

WHAT IS IT?

Thyroid cancer is the growth of malignant cells in the thyroid, a gland comprising two large lobes flanking the windpipe (trachea) at the base of the neck. There are four basic types of thyroid cancer: papillary, follicular, anaplastic, and medullary. Papillary carcinoma accounts for over 80 percent of thyroid cancers and fortunately is the least malignant; such tumors tend to grow very slowly and often take years to spread to other sites. Follicular carcinoma, the second most common type, is also slow growing, but it may spread more quickly, especially to the lungs and to bone tissue. Medullary carcinomas are considerably more rare; they are aggressive but highly curable if detected and treated while still confined exclusively to the thyroid. Anaplastic carcinomas (giant cell variety) are highly malignant—death usually occurs within six months of diagnosis. They are very rare in younger people but a frequent type of thyroid cancer in older people. The majority of cases of thyroid cancer occurs between the ages of 25 and 65, and women are more commonly affected than men. While prognosis depends heavily upon the type of malignancy involved and the age of the patient, outlook is generally quite good, and the mortality rate is low.

WHAT CAUSES IT?

• The cause of thyroid cancer is unknown, but previous radiation therapy to the thyroid area (for acne, enlarged thymus gland, tonsils, or adenoids) is a significant risk factor, especially when it has been administered during infancy or early childhood. Malignancies may appear as early as five or as late as 30 years after radiation.

• Exposure to radioactive fallout is associated with an increased incidence of thyroid cancer.

• Medullary carcinoma frequently occurs as a genetic disorder in members of the same family. Familial medullary carcinoma is often associated with a type of adrenal tumor (see Pheochromocytoma) and overgrowth of the parathyroid glands (see Hyperparathyroidism).

• Papillary and follicular carcinoma (the two most common types) also appear to be linked to hereditary factors.

PREVENTION

• Avoid x-rays to the neck or upper chest areas as much as possible.

• Frequent screening for thyrocalcitonin levels (see Diagnosis below) in those with a family history of medullary cancer is advised to detect cancer at the earliest stage.

DIAGNOSIS

• Patient history should include any childhood x-rays or other radiation treatments, as well as any family history of thyroid cancer.

• Physical examination of the nodule to identify whether it is solitary or part of a cluster, common in benign goiters.

• A fine-needle biopsy (use of a small-gauge needle and syringe to take a tissue sample for examination under a microscope) is done to identify malignant cells.

• When medullary carcinoma is suspected, blood levels of thyrocalcitonin, a thyroid hormone, are measured, often following intravenous administration of pentagastrin, a synthetic form of a hormone that stimulates the secretion of stomach acid. High levels of thyrocalcitonin indicate medullary carcinoma.

• Radioiodine thyroid scanning may be used to determine if the nodule is "cold," or nonfunctioning; 20 percent of cold nodules are malignant.

• Ultrasound may determine the consistency of the tumor or mass.

SYMPTOMS

• A firm or hard, usually painless lump in the front of the neck.
• Swelling in the neck.
• Swallowing difficulty.
• Hoarseness or changes in the voice.
• Cough, possibly bloody.
• Breathing difficulty.
• Unexplained bone fractures (occurs with follicular carcinoma).
• Severe diarrhea (occurs with medullary carcinoma).

Thyroid Cancer *continued*

• Suppressive doses of thyroid hormone may be given to see whether the nodule shrinks or disappears, indicating a benign tumor.

HOW TO TREAT IT

• Partial or often near-total surgical removal of the thyroid (thyroidectomy) is done in almost all cases. Removal of surrounding lymph nodes and other tissues may also be warranted.

• The absence of thyroid tissue following thyroidectomy requires lifetime supplementation with thyroid hormone (thyroxine), which also reduces the risk of cancer recurrence.

• Radioactive iodine therapy may be used to destroy malignant thyroid tissue left behind after thyroidectomy or to treat thyroid cancer that has spread to the lungs or bone.

• Treatment for rare anaplastic carcinoma primarily involves supportive therapy to make the patient as comfortable as possible.

WHEN TO CALL A DOCTOR

• Call a doctor as soon as you detect an unusual lump in your neck, especially if it rapidly increases in size. While thyroid cancer is rare, all such growths warrant examination.

Thyroid Nodules

WHAT IS IT?

Thyroid nodules are solid lumps arising in the thyroid gland. The thyroid, consisting of two large lobes on either side of the windpipe at the base of the neck, produces thyroid hormone, which regulates body growth and metabolism. Nodules usually grow slowly over many years. They appear singularly or in clusters (benign nodular goiter) and usually are not detectable until they have grown to at least one centimeter in size. The greatest concern of a solitary nodule is the possibility of cancer, although this is uncommon. The vast majority of solitary nodules are cysts or benign tumors (adenomas) and affect about 4 percent of the adult population. Nodules are classified according to their production of thyroid hormone. "Warm" nodules mimic normal thyroid cells in this regard. "Hot" nodules overproduce thyroid hormone (see Hyperthyroidism). "Cold" nodules are nonfunctioning and represent a greater cancer risk (see Thyroid Cancer). Determining whether a nodule is hot, warm, or cold is generally the first step in determining subsequent treatment.

SYMPTOMS

- A solid, usually painless lump in the front of the neck, near the windpipe or Adam's apple.
- Possibly, symptoms of hyperthyroidism (see Hyperthyroidism) in the case of "hot" nodules.
- Substantial swelling in the neck in cases of benign nodular goiter.
- Breathing or swallowing difficulty, if nodules grow large enough to become obstructions (rare).

WHAT CAUSES IT?

- The cause of thyroid nodules is unknown, but incidence is higher among people who received x-ray treatment to the thyroid area in infancy or childhood. Women are affected more often than men.

PREVENTION

- There is no known way to prevent thyroid nodules.

DIAGNOSIS

- Patient history including any x-ray treatments in infancy or childhood.
- Physical examination to determine whether the lump is solitary or in a cluster.
- A thyroid scan with radioactive iodine or technetium to identify if the nodule is hot, warm, or cold.
- Thyroid-function tests to measure thyroid hormone production and iodine uptake levels.
- Ultrasound scans to identify cysts.
- If the nodule is cold, fine-needle biopsy (use of a small-gauge needle and syringe to take a tissue sample for examination under a microscope) is used to rule out cancer.

HOW TO TREAT IT

- If a needle biopsy shows no evidence of cancer and thyroid-function tests are normal, regular follow-up with thyroid-function tests is all that is required.
- If the nodule is a fluid-filled cyst, needle drainage may be done.
- Hot nodules associated with hyperthyroidism are treated with radioactive iodine or surgery.
- Partial or near-total thyroidectomy is recommended if cancerous cells are detected in a needle biopsy.
- Treatment for hypothyroidism may subsequently be needed if excess thyroid tissue is removed or destroyed by radioactive iodine therapy (see Hypothyroidism).
- If the findings are equivocal on fine-needle biopsy, thyroid hormone may be administered to observe whether the nodule shrinks over the ensuing six to 12 months.

WHEN TO CALL A DOCTOR

- Call a doctor as soon as possible if you detect an unusual lump in your neck. A complete evaluation is imperative.

Thyroiditis

WHAT IS IT?

Thyroiditis is inflammation of the thyroid, the gland at the base of the neck that produces thyroid hormone (thyroxine), crucial in the regulation of body growth and metabolism. There are three types of thyroiditis: acute, subacute, and chronic. Although inflammation of the thyroid gland is common to all three, they differ significantly in terms of symptoms, cause, and outcome. Acute thyroiditis is extremely rare. Subacute thyroiditis is self-limited, meaning it resolves spontaneously without treatment, usually in a matter of months. Chronic thyroiditis, the most serious of the three, may lead to tissue destruction and scarring of the thyroid; indeed, it is the leading cause of insufficient thyroid hormone production in adults (see Hypothyroidism).

SYMPTOMS

- Acute thyroiditis: fever; swelling, pain, or tenderness in the front of the neck.
- Subacute thyroiditis: pain and tenderness in the front of the neck, especially upon swallowing or the application of pressure; fever; local swelling; pain in one or both ears. Symptoms may develop gradually or come on suddenly.
- Chronic thyroiditis: painless swelling in the neck (see Goiter); symptoms of hypothyroidism (see Hypothyroidism), including fatigue, unexplained weight gain, constipation, dry skin, and intolerance to cold.

WHAT CAUSES IT?

- Acute thyroiditis is rare, resulting from direct infection of the thyroid following a penetrating neck wound or, more rarely still, a bacterial infection elsewhere in the body that spreads to the thyroid via the bloodstream.
- The cause of subacute thyroiditis is unknown, although it is often preceded by a viral infection of the upper respiratory tract, suggesting some association with the body's response to infection.
- The cause of chronic thyroiditis is also uncertain, but evidence is strong that it involves autoimmune activity (an attack by the body's defenses on its own healthy tissue). Hereditary factors may play a role.
- A painless and typically temporary form of thyroiditis affects about one in 20 women after they give birth (postpartum thyroiditis). Either hyper- or hypothyroidism may occur transiently.

PREVENTION

- There is no known way to prevent thyroiditis.

DIAGNOSIS

- Patient history and physical exam are necessary.
- Blood levels of thyroid hormone, thyroid-stimulating hormone, and antibodies to the thyroid gland are measured.
- A scan of the thyroid may be taken after administration of radioactive iodine to evaluate thyroid function.
- A fine-needle biopsy, extracting tissue directly from the thyroid, may be done to rule out thyroid cancer in patients with chronic thyroiditis.

HOW TO TREAT IT

- Antibiotics are use to treat the infection associated with acute thyroiditis.
- Because subacute thyroiditis resolves on its own, treatment is aimed at relieving symptoms only. Aspirin or other pain relievers may ease inflammation and tenderness. In more severe cases the drug triiodothyronine may be prescribed; it usually brings an end to symptoms within a month. Corticosteroids such as prednisone may sometimes be used.
- Some patients with subacute thyroiditis may develop transient hyper- or hypothyroidism, which may require brief periods of treatment with, respectively, either an antithyroid medication or thyroid hormone.
- Treatment for chronic thyroiditis primarily consists of thyroid hormone (thyroxine) replacement to correct hypothyroidism (see Hypothyroidism for more).

WHEN TO CALL A DOCTOR

- Call a doctor if you suffer from pain or swelling in the neck; pain in the ears, lower jaw, or back of the head; fatigue, unexplained weight gain, or other symptoms of hypothyroidism.

Tics

WHAT IS IT?

Tics are abrupt, involuntary, repeated movements (motors tics) or vocalized sounds (vocal or phonic tics). They usually develop during childhood and may gradually disappear with time or persist into adulthood. Their nature, severity, and frequency vary from case to case. With effort, tics can usually be suppressed for short periods of time. They tend to become more pronounced during periods of stress or excitement and disappear when the person is distracted or deeply absorbed. The most common and severe condition that causes tics is called Gilles de la Tourette's syndrome. More common among boys

SYMPTOMS

- Repetitive movements or sounds, usually first appearing during childhood. Motor tics usually involve one or more muscles groups in the face, shoulders, or arms, but other parts of the body may be affected. They may be simple (blinking, raising the eyebrows, nose or mouth twitching, head turning, shoulder shrugging, or a specific facial grimace) or complex (leg kicking, jumping). Vocal or phonic tics also vary in complexity from sniffing or throat clearing to echolalia (compulsive repeating of words or phrases uttered by other people) or coprolalia (compulsive swearing and repeating vulgar phrases).
- Symptoms of Tourette's syndrome: multiple, complex motor tics; grunting, barking, or coprolalia; obsessive compulsive behavior, poor attention span, learning difficulties, and sleep disorders.

than girls, Tourette's syndrome is usually a lifelong illness that normally begins before the age of 21. It is characterized by frequent, multiple motor and vocal tics that may wax and wane throughout the course of the illness. Tourette's syndrome may also be accompanied by behavioral disturbances, such as

obsessive-compulsive disorder, attention and learning difficulties, or sleep disorders. Treatment of tics varies considerably depending on the nature and severity of the individual case. Mild cases require no treatment or can be treated with behavioral therapy. Tics that cause discomfort or embarrassment, or that otherwise interfere with daily life, may be treated with one of several drugs. Tourette's syndrome usually requires lifetime drug treatment.

WHAT CAUSES IT?

- The cause of simple tics is unknown. They may develop as a means of relieving psychological tension.
- Tourette's syndrome is usually genetically inherited.

PREVENTION

- There is no known way to prevent tics or Tourette's syndrome.

DIAGNOSIS

- Medical history and physical examination are necessary.

HOW TO TREAT IT

- In people with simple, transient tics, symptoms usually disappear without treatment within one to several years.
- Mild cases may be treated with behavioral therapy, during which the patient learns to control the tic.
- Drug therapy is indicated in more severe, persistent cases (such as Tourette's syndrome), when tics cause physical or social discomfort. Several types of medications can be effective, including anticonvulsants, antipsychotic drugs, tranquilizers, antidepressants, and the antihypertensive drug clonidine. These are all powerful drugs that may produce bothersome side effects.

WHEN TO CALL A DOCTOR

- If you or your child develops a simple tic or multiple tics, make an appointment with a doctor. You may be referred to a behavioral therapist or other specialist for further examination or treatment.

Tinnitus

WHAT IS IT?

Tinnitus is the perception of sound when there is no external source of the sound in the environment. The perceived sound is variously described as ringing, buzzing, hissing, or even roaring, whistling, or pounding. Almost everyone experiences intermittent tinnitus once in a while (especially in a quiet room), and it is nothing to worry about. Persistent tinnitus, however, can be extremely distressing psychologically, may interfere with sleep, and is sometimes a sign of a more serious underlying disorder. Treatment depends upon identifying the underlying problem.

SYMPTOMS

- Persistent or intermittent noises in one or both ears (described as ringing, buzzing, hissing, humming, whistling, roaring, pounding, etc.)
- Hearing loss.
- Sleep disturbances.
- Emotional distress.

WHAT CAUSES IT?

- Tinnitus can be associated with all types of hearing loss and may be a symptom of almost any ear disorder, including labyrinthitis, Ménière's disease, otitis media, otosclerosis, acoustic trauma, and presbycusis (see these disorders for more information).
- Certain conditions can produce an actual sound near the ear that an examiner can hear with a stethoscope. This phenomenon is known as objective tinnitus and can be caused by increased intracranial pressure, an aneurysm, temporomandibular jaw disorders, normal blood flow through an artery or vein, or a tumor pressing on a blood vessel or nerve.
- Drugs such as caffeine, aminoglycosides, aspirin, propranolol, levodopa, and quinidine can cause tinnitus.
- In some cases no cause can be established.

PREVENTION

- Prompt antibiotic therapy can avert the disorder in cases of otitis media or other ear infections.
- Noise-induced tinnitus can be prevented by avoiding loud noise or using ear plugs or muffs.
- Drug-induced tinnitus can be prevented by avoiding the drugs mentioned above.

DIAGNOSIS

- A patient interview and physical examination, including a detailed description of the sounds and when they occur.
- Audiometry (hearing tests) may be used to measure any hearing loss.
- X-rays or ultrasound scans may be used to detect a tumor or other abnormality.

HOW TO TREAT IT

- Background sound from a radio or television may successfully mask tinnitus and help sufferers to fall asleep.
- Sedatives may be prescribed to alleviate chronic sleep disturbance.
- Hearing aids can amplify ambient sound and drown out tinnitus.
- In more severe cases tinnitus masking may be prescribed by an otolaryngologist (ear, nose, and throat specialist). Masking utilizes white noise or a more pleasant sound that often successfully inhibits tinnitus for several hours after use.
- Tinnitus clinics and support groups are available in most major cities.
- Surgery may be used to correct an underlying disorder, such as a tumor, but usually is ineffective in eliminating the tinnitus.

WHEN TO CALL A DOCTOR

- Call a doctor if ringing, buzzing, or other sounds disrupt daily activities or sleeping habits. Your physician may refer you to an otolaryngologist for further evaluation and treatment.

Tongue Disorders

WHAT IS IT?

Tongue disorders are characterized by changes in the texture and appearance of the tongue's surface. They may result from poor oral hygiene or indicate a medical problem. Glossitis is inflammation of the tongue, in which the whole tongue becomes extremely smooth, swollen, red, and painful. Geographic tongue also involves inflammation, but in small, painless, migrating patches. Macroglossia is an abnormally enlarged tongue, caused by an underlying disorder

---

SYMPTOMS

- A painful, red, swollen tongue that glistens and is extremely smooth (glossitis).
- Painless red patches that heal then reappear on other parts of the tongue (geographic tongue).
- Elongated papillae that make the tongue look hairy (hairy tongue).
- A painless, raised white patch that may become firm or rough (leukoplakia).
- Discoloration of the tongue ranging from yellowish white to brown-black.
- Bad breath.
- Excessive salivation.
- Difficulty swallowing.
- Stiffness of the tongue.

---

such as Down's syndrome. Hairy tongue and discolored tongue are more unsightly than painful, and both can usually be remedied by good oral hygiene. Tongue cancer, the most serious disorder, primarily affects people over 40. A small ulcer or a raised white patch of thickened tissue (leukoplakia) may be the earliest sign of cancer, although most leukoplakias do not become malignant. Tongue cancer may spread rapidly to surrounding tissues in the gums, lower jaw, or lymph nodes in the neck; detection before cancer spreads is essential for a favorable prognosis.

WHAT CAUSES IT?

- Hairy tongue and discolored tongue (in which papillae, the small projections on the tongue, become elongated or darkened) may be caused by tobacco, foods, or medications such as antibiotics. Poor oral hygiene is a contributing factor.

- Tongue disorders may be a sign of an underlying ailment, such as lupus, candidiasis, psoriasis, or syphilis. Disorders associated with glossitis include a deficiency of vitamin B_{12} (pernicious anemia) or other B vitamins, scarlet fever, toxic shock syndrome, and infection (particularly herpes simplex, which may also cause cold sores on the tongue). Down's syndrome, intrauterine hypothyroidism (cretinism), and overproduction of growth hormone by a pituitary tumor (see Hyperpituitarism) can cause macroglossia.
- Chronic irritation due to smoking, alcohol, jagged teeth, or dentures can cause leukoplakia or glossitis.
- Tongue cancer is often associated with smoking and heavy alcohol use (especially in combination).
- Hairy leukoplakia may be a complication of AIDS.

PREVENTION

- Brush or scrape the tongue when you brush your teeth to promote good oral hygiene.
- See a dentist at least once a year.
- Avoid tobacco (especially smokeless) and excessive use of alcohol. Reduce exposure to acidic or spicy foods that cause discomfort.

DIAGNOSIS

- Examination and patient history are often sufficient.
- Tongue biopsy (removal of a small tissue sample for analysis) may be performed when cancer is suspected.

HOW TO TREAT IT

- Treatment is directed at the underlying cause. For example, if a tongue disorder is caused by a vitamin deficiency, dietary guidelines or vitamin supplements may be recommended. Ill-fitting dentures or jagged teeth should be remedied by a dentist.
- A mild salt solution, antiseptic mouthwash, or topical ointment may soothe discomfort or kill germs.
- Antibiotics may be used when the disorder includes minor bacterial infections (as in glossitis).
- Tongue cancer may require surgical excision of all affected tissue and radiation therapy. Tumors that have spread may also require chemotherapy.

WHEN TO CALL A DOCTOR

- Call a doctor if your tongue is sore, swollen, or stiff, or if symptoms persist for more than three days.

Tonsillitis

WHAT IS IT?

Tonsillitis is inflammation of the tonsils—the infection-fighting lymph tissue located on either side of the back of the mouth—due to infection. It is most common in children between the ages of five and 15 (although it can occur at any age) and is characterized by a severe sore throat. The tonsils, once considered a nuisance and frequently removed surgically, are now known to serve an immune system role. They are also the respiratory system's first line of defense, trapping and neutralizing infectious agents before they can penetrate to the bronchial passages. For extra protection, children's tonsils are normally large; they reach their maximum size at around age six or seven and then start to shrink. Because of their continuous exposure to infectious agents, the tonsils sometimes become overwhelmed by infection, resulting in tonsillitis. Although tonsillitis usually goes away on its own within a week, it still warrants a physician's attention to identify the infectious agent. Bacterial infections, particularly strep throat, require prescription medication; an immunologic reaction to products formed by group A streptococci cause glomerulonephritis or rheumatic fever (see these disorders for more information). A serious infection can also develop into peritonsillar abscess, an accumulation of pus in the tissues around the tonsils. Chronic, recurrent tonsillitis may require surgery (tonsillectomy).

WHAT CAUSES IT?

• Viruses are the most common cause; bacteria account for some 40 percent of cases. Germs that cause tonsillitis are usually spread via hand-to-hand and hand-to-mouth contact.

PREVENTION

• Normal infection-fighting measures can help reduce the incidence of tonsillitis. Chief among these is frequent hand washing, especially in winter when germs are spread more easily owing to close indoor contact. Young children should be taught to cover their mouths when they sneeze or cough.
• Prompt treatment will limit transmission to others.

DIAGNOSIS

• Patient history and physical examination are necessary. Streptococcal tonsillitis cannot be distinguished from viral causes by its clinical features.
• Throat swabs are cultured to identify the underlying infectious agent and so determine the proper treatment.
• More rapid tests are available to quickly identify group A streptococci.

HOW TO TREAT IT

• Antibiotics are prescribed for streptococcal (or other bacterial) infections and must usually be taken for at least 10 days.
• Acetaminophen or other nonprescription pain-relieving and fever-reducing medications are recommended to relieve discomfort. Do not give aspirin to those under 16 years of age, however, as it may trigger a potentially life-threatening disorder (see Reye's Syndrome).
• Gargling with a salt-water solution several times a day may relieve sore throat.
• Surgical drainage may be required if an abscess develops.
• If tonsillitis becomes chronic, or tonsil size interferes with breathing or swallowing, surgical removal of the tonsils (tonsillectomy) may be recommended. This procedure is often done on an outpatient basis.

WHEN TO CALL A DOCTOR

• Call a doctor if a sore throat does not go away within 48 hours, especially if accompanied by fever.
• Call a doctor if a sore throat worsens, especially on one side, despite antibiotic therapy.

SYMPTOMS

• Sore, red, raw throat; swallowing difficulty.
• Gray or white patches on the tonsils or soft palate.
• Fever.
• Headache.
• Swollen lymph nodes in the jaw and neck.
• Nausea, vomiting, and abdominal pain (common in children).

Tooth Abscess

WHAT IS IT?

A tooth abscess is a pus-filled sac that forms in the tissues surrounding the root of a tooth. It usually occurs when bacteria penetrate the hard outer layers of a tooth and spread to the pulp—the blood vessels and nerves that make up the soft core of each tooth—causing the pulp to die. Bacteria and dead pulp tissue form pus, which may spread to the surrounding tissue, resulting in a painful abscess. If left untreated, the abscess may erode a channel through the jawbone to the gum, forming a boil. The boil may eventually burst; this relieves the pain but allows infection to spread to other parts of the body. The abscess may also cause swelling in the side of the face or the lymph nodes in the neck.

WHAT CAUSES IT?

• The most common cause of an abscess is tooth decay, which erodes the outer layers of the tooth, allowing bacteria to enter the pulp.
• An abscess may result when gingivitis or periodontitis goes unchecked, as bacteria proliferate in gaps between the teeth and gums.
• An abscess may develop after injury to a tooth.
• Occasionally, tooth pulp dies spontaneously for no apparent reason, resulting in pus that may form an abscess.

DIAGNOSIS

• Dental examination and x-rays.

SYMPTOMS

• Persistent aching or painful throbbing in the affected tooth. Biting or chewing usually causes severe pain.
• Sensitivity to hot or cold foods and drinks.
• Tenderness, redness, or swelling in the gum around the affected tooth.
• A foul taste in the mouth if the abscess forms a boil and bursts.
• Swelling and tenderness of the lymph nodes in the side of the face.
• Fever and general malaise.

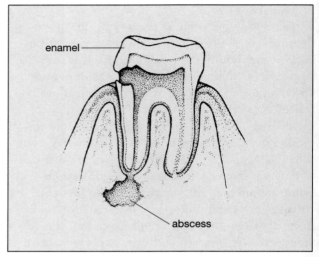

An abscess may result when plaque eats through the tooth's outer protective enamel, allowing bacteria to invade the soft inner tissues.

PREVENTION

• Practice careful oral hygiene (see Gingivitis for more information) and see a dentist at least once a year for a routine cleaning and checkup.

HOW TO TREAT IT

• Rinse with warm salt water to ease pain until you can see a dentist.
• Aspirin or another pain reliever can help reduce pain. Stronger analgesics such as codeine may be prescribed in more severe cases.
• The dentist may drill a small hole through the crown of the infected tooth into the pulp, to release the pus. The pulp cavity and root canals are cleaned out and disinfected (root canal procedure). After the infection has subsided, the cavity is filled and the tooth is fitted with a crown.
• Antibiotics may be given to fight infection.
• If the tooth cannot be saved, it will be extracted.

WHEN TO CALL A DOCTOR

• The pain of a tooth abscess usually prompts the sufferer to see a dentist as soon as possible. But if pain eases as an abscessed boil bursts, or if swelling has spread to the face or neck, see a dentist immediately.

Tooth Decay

WHAT IS IT?

Tooth decay is caused by bacteria that normally dwell inside the mouth. These bacteria combine with food particles and mucus to form dental plaque, a sticky, colorless film that builds up on the teeth. The bacteria in plaque breaks down sugars to produce acids that, without proper oral hygiene, may gradually eat away and form cavities in the tooth's hard protective layer of enamel. Once the acids have penetrated the enamel, they can then attack the softer layers of tissue inside the tooth (the dentin and the pulp, which contain nerves and blood vessels), resulting in a toothache. Eventually, bacteria may invade the dentin and pulp, causing an infection that leaves the tooth vulnerable to a potentially dangerous abscess, characterized by severe pain and infection of the jaw.

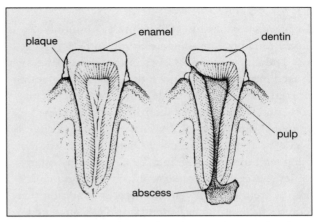

Dental plaque may erode the tooth's outer protective enamel so that bacteria can invade the soft dentin and pulp, leading to an abscess.

WHAT CAUSES IT?

• Poor dental hygiene causes tooth decay
• Sugary and starchy foods and drinks may promote tooth decay.

SYMPTOMS

• Increased sensitivity of the teeth to heat and cold.
• Toothache, especially after eating sweet or sour foods. Pain may grow more intense and persistent as decay worsens.
• Bad breath and an unpleasant taste in the mouth.

DIAGNOSIS

• A dental examination is performed.
• Dental x-rays are taken.

PREVENTION

• Brush your teeth using a soft bristle toothbrush and a fluoride toothpaste. Scrub with a gentle circular motion, then whisk the brush vertically, away from the gums. Brush your tongue too; it collects the same bacteria that stick to the teeth.
• Floss after brushing. Ease the floss between the teeth, forming a crescent against one side of a tooth.

Gingerly scrape up and down, from just under the gum line to the top of the teeth.
• Nonprescription fluoride mouth rinses offer extra protection. Two strengths are available—one for daily use and one for weekly use.
• Ask your dentist about the benefits of irrigation devices such as Waterpik or plaque removal devices such as Interplak.
• Schedule a dental checkup at least once a year.
• Limit your consumption of sugary drinks and sweet, starchy, or sticky foods.

HOW TO TREAT IT

• For a toothache, use ice packs, aspirin, or acetaminophen until you receive professional help.
• The decayed section of tooth will be drilled away and filled with a metal alloy or plastic resin.
• If a tooth is severely decayed and in danger of being lost, a root canal may be needed. The nerve and pulp of the tooth are removed leaving only the hollow tooth and roots. The cavity is then sterilized and filled with cement, and the tooth is fitted over with a metal or porcelain crown.
• In the case of an abscess, tooth extraction may be required.

WHEN TO CALL A DOCTOR

• See a dentist as soon as possible if you experience a toothache.

Toxic Shock Syndrome

WHAT IS IT?

Toxic shock syndrome (TSS)—most commonly linked to tampon use—is a reaction to bacterial toxins. The number of TSS cases in the United States peaked in the late '70s and early 1980s among young women using certain brands of superabsorbent tampons, and it has dropped dramatically since these tampons were taken off the market. The majority of TSS cases today still occurs in menstruating women using tampons, but TSS may be triggered by other causes and can affect older women, men, and children as well. It is a potentially serious condition that requires prompt medical attention; if left untreated, TSS can produce complications, such as a severe drop in blood pressure (shock), or liver or kidney failure. Most patients recover fully with treatment in one to two weeks, but TSS can recur (with subsequent menstrual periods for example), and, in rare cases, it can be fatal. Overall incidence of TSS is now low, and in general, judicious tampon use is safe. However, women who use tampons during menstruation should be aware of the typical symptoms of TSS and should seek immediate medical attention if any of these symptoms appears.

WHAT CAUSES IT?

• Toxic shock syndrome is caused by *Staphylococcus aureus* bacteria, which produce toxins that are absorbed into the bloodstream. The precise association between tampons and TSS is still in question; it is believed that tampon insertion may cause tiny breaks in the skin, which become infected, or that superabsorbent tampons that are left in place too long may trap the bacteria in the vagina and provide a favorable environment for bacterial growth.

• Some cases of TSS have been linked to the use of contraceptive sponges or diaphragms.

• TSS may result from other *Staph. aureus* infections, occurring in association with infected scrapes or burns, abscesses, osteomyelitis, or postsurgical infections.

PREVENTION

• Change tampons several times a day, or alternate tampons with sanitary napkins. Never use a tampon overnight or between menstrual periods.

• Use lower-absorbency tampons.

• If you have experienced TSS in the past, avoid using tampons altogether.

• Clean and disinfect surface cuts and scrapes, and cover them with an antibiotic cream.

DIAGNOSIS

• Patient history (including tampon usage) and physical examination are necessary.

• Blood tests help to rule out other disorders that can cause similar symptoms.

• Vaginal tissue or discharge may be cultured to confirm the diagnosis.

HOW TO TREAT IT

• A tampon, if present, must be removed immediately.

• In most cases hospitalization and intravenous administration of antibiotics are required.

• Intravenous fluid replacement is necessary for patients who have gone into shock.

• Further treatment may be necessary for the complications of TSS, such as renal failure.

WHEN TO CALL A DOCTOR

• **EMERGENCY** Seek medical help immediately if you experience the symptoms of TSS.

SYMPTOMS

• Sudden, high fever (above 102°F).

• Vomiting and diarrhea.

• A deep red rash, most often on the palms of the hands or soles of the feet. After one to two weeks, the skin begins to peel.

• Aching or severe muscle pain.

• Headache.

• Bloodshot eyes.

• Sore throat.

• Vaginal bleeding or discharge.

• Dizziness, weakness, disorientation, or fainting.

Transient Ischemic Attack

WHAT IS IT?

A transient ischemic attack (TIA) occurs when blood flow to part of the brain is interrupted by a temporary blockage in an artery supplying the brain. The pathological mechanism of a TIA is identical to that of certain kinds of stroke, except that normal circulation is restored within 24 hours, and no permanent brain damage occurs; indeed, most TIAs resolve within a few minutes to an hour. Symptoms occur suddenly and vary considerably depending on the part of the brain affected. Although symptoms of TIAs disappear completely without treatment, they frequently recur. Prompt medical attention is important since TIAs are a warning sign of an impending stroke.

SYMPTOMS

- Sudden weakness, tingling, or numbness, usually affecting only one side of the body.
- Double vision or temporary blindness in one eye.
- Speech difficulty.
- Dizziness and loss of balance or coordination.
- Lightheadedness, confusion, or amnesia.
- Hearing loss.
- Headache or eye pain.

WHAT CAUSES IT?

- The majority of TIAs are associated with atherosclerosis, a buildup of plaques in the walls of the arteries. A TIA may develop when a plaque becomes substantial enough to reduce blood supply locally in an artery supplying the brain. More commonly, however, a TIA occurs when a small fragment of a plaque that has broken off from a blood vessel, or a blood clot (embolus), usually from the heart, travels to an artery supplying the brain and lodges in a site already narrowed by atherosclerosis.
- Major risk factors for TIAs include high blood pressure, heart disease, diabetes, smoking, and aging.

PREVENTION

- Seek treatment for any predisposing condition, such as high blood pressure, diabetes, or heart disease.
- Don't smoke.
- Lose weight if you are overweight.

DIAGNOSIS

- Patient history and physical examination are needed to rule out other disorders such as epileptic seizures and migraines.
- Blood tests are taken to rule out disorders like hypoglycemia.
- Imaging studies may be done, such as magnetic resonance imaging (MRI) of the brain or ultrasound scans of the carotid arteries.
- Cerebral arteriography (injection of a contrast material into the blood vessels supplying the brain to highlight them during x-ray imaging) may be performed in some cases.

HOW TO TREAT IT

- Anticoagulant drugs, which inhibit blood clot formation, may be prescribed. Aspirin—the most commonly used anticoagulant—is usually tried first. More powerful anticoagulants such as warfarin and heparin may be warranted in some cases.
- Measures to control hypertension and blood cholesterol levels (including drug therapy) are undertaken if needed.
- Patients who have experienced one or more TIAs, who are healthy enough to have surgery, and who show evidence of substantial atherosclerotic narrowing in the carotid arteries (the two main blood vessels in the neck supplying the brain) may be good candidates for carotid endarterectomy—a surgical procedure to clear away plaque deposits in the arteries. This technique is not appropriate for all patients, but in those who do qualify, it has been shown to reduce the risk of having a stroke in the future.

WHEN TO CALL A DOCTOR

- If you experience the symptoms of a TIA, see a doctor immediately. Do not ignore symptoms just because they go away by themselves.

Trench Mouth

WHAT IS IT?

Trench mouth is a painful gum infection that was widespread among soldiers in the trenches during World War I, hence its name. Also known as necrotizing ulcerative gingivitis or Vincent's disease, trench mouth is a noncontagious, relatively rare condition that usually affects young adults, ages 15 to 35, though it can occur at any age. Symptoms generally appear suddenly over the course of one to two days, and they can be mild or severe. The infection destroys gum tissue, usually the gum tips between the teeth (papillae). Craterlike ulcers that bleed spontaneously may form where the papillae have been damaged, and gums may become so painful that eating is difficult. A grayish film of decayed gum tissue develops over the damaged areas. Severe or recurrent trench mouth can damage the underlying supporting bone and tissue in the mouth and lead to eventual tooth loss. In most cases prompt treatment results in marked improvement within five days. However, if follow-up dental care is not maintained after an acute episode of trench mouth, recurrence and eventual tooth loss is possible.

SYMPTOMS

- Red, swollen, painful gums.
- Highly sensitive gums that may bleed profusely with even slight pressure.
- A grayish film over the gums.
- Bleeding ulcers on the gums.
- Bad breath and a foul taste in the mouth.
- Fever and general malaise.
- Swelling in the lymph nodes under the jaw.

WHAT CAUSES IT?

- Trench mouth is caused by infection from bacteria that normally inhabit the mouth in harmless numbers. It may occur when gingivitis or periodontitis is left untreated, allowing bacteria to proliferate.
- Smoking, lack of sleep, inadequate nutrition, poor dental hygiene, and emotional stress increase the risk of getting trench mouth.
- Trench mouth may strike when the immune system is weakened by a more serious disease, such as leukemia or AIDS.

PREVENTION

- Practice careful oral hygiene (see Gingivitis for more information) and see a dentist at least once a year for a routine cleaning and checkup.
- Do not smoke.
- Eat a balanced, nutritious diet.
- Get adequate amounts of rest.

DIAGNOSIS

- Examination of the teeth and gums by a dentist is necessary.

HOW TO TREAT IT

- A topical anesthetic is applied, and the gums are cleaned thoroughly; bacteria and dead tissue are removed from the gum surface. The mouth is then flushed with warm water or saline.
- At a later visit, the dentist will remove surface plaque and calculus—a buildup of minerals and bacterial products—from the teeth (dental scaling).
- Antibiotics may be prescribed to fight bacteria.
- Frequent rinsing with a dilute hydrogen peroxide mouthwash is recommended.
- Take aspirin or another pain reliever to help ease pain.
- In severe cases when infection has spread to other parts of the body, hospitalization and intravenous antibiotics may be required.
- During recovery, avoid hot, spicy foods, alcohol, and tobacco; get plenty of rest; eat a well-balanced diet; and brush teeth gently and cautiously.
- A series of follow-up dental visits may be required.

WHEN TO CALL A DOCTOR

- If you suspect you have trench mouth, especially if your symptoms are accompanied by a fever, see a dentist immediately.

Trichinosis

WHAT IS IT?

Trichinosis is a parasitic disease often spread through raw or undercooked meat, especially pork. Most cases are mild and cause few if any symptoms. Trichinosis is transmitted to humans who ingest the larvae of a parasitic roundworm found in the muscles of infected animals. These larvae mature into adult worms in the lining of the intestine. The fertilized female can produce thousands of larvae that may migrate throughout the body and form cysts in the muscles of the host. Once formed, these cysts can persist indefinitely. If symptoms do occur, those resulting from infestation of the intestine generally begin within one to two days after eating the infected meat. Symptoms

SYMPTOMS
- Early symptoms (within a few days of ingestion): nausea and vomiting; diarrhea and abdominal pain or cramps; fever; sometimes prostration.
- Later symptoms (one to three weeks after ingestion): swelling around the eyes; red eyes; muscle pain and tenderness; severe weakness; fever; itching or burning skin.
- Possible more serious symptoms: coughing up bloody phlegm, paralysis, delirium, coma, heart failure.

due to muscle involvement typically begin a week later and subside gradually after a few weeks, but they sometimes last for several months. Severity depends on the number of larvae consumed and the condition of the host's immune system. In many people, trichinosis resolves on its own; however, treatment is necessary if larval cysts in the muscles of the host produce significant muscle inflammation. Rarely, the infection may cause serious, even fatal, complications involving the heart, lungs, or central nervous system. The incidence of trichinosis in the United States has dropped greatly over the past few decades thanks to public health regulations, but it is still important to cook all meat thoroughly, particularly pork and pork products, as well as wild game (such as bear, wolf, coyote, fox, horse, and rabbit).

WHAT CAUSES IT?

- Trichinosis is caused by the roundworm *Trichinella spiralis,* which lives in the intestines and muscles of many species of meat-eating animals. The disease is transmitted to humans by ingestion of undercooked meat from such animals. Larvae from intestinal worms enter the bloodstream and muscles where they form cysts that can induce an inflammatory response. This may lead to damage to the heart, lungs, and brain.

PREVENTION

- Cook pork and other meat thoroughly. Pork should be cooked until all pink portions turn white or gray. As an alternative precaution, freeze meat at 15°C for at least 20 days before cooking it.

DIAGNOSIS

- Patient history (including recent food consumption history) is taken. Physical examination may reveal characteristic signs of trichinosis infection.
- Blood tests will reveal an elevated eosinophil count and antibodies against *Trichinella.*
- Stool analysis may detect worms and larvae.
- The most definitive test is a muscle biopsy to detect the presence of the *Trichinella spiralis* larvae.
- If possible, a portion of the suspect meat is analyzed.

HOW TO TREAT IT

- In mild cases treatment may not be necessary.
- The drugs thiabendazole or mebendazole may be prescribed to kill the worms and so relieve symptoms. Mebendazole can kill larvae as well as adult worms and has less risk of side effects than thiabendazole, but it should not be used in children or pregnant women.
- Acetaminophen or aspirin may be used to reduce fever and ease discomfort.
- When the heart is affected, bed rest is necessary until symptoms subside.
- Corticosteroid drugs may be prescribed to reduce inflammation in severe cases, or for patients who have an allergic response to the parasite.

WHEN TO CALL A DOCTOR

- If you experience the symptoms of trichinosis, especially if you have eaten pork within the past several weeks, see a doctor as soon as possible.

Tuberculosis

WHAT IS IT?

Tuberculosis, also known as TB, is a chronic infection with a specific type of bacterium *(Mycobacterium)* that usually affects the lungs. Although contagious, TB is not as easy to catch as other respiratory infections, since repeated and prolonged exposure to airborne particles from coughing or sneezing is necessary to permit sufficient numbers of the bacteria into the lungs. Overcrowded, impoverished living conditions and frequent contact with others infected with TB are significant risk factors. The infection has two distinct stages. First, bacteria are inhaled into the lungs, where most are destroyed by the immune system. Bacteria that are not destroyed are trapped by

---

SYMPTOMS

- Persistent cough, possibly with bloody sputum.
- Chest pain.
- Shortness of breath.
- Fever.
- Fatigue.
- Night sweats.
- Loss of appetite; weight loss.

---

the immune system inside hard, walled capsules, known as tubercles, which are composed of a number of different types of cells. TB bacteria cannot cause damage or symptoms while encased in the tubercles, and in many people the disease never progresses beyond this point. Only a small fraction of those infected will develop active disease, the second stage of TB. Active disease appears if the bacteria break out of the tubercles and infect other sites in the lungs. Bacteria may also invade the bloodstream and the lymphatic system and spread throughout the body. A few people develop active disease within weeks of the initial infection, but in most cases the second stage does not appear until years or decades later. Factors such as aging, a weakened immune system, and poor nutrition increase the risk that the bacteria will break through the tubercle walls. Most commonly, active TB destroys lung tissue and severely impairs breathing, but it may also affect

other parts of the body, including the brain, heart, kidneys, and gastrointestinal tract. Untreated TB may be fatal.

Sometimes known as the white plague for the ashen complexion of its victims, TB was a leading killer worldwide until the development of an effective drug treatment. Unfortunately, the disease has once more become a serious public health threat: after a period of steady decline, the number of cases in the United States has risen dramatically since 1985. Perhaps the most significant factor is that, although TB can be cured, treatment is lengthy, and many do not adhere to it. A combination of drugs must be taken daily for up to one year to cure TB. These drugs kill the weakest bacteria first; stronger, more resistant bacteria survive the initial assault and must be attacked steadily over time. However, since symptoms fade after a few weeks, many people do not complete the entire course of treatment. This practice may lead to a relapse with an even more deadly form of the disease. Taking the medication for only a few weeks or months favors survival and growth of the strongest bacteria, creating an infection resistant to some or all drug therapy. To fight TB effectively, and to prevent the growth of drug-resistant strains of the bacteria, it is important that proper preventive measures and courses of treatment are strictly followed. Another major contributor to the resurgence of TB is the AIDS epidemic, since the weakened immune defenses of AIDS patients result in the rapid spread of bacteria after an infection.

WHAT CAUSES IT?

- Bacterial infection causes tuberculosis.
- TB is spread through the air by the sneeze or cough of an infected person.
- Those who live in crowded or unsanitary areas, including the poor, migrant farm workers, and the homeless, are at higher risk for TB.
- People with weakened immune systems, such as those infected with the human immunodeficiency virus (HIV) or undergoing treatment for cancer, are at greater risk for TB.
- Others at high risk for TB include infants, the elderly, diabetics, substance abusers, the malnourished, recent immigrants from countries where TB

Tuberculosis *continued*

is common, health care workers, prison guards, and family members of those with TB.
• TB spreads more easily in confined, poorly ventilated spaces, including jails, nursing homes, tenements, homeless shelters, and even hospitals (which are ill-equipped to deal with the current resurgence in TB).

PREVENTION
• People in high-risk groups may be immunized against TB with what is known as the BCG vaccine. Recent work has shown the value of BCG in preventing TB, but the vaccine has not been recommended generally because it leads to a positive tuberculosis test and thus may negate one of the most important screening tests for the disorder.
• The antibiotic isoniazid may be administered to people who test positive for TB but have no evidence of active disease. Isoniazid prevents development of the second stage disease by destroying the bacteria trapped within the tubercles. The medication must be taken for six to nine months.

DIAGNOSIS
• Patient history and physical examination.
• Chest x-rays.
• Tuberculin skin test. A small amount of protein derived from mycobacteria is injected into the skin on the arm, and the area is examined after a day or two. A slightly raised, hard, red patch of skin at the site indicates the presence of TB (although not necessarily active disease). However, a positive TB skin test may also result from prior immunization with BCG.

• Sputum culture. The results of the culture may take up to six weeks to develop. A positive culture is essential for diagnosis.
• Blood tests.
• Bronchoscopy (the use of a thin, hollow, flexible tube passed through the mouth into the windpipe to view the main bronchial passages).
• Bone marrow biopsy. A sample of bone marrow is usually taken from the hip bone.

HOW TO TREAT IT
• A combination of two antibiotics—isoniazid and rifampin, the most effective drugs against tuberculosis—is prescribed for nine to 12 months. The antibiotics must be taken for the full term prescribed, both to cure the infection and to prevent the development of drug-resistant TB strains.
• Resistant strains of bacteria may require treatment with a combination of additional drugs.
• Patients should get plenty of rest until symptoms subside.
• TB sufferers should sneeze or cough into disposable tissues to prevent the spread of infection.
• Hospitalization in an isolation room with adequate ventilation may be necessary to treat and prevent the spread of drug-resistant strains of TB.
• Surgery to remove damaged lung tissue may be performed in advanced cases.

WHEN TO CALL A DOCTOR
• Call a doctor if you develop a persistent cough, chest pain, night sweats, and shortness of breath.

Typhoid Fever

WHAT IS IT?

Typhoid fever is a contagious bacterial infection that involves the intestine and lymphatic system. Now rare in the United States, typhoid fever remains common in developing countries, especially in areas with poor sanitation. Symptoms develop gradually over three weeks, with fever, chills, and headache occurring first. Left untreated, typhoid fever may result in life-threatening intestinal perforation and bleeding. Some people become symptom-free carriers of the disease when the typhoid bacteria lodge in the bile or in gallstones. The bacteria may then periodically migrate to the bowel and be excreted in the feces, thereby contaminating ground water or vegetation fertilized with human waste. Typhoid fever responds well to antibiotics, and severe symptoms are unlikely with early treatment, although about one in five patients relapses.

WHAT CAUSES IT?

• Typhoid is most often caused by *Salmonella typhi,* a bacterium that invades the wall of the small intestine. Other salmonella species may also cause typhoid fever.
• Typhoid fever is spread by water and food contaminated with the fecal matter of an infected person.
• Nearly 5 percent of former patients become chronic carriers—people who carry the bacteria and spread the disease but have no symptoms themselves.

SYMPTOMS

• Persistent fever and chills. Fever is higher in the morning.
• Headache.
• Abdominal pain.
• General feeling of poor health.
• Muscle aches.
• Nausea and vomiting.
• Constipation or diarrhea.
• Loss of appetite and weight.
• Pale, reddish skin rash ("rose spots") on the shoulders, chest, and back, lasting for three to four days.
• Nosebleeds.
• Personality changes and delirium; coma; seizures in children.

• Flies may spread the bacteria and cause epidemics; this is more common in areas with poor sanitation.

PREVENTION

• Wash hands with soap and warm water often, especially after using the toilet or before handling food.
• Typhoid vaccine (while only partially effective) should be obtained before traveling to high-risk areas.
• When traveling abroad or in areas with poor sanitation, drink only bottled water or other bottled beverages, and eat only well-cooked foods and peeled fruit. Do not use ice.
• Infected persons and carriers should use a separate toilet if possible and be extremely cautious when handling food that may be consumed by others.

DIAGNOSIS

• Blood and stool cultures to identify the bacterium.

HOW TO TREAT IT

• Do not take aspirin or other over-the-counter pain relievers for typhoid fever unless prescribed by your doctor. These medications may lower blood pressure, and aspirin may also promote gastrointestinal bleeding.
• The antibiotic chloramphenicol is most often prescribed to treat typhoid fever. Other antibiotics or sulfa drugs, such as trimethoprim-sulfamethoxazole, can also be effective.
• Intravenous fluids and electrolytes (mineral salts) may be administered to prevent or treat dehydration.
• Antidiarrheal drugs or narcotics may be warranted to relieve diarrhea and cramps.
• Blood transfusions may be necessary in the event of intestinal bleeding.
• Dexamethasone, a corticosteroid drug, may be used in severe cases involving the central nervous system to treat delirium, seizures, or shock.
• Emergency surgery may be necessary to repair intestinal perforation.
• Months of antibiotic treatment may eliminate bacteria from chronic carriers, but surgical removal of the gallbladder (cholecystectomy) may also be warranted.

WHEN TO CALL A DOCTOR

• Call a doctor if you develop persistent fever and chills along with other symptoms of typhoid fever.

Urethritis

WHAT IS IT?

Urethritis is an inflammation of the urethra, the thin tube that carries urine out of the body from the bladder. Often caused by a bacterial infection, urethritis may produce distinctly different symptoms in men and women. Infectious agents (including chlamydia, gonorrhea, and herpesvirus) transmitted during sexual activity may cause urethritis in both men and women, but women may not exhibit any symptoms. In symptomatic women, urethritis may be difficult to distinguish from a bladder infection; however, treatment is similar in either case (see Bladder Infection for more information). Urethritis may also be caused by nonsexually transmitted infections; such infections are most common among women.

SYMPTOMS

- Burning on urination.
- Frequent urination with only small amounts of urine passed on each occasion.
- Urgent need to urinate.
- Blood in the urine.
- Yellowish discharge from the urethra.
- Lower abdominal pain.
- Painful sexual intercourse (dyspareunia) in women.

WHAT CAUSES IT?

- In women, urethritis often results from an infection caused by bacteria that normally inhabit the anal area with no ill effect. If these bacteria enter the urinary tract, urethritis may ensue.
- Urethritis may result from sexual transmission of the herpesvirus or the bacteria that cause chlamydia or gonorrhea.
- Prolonged use of a urinary catheter increases the risk of urethritis.
- Sexual activity may bruise the urethra in women and promote inflammation.
- Some soaps, bath oils, and vaginal douches may irritate the urethra.

PREVENTION

- Use condoms during sexual intercourse to help decrease the risk of infection.
- Good hygiene is recommended, especially prior to sexual activity. Use mild, unscented soap. Showers are less likely to promote urethritis than baths.
- To flush bacteria from the vaginal tract, women should drink some water prior to intercourse and urinate within 15 minutes afterward, and, if necessary, use a water-soluble lubricant (not petroleum jelly) to decrease the risk of bruising during intercourse.
- After using the bathroom, women should wipe from front to back to avoid spreading fecal bacteria to the urethra.
- Women should not douche unless otherwise instructed by a doctor.
- People who have recurrent episodes of urethritis should drink at least eight glasses of liquid a day and should avoid caffeine and alcohol, which may irritate the bladder.

DIAGNOSIS

- Patient history and physical examination.
- Microscopic examination and culture of urethral discharge and urine.

HOW TO TREAT IT

- Antibiotics, prescribed to treat bacterial infections, should be taken for the full term as directed; stopping the medication too early may result in a more serious and more difficult-to-treat rebound infection. For sexually transmitted diseases, only one partner may exhibit symptoms, but it is likely that the symptomless partner is also infected. Therefore, both partners need to be treated to prevent a self-perpetuating cycle of reinfection.
- Analgesics may be administered to relieve pain.
- Cranberry juice can increase the acidity of urine and enhance the effectiveness of some medications for urinary tract infections.

WHEN TO CALL A DOCTOR

- Call a doctor if you or your partner experiences painful, frequent urination, or if you notice an abnormal discharge from the vagina or penis.

Urinary Incontinence

WHAT IS IT?

Urinary incontinence, the partial or complete inability to control the urge to urinate, is a very common problem in older people (and twice as common in women). Incontinence is not, however, an inevitable consequence of aging; it is caused by some underlying disorder. There are different types of incontinence: stress and urge incontinence are two of the most common. Stress incontinence occurs when some activity—coughing, laughing, or lifting, for example—temporarily increases the pressure on the bladder, causing a small amount of urine to be released. Urge incontinence occurs when a sudden urge to urinate is accompanied by an inability to control the bladder, sometimes releasing large amounts of urine. Incontinence causes embarrassment, depression, and social isolation, and is often the final reason why people are placed in nursing homes. Specific treatment measures and the degree of success achieved with treatment depend on the underlying cause, but in most instances, incontinence can at least be controlled if not eliminated.

SYMPTOMS
- Urine leakage when coughing or during lifting, or other activities that increase pressure on the bladder.
- Partial or complete inability to control the bladder.
- Involuntary, unpredictable urination.

WHAT CAUSES IT?
- Abnormalities of the detrusor muscle, which contracts to force urine out of the bladder.
- Weakness, due to childbirth, of the muscles of the pelvic floor that support the bladder and control urine flow.
- Age-related changes in the urinary tract, such as bladder shrinkage.
- Atrophy of the urethra due to decreased estrogen production in postmenopausal women.
- Drugs including diuretics, sleeping pills, and tranquilizers.
- Urinary tract infections.
- Damage to the nerves that control bladder function, causing either excessive contraction of the bladder or loss of sensation governing the urge to urinate.
- Surgery or radiation therapy of the pelvic area.
- Obstruction of the flow of urine, for example, due to an enlarged prostate or urethral stricture.
- Psychological disorders including depression.

PREVENTION
- Hormone replacement therapy may be prescribed for postmenopausal women.

DIAGNOSIS
- Patient history and physical examination.
- An "incontinence chart" or voiding record of the time, amount, and circumstances of urination.
- Catheterization of the bladder to measure amount of urine remaining in the bladder after urination.
- Observation of the effects of filling the bladder with a catheter.
- Microscopic examination and culture of urine.

HOW TO TREAT IT
- Education is important. Sometimes mere interpretation of the incontinence chart will lead to complete or greatly improved bladder control.
- In many cases bladder control can be regained with techniques known as bladder training (for urge incontinence) and Kegel exercises (for stress incontinence). Bladder training begins by scheduling a bathroom visit every two hours, whether the patient needs to go or not. The interval is gradually increased by a half hour at a time, toward a goal of four-hour intervals. In many cases the body adapts to this schedule, eliminating incontinence. Kegel exercises involve repetitive contractions of the pelvic-floor muscles to strengthen them and prevent stress incontinence.
- Biofeedback—a technique using electronic equipment that provides visual and auditory feedback to increase patient awareness and control of the bladder muscles—may improve or even cure incontinence in certain patients.
- Anticholinergic drugs (which block the neurotransmitter acetylcholine), imipramine, and estrogen are sometimes helpful in treating incontinence.

Urinary Incontinence *continued*

• Antibiotics may be prescribed to treat an associated bacterial infection.

• Consult your doctor if you believe that any medications may be contributing to incontinence.

• Adult diapers and pads may actually promote complications, so they are not recommended for anything but very short-term use unless otherwise advised by a doctor.

• A bedside toilet may help with nighttime urgency. Avoid drinking excess fluids for two to three hours prior to going to bed.

• Surgery may be used to relieve pressure on bladder nerves, reduce blockage of the urethra, or repair damaged muscles or other structures.

• In rare, severe cases, an indwelling catheter may be indicated.

WHEN TO CALL A DOCTOR

• Call a doctor if you experience any bladder control problems.

Uterine Cancer

WHAT IS IT?
Uterine cancer is the growth of malignant cells in the uterus. The term uterine cancer is often used interchangeably with endometrial cancer, since malignancy typically develops in the endometrium, or uterine lining. Malignant tumors may also develop in the muscular wall of the uterus, although this is quite rare. Endometrial cancer is the most common pelvic gynecological cancer; it almost always affects postmenopausal women between the ages of 50 and 70. With early detection and treatment, endometrial cancer is highly curable, since it tends to grow and spread slowly.

SYMPTOMS
- Vaginal bleeding after menopause.
- Heavy, persistent, or unusual (sometimes watery or blood-streaked) vaginal bleeding.
- Lower abdominal pain and weight loss in advanced stages.

WHAT CAUSES IT?
- The cause of uterine cancer is unknown.
- Obesity, hypertension, diabetes mellitus, polycystic ovary disease, endometrial hyperplasia, and endometrial polyps may increase the risk of uterine cancer (see these specific disorders for more information).
- Long-term use of unopposed (without progesterone) estrogen replacement therapy in postmenopausal women is associated with a higher incidence of endometrial cancer.
- Tamoxifen, a drug used in the treatment of breast cancer, may increase the risk of uterine cancer.
- Endometrial cancer is more common in women who have had few or no children; it is less frequent in those who have used oral contraceptives.

PREVENTION
- There is no way to prevent uterine cancer, but regular pelvic examinations during and after menopause are advised to aid in early detection and treatment of any abnormalities.
- Postmenopausal estrogen replacement should be accompanied by a progestational agent or frequent endometrial biopsies.

DIAGNOSIS
- Patient history and gynecological examination.
- Diagnosis of endometrial cancer requires an endometrial biopsy or D&C (dilatation and curettage). In these procedures the cervix is widened so that biopsies can be taken from the endometrium and cervix.
- Pelvic ultrasound scans may be done to detect tumors (whether benign or malignant).
- A Pap smear (performed during a pelvic examination) may reveal the presence of malignant cells in the cervix (see Cervical Cancer), but it is not a reliable way to detect endometrial cancer.

HOW TO TREAT IT
- The primary treatment for uterine cancer is a total hysterectomy (surgical removal of the uterus), in addition to removal of the cervix, fallopian tubes, both ovaries, a portion of the upper vagina, and neighboring lymph nodes. Cancers in their earliest stage may be treated by hysterectomy alone, without further measures.
- If cancer is believed to have advanced beyond the earliest stage, radiation therapy is initiated in addition to surgery. Both external and internal radiation may be used; in internal radiation, small radioactive pellets are implanted in or near the tumor site for 48 to 72 hours at a time.
- Progestational agents are used in the treatment of endometrial cancer; chemotherapy has not usually proved to be effective.

WHEN TO CALL A DOCTOR
- Call a gynecologist if you develop heavy vaginal bleeding or if you experience vaginal bleeding between periods or after menopause.

Uterine Prolapse

WHAT IS IT?

Uterine prolapse is a protrusion of the uterus into the vagina. Normally, the uterus is held in place by the pelvic muscles and supporting ligaments. Uterine prolapse occurs when these structures become injured or weakened. In mild prolapse a portion of the uterus descends into the top of the vagina. In more severe cases the uterus may even protrude through the vaginal opening. Uterine prolapse is often accompanied by a bulging of the bladder (cystocele) or the urethra (urethrocele) into the front wall of the vagina, or a bulging of the rectum into the back wall of the vagina. Mild cases of uterine prolapse may not require treatment. If symptoms become more pronounced, treatment options include special exercises, a device that physically supports the uterus (a pessary), and surgery.

WHAT CAUSES IT?

• Injury or weakness of the pelvic muscles, usually due to multiple childbirths, is the most common cause of uterine prolapse.
• Obesity, uterine cancer, ascites, diabetes mellitus, chronic bronchitis, asthma, and a retroverted uterus (uterus is tipped toward the back of the body) increase the risk of uterine prolapse.
• Heavy lifting or straining may contribute to uterine prolapse if pelvic muscles are already weakened.
• Rarely, uterine prolapse may appear in infants.

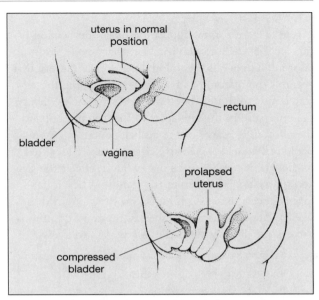

A slackening or stretching of the pelvic muscles may cause the uterus to prolapse and slide into the vaginal canal, compressing the bladder.

PREVENTION

• Kegel exercises to strengthen the muscles supporting the uterus may be recommended after childbirth.
• If necessary, weight reduction may be advised.
• Estrogen replacement may be recommended for postmenopausal women.

DIAGNOSIS

• Gynecological examination.
• A dilatation and curettage, or D&C, may be performed to obtain uterine tissue samples.

HOW TO TREAT IT

• Avoid tight pants, belts, or girdles.
• Do not strain during urination or bowel movements.
• A small plastic, rubber, or silicone ring known as a pessary may be used to provide support for a mildly prolapsed uterus or when surgery is warranted but the patient cannot endure it. The pessary is inserted into the vagina and positioned against the cervix.
• Surgery (hysterectomy) may be performed to remove a severely prolapsed uterus.

WHEN TO CALL A DOCTOR

• Call a doctor if you develop pelvic pain or discomfort or unusual vaginal discharge.

SYMPTOMS

• In many women, no symptoms.
• Discomfort, pain, or a sensation of heaviness or fullness in the lower abdomen and vagina.
• Abnormal vaginal discharge or bleeding.
• Excessive menstrual bleeding.
• Painful sexual intercourse.
• Pain in the lower back.
• Anal pain or a sensation of "sitting on a ball."
• Constipation.
• Urinary urgency or frequency.
• Visible protrusion of the uterus through the vaginal opening (in severe cases).

Uveitis and Iritis

WHAT IS IT?

Uveitis is an inflammation of the uvea, the portion of the eye that includes the iris, the ciliary body, and the choroid. The iris is the colored portion of the eye that controls the opening and closing of the pupil; the ciliary body is a muscle behind the iris that helps change the curvature of the lens so as to focus light rays; and the choroid is a layer of the eyeball containing essential blood vessels. When uveitis is primarily localized in the iris, it is called iritis or—when it affects the iris and the ciliary body—anterior uveitis. When it primarily affects the choroid, it is known as posterior uveitis. Attacks of anterior uveitis, the most common variety, usually subside within a few days to a few

---

SYMPTOMS

- Moderate to severe eye pain.
- Aversion to light.
- Blurred vision.
- Spots in the field of vision.
- Redness in the eye.
- Pupil contraction.
- Copious tearing.

---

weeks with no permanent damage; however, recurrence is common. On the other hand, posterior uveitis may persist for months or years even with treatment and cause irreversible scarring of delicate structures within the eye, including the retina (the layer of nerve cells that converts light rays into nerve impulses). If left untreated, uveitis of either type may lead to permanent vision loss and complications, including glaucoma, cataracts, and retinal detachment. A rare form of uveitis occurs when an injured eye that is severely inflamed for several weeks triggers inflammation of the uvea in the uninvolved eye. This condition, known as sympathetic ophthalmia, can result in severe vision loss in both eyes; therefore, acute uveitis in one eye that does not respond to treatment may warrant preemptive removal of the affected eye before it spreads to the other eye. Uveitis is a relatively rare disorder and most often affects young adults.

WHAT CAUSES IT?

- In most cases, the cause of uveitis is unknown.
- An autoimmune reaction (in which the body's natural defenses inappropriately attack healthy tissue) may be responsible.
- Bacterial, viral, and fungal infections are potential causes.
- Systemic disorders (those affecting entire organ systems of the body) such as rheumatoid arthritis, ankylosing spondylitis, toxoplasmosis, Crohn's disease, ulcerative colitis, and sarcoidosis may cause uveitis.

DIAGNOSIS

- A thorough examination by an ophthalmologist is necessary.

PREVENTION

- There is no known way to prevent uveitis.

HOW TO TREAT IT

- A cycloplegic ("eye-paralyzing") drug such as atropine sulfate may be administered. Immobilizing the inflamed iris and ciliary body may prevent scarring and alleviate pain somewhat. When such drugs are used, the pupil remains constantly dilated in one position, making the eye extremely sensitive to light; dark glasses are therefore recommended during the treatment period, even while indoors.
- Topical anti-inflammatory corticosteroid eye drops are usually prescribed. For more severe cases, oral or injected steroids may be required.
- Long-term steroid use increases the risks of cataracts and glaucoma, so frequent monitoring by an ophthalmologist is essential.
- Aspirin may help reduce inflammation and eye pain.
- Warm compresses, applied several times a day, may ease pain.

WHEN TO CALL A DOCTOR

- Any persistent or serious eye pain and even the slightest loss of vision warrant a prompt examination by an ophthalmologist.

Vaginal Cancer

WHAT IS IT?

Vaginal cancer—the growth of malignant cells in the vagina—is rare, representing less than 2 percent of all gynecologic cancers. Most cases of vaginal cancer occur in women over the age of 50. However, some types may affect young women during adolescence or early adulthood, and one very rare type appears in children under five. Vaginal cancers are highly treatable and often curable; outlook is most optimistic with early detection and treatment.

WHAT CAUSES IT?

• The cause of vaginal cancer is unknown.
• Women whose mothers took the synthetic hormone DES (diethylstilbestrol) during pregnancy are at greater risk for vaginal cancer.
• Previous radiation therapy to the pelvic region carries a higher risk of vaginal cancer.
• Women who have undergone a hysterectomy have an increased risk of vaginal cancer.
• A history of untreated genital warts is associated with vaginal cancer.

SYMPTOMS

• Vaginal bleeding between menstrual periods or after menopause.
• Firm, raised ulcer or bump in the vagina.
• Vaginal pain or itching. Pain may be worse upon urination and during sexual intercourse.

PREVENTION

• There is no way to prevent vaginal cancer, but regular pelvic examinations and Pap smears are advised to aid in the early detection and treatment of any abnormalities.
• Women whose mothers took the drug DES during pregnancy should have Pap smears of the vagina as well as the cervix at least once a year.

DIAGNOSIS

• Patient history and gynecologic examination are necessary.
• A Pap smear (involving the scraping of a small sample of cells from the cervix and vagina for microscopic inspection) may reveal the presence of malignant cells.
• Colposcopy (use of a special magnifying scope designed to examine the female reproductive system) may be used to view the vagina in detail. A biopsy may be taken at the time of the colposcopy.

HOW TO TREAT IT

• In the very earliest stage of vaginal cancer, a cream containing the chemotherapeutic medication fluorouracil may be applied intravaginally for five to 10 days.
• Laser surgery may be performed to eliminate a single tumor that has not spread.
• Radiation therapy may be used in addition to or instead of surgery to destroy cancerous cells. Both external and internal radiation may be administered; in internal radiation, small radioactive pellets are implanted in the body near the tumor site for 48 to 72 hours at a time.
• Conventional surgery may be performed to remove the cancerous region of the vagina and some neighboring tissue. If a large portion of vaginal tissue is to be removed, a skin graft and plastic surgery can be performed to reconstruct a functional vagina. In more severe cases a hysterectomy (removal of the cervix and uterus) or a radical hysterectomy (removal of the cervix and uterus in addition to the upper vagina, fallopian tubes, neighboring lymph nodes, and possibly the ovaries) may be advised.

WHEN TO CALL A DOCTOR

• Call a gynecologist if you develop abnormal vaginal itching, bleeding, or pain.

Vaginitis

WHAT IS IT?

Vaginitis is a common inflammation of the vaginal lining and the vulva, the folds of skin surrounding the vaginal opening. It is often a result of infection by one of various microorganisms, but vaginitis may also be caused by irritation from soaps or medications, an allergic reaction, or by hormonal changes. Three of the most common types of vaginitis are due to infections: candidiasis (yeast infection), trichomoniasis (infection by a tiny, one-celled organism), and bacterial vaginosis or nonspecific vaginitis (infections caused mainly by various types of bacteria). Although irritating, vaginitis is not a serious health risk, and it subsides quickly with treatment (although recurrence is common).

SYMPTOMS

- Profuse vaginal discharge. Discharge may be heavy, white, thick, and odorless (candidiasis); greenish yellow, frothy, and foul-smelling (trichomoniasis); white or gray, and fishy-smelling (bacterial vaginosis); thin, white or blood-streaked, and foul-smelling (atrophic vaginitis).
- Vaginal and vulvar pain or itching. Pain may be worse upon urination and during sexual intercourse.
- Bright reddish color to the vulva.

WHAT CAUSES IT?

- Fungal, parasitical, or bacterial infection causes vaginitis.
- Trichomoniasis may be spread by sexual intercourse.
- An allergic reaction to or irritation by substances in spermicides, douches, soaps, or bath oils may produce vaginitis.
- Oral corticosteroids, antibiotics, and oral contraceptives may make vaginitis more likely.
- Certain conditions including pregnancy, malnutrition, poor health, and diabetes mellitus carry a greater risk of vaginitis.
- A decrease in estrogen levels in postmenopausal women may thin the vaginal lining and cause atrophic vaginitis.

PREVENTION

- Shower daily, using a mild, unscented soap in the vaginal area.
- Use condoms during sexual intercourse to help decrease the risk of infection.
- Wear cotton undergarments and pantyhose with a cotton crotch, to prevent excess moisture accumulation. Avoid nylon undergarments that do not breathe. Do not share underwear, towels, or swimsuits.
- After a bowel movement, wipe from front to back to prevent the bacteria that normally inhabit the anal area from contacting the vagina.
- Do not use vaginal douches unless otherwise advised by your doctor.

DIAGNOSIS

- Pelvic examination.
- Microscopic examination or culture of vaginal discharge.

HOW TO TREAT IT

- An antifungal medication, such as miconazole or clotrimazole, is prescribed in the form of vaginal suppositories or cream to treat candidiasis (yeast infection). These medications are now available over-the-counter. Oral antifungal medication such as ketoconazole may be prescribed in severe cases that do not respond to topical therapy.
- Metronidazole, a microbicidal drug, is administered to both sexual partners for trichomoniasis and should be taken for the full term prescribed. Only one partner may exhibit symptoms, but both need to be treated to prevent a perpetual cycle of reinfection.
- Metronidazole or various antibiotics may be prescribed to treat bacterial vaginosis.
- Topical or oral estrogens may be prescribed for atrophic vaginitis.
- If a medication is suspected as the cause of vaginitis, a change in prescription may be warranted.
- Abstinence from sexual intercourse may be advised until treatment is completed.

WHEN TO CALL A DOCTOR

- Call your gynecologist if you experience vaginal itching, burning, or pain, or if you notice any abnormal vaginal discharge.

Valvular Heart Disease

WHAT IS IT?

Valvular heart disease is characterized by damage to or a defect in one of the four heart valves: the mitral, aortic, tricuspid, and pulmonary. The mitral and tricuspid valves control the flow of blood between the atria and the ventricles (the upper and lower chambers of the heart). The pulmonary valve controls the flow of blood from the heart to the lungs, and the aortic valve governs blood flow between the heart and the aorta, and thereby the blood vessels to the rest of the body. The mitral and aortic valves are the ones most frequently affected by valvular heart disease. Normally functioning valves ensure that blood flows with proper force in the proper direction at the proper time. In valvular heart disease, the valves become too narrow and hardened (stenotic) to open fully, or are unable to close completely (incompetent). A stenotic valve forces blood to back up in the adjacent heart chamber, while an incompetent valve allows blood to leak back into the chamber it previously exited. To compensate for poor pumping action, the heart muscle enlarges and thickens, thereby losing elasticity and efficiency. In addition, blood pooling in the chambers of the heart has a greater tendency to clot, increasing the risk of stroke or pulmonary embolism (see Stroke or Pulmonary Embolism for more information). The severity of valvular heart disease varies. In mild cases there may be no symptoms, while in advanced cases, valvular heart disease may lead to congestive heart failure (see Congestive Heart Failure for more information) and other com-

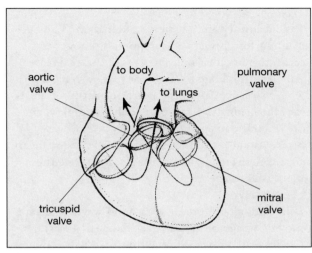

When the heart's ventricles contract, the aortic and pulmonary valves open to allow blood to be pumped out to the body and lungs, respectively. As the ventricles relax between beats, the aortic and pulmonary valves close, while the mitral and tricuspid valves open, allowing the ventricles to fill with blood again before the next contraction.

plications. Treatment depends upon the extent of the disease.

WHAT CAUSES IT?

• Rheumatic fever may cause valvular heart disease.
• Bacterial endocarditis, an infection of the inner lining of the heart muscle and heart valves (endocardium), is both a cause and a risk of valvular heart disease.
• High blood pressure and atherosclerosis may damage the aortic valve.
• A heart attack may damage the heart valves.
• Congenital abnormalities of the heart valves may be present.
• Heart valve tissue may degenerate with age.
• Other disorders such as carcinoid tumors, rheumatoid arthritis, systemic lupus erythematosus, or syphilis may damage one or more heart valves (see these specific disorders for more information).
• Methysergide, a medication used to treat migraine headaches, may promote valvular heart disease.
• Radiation therapy (used to treat cancer) may be associated with valvular heart disease.

PREVENTION

• A heart-healthy lifestyle is advised to reduce the risks of hypertension, atherosclerosis, and heart attack.

SYMPTOMS

• Symptoms of congestive heart failure: shortness of breath and wheezing after limited physical exertion; swelling of feet, ankles, hands, or abdomen (edema).
• Palpitations.
• Chest pain (may be mild).
• Fatigue.
• Dizziness or fainting (with aortic stenosis).
• Fever (with bacterial endocarditis).

Valvular Heart Disease *continued*

DIAGNOSIS

• Patient history and physical examination. The doctor listens for distinctive heart sounds, known as heart murmurs, that indicate valvular heart disease.

• An electrocardiogram (ECG or EKG), to measure the electrical activity of the heart, regularity of heartbeats, thickening of heart muscle (hypertrophy), and heart-muscle damage from coronary artery disease.

• Stress testing (measurement of blood pressure, heart rate, ECG changes, and breathing rates while the patient walks on a treadmill).

• Chest x-rays.

• Echocardiogram (use of ultrasound waves to create a moving image of the valves as the heart beats).

• Cardiac catheterization: the threading of a catheter into the heart chambers to measure pressure irregularities across the valves (to detect stenosis) or to observe backflow of an injected dye on an x-ray (to detect incompetence).

HOW TO TREAT IT

• Don't smoke; follow prevention tips for a heart-healthy lifestyle. Avoid excessive alcohol consumption, nasal decongestants, excessive salt intake, and diet pills—all of which may raise blood pressure.

• Your doctor may adopt a "watch and wait" policy for mild or asymptomatic cases of valvular heart disease.

• A course of antibiotics is prescribed prior to surgery or dental work for those with valvular heart disease, to prevent bacterial endocarditis.

• Long-term antibiotic therapy is recommended to prevent a recurrence of streptococcal infection in those who have had rheumatic fever.

• Antithrombotic (clot preventing) medications such as aspirin or ticlopidine may be prescribed for those with valvular heart disease who have experienced unexplained transient ischemic attacks, also known as TIAs (see this disorder for more information).

• More potent anticoagulants such as warfarin may be prescribed for those who have atrial fibrillation (a common complication of mitral valve disease) or who continue to experience TIAs despite initial treatment. Long-term administration of anticoagulants may be necessary following valve replacement surgery, since prosthetic valves are associated with a higher risk of blood clots.

• Balloon dilatation (a surgical technique involving the insertion into a blood vessel of a small balloon that is led via catheter to the narrowed site and then inflated) may be performed to widen a stenotic valve.

• Surgery to replace a damaged valve may be necessary (valvuloplasty). Replacement valves may be artificial (prosthetic valves) or made from animal tissue (bioprosthetic valves). The type of replacement valve selected depends on the patient's age, condition, and the specific valve affected.

WHEN TO CALL A DOCTOR

• **EMERGENCY** Call an ambulance if it is the first time you have experienced severe chest pain.

• Call a doctor if you develop persistent shortness of breath, palpitations, or dizziness.

Varicocele

WHAT IS IT?

A varicocele is an enlarged, knotty, swollen (varicose) vein in the scrotum. Veins are the vessels that return blood to the heart after oxygen has been delivered to the body's tissues. All along the walls of the veins are valves that permit blood to flow in only one direction. Varicose veins occur when these valves become weak or defective, allowing blood to flow backward or stagnate within the vein. Varicoceles are simply varicose veins in the scrotum; they are not a serious health risk and in many cases do not require treatment. However, varicoceles may lead to infertility in some men. It is thought that the pooled blood in the engorged vein may increase testicular temperature and impair blood flow; both can inhibit sperm cell production. In such cases, fertility may improve when the varicocele is surgically treated. Varicoceles are quite common, affecting about 10 percent of all men.

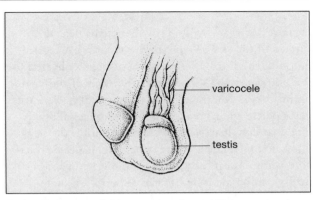

Each testis is suspended from a spermatic cord. Varicose veins along the spermatic cord produce a knotty, swollen varicocele.

SYMPTOMS

- Painless swelling on one side of the scrotum (almost always the left) that may disappear when lying down. The swollen area may feel like a mass of soft tubes or worms when pressed gently.
- Pain or sensation of heaviness in the scrotum during hot weather or after strenuous physical activity.

WHAT CAUSES IT?

- Weak or defective valves in the veins leading from the testicles may produce a varicocele.
- Infrequently, an obstruction of the vein due to a tumor or blood clot may lead to a varicocele.

PREVENTION

- There is no known way to prevent varicocele.
- Regular testicular examination aids in early diagnosis and treatment of any abnormalities (see Testicular Cancer for more information on testicular examination).

DIAGNOSIS

- Testicular examination, involving gentle palpation of the testicles and scrotum, is performed by the doctor to determine the size and consistency of any lumps.
- A special bright light can be shined through the scrotum to aid in diagnosis; varicoceles are opaque and do not allow the light to shine through, while other abnormalities (such as a hydrocele or a spermatocele) appear translucent.
- An ultrasound examination may be performed to confirm the diagnosis.
- Seminal fluid is analyzed in infertile men.

HOW TO TREAT IT

- In many cases treatment is unnecessary.
- Wear an athletic supporter or snugly fitting jockey shorts to provide extra support for the scrotum and to relieve pain.
- Surgery to remove the enlarged veins through a small incision in the scrotum may be performed (either on an outpatient basis or with an overnight hospital stay) to improve fertility. Other remaining veins compensate for the absent one(s).

WHEN TO CALL A DOCTOR

- Call a doctor if you feel an unusual lump in the scrotum. While a varicocele is not a serious health risk, all such lumps should be examined by a doctor to rule out cancer.
- Call a doctor if you are concerned that a varicocele may be impairing fertility.

Varicose Veins

WHAT IS IT?

Varicose veins are twisted, swollen veins near the surface of the skin. Veins are the vessels that return blood to the heart after oxygen has been delivered to the body's tissues. Valves along the walls of the veins permit blood to flow in only one direction. Varicose veins occur when weak or defective valves allow blood to flow backward or stagnate within the vein. Chronic obstruction of the veins can also cause varicose veins, but in most cases no underlying abnormality can be identified. Varicose veins are quite common, and women are affected at least two times more often than men. Usually appearing in the legs, varicose veins may also occur in the anus, where they are known as hemorrhoids (see Hemorrhoids for more information). While not a serious health risk, varicose veins can be eliminated for cosmetic reasons or if they cause discomfort.

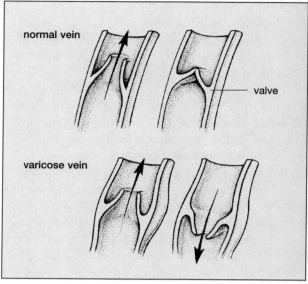

In a normal vein, valves permit blood to flow in only one direction. In a varicose vein, defective valves never fully close, allowing backflow.

SYMPTOMS

- Enlarged, swollen, knotted clusters of purple veins.
- Edema (swelling in the legs).
- Aching or a sensation of heaviness in the legs.
- Itching skin above the affected veins.
- Skin discoloration and ulcers on the inner aspect of the ankles (in advanced cases).

WHAT CAUSES IT?

- In most cases the cause of varicose veins is unknown.
- Chronic venous (vein) obstruction can be a cause.
- Hereditary factors may play a role. People of Irish or German descent are at highest risk.
- Other risk factors include pregnancy, prolonged standing or sitting, obesity, lack of exercise, and increased age.

PREVENTION

- Maintain a healthy weight and get regular, moderate exercise.
- Avoid standing or sitting for long periods.
- Elevate the legs above hip level periodically throughout the day. Do not cross the legs when sitting.
- Avoid tight shoes, belts, or other restrictive clothing.

DIAGNOSIS

- Diagnosis may be made by observation of veins and does not require a doctor.
- In some cases x-rays may be taken after a contrast medium is injected into the veins (venography) to highlight them.

HOW TO TREAT IT

- Follow prevention tips.
- Special elastic support stockings that prevent blood from pooling in the veins may be recommended.
- Raise the foot of your bed from two to four inches with blocks to aid circulation at night.
- Avoid scratching itchy skin above varicose veins, since this may cause ulceration or profuse bleeding.
- For superficial varicose veins, sclerotherapy (injection of chemicals that harden and shrink the vein) is an option. Blood is then rerouted through other veins.
- Surgical ligation (tying off) and removal (stripping) of the varicose vein is the definitive therapy in severe cases. Other veins compensate for the absent one(s).

WHEN TO CALL A DOCTOR

- Call a doctor if symptoms of varicose veins interfere with normal activities, or if you develop skin ulcers over the veins.

Vitiligo

WHAT IS IT?

Vitiligo is the patchy depigmentation of skin due to loss of melanocytes in the skin. Melanocytes, located in the epidermis (the surface layer of the skin) and eyes, are cells that produce melanin, a dark pigment that gives skin its color and protects against ultraviolet radiation. People with darker skin produce more melanin than those with pale skin. In vitiligo, melanocytes gradually stop producing melanin, causing pale spots. Eventually, melanocytes disappear from these sites completely, resulting in irregular patches of depigmented, ivory-colored skin. Some people may exhibit just a few small depigmented patches, while others may have widespread depigmentation. The cause of vitiligo is unknown; however, it may be an autoimmune disorder, in which the body's defenses mistakenly destroy some of its own cells—in this case, melanocytes. People of any skin color may be affected, but the condition is more apparent in those with darker skin. Vitiligo is a relatively common condition that does not pose a health risk, but it may be quite psychologically distressing.

SYMPTOMS

- Irregular patches of depigmented, white skin. Patches are commonly located on the hands, face, groin, and folds of skin, and may be symmetrically distributed on the body. Patches may slowly spread to cover large areas of the body.
- White hairs within depigmented patches.

WHAT CAUSES IT?

- Vitiligo may be an autoimmune disorder. The underlying cause is unknown, but hereditary factors play a role.
- Vitiligo is associated with other disorders, such as diabetes mellitus, adrenal insufficiency, pernicious anemia, and hyperthyroidism.
- Skin injury, burns, and inflammatory skin disorders may cause loss of pigment.

PREVENTION

- There is no known way to prevent vitiligo.

DIAGNOSIS

- Patient history should include exposure to any caustic chemicals or solvents.
- Diagnosis can usually be made solely by observation of characteristic skin changes.
- A special light (Wood's lamp) may be shined on the skin in a dark room to identify vitiliginous patches in fair-skinned patients.

HOW TO TREAT IT

- To keep skin as evenly pigmented as possible, try to avoid exposure to direct sunlight between the hours of 10:00 AM and 2:00 PM. Block the sun's rays by wearing protective clothing, such as hats and long sleeves, whenever possible. A half hour before going outside, apply a sunscreen lotion containing PABA (para-aminobenzoic acid) that has a sun protection factor (SPF) of 15 or higher. Reapply often, especially after swimming or perspiring heavily.
- Over-the-counter cosmetic creams and dyes are available to cover depigmented areas with a color that matches your skin tone.
- Controlled exposure to ultraviolet A (UVA) light, in combination with psoralens such as trioxsalen or methoxsalen—drugs that increase the skin's sensitivity to UVA wavelengths—may be used to stimulate skin repigmentation. A minimum of two sessions per week is necessary, and many sessions may be required before any improvement is seen.
- Creams containing fluorinated steroids may be prescribed to stimulate repigmentation of the skin.
- In cases of widespread vitiligo, bleaching the unaffected skin with hydroquinone to match depigmented areas may be considered.

WHEN TO CALL A DOCTOR

- Make an appointment with a doctor if you find mere cosmetic coverage of vitiliginous patches of skin to be unsatisfactory.

Von Willebrand's Disease

WHAT IS IT?

Von Willebrand's disease is the most common inherited blood coagulation disorder, caused by a deficiency in a blood clotting factor known as von Willebrand's factor. Von Willebrand's factor promotes clotting in two ways: first, it is an essential component in the mechanism that causes platelets to gather and adhere to one another at the site of an injury; second, it acts as a carrier for Factor VIII (also known as antihemophilic factor), a crucial protein in the process of clot formation. A deficiency in von Willebrand's factor thus results in uncontrolled bleeding due to inadequate platelet activity and decreased levels of active Factor VIII. Von Willebrand's disease affects both men and women alike (unlike hemophilia, which only leads to bleeding in men; see Hemophilia for more information). The severity of symptoms varies widely—most cases are mild, with episodes of excessive bleeding presenting a risk only after surgery. Unlike hemophilia, most people with von Willebrand's disease need not limit their level of physical activity. Treatment of bleeding episodes consists of transfusions of essential clotting factors from donated blood, or administration of a medication that stimulates the release of von Willebrand's factor into the blood.

SYMPTOMS

- Easy bruising.
- Frequent nosebleeds.
- Heavy bleeding from cuts, during menstrual periods, and after surgery or tooth extraction.
- Blood in the urine or stool.
- Swollen, painful joints (uncommon compared to hemophilia).

WHAT CAUSES IT?

- A genetic deficiency of von Willebrand's factor, a clotting factor in the blood, causes von Willebrand's disease. This condition is a genetically dominant trait, meaning it can be inherited by offspring if even only one parent carries the affected gene.
- Severe bleeding occurs only in those who inherit an abnormal gene from both parents.

PREVENTION

- There is no way to prevent von Willebrand's disease, although those with a family history of it may benefit from genetic counseling when considering having a child.

DIAGNOSIS

- Patient history (including family history) and physical examination.
- Blood tests to measure clotting time and blood levels of von Willebrand's factor and Factor VIII.

HOW TO TREAT IT

- Do not use medications such as aspirin that promote bleeding.
- Infusions of cryoprecipitate, a product containing concentrated clotting factors derived from donated blood, may be administered.
- Infusions of desmopressin (DDAVP), a medication that stimulates the release of von Willebrand's factor and Factor VIII from blood vessel walls, may be administered to stop bleeding.
- For women with a severe form of von Willebrand's disease, oral contraceptives may be prescribed to suppress unusually heavy menstrual bleeding.
- Patients may be advised to wear a Medic-Alert bracelet identifying them as having a blood clotting disorder.
- Surgeons or dentists should be informed of the condition prior to surgery or tooth extraction, so that cryoprecipitate can be given and other precautions taken to prevent uncontrolled bleeding during and after the procedure.

WHEN TO CALL A DOCTOR

- All blood relatives of someone with von Willebrand's disease may wish to be tested for the disorder.
- **EMERGENCY** Call an ambulance for any episode of prolonged, uncontrolled bleeding.

Warts

WHAT IS IT?

Warts are common, benign skin growths caused by a viral infection. Commonly appearing on the hands, elbows, face, and soles of the feet, warts may also be located on the genitals, where the infection is more serious (see Genital Warts for more information). Nongenital warts are harmless and only mildly contagious. There are a number of different types of warts, named for their location on the body and their appearance: common warts (verrucae vulgaris) are most often seen on the hands and fingers; plantar warts are located on the soles of the feet (see Plantar Warts); periungual warts are located around the nails of fingers and toes; digitate warts are small fingerlike projections that appear on the scalp; filiform warts are thin, threadlike projections commonly found around the face and neck; flat warts occur in groups of up to several hundred at a time. Many warts disappear spontaneously within one or two years. Warts may also be removed by a variety of treatments. However, recurrence is common, since the virus may be present in neighboring tissues. Warts are more common among children and adolescents; most people develop immunity as they grow older.

SYMPTOMS

- Bumps or lesions on the skin. Warts may be pale or dark, rough or smooth, raised or flat; appearance depends on the location of the wart and the human papillomavirus type.
- Clusters of multiple warts.
- Thin hornlike projections.
- Bleeding or itching (in some cases).

WHAT CAUSES IT?

- Warts are caused by the human papillomavirus (HPV), of which there are more than 60 types. The virus enters the skin through tiny breaks and can be transmitted by direct physical contact with another person, or from contact with shed skin from a wart found on a shower room floor, for example. For the most part, warts are only mildly contagious (with the exception of genital warts).

- People with weakened immune systems—such as those infected with the human immunodeficiency virus (HIV) or undergoing treatment with immuno-suppressant drugs following organ transplant—have a higher risk for widespread, persistent warts.
- Contrary to popular belief, you cannot get warts from handling frogs or toads. The wartlike bumps on these amphibians contain poison to protect against enemies, but are unrelated to actual warts, which are caused by a virus found only in humans.

PREVENTION

- An electric razor or depilatory may be used in lieu of a conventional razor to prevent nicks that may promote the spread of warts on the face.
- Do not scratch existing warts.

DIAGNOSIS

- Diagnosis may be made by observation of the characteristic appearance and does not require a doctor.

HOW TO TREAT IT

- Wart removal preparations containing salicylic or lactic acid are available over the counter. Do not use these wart removal preparations to remove facial or genital warts; such preparations are too harsh for sensitive facial and genital skin.
- Warts may be removed by freezing them off with liquid nitrogen (cryosurgery), by laser surgery, or by electrocautery (burning warts off with an electric current).
- Topical tretinoin (Retin-A), a vitamin A derivative, may be prescribed to treat flat warts.
- Your doctor may apply caustic chemical solutions, such as cantharidin or trichloroacetic acid, to destroy the warts.

WHEN TO CALL A DOCTOR

- Make an appointment with a doctor or dermatologist if you wish to have warts removed.
- Call a doctor if you are over 45 and you develop warts. New or unusual skin growths should be evaluated to rule out skin cancer.
- Make an appointment with a doctor if you or your sexual partner develops genital warts.

Whooping Cough Pertussis

WHAT IS IT?

Whooping cough, also known as pertussis, is a highly contagious, potentially serious, bacterial infection of the respiratory tract. Symptoms occur in three distinct stages, each lasting several weeks. The disease may affect anyone, but it is most dangerous when severe coughing interferes with breathing in children and infants; pneumonia can be a serious complication in young infants. Fortunately, the incidence of whooping cough has declined sharply in the United States since the introduction of the pertussis vaccine in the 1940s. The vaccine does not provide indefinite immunity (its effectiveness wears off after four to 12 years), but it protects children during the ages when they are most at risk.

SYMPTOMS

- First or catarrhal stage (resembling an ordinary cold and lasting 10 days to two weeks): nasal discharge; sneezing; mild cough; low-grade fever; general feeling of poor health.
- Second or paroxysmal stage (lasting four to six weeks): episodes of severe coughing, sometimes followed by a characteristic "whoop" as air is inhaled sharply and desperately at the end of a coughing spasm; bulging eyes and neck veins; blue tinge to the skin during a coughing spasm due to lack of oxygen; vomiting induced by efforts to expel thick sputum; seizures (rare).
- Third or convalescent stage: coughing spasms that become milder and less frequent.

WHAT CAUSES IT?

- An infection with the bacterium *Bordetella pertussis* causes whooping cough.
- Whooping cough is spread through the air by the sneeze or cough of an infected person. The infection may spread easily in families, schools, and day-care centers; those living in overcrowded or unsanitary conditions are at heightened risk.

PREVENTION

- A combination vaccine that protects against diphtheria, tetanus, and pertussis, known as DTP, provides immunity from pertussis for a number of years. Children should receive the DTP vaccine at two, four, six, and 18 months of age. A DTP booster shot is given between the ages of four and six years, just before the child starts school.
- Infants with a history of seizures or other neurologic disorders should receive the vaccine only with a doctor's permission.
- A 14-day course of preventive antibiotics may be administered to household members or schoolmates if a child develops whooping cough. Children under seven years of age who have received four doses of DTP vaccine may be given a booster shot; younger children should be continued on their regular vaccination schedule.

DIAGNOSIS

- Patient history and physical examination during the paroxysmal stage usually establishes the diagnosis.
- Throat culture.
- Chest x-ray if pneumonia is suspected.

HOW TO TREAT IT

- Treatment with antibiotics during the first stage may limit or prevent more severe symptoms. Antibiotics administered during the second stage do not alter the course of the infection but can reduce the degree of contagion. Antibiotic therapy may be necessary for 14 to 21 days and should be continued for the full term prescribed.
- Supportive care is aimed at making the patient as comfortable as possible. Plenty of fluids and frequent small meals are recommended.
- Hospitalization in an isolation room may be necessary for infants, especially those younger than six months of age. Oxygen and intravenous fluids and nutrients may be administered.

WHEN TO CALL A DOCTOR

- Call a doctor if a child's cold persists or worsens.
- **EMERGENCY** Call an ambulance if a child turns blue or stops breathing.

Wilson's Disease

WHAT IS IT?

Wilson's disease is a rare inherited disorder marked by a defect in the body's ability to excrete copper. Consequently, the excessive accumulation of copper in body tissues—primarily the liver and brain—causes organ damage and a myriad of possible symptoms and complications. The disorder is present at birth, but symptoms are rare before age six. Half of those affected remain asymptomatic through adolescence or, more rarely, early adulthood. Treatment is essential whether or not symptoms are present. Untreated Wilson's disease can lead to hepatitis, cirrhosis, and brain damage, often before age 20, and is ultimately fatal. Early detection and treatment of Wilson's disease can prevent symptoms and complications entirely. Children in high-risk families should be tested at birth. With lifelong treatment, prognosis is excellent.

WHAT CAUSES IT?

• An unexplained genetic defect prevents the normal excretion of copper in the bile and leads to excess storage of copper.

SYMPTOMS

• Fatigue, weakness, loss of appetite, and jaundice, resembling viral hepatitis.
• Swelling and fluid accumulation in the abdomen.
• Vomiting of blood.
• Muscle rigidity, spasms, and tremors.
• Walking difficulty.
• Swallowing difficulty; drooling.
• Progressive intellectual impairment; speech difficulties; psychological deterioration; personality changes; bizarre behavior.
• In advanced stages, symptoms due to chronic active hepatitis or cirrhosis (see Hepatitis, Acute, and Cirrhosis for more information).
• Lightheadedness; pallor; heart palpitations, chest pain, or shortness of breath on exertion (due to associated anemia).
• Cessation of menstruation (amenorrhea).

PREVENTION

• There is no way to prevent Wilson's disease, but a family history of the disorder warrants diagnostic testing so that symptoms and complications may be prevented by early detection and treatment.

DIAGNOSIS

• Patient and family history; physical examination.
• Blood tests show low levels of the copper-carrying protein ceruloplasmin, as well as anemia.
• Urine tests may show increased levels of copper.
• Diagnosis is confirmed by a liver biopsy (removal of a small sample of liver tissue) showing excessive levels of copper.
• Detection of a Kayser-Fleisher ring—a green or golden deposit of copper in the cornea—may require a slit lamp examination by an ophthalmologist.

HOW TO TREAT IT

• Treatment with penicillamine, a medication that binds copper, removes copper from the body by increasing its excretion in the urine. In a substantial minority of patients, pronounced sensitivity to penicillamine may produce side effects that require the administration of prednisone in addition to penicillamine. If penicillamine sensitivity persists despite prednisone treatment, trientine or zinc acetate—alternative medications that promote copper excretion—may be prescribed.
• Since penicillamine counteracts vitamin B_6 (pyridoxine), supplements of pyridoxine are given to avoid damage to the nervous system.
• Intake of foods high in dietary copper—including mushrooms, nuts, dried fruit, liver, shellfish, and chocolate—may be restricted.
• Regular lifelong checkups are necessary to detect for side effects of the medication and to monitor the effectiveness of therapy by measuring copper levels in the urine.
• In advanced cases where cirrhosis of the liver is extensive, a liver transplant may be advised.

WHEN TO CALL A DOCTOR

• Call a doctor if you or your child develops tremors, psychological changes, fatigue, or jaundice, especially if there is a family history of Wilson's disease.

Index